Introduction to Emotional and Behavioral Disorders

Recognizing and Managing Problems in the Classroom

Mary M. Jensen
Western Illinois University

PEARSON

Merrill
Prentice Hall

Upper Saddle River, New Jersey
Columbus, Ohio

Vice President and Executive Publisher: Jeffery W. Johnston
Acquisitions Editor: Allyson P. Sharp
Editorial Assistants: Penny Burleson and Kathleen S. Burk
Production Editor: Linda Hillis Bayma
Design Coordinator: Diane C. Lorenzo
Photo Coordinator: Cynthia Cassidy
Cover Designer: Jason Moore
Cover image: Corbis
Production Manager: Laura Messerly
Director of Marketing: Ann Castel Davis
Marketing Manager: Autumn Purdy
Marketing Coordinator: Tyra Poole

This book was set in by Novarese Book by Carlisle Communications, Ltd. It was printed and bound by R.R. Donnelley & Sons Company. The cover was printed by Phoenix Color Corp.

Photo Credits: Scott Cunningham/Merrill, p. 133; George Dodson/PH College, p. 81; Dan Floss/Merrill, p. 341; Larry Hamill/Merrill, p. 163; KS Studios/Merrill, p. 23; Anthony Magnacca/Merrill, pp. 3, 39, 165, 221, 309, 311, 343; Gail Meese/Merrill, p. 279; PH College, pp. 61, 181; Page Poore/PH College, p. 199; Susan Rosenberg/PH College, p. 253; Silver Burdett Ginn, p. 219; Anne Vega/Merrill, pp. 1, 59, 113.

Pearson Education Ltd.
Pearson Education Singapore Pte. Ltd.
Pearson Education Canada, Ltd.
Pearson Education—Japan

Pearson Education Australia Pty. Limited
Pearson Education North Asia Ltd.
Pearson Educación de Mexico, S.A. de C.V.
Pearson Education Malaysia Pte. Ltd.

10 9 8 7 6 5 4 3 2 1
ISBN: 0-13-096236-8

This book is dedicated to my parents, William Jensen and Gerry Murphy Jensen. Your consistent support and encouragement is the source of all success in my life!

ABOUT THE AUTHOR

Mary Jensen is a professor in the Department of Special Education at Western Illinois University (WIU). She teaches classes in the area of behavioral disorders and behavior management for undergraduate and graduate education majors and others who plan to work with youth and adolescents in a professional capacity. Dr. Jensen was the 1994 recipient of the Outstanding Teacher of the Year Award for the College of Education at WIU as well as 1995 and 1996 Faculty Excellence Awards. Her main areas of research interest and expertise are proactive and positive management strategies for students who are aggressive and noncompliant and youth gangs.

Before teaching at the university level, Dr. Jensen taught students with learning and behavioral disorders for 10 years in the public schools and in residential treatment. Today, she actively collaborates on practical research projects with classroom teachers and all of their students. Her interest in youth gangs and management strategies developed as educators and parents voiced a need for practical management strategies to apply at school, in the community, and at home. Dr. Jensen makes a variety of presentations at conferences, school in-services, and workshops on proactive behavior management strategies, management of aggressive and/or hostile behaviors, crisis intervention, and many types of behavioral disorders, including youth gangs.

Dr. Jensen also coauthored *Gangs: Straight Talk, Straight Up*, published by Sopris West. This book provides practical information to educators, parents, and other professionals who work with youth and adolescents about youth gang characteristics, proactive management strategies, and crisis intervention planning.

PREFACE

The purpose of this text is to serve as a practical manual to help general education and special education teachers (PreK–12) recognize the behavior problems common to some children and youth in their classrooms. If unaddressed, these problems might lead to the development of academic underachievement and emotional and/or behavioral disorders (E/BD). Academic and behavioral problems often lead to placement in special education classes. This text is designed to help teachers become familiar with and manage problems effectively at early stages. The goal is for teachers to learn to use proactive and positive methods to reduce problem behavior, increase academic achievement, and improve social behavior.

This book presents the characteristics and observable symptoms of a variety of E/BD that may be observed in school-age children and youth. Teachers must be aware of the disorders in order to reduce problem behavior and increase socially appropriate behavior and academic achievement at school. Many teachers view emotional and behavioral disorders as willful disruptive behavior. With that frame of reference, many simply punish these students. Punishment is not productive. Students who are only punished never learn appropriate replacement behaviors or alternatives to their problem behavior.

Organization of the Text

The categories of problem behavior presented are not necessarily limited to legal special education divisions. Topics of current interest, such as gangs, school violence, eating disorders, substance abuse, depression, and Tourette syndrome, are included among more traditional categories such as conduct disorder, autism, prenatal substance abuse, and Attention Deficit Disorder/Attention Deficit Hyperactivity Disorder. The characteristics of each disorder are presented in detail. Observable behaviors and assessment methods are provided for each category. Suggested classroom management methods are all proactive and positive. All of the strategies are designed to help children and youth learn appropriate replacement skills for problem behavior to help them learn to be more successful in school and life. At the end of each chapter, excluding the final chapter, is a section titled "Implications for Working with Youth and Adolescents" that provides suggested proactive and positive methods for effectively managing each behavior problem category.

The text is organized into six parts. **Part 1,** "Foundational Issues," covers the background and a brief historical overview of school-age students with emotional and behavioral disorders. IDEA 1997, common characteristics and overlapping problems, and causes of E/BD are presented in Chapter 1.

Chapter 2 introduces the process of assessment. This overview of assessment methods is presented in a general format because an entire assessment class is a required component of every university special education teacher training program. Readers are directed to specific texts and university courses for in-depth assessment information. The second part of Chapter 2 describes models of intervention, with emphasis on the behavioral model. The behavioral model has been the most successful research-based method for reducing problem behavior and teaching individuals appropriate replacement behaviors.

Chapter 3 covers an array of educational options for students with E/BD. The least restrictive environment mandate of IDEA 1997 is discussed, along with various alternatives to public school placements.

Part 2, "Social, Cultural, and Environmental Issues," covers a variety of topics related to school-age students. Chapter 4 presents information on prenatal drug and alcohol exposure. Fetal alcohol syndrome (FAS) and fetal alcohol effects (FAE), as well as other prenatal drug exposure, are described.

Chapter 5 presents information about substance abuse and related problems in youth and adolescents. Chapter 6 and Chapter 7 discuss topics that are relatively new on the education scene—school violence and gangs—that often produce tragic results if educators, students, and parents are not adequately educated and prepared to deal with the problems that can accompany these two areas. Chapter 6 presents information about and methods of preventing school violence. Chapter 7 provides information on gang identifiers, including prevention and management strategies.

Part 3, "Categories of Internalized Disorders," covers a variety of problem areas. Chapter 8 begins this section with information on an array of anxiety disorders along with management methods for teachers and parents.

Chapter 9 describes symptoms and characteristics of youth and adolescents with depression. Signals of potential suicidal behaviors are also presented. Bipolar and seasonal affective disorder, along with numerous treatment options, are discussed.

Chapter 10 discusses eating disorders, an area not typically covered under behavioral disorders. However, eating disorders can cause behavioral and emotional problems in youth and adolescents. Definitions, characteristic behaviors, and treatment options for anorexia and bulimia are presented.

Part 4 is titled "Categories of Externalized Disorders." Chapter 11, "Attention Deficit Hyperactivity Disorder (ADD)," discusses the typical characteristics associated with students who have attention deficits.*

Chapter 12 provides information on Tourette syndrome (TS). TS is not technically a behavioral or emotional disorder according to IDEA 1997. It is considered a neurological disorder of unknown cause. However, the tics associated with TS often have such a negative social stigma that individuals with TS often develop social and emotional problems. The background and a brief historical overview of TS are presented, along with characteristics, a detailed checklist for teachers and parents, treatment options, and intervention strategies.

Chapter 13 provides information on conduct disorders and bully behavior. Conduct disorders may be the most common pattern of behavior in youth and adolescents with EB/D. Bully behavior has become all too common, with very tragic results in schools across the country. Characteristics and intervention methods are also provided in this chapter.

Part 5, "Categories of Pervasive Developmental Disorders," includes Chapter 14, "Autism Spectrum Disorders and Schizophrenia." Autism and related disorders are not categorized as true emotional and behavioral disorders under IDEA 1997. However, because of the nature of the typical problems, youth and adolescents with autism spectrum disorders are often educated in E/BD classrooms. This chapter also provides information about Asperger syndrome, a condition that is closely related to autism. Characteristics, treatment options, and intervention strategies are provided.

Part 6, "The Future of Special Education," has one main objective. Chapter 15 emphasizes the incredible importance of using a proactive and positive approach when working with youth and adolescents with E/BD. The main objective is to reduce problem behavior and teach students appropriate and positive replacement behaviors and alternatives to their old problem behavior. Social skills are presented as life skills. These are skills that, along with satisfactory academic skills, will help students graduate from high school and go on to become productive, well-adjusted adults.

Acknowledgments

It would be absolutely impossible to write a textbook without the assistance and support from a number of incredibly helpful people.

*This text follows the policy set in 1991 by the U.S. Department of Education and uses the term *attention deficit disorder* (ADD) for both ADD and *attention deficit hyperactivity disorder* (ADHD).

Thank you to Ann Davis for all the good advice and for helping me to get started on this book writing adventure.

Thank you to Allyson Sharp for having the patience of a saint and the optimism and perseverance to help me through all the edits, revisions, and final details of the book.

I extend my sincere thanks for the reviewers: Brent A. Askvig, Minot State University; Amelia E. Blyden, The College of New Jersey; Marion Boss, the University of Toledo; E. Paula Crowley, Illinois State University; Charlotte Erickson, University of Wisconsin; James Krouse, Clarion University; and Martha J. Meyer, Butler University.

Thank you to the following Western Illinois University faculty and staff who have been incredibly helpful: Kathy Dahl, reference librarian, for helping to complete tons of research; Dr. Sharon Maroney (Chapter 1), Dr. Donald Healy (Chapter 3), and Dr. Darlos Mummert (Chapter 4) for researching and writing contributions; and Cheryl Hutchins, the world's best secretary, for all the typing and pep talks.

Thank you to my friend, Al Valdez, for providing encouragement and updated information on gangs and drugs.

Thanks to my family for believing in me. To Bryan for always being proud of my accomplishments. To Bart, Champ, Haley, Catch Me, and Magic for always being so patient and happy to see me even when I was very late.

DISCOVER THE COMPANION WEBSITE
ACCOMPANYING THIS BOOK

The Prentice Hall Companion Website: A Virtual Learning Environment

Technology is a constantly growing and changing aspect of our field that is creating a need for content and resources. To address this emerging need, Prentice Hall has developed an online learning environment for students and professors alike—Companion Websites—to support our textbooks.

In creating a Companion Website, our goal is to build on and enhance what the textbook already offers. For this reason, the content for each user-friendly website is organized by topic and provides the professor and student with a variety of meaningful resources. Common features of a Companion Website include:

For the Professor—

Every Companion Website integrates **Syllabus Manager**™, an online syllabus creation and management utility.

- **Syllabus Manager**™ provides you, the instructor, with an easy, step-by-step process to create and revise syllabi, with direct links into Companion Website and other online content without having to learn HTML.

- Students may logon to your syllabus during any study session. All they need to know is the web address for the Companion Website and the password you've assigned to your syllabus.

- After you have created a syllabus using **Syllabus Manager**™, students may enter the syllabus for their course section from any point in the Companion Website.

- Clicking on a date, the student is shown the list of activities for the assignment. The activities for each assignment are linked directly to actual content, saving time for students.

- Adding assignments consists of clicking on the desired due date, then filling in the details of the assignment—name of the assignment, instructions, and whether it is a one-time or repeating assignment.

- In addition, links to other activities can be created easily. If the activity is online, a URL can be entered in the space provided, and it will be linked automatically in the final syllabus.

- Your completed syllabus is hosted on our servers, allowing convenient updates from any computer on the Internet. Changes you make to your syllabus are immediately available to your students at their next logon.

For the Student—

- **Overview and General Information**—General information about the topic and how it will be covered in the website.

- **Web Links**—A variety of websites related to topic areas.

- **Content Methods and Strategies**—Resources that help to put theories into practice in the special education classroom.

- **Reflective Questions and Case-Based Activities**—Put concepts into action, participate in activities, examine strategies, and more.

- **National and State Laws**—An online guide to how federal and state laws affect your special education classroom.

- **Behavior Management**—An online guide to help you manage behaviors in the special education classroom.

- **Message Board**—Virtual bulletin board to post and respond to questions and comments from a national audience.

To take advantage of these and other resources, please visit the *Introduction to Emotional and Behavioral Disorders* Companion Website at

www.prenhall.com/jensen

EDUCATOR LEARNING CENTER: AN INVALUABLE ONLINE RESOURCE

Merrill Education and the Association for Supervision and Curriculum Development (ASCD) invite you to take advantage of a new online resource, one that provides access to the top research and proven strategies associated with ASCD and Merrill— the Educator Learning Center. At **www.EducatorLearningCenter.com** you will find resources that will enhance your students' understanding of course topics and of current educational issues, in addition to being invaluable for further research.

How the Educator Learning Center Will Help Your Students Become Better Teachers

With the combined resources of Merrill Education and ASCD, you and your students will find a wealth of tools and materials to better prepare them for the classroom.

Research

- More than 600 articles from the ASCD journal *Educational Leadership* discuss everyday issues faced by practicing teachers.
- A direct link on the site to Research Navigator™ gives students access to many of the leading education journals, as well as extensive content detailing the research process.
- Excerpts from Merrill Education texts give your students insights on important topics of instructional methods, diverse populations, assessment, classroom management, technology, and refining classroom practice.

Classroom Practice

- Hundreds of lesson plans and teaching strategies are categorized by content area and age range.
- Case studies and classroom video footage provide virtual field experience for student reflection.
- Computer simulations and other electronic tools keep your students abreast of today's classrooms and current technologies.

Look into the Value of Educator Learning Center Yourself

A four-month subscription to Educator Learning Center is $25 but is **FREE** when ordered in conjunction with this text. To obtain free passcodes for your students, simply contact your local Merrill/Prentice Hall sales representative, who will give you a special ISBN to give your bookstore when ordering your textbooks. To preview the value of this website to you and your students, please go to **www.EducatorLearningCenter.com** and click on "Demo."

BRIEF CONTENTS

CONTENTS

PART 2
SOCIAL, CULTURAL, AND
ENVIRONMENTAL ISSUES 59

Chapter 4
PRENATAL DRUG AND ALCOHOL EXPOSURE 60

Chapter 5
SUBSTANCE ABUSE IN YOUTH AND
ADOLESCENTS 80

PART 3
CATEGORIES OF INTERNALIZED
DISORDERS   163

Chapter 8
ANXIETY DISORDERS   164

Chapter 9
DEPRESSION AND SUICIDE   180

Chapter 12
TOURETTE SYNDROME   252

Chapter 13
CONDUCT DISORDER   278

FOUNDATIONAL ISSUES

1

OVERVIEW OF EMOTIONAL AND BEHAVIORAL DISORDERS

After completing the chapter, the reader will be able to identify:

- The definition of emotional and behavioral disorders (E/BD).
- Effects of poverty on E/BD.
- General characteristics of E/BD.
- The various labels used for students with E/BD.
- Causes and prevalence of E/BD.
- Implications for educators, parents, and other professionals who work with youth and adolescents.

Introduction

Most of us believe we can recognize tough or difficult students. To have one in your classroom is to recognize one. They can make our teaching life miserable and single-handedly disrupt a classroom. They hurt others. They are disruptive. They do not learn easily. They are not well-liked. (Rhode, Jenson, & Reavis, 1992, p. 3)

Emotional and Behavioral Disorders (E/BD)

The purpose of Chapter 1 is to provide an overview of the category of emotional and behavioral disorders (E/BD). Topics including definition, labeling, prevalence, laws, and implications for educators are covered. A variety of terms are used to identify students with behavioral problems. For the purposes of this text, the term *emotional and behavioral disorders* (E/BD) is used.

Students with diagnosed E/BD demonstrate problems on a consistent basis that are much more severe, intense, and of longer duration than the more transient, but typical problems many children experience as they grow up. The main difference is that students with true E/BD show chronic problems that significantly interfere with academic achievement and the establishment of appropriate social relationships at home, at school, and in the community (Gargiulo, 2003; Hallahan & Kauffman, 2003; Heward, 2003; Kirk, Gallagher, & Anastasiow, 2003; Turnbull, Turnbull, Shank, Smith, & Leal, 2002). If a behavior problem is evident for at least 6 months and seems to be highly resistant to intervention, it may be diagnosed as an E/BD (Kerr & Nelson, 2002; Morgan & Jenson, 1988).

Definition of E/BD

Students with E/BD are often challenging for teachers to manage in the classroom. Many teachers report that they can spot a child with E/BD a mile away. That probably is true! The most typical student with an E/BD is an acting-out, aggressive, conduct disorder-type, male student (Hallahan & Kauffman, 2003; Heward, 2003; Morgan & Jenson, 1988; Rhode et al., 1992; Vaughn, Bos, & Schumm, 2003).

Two official sets of criteria are used to define the characteristics of children with behavior problems that negatively affect academic achievement and social relationships. One definition comes from the federal government (IDEA, 1997), and the other definition was produced by a consortium of mental health professionals called the National Mental Health and Special Education Coalition (NMHSEC, 1990). Although they are slightly different, the two definitions do have common features. They show general agreement on the following three factors related to behavior problems:

1. The behavior problem is extreme. It is not just a little more serious than the usual problems children experience.
2. The behavior problem is chronic. It seems to be resistant to intervention and is not a stage or a phase.
3. The behavior problem is in direct opposition to the accepted social, cultural, and moral values of society (Hallahan & Kauffman, 2003).

The first definition comes from IDEA and originally stems from the Education for All Handicapped Children law, passed in 1975. This law and the most recent amendment were passed to ensure that all students with handicapping conditions receive a free and appropriate education in the least restrictive environment.

IDEA Definition of Emotional Disturbance

IDEA 1997 provides the following criteria to describe *emotional disturbance*:

1. The term means a condition exhibiting one or more of the following characteristics over a long period of time and to a marked degree that adversely affects educational performance:
   a. An inability to learn which cannot be explained by intellectual, sensory, and health factors;
   b. An inability to build or maintain satisfactory interpersonal relationships with peers and teachers;
   c. Inappropriate types of behavior and feelings under normal circumstances;
   d. A general, pervasive mood of unhappiness or depression; or
   e. A tendency to develop physical symptoms or fears associated with personal or school problems.
2. The term includes schizophrenia. The term does not apply to children who are socially maladjusted, unless it is determined that they have an emotional disturbance.

The IDEA definition refers to three main points: (a) *chronic behavior*: occurs over a long period, (b) *severe behavior*: occurs to a marked degree, and (c) *difficulty in school*: occurs so often that it interferes with educational achievement. The definition seems adequate at first glance. However, a common criticism is that the definition is too vague. A number of questions come to mind:

- First, exactly how long is a *long* period of time?
- Second, related to disruptive behavior, what exactly does occurs to a *marked* degree mean?
- Third, there are many ways that *interferes* with educational achievement can be interpreted.

Much of the language interpretation in the definition is left to the subjective opinion of the reader. In addition, interpretation of the criteria can vary from one school district to another and from state to state (Heward, 2003; Vaughn et al., 2003).

Schizophrenia Is Included   *Schizophrenia* refers to a condition where the individual has a severe mental disorder that is characterized by specific and maladaptive behavioral patterns. Characteristics include distorted thought processes, abnormal perceptions, fantasies, delusions, and generally being out of touch with the true reality of the individual's environment (Hallahan & Kauffman, 2003; Vergason & Anderegg, 1997).

Social Maladjustment Is Excluded from Services Under IDEA   A controversial point related to the IDEA definition refers to the classification of *social maladjustment* (SM). This condition refers to an individual's persistent refusal or inability to follow expectations, rules, and the laws of society. Individuals with social maladjustment may demonstrate any of the following types of behavior: (a) destroys or vandalizes the property of others; (b) bullies, intimidates, or takes things from others by force; (c) blames others and refuses to take responsibility for actions; (d) shows aggression and inappropriate social interaction skills with peers and adults (Vergason & Anderegg, 1997).

The ineligibility of students with social maladjustment for special education services under IDEA (1997) continues to be hotly debated. The argument about inclusion or exclusion of these students pivots around the issue of behavior patterns of SM being so similar to E/BD and conduct disorder that it is realistically impossible to differentiate one from the other.

Some psychologists argue that the behavior of students with SM is willful while E/BD is not. Others suggest that including all students who show the behavior patterns of SM will overburden the schools with high numbers of students in the special education classrooms. Prevalence figures actually show that E/BD is an underserved category (Vaughn et al., 2003). Conversely, the following NMHSEC definition *does* include students with SM.

MNHSEC Definition of E/BD

The second definition of E/BD was devised in 1990 by the National Mental Health and Special Education Coalition (NMHSEC). This professional organization is composed of individuals from more than 30 professional, educational, and child advocacy groups. In addition, this definition of E/BD has been proposed to replace IDEA terminology used in federal laws and regulations (Hallahan & Kauffman, 2003; Heward, 2003). NMHSEC wrote and promotes its version as opposed to the IDEA definition because the group thinks that it is a more precise and objective description of the children whose behavior causes problems at home, at school, and in the community.

The definition proposed by MNHSEC is gaining credibility among professionals in special education. MNHSEC has officially adopted the terminology of E/BD as opposed to emotionally disturbed (ED) as a label. They provide three main reasons for the new terminology:

1. E/BD has a less negative stigma than a label of ED.
2. It is a more representative name for students who experience problems in daily life primarily due to behavior.
3. It does not suggest either a cause or any particular intervention.

Research on teacher perception has reported that teachers do perceive student problems to be much more severe when labeled with emotional disturbance (ED) as compared with behavior disorders (BD). Teachers seem to be more comfortable with the behavior disorder label. The teachers thought that students labeled BD were more "teachable" and more likely to be successful (Turnbull et al., 2002; Vaughn et al., 2003).

MNHSEC Definition

1. The term *emotional or behavioral disorders* means a disability that is …
   a. Characterized by behavioral or emotional responses in school programs so different from appropriate age, cultural, or ethnic norms that the responses adversely affect educational performance, including academic, social, vocational, or personal skills;
   b. More than a temporary, expected response to stressful events in the environment;
   c. Consistently exhibited in two different settings, at least one of which is school-related; and
   d. Unresponsive to direct intervention applied in general education, or the condition of the child such that general education interventions would be sufficient.
2. The term includes such a disability that coexists with other disabilities.
3. The term includes a schizophrenic disorder, affective disorder, anxiety disorder, or other sustained disorder of conduct or adjustment, affecting a child if the disorder affects educational performances as described in paragraph (1).*

Characteristics of E/BD

Students with E/BD usually show a wide range of problem behaviors. These behaviors can be generally classified as externalizing and internalizing behaviors (Kerr & Nelson, 2002; Rhode et al., 1992; Vaughn et al., 2003).

Externalizing Behaviors

Externalizing behaviors are hard to miss. They are loud, disruptive, and often annoying. They are more overt; on the outside of the person. They are often reactive or impulsive. Students who show these behaviors seem to lack self-control. Examples of externalizing behaviors are inappropriate acting-out behaviors like noncompliance, aggression, hostility, bully behavior, oppositional behavior, and defiance.

This group of externalizing behaviors is also called *excessive behaviors*. Students who show excessive

*A New Proposed Definition and Terminology to Replace 'Serious Emotional Disturbance' in the Individuals with Disabilities Act by S. Forness and J. Kinzer, 1992, *School Psychology Review*, 21(1), p. 13. Copyright 1992 by the National Association of School Psychologists. Adapted with permission of the publisher.

behaviors have too many of the problem behaviors that cause disruptions. Students who have excessive behaviors tend to demonstrate higher rates of inappropriate, problem behaviors at school, at home, and in the community.

Internalizing Behaviors

Internalizing behaviors are the opposite of acting-out, aggressive behaviors. Internalizing behaviors are more on the inside of the person. They are *covert* or undercover. Students who have internalizing behavioral patterns are typically more shy, quiet, dependent, helpless, anxious, depressed, possibly suicidal, and frequently victimized. They might be overlooked in the screening and evaluation process because they are so quiet and do not usually cause overt behavior problems.

Behavioral Deficits

Students with externalizing and internalizing problem behaviors tend to have behavioral deficits. A behavioral deficit means students do not have enough necessary skills in certain areas that will help them to be successful at school working with peers and teachers, at home with their families, or in activities or with groups in the community.

Behavioral excesses and deficits function like a teeter-totter. When one side is up, the other side is down. When a child has a high rate of externalizing types of aggressive, antisocial behaviors, he will logically have fewer socially appropriate positive behaviors. The teacher's goal is to reduce the behavioral excesses. That means the students must learn what to do instead of their habitual problem behaviors, which seem to always end up with TROUBLE!

Examples of deficit behaviors include organization and time management, task completion, social skills, reading skills, general compliance skills, on-task skills, and perseverance. Educators must use proactive behavioral intervention plans to systematically reduce excessive student behavior and build up deficit skills.

IQ and Achievement

Students with E/BD generally score in the average to above average IQ range (Hardman, Drew, & Egan, 2002; Heward, 2003; Kerr & Nelson, 2002). However, their actual achievement may not always reflect IQ level. It seems that their inappropriate behaviors often have a negative influence on academic achievement. This means their misbehavior interferes with the learning process. The average sixth grader with a behavioral disorder is already 2 years behind academically. The performance demand increases for all students as they transition from elementary school to middle school to high school. More academic skills, more social skills, and more independent skills are required at each level. Without a proactive, consistent behavioral intervention plan, students with E/BD tend to fall further and further behind academically and socially as they go through school (Morgan & Jenson, 1988).

Students with E/BD do not have very many, if any, friends. They tend to associate with two particular groups: younger children whom the student with E/BD can dominate and boss around or children who have similar types of behavioral problems. They are often excluded or isolated from the average peer group (Rhode et al., 1992; Sheridan, 1995). Kauffman (2001) relates that being a peer group isolate as a child is the primary predictor of future adult adjustment problems. Other children don't like them, don't want to play with them or include them in groups, don't want to work on projects or teams with them, and don't invite them over to play after school or to sleepovers on the weekends. As a result of social and academic deficits, there is a higher than average school dropout rate for students with E/BD.

Overlapping Problems with E/BD

Researchers have identified a variety of coexisting disorders within the population of students with E/BD. It does not appear that any youth or adolescents simply have behavioral disorders and no other problems. Overlapping conditions included attention deficit disorder (ADD), learning disabilities, delinquency, drug and alcohol addiction, gang activity, mood disorders, depression and anxiety disorders, and family dysfunction (Goldstein, 1990; Hallahan & Kauffman, 2003; Heward, 2003; Jensen & Yerington, 1997; Kerr & Nelson, 2002; Kirk et al., 2003; Rhode et al., 1992). Educators who teach students with E/BD must be prepared to deal with overt excessive behavior problems, covert internalizing problems, and academic deficiencies in addition to a host of complicating factors.

Depression

Depression is inordinately common in students with E/BD. Researchers have reported that as many as 50% of adolescents with E/BD also experience depression (Coleman & Webber, 2002; Hallahan & Kauffman, 2003; Kirk et al., 2003). This compares to about 18% of the general population of adolescents. The problem behaviors demonstrated by students with E/BD can usually be traced to a variety of factors.

School Problems

Many students with E/BD find school to be an aversive and frustrating environment. Educators must be aware of these overlapping problems to provide the most appropriate programming for students with E/BD. Some students have so many problems at school that they simply choose not to attend. Tardiness and truancy rates skyrocket. Dropout is a major impediment for students with E/BD. Dropout usually causes lifelong negative effects for the individual and for society (Lovitt, 2000).

Dropout and E/BD

The following comment was made by an incarcerated juvenile when asked how truancy from school affected adolescents:

> If he ain't learning, he gonna do crime. . . . The kid is going to get stupider and stupider. They gonna go out there and do something stupid. He ain't gonna know how to read, he gonna read the sign

backward and get hit by a car while he crosses the street. He gonna get a crack paper that says don't use crack. He'll think it says use crack. If it says don't sell drugs, he'll probably do it. (Goldstein, 1990, p. 56)

The prognosis for academic success for students with E/BD is poor. Heward (2003, p. 287) reported the following dismal statistics gathered from various educational sources, including the Chesapeake Institute (1994); Valdes, Williamson, and Wagner, (1990); and the U.S. Department of Education (1998, 1999):

- Two thirds of students with E/BD cannot pass competency exams for their grade level.
- Students with E/BD have the lowest GPA of all students with disabilities even though IQ. levels are typically average or above average.
- Students with E/BD have the highest rate of absenteeism as compared with any other group of students.
- About 20 to 25% of students with E/BD actually earn a high school diploma compared with 50% of other students with disabilities and 76% of the general student population.

Statistics indicate that 50 to 65% of students with E/BD drop out of high school. To top that, delinquency statistics document that 41% of those dropouts with E/BD are arrested within 1 year of separating from school (Coleman & Webber, 2002; Hardman et al., 2002; Heward, 2003; Rhode et al., 1992). Educators must concentrate on positively oriented behavior intervention programs designed to reduce problem behavior, teach appropriate replacement behaviors, and educate students with E/BD so they graduate and are more likely to be able to successfully go on to further schooling, vocational training, or employment.

Additionally, postgraduation histories of students with behavioral disorders are very poor compared with those of both other students with disabilities and nondisabled peers (Wagner, 1995). A review of postschool employment histories compiled by Maag and Katsiyannis (1998) indicated that postschool employment statistics for individuals with E/BD lagged way behind nondisabled peers and peers with other disabilities. The unemployment rate for students with E/BD who obtained a high school diploma was 25% as compared with only 2% of nondisabled peers.

Labels for Students with E/BD

The actual labels used to designate E/BD often vary from one school district to another and from state to state. No consistent label is used. The variety of labels include (a) emotional disturbance, (b) behavioral disorders, (c) serious emotional disturbance, (d) social and emotional disorders, (e) behavioral handicap, and (f) emotional and behavioral disorders. Sometimes the behavior of these children is described as psychotic or bizarre (Heward, 2003). The U.S. Office of Education's official label for these students is emotionally disturbed (ED) (IDEA, 1997).

Benefits of Labels

As discussed previously, students with E/BD have a wide assortment of internalized and externalized behavior problems. Because there is no commonly used label, students in this group may be tagged with a variety of labels. There are advantages and disadvantages to labels. The application of a label has three benefits:

1. A label or diagnosis is usually necessary to qualify for special services at school.
2. Labels group or categorize individuals with a disability or handicap, which in turn helps researchers and other professionals to understand their learning and behavioral needs.
3. A label or diagnosis also assists researchers who study certain groups of individuals to classify, categorize, or label similar groups of characteristics for investigation purposes.

Disadvantages of Labels

The main disadvantage of a label is that it usually is negative. Some people may look at the child with a label of E/BD and see a *problem* rather than a *child*. The Council for Children with Behavioral Disorders (CCBD) is a division of the Council for Exceptional Children (CEC), the major professional organization for practitioners, researchers, parents, and others interested in the field of special education. CCBD professionals are specifically interested in youth and adolescents with E/BD. CCBD advocates for politically correct language regarding people and handicaps. A correct and sensitive label can help reduce the negativity too often associated with a handicapping condition. CCBD refers to this group of students as having E/BD.

Name Person First and Handicap Second   CCBD officially supports naming the person first and the problem second in all references to individuals with disabilities. Rather than referring to a student as *one of the E/BD students*, he or she would be called a *student with E/BD.* This standard is in place for all references to individuals with all types of disabilities.

Prevalence Rates of Students with E/BD

E/BD is the fourth largest disability area that qualifies children for special education services at school. This is close to 9% (8.7%) of all students with disabilities (Turnbull et al., 2002). Following are statistics documenting numbers of students and percentages of the total special education categories of the five largest categories for comparison purposes (U.S. Department of Education, 1998):

Category	Number	Percentage
Learning disabilities	2,676,299	51.1
Speech/language	1,050,975	20.1
Mental retardation	594,025	11.4
Emotional disturbance	447,426	8.8
Multiple disabilities	99,638	3.1

The prevalence rate of students with E/BD is not a simple figure to report. There appears to be much disparity in statistics provided (Hallahan & Kauffman, 2003; Hardman et al., 2002; Heward, 2003; Kauffman, 2001; Turnbull et al., 2002). Reports range from about 0.5% up to a whopping 20% or more of the total school population. Hallahan and Kauffman (2003) reviewed a number of research studies from the United States and other countries. They concluded that about 6 to 10% of all school-age children show "serious and persistent emotional/behavioral problems" (p. 229).

The U.S. Office of Education has estimated that about 1 to 2% of the student population should be identified as having E/BD. However, actual data provided over a number of years document that only about half that projected figure are actually identified in schools across the country. This means 1% or less of students in U.S. schools are formally identified as having E/BD on an annual basis.

During the 1996–1997 school year, there were 447,426 children diagnosed with E/BD. This is actually only 0.7% of all school-age students. Ironically, this statistic marks the greatest number of students ever identified as served in this category. In truth, E/BD is an underserved category. Since estimates of prevalence and actual statistics on the numbers of students served have been so divergent, the U.S. government has eliminated the practice of projecting estimates (Hallahan & Kauffman, 2003; Kaufman, 2001).

Variance in Prevalence Rates

Kauffman (2001) reports that there is extreme variation in E/BD rates from state to state and among school districts; it is "one of the most variable categories of special education in terms of differences among states" (p. 50). Why is there such a discrepancy in prevalence of E/BD? There are three primary reasons:

1. The main problem is the ambiguous definition of E/BD. According to Kauffman (2001), "It is difficult, if not impossible, to count the instances of a phenomenon that has no precise definition" (p. 44).
2. There is controversy revolving around eligibility/ineligibility of behavioral patterns such as social maladjustment, affective disorders, anxiety disorders, conduct disorders, and other overlapping conditions. There are many differences of opinion regarding problem behaviors some schools consider acceptable for special education services and the behavior that others don't. Due to the lack of consistent agreement, a particular student might qualify for special education services at one school, but not at another. A school district that accepts a wider range of students with problems will logically have more students with E/BD than another district with narrower criteria.
3. Assessment and data collection procedures vary between schools. Different schools use different assessment devices. Different professionals interpret test results differently. The process results in a less than optimal method of determining which students are eligible for special services.

Reasons E/BD Is an Underserved Category

There are a number of reasons many students with E/BD are not formally identified and provided with special education services. The reasons are based on philosophical differences of opinion related to eligibility criteria, funding dilemmas, and personnel concerns (Hardman et al., 2002; Kauffman, 2001; Peacock Hill Working Group, 1991):

- The label *emotionally disturbed* has a negative connotation. Parents and professionals shy away from applying that label, if possible.
- Since there is no clear definition of E/BD, states interpret the criteria differently, which results in wide variation of numbers of students served.
- States and school districts lack uniformity in assessment and evaluation procedures to

identify E/BD. There is little research to document most appropriate practices to assess, label, and place students with E/BD.

- When states experience funding constraints, only students with the most severe, acting-out, aggressive behavior problems are identified.
- If an appropriate E/BD program and teacher are not available in the community school, school districts simply may not classify any students as having E/BD.
- IDEA (1997) specifically excludes students with SM. Since there is so much confusion about the meaning of SM compared with E/BD, some students simply are not identified and provided with necessary special education services.

Gender Differences in E/BD Prevalence Rates

Sources document that boys outnumber girls in E/BD classes about 5:1 (Hallahan & Kauffman, 2003; Hardman et al., 2002; Heward, 2003; Kauffman, 2001; Turnbull et al., 2002). Incidentally, prevalence is greater for males in almost all areas of externalizing behavioral disorders. Girls display more problems with a few internalizing disorders such as depression and eating disorders.

Biological Factors Wicks-Nelson and Israel (2000) reported the biological and societal factors that accounted for boys being affected more than girls. The differences seem to be apparent from the moment of conception. Boys are more fragile and biologically vulnerable than girls. The male fetus shows higher death rates through prenatal development and the birth process. A variety of genetically linked disorders are transferred through the Y chromosome carried by males but not by females.

Societal Factors As children grow up, societal expectations, gender role stereotypes, and socialization may put pressure on boys and girls to act in different ways. Boys are expected to act in a more tough, less emotional, and more aggressive manner, while females are conditioned to be more quiet, "ladylike," dependent, and submissive. Unfortunately, these expectations increase the chances that girls will develop more internalizing disorders such as depression, anxiety, helplessness, and eating disorders.

Causes of E/BD

Multiple Causes

E/BD is a multiply caused disorder (Coleman & Webber, 2002; Hallahan & Kauffman, 2003; Heward, 2003; Kirk et al., 2003; Rhode et al., 1992). In many cases, it is hard to tell what actually triggers the maladaptive patterns of behavior. There might not be a single cause. Sometimes any number of contributing factors increase the chances that an individual will develop an emotional or behavioral disorder. However, it is not always necessary to know exactly what causes a disorder for the individual to learn to cope with or manage the problem.

The determination of cause is valuable when the information is used for program planning for the individual. It is most important to look at the outward behavior problems and determine what must be changed so that the student can achieve academically and show appropriate social behavior. The ultimate goal of education should be focused on self-management or independence and successful adjustment of students as adults. The literature describes two main causes of behavioral disorders: biological and environmental (Hallahan & Kauffman, 2003; Hardman et al., 2002; Heward, 2003; Kauffman, 2001; Kirk et al., 2003; Turnbull et al., 2002).

Biological Causes

Biological causes of E/BD may be related to either organic conditions within the body or possibly an illness or disease that affects the central nervous system (CNS). [Organic conditions are congenital.] According to biological theorists, behavior problems are a function of a physiological, neurological, biochemical imbalance or of the illness, accident, or injury the individual suffered.

Researchers suggest that the behavior problems associated with E/BD often begin at a very young age and persist in a very stable pattern into adulthood (Gargiulo, 2003; Landrum & Tankersley, 1999). Studies have indicated that many children are simply born with a difficult temperament, meaning they have a personality that was often difficult for parents, other caregivers, and teachers to deal with (Chess & Thomas, 1983; Coleman & Webber, 2002; Gelfand, Jenson, & Drew, 1988). Research on temperament and behavior indicated that an inordinate number of babies who had difficult temperaments grew up to have behavior problems. Chess and Thomas followed a group of 136 babies from infancy through adulthood. The largest sample of the baby population (40%) was categorized as *easy children* because they exhibited regularity, adaptability, and a positive approach to new stimuli. Of the sample population of babies who participated in the study, *difficult temperament children* actually made up the smallest sample group of 10%. These babies showed irregularity in biological functions, poor adaptability, negative and intense mood, and hypersensitivity to environmental changes. As the study progressed into adolescence and young adulthood, the typing of temperament was astonishingly accurate in predicting future adult adjustment problems. Later in life, 70% of the difficult temperament children developed E/BD as compared with only 18% of the easy temperament babies. Consequently, E/BD can be considered a biological disorder. Gelfand et al. reported an interesting, true story related to temperament and resiliency:

> However, a report by de Vries (cited by Chess & Thomas, 1983) illustrates why a difficult temperament may benefit some children in some situations. In the study by de Vries, the temperament of the children of the Masai tribe (a tribe of herders in the sub-Sahara region of Kenya) was studied. de Vries assessed the infants with the most easy temperament and 10 infants with the most difficult temperament. He returned to the tribe 5 months later and found that a severe drought had killed 97 percent of the tribe's cattle herd. When he tried to locate the families of the children he had assessed for temperament, he found seven of the families with easy babies and six of the families with difficult ones. The families of the other infants had moved away to escape the drought. Interestingly, of the seven easy infants, five had died, and of the difficult infants, all had survived. When times get difficult, there may be survival value in being a difficult infant; in other words, the "squeaky wheel" (infant) may get the grease (milk). (1988, p. 143)

Genetic Causes

Two types of E/BD, schizophrenia and depression, have been directly linked to physiology or genetics. Researchers do not know exactly why or how the genetic transmission occurs in the development of behavioral disorders, but they have studied enough family members who have a biochemical imbalance or abnormality in the central nervous system (CNS) to support the theory that transmission is hereditary in many cases (Kirk et al., 2003; Turnbull et al., 2002).

Environmental Causes

A number of environmental conditions could lead to the development of E/BD in some children (Coleman & Webber, 2002; Hallahan & Kauffman, 2003; Hardman et al., 2002; Heward, 2003; Kauffman, 2001; Kirk et al., 2003; Turnbull et al., 2002). Environmental stress that is severe and chronic can cause an imbalance in the delicate neurological system that regulates behavior. The stress can come from a variety of sources, including a significant loss such as death or divorce.

Other environmental contributors to the development of E/BD in children include socioeconomic status, child abuse and neglect, and traumatic brain injury. In some cases, the home situation can promote behavior problems in children (Kerr & Nelson, 2002; Kirk et al., 2003).

Ineffective parenting practices, alcohol and/or drug-addicted parents and/or siblings, exposure to firsthand or media violence, having many children closely spaced in age, and birth order may also be contributing factors (Kerr & Nelson, 2002; Kirk et al., 2003; Rhode et al., 1992; Turnbull et al., 2002).

Traumatic Brain Injury

Injury to the brain can cause behavior problems in children. Traumatic brain injury (TBI) is a separate special education category recognized by IDEA (1997). Kauffman (2001) describes TBI in great detail. The cause of TBI can be either open or closed head injuries. *Open head injuries* involve a penetrating head wound that might be the result of a car accident, fall, gunshot, other assault, or surgery. *Closed head injuries* occur when there is no penetrating damage. The damage occurs through injury to the brain from incidents such as falls, assaults, accidents, or violent shaking. Students with TBI often exhibit both academic as well as social and behavioral difficulties.

Consequently, they may be placed in classrooms for students with E/BD. The typical problem behaviors associated with TBI reflect those of students with E/BD. Examples include (a) inappropriate behaviors; (b) failure to understand the dynamics of social situations; (c) tendency to became easily angered, frustrated, or irritated; (d) lack of energy; (e) unreasonable fears or anxiety; and (f) depression and exaggerated mood swings. Educational problems associated with TBI include cognitive processing problems related to attention, memory, reasoning, and problem solving. Kauffman (2001, p. 208) provides the following descriptors for TBI:

- There is injury to the brain caused by an external force.
- The injury is not caused by a degenerative or congenital condition.

- There is a diminished or altered state of consciousness.
- Neurological or neurobehavioral dysfunction results from the injury.

A combination of medical and behavioral therapy is used as intervention for TBI. Medication cannot cure the effects of TBI or make it go away. The medication is used to reduce symptoms while behavioral therapy teaches more appropriate alternatives to maladaptive behavior.

Child Abuse

Children who are emotionally, sexually, or physically abused or neglected suffer increased feelings of stress. This cycle of abuse increases the potential for physical and psychological injury, which can lead to the formation of behavioral disorders. Child abuse and neglect is more prevalent for children with disabilities, occurring almost twice as often as it does for children without disabilities (Hallahan & Kauffman, 2003; Hardman et al., 2002; Kirk et al., 2003). According to a nationwide survey (Turnbull et al., 2002), teachers of students with E/BD reported a higher than average rate of child abuse and neglect. Statistics indicated that 38% of teachers reported that their students with E/BD had been physically or sexually abused, 41% had been neglected, and 51% had suffered emotional abuse. Hardman et al. (2002) report that child abuse and neglect is now the leading cause of physical and psychological injury and death among children. It is estimated that about half of all child abuse and neglect cases are perpetrated by parents and other adult caregivers who have substance abuse addictions.

Socioeconomic Status May Contribute to E/BD

The following comment was made by an incarcerated juvenile when he was asked if low socioeconomic status promoted delinquency problems in children:

. . . They can't get the things they want from their families, so they probably said, "So if I can't have that, I'll go out and rob a rich person and rob stores." And they probably tell all their friends when they come back with a lot of jewelry that they bought this and bought that . . . . But they really didn't. (Goldstein, 1990, p. 55)

Low socioeconomic level is frequently, but not always, associated with academic and/or behavioral problems (Kerr & Nelson, 2002; Kirk et al., 2003). It can have a harmful effect on the development of E/BD in children. Turnbull et al. (2002) provided results from a nationwide longitudinal study indicating that 38% of students with E/BD live in households with an annual income under $12,000. Another 32% of students came from the $12,000 to $24,000 income bracket. Accordingly, 70% of children with E/BD live in lower income households. Low income is also closely linked with single-parent status, which may also be a precursor for the development of E/BD because many children who live in a single-parent household are unsupervised for extended periods. Prime time for children to get into trouble on the street with criminal behaviors, inappropriate sexual behavior, drug and alcohol abuse, juvenile delinquency, and gang membership is from 3:00 P.M. to 10:00 P.M. on weeknights and all day on weekends (Walker, Colvin, & Ramsey, 1995). Table 1–1 provides a summary of environmental and organic causes of E/BD in youth and adolescents.

Poverty and the Development of E/BD

I think kids get into trouble because, while they are growing up, their parents have low income jobs and housing, and they see that they are not getting enough. And they see other people making money, and they have nowhere to turn, so they think the only way to get the things they want to get is by robbing and stealing. And they think if they steal, it will make them feel higher. So that is what they rob for. (Goldstein, 1990, p. 54)

This statement was made by an incarcerated juvenile when asked if poverty had an effect on children getting into trouble. To a child, the definition of poverty is one based more on what you do not have rather than on what you do have. Many children who live in poverty do not have enough food, warm clothing, or a bed of their own. They also do not have opportunities to see the newest movie, wear the popular styles of clothes, or have the required new school supplies on the first day of school. Through the eyes of a child in a country that emphasizes materialism, being poor means not having what regular kids have. "Being poor is about being left out of what your society tells people they could expect if they were included" (Garbarino, 1996, p. 29).

Poverty and E/BD Children and youth living in poverty in America are highly susceptible to serious academic, social, emotional, behavioral, and physical problems. The cumulative effects of many diverse

TABLE 1–1 Summary of Causes of E/BD

Environmental Causes	Organic Causes
Stress	Physiological, neurological, biochemical imbalances present at birth
Significant loss such as death or divorce	Allergies or sensitivities to environmental toxins
Single-parent family	Illness, accident, or injury to the CNS
Ineffective parenting	Traumatic brain injury
Drug- and/or alcohol-addicted parents	Mood disorders/depression
Many children closely spaced in age	ADD/ADHD
Socioeconomic status	Learning disabilities
Poverty and hunger	
Child abuse, neglect, violence	
Exposure to media violence	

factors put this group at risk and make it very difficult for children and youth living in poverty to be successful in school. Students from impoverished backgrounds are consistently identified by teachers as displaying learning, social, behavioral, and emotional problems (Kirk et al., 2003; Turnbull, Turnbull, Shank, & Smith, 2004). Externalized behavior problems, such as noncompliance, aggression, or delinquency, and internalizing behaviors, such as depression and withdrawal, in addition to below grade level school performance, are the most frequently identified problems linking poverty and E/BD. In some cases, E/BD may be an outcome of poverty and that is discussed in detail later in the chapter.

Young Children in Poverty   Most educators will have one or more students in the classroom who live in families at the low-income socioeconomic level or at the poverty level. The education of these children must address the potential damaging effects of poverty on academic, emotional, and social development. The U.S. child poverty rate is substantially higher (often two to three times higher) than that of most other major western industrialized nations. According to the National Center for Children in Poverty (NCCP, 2003), 16% of all children (almost 12 million) live in poverty.

Poverty is described in financial terms as families with incomes at or below $18,400 for a family of four in 2003. However, the NCCP reported that in most areas of the United States a family of four requires about double the income designated as the poverty level in order to obtain basic life necessities such as housing, health care, and food. Extreme poverty is described as families with incomes 50% below the poverty line—about $9,200 for a family of four. Low-income statistics indicate an ongoing problem for many children in minority as well as White families in the United States. While the low-income rate is highest for Latinos (64%) and African Americans (57%), it is also exceptionally high for Whites (34%). Seven percent of America's children live in extreme poverty; 8% of U.S. children under age 6. Not having enough money for food, shelter, and basic health care causes stress and anxiety for not only the parents but the children in the family as well. Living in poverty during the first 5 years of life has especially damaging effects on a child's future life chances and opportunities (NCCP, 2003).

Poverty and the Behavior Problems of Children

Poor kids have nothing to lose, so they do crazy things to purposely get looked up to. Rich kids got too much to lose. (Goldstein, 1990, p. 66)

This statement was made by an incarcerated juvenile when asked if being rich or poor had an effect on children and problems. Living in poverty does appear to trigger the development of behaviors characteristic of E/BD. Children who were poor before age 5 had significantly high levels of depression, which is extremely common in students with E/BD. The children maintained these high levels of depressed behaviors regardless of their poverty status in future years.

Both persistently poor children and transiently poor children show higher rates of antisocial behavior when compared with normative data of children. The number of years living in poverty correlated with the rates of antisocial behavior. Persistently poor children had the highest rates of antisocial behavior with the steepest slopes of problem behavior increase (McLeod & Shanahan, 1996).

Hunger and E/BD

Kleinman et al. (1998) note that while the status of hunger or the history of being hungry affects a child's emotions and behavior, so might the stress and anxiety experienced by children who are fearful of being hungry. Hungry children were found to be 7 to 12 times more likely to exhibit signs of conduct disorders than were children at-risk for hunger or not hungry. Hungry children also were found to have higher ratings of oppositional behavior, aggression, irritability, and anxiety (Kleinman et al., 1998).

Children who live in or have lived in homes without adequate food develop stress related to the uncertainty of the future availability of food. As might be expected, these children exhibit more oppositional and aggressive behavior as a response to this stress. For the many Americans who experience stress associated with having too much food and eating more than they should, the effects of hunger and the stress related to being hungry experienced by many children living in poverty may not be readily acknowledged.

Poverty and Effective Parenting

Parents who live in persistent poverty experience high levels of stress related to limited economic resources. Additional environmental factors, including living in dangerous neighborhoods often with gang activity, inadequate health care, substandard educational resources, and exposure to environmental toxins such as lead, increase the stress experienced by parents.

Parental stress can lead to the use of harsh, ineffective, and inconsistent parenting practices. Harsh or punitive parenting may serve as a model of aggression and antisocial behavior for children. It is not surprising that children living in poverty display more depressed and antisocial behavior than children who do not live in poverty. It also is not surprising that the antisocial behavior of poor children increases the longer they live in poverty (McLeod & Shanahan, 1996).

Family Interaction Patterns   Family interaction patterns may lead to the inception of E/BD. One usually thinks of the parents as being the culprits in this situation. However, it is important to remember that interaction between parents and children is a two-way street. Kauffman (2001) compares two schools of thought to illustrate this pattern. Some ask, "What type of families produce children with E/BD?" He then turns the question around and asks, "What kinds of families do children with E/BD produce?" (p. 232).

E/BD is the only handicapping condition where children with a disability or their parents are blamed for their problems. No one would think of blaming a little child with Down syndrome for having mental retardation. No one blames a child with dyslexia for not being able to read. However, children with E/BD are frequently blamed for what is believed to be willful behavior. Many people think this child could just "shape up and behave"

. . . if he really wanted to. People point fingers at parents and blame their child's disability on ineffective parenting. The child with E/BD cannot simply behave, any more than the child with dyslexia could just read . . . if he really wanted to.

Granted, some parents do not have effective parenting skills. Parents who base their child-rearing techniques on punishing and aversive methods can inadvertently cause their children to develop problems. Harsh and inconsistent discipline is confusing and worse than no discipline at all for many children (Morgan & Jenson, 1988). Other parents suffer from drug and alcohol addictions that render them incapable of being competent parents. Single parents may have a difficulties with children who have the potential to develop E/BD simply because of time factors. Only one person is trying to both support the household and be a parent.

Children learn a great deal through observation and imitation. Many children learn aggressive forms of social interaction from imitating their parents and other family members. Children with E/BD behave in a manner that is reactive and impulsive. They do not seem to be able to think ahead to the consequences of their behavior. They do not usually stop and think about alternatives. Why is this such a common form of misbehavior? They tend to use strategies that are familiar and easy (Kaplan, 1995). They frequently observe other family members screaming, hitting, fighting, drinking or abusing drugs, or walking out and slamming the door as a method of solving differences. Consequently, children tend to imitate those solutions because they are familiar. The poem titled "Children Learn What They Live" precisely demonstrates how children are affected by the attitudes, behaviors, and environments in which they live.

Children Learn What They Live

If children live with criticism, they learn to condemn.
If children live with hostility, they learn to fight.
If children live with fear, they learn to be apprehensive.
If children live with pity, they learn to feel sorry for
    themselves.
If children live with ridicule, they learn to feel shy.

If children live with jealousy, they learn to feel envy.
If children live with shame, they learn to feel guilty.
If children live with encouragement, they learn
  confidence.
If children live with tolerance, they learn patience.
If children live with praise, they learn appreciation.
If children live with acceptance, they learn to love.
If children live with approval, they learn to like
  themselves.
If children live with recognition, they learn it is good to
  have a goal.
If children live with sharing, they learn generosity.
If children live with honesty, they learn truthfulness.
If children live with fairness, they learn justice.
If children live with kindness and consideration, they
  learn respect.
If children live with security, they learn to have faith in
  themselves and in those about them.
If children live with friendliness, they learn the world is a
  nice place in which to live.[†]

Dorothy Law Nolte

IDEA 1997 and Controversial Discipline

Basic Assumptions of IDEA 1997

IDEA 1997 generated six major assumptions that describe educational delivery and describe the rights of children with exceptional educational needs. Those six assumptions were succinctly described by Turnbull et al. (2002) as follows:

1. Zero reject: Individuals all deserve a free and appropriate public education no matter how severe the disability.

[†]Excerpted from the book *Children Learn What They Live*, Copyright 1998 by Dorothy Law Nolte and Rachel Harris. The poem "Children Learn What They Live" on page vi, Copyright © 1972 by Dorothy Law Nolte. Used by permission of Workman Publishing Co., Inc., New York. All Rights Reserved.

2. Nondiscriminatory evaluation: Each individual will be fairly assessed to determine the nature, scope, and severity of the disability.
3. Appropriate education: Schools must provide an individualized education to all students with disabilities based on evaluation results, current level of performance, and augmented with any necessary related services and supplementary aids and devices.
4. Least restrictive environment: Each student with a disability must be educated with students who do not have disabilities to the maximum amount possible and appropriate.
5. Procedural due process: This is a process that safeguards students' and their families' rights and allows them to challenge school decisions and policies through legal channels.
6. Parental and student participation: This rule requires collaboration between the school, parents, and adolescent students to design and implement Individualized Education Plans (IEPs).

Manifest Determination

As IDEA 1997 was passed into law, a controversial discipline component immediately came to light. The law states that exclusionary discipline procedures (suspension or expulsion) cannot be used for students with disabilities if the deviant behavior is a direct result of the diagnosed disability. Any special education student who has an IEP is eligible to be considered under this process. The IEP is required for all students in special education and documents academic and behavioral goals and objectives for a particular student for the current school year. For a complete explanation of the discipline process mandated by IDEA 1997, read Zurkowski, Kelly, and Griswold's article in the September, 1998 issue of *Intervention in School and Clinic*.

[When a student in special education commits an offense that could result in suspension or expulsion, schools must now go through a process to determine whether a student's behavioral problems are a manifestation of the disability. The procedure is called *manifest determination.*]The team of individuals charged with this responsibility includes special educators, general educators, administrators, parents, the student when appropriate, and other qualified professionals. All students in special education should have IEPs, functional behavioral assessments, and behavioral intervention plans in place.

Functional Behavioral Assessment The purpose of a *functional behavioral assessment* (FBA) is to evaluate the function or purpose of specific observable student behavior (in this case, a maladaptive or problem behavior) using direct observation, behavioral checklists, interviews, and possibly an ecological evaluation of the school environment (Kauffman, 2001; Kerr & Nelson, 2002).

The FBA is then used to develop a *behavioral intervention plan* (BIP). The purpose of the BIP is to identify an individual student's problem behaviors, determine their purpose or function, and then teach the student new, alternative behaviors that serve the same purpose or function as the old problem behavior. This is based on the assumption that all behavior is learned and purposeful. The student learns a new, appropriate, and positive replacement for an old problem behavior. The goal of this process is for educators to learn to use proactive and positive strategies to deal with behavior problems.

When Is a Manifest Determination Review Completed? Three different situations at school might be used as the basis for instituting a manifest determination review:

1. A student is being considered for an individualized alternative education setting (IAES) because of weapon or drug policy violations.

2. The student shows behavior that is harmful to self or to others.
3. The student shows behavior that violates school rules of conduct.

When a problem occurs, the team convenes and reviews pertinent information about the student and the problem behavior incident(s). They must make a decision as to whether the problem behavior was directly related to the student's diagnosed disability. There are two possible outcomes:

1. If the team decides that the problem behavior *was* a manifestation of the disability, no disciplinary consequences can be imposed. However, at this time the team can decide that the student needs a change in services or placement.
2. The team can decide that the problem *was not* a manifestation of the disability. In this case, the usual school discipline policy is activated.

When activating normal school discipline policies, another relevant point must be considered. Suspensions for students in special education are limited to 10 cumulative days in the entire school year. If regular school discipline policies are to be implemented, three criteria must be met:

- The student's IEP and special education placement was appropriate. All necessary related services and behavioral intervention strategies of the BIP were being implemented.
- The student's disability did not impair his or her ability to understand the behavior's impact and consequences.
- The student's disability did not impair his or her ability to control the behavior of concern.

Ironically, even if the school can provide evidence that the inappropriate behavior is not in any way related to or caused by the disability, the school usually is required to provide an alternative educational setting to the student during the suspension period. Discipline of students in special education classes continues to be a controversial and hotly debated topic (Kerr & Nelson, 2002; Kirk et al., 2003). School district attorneys have warned that, "Whether particular conduct is a manifestation of or related to a particular disability may depend on which expert the group chooses to believe. In cases involving emotional disabilities, one may never be able to say that particular misconduct is unrelated to the disability" (Arnold & Szeptycki, 1994, p. 37).

Implications for Working with Youth and Adolescents

Based on research of successful behavior intervention plans for students with E/BD, programs must be positive. Summaries of many research projects indicate the proactive method of behavioral intervention for students with E/BD as being the most successful in reducing problem behavior and teaching appropriate replacement behavior. It is imperative that educators consistently work to reduce socially inappropriate behaviors that keep students from achieving academically and forming appropriate social relationships. In turn, students must learn what to do instead of the problem behavior. They must learn appropriate alternative behaviors to replace the old problems.

It has been continually demonstrated that punishment does not change problem behavior over the long term. Many students with E/BD have experienced every type of punishment available. They do not seem to learn from past mistakes or from punishment. A wide range of problem behaviors are associated with E/BD. All students with E/BD, whether they demonstrate externalizing types of aggression problem behavior or more covert, internalizing problem behavior, will benefit from proactive academic instruction and behavior change methods. The chapters in the remainder of this text focus on characteristics of specific types of behavioral disorders, assessment methods, and research-based proactive approaches teachers can use in the classroom.

References

Arnold, J. B., & Szeptycki, L. F. (1994). Handling discipline of disabled pupils within the law. *The School Administrator, 51*, 36–38.

Chesapeake Institute. (1994, September). *National agenda for achieving better results for children and youth with serious emotional disturbance.* Washington, DC: U.S. Department of Education.

Chess. S., & Thomas, A. (1983). *Origins and evolutions of behavior disorders: From infancy to early adult life.* New York: Brunner/Mazel.

Coleman, M. C., & Webber, J. (2002). *Emotional and behavioral disorders: Theory and practice* (4th ed.). Needham Heights, MA: Allyn & Bacon.

Council for Exceptional Children. (1997). Strategies to meet IDEA 1997's discipline requirements. CEC *Today, 4*, 1–15.

Forness, S., & Kinzer, J. (1992). A new proposed definition and terminology to replace "serious emotional disturbance" in the Individuals with Disabilities Act. *School Psychology Review, 21*, 12–20.

Garbarino, J. (1996). Children and poverty in America. *Phi Kappa Phi Journal, 78*(3), 28–31, 42.

Gargiulo, R. M. (2003). *Special education in contemporary society: An introduction to exceptionality.* Belmont, CA: Wadsworth/Thomson Learning, Inc.

Gelfand, D. M., Jenson, W. R., & Drew, C. J. (1988). *Understanding child behavior disorders* (2nd ed.). Fort Worth, TX: Holt, Rinehart, Winston.

Goldstein, A. P. (1990). *Delinquents on delinquency.* Champaign, IL: Research Press.

Hallahan, D. P., & Kauffman, J. M. (2003). *Exceptional learners: Introduction to special education* (9th ed.). Needham Heights, MA: Allyn & Bacon.

Hardman, M. L., Drew, C. J., & Egan, M. W. (2002). *Human exceptionality: Society, school, and family* (7th ed.). Needham Heights, MA: Allyn & Bacon.

Heward, W. L. (2003). *Exceptional children: An introduction to special education* (7th ed.). Upper Saddle River, NJ: Merrill/Prentice Hall.

Jensen, M. M., & Yerington, P. C. (1997). *Gangs: Straight talk, straight up.* Longmont, CO: Sopris West.

Kaplan, J. S. (with Carter, J.). (1995). *Beyond behavior modification* (3rd ed.). Austin, TX: Pro-Ed.

Kauffman, J. M. (2001). *Characteristics of emotional and behavioral disorders of children and youth* (8th ed.). Upper Saddle River, NJ: Merrill/Prentice Hall.

Kerr, M. M., & Nelson, C. M. (2002). *Strategies for addressing behavior problems in the classroom* (4th ed.). Upper Saddle River, NJ: Merrill/Prentice Hall.

Kirk, S. A., Gallagher, J. J., & Anastasiow, N. J. (2003). *Educating exceptional children* (10th ed.). Boston: Houghton Mifflin.

Kleinman, R. E., Murphy, J. M., Little, M., Pagano, M., Wehler, C. A., Regal, K., et al. (1998). Hunger in children in the United States: Potential behavioral and emotional correlates. *Pediatrics, 101*(1). Retrieved from http://www.pediatrics.org

Knitzer, J., & Lawrence, A. (1995). Young children in poverty: Facing the facts. *American Journal of Orthopsychiatry, 65*(2), 174–176.

Landrum, T. J., & Tankersley, M. (1999). Emotional and behavioral disorders in the new millennium: The future is now. *Behavioral Disorders, 24*(4), 319–330.

Lovitt, T. C. (2000). *Preventing school failure* (2nd ed.). Austin, TX: Pro-Ed.

Maag, J., & Katsiyannis, A. (1998). Challenges facing successful transition for youths with E/BD. *Behavioral Disorders, 23,* 209–221.

McLeod, J. D., & Shanahan, M. J. (1996). Trajectories of poverty and children's mental health. *Journal of Health and Social Behavior, 37*(3), 207–220.

Morgan, D. P., & Jenson, W. R. (1988). *Teaching behaviorally disordered students: Preferred practices.* Upper Saddle River, NJ: Merrill/Prentice Hall.

National Center for Children in Poverty. (2003, July). Low-income children in the United States. Retrieved from http://www.nccp.org/pub_cpf03.html

Peacock Hill Working Group. (1991). Problems and promises in special education and related services for children and youth with emotional or behavioral disorders. *Behavioral Disorders, 16,* 299–313.

Rhode, G., Jenson, W. R., & Reavis, H. K. (1992). *The tough kid book.* Longmont, CO: Sopris West.

Sheridan, S. M. (1995). *The tough kid social skills book.* Longmont, CO: Sopris West.

Turnbull, A., Turnbull, R., Shank, M., Smith, S., & Leal, D. (2002). *Exceptional lives: Special education in today's schools* (3rd ed.). Upper Saddle River, NJ: Merrill/Prentice Hall.

Turnbull, R., Turnbull, A., Shank, M., & Smith, S. (2004). *Exceptional lives: Special education in today's schools* (4th ed.). Upper Saddle River, NJ: Merrill/Prentice Hall.

U.S. Department of Education. (1998). *Twenty-first annual report to Congress on the implementation of the Individuals with Disabilities Education Act.* Washington, DC: Author.

U.S. Department of Education. (1999). Assistance to states for the education of children with disabilities and the early intervention program for infants and toddlers with disabilities. Final regulations. *Federal Register, 64*(480CFR parts 300 and 303).

Valdes, K. A., Williamson, C. I., & Wagner, M. (1990). *The national transition study of special education students: Vol. 3. Youth categorized as emotionally disturbed.* Palo Alto, CA: SRI International.

Vaughn, S., Bos, C. S., & Schumm, J. S. (2003). *Teaching exceptional, diverse, and at-risk students in the general education classroom* (3rd ed.). Needham Heights, MA: Allyn & Bacon.

Vergason, G. A., & Anderegg, M. L. (1997). *Dictionary of special education and rehabilitation* (4th ed.). Denver, CO: Love.

Wagner, M. (1995). Outcomes for youths with serious emotional disturbance in secondary school and early adulthood. *The Future of Children, 5,* 90–112.

Walker, H. M., Colvin, G., & Ramsey, E. (1995). *Antisocial behavior in schools: Strategies and best practices.* Pacific Grove, CA: Brooks/Cole Publishing.

Wicks-Nelson, R., & Israel, A. C. (2000). *Behavior disorders of childhood* (4th ed.). Upper Saddle River, NJ: Merrill/Prentice Hall.

Zurkowski, J. K., Kelly, P. S., & Griswold, D. E. (1998, September). Discipline and IDEA 1997: Instituting a new balance. *Intervention in School and Clinic, 34*(1), 3–9.

2 ASSESSMENT METHODS FOR E/BD

After completing the chapter, the reader will be able to identify:

- General types of assessment for E/BD.
- Models of intervention for E/BD:
  Biophysical
  Psychodynamic
  Behavioral
  Ecological
  Social learning theory
- Implications for educators, parents, and other professionals who work with youth and adolescents.

Introduction

A teacher might ask, "Why is assessment necessary for Tough Kids? To have one in your class is to know one." (Rhode, Jenson, & Reavis, 1992, p. 9)

The process of assessment is simply a structured method of collecting data on a student's academic or social behavior. Assessment in and of itself is not particularly useful. The ultimate purpose of assessment is to gather information concerning a student's skills and then use it to plan the most effective educational program. Rhode et al. (1992) have provided three main reasons to specify the importance of accurate assessment of the behavior of tough kids:

- Assessment helps to accurately identify a student's strengths and areas of need when requests or referrals for special services are made.
- Assessment helps to determine the specific problem behaviors that will require intervention.
- Assessment provides quantitative data that can be used to accurately chart progress toward behavior change.

The main purpose of this chapter is to provide a general explanation of the assessment process and models of intervention for students with E/BD. Since there are entire texts written on assessment for students with special needs, this chapter is simply an overview of the types of methods that can be used to assess the strengths and areas of need for students with E/BD. Screening methods, behavior rating scales, and the process of functional assessment are covered. A discussion of the five main models of intervention is presented. The models provide a theoretical foundation on which to design proactive and positive behavior intervention plans for students with E/BD.

Assessment of Students with EB/D

Students who show chronic and severe problems are referred to the educational team responsible for further testing. This team may consist of educators; parents and other guardians; and mental health, medical, and social service personnel who complete evaluations in their respective areas of expertise. Individuals on the team have two main responsibilities. First, based on test results, the team determines whether a handicapping condition exists. Second, they decide whether the condition is a disability indicating the need for special education services. An individual can have a handicapping condition but may function in such a satisfactory manner that there would be no need for any type of formal special education services. As discussed in Chapter 1, IDEA (1997) suggests 504 Plans, which are written plans to provide academic and behavioral accommodations and modifications to help students succeed in the general education classroom. Students with more severe problems will require a special education placement and an Individualized Education Plan (IEP). The IEP will document specific services that will be provided on an annual basis at school.

General Assessment Procedures

The battery of assessments may include any of the following: (a) standardized IQ tests, (b) achievement tests, (c) behavior rating scales or checklists, (d) social skills/peer relations assessments, (e) direct interviews, (f) student self-reports, and (g) direct observations of the student's behavior in various environments (Kauffman, 2001). It is important for the team to complete an array of assessments with a variety of professionals and family members to obtain the most accurate indication of a student's academic and behavioral strengths and areas of need.

The various assessments are given by different members of the evaluation team. The school psychologist is usually the person who administers IQ and academic achievement tests. The special education teacher can conduct behavior rating scales, social skills assessments, observations, and interviews. Prereferral methods, mandated by IDEA, are usually completed and documented before referring a student for special services.

Prereferral Methods

A number of assessment methods can be used to determine the scope and severity of behavior problems in children. Ideally, before any referral or assessment procedures, teachers and parents will team up to generate *prereferral* methods of intervention. Prereferral methods are used by general educators, special educators, and parents in an attempt to make adjustments at school and at home that will negate the need for a formal referral for special education assessment. Examples of prereferral methods include preferential seating, assistance with note taking, organization and time management methods, social skills instruction, or an individualized behavior plan to deal with students' unique problems.

Ecological Approach

It is important to take an ecological approach to assessment. Individuals from home, school, and community may be invited to participate in the assessment process. Including a variety of individuals from the child's environment can give a more well-rounded picture of the student's ability to function in various environments. The purpose is to compare the target student's behavior with a range of behaviors considered to be normal. The assessment results are used to determine the scope and severity of problem behavior. Those results are then used as the foundation to design and implement an individualized behavioral intervention program.

The main purpose of conducting behavioral assessments is to determine the specific behavioral problems that are occurring and their severity level. Then the information can be used to plan an appropriate and individualized intervention program.

Procedural Suggestions

Sheridan (1995) provided the following six suggestions to use as a foundation for successful assessment procedures:

- Obtain signed, informed consent from parents before beginning the assessment process.
- Use an ecological approach by collecting assessment information from teachers, parents, the target student, peers, and other professionals who have a relationship with the student. Use an assessment tool that includes multiple forms for the different groups.
- Explain the purpose, procedure, and format of the assessment carefully before anyone begins to complete it.
- Score the completed assessments carefully.
- Double-check everything—twice! This includes student identification information, math used to compute scores, transfer of scores from tables or charts, graphing scores, summary, and recommendations.
- Personally thank everyone who helped in the assessment process.

Screening

The initial evaluation method suggested is usually a *screening* technique. Screening is a method by which the evaluator takes a quick look at every student in a school or other program to determine which ones need more in-depth testing to determine specific areas of need. In other words, a screening is a large-scale survey method to decide which individuals in the population would benefit from more detailed testing (Vergason & Anderegg, 1997).

Behavior Rating Scales

The types of assessments completed by the special educator in the area of E/BD are usually behavior rating scales or behavior checklists. Teachers, parents, other family members, coaches, peers, and even the student can provide valid information on behavioral checklists. Student self-reports—where a student provides perceptions of his own behavior—are a component of some behavior rating scales (Achenbach & Edelbrock, 1991; Brown & Hammill, 1990; Reynolds & Kamphaus, 1992). The results and information gathered from this component of the evaluation can provide interesting and relevant insight to the student's problems in academic and social and behavioral areas.

Student Self-Reports Test administrators are advised to use some caution when interpreting the results of student self-reports. There are three main scenarios to consider. First, some students will be very honest and provide an accurate picture of their feelings and perceptions of their abilities. Second, some students may be so desperate to please an adult, and intensely desire to be viewed in a positive light, that they will say whatever they think the test giver wants to hear. Third, some students will lie because they wish to present an image different from their real self. In summary, the test giver must interpret student self-reports with a grain of salt. Student self-reports can be compared with results obtained through interviews with other professionals and family members and direct observations of the student in various environments.

Completing the Behavior Rating Scale A person who has a relationship with a student and is familiar with his typical behavioral patterns simply rates the given behaviors on a scale that might include three or four categories of response such as:

- Always does the behavior
- Usually does the behavior
- Sometimes does the behavior
- Never does the behavior

- Very much like my child (student)
- Like my child (student)
- Not much like my child (student)
- Not at all like my child (student)

Results from behavior rating scales are usually plotted on a profile. The profile depicts the level of behavior indicated by each person who has completed the assessment. This can be used to compare the student's behavior with the behavior of students who do not have behavior problems and other students who do. The results on the profile provide an idea of the severity level of behavior compared to the average.

Behavioral Perceptions May Differ It is likely that different persons who interact with the student will have different perceptions of his behavior. Some people will observe more severe problems and others will see only mild to moderate problems. The disparity in results may be due to several factors. First, teacher and student personality components may come into play. Some teachers work more effectively and productively with students who have learning or behavioral problems. Students are going to show more appropriate responses to a teacher who is positive and rewarding and in a classroom where the curriculum is motivating and relevant (Rhode et al., 1992). Second, some teachers have stronger classroom management skills, resulting in more highly structured, predictable classroom routines. Most students who experience difficulty in school experience more success with organization of this type in a classroom. Third, some teachers have more effective behavior management skills than others. Behavior management plans that are proactive and positive are usually more successful with students who have E/BD. The variety of responses provided by evaluators will assist educators in planning the most appropriate education program for the student with E/BD.

Examples of Behavior Rating Scales Three annotated behavior rating scales detailed in Kauffman (2001) that might be used by the evaluation team to assess emotional and behavioral disorders in school-age students are as follows:

Behavior Rating Profile (BRP) (Brown & Hammill, 1990)
    The BRP consists of four subtests: one for teachers, one for parents, a sociogram, and a student self-report survey. It is normed for students aged 6 to 18 and can be used to classify the target student's behavior in either the normal range or the deviant range.

Behavior Assessment System for Children (BASC) (Reynolds & Kamphaus, 1992)
    The BASC is a very comprehensive evaluation system. Its purpose is to evaluate, diagnose, and plan treatment programs for students with developmental learning and behavioral disorders. The BASC consists of a teacher report form, a parent report form, a student self-report form, a structured developmental history report form, and a format for direct observation of student behavior.

Child Behavior Checklist (CBC) (Achenbach & Edelbrock, 1991)
    The CBC consists of a teacher checklist, a parent checklist, and a student self-report checklist. Each behavior on the checklist is rated on a 3-point scale ranging from "not true," "somewhat or sometimes true," to "very true or often true." It is normed for students aged 5 to 18. Results are plotted on a profile that relates specific problem behaviors and specific appropriate behaviors to categories. Problem behavior might be grouped as aggression, hyperactivity, self-destruction, or obsessive-compulsive disorder. On the profile, appropriate behaviors might fall into the categories of *working hard, behaving appropriately, learning,* or *being happy.*

Social Skills Assessments

A *multigating assessment procedure* for the assessment of social skills is suggested by Sheridan (1995). A multigating assessment is based on three steps:

    Step 1: Narrative information is obtained from parents, teachers, and peers.
    Step 2: Rating scales and/or checklists are completed by professionals, educators, and possibly the student.
    Step 3: In-depth interviews are conducted with a variety of persons who have a relationship with the student to collect detailed information on the student's strengths and weaknesses.

    The first step of the multigating approach may be compared to screening. All students are considered to determine who might need more detailed assessment. At the second step, social skill deficits are specifically identified through rating scales. A social skill deficit is an area of weakness where the student needs instruction to master the skill. During Step 3, specific, detailed information about the student's unique social behaviors, strengths, and deficits are pinpointed by conducting interviews and observations.

    Three social skill rating scales (Sheridan, 1995) that may be used to evaluate and provide program planning options are as follows:

Social Skills Rating Scale (SSRS) (Gresham & Elliott, 1990)
    This assessment is appropriate for children in preschool through Grade 12. Forms are available for parent, teacher, and student responses. Social skills, problem behavior, and academic competence are the three subtests included. The specific social skills covered include cooperation, assertion, self-control, responsibility, and empathy.

Walker-McConnell Scale of Social Competence (Walker & McConnell, 1988)
    This assessment is completed only by the teacher and is appropriate for students in

kindergarten through sixth grade. It is composed of one major scale on social competence with three subscales, including teacher-preferred social behavior, peer-preferred social behavior, and school adjustment. There are 43 items that are scored on a 5-point Likert scale.

School Social Behavior Scales (SSBS) (Merrell, 1993)
This assessment is completed by the teacher and is appropriate for students in kindergarten through twelfth grade. There are two major scales: social competence and antisocial behavior. The social competence portion of the assessment includes subtests on specific skills, including interpersonal skills, self-management, and academic skills. The antisocial behavior scale includes the following specific subtests: hostile-irritable, antisocial-aggressive, and disruptive-demanding.

These scales are examples of social skill rating scales that would be helpful in pinpointing students' deficits. Specific social behaviors are rated on Likert scales to determine individualized strengths and weaknesses for further instructional planning.

Interviews and Direct Observations

Interviews and direct observations can be used to gather specific in-depth information about an individual's behavior. The interviews can be used with any individual who is familiar with the student's behavior and who has the ability to comment on behavior in a way that will help identify individualized strengths and weaknesses. The goal is to obtain information about social behavior and problem behavior that might indicate typical patterns.

Assessment Summary

It is important to accurately determine the student's behavioral strengths and areas of need in order to plan the most effective intervention plan. Different types of assessment instruments can be used. The screening process, usually the first step, takes a

quick look at all students to determine who might have behaviors that warrant more in-depth assessment. Following the screening, an evaluation team plans a battery of assessments to obtain an ecological view of the student's ability to function in school, at home, and in the community. Educators, other professionals who work with the student in some capacity, and parents or other family members may be asked to complete assessments. Some examples that might be included in the complete battery are IQ or achievement tests, behavior rating scales, interviews, and direct observations. When results are tabulated, recommendations are made for an individualized behavior intervention plan. The goal of the plan is to reduce the student's problem behavior and increase relevant functional skills. These are the socially appropriate skills that will help the student show more appropriate behaviors and increase academic achievement.

Intervention Models

There is no "silver bullet" to effectively deal with behavior problems. (Morgan & Jenson, 1988)

Remember how the silver bullet always killed the werewolf in the old scary movies? That strategy was consistently successful. Unfortunately, there is no silver bullet strategy to deal with misbehavior in the classroom. Educators must individualize research-based behavior management strategies. Research-based means that the intervention is built on a treatment model that has been tested, replicated, and shown to be successful in dealing with a certain problem. That way, teachers can set up the most effective behavior management programs to deal with each student's unique problem behaviors. However, even when using research-based methods, it is important to remember that a method that works for one student may not work for all students or even for any other student in the classroom. In fact, what works for a particular student one day may be ineffective the next day based on environmental or individual circumstances. Teachers must be flexible and have a variety of proactive behavior management methods to implement in the classroom.

Intervention for E/BD can be based on a number of theoretical models. There is no one best model that will be highly beneficial to all students or any student with a problem. An eclectic plan can be set up where the teacher uses bits and pieces from any or all of the different models. Each plan must be individualized based on a student's current level of functioning, areas of strength or positive behaviors, and areas of need or problem behaviors.

Be Proactive Regardless of what model is used, the intervention plan should use *proactive methods* to teach the student new, positive, and appropriate alternatives to problem behavior. This proactive approach focuses on the reduction or elimination of problem behavior while providing redirection or teaching new, appropriate, socially acceptable behaviors. Educators who are proactive think ahead, plan, and analyze how to set up positive classroom management programs and behavioral intervention plans so that students are most likely to be successful. This is the opposite of *reactive management*, which means that the teacher waits for problems to happen and then deals with them.

A real-life example of a reactive profession is fire fighting. Firefighters wait for fires to begin; then when the alarm sounds, they rush to the scene and put out the fire. Instead of passively waiting for behavior problems to occur, proactive educators analyze, plan, and prepare for situations that might cause problems for students. Teachers must consider *antecedents* for problem behavior in the classroom. An antecedent is an event that occurs just before a specific behavior and may actually be a cause or trigger for that problem. A teacher who is proactive and identifies antecedents may be able to reduce or eliminate those triggers. Eliminating the cause of misbehavior will often prevent the occurrence of the problem behavior. That way there is no "fire" for the teacher to put out. Teachers can spend

more time teaching, and students will spend more time on-task and actively engaged in learning.

Proactive management strategies actually reduce the incidence of problem behavior by using positive methods to teach students alternative behaviors to replace the old problem behaviors (Rhode et al., 1992). That means the students learn new behaviors and consequently are not making the same mistakes over and over. Rather than simply being punished, the students are learning behavioral strategies that will help them be more successful over the long term.

There are advantages and disadvantages to each of the intervention models. It is important for educators to take an eclectic approach to using the models to intervene with problem behavior. This means the teacher might use a combination of strategies from two or more of the models to plan and implement a treatment program. Coleman and Webber (2002) provided a highly detailed account of the different theoretical models of intervention. A summary of the intervention models follows.

Biophysical Model

The biophysical or medical model is based on the premise that there is something physically wrong with the individual. Medical personnel such as doctors, nurses, and psychiatrists are the primary interventionists. The assumption is that since there is some type of physiological or biological abnormality, medicine can be prescribed to cure the condition. The advantage to taking the appropriate medicine in the correct dosage on a consistent schedule is that it can reduce debilitating symptoms quickly.

Medication Is Not a Cure for Behavior Problems It is important to remember that medicine does not cure problem behavior. The medicine simply reduces aberrant symptoms associated with a disorder. For example, haloperidol decreases the tics of Tourette syndrome, Ritalin reduces hyperactivity associated with attention deficit hyperactivity disorder (ADHD), and lithium balances the manic highs and depressive lows of bipolar disorder. The positive effects of the medicine last only as long as the individual takes the medicine as prescribed. There is no cure-all behavior pill. In most cases, it is important for a medical regimen to be paired with behavioral therapy. The medicine may help to decrease symptoms to a much reduced level, while behavioral therapy can be used to teach the individual self-management skills and coping strategies. Research supports the medical model as a means to reduce physical symptoms associated with problem behavior (Coleman & Webber, 2002).

Psychodynamic Model

The psychodynamic model is mental health system–oriented. Psychologists, psychiatrists, counselors, and therapists are the professionals who are responsible for treatment and behavior change based on this model. Intervention is focused primarily on talk therapy to gain insight to the cause of a problem. The fundamental assumption is that the individual is experiencing *interpsychic conflict*, which is described as the good conscience and the bad conscience waging an ongoing dispute. It could be compared to having an angel on one shoulder and the devil on the other. When the person is trying to decide whether to demonstrate a particular behavior, the angel whispers, "Better not, you'll get caught; you'll get in trouble; it is not a smart, responsible thing to do. . . ." On the other shoulder, the devil is hissing, "Ahhh, but it will be so fun, you'll like it, just try it, you can get away with it, no one will catch you!" This conflict is the source of the individual's inner struggle. Each person must make a conscious decision to act out behaviors that are socially acceptable according to values of the society or to simply do what the individual wants to do. These behaviors may be in direct violation of moral values of the society.

Development Is Stepwise   Psychodynamic theorists believe that all development takes place in a stepwise fashion. The individual must master each step before going on to the next step. Consequently, this model suggests that behavior problems result from lags in development or getting stuck on a particular step for long periods. Talk therapy or counseling is aimed at helping the individual move up the steps of development. Although counseling can be highly beneficial in helping people to better understand the cause of their problems, research does not support this model as a sole means of behavior change. Simply talking to individuals with E/BD does not change their behavior (Rhode et al., 1992). The verbal counseling approach must be paired with behavioral modification to teach the individual more appropriate alternatives to maladaptive behavior.

Behavioral Model

The behavioral model theory is based on three major assumptions. First, all behavior is learned. Second, all behavior is functional. Third, consequences from the environment shape and maintain behavior. Beginning at a very young age and continuing throughout the life span, individuals learn and maintain certain behaviors for a reason; the behaviors are *functional*, meaning they serve a purpose. As children grow, they often learn inappropriate behaviors as easily as they learn appropriate, positive, socially acceptable actions. Inappropriate behavior can serve a purpose in the child's life. It can help satisfy a want or a need that has not been met through more appropriate channels. When students chronically show maladaptive or deviant behavior to meet wants or needs, they usually end up in trouble and eventually are referred for special services.

Consequences Shape Behavior   The behavioral model asserts that consequences from the environment shape and maintain behaviors. Behaviors that are followed by positive reinforcement are most likely to continue or increase. Conversely, any behavior that is followed by negative consequences such as punishment, should theoretically decrease. However, research has not shown punishment to be an effective means of behavioral intervention. The main reason is that it simply works to stop misbehavior. In fact, it usually stops misbehavior only while the punisher is actually present.

A behavioral phenomenon called *contingency-governed behavior* may begin to develop at this time. Rule-governed behavior simply means an individual follows the rules and obeys the laws just because he has a moral character and rules are rules and laws are laws. Both are meant to be obeyed. Contingency-governed behavior means that an individual's behavior depends on the next consequence he perceives may be coming from the environment. In plain English, this means that a person will try to get away with an inappropriate behavior if he thinks he will not get caught. Consequently, if the student believes the punisher will not see him or catch him in the misbehavior, he will try to get away with it. The problem behavior cycle escalates. If the student does not get caught, he feels successful, which is a form of positive reinforcement, so he continues the pattern of problem behavior.

Punishment procedures do not teach any appropriate alternatives or replacements for the problem behavior. For behavior change to be effective and long-lasting, the methods must be mostly positive (Jensen & Yerington, 1997; Kaplan, 1995; Rhode et al., 1992). Research strongly supports the use of proactive and positive procedures as the most long-term, durable means of behavior change. The behavioral model is the most widely used model of intervention to change maladaptive behavior in schools, clinics, and other types of treatment centers and agencies.

Process of Behavior Change The student with E/BD is usually referred for special education services because he or she has out-of-control problem behaviors that are interfering with academic achievement and social adjustment (Jensen & Yerington, 1997). General education teachers are the main source of student referrals for special services. The two most common behaviors that result in referral are noncompliance and aggression (Rhode et al., 1992). When students demonstrate these behaviors on a chronic or consistent basis, they are often so disruptive in the classroom that it becomes difficult for the teacher to teach and for the other students to learn.

Out-of-control behavior often results in a special education placement. After a special education placement has been made, it is the teacher's job to bring those problem behaviors under control. The next step in the process is to teach self-management or self-control to the student. Once the problem behaviors can be self-managed on a consistent basis and the student's academic achievement is consistent with curriculum content requirements, then it is appropriate to mainstream into the general education classroom (Jensen & Yerington, 1997).

Problems with Punishment Research does not support the use of punishment as a viable means of behavior change (Jensen & Yerington, 1997; Kaplan, 1995; Rhode et al., 1992). There are a number of cautions attached to using punishment to deal with problem behavior:

- Simply punishing an inappropriate behavior does not teach an alternative, more appropriate behavior.
- Effects of punishment tend to last only as long as the punisher is present.
- Children learn aversive, aggressive methods of social interaction from punishers.

Unfortunately, many school systems depend only on a system of punishment to deal with problem behavior, namely, detention, suspension, or expulsion. Those exclusionary methods remove students from school for various periods. But when students return to school, they go back with the same problem behaviors that got them into trouble. Many students with E/BD do not learn from past mistakes. They tend to show the same problem behaviors over and over. Educators must actively teach appropriate and positive alternatives to the old problem behavior (Jensen & Yerington, 1997).

Redirection Strategy Proactive educators will be successful at teaching their students socially acceptable alternative behaviors using the following method. It is vitally important in every case of misbehavior that educators use a four-step process to deal with behavior problems (Jensen & Yerington, 1997; Kaplan, 1995; Rhode et al., 1992).

When problem behavior is simply punished, individuals tend to keep on making the same mistakes. Using this proactive strategy, educators will plan ahead and be prepared to teach students skills that will help them to be more successful in the future. It does take a small investment of time to plan ahead and be prepared to use the redirection strategy. However, the investment will pay off. When used consistently, this procedure usually means the teacher can spend more time teaching and students will spend more time engaged and on-task during lessons (Jensen & Yerington, 1997):

1. Confront the student with the problem behavior. This means the teacher will describe what the student is doing wrong and why it is not appropriate or acceptable behavior.
2. The educator will teach the student an appropriate alternative to the problem behavior. This is a behavior the student can do that fulfills the function of the old problem behavior in a socially acceptable manner. This step requires that the teacher be highly observant and to analyze to determine *why* the student is behaving in a certain manner.
3. Prompt practice opportunities to help the student learn and internalize the new replacement behavior. Give many opportunities to practice. Consider giving students points or some type of bonus to motivate the student to show the new behavior. If the student lost points for the old problem behavior, consider refunding half the points if she responds to the positive redirection. This method can provide an incentive to help the student get back on a positive roll.
4. Heap on the positive reinforcement for following through and using the good new behavior. Educators need to give about four to six good, genuine positive reinforcement praise statements for every reprimand used in the classroom (Rhode et al., 1992).

It is vitally important that adults focus mainly on the use of redirection with positive reinforcement as a consequence to intervene with maladaptive behavior. Using this four-step process (see Table 2–1), educators can help students learn to think, make good choices, and learn to change their habitual problem behavior. Students will need encouragement, support, consistent reminders, and much positive reinforcement to be successful at demonstrating the new behaviors. (Think how hard it is to change one of your own old problem behaviors!) The long-term goal of the positive redirection strategy is independence and self-management (Jensen & Yerington, 1997).

TABLE 2–1 Steps for Proactive Behavioral Intervention

	Steps	Behavior
1	Confront the student's problem behavior	Tell student what he is doing wrong and why
2	Teach the student a new appropriate replacement behavior	Give options or alternatives that will be functional and serve a purpose
3	Prompt or set up practice opportunities for the new behavior	Make sure the student knows, understands, and can do the new behavior
4	Heap on the positive reinforcement to motivate the student	Behaviors that are followed by positive reinforcement are likely to be repeated

Note. *From Gangs: Straight Talk, Straight Up by M. M. Jensen and P. C. Yerington, 1997, Longmont, CO: Sopris West. Copyright 1997 by Sopris West. Reprinted with permission.*

Parent/Teacher Collaboration Collaboration with parents is beneficial in providing students with a pervasive and consistent behavior intervention program that is designed to reduce problem behavior and increase socially acceptable alternatives. Parents must feel welcome and comfortable to meet with the teacher and implement the intervention program in order to carry it out on a consistent basis at home. Teachers can set up support group meetings and training sessions to help parents become more effective behavior managers. Teachers also must set up daily or weekly communication systems with parents. Home notes (Jenson, Rhode, & Reavis, 1996; Rhode et al., 1992) are an excellent means of consistent communication between home and school. In addition, teachers might encourage parent visits and volunteers in the classroom.

Cycle of Problem Behavior Most students are referred for special education services at school because they have some sort of out-of-control behavior, either academic or behavioral. Once they start receiving special services, the teacher works to bring that behavior under teacher control. The teacher eventually gains external control over the problem behavior. This is the point at which many teachers stop the behavior plan. The teachers reason that as long as they can control the problem behavior, the student has mastered the problem behavior. However, to internalize control, teachers must proceed one step further. They must teach the student self-control. Thus the cycle runs through the following stages:

- Student demonstrates out-of-control behavior that may result in a referral for special services.
- Using a behavior intervention plan, the student behavior is brought under teacher control.
- The educator teaches and reinforces the self-management methods until the new behavior is internalized and student behavior is under self-control (Jensen & Yerington, 1997).

Teaching Students Self-Control Self-control is crucial for lifelong successful adjustment. According to the behavioral model, teaching self-control has three steps:

- Self-assessment
- Self-monitoring
- Self-reinforcement

Self-Assessment Self-assessment takes place when the student learns to recognize occurrence or nonoccurrence of his or her own *target* behavior. A target behavior is defined as the new appropriate alternative that the student is learning to do in place of the old behavior. It is essential that the student be able to recognize when he is doing the behavior as opposed to when he is not.

Self-Monitoring After mastering self-assessment, the student learns to self-monitor or mark his or her behavioral chart. This process of concrete data collection and tallying of behavioral responses helps to make the student aware of personal behavioral patterns.

Self-Reinforcement Finally, the student learns to evaluate and self-reinforce his own behavior. This is the step where educators can teach students to set goals, master goals, and give themselves rewards for achievement.

Observation and Analyzation of Student Behavior Is Important

To use the positive redirection strategy effectively, teachers must become astute observers of student behavior. By closely observing and analyzing signal behavior, including body language, facial expression, eye contact, and attitude, educators will be better informed of students' emotional levels and communicative intents. Many students with E/BD do not have adequate communication skills or social interaction skills. They do not have the ability to ask for help in problem solving when they need it. When teachers observe a problem behavior indicator, they can use the proactive redirection strategy to prompt more effective communication skills and teach students alternative behaviors.

The behavioral model is the most widely used model of intervention for students with E/BD. When used correctly and consistently, research supports this model as the most effective means of long-term, durable behavior change. The following anecdotal story from a third grade general education teacher, Mrs. Christy Glick, relates a proactive behavior management method she created to deal with a chronic behavior problem in her classroom. This is an example of a simple, individualized behavior plan any teacher could implement in the classroom.

Christy Glick

I am a general education teacher and have been taking classes to learn more about students who have learning disabilities and behavior problems. I took a graduate-level class with Dr. Mary Jensen called Behavior Management in the Classroom. When I first went into the class, I was not sure how much of the information I would be able to use since I taught in a second grade general education classroom. After listening to the lectures and thinking of my class, I soon found out that I was wrong. There were many things that I could apply to my classroom even though it was not a special education classroom.

I had one student in my second grade class, whom I will call James. It seemed like James was consistently talking out. He would hardly ever raise his hand to speak. When James did raise his hand, he would blurt out the answer before he was called on. I found this student difficult and frustrating to work with because he had such a high rate of talk outs.

I calculated the average number of times per minute that James talked out one day. He blurted out some type of verbal response about once every 2 minutes. This may not sound like much at first thought. However, this means he is calling

out a comment about 20 times each 40-minute class period. In comparison, the other students talk out without permission maybe once or twice if at all.

I remember trying to think of ways I could help this student learn to raise his hand and wait to be called on. I felt that if I could help him with this behavior then my classroom would be a more positive atmosphere for him, me, and the rest of the students. We had an assignment in my behavior management class to design a behavior intervention plan, so I decided to make a behavior intervention plan for James.

The behavior plan was not difficult to make or to use. I wrote an objective to state student learning outcome. The objective states what behavior I would like the student to be able to do at the conclusion of the behavior intervention plan. It tells the skill the student will learn. In the objective, I defined the new target replacement behavior, which was for James to raise his hand and wait to be called on before speaking. Then I set a mastery goal for the student to work for. My criterion was for James to raise his hand and wait to be called on 90% of the time over a 5-day period. It was obvious to me that this would take a lot of time and I would have to be very patient. I had to remind myself that his behavior would not change overnight.

I then made a contract for James and set up menu reinforcers for him to work for. James and I thought up things that he wanted to work for. I would then set a price for the item on the reinforcement menu. Some of his reinforcers consisted of a soft drink, candy bar, computer time, or time with a friend. The prices on the items helped James to know what he had to do to earn the desired prize.

I then made tickets for James to earn. During the first week, I would give him a ticket every time he raised his hand and waited to be called on. I had decorated an envelope and taped it to the side of James's desk. Anytime he earned a ticket, I would put the ticket in the envelope. I was able to do this while I was teaching, and it was not distracting to the other students either. In fact, the other students were very supportive and helped James remember to raise his hand.

At the end of each day, James would count the number of tickets that he had earned. I would then record it on his contract so that we could compare it to the preceding days. After James had counted the tickets, he could choose to spend the tickets on a prize or he could save them for something that cost more tickets. I was surprised at how James would save his tickets for different prizes. His favorite prize was a can of pop.

The second week of the behavior intervention plan, I didn't give James a ticket every time he raised his hand. However, I did use verbal praise every time. If he did forget, I reminded him and he would shoot his hand up and wait for me to call on him! I began to slowly get away from rewarding him every time. I would randomly give him tickets for raising his hand. James's behavior was really starting to improve and he seemed to like the plan that I had set up.

Over the next few weeks, I continued to give the tickets randomly while using a lot of verbal praise. Other teachers in the building were noticing James's improved behavior. In fact, one day after Mrs. Pensinger, the music teacher, complimented James on his hand-raising behavior, he proceeded to tow her by the hand down to my classroom so she could personally relate to me how well James was doing in music class. He was so proud of himself!

James's mother also noticed a positive change in his behavior at home. He was getting so much positive attention, it seemed to be improving his self-confidence! We continued to count the tickets daily and James chose more and more often to save his tickets rather that buy a prize. He wanted to see how many he could accumulate. By the end of the program he had hundreds! He was very proud of that. We eventually discontinued the tickets but kept up with the positive praise statements. This situation gave me the opportunity to gain firsthand experience seeing the great benefits of using consistent positive reinforcement in my classroom. I use it with all my students. It makes my classroom such a pleasant place!

I was amazed at how positive and encouraging the other students were with James. They urged him to remember to raise his hand. They also asked him for updates on how many tickets he had earned so far. None of the other students complained that the situation was unfair because they were not getting tickets. I think there were two reasons for this. First, I try to make my classroom very positive and give all the students a lot of positive reinforcement. Second, I think the students were just so happy that James was not calling out all the time and disrupting the classroom. They wanted to see the new hand-raising behavior continue. The students have been more positive, kind, and helpful to each other since I started the program with James. It was certainly worth the time and preparation I put in planning the behavior intervention program. I believe any general education teacher can make a plan of this type to help students change their problem behaviors.*

Ecological Model

The ecological model is based on an interesting hypothesis. The main assumption of the model is that the individual's problem behavior results from a mismatch between his or her abilities and the performance demands from the environment. Essentially, the behavior problem does not lie within the child, so the goal is not to "fix" the child. The goal is to make the child's whole ecosystem fit smoothly together. The basic theory underlying the ecological model is that the individual as well as the environment may need to make behavioral and attitudinal modifications.

Project Re-ED Project Re-ED (Hobbs, 1966) was an early educational program designed to remediate behavior problems based on the ecological model (Coleman & Webber, 2002). The goal was to replace psychiatric, institutional-type placements for students with problems. The program was set up to provide children with E/BD a weekly residential

*Reprinted with permission of Christy Glick.

treatment program with the goal of promoting behavior change. Teacher-counselors manage school-based intervention programs with students during the residential program. Liaison teacher-counselors assess the home, school, and community environments to help them prepare for the student's transition from the residential program back to the home. In addition, the staff works with the family and other important persons in the child's environment to help them to make necessary behavioral and attitudinal adjustments. The child would then return home on the weekends to interact with family and significant others. In summary, the assumption is that behavior change of the individual, as well as the home and community environment and significant others, will result in a more smoothly functioning ecosystem.

Hobbs (1966) referred to the self-fulfilling prophecy in his disenchantment with hospital-type settings in stating that hospitals often make children feel as if there were something wrong with them; that the hospital can make a child feel sick. The self-fulfilling prophecy states that you usually get what you expect. In this case, students feel like they are sick because someone put them in the hospital. Consequently, they start acting sick.

In the mid 1960s, Hobbs opened two Project Re-ED campuses in Tennessee and North Carolina. The treatment program provided a short-term residential placement and ecological intervention directly to the student's family, neighborhood school, social service agencies, and community. The philosophy of the program placed confidence in each individual's ability to learn self-management skills and to make appropriate behavioral changes. Intervention was provided to help the children learn to trust adults, to show academic achievement at school, and to master life skills.

The outdoor adventure programs were a vital component of Project Re-ED designed to help the students learn life skills. Participation in outdoor adventure programs may result in an increase in self-confidence, social skills, physical strength and dexterity, and trust in others. More simply, being outdoors may provide an experience for students to explore and appreciate nature. Outdoor adventure activity programs range from simple games to problem-solving and confidence-building activities; to ropes courses; to recreational activities such as camping, hiking, canoeing, and rock climbing; to advanced outdoor camping, hiking, adventure, and other wilderness survival types of activities.

Social Learning Theory Model

Kaplan (1995) explained the main points of the social learning theory model. The basic assumption states that human behavior results from a combination of variables: (a) the individual's internal variables, (b) the external environment where behavior takes place, and (c) the behavior itself. Personal variables include factors such as beliefs, perceptions, values, problem-solving abilities, emotions, social skills, self-management skills, and physiological characteristics. Examples of environmental variables are people, events, antecedents, and consequences. Personal and environmental variables work in combination to produce the individual's own pattern of behavior.

Social learning theorists claim that all behavior is learned through either direct social interactions with peers and adults or observation of the results of others' interactions. The theorists then attempt to decide which, if any, of the individual's personal variables influence his or her behavioral habits.

While the behavioral models focus on overt or observable behavior, social learning theory goes one step beyond and tries to determine how a person's own internal variables and the environmental variables combine to promote certain types of behavior. The social learning theory intervention plan is individualized based on the person's internal variables rather than simply overt or observable behavior. It attempts to change the individual's thinking patterns and emotional responses to certain antecedents in the environment. The ultimate goal is self-management or independence (Kaplan, 1995).

Implications for Working with Youth and Adolescents

A variety of assessments can be used to evaluate the specific problems and severity of emotional and behavioral disorders. The evaluation team plans a battery of assessments to determine the exact nature of the student's problems. The results of the assessment battery can then ideally be used as a means to plan an effective and individualized education plan.

Behavior plans may be based on theoretical models of intervention. The models all have advantages and disadvantages. Educators must take an eclectic approach to use components of each model to plan a proactive program that is most effective, reduces problem behavior, and teaches new alternative replacement behavior for each student.

References

Achenbach, T. M., & Edelbrock, C. S. (1991). *Child Behavior Checklist*. Burlington, VT: University Associates in Psychiatry.

Brown, L. L., & Hammill, D. D. (1990). *Behavior Rating Profile: An ecological approach to behavioral assessment* (2nd ed.). Austin, TX: Pro-Ed.

Coleman, M. C., & Webber, J. (2002). *Emotional and behavioral disorders: Theory and practice* (4th ed.). Needham Heights, MA: Allyn & Bacon.

Gresham, F., & Elliott, S. (1990). *Social Skills Rating Scale (SSRS)*. Circle Pines, MN: American Guidance Services.

Hobbs, N. (1966). Helping disturbed children: Psychological and ecological strategies. *American Psychologist*, 21, 1105–1115.

Jensen, M. M., & Yerington, P. C. (1997). *Gangs: Straight talk, straight up*. Longmont, CO: Sopris West.

Jenson, W. R., Rhode, G., & Reavis, H. K. (1996). *The tough kid toolbox*. Longmont, CO: Sopris West.

Kaplan, J. S. (with Carter, J.). (1995). *Beyond behavior modification* (3rd ed.). Austin, TX: Pro-Ed.

Kauffman, J. M. (2001). *Characteristics of emotional and behavioral disorders of children and youth* (8th ed.). Upper Saddle River, NJ: Merrill/Prentice Hall.

Merrell, K. (1993). *School Social Behavior Scales (SSBS)*. Eugene, OR: Castalia.

Morgan, D. P., & Jenson, W. R. (1988). *Teaching behaviorally disordered students: Preferred practices*. Upper Saddle River, NJ: Merrill/Prentice Hall.

Reynolds, C. R., & Kamphaus, R. W. (1992). *Behavioral Assessment System for Children. (BASC)* Circle Pines, MN: American Guidance Service.

Rhode, G., Jenson, W. R., & Reavis, H. K. (1992). *The tough kid book*. Longmont, CO: Sopris West.

Sheridan, S. M. (1995). *The tough kid social skills book*. Longmont, CO: Sopris West.

Vergason, G. A., & Anderegg, M. L. (1997). *Dictionary of special education and rehabilitation* (4th ed.). Denver, CO: Love.

Walker, H. M., & McConnell, S. (1988). *Walker-McConnell Scale of Social Competence*. Austin, TX: Pro-Ed.

3
EDUCATIONAL PLACEMENT OPTIONS

After completing the chapter, the reader will be able to identify:

- Inclusion practices for students with behavioral disorders.
- The concept of least restrictive environment (LRE).
- Legal educational definitions and practices regarding students with behavioral disorders.
- A variety of alternative education service models for students with behavioral disorders.
- Implications for educators, parents, and other professionals who work with youth and adolescents.

Introduction

I was in a lock up before this place. I didn't have to go to school there—I didn't have to do nothin'. I lifted [weights], I hung out with my homies. After I got outa there, I got in trouble again and I got sent to this place. Here, I have to go to school, an' my social worker here and my teacher, they really try to help us. We have to work on goals. My teacher, she tries to tell us about what's out there in the world. She takes us to places and shows us real stuff, ya know? She has a lot of people come in and talk about their jobs—and we go see some—so we know what kinds of jobs they do—and maybe learn more about what jobs we want. I want to get a good job. I want people to respect me for what I do—not for my rep—like I used to. I don't want to be in jail. This place is helping me get my education. I want to be somebody .... Somebody good. (Jensen & Yerington, 1997, p. 202)

The preceding comment was made by Justin, age 17. He was a student in a residential treatment center who had previously been involved in gang and other criminal activities. As a result, Justin had spent the last several years in and out of detention and corrections. The interviewer asked whether Justin thought the treatment center where he was in residence helped to prepare the students for successful transition to their home schools after discharge. It is interesting to note that the structured program of the treatment center and the caring teacher who was working to prepare the students for real life were having a very positive impact on Justin's future choices.

This chapter discusses educational placement options for youth and adolescents with emotional and behavioral disorders (E/BD). These students may be placed in a range of educational settings described as the *least restrictive environment* (LRE) by IDEA 1997. LRE is a legal mandate stating that all students should be placed in the setting that most closely resembles the general education classroom while still meeting their exceptional education needs (Heward, 2003). Students with E/BD may need an alternative classroom environment because of academic underachievement and because their behaviors are too disruptive to allow them to stay in the general classroom.

A variety of alternatives are available based on various theoretical models. All have advantages and disadvantages. The most important consideration is that the program is truly a source of effective education that will best prepare adolescents to transition successfully back to their home schools. The individuals need both an individualized academic plan and a behavioral intervention plan that will reduce old problem behaviors and teach socially appropriate and functional replacement behaviors. The ultimate goal is for all of these students to graduate so they can become productive adults.

History of Educational Placement Options

There is a long history of educational options for students who do not seem to fit into the mainstream of education. In the early 1900s, William Healy (1915) had already been developing a comprehensive educational service strategy for delinquent boys living in Chicago slums. By 1935, behavior problems were so rampant in schools throughout industrialized areas in the United States that Baker and Traphagen (1935) published a textbook describing a comprehensive diagnostic instrument designed to help school districts categorize and prioritize students most at risk for academic failure due to behavior problems. Historically, it seems that these students have always been a challenge for the American education system. What has changed over time, however, is the legal mandate to provide students with E/BD with a free and appropriate education, no matter what the severity level of the disability.

Alternative education placements for students with E/BD outside the general education classroom are discussed in this chapter. Inclusion and mainstreaming models are presented. The concept of least restrictive environment (LRE) is reviewed. Finally, educational service models including self-contained classrooms, alternative day schools, residential treatment centers, and juvenile corrections are presented.

Mainstreaming and Inclusion

Many schools are now attempting to shift students with E/BD out of self-contained classes and into the mainstream of general education. This process must be implemented on an individualized basis for all students with special needs. Students with E/BD were placed in special education classrooms to receive special services based on the fact that their problem behavior hindered their own academic achievement and was disruptive in the general classroom learning process. If not fully prepared to be successful on return to the general education classroom, their behavior may again keep teachers from teaching and other students from learning.

Mainstreaming

Mainstreaming and inclusion practices can both be used to provide students with special education needs instructional time in the general education classroom. They are based on two different theoretical models. When a student is mainstreamed, he may spend some of the school day in a special education classroom and another portion of the day in a general education classroom. The idea is to set up an individualized plan that will best fit the unique needs of each student.

Planning and preparation is a crucial component to ensure that the student with special education needs is ready to go out to the general

education classroom and be successful both socially and academically. In addition, the general education classroom teacher may need training or other preparation to best meet the needs of the exceptional student. Such training may consist of making modifications or adaptations to academic assignments or learning behavior management strategies. Mainstreaming can be a very effective means of assisting students with special needs to be reintegrated to the general education classroom. The key to success is individualized preplanning and preparation for students and teachers.

Inclusion

The pure inclusion model dictates that *all* students with special needs receive *all* of their education in the general education classroom. A major assumption of this model is that there would be no more separate special education classes. Turnbull, Turnbull, Shank, Smith, and Leal (2002) indicate that inclusion reaches far beyond just the classroom. Full inclusion means that all exceptional students would be integrated into the same school, community, and recreation activities and home settings as students who do not have disabilities. The pure inclusion model means that there would be no more segregated special education class, no more special services, no more special schools, no more special transportation services, and no more special living arrangements.

I am not in favor of the pure inclusion model. The inclusion model takes special education back to the days prior to 1975, before the Education for All Handicapped Children Act was passed. That law gave all children with handicaps, no matter how severe, the right to a free and appropriate public education. Some exceptional students *need* to be in a separate classroom, with specially trained teachers, to have special educational services, and to have special transportation or living services in order for them to be able to progress academically and socially.

Problems with Inclusion and Students with E/BD

Due to typical excessive behaviors demonstrated by students with E/BD, including noncompliance, aggression, and other antisocial behaviors, the inclusion process is often fraught with controversy and emotional upheaval for staff and students alike. E/BD placements seem to have more inherent problems with the inclusion and mainstreaming process as compared to other categories of disability. Social skills are such a major deficit area for these students that they seem to have a difficult time simply getting along with peers and teachers. They need to be systematically taught appropriate social interaction skills. In addition, many students with E/BD have academic deficits. Content areas that require satisfactory reading and math skills pose particular problems for students with E/BD. Before they are placed in general education classes, they must be taught the academic skill foundations necessary for success in the general education classroom. In particular, reading and mathematics are two primary areas where students with E/BD tend to get for behind their same-age peers. The lack of reading and math skills is going to negatively impact virtually every academic area these students will encounter.

Professionals who specialize in educational programs for students with E/BD believe that inclusion services are not always the most appropriate placement for all students. For example, Kauffman (2001) has repeatedly spoken against the inclusion model and noncategorical placements for students with E/BD. He described the full inclusion movement as nothing but a thinly disguised attempt by the government to dismantle special education as a categorically funded educational service delivery system. He takes offense to the comparisons that some inclusion proponents have drawn between special placements on the basis of exceptionality with past racial segregation practices. Kauffman (2001) further stated that equating categories of race with disability "has immediate emotional appeal but actually denigrates the spirit of racial equality issues and makes affirmative action, compensatory programs, and special education accommodation impossible" (p. 264).

To simply place all students with special needs back into the mainstream of general education without individual preparation for both the students and the teachers is doing a great disservice to both groups. In effect, the student with special needs is losing the necessary special service for which he qualified. The general education teacher is then required to work with a student who has special learning needs with little or no preparation or training. This is nothing more than a lose-lose situation.

Following is a quote from a student who had been mainstreamed (included) in a classroom where he was not experiencing success (Jensen & Yerington, 1997, p. 219):

> I like history, I like to hear about what all those old guys used to do. But I've been ditchin' class. All we do is read to ourselves and write answers. I had teachers before who made it real interesting, but not this one.... Man, I can't do all that readin'. I don't get it. Last time, the teacher in there, man, he put me down. Told me I'd never be nothin'— just 'cause I didn't do the homework. I couldn't do it. I didn't get it. I need help with the readin'. But I'm never goin' back to that class again, man, never.... (Ramon, age 16)

As can be imagined, in some cases, like the case with Ramon, a student with E/BD who is not ready or has not been prepared to be successful in the general education classroom will fail miserably. The general education teacher may have a very difficult time teaching. Other nondisabled peers may find it very disruptive and hard to learn. The inclusion process may be doing an injustice to students with E/BD, general teachers, and peers. It is not fair to take the incredibly necessary and beneficial services away from the students who need them. Inclusion, like mainstreaming, must be implemented in an individualized manner to best meet the unique needs of each and every student and teacher impacted by the process.

To summarize, inclusion is often a difficult process for students with E/BD. They are more likely to succeed in a mainstreaming program where they are specifically prepared for one or more general education classroom placements and then return to the resource room for extra assistance and monitoring by the special education teacher. The time spent in general education classes can be gradually increased on an individualized basis for each student.

Least Restrictive Environment

Definition

One of the major educational provisions of IDEA 1997 is least restrictive environment (LRE). LRE refers to the mandate that all students with exceptional education must be educated to the maximum extent appropriate with students who do not have disabilities and in the most normal type of educational setting. Since Public Law 94-142 was passed in 1975 and the Individuals with Disabilities Education Act (IDEA) Amendments of 1997 were approved, LRE has been defined as:

> That to the maximum extent appropriate, children with disabilities, including children in public or private institutions or other care facilities, are educated with children who are nondisabled, and that special classes, special schooling, or other removal of children with disabilities from the regular education environment occurs only when the nature or severity of the disability is such that education in regular classes with the use of supplementary aids and services cannot be achieved satisfactorily. (IDEA, 20 U.S.C. § 1412)

This provision is written in terms that are "purposefully vague." The original intent was to allow school districts latitude in determining the best "mix" of access to the general education setting while maintaining special education service provisions for those students in need. In fact, it was noted in the Federal Register regarding IDEA 1997 that:

> The committee supports the longstanding policy of a continuum of alternative placements designed to meet the unique needs of each child with a disability. Placement options available include instruction in regular classes, special classes, special schools, home instruction, and instruction in hospitals and institutions. For disabled children placed in regular classes, supplementary aids and services and resource room services or itinerant instruction must also be offered as needed. (H. Rep. 105–95, p. 91, 1997)

The *continuum of placements* means that there is a series of educational settings available to students with exceptional needs (see Figure 3–1). The student should be placed in the setting that will afford the most appropriate services to fit the exceptional needs. A picture of the LRE continuum of services is often diagrammed as an upside-down triangle. General education classrooms are at the top, in the biggest part of the triangle, indicating that the majority of students should be placed in the upper services areas. Numbers of students in more restrictive placements should be reduced as one progresses to the pointed end of the triangle. The largest percentage of the student population is in the top area, with the smallest percentage of students with more severe behavioral and academic problems in the bottom end of the triangle.

Inclusion Model

Kirk, Gallagher, and Anastasiow (2003) suggest that the Inclusion Model has been the most significant movement in special education during the past two decades. School districts across the country are moving steadily toward adopting the Inclusion Model as a special education option. This means schools will experience more pressure to place all students with special needs in the LRE.

Placement Options from Least to Most Restrictive	Services Provided
General Education Classroom in Public School	All students receive the same academic instruction and assistance.
Inclusion Classroom in Public School	The exceptional student receives the same academic instruction as the general education students with individualized academic and behavior management services as needed.
Special Education Resource Room	The exceptional student receives academic instruction in both the general education classroom and the special education resource room. The division of time is based on the student's individualized academic and behavioral needs.
Special Education Self-Contained Classroom	The exceptional student receives all educational services in the special education classroom.
Alternative Day School in the Community	The exceptional student receives all educational services in a setting that is separate from the regular public school. The alternative school is specially designed for students who have academic and/or behavioral problems that are too severe or disruptive for the public school setting.
Residential Treatment Center	The exceptional student receives all educational services in a residential facility providing 24-hour care for a time period ranging from a number of months to a year or more, depending on the severity of the problem.
Juvenile Corrections	All educational and rehabilitation services are provided for an established time period determined by the juvenile court system for juvenile offenders.
Psychiatric Hospital Placement	Individualized assessment, intervention, and medical and educational services are provided in a hospital setting for students with severe psychological and/or medical problems that cannot be managed on an outpatient basis.
Homebound Instruction	Individualized educational services are provided in the student's home when he/she is unable to attend school for medical, behavioral, or other reasons.

FIGURE 3–1 Least Restrictive Environment

Note. *Kirk et al, Educating Exceptional Children, Tenth Edition. Copyright © 2003 by Houghton Mifflin Company. Adapted with permission.*

That is, schools must provide students with disabilities every opportunity to demonstrate that they can be successful in the LRE, given all necessary supplemental aids and services, *before* a more restrictive placement is implemented. Villa (1996) made the suggestion that special education be thought of as a "process" rather than a "place to go." The proliferation of inclusion models in many schools reflects the growing judicial opinion that a disability alone should not be enough justification to exclude a student from equal access to the same educational opportunities as the nondisabled classmates.

The current status of the debate on the relationship between LRE, inclusion, and mainstreaming is well summarized by Katsiyannis and Maag (1998). They describe the four basic themes apparent in the IDEA discipline provisions that schools are obligated to provide to all students:

1. All students, with and without disabilities, deserve to be educated in safe, well-disciplined schools and orderly learning environments.
2. School personnel should have effective techniques and methodologies to prevent behavior problems and to deal with them positively if they occur.
3. A balanced approach to discipline must exist in which the order and safety of schools is maintained while at the same time the rights of students with disabilities to receive a free, appropriate education are protected.
4. IEPs must contain behavior intervention strategies that will contribute to a reduction in school discipline problems. (p. 279)

Katsiyannis and Maag (1998) note that the optimal educational placement option for students with E/BD may be one that has been most productive and successful for increasing academic achievement and improving social behavior during the past 20 years: the self-contained E/BD classroom.

Educational Placement Options for Students with E/BD

Turnbull et al. (2002) provided statistics on education placements for students with E/BD. Over half of all students identified with E/BD are placed in either segregated classrooms or special schools. Although students with E/BD represent less than 10% of the total special education population, they make up more than half of the total population of persons with disabilities in residential facilities. Of all the placement options available in the traditional continuum of services, the self-contained classroom is the most likely placement for students with E/BD. More than one of three students with behavior disorders will be in such a placement. The main reason students with E/BD are placed in more restrictive settings is that their behaviors can be very challenging, and often intimidating to teachers. These students can be downright frustrating to teach. I was asked several times when I was a "real" E/BD teacher (as opposed to being a university professor) why I wasted my time with "those" kids. The answer? "Those kids are not a throw-away group. They are smart, capable, and have a ton of potential! The right teacher just has to find the right way to motivate and teach them." Some of these students have a less than stellar reputation that precedes them. Sometimes other teachers do not give them a fair chance. Following is a quote from Robert, age 15, a very capable student with E/BD (conduct disorder) who has a sparkling personality—when you get to know him:

> Last year when I was a freshman, we were going up and down the rows saying what we wanted to be when we got out of school. And it got to me and I said I wanted to be a singer, or whatever, and Miss Clark told me that was never going to be …. And then she started cutting me down …. Made me look bad …. I just walked out of the room. I was embarrassed—made me feel bad. (Jensen & Yerington, 1997, p. 223)

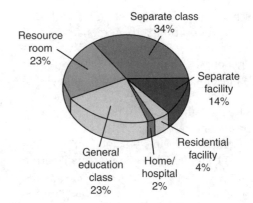

FIGURE 3–2 Statistics on Education Placements of Students with E/BD

Note. *From* To Assure the Free Appropriate Public Education of All Children With Disabilities: Twenty-first Annual Report to Congress on the Implementation of the Individuals with Disabilities Education Act, *1999, Washington, DC: U.S. Department of Education.*

Figure 3–2 documents data on placements regarding settings where students with E/BD receive the majority of their education.

Special Education Continuum of Services in Public Schools

Resource Rooms

There are usually two types of special education classrooms in public schools. The least restrictive is called a resource classroom. The resource room is staffed by special educators. Students with diagnosed special education needs attend classes in the resource room for a part of the school day. During the rest of the school day they are mainstreamed into general education classes where they can be successful. The resource room teacher may provide individualized instruction in academic content areas, implement social/behavioral management programs, and assist the student with assignments from the general education classes.

Self-Contained Classrooms

Following is a quote from Marshall, age 15, a student with E/BD. He was asked to tell about his favorite teacher and to provide an example of what made this teacher a "good" teacher:

> I had this teacher when I was in the fifth grade in St. Louis. He was like, he always knew I could be something better than what I was aiming for. He used to always take time to help me—it was with reading. He'd even take his own lunchtime and that meant a lot to me. (Jensen & Yerington, 1997, p. 224)

Teacher attention can be an incredibly important motivator and a source of positive reinforcement in the classroom. Teachers in self-contained classrooms usually have smaller numbers of students. This can allow them to provide more one-to-one time for students, who will readily benefit from the individualized attention.

Students with E/BD have a great deal of potential for negative impact on other students and teachers. As a result, students with E/BD are more likely to be isolated from the mainstream in more restrictive placements designed to prevent disruption and facilitate the educational process for all students and teachers. It has been reported that variables such as age, level of academic abilities, and the presence of externalizing behavioral symptoms were the most accurate predictors of a more restrictive placement (Glassberg, 1994; Heward, 2003; Kirk et al., 2003).

The self-contained classroom is more restrictive than the resource room. Students who are placed in self-contained classrooms tend to have more severe and disruptive behaviors than students who are placed in resource rooms. Students who are not yet prepared to be mainstreamed attend the self-contained classroom for the entire school day. The special education teacher in the self-contained classroom is responsible for planning and teaching all required academic content areas as well as planning and implementing behavior change programs for the students. These students will work their way up to the resource room by showing improved academic skills and increased levels of self-control and appropriate behavior.

Self-Contained Classrooms Are Necessary

Even though schools are adopting the Inclusion Model, there is a need to maintain self-contained classrooms for students who are at the stage where they would benefit from that type of restrictive setting. Self-contained classrooms can be used to provide one-to-one and small group lessons to effectively prepare students with E/BD to return to the mainstream of general education. Special educators can use the setting to build trust with students who frequently have had mainly aversive interactions with teachers. They can fill in the knowledge gaps and raise academic achievement levels. They can improve social skills to boost self-esteem and increase appropriate peer interactions. Improving behavior and increasing academic achievement for mainstreaming should be the goals of the self-contained classroom.

The self-contained classroom is not meant to be a form of punishment. It is an educational opportunity for students who have E/BD to learn new behaviors that will reduce problems while learning new, socially appropriate replacement behaviors. The special educators who teach in self-contained classrooms receive training in specific classroom and behavior management strategies to plan and implement behavioral intervention plans while increasing academic achievement. A proactive program that encourages collaboration among parents, teachers, coaches, and community recreation, church, and social service personnel will help to provide the most beneficial and consistent treatment options for students with E/BD.

The Alternative Day School

Students who have special education needs that cannot be met effectively in the public school setting often attend a local alternative day school. For students with E/BD, alternative school placements may be recommended due to behaviors that are highly disruptive and cannot be effectively managed in a self-contained classroom. These behavior problems may include aggression, noncompliance, hostility, and antisocial behaviors such as repetitive acts of rule violation and delinquency (Jensen & Yerington, 1997; Rhode, Jenson, & Reavis, 1992; Rosenberg, Wilson, Maheady, & Sindelar, 1997). Approximately 14% of students with E/BD are educated outside the public school system (Turnbull et al., 2002).

Alternative school programs designed for students with E/BD have a wide range of mission statements. Some emphasize conformity to rules and authority figures, while others attempt to furnish a truly therapeutic environment to provide "constructive activity, kindness, minimum restraint, structure, routine, and consistency in treatment" (Kauffman, 1997, p. 71). The treatment emphasis of alternative day schools is varied. School administrators may choose to accentuate any number of program components, including but not limited to academic skills, proactive behavioral intervention, vocational skills, social skills, survival skills, adaptive skills, outdoor adventure skills, and humanistic principles of personal empowerment (Brendtro & Brokenleg, 1993; Rosenberg et al., 1997). The most common elements of alternative school programs include academic, behavior change, and vocational components.

Many alternative day school programs narrowly define the specific type of behavioral disorders they can work with and accept only students with those problems. The intake criteria result in a group of students with relatively homogeneous problems. Research and follow-up has documented that these schools have more success in remediating problems than schools that accepted students with wide-ranging problems (Coleman & Webber, 2002).

The alternative day school, with specially trained staff, is often much better prepared to provide comprehensive services for the student with E/BD as compared to public school settings. Staff are specially trained to work toward a common goal with the students. There is much backup and support for staff. Students find consistency in behavior and classroom management strategies that is often lacking in the public school system.

Longitudinal studies have documented the success of alternative day schools. After discharge, student outcomes demonstrate improvements in specific emphasized academic and behavioral skills and more positive student experiences as compared with student outcomes in public school special education classrooms. Ironically, there was not a significant reduction in the level of delinquent behaviors of students at alternative day schools. In fact, some evidence suggests that combining predelinquent students with those already involved in the juvenile court system actually increased the rate of delinquent behaviors of students who attended alternative schools (Rosenberg et al., 1997).

Alternative Day School Models

Birchwood School (Buchweitz, 1993) in upstate New York is an example of an effective alternative day school. It is one part of a continuum of services in the school district for students with E/BD who have behavior problems that are too severe to be managed in self-contained classrooms in the local public schools. Students from outside the district may also attend on a tuition basis. Some students also attend who have recently been discharged from residential placements as a transition back to their local public school. In effect, numerous schools, agencies, and districts within a given eligibility area pool financial resources to fund this alternative day school. This procedure may be called an interdistrict, cooperative, or tuition-based program.

A significant statistic associated with Birchwood was the extremely low dropout rate of the high school students. Over a 10-year period, only 0.005% of the 400+ Birchwood students dropped out of school. Across the nation, dropout rates for students with E/BD range from 45 to 65% (Buchweitz, 1993; Rhode, Jenson, & Reavis, 1992).

Newhaus, Mowrey, and Glenwick (1982) described an alternative school model that combined strict behavior management strategies with environmental education experiences and comprehensive health services. This Cooperative Learning Program involved a local community mental health center, 10 cooperating school districts, and various institutions of higher education in Ohio. The agencies worked cooperatively to develop referral, treatment, and discharge procedures to serve over 80 students with severe E/BD. Discharge statistics indicated academic gains above expectations as well as successful transition back to school and/or work by a majority of the secondary students. This study serves as a relevant example of how agencies can pool resources to provide comprehensive services via the alternative day school model.

The alternative day school can provide effective educational programming for students with E/BD. Each school must have reasonable control over the intake process, establish a philosophical base to make program decisions, provide individualized behavioral and academic intervention strategies, and cooperate with other schools and agencies. Finally, alternative schools need a strong transition program. The school must make a plan to successfully reintegrate students who have met treatment goals into less restrictive settings.

Residential Schools

This comment was made by an incarcerated juvenile when asked whether a nurturing, caring environment would have a positive effect on reducing delinquency:

> Yes… because you can say, for instance, like say your mother is alcoholic; she's always abusing you, you have no father, you have nobody there to look out for you, and the next thing you know you're out there robbing. Your mother's in there on the couch—on the sofa—sleeping with a cigarette in her hand. Next thing you know, you come in late, she wakes up, she beats you with the belt, you're in your room crying, have marks all over your body, and it encourages you to go out there and say, I want to be put away. I don't want to be living with my mother because she abuses me. I want to be with somebody that cares about me. (Goldstein, 1990, p. 39)

Students with extreme levels of E/BD such as conduct disorder, rule-breaking and law-violating behavior, behavior that is dangerous to self and others, delinquency, and other antisocial behavioral disorders are most likely to receive services in a residential facility. They demonstrate maladaptive behavior that is too severe, intense, and highly resistant to intervention to allow placement in a less restrictive setting.

The student may be referred for a residential placement if problems persist over a long period and local educational or social service agency programs have not been able to remediate the problem satisfactorily. In some cases, if a precipitating episode such as a suicide attempt or other dangerous, out-of-control behavior occurs, residential programming may be recommended. Some residential treatment centers admit students who have a wide range of behavioral problems. In addition to E/BD, they might also accept students with overlapping conditions including but not limited to depression and suicidal tendencies, developmental delays, mental retardation, autism, Tourette syndrome, eating disorders, learning disabilities, other school-related problems, drug and alcohol addiction, sexual abuse victims or perpetrators, and other impairments. (Aman, Sarphare, & Burrow, 1995). There are high rates of ADHD and learning disabilities in students referred for residential treatment. Persistent noncompliance and aggression are common problems at the time of referral for residential treatment. Symptoms of ADHD are highly similar to those of conduct disorder (Warr-Leeper, Wright, & Mack, 1994). Environmental stressors, including poverty, divorce, negative peer influences, family alcohol problems, family drug problems, physical abuse, incest, and other types of sexual abuse, were found to be two to six times more likely to occur in the case histories of over 3,600 adolescents placed in residential facilities as compared with students not referred (Epstein, Cullinan, Quinn, & Cumblad, 1994; Minnesota State Department of Education, 1991). As with alternative day schools, residential treatment centers that limit the scope of student handicapping conditions are often much more successful in remediating problems as compared with centers that deal with a very diverse population with a wide variety of needs.

Treatment center schools often have the "luxury" of developing a treatment model to remediate specific problems of the student population served. Low student-to-staff ratios and consistent support for student problems often result in very positive relationships between educators and students. Educators in residential treatment centers often express feelings of having opportunities to make a very positive impact on students. Plus, treatment centers have a 24-hour captive audience. The students are not faced with a chaotic or aversive neighborhood or home situation every afternoon and evening. Many times the gains teachers make with students in day programs are erased daily during the afternoon and evening hours when these students live in less than desirable environments (Aylward, Schloss, Alper, & Green, 1995; Butler & Fontenelle, 1995; Cambone, 1994).

Students who have spent 9 months to a year or even longer in residential treatment may have felt comfortable or safe in that environment. For many students, the treatment center provided a supportive staff, a warm and safe bed, consistently good and plentiful food, an adequate supply of clothing, and a school where they experienced a level of success that they did not have in their home or school environment. Residential treatment centers often have smaller, on-grounds classrooms staffed by teachers who choose to work with students who have E/BD. There is often a great deal more positive and consistent care and concern demonstrated by staff members for the students than in any other school, community, or home situation they have experienced.

This comment was made by an incarcerated juvenile when asked whether treatment centers helped to reduce delinquency:

> To tell you the truth, I think placements now, the homes and stuff, I think they're treating kids too good. I think they have to treat them—treat them with respect, but like you're giving them too much, too much freedom and you know that's what they want. Like you're up there [at the treatment center] and you're happy. It's like a camp, like you're just going away to summer camp. They get to go off grounds like to movies. Even if their behavior is good, give them something else, but keep them on grounds. It's like they're living too good. (Goldstein, 1990, p. 113)

The basic goal of residential treatment is to reduce problem behaviors and teach socially appropriate replacement behaviors. This is a proactive strategy designed to help prepare students to be successful after discharge from the treatment center. The residential school may be the best environment in which to build a type of therapeutic rapport with students who have very severe problems. The focus of this section is on common elements of residential schools. Various types of residential facilities including treatment center schools, schools affiliated with hospitals or psychiatric institutions, privately funded schools, and schools for adjudicated delinquents are presented.

Residential School Models

There are many different types of residential schools. Each has specific defining characteristics and behavior change programs. Approximately 6% of students with E/BD spend some time in residential treatment (Turnbull et al., 2002). The index entitled *Caring for Kids with Special Needs: Residential Programs for Children and Adults* lists 817 separate facilities in the United States for students with E/BD. Many of the treatment centers include elaborate program descriptions that, in a very real sense, functioned as "advertisements" for their programs (Peterson's Guides, 1993).

All treatment center schools should have effective transition plans in place to facilitate discharge of students. Otherwise, students may feel abandoned after release from the treatment center. They may strongly feel the loss of positive support and the relationships they established in the treatment center. At discharge they are separated from the friendships made with teachers and peers at the treatment center. They lost not only the support of the educators, but also the 24-hour staff support services and the safety factors inherent in effective residential treatment settings. More likely than not, these students will end up as recidivism statistics. They will get into further serious trouble or criminal activities, resulting in their re-placement into some type of residential facility. Thus, residential treatment outcomes are further compromised. Effective transition plans are a critical component for all residential treatment facilities.

Arrowhead Ranch, Coal Valley, Illinois Arrowhead Ranch, Coal Valley, Illinois, is an excellent example of a treatment program with a well-developed transition plan. Transition services are provided for as long as necessary after a boy is discharged. Initially, boys are required to return on a frequently scheduled basis for follow-up services. Then transition is phased into a program that includes periodic weekends back at the ranch. The year-round school curriculum for boys with severe delinquency problems has a strong focus on academics as well as a vocational component. The program also emphasizes community service. Family counseling is provided throughout treatment.

Arrowhead has an extremely high success rate. One reason is that the school administrators carefully screen prospective students for the program. Only male students with average IQ and severe delinquency problems are included. Arrowhead is based on positive peer culture.

Positive peer culture (PPC) is an example of a program format that is used in residential settings. PPC stresses peer group accountability through cooperative group living and decision making (Ragan, 1993). The focus of PPC is on social skills, life skills, making good choices, and problem solving. Although students learn to take responsibility for improving their own behavior, intergroup cohesiveness is emphasized. Groups function as a unit. They live together, eat together, and go to school together. A major responsibility of the group is to help each other solve problems. This structure requires residents to become totally involved with the program as they learn to show care and concern for one another (Arrowhead Ranch Information Handbook, 1995; Moore, McCarty, & Jelin, 1994; Wasmund & Copas, 1994).

Father Flanagan's Girls and Boys Town Father Flanagan's Girls and Boys Town provides treatment and care to boys and girls and their families. The headquarters and its largest childcare facility are located in Omaha, Nebraska. Satellite campuses are located in communities across the country. The home was started in 1917 by Father Edward J. Flanagan. His goal was to provide a means for troubled young boys to get off the streets, away from crime, and to learn to lead successful lives. During the 1920s and 1930s, Father Flanagan changed the way Americans thought about troubled children as he engineered a program that provided an alternative form of education instead of prison for youth with serious problems. Services are provided regardless of race, color, creed, gender, national origin, or ability to pay. Direct care and treatment has been provided to more than 24,000 children and direct assistance given to 575,000 through the Girls and Boys Town National Hotline. Admission requests can be made by families, relatives, friends, teachers, clergy, juvenile courts, or social service agencies.

Children from age 9 to 19 are admitted. The average stay is about 20 months. Groups of six to eight youth (either girls or boys) live together with their teaching parents on campus in single-family dwellings. All of the teaching parents are formally trained and certified as professional family teachers. They can have their own children and pets in the teaching home. The family teachers have no other job. This is a 24 hours a day, seven days a week vocation. The group lives together as a family. The children are required to help with routine chores. Each home has a daily family conference where the children help make decisions related to the home and their individual responsibilities. This is not a "lockup" type of facility. There are no fences. The only children who are not admitted to Girls and Boys Town are those who do not want to live there. Homeless, runaway, or street children have been known to find their own way to Girls and Boys Town. No boy or girl coming in off the streets who wants assistance is ever turned away.

There are two schools at Girls and Boys Town: a middle school and a high school. The school is in session year-round with half-day classes during the summer months. The core curriculum is set by the state of Nebraska. In addition to the core curriculum, all students take keyboarding, computer literacy, employment skills, and home maintenance. Students may elect to take advanced placement courses for college as well as employment training courses. An extensive 4-H training program in horse and farm field operations is available. Most boys and girls work on the farm at some time during their stay as part of the employment skills program.

Intervention strategies used consistently in the home and at school to help the youth at Girls and Boys Town include (a) direct instruction of social skills; (b) consistent behavior management principles; (c) an absolute prohibition on aversive or physical punishment; (d) low student–staff ratios; (e) a token economy system based on daily points; (f) and extensive academic interventions with a heavy emphasis on transition and vocational opportunities. The Girls and Boys Town high school graduation rate of 84% is well above expectations for this population.

Girls and Boys Town is an incorporated village in the state of Nebraska. It consists of 76 family homes, a U.S. post office, a fire department, and a police department. It has Catholic and Protestant chapels, two schools, and a working farm. The village is run by a board of trustees (www.boystown.org; Jendryka, 1994).

Various components of the Girls and Boys Town programs have been implemented in the public schools. The Girls and Boys Town model has been replicated in both residential and community-based programs for students with behavioral disorders. Public schools are able to adapt and implement the program. Training is provided by Girls and Boys Town staff (www.boystown.org).

Outdoor Adventure Programming

Outdoor adventure programs have been specifically designed for students with E/BD and are often an important component of residential treatment programs. Outdoor adventure programs attempt to use aspects of the humanistic treatment philosophy, combined with wilderness experiences, to teach students with E/BD thinking and decision-making skills, group cooperation, self-reliance, and social skills. Students who participate in these activities are taught to appreciate mutual interdependency with peers and staff and oftentimes shed the traditional roles they play in their regular home and school settings. Although safety considerations are factored in, there is a certain element of risk involved in some of the activities, which lends

to its appeal to students with E/BD characteristics as well (Johnson, 1992). Outdoor adventure programs may be provided through alternative day and residential schools and private agencies.

Correctional Facilities

The following statement was made by an incarcerated juvenile who was asked what might be done to keep kids from getting into trouble:

> Well, my way would be to catch them, you know sentence them. Give them some time to let them know what it feels like to be locked up. And let them know what it feels like to be away from your family, your girlfriend, you know, people you love. (Goldstein, 1990, p. 112)

Definition

Juvenile corrections is comparable to the adult prison system but inmates there are under the age of 18 to 21 years. A juvenile who commits a crime is arrested, goes through the juvenile court system, and may then be labeled an adjudicated delinquent. Adolescents who are found guilty of criminal activities may be sentenced to a juvenile corrections institute for a specific period.

Difference Between Treatment and Corrections

Corrections is different from residential treatment in one major way. Residential treatment settings typically identify behavioral and academic goals and objectives that students must master before discharge from the facility. In corrections, inmates are sentenced to a certain amount of time in the facility to make restitution for the crime committed. Corrections facilities do have on-grounds schools, but not as much emphasis is placed on school attendance, school achievement, and behavior change as compared with residential treatment. Students who are placed in treatment usually receive more individualized, specific services designed to improve problem behaviors. Hence, students who spend time in residential treatment are likely to leave with increased academic skills and more improved, socially appropriate behaviors. However, students are discharged from corrections with pretty much the same set of problems behaviors they had at intake. Corrections education for juveniles is still in an emerging state.

The great majority of persons under 18 years are served in state facilities, not federal corrections facilities. No cookbook approach can be used to describe an effective corrections setting for adjudicated youth. Corrections situations may include training schools, ranches, camps, farms, group homes, residential facilities, foster care facilities, detention facilities, diagnostic facilities, and/or community supervision programs (Dedel, 1998).

Corrections and Special Education Services

Many juveniles in corrections centers have special education learning problems, primarily E/BD, learning disabilities, and mild mental retardation. To illustrate, LaCoste (1989) reported that 25% of the 247 juveniles scheduled to be sentenced had identified special education handicaps (compared to 10% of the general population). When the judge was provided with the a case history on each of those students, including information demonstrating the link between handicapping conditions and problematic behaviors, four of five students with handicaps were placed in a residential treatment center rather than in corrections. Corrections placements often do not provide the strong academic program necessary to meet the special educational needs of adjudicated delinquents.

Special education services do not appear to be the main priority once a student is incarcerated. To improve this situation, corrections agencies need to provide academic programs to meet the educational needs of juvenile inmates. Suggested services for an effective program include (a)

completing high school equivalency degree (GED) requirements, (b) vocational and life skills training, and (c) systematic transition strategies to return to the community as a more self-sufficient person. These services are typical of the plans in place of virtually all of the IEPs of students with severe E/BD in the other less restrictive educational settings.

Discharge and Transition from Corrections

Briscoe and Doyle (1996) emphasized the importance of coordinating transition services when students with E/BD were discharged from corrections. The three major "players," including the juvenile justice, mental health, and educational agencies, must provide strong transition services and a continuum of services based on education, socialization, and job training.

More punitive approaches toward juvenile crime seem to be gaining political favor in this country. It remains important to attempt to improve the intake, programming, and discharge procedures for incarcerated juveniles, particularly considering the high percentages of those individuals with identified handicaps. Dedel (1998) reported that a minimum of 77,000 juveniles were placed in corrections across the country. Further research is needed to gather information and identify the most optimal educational and rehabilitative programs available for incarcerated youth.

Boot Camps

At last, the drill instructors have quit yelling, and the 10 young members of B Company are seated rigidly at their desks in a classroom trailer. The boys rose this morning to a 5 o'clock bugle call, made their beds, showered, marched to breakfast, ran three miles, and mopped their barracks. Now, they watch intently as…. He asks the boys—all in their third week of detention in one of America's three federally funded juvenile boot camps—to describe the role discipline has played in their lives…. "Sir," says recruit Philip, a 15 year old convicted of criminal mischief, "All this waking up at

5 in the morning, marching, and push ups—that can't change our environment when we get back out, Sir." A consensus emerges: The boys just don't understand the link between the Environmental Youth Corps's daily rigors and their hoped for transformation into law-abiding teenagers. (Simons, 1994)

Militaristic approaches to incarceration date back to the 1800s. It was not until the early 1980s that using boot camps to deal with youthful offenders became popular. Boot camps were suggested as a means to punish the crime and reduce recidivism rates. It was thought the boot camp experience would teach improved behavior and inspire stronger moral behavior. The goal was to instill a sense of strong self-discipline and respect for authority in each recruit (Zhang, 1998). The boot camp approach is gaining popularity in the private sector. As many as 2,000 private agencies are currently embracing the boot camp mind-set to deal with recalcitrant teenagers at their parents' request. Some focus on areas such as counteracting drug or alcohol abuse, improving behavioral compliance, and rule-following behavior. There are some that attempt to induce lifestyle changes, such as forcing homosexual children back to heterosexuality (Cohen, 1998).

However, a review of such programs indicates that there are no quick and easy answers to the issue of dealing with a population of individuals who have such complex needs. The lack of solid research connecting boot camp programs to positive outcomes, along with a lack of consistent strategies in examining treatment effects, appears to make the boot camp approach less successful in changing behavior than more traditional forms of juvenile corrections (Zhang, 1998). Currently, the dwindling status of boot camps indicates that this is becoming more and more evident.

There do seem to be some positive guidelines emerging as to how to provide a more comprehensive array of treatment services to meet the needs of incarcerated youth in boot camps. Sharp (1995) strongly suggests that numerous points were necessary for a boot camp to accomplish specific goals:

- Communicating a mission statement based on achievable goals
- Systematically evaluating program goals
- Determining key program components to meet treatment goals
- Reinforcing and acknowledging mastery of program goals
- Designing an effective transition/aftercare treatment program
- Limiting participation to specific E/BD
- Proper training/supervision/evaluation of program staff
- Community collaboration and mentorship

Boot camp programs should have more emphasis on rehabilitation and less emphasis on punishment for youth with severe E/BD who are sentenced for short (or long) periods. If students who commit crimes are to be placed in these facilities, there must be clear-cut goals and objectives stating what academic and behavioral skills the students will have gained upon discharge from the facility. In addition, follow-up must done for successful transition and student outcome following completion of the boot camp program.

Implications for Working with Youth and Adolescents

There is no doubt that educators are being asked to teach an increasingly difficult population of students. Some teachers will choose to educate students with E/BD in settings outside the public school classroom. Administrators and teachers are charged with the responsibility of making those alternative settings a truly educational placement, whether a day school, a residential treatment center, or corrections.

Alternative educational settings that are simply holding tanks or glorified baby-sitting situations hinder the student's future ability to be a productive member of society. The youth of this country must be well prepared to be productive members of society.

Educators must take the lead in providing relevant and motivating curricula that will prepare the students for high school graduation. It is critically important that all students with E/BD be well prepared to go on to higher education, further training, or a role in the adult workforce. Effective programming, transition, and discharge services must be in place for every alternative education setting. Otherwise, the United States may end up with "safe schools" at the cost of safe communities and a safe nation.

References

Aman, M., Sarphare, G., & Burrow, W. H. (1995). Psychotropic drugs in group homes: Prevalence in relation to demographic/psychiatric variables, *American Journal on Mental Retardation* 99(5), 500–509.

Arnold, J. B., & Szeptycki, L. F. (1994). Handling discipline of disabled pupils within the law. *The School Administrator*, 51, 36–38.

Arrowhead Ranch Information Handbook. (1995). *Information handbook: Helping troubled boys become responsible men.* (Available from Arrowhead Ranch, 12200 104th Street, Coal Valley, IL 61240. Phone: 309-799-7044.)

Aylward, A., Schloss, P., Alper, S., & Green, C. (1995). Improving direct-care staff consistency in a residential treatment program through the use of self-recording and feedback. *International Journal of Disability, Development and Education*, 43, 43–53.

Bader, B. D. (1997). Schools, discipline, and students with disability: The AFT responds. Paper presented at the 75th Annual Convention of the Council for Exceptional Children, Salt Lake City, UT. (ERIC Document Reproduction Service No. 408 737, p. 21.)

Baker, H., & Traphagen, V. (1935). *The diagnosis and treatment of behavior-problem children.* New York: Macmillan.

Berrick, J., & Duerr, M. (1996). Maintaining positive school relationships: The role of the social worker vis-a-vis full service schools. *Social Work in Education*, 18, 53–57.

Billings, L., & Wolford, B. (1996). Promoting the successful transition of Kentucky's state agency children. *Preventing School Failure*, 40, 77–81.

Boys Town Group Home/Residential Services. (1999). *Effectively meeting the needs of the increasing number of youth in out-of-home placements.* Retrieved from www.boystown.org

Boys Town: Questions and answers. (Brochure available from Father Flanagan's Boy's Home, Boys Town, NE, 68010. Phone: 402-498-1111.)

Braaten, S., Kauffman, J. M., Braaten, B., Poslsgrove, L., & Nelson, C. (1988). The regular education initiative, Patent medicine for behavioral disorders. *Exceptional Children*, 55, 21–27.

Brendtro, L., & Brokenleg, M. (1993). Beyond the curriculum of control. *Journal of Emotional and Behavioral Problems*, 1, 5–11.

Briscoe, R., & Doyle, J. (1996). Aftercare services in juvenile justice: Approaches for providing services for high-risk youth. *Preventing School Failure*, 40, 73–76.

Buchweitz, S. (1993). Birchwood: An exemplary educational program for children with emotional disabilities. *Social Work in Education*, 15, 241–246.

Butler, S., & Fontenelle, S. (1995). Cognitive-behavioral group therapy: Applications with adolescents who are cognitively impaired and sexually acting out. *Journal for Specialists in Group Work*, 20, 121–127.

Cambone, J. (1994). *Teaching troubled children: A case study in effective educational practice.* New York: Teachers College Press.

Carlson, E., & Parshall, L. (1996). Academic, social, and behavioral adjustment for students declassified from special education. *Exceptional Children*, 63, 89–100.

Carr, V. (1995). *The Garrison Model: An effective program for managing the behaviors of students with behavioral disorders.* Paper presented at the Annual International Convention of the Council for Exceptional Children, Indianapolis, IN. (ERIC Document Reproduction Service No. 384–164, p. 14.)

CEC Today. (1996). *States act to include students with disabilities in standards.* (Vol. 3, 1–9). Reston, Virginia.

CEC Today. (1997). *Strategies to meet IDEA 1997's discipline requirements.* (Vol. 4, 1–15). Reston, Virginia.

CEC Today. (1998). *Alternative schools—Hope or heartache?* (Vol. 5, 1–15). Reston, Virginia.

Cohen, A. (1998). Is this a camp or jail? *Time*, 151, 56–57.

Coleman, M. C., & Webber, J. (2002). *Emotional and behavioral disorders: Theory and practice* (4th ed.). Needham Heights, MA: Allyn & Bacon.

Council for Children with Behavior Disorders & Council of Administrators of Special Education, Inc. (1995). A *Joint Statement on Violence in the Schools.* Issue Paper. Reston, Virginia. (ERIC Document Reproduction Service No. 386–878, p. 4.)

Council on Children at Risk. (1985). Behavior day treatment program training manual. Unpublished Manual. Moline, IL: Council on Children at Risk.

Dedel, K. (1998). National profile of the organization of state juvenile corrections systems. *Crime & Delinquency, 44*, 507–525.

Doyle, W. (1980s). *Classroom management.* West Lafayette, IN: Kappa Delta Pi.

Dryfoos, J. G. (1993). *Full-service schools: A revolution in health and social services for children, youth, and families.* San Francisco: Jossey-Bass.

Eber, L., Nelson, M., & Miles, P. (1997). School-based wraparound for students with emotional and behavioral challenges. *Exceptional Children, 63*, 539–555.

Epstein, M., Cullinan, D., Quinn, K., & Cumblad, C. (1994). Characteristics of children with emotional and behavioral disorders in community-based programs designed to prevent placement in residential facilities. *Journal of Emotional and Behavioral Disorders, 2*, 51–57.

Forness, S., Kavale, K., King, B., & Kasari, C. (1994). Simple versus complex conduct disorders: Identification and phenomenology. *Behavioral Disorders, 19*, 306–312.

Frey, L., & Lane, C. (1995). *Promoting home school inclusion through a continuum of services.* Paper presented at the Annual International Convention of the Council for Exceptional Children, Indianapolis, IN. (ERIC Document Reproduction Service No. 383–144.)

Fuchs, D., Fuchs, L., Fernstrom, P., & Hohn, M. (1991). Toward a responsible reintegration of behaviorally disordered students. *Behavioral Disorders, 16*, 133–147.

Gelfand, D. M., Jenson, W. R., & Drew, C. J. (1988). *Understanding child behavior disorders* (2nd ed.). Fort Worth, TX: Holt, Rinehart, and Winston.

Glassberg, L. (1994). Students with behavioral disorders: Determinants of placement outcomes. *Behavioral Disorders, 19*, 181–191.

Goldstein, A. P. (1990). *Delinquents on delinquency.* Champaign, IL: Research Press.

Gronna, S., Jenkins, A., & Chin-Chance, S. (1998). Who are we assessing? Determining state-wide participation rates for students with disabilities. *Exceptional Children, 64*, 407–418.

Hardman, M. L., Drew, C. J., Egan, M. W., & Wolf, B. (1993). *Human exceptionality: Society, school, and family.* Needham Heights, MA: Allyn & Bacon.

Healy, D. (1992). *A qualitative analysis of the strategies employed by intermediate elementary teachers instructing mainstreamed exceptional children* (pp. 263–264). Unpublished doctoral dissertation, University of Iowa, Iowa City.

Healy, W. (1915). *The individual delinquent.* Boston: Little, Brown.

Heward, W. L. (2003). *Exceptional children: An introduction to special education* (7th ed.). Upper Saddle River, NJ: Merrill/Prentice Hall.

Hewett, F. (1967). Educational engineering with emotionally disturbed children. *Exceptional Children, 33*, 459–467.

Hobbs, N. (1966). Helping disturbed children: Psychological and ecological strategies. *American Psychologist, 21*, 1105–1115.

Individuals with Disabilities Education Act. (1986). 20 U.S.C. § 1412.

Individuals with Disabilities Education Act Amendments of 1997, Pub. L. No. 105-95, 105th Congress.

Jendryka, B. (1994). Flanagan's Island. *Policy Review, 69*, 44–51.

Jensen, M. M., & Yerington, P. C. (1997). *Gangs: Straight talk, straight up.* Longmont, CO: Sopris West.

Johnson, J. (1992). Adventure therapy: The ropes-wilderness connection. *Therapeutic Recreation Journal, 26*, 17–26.

Jones, V. (1996). In the face of predictable crises: Developing a comprehensive treatment plan for students with emotional or behavioral disorders. *Teaching Exceptional Children, 29*, 54–59.

Karlin, S., & Harnish, D. (1995). *An evaluation: Assessment of the crossroads alternative schools in Georgia.* Atlanta, GA: Georgia State Department of Education, Office of Research, Evaluation, and Assessment. (ERIC Document Reproduction Service No. 393-239 p. 60.)

Katsiyannis, A., & Maag, J. (1998). Disciplining students with disabilities: Issues and considerations for implementing IDEA '97. *Behavioral Disorders, 23*, 276–289.

Kauffman, J. (1989). The regular education initiative as Reagan–Bush education policy: A trickle-down theory of education of the hard to teach. *Journal of Special Education, 23*, 256–278.

Kauffman, J. (1997). *Characteristics of emotional and behavioral disorders of children and youths* (6th ed.). Upper Saddle River, NJ: Merrill/Prentice Hall.

Kauffman, J. (2001). *Characteristics of emotional and behavioral disorders of children and youths* (7th ed.). Upper Saddle River, NJ: Merrill/Prentice Hall.

Kirk, S. A., Gallagher, J. J., & Anastasiow, N. J. (2003). *Educating exceptional children* (10th ed.). Boston: Houghton Mifflin.

Knitzer, J., Steinberg, Z., & Fleisch, F. (1990). *At the schoolhouse door: An examination of the programs and policies for* children with behavioral and emotional problems. New York: Bank Street College of Education.

LaCoste, L. (1989). Implementation of alternative sentencing for the handicapped child and adolescent through cooperative judiciary training. Fd. D. Practicum, Ft. Lauderdale, FL: Nova Southeastern University. (ERIC Document Reproduction Service No. ED 316-970, p. 67.)

Maag, J., & Katsiyannis, A. (1998). Challenges facing successful transition for youths with E/BD. Behavioral Disorders, 23, 209–221.

Mank, D., Cioffi, A., & Yovanoff, P. (1998). Employment outcomes for people with severe disabilities: Opportunities for improvement. Mental Retardation, 36, 205–216.

Martin, K., Lloyd, J., Kauffman, J., & Coyne, M. (1995). Teachers' perceptions of educational placement decisions for pupils with emotional or behavioral disorders. Behavioral Disorders, 20, 106–117.

Mattison, R., Spitznagel, E., & Felix, B. (1997s). Enrollment predictors of the special education outcome for students with SED. Behavioral Disorders, 23, 243–256.

Meadows, N., Neel, R., Scott, C., Parker, G. (1994). Academic performance, social competence, and mainstream accommodation: A look at mainstreamed and nonmainstreamed students with serious behavior disorders. Behavioral Disorders, 19, 170–180.

Minnesota State Department of Education. (1991). A report on special populations. Alternate schools area learning centers, correction/detention centers, residential treatment centers. (Minnesota Student Survey). (ERIC Document Reproduction Service No. 376-097 p. 82.)

Moore, G., McCarty, A., & Jelin, G. (1994). Children's village: A safe haven for children of stress and violence. Project Proposal. (ERIC Document Reproduction Service No. 378-770, p. 55.)

Newhaus, S., Mowrey, J., & Glenwick, D. (1982). The cooperative learning program: Implementing an ecological approach to the development of alternative psychoeducational programs. Journal of Clinical Child Psychology, 11, 151–156.

Nichols, P. (1992). The curriculum of control: Twelve reasons for it, some arguments against it. Beyond Behavior, 3, 5–11.

Osborne, A., & Dimatta, P. (1994). The IDEA's least restrictive environment mandate: Legal implications. Exceptional Children, 61, 6–14.

Osborne, J., & Byrnes, D. (1990). Identifying gifted and talented students in an alternative learning center. Gifted Child Quarterly, 34, 143–146.

Peterson's Guides. (1993). Caring for kids with special needs: Residential programs for children and adults. Princeton, NJ: Author.

Ragan, P. (1993). Cooperative learning can work in residential care settings. Teaching Exceptional Children, 25, 48–51.

Rhode, G., Jenson, W. R., & Reavis, H. K. (1992). The tough kid book. Longmont, CO: Sopris West.

Rockwell, S., & Guetzloe, E. (1996). Group development for students with emotional/behavioral disorders. Teaching Exceptional Children, 29, 38–43.

Rosenberg, M. S., Wilson, R., Maheady, L., & Sindelar, P. T. (1997). Educating students with behavior disorders (2nd ed.). Needham Heights, MA: Allyn & Bacon.

Sack, J. (1999). Florida district criticized for moving students out of special centers. Education Week, 28, 6.

Scruggs, T., & Mastropieri, M. (1996). Teacher perceptions of mainstreaming/inclusion, 1958–1995: A research synthesis. Exceptional Children, 63, 59–74.

Sharp, D. (1995). Correctional options boot camps—punishment and treatment. Corrections Today, 57 (unpaginated special insert).

Simons, J. (1994). A wayward boys' "shock incarceration" camp. U.S. News and World Report, 116, 20.

Snell, M. (1991). Schools are for all kids: The importance of integration for students with severe disabilities and their peers. In J. Lloyd, N. Singh, & A. Repp (Eds.), The regular education initiative: Alternative perspectives on concepts, issues, and models (pp. 133–148). Sycamore, IL: Sycamore Publishing.

Turnbull, R., Turnbull, A., Shank, M., Smith, S., & Leal, D. (2002). Exceptional lives: Special education in today's schools. Upper Saddle River, NJ: Merrill/Prentice Hall.

U.S. Department of Education. (1993). Data analysis systems (DANS). Washington, DC: Office of Special Education Programs.

Villa, R. (1996). Creating inclusive schools and classrooms practical strategies and ideas (Grades K–12): A resource handbook. Bellevue, WA: Bureau of Education and Research.

Wagner, M. (1995). Outcomes for youths with serious emotional disturbance in secondary school and early adulthood. The Future of Children, 5, 90–112.

Warr-Leeper, G., Wright, N., & Mack, A. (1994). Language disabilities of antisocial boys in residential treatment. Behavioral Disorders, 19, 159–169.

Wasmund, W., & Copas, R. (1994). Problem youths or problem solvers? Building resilience through peer helping. Journal of Emotional and Behavioral Problems, 3, 50–52.

Weinberg, L., & Weinberg, C. (1990). Seriously emotionally disturbed or socially maladjusted? A critique of interpretations. *Behavioral Disorders, 15,* 149–158.

Wolfe, T. (1929). *Look Homeward, Angel.* New York: Random House.

Yell, M. (1998). *The law and special education.* Upper Saddle River, NJ: Merrill/Prentice Hall.

Zhang, S. (1998). In search of hopeful glimpses: A critique of research strategies in current boot camp evaluations. *Crime & Delinquency, 44,* 314–344.

Zutter, T. (1996). Serving students in a co-facility: A needed alternative to full inclusion. *Canadian Journal of Special Education, 11,* 51–67.

2
SOCIAL, CULTURAL, AND ENVIRONMENTAL ISSUES

4 PRENATAL DRUG AND ALCOHOL EXPOSURE

After completing the chapter, the reader will be able to identify:

- The impact of prenatal drug and alcohol exposure on children.
- Prevalence statistics of prenatal drug and alcohol exposure on children.
- Characteristics of children with prenatal drug and alcohol exposure.
- Characteristics of fetal alcohol syndrome and fetal alcohol effects.
- Lifelong cognitive, behavioral, and economic impacts of prenatal drug and alcohol exposure on children.
- Best practices for effective home and school management of cognitive and behavioral disabilities associated with prenatal drug and alcohol exposure on children.
- Implications for educators, parents, and other professionals who work with youth and adolescents.

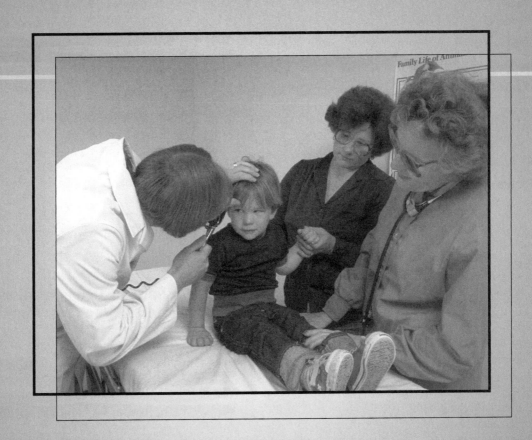

Introduction

Always bear in mind that they may not know how to behave. They must be taught—by you—to do nearly everything. (Odom-Winn & Dunagan, 1991, p. 95)

It took over 8 months for two highly experienced teachers (Odom-Winn & Dunagan, 1991) to teach six children aged 8 to 10 years a skill most people take for granted. The skill was to "stop" at the stop sign before crossing the street. The small group of children finally mastered the skill of "stopping" at the sign due to the teacher's persistence, repetition, blood, sweat, and tears! Since then, not one person has been able to successfully teach those children the concept of "safe to go." All of the children in this group had been prenatally exposed to drugs or alcohol.

Think about that! The language and vocabulary concepts they would have to understand before learning "go" include the words "don't," "go," "until," "road," and "clear." The children would also need to conceptualize the abstract meaning of the actions "go" and "is coming." After those tasks were accomplished, these children would have to be taught to concretely recognize every color car; then move to trucks, buses, eighteen-wheelers, motorcycles, bicycles, mopeds, vans, trash trucks, and every other vehicle on the road!

The amount of time necessary to teach this one safety concept is almost unimaginable. The difficulty and frustration inherent in teaching prenatally drug-exposed children lies in their inability to think abstractly. Their cognitive processing skills are severely limited. They usually perceive only the most concrete ideas. Successful teachers of prenatally exposed children must be well versed in consistent proactive and positively oriented behavior management techniques. The classroom must be structured yet flexible and responsive to the individual and unique needs of each child.

Treat All Students as Individuals

It is important for educators and other professionals who work with youth and adolescents not to stereotype students who were prenatally exposed to drugs. This might lead to misconceptions about a student's actual abilities and potential. A child who was prenatally exposed may be at risk for certain learning and behavioral disorders, and it is good to be on the lookout for those things. However, many other children are also susceptible to those very same problems at school, at home, and in the community. Children who suffer from abuse and neglect, who have parents who abuse drugs and alcohol, who witness violence, or who live in poverty may be at risk for the very same type of problems as children who were prenatally exposed (Barth, 1991). For these reasons, all students must be treated as individuals in the classroom.

No Amount of Drugs or Alcohol Is Safe for a Pregnant Woman

Medical researchers state that *no* amount of alcohol or illegal drug is safe for a fetus. However, current research results cannot articulate with any certainty exactly what impact maternal drug use of any amount will have on the developing fetus. Systematic research must continue in medical and educational domains to learn more about the lifelong behavioral, intellectual, social, and physiological impact of prenatal drug and alcohol exposure and about best methods for educating children who are innocent victims of this incurable and lifelong affliction.

For the purposes of this chapter, the term *prenatal drug exposure* relates to the use of both illegal drugs and alcohol by a woman who is pregnant. The concepts covered in this chapter explore

(a) background information on prenatal drug and alcohol exposure; (b) what behavioral, emotional, and cognitive characteristics are common to prenatally exposed children; and (c) effective interventions for teachers, parents, professionals, and other caregivers who work with prenatally exposed children.

Prenatal Drug Exposure Is a Complicated Problem

Drug and alcohol abuse is not a new or recent phenomenon. Prenatal drug exposure knows no economic, cultural, geographic, or social boundaries. This is not a unique problem, as some think, just for the poor, the ignorant, or the uneducated. Children prenatally exposed to drugs and alcohol come from all strata of society. The lifelong challenges the victims of prenatal drug exposure face will vary significantly from mild to moderate to severe. The severity of the symptoms and negative impact on the child depends on how much, how frequently, and at what points in fetal development the pregnant woman abused drugs and/or alcohol. The exact outcome for the child of any drug abuse during pregnancy is difficult for researchers to specify. Although maternal drug abuse has been a longtime concern, medical research on prenatal and postnatal effects and educational research on best educational practices are in an emerging state. Three major complicating factors make it difficult to study the consequences of prenatal exposure to drugs and alcohol on children.

Complicating Research Factors

First, pregnant women cannot be used as subjects for scientific studies. Moral ethics of society vehemently preclude the use of illegal drugs or alcohol by pregnant women simply to allow researchers to study the effects of those substances on children.

Second, the use of illegal drugs and alcohol abuse carry a very negative stigma. Over the ages, women have been verbally warned by medical personnel and warnings have appeared in print about the potential consequences for children when pregnant women use drugs and alcohol. Most women are secretive and will not admit to using drugs or drinking alcohol while pregnant. Unless there is firsthand documentation or direct observation of substance abuse, it may be difficult to diagnose later difficulties. Burgess and Streissguth (1992) relate a quote from one mother who described her own experience with the secrecy and denial associated with drinking during pregnancy:

> My 15-year-old daughter has fetal alcohol syndrome (FAS) because I drank heavily while I was pregnant with her. She was born 2 1/2 months early and weighed 2 pounds 8 ounces. Her medical records include a multitude of tests, but there was no mention of my drinking habits. Who would have asked a middle-class professional woman, who appeared to be successfully moving through the world, if she had a drinking problem? (p. 24)

The third and final complicating factor relates to the diversity of problems experienced later in life by children who were prenatally exposed. A specific set of observable characteristics or behavioral problems cannot be predicted that would be consistent from one prenatally exposed child to another. At birth, each infant is affected differently based on biological sensitivity and time during fetal development that the drug or alcohol ingestion occurred.

As children grow up, the impact of prenatal drug exposure will differ according to inherited genetics, personal biology, educational opportunities, and the home and family environment in which each lives. For example, two children in one household may both be exposed to chickenpox. One child may run the course of the illness without complications while the other develops much more serious symptoms and complications and ultimately requires medical attention. Researchers have reported differences in effects of prenatal drug and alcohol exposure that can be explained only by individual biological differences.

Multidrug Use

An additional problem for researchers is the fact that individuals with addictions are frequently *multidrug* users. Multidrug use means that one individual uses a variety of drugs and possibly alcohol. For example, crack cocaine is seldom used alone. Other illegal substances such as alcohol, marijuana, and tranquilizers are commonly abused by crack cocaine addicts (Lesar, 1992). MacDonald (1992) reported results from a study completed in New York. Findings indicated that addicts often had an illegal drug of choice, but also used a variety of drugs, tobacco, and alcohol in whatever combination was available.

It is difficult for medical personnel or researchers to separate the effects of different drugs. The possible combination of substances abused and the potential *synergistic* effects of various drug and alcohol combinations compound the difficulty of identifying the explicit dangers for pregnant women and possible outcomes for children who were prenatally exposed to drugs. Synergistic means that taking a combination of drugs and/or alcohol can have a different or unpredictable effect on an individual than the sum of their effects would have been if taken independently. Multidrug use can produce unique effects depending on combinations and amounts used.

Prenatal Effects

Prenatal drug and alcohol exposure on the fetus and postnatal effects on the infant, developing child, adolescent, and adult have been highly studied (Burgess & Streissguth, 1992; Chasnoff, 1989; Chasnoff et al., 1998; Cone-Wesson & Wu, 1992;

Lesar, 1992; MacDonald, 1992; Rivers & Hedrick, 1992). The real difficulty in understanding the prenatal effects of exposure to illegal drugs is that approximately two thirds of drug abusers use multiple substances (MacDonald, 1992). As one reads research reports about the effects of illegal drug exposure on human subjects, it is important to keep in mind that the physiological and cognitive results probably are based on actual exposure to more than one drug. In addition, many illegal drugs are not pure. Most are cut with a variety of additives from baking soda to talcum powder to cleanser to drain cleaner. Researchers cannot always identify what hidden substances were in drugs taken by an addict. Since it is so difficult to determine how many, what amount, or in what combination additives were included in illegal drugs, much is likely to remain a mystery in terms of exactly what effects can be expected. Research at this point suggests that prenatal exposure during early gestation may produce the most negative outcomes for children (Hallahan & Kauffman, 2003). This is because the majority of central nervous system (CNS) and neurological development takes place during the first trimester of pregnancy.

Quality of Life

The impact of a pregnant woman's pattern of substance abuse is further complicated and compounded by how significantly her quality of life was altered by drug and/or alcohol use. The fetus is affected by the mother's nutrition, general health, stress level, and quality of prenatal care. The following parameters influence the severity of effects on both the mother and the unborn child:

- Maternal health and nutrition before and during pregnancy
- Access to and quality of prenatal care
- Ability to continue normal daily routine with family, job, and friends while pregnant
- Exposure to stress and emotional or physical violence in the environment while pregnant

- Emotional maturity and ability to care for the newborn infant

Responses to the preceding points will vary widely for each pregnant woman. Data gathered on the parameters may allow predictions as to the severity of physical, developmental, behavioral, and academic problems experienced by children prenatally exposed to drugs and alcohol.

Demographic Changes in Drug Abuse

It is commonly known that drug abuse is not a new bad habit for humankind. In the past, it was customary to think of drug abuse as a problem of unemployed, uneducated, derelict-type males. Until the epidemic rise in street sales of crack cocaine in the 1980s, drug addiction primarily affected single males. Dramatic shifts in the demographics of drug addiction have taken place in recent years, particularly since crack cocaine became easy to obtain.

Demographic changes have been observed in a number of categories (see Table 4–1). First, the gender of addicts has changed. It is well known that there were female substance abusers in the past. Currently, researchers report a rise in the number of female drug abusers. As a result of the widespread availability, relatively low cost, and ease of use, the number of female users has increased.

Second, Haymes Rice, director of Howard University Hospital in Washington, D.C., noted that "Where the current problem differs from the historical problem is the reach of drug abuse across multiple generations; we're seeing 29- to 35-year-old grandmothers who are themselves drug abusers ... in the mothers themselves, there is increasing use and abuse of drugs during their pregnancy and right up to the date of delivery in some cases" (U.S. Congress, House Select Committee on Children, Youth, and Families, 1989, p. 43).

The third demographic change in drug abuse concerns the age of identified addicts. Drug abuse has shifted to an ever-younger age group. The 2000 Monitoring the Future Study reported that 54% of high school seniors, 45.6% of tenth graders, and 26.8% of eighth graders concede to using illicit drugs. The good news about these statistics is that there has been a slight reduction at all three grade levels for each of the past 4 years.

The fourth change relates to the speed at which illegal drugs become an addiction for individuals. The addictive behavior patterns are forming much more quickly than with previous drugs, especially with crack cocaine. This is attributed mainly to the easy availability of crack cocaine on the street. Because of the intense high experienced by crack users, it is thought to be almost immediately addictive.

The final demographic change is the fact that popular illegal drugs such as marijuana and crack are relatively inexpensive. A lot more people can easily buy these drugs as compared to buying any other illicit drug in the past. An individual can make a purchase with as little as three dollars for a rock of crack or a vial of cocaine (U.S. Department of Health and Human Services, 1997). The low cost means school-age students often become the buyers as well as the drug sellers, making crack readily available to teenagers and others. Even though it is an

TABLE 4–1 Demographic Changes in Drug Abuse

Change #1	Increase in number of female drug abusers
Change #2	Drug abuse patterns are becoming generational
Change #3	Drug addiction is occurring at younger ages
Change #4	Drugs are more quickly addictive
Change #5	Popular drugs are relatively inexpensive, widely available, and easy to use

Note. From Developmental Problems of Drug-Exposed Infants, by S. Lesar, 1992, San Diego, CA: Singular.

inexpensive drug, crack addiction forms quickly, the body becomes tolerant, and the individual needs an ever-increasing supply to achieve the same high. Ultimately, the addict's life begins to revolve around obtaining and using the drugs. At that point, drug abuse can become an incredibly expensive habit.

As a result of these demographic changes, society will experience a dramatic surge in the human and financial resources needed to serve children who have been prenatally drug-exposed. The Robert Wood Johnson Foundation (National Institute on Drug Abuse [NIDA] InfoFacts, 1998) estimated the total economic cost of drug abuse at $67 billion in 1990, up $23 billion from 1985. The figures do not include the cost to society from alcohol abuse. Alcohol abuse costs would add an estimated $99 billion to the total amount figured by the Robert Wood Johnson study.

Prevalence of Drug Abuse Among Pregnant Women

One substance-exposed infant is born every 90 seconds. (Schipper, 1991)

There are conflicting statistics reported on the number of prenatally exposed infants born annually in the United States. Despite all the medical attention directed to "crack babies," marijuana remains the most widely used illicit drug. Estimates are that from 3 to 20% of babies are born prenatally exposed to marijuana (Gomby & Shiono, 1991; MacGregor, 1990). Prenatal exposure to alcohol is much higher than exposure to any of the illegal drugs (Gomby & Shiono, 1991). Estimates indicate that more than 2.6 million babies with prenatal exposure to alcohol are born each year, which translates to approximately 2 per every 1,000 live births in the United States. NIDA estimated that 5 to 6 million women of childbearing age were illicit drug users. NIDA also reports that

as many as 60% of females drink alcohol while pregnant (MacDonald, 1992). Researchers report that anywhere from 11 to 25% of pregnant women abuse chemical substances during pregnancy (MacDonald, 1992). Survey results gathered by Lesar (1992) reported the following statistics related to pregnancy and substance abuse:

- Houston, TX: Rate of prenatal exposure increased from 2% in 1980 to more than 89% in 1989
- San Francisco, CA: Substance abuse affected 16% of babies in 1988
- Philadelphia, PA: Rate of prenatal exposure increased from 4% in 1987 to more than 15% in 1988
- Fort Lauderdale, FL: 20% of infants born in 1987 tested positive for cocaine
- California: 40 babies a month were born drug-addicted in suburban areas in 1989

In 1994, NIDA estimated that 221,000 children were prenatally exposed to drugs annually; approximately 45,000 of them probably were exposed to cocaine (Chasnoff et al., 1998). Elizabeth Graham, New York Assistant Health Commissioner, stated that cocaine abuse had increased 300% between 1976 and 1986 and increased another 340% from 1989 to 1990 (Rist, 1990).

Additional Risks of Addiction for Pregnant Women

The dangers inherent in drug addiction affect both the mother and the developing fetus. First, there are significant physiological and emotional dangers of substance abuse for the pregnant female. Second, the risks for exposure to sexually transmitted diseases, including HIV and AIDS, tuberculosis, and hepatitis B, are dramatically increased. In addition, the search for a supply of drugs may place a woman at risk for physical and emotional violence in social situations and on the streets (Little, Snell, Gilstrap, & Johnson, 1990; MacDonald, 1992). All of these dangers negatively impact the child before and after birth.

Effects of Drug Addiction on Mother and Fetus

Illegal drug use and alcohol consumption often result in elevated body temperature, very rapid heart rate (*tachycardia*), and increased blood pressure. *Vascular constriction* can have a major negative effect on the developing fetus. Vascular constriction means the diameter of blood veins and arteries becomes smaller or narrower. The combination of increased blood pressure and vascular constriction can be dangerous and sometimes fatal to the developing fetus. The result is a decrease in the blood flow to the mother's uterus and ultimately a decrease in oxygen to the fetus (Chasnoff et al., 1998; Hallahan & Kauffman, 2003). Lack of oxygen to the fetus may cause fetal stroke, seizure, brain damage, and spontaneous abortion.

Vascular constriction and the sharp rise in blood pressure that follows may lead to a condition called *abruptio placentae,* in which the placenta pulls away from the uterine wall. This situation can cause spontaneous abortions among drug and alcohol users. In addition, the disruption in the placenta may cause a loss of blood and oxygen flow to the fetus, a potentially life-threatening or life-altering occurrence.

An ordinary pregnancy for a woman in good health places considerable stress on her body. The additional burden of drug abuse on the mother produces a life-threatening environment for the fetus. An explanation of how an illicit drug or alcohol affects the fetus follows.

After the drug or alcohol is ingested and absorbed into the bloodstream, it is metabolized in the kidneys. Because the pregnant woman's kidneys are working for two, it takes longer for her system to become free of the drug or alcohol.

The fetus is exposed to the drug as it crosses the placenta. The fetus has a limited ability to metabolize and eliminate whatever the mother takes in. Consequently, the tiny fetus maintains dangerous and possibly toxic levels of drugs and/or alcohol for hours or days longer than the mother does. A drug that the mother may not feel after half an hour and which is clinically undetectable (in the mother) after a day may affect the fetus for hours or days afterward (Mastrogriannis, Decavales, Verma, & Tejani, 1990).

The exact quantity and quality of effect on fetal development are not known. If the mother is taking drugs or drinking alcohol regularly, her fetus probably is receiving overlapping doses of the drug. The fetus not only is attempting to metabolize the most recently used drug but also is still dealing with the effects of the drug the mother used yesterday. The fetus, in effect, may be exposed to a much larger concentration of the drug at one time than the mother is.

The potential lifelong fetal effects of prenatal drug exposure vary depending on the time frame of specific physiological development in the fetus. Whatever organ or neurological system is developing at the time of drug and/or alcohol exposure may be damaged. Researchers report that they cannot say for sure how severe the damage will be, but they are 100% certain that drug ingestion will adversely affect prenatal development to some degree.

Postnatal Effects on Drug-Exposed Infants

Research suggests that at birth some infants prenatally exposed to illegal drugs go through a withdrawal period showing symptoms of hypersensitivity to light, sound, touch, or any other change in the environment (Parietti, 1992). The hypersensitive behavior is demonstrated through chronic crying, gaze aversion of the infant with the adult caregiver, and resistance to cuddling or holding. A major problem associated with these maladaptive infant behaviors is that the bonding process with caregivers is often delayed or nonexistent.

One of the clusters of postnatal abnormal behavior observed in some drug-exposed infants is called *difficulty in state regulation.* State regulation is the ability of an infant to calm himself when there are environmental changes or to wake himself gently. It is normal behavior for infants who are overloaded with stimulation from the environment or just sleepy to suck a thumb, rock slightly, or want to cuddle with a caregiver. Infants with prenatal drug exposure do not seem to have this ability. In fact, they often actively resist physical contact, cuddling, or soothing from the caregiver. As previously stated, these irritable, hypersensitive behaviors are likely to disrupt the bonding or attachment process between caregiver and child. Bonding is the earliest social skill and is necessary for children to feel safe and secure. It helps them interact appropriately with and relate well to others throughout their lives. Mothers with addictions often have difficulty bonding and providing the consistently nurturing care an at-risk infant needs. These women often need specific training to learn how to deal calmly and effectively with the hyper-irritable and hypersensitive behaviors common in prenatally drug-exposed infants.

Swaddling

One strategy that Chasnoff (1988) has promoted to soothe and quiet babies is called *swaddling*, or wrapping the babies securely in a blanket. This seems to have a calming effect, helps the babies to stop crying, and makes the infants feel safe and secure. Apparently, this strategy helps to quiet the babies so that caregivers have a better chance of bonding. As one can imagine, it is much easier to bond with a quieter, calmer baby. Since this procedure does seem to help the babies calm down, the technique also reduces the adult frustration of dealing with an inconsolable infant who is chronically crying and distraught.

Fetal Alcohol Syndrome (FAS) and Fetal Alcohol Effects (FAE)

Fetal alcohol syndrome (FAS) and fetal alcohol effects (FAE) refer to a cluster of neurological and physiological birth defects that result when a woman drinks alcohol during pregnancy. FAS is recognized as the leading cause of mental retardation in children in the United States. Approximately 80% of children prenatally exposed to alcohol will have some form of mental retardation (Burgess & Streissguth, 1992). The level of mental retardation can range from mild to moderate to severe and profound. Currently, there is no standardized psychological or behavioral assessment device to evaluate the characteristics of FAS and FAE. The diagnosis must be made by a physician who has been trained to recognize the specific symptoms.

The first trimester of pregnancy may be the most critical developmental period because that is when the brain of the fetus is forming and is especially sensitive to alcohol ingestion by the mother. In the second trimester, miscarriage is a major risk factor. In the third trimester, fetal growth of organ systems, neurological development, and central nervous system (CNS) development are all highly susceptible to alcohol poisoning (Lesar, 1992). Women who drink alcohol during pregnancy are at significantly increased risk for miscarriage and stillbirth. Burgess and Streissguth (1992) report that researchers unequivocally state that there is neither a safe time for drinking nor a safe amount of alcohol that could be consumed by a pregnant woman.

Research studies in animals indicate that alcohol concentration rather than the actual number of days or times a drink is taken may have more severe effects on a developing fetus. Consequently, even one incident of binge drinking can have a critical and lifelong impact on a child (Streissguth, 1997).

General Characteristics of FAS and FAE

General characteristics of FAS and FAE include physical growth deficiencies, organ system dysfunctions, and CNS dysfunctions (Burgess & Streissguth, 1992). The lifelong impact of fetal alcohol exposure may result in a very wide range of problems (see Table 4–2). These include learning disabilities, behavioral disorders, mental retardation, cognitive processing problems, deformities of the face and cranial areas, organ system problems, and fine and gross motor skill deficiencies. Individuals with FAS and FAE may also experience social, emotional, and behavioral problems that last a lifetime. There is no cure for the problems that these victims suffer. It is a well-known fact, however, that FAS and FAE are 100% preventable. If pregnant women totally abstained from alcohol, there would be no more FAS or FAE.

Medical Criteria for the Diagnosis of FAS

Fetal alcohol syndrome (FAS) was first defined in 1973 by Jones and Smith. FAS can be accurately diagnosed by observable physical malformations of the head and face. Medical researchers have also identified specific behavioral and growth problems that are caused by maternal alcohol consumption. The medical criteria for a diagnosis of FAS include (a) growth retardation, (b) CNS damage, and (c) deformities of the head and face. To be diagnosed with FAS, a child must have at least one characteristic from each of the three categories.

Growth Retardation   In the first category, characteristics of growth retardation include low birth weight, short body length, and small head circum-

TABLE 4–2   Criteria for FAS/FAE Diagnosis

Fetal Alcohol Syndrome (FAS)

- Premature birth
- Low birth weight
- Small head circumference
- Lower than 10th percentile for gestational age
- Distinctive pattern of facial abnormalities
- Some degree of neurological damage which may include:
  - Mild, moderate, or severe mental retardation
    - Learning disabilities
  - Cognitive reasoning difficulties
    - Impulsivity
    - Hyperactivity   ↓ alcohol tolerance
      - ADD/ADHD
  - Gross motor problems
  - Fine motor problems
  - Developmental delays
- Behavioral disorders
  - Lack of moral reasoning behavior
  - Lack of rule-following behavior

Fetal Alcohol Effects (FAE)

- Must have direct, firsthand knowledge of maternal alcohol use
- Possible low birth weight
  - Lower than 10th percentile for gestational age
- Possible facial feature abnormalities
- Various degrees of
  - Mental retardation
  - Learning disabilities
  - Motor skill deficits or dysfunctions
  - Hyperactivity
  - ADD or ADHD
  - Behavioral disorders
    - Lack of moral reasoning behavior
    - Lack of rule-following behavior

Note. From Fetal Alcohol Syndrome: A Guide for Families and Communities, by A. Streissguth, 1997. Baltimore, MD: Brookes.

ference (microcephaly) at birth. These children tend to continue to score below the 10th percentile for height and weight throughout their developmental years (Parent-Teacher Information Packet on FAS/FAE, 1992).

Central Nervous System Damage In the second category, CNS damage, the characteristics relate to neurological problems. Head circumference tends to be smaller than average due to delays in brain development. Because of the developmental delays, the infants often have neurological problems. The brain of the drug-exposed baby often is not fully formed or mature at birth. Intellectual development is stunted and mental retardation at various levels is common. Children usually have developmental delays in vision, hearing impairments, and poor motor coordination. Neurobehavioral dysfunctions including hyperactivity, motor problems, attention deficits, and cognitive disabilities are common.

Head and Facial Deformities The third category for diagnosis of FAS relates to head and facial deformities. As stated previously, the infants are born with smaller than average heads (microcephaly). The area around the midface looks flat with no definition. There usually is what looks like too large a space between the eyes. The problem actually relates to the length of the eye as compared to the space between the eyes. The length of each eye slit, when measured from inner corner to outer corner, is shorter than average (short palpebral fissures). Eyelids often look droopy (epicanthal folds). The chin is often receding (micrognathia), teeth may be smaller than average with malalignment and malocclusions. These terms mean that the teeth are crooked and do not close properly. The nose appears short with a low or flat bridge at the top, and there may be minor ear shape abnormalities. The ears might look like they are not attached evenly or may stick out at an abnormal angle. Children with FAS also may lack a *philtrum*, the two vertical lines located centrally between the nose and the top lip. Often times the top lip is very thin to nonexistent (Burgess & Streissguth, 1992; Streissguth, 1997).

Diagnostic Criteria for FAE

Children who do not meet the medical criteria for FAS but have been affected by prenatal alcohol exposure are considered to have fetal alcohol effects (FAE). FAE is also sometimes referred to as alcohol-related birth defects (ARBD). There is no medical diagnosis for FAE at this time. Physicians use the term to describe children who have at least one symptom from the three categories required for FAE diagnosis plus knowledge of maternal drinking during pregnancy. That means there was definite prenatal exposure to alcohol but the child suffered less severe physical or observable effects as compared with the infant born with FAS (Burgess & Streissguth, 1992). The mother of a baby with FAE did not necessarily drink less than the mother of a child with FAS, but for a currently unknown biological reason, the baby with FAE was not as severely physically, or outwardly, affected as the baby with FAS. Researchers *do* know that children with FAE may have problems that are just as severe as those associated with FAS. However, they may be more difficult to diagnose early because children with FAE lack the physical features used to make an immediate dignosis of FAS. Both FAS and FAE are likely to cause learning and behavioral difficulties for children in school.

Lifetime Costs of FAS and FAE

The effects of prenatal alcohol exposure are not reversible. There is no cure. Victims of FAS and FAE are likely to need lifelong support and care. The prognosis for independent living skills in adult victims is poor. The financial estimate for treating a child with FAS is anywhere from $1 million to $1.5 million over a lifetime (Abel & Sokol, 1987; Parent-Teacher Information Packet on FAS/FAE, 1992). The costs include fees for medical, educational, vocational, and mental health services.

Individuals with prenatal alcohol exposure often have poor reasoning skills. They do not understand the relationship between cause and effect.

Consequently, it is very difficult for most of them to learn anything from past behavior or the mistakes they made. Many people with FAS will not ever be able to live independently. They do not have the ability to process information and solve problems appropriately. Because they tend to be vulnerable and easily misled into problem behavior, many end up committing crimes and are incarcerated (Parent-Teacher Information Packet on FAS/FAE, 1992). Tax dollars are then required to pay the rehabilitation costs of food, clothing, shelter, and recreation for these individuals while they are in jail or prison.

Physiological Complications for Prenatally Drug-Exposed Children

Low Birth Weight

There are physiological symptoms of drug-exposed babies that are easily observed by medical personnel immediately after birth. Many babies will have *low birth weight*. This is also referred to as intrauterine growth retardation. Low birth weight is considered to be below 5.5 pounds. Medical research (MacDonald, 1992) indicates that prenatal growth retardation is most likely due to the reduction in blood flow through constricted veins and arteries to the developing fetus. The result is a decrease in the required nutrients and oxygen that the fetus needs to develop normally. It can be compared to malnutrition in later life stages. Babies who are very small in size at birth may have a variety of physical and sensory disabilities and organ system dysfunctions because they are so tiny. However, low birth weight alone is not always an indicator of future problems. Some newborns are simply smaller than average and develop quite normally during childhood and adolescence with no problems at all during their lifetime.

Small Head Circumference Measurement

Prenatally exposed babies may be born with a smaller than average head circumference. The main problem associated with smaller head circumference is that the brain has not yet developed to the size or stage it should be for the developmental level of the average newborn. This often leads to a multitude of neurological problems, problems with the CNS, and mental retardation. The observable behavioral characteristics of babies with CNS dysfunction are jitteriness, irritability, feeding difficulties, reduced interactive behaviors, and hypersensitivity to the environment (MacDonald, 1992).

Premature Birth

Being born prematurely is also a problem for drug-exposed infants. Premature birth usually results in the babies being small in length and weight for their gestational age (Bingol, Fuchs, Diaz, Stone, & Gromisch, 1987; Brady, Posner, Lang, & Rosati, 1994; Chasnoff, 1989). These factors are indicators of a baby at risk for ongoing problems through childhood.

One of the prenatal dangers to the fetus when the mother is abusing drugs is *abruptio placentae*. This means that the placenta, which surrounds the developing fetus, begins to tear away and detach from the wall of the uterus. This may cause premature birth or spontaneous abortion.

Learning and Behavioral Problems

In addition to the fact that prenatally drug-exposed babies tend to be more physiologically fragile due to their less than optimum prenatal development, low birth weight and small head circumference are also predictors of future learning and behavioral problems (Lesar, 1992; MacDonald,

1992). Babies with small head circumference lack brain development and often experience cognitive delays and functioning impairment, which tend to be very apparent in the areas of attention, memory, reading, and math skills. In studies of premature children, low birth weight correlated with lower scores on ability tests (Brady et al., 1994). Low birth weight is also related to difficulties in reading, language, speech, handwriting, and spelling (Brady et al., 1994). There are also indicators that some infants with low birth weight who have normal cognitive functioning exhibit difficulties in perception, memory, and motor skills (Odom-Winn & Dunagan, 1991). The ability to think in abstract terms seems to be difficult for prenatally exposed children (Odom-Winn & Dunagan, 1991). Abstract thinking is necessary for academic learning as well as internalizing moral values and showing socially acceptable behavior. Prenatally exposed children may also have difficulty controlling impulses and managing their own behavior. Later in life, prenatally exposed adolescents may show higher than average levels of externalizing behaviors, which may include antisocial, aggressive, or delinquent behavior, attention problems, and social skill deficits (Chasnoff et al., 1998).

Chasnoff et al. (1998) described the relationship between the variables of prenatal drug exposure and the home environment with the child's behavioral problems later in life related to level of intelligence. Results indicated that there was a correlation between a home environment that was chaotic and unstructured, where the mother continued to abuse drugs and/or alcohol, and a lower IQ and a higher rate of behavior problems demonstrated by the child. The quality of the home environment was assumed to be negatively affected by the mother's continued use of drugs. The child's IQ level and behavioral difficulties seemed to be directly related to prenatal drug exposure and the character of the home environment in which the child grew up.

Implications for Working with Youth and Adolescents

Learning and Behavioral Disorders

A major concern related to prenatal drug exposure relates to future and often lifelong learning and behavioral disorders. Research in this area is still in an emerging stage. There are a number of anecdotal reports about teachers' experiences, but empirical studies (replicable studies that follow the rules of scientific research) still need to be conducted. Much of the current research on teaching strategies comes from early intervention and preschool teachers (Lesar, 1992; Odom-Winn & Dunagan, 1991, 1994).

Social and behavioral patterns of preschool children exposed to drugs indicate difficulty in three main areas that negatively affect academic and behavioral progress at school. The three areas include (a) difficulties with attention, concentration, and memory; (b) social skill deficits; and (c) the lack of appropriate play behaviors. Play is really the work of children. Children with prenatal drug or alcohol exposure often do not know how to play alone or with other children. Consequently, as infants and toddlers, the children begin demonstrating learning and behavior problems that cause later school-related deficiencies. The problems are directly related to the prenatal exposure and the ongoing problem for some children of being cared for by a drug-addicted mother and living in a chaotic, unstructured, inconsistent home environment (Lesar, 1992; MacDonald, 1992; Rist, 1990).

A highly structured and predictable educational environment is most effective and beneficial for these students. Support staff such as pediatricians, psychologists, social workers, and speech and language therapists are able to provide an extensive and comprehensive program for the children and their families. Programs that provide consistent daily routines and promote strong and positive bonds between the children and their teachers have been effective. The consistency of the classroom routine and the positive rapport with teachers seem to help the children feel more secure in the school environment. The programs must emphasize treating each child as a unique individual. Programs that provide parent training and support also seem to be successful in helping to remediate family problems (Lesar, 1992).

An interesting but sad anecdote was provided by Ms. Carol Cole, who was a teacher at the Slavin School in California. This was a special school for students with prenatal drug exposure. The school was conducted as a pilot program connected with UCLA. Ms. Cole testified before Congress about her experiences with a class of 3- and 4-year-old prenatally exposed children:

> Let me share some scenes from my classroom. In the sandbox, Lonnie and Timmy are cooking. Lonnie gets upset, reaches into her sock, pulls out a pretend knife, and wields it in Timmy's face.
>
> Marta gets off the bus and her reply to my "good morning" is shouting, "Leave me alone. I don't want to talk to you." Later, Marta seems disoriented as she unexpectedly walks right into a wall. At snack time she spills her milk. During the afternoon, Marta seems to have no concept of how to do the puzzles she easily completed yesterday. On occasion she stares off vaguely into space.
>
> While reading a familiar and favorite book, *The Hungry Caterpillar*, to my class, I asked if they could remember the special name of that special house that caterpillars make before they become beautiful butterflies. You could see them thinking. I tried giving them a little prompt, "Coooo …", to help them remember the word *cocoon*. Allen blurts out with enthusiasm, "Cocaine!" (U.S. Congress, House Select Committee on Children, Youth, and Families, 1989).

Prenatal Drug Exposure and School Behavior

While students prenatally exposed to drugs may exhibit learning and behavioral problems at school, research evidence does not suggest that they are a homogeneous group. Unfortunately, there is no cookbook procedure that describes an effective approach for all children born with these problems. Additionally, there is no one best approach for educating them. These students are going to have a multitude of wide-ranging and varied behavior problems throughout childhood. Some examples that are typical of the range and variety include aggressive behaviors, withdrawal and anxiety, attention and memory difficulties, learning problems, hyperactivity, social skill problems with peers and adults, and language deficits.

Consequently, there are few assumptions that educators can make regarding a typical pattern of behavior. To assume that "crack kids all behave like this" or "FAS kids behave like that" is a misconception. Students who were prenatally drug-exposed need to be individually assessed to determine the most appropriate education program to meet their academic and behavioral areas of weakness and areas of strength.

Teach Appropriate Alternatives for Misbehavior

A general proactive management method is for the teacher to approach challenging behaviors in children with prenatal exposure by using mainly positive reinforcement for appropriate behavior. There is a three-step process that the teacher can use to help teach the children what to do instead of the problem behaviors:

- First, the teacher will need to confront the problem behavior and give a short, concise explanation telling why it is not appropriate.
- Second, it is imperative that the teacher provide the child with a positive, socially acceptable replacement for the problem behavior. Most children will continue to misbehave and make the same mistakes over and over if they are not systematically taught what to do instead.
- Third, the teacher must prompt the child to practice the new replacement behavior. Each

time the child demonstrates the new behavior, the teacher should consistently provide social praise and reinforcement. Teachers, parents, and other professionals need to focus on proactive and positive behavior change methods that emphasize the use of positive reinforcement to teach appropriate new behaviors for the old maladaptive behaviors. Rhode, Jenson, and Reavis (1992) suggest that the adult make about four to six genuine positive reininforcement comments for each negative or reprimand given.

Specific Behavioral Symptoms of Prenatal Exposure

The Peoria [Illinois] Association for Retarded Citizens (PARC) disseminates a packet of information on prenatal exposure to drugs and alcohol (Parent-Teacher Information Packet on FAS/FAE, 1992). One component of the packet includes lists of behaviors that are common to individuals who are victims of prenatal exposure. PARC credits Dr. Donna Burgess and Dr. Robin LaDue (University of Washington–Seattle) and Doris (1989) as sources for this information. The lists of characteristic behaviors with recommendations for management are divided by age groups. This information should be very helpful for parents and educators and other professionals to read and use to effectively deal with prenatal exposure in children and adolescents. As with any type of behavior problem at home, in the classroom, or in the community, there is no "cookbook" approach to management that will be effective for all individuals. The methods suggested are based on a positive and proactive approach designed to teach youth and adolescents skills for successful life adjustment.

It is essential that parents, teachers, and other professionals recognize the need for ongoing support and structure of the individual victims of prenatal exposure. Following are the lists of observable behaviors and suggestions for management and education. The age-group categories include infancy and early childhood, elementary school age, and adolescence.

Behavioral Characteristics of Prenatally Exposed Children During Infancy and Early Childhood

- Failure to thrive
  - Medically fragile
  - 25 hospitalizations during the first year is common
- Developmental delays
  - Poor sucking response
  - Walking and talking
  - Toilet training
  - Don't distinguish familiar persons from strangers
- Language deficiencies
  - Receptive and expressive
  - Difficulty understanding and following directions
- Disobedience
  - Temper tantrums
- Sleep disturbances
  - Exhaustion and irritability
- Distractibility and hyperactivity
  - Don't recognize relationship between cause and effect
    - Often dangerous to themselves and to others

(Parent-Teacher Information Packet on FAS/FAE, 1992)

Recommendations for Infancy and Early Childhood Years

Early identification and diagnosis of prenatal drug and/or alcohol exposure is critical as a first step to assist the parents and other caregivers of the child to learn to manage the symptoms of the condition. The caregivers will often need training and instruction from social service agencies and medical personnel to deal with specific problems. The social service agencies can work with the parents to design a case management plan for coordination of education, medical, and social services to be provided. Early educational intervention must be provided at this stage. Careful monitoring of health and physical development is important. The prenatally drug-exposed child can be unusually demanding of the parents' time and attention. Parents should receive instruction on and be provided with respite care services. Respite care is like having an exceptionally skilled baby-sitter, someone who is specially trained to deal with the unique problems and challenges of children with special needs.

Behavioral Characteristics of Prenatally Exposed Children During the Elementary Grades

- Hyperactivity and impulsive behavior
- Attention and memory deficits
- Easily influenced and misled by peers
- Does not understand cause and effect
- Is not able to think ahead to consequences
- Often gives the appearance of having expressive language capability without having the actual receptive language skills
- Poor comprehension of societal rules, expectations, and moral behavior
- Uses swear words and other inappropriate language
- Coercive behaviors including arguing, noncompliance, defiance, disobedience, temper tantrums, lying, and stealing
- Delayed physical and cognitive development

(Parent-Teacher Information Packet on FAS/FAE, 1992)

Recommendations for the Elementary School Years

Parents and other caregivers must provide an environment that is structured, safe, consistent, and stable for children who experienced prenatal drug exposure. Routines are especially important at both home and school. Parents and teachers should use similar language to remind the child of rules and expectations. Parents at home, educators at school, and other professionals in the community need to work cooperatively, think ahead, and plan for the child's future systematically. Each child must have an appropriate educational placement in a classroom that best meets his or her unique needs. Some children with mild symptoms will be able to make satisfactory progress in a general education class. Some children with more severe symptoms will need a special education class. Some children will need to have a residential school placement with 24-hour care. Parents and social service providers must make sure that both educational and health issues are being closely monitored.

Brady et al. (1994) noted that behavioral problems such as lying, oppositional behavior, stealing, hyperactivity, and impulsivity were exhibited by children prenatally exposed that were more extreme in number and kind than those found in other children with mental retardation. Although a prenatally exposed child might have a cognitive profile similar to that of another child with mental retardation, problem behaviors are likely to be significantly more intense and severe. Prenatally exposed children may display a fearlessness that is unresponsive to verbal warnings. A strategy to teach safe behavior is to give brief verbal directions, to be very consistent with expectations and rules, and to be persistent in working with challenging behaviors.

Children with prenatal drug exposure often demonstrate a discrepancy between their *receptive* language skills and their *expressive* language skills. Receptive language relates to hearing, and expressive language relates to speaking. In some prenatally exposed children and adolescents, expressive language skills *appear* to be more advanced than receptive language skills. The key word is *appear*. In effect, even though it seems as though these children can express themselves well, their language is more like parroting than true thought. PARC (Parent-Teacher Information Packet on FAS/FAE, 1992) reported that prenatally exposed individuals may understand only about one third of what is said to them. Try dropping out every third word of reading or conversation and see how much you understand! It is very confusing. They do not have the ability to communicate thoughts, wants, and needs effectively (personal communication, Colleen Matterelli, 1998).

Communicative Intent   Adults need to learn to recognize the *communicative intent* of speech and actions of the children who have expressive language deficits. Recognizing communicative intent means being able to interpret what an individual wants or needs by closely observing behavior, how the individual acts, or what he does, rather than what he actually says. For example, acting out with aggression or hostility might be a result of a child's need for attention. Incidents of lying or stealing might actually be the result of a child trying to please another person.

Social Skills   Social skills are another problematic area for children with prenatal exposure. The development of friendships requires trust and predictability of behavior. It is no wonder that it is difficult for peers to trust another child who does not understand consequences, is often impulsive or aggressive with others, and may lie, cheat, and steal.

Generalization of Skills   Educators and parents will need to consistently teach and reinforce appropriate social skills. Most children will also need extra instruction in the area of adaptive skills such as adjusting to transitions during a school day, dealing with multiple adults, or learning how to get from one place to another in a school building within the time allotted. Teachers will also have to actively teach students to generalize what they have learned in one classroom to other settings in the school, home, or community. A child who is able to say no to negative peer pressure in Mr. Smith's class may not be able to do so in a less structured social situation. The child who is able to recognize that his classmates' materials may be used only with their permission often does not make the same connection at the local discount store. This means that the teacher must require the student to use the skills in settings outside the classroom. Two social skills curricula, *Skillstreaming the Adolescent* (Gold-

stein & McGinnis, 1984) and *The Tough Kid Social Skills Book* (Sheridan, 1995) provide excellent methods for teaching and generalizing social skills.

Behavioral Characteristics of Prenatally Exposed Children During Adolescence (Ages 12–17)

- Students reach academic ceiling
  - School dropout
- Individuals experience problems in the area of moral behavior
  - Inappropriate sexual behavior
    - Easily exploited sexually
  - Easily misled into criminal behavior

(Parent-Teacher Information Packet on FAS/FAE, 1992)

Recommendations During Adolescence

PARC (1992) reported that the average IQ for an individual with prenatal exposure is about 70, which is borderline for mental retardation. An IQ of 70 is considered *mild mental retardation*. More than 80% of individuals who were specifically prenatally exposed to alcohol exhibit mild to moderate mental retardation. As many as 85% of these children also have attention deficit hyperactivity disorder (ADHD). Streissguth, Randels, & Smith (1991) noted that as these children grow up, the young adults who had cognitive deficits maintained below-average intellectual functioning. They tended to exhibit specific arithmetic difficulties, which included problems with abstractions with time and space. Difficulties with attention, concentration, memory, judgment, and abstract reasoning also continued to be problematic through young adulthood.

Even as chronological age increases, cognitive and social functioning seems to reach a ceiling level similar to a child of 7 to 9 years of age. For the average individual with prenatal exposure, the grade level equivalent that most will be able to achieve for reading is about fourth grade and around the second to third grade for math skills. Logically, the majority of these individuals will not be able to live independently.

A teacher with a student with prenatal exposure may work to promote more independence by providing safe, structured choices, which help instill problem-solving and decision-making skills. The idea is to let the student choose between two options that are both safe and appropriate. Later, students can be taught to think through alternative options and to think ahead to the consequences of each.

Memory and attention difficulties may be particular problems for adolescents with prenatal exposure. Using a variety of methods to teach and motivate the student will help keep up his or her interest. Modeling while providing verbal instruction will help children to more easily grasp new concepts. Try breaking a task into small pieces. This method will help the child avoid feeling overwhelmed, and it will foster a feeling of accomplishment as each component of the task is mastered. Use lots of specific positive reinforcement. Two books, *The Tough Kid Book* (Rhode, Jenson, & Reavis, 1992) and *The Tough Kid Toolbox* (Rhode, Jenson, & Reavis, 1994), provide a wealth of positive and proactive management information for teachers and parents to motivate and reinforce students using extremely unique and innovative methods. The need for change (to keep things interesting) and routine may seem contradictory but both are important for students with prenatal exposure. Warning the child if a routine is to be disrupted may be helpful.

Discipline procedures at home and in the classroom should be consistent for children with prenatal exposure. Consistent consequences must be established for misbehavior. It may be necessary to review consequences for breaking rules many times and to ask the child to repeat the rules and the consequences. As with any child, it is helpful to avoid verbal confrontation or threats and to remember to comment when the child is behaving appropriately.

Children and young adults with prenatal exposure may be highly at risk for exploitation. Because of their cognitive processing deficits and poor decision-making skills, they may be led very easily into crime and other dangerous or harmful behaviors. The combination of impulsivity, challenges in thinking ahead and recognizing the consequences of behavior, and the language difficulties that may be present make it very easy for a child to be led into misbehavior. Parents and teachers will need to be vigilant to protect the child and teach age-appropriate life skills.

Conclusion

Children with prenatal exposure need consistent and comprehensive planning to lead independent and productive lives. Systematically teaching social skills, daily living skills, self-esteem, and decision-making skills will provide cornerstones of effective interventions that foster independence.

Unfortunately, even with appropriate educational and home intervention, many individuals with prenatal exposure need lifelong supervision. The transition process, which by federal mandate becomes part of the IEP by age 14, should address the need for any student with prenatal exposure to connect with local, state, and federal agencies that provide sheltered living and employment services. In addition, parents may wish to begin to consider trusts or wills, which can provide protective services and make alternate living and guardianship arrangements for the child in the event of their death. The specific needs of each child will be different, but the need to construct a long-term plan that can be adjusted according to changing needs is crucial.

The incurable problems faced by individuals prenatally exposed to drugs and alcohol are 100% preventable. The challenges that the children present educationally and socially are expensive, time-consuming, and, for many, will last a lifetime. Research on prenatal drug and alcohol exposure is relatively new. Information for educators regarding the most effective educational practices is in an emerging state. As research becomes more established and the connections between drugs, lifestyle, environment, and birth defects or deficits become more clearly defined, improved teaching methods and more appropriate interventions will be developed. Educators who work with students prenatally exposed to drugs and alcohol must be continually aware of ongoing research in order to learn the most effective teaching methods. Regardless of any breakthroughs that may appear on the horizon during the coming years, education and information on the dangers of taking drugs or drinking during pregnancy must be disseminated to adolescents. All must comprehend the fact that drinking or using drugs during pregnancy is a risky proposition.

References

Abel, E., & Sokol, R. (1987). Incidence of fetal alcohol syndrome and economic impact of FAS-related anomalies. *Drug and Alcohol Dependence*, 19, 51–70.

Barth, R. (1991). Educational implications of prenatally drug-exposed children. *Social Work in Education*, 13, 130–136.

Bingol, N., Fuchs, M., Diaz, V., Stone, R., & Gromisch, D. (1987). Teratogenicity of cocaine in humans. *Journal of Pediatrics*, 111(1), 93–96.

Brady, J. P., Posner, M., Lang, C., & Rosati, M. J. (1994). *Risk and reality: The implications of prenatal exposure to alcohol and other drugs*. The Educational Developmental Center, Inc. Retrievable from http://www.evalustats.com//drugkids.htm

Burgess, D. M., & Streissguth, A. P. (1992). Fetal alcohol syndrome and fetal alcohol effects: Principles for educators. *Phi Delta Kappan*, 74(1), 24–30.

Chasnoff, I. (1988). *Cocaine's children* [Video recording]. March of Dimes Birth Defects Foundation, White Plains, NY. (Available from the Illinois Early Childhood Intervention Clearing House, 830 South Spring Street, Springfield, IL 62704, 1-800-852-4302.)

Chasnoff, I. (1989). Cocaine, pregnancy, and the neonate. *Women and Health*, 15(3), 23–35.

Chasnoff, I., Anson, A., Hatcher, R., Stenson, H., Laukea, K., & Randolph, L. (1998). Prenatal exposure to cocaine and other drugs. *Annals of the New York Academy of Science*, 846, 314–328.

Cone-Wesson, B., & Wu, P. (1992). Audiologic findings in infants born to cocaine-abusing mothers. In L. M. Rosetti (Ed.), *Developmental problems of drug-exposed infants* (pp. 25–35). San Diego, CA: Singular.

Dorfman, A. (1986). Alcohol's youngest victims. *Time*, 134, 58.

Doris, M. (1989). *The broken cord*. New York: Harper & Row.

Goldstein, A. P., & McGinnis, E. (1997). Skillstreaming the adolescent (2nd ed.). Champaign, IL: Research Press.

Gomby, D., & Shiono, P. (1991, Spring). Estimating the number of substance-exposed infants. *The Future of Children*, 1(1), 17–25.

Hallahan, D. P., & Kauffman, J. M. (2003). *Exceptional learners: Introduction to special education* (9th ed.). Needham Heights, MA: Allyn & Bacon.

Johnson, M., & Scruggs, T. (1981). *All our children: Handicapped and normal*. (Report No. E 142 762). Paper presented at the Third National Indian Child Conference, Albuquerque, NM. (ERIC Document Reproduction Service No. ED 217 674)

Jones, K. L. (1986). Fetal alcohol syndrome. *Pediatrics in Review*, 8, 122–126.

Jones, K. L., & Smith, D. (1973). Recognition of the fetal alcohol syndrome in early infancy. *Lancet*, 2, 999–1001.

Lesar, S. (1992). Prenatal cocaine exposure: The challenge to education. In L. M. Rosetti (Ed.), *Developmental problems of drug-exposed infants* (pp. 37–52). San Diego, CA: Singular.

Little, B., Snell, L. M., Gilstrap, L. D., & Johnson, W. L. (1990). Patterns of multiple substance abuse during pregnancy: Implications for mother and fetus. *Southern Medical Journal*, 83(5), 507–509.

MacDonald, C. C. (1992). Perinatal cocaine exposure: Predictor of an endangered generation. In L. M. Rosetti (Ed.), *Developmental problems of drug-exposed infants* (pp. 1–12). San Diego, CA: Singular.

MacGregor, S. (1990). Prevalence of marijuana use during pregnancy: A pilot study. *The Journal of Reproductive Medicine*, 35(12), 1147–1149.

Mastrogriannis, D. S., Decavales, G. O., Verma, U., & Tejani, N. (1990). Perinatal outcome after recent cocaine usage. *Journal of Obstetrics and Gynecology*, 76(1), 8–11.

May, P. A. (1981). *Report on outreach efforts and analysis of approach: A pilot project on fetal alcohol syndrome for American Indians*. (Report No. RC013226). All Indian Pueblo Council, Albuquerque, NM. (ERIC Document Reproduction Service No. ED 213 561)

Monitoring the Future Study. (2000). University of Michigan–Ann Arbor. Retrievable from www.monitoringthefuture.org

National Institute on Drug Abuse InfoFacts. (1998). *Costs to society*. (NIH Publication No. 038). Retrievable from http://www.nida.nih.gov/

Odom-Winn, D., & Dunagan, D. E. (1991). *Prenatally exposed kids in school: What to do and how to do it*. Freeport, NY: Educational Activities.

Odom-Winn, D., & Dunagan, D. E. (1994). *Teaching the tough ones*. Freeport, NY: Educational Activities.

Parent-Teacher Information Packet on FAS/FAE (1992). (Available from the Peoria Association for Retarded Citizens [PARC], 1913 West Townline Road, P.O. Box 3418, Peoria, IL 61612, 309-691-3800.)

Parietti, J. (1992, November 3). Saving drug affected infants. *Family Circle Magazine*.

Rhode, G., Jenson, W. R., & Reavis, H. K. (1992). *The tough kid book*. Longman, CO: Sopris West.

Rhode, G., Jenson, W. R., & Reavis, H. K. (1994). *The tough kid toolbox*. Longmont, CO: Sopris West.

Rist, M. C. (1990, January). The shadow children. *American School Board Journal*, 177(1), 18–24.

Rivers, K. O., & Hedrick, D. L. (1992). Language and behavioral concerns for drug-exposed infants and toddlers. In L. M. Rosetti (Ed.), *Developmental problems of drug-exposed infants* (pp. 63–71). San Diego, CA: Singular.

Sattler, J. M. (1992). *Assessment of children* (3rd ed.). San Diego, CA: Jerome M. Sattler Publishing.

Schipper, W. (1991). *Testimony before the U.S. House of Representitives Select Committee on Narcotics Abuse and Control*. Retrievable from www.naic.com/naic/pubs/s_drug.htm

Sheridan, S. M. (1995). *The tough kid social skills book*. Longmont, CO: Sopris West.

Streissguth, A. (1997). *Fetal alcohol syndrome: A guide for families and communities*. Baltimore, MD: Brookes.

Streissguth, A., Randels, S., & Smith, D. (1991). A test-retest study of intelligence in patients with fetal alcohol syndrome: Implications for care. *Journal of the American Academy of Adolescent Psychiatry*, 30(4), 584–587.

U.S. Congress. House Select Committee on Children, Youth, and Families. (1989). *Born hooked: Confronting the impact of perinatal substance abuse*. Washington, DC: U.S. Government Printing Office.

U.S. Department of Health and Human Services. (1997). *Drug use survey shows mixed results for nation's youth*. Retrievable from http://www.hhs.gov/

SUBSTANCE ABUSE IN YOUTH AND ADOLESCENTS

After completing the chapter, the reader will be able to identify:

- Most commonly abused substances.
- History of substance abuse.
- Current statistics on adolescent substance abuse.
- Substance abuse categories and their effects:
  Stimulants
  Club drugs
  Depressants
  Hallucinogens
  Narcotics
- Other abused substances:
  Steroids
  Inhalants
  Prescription drugs
- Risk factors for adolescent drug abuse.
- Problems related to adolescent drug abuse.
- Prevention and intervention for adolescent substance abuse;
  drug paraphernalia
- Implications for educators, parents, and other professionals who work with youth and adolescents.

Introduction

One beer is too much, a thousand will never be enough. (personal communication, anonymous adoptive parent, 1998)

An adoptive parent related this comment when discussing her son's teenage alcoholism. The statement related to his sensitivity to alcohol and inability to control his drinking. Use of alcohol and other illegal drugs is higher among American youth than in any other industrialized nation. Monitoring the Future is a nationwide survey that investigates trends in lifetime prevalence of use of various drugs and alcohol for 8th, 10th, and 12th graders. The 2002 results indicate that 53% of 12th graders have tried an illict drug (includes alcohol). This is a 0.9% decrease from the recent high of 54.7% in 1999 (Johnston, O'Malley, & Bachman, 2003).

This chapter is divided into eight sections and provides the reader with the following information on adolescent drug abuse. First, a brief history of drug abuse is presented. Second, an explanation with sample statistics from the annual Monitoring the Future survey is provided. Then the four main categories of abused drugs and their physiological and psychological effects are addressed. The fourth section discusses risk factors for adolescent drug abuse. In the fifth section, a short history of various abused drugs is provided. Specific drug identifiers are presented in a chart format. In the sixth section, specific school problems and related lifelong problems are reviewed. In the seventh section, illegal drugs and the consequences of their use by adolescents regarding state and federal law are discussed. Finally, some prevention and intervention programs for adolescent drug abuse are presented.

Adolescence Is a Stressful Period

Many individuals of all ages have problems with substance abuse and addiction. Adolescents have their share of problems. Adolescence is described as the period between 11 and 21 years of age. This is usually a turbulent period when children experience pressure from both the family and society at large to "grow up" and to take on more adult responsibilities. There seems to be ever-increasing peer and societal pressure for adolescents to show more adultlike behaviors and grow up faster as compared to a generation or two ago. Consequently, many children are faced with difficult and stressful choices at much younger ages. The hurried childhood and the decisions made often cause problems and increased levels of stress and anxiety for these children (Kaplan, 1995).

Some youth and adolescents turn to substance abuse in response to peer pressure, environmental factors, and an inability to cope with the stress experienced in life. Substance abuse may provide a means to fit in and be accepted by the peer group or simply to escape the stress they are unable to handle in a socially acceptable manner. The term *substance abuse* is often used as opposed to *drug abuse* because there are a variety of chemicals that can be abused, not just illicit drugs (Kauffman, 2001). Other substances often abused include alcohol, cigarettes, other tobacco products, glue, gasoline, cleaning products, aerosols, and other chemical products. It is known that students with emotional and behavioral disorders (E/BD) are at higher risk than the general population for substance abuse problems (Coleman & Webber, 2002; Kauffman, 2001).

Three Most Commonly Abused Substances

When referring to adolescent drug abuse, many people simply assume that the term *drugs* relates to the illegal narcotics and stimulants such as crack, cocaine, and heroin. However, the most commonly abused substances are much more ordinary and easy for teenagers to get. Alcohol, tobacco, and marijuana are the three most often abused substances for adolescents (Johnston, O'Malley, & Bachman, 2000a, b; National Institute on Drug Abuse [NIDA],

2003). Preteen adolescents typically move through an experimental sequence that begins with cigarettes, moves to alcohol, and then progresses to marijuana. This pattern has been identified in the great majority of long-term substance abusers. The risk to move on to marijuana from smoking and drinking is 65 times greater than for those who never smoke or drank. The risk for trying cocaine is 104 times greater for those who experimented with marijuana than for individuals who never tried it (NIDA, 1997).

Why these three products? They are relatively inexpensive and most teenagers find easy access in their own home or friends' homes. If not found at home, teens can often locate a willing accomplice to purchase the products for them. Since substance abuse is a relatively common pattern of behavior during the adolescent years, teachers, parents, and other professionals must be vigilant about watching for the signs and symptoms of illegal drug, alcohol, and other substance abuse. The harmful consequences of substance abuse can create lifelong complications.

Historic Use of Illicit Drugs

A number of researchers and agencies (Ebron, 1997; National Child Safety Council [NCSC], 1999; National Clearinghouse for Alcohol and Drug Information [NCADI], 1997; U.S. Department of Education [USDE], 1998; U.S. Drug Enforcement Administration [DEA], n.d.) have chronicled a complete history of drug abuse practices beginning with the Greek physician Hippocrates, who wrote about the use of opium during the 5th century. The history documents events through the present-day war waged on the epidemic abuse of illegal drugs by individuals from all walks of life. Drug abuse is a rampant and ever-increasing problem that knows no socio-economic or ethnic boundaries.

Tribal Shaman

It is thought that during prehistoric times the medicine men or women, often called the tribal shaman,

probably learned the medicinal value and curative powers of herbs, berries, roots, and bark of the local vegetation. Through ongoing experimentation, the tribal shaman also discovered the toxic, addictive side of the drugs. Two examples follow. The coca leaf (naturally occurring form of cocaine) was chewed by the Andean Indians during 1500 B.C. to reduce feelings of hunger, cold, and fatigue. Marijuana was used in ancient China as an anesthetic for pain.

Tonics, "Cure-Alls," and Coca-Cola

During the early part of the 20th century, stimulant drugs were both cheap and plentiful. Different tonics were promoted as "cure-alls." For example, Dr. Agnew's Catarrh Powder, a remedy for the common cold, contained 10 grams of pure cocaine per ounce. Adamson's Botanic Cough Balsam used heroin as an ingredient. Dr. Brutus Shiloh's Cure for Consumption combined heroin with chloroform in its recipe. The Sears Roebuck catalogue advertised 2-ounce bottles of laudanum, a tincture of alcohol and opiates for $.18. If one wished to purchase a larger supply, a 1.5 pint bottle could be purchased for $2. The new soda sensation, Coca-Cola, contained a derivative of the coca plant (cocaine).

Just before 1906, when Congress passed the Pure Food and Drug Act, the Coca-Cola Company adjusted the recipe for the popular soft drink by removing the derivative from the coca leaf and replacing it with a safer ingredient, caffeine. One mandate of the Food and Drug Act of 1906 prohibited interstate shipment of any food or soda water that contained cocaine.

Heroin was first synthesized from morphine in 1874. Illicit dealing in opium, heroin, and morphine began to increase. During the early 19th century, heroin was commercially produced as a pain remedy. It was widely accepted by physicians, who at that time were unaware of its highly addictive nature.

A few years later, after the Spanish-American War, President Theodore Roosevelt began taking steps to control the internal traffic of narcotics. The Harrison Narcotic Act of 1914 established the first effort to comprehensively control the possession, distribution, and use of narcotics. The Harrison Act controlled the manufacture and distribution of opium, morphine, heroin, and coca products. Use of these drugs was limited to medical intervention. During this time small-time smuggling of these drugs became a booming business.

Gangsters and Drugs

During Prohibition and the Roaring Twenties, small-time smugglers were overcome by organized crime syndicates, the Mob, and gangsters such as Al Capone in Chicago and Dutch Schultz in New York. Even though gambling and alcohol were their main sources of income, the gangsters were not ignorant of the profits to be made in the illegal drug trade. Currently gangsters still control much of the street trade in illegal drugs (Jensen & Yerington, 1997). The present-day street gangs are thought to be the primary agents responsible for the epidemic sales of street drugs such as crack cocaine readily available in communities of all sizes across the country. Unfortunately, the competition surrounding street sales of illegal drugs by the gangs has also resulted in an incredible increase in violent turf battles and other brutal and vicious gang-related activity.

Over-the-Counter Medications

Amphetamine (a stimulant) was widely sold and distributed in various forms before its highly addictive properties were recognized. Amphetamine was first marketed in the 1930s as a drug called Benzedrine®. It was sold in over-the-counter inhalers to treat nasal congestion until the 1970s. In 1937, another form of amphetamine was marketed by prescription in a tablet to treat sleep disorders, asthma, and a behavioral syndrome that was then called minimal brain dysfunction (MBD). During World War II, soldiers were given amphetamines to keep up their energy level. Blue-collar factory workers were also provided with amphetamines to ensure longer work days, which contributed significantly to the war effort. The Japanese government distributed amphetamines to soldiers and workers to increase labor output. In fact, when the war was over, Japan had huge stockpiles of this wonder drug hailed to be a "miracle of modern chemistry." The common use of this drug is said to have been very influential in helping Japanese workers rebuild their country because it added several hours a day of production for each worker. During the 1950s, the easy accessibility of amphetamines and the mind-set of society led to the pervasive and epidemic drug culture of the 1960s.

As dextroamphetamine (common name Dexedrine®) and methamphetamine (Methedrine®) became readily available, abuse of the drug became widespread. Amphetamines were used by over-the-road truck drivers to stay awake for abnormally long periods of time, by the obese for weight control, by athletes to enhance performance, and by individuals attempting to deal with symptoms of depression. During the same time frame, a subculture of "speed freaks" developed. These were addicts who injected amphetamines intravenously.

Methamphetamine

Legislation was enacted in 1965 with amendments to federal food and drug laws attempting to reduce and eliminate the black market activities in amphetamines. In 1968, a derivative of amphetamine called methamphetamine appeared on the West Coast. It was a stimulant drug chemically related to amphetamine but with stronger effects on the central nervous system (CNS). In response to the crackdown on amphetamine distribution, clandestine methamphetamine laboratory production escalated to epidemic proportions across the nation. Currently most black market methamphetamine is produced in these makeshift laboratories. They are most commonly found in rural areas because of one very important chemical required to make *meth*. The ingredient is called anhydrous ammonia, a chemical used on farm fields. The only way to get it if one is not a licensed farmer is to steal it from tanks in farm fields. The drug task forces in rural areas are working overtime to battle this epidemic problem. Another part of their mission is to educate the public on the signs to watch for that may indicate the presence of meth labs (personal communication, Sgt. Michael Inman, District 14, Illinois State Police, 2002).

The Monitoring the Future Survey

Current Statistics on Illicit Drug Use

Monitoring the Future (MTF) is a national survey produced since 1975 by the University of Michigan–Ann Arbor, Institute for Social Research. Each year the survey is conducted with a nationally representative sample of adolescents in 8th, 10th, and 12th grades from public and private schools in the United States to provide reliable statistics on adolescent substance abuse (Johnston et al., 2003). This survey is sponsored by research grants supported by the National Institute on Drug Abuse (NIDA). NIDA is one of the National Institutes of Health in the U.S. Department of Health and Human Services. In the spring of 2002 (latest year results were available), almost 44,000 students in nearly 400 different schools completed the survey. Results are categorized for practically every known illicit drug, for alcohol, and for tobacco. Each of those categories is then further sorted into (a) lifetime use, (b) annual use, and (c) use in the past 30 days.

Adolescent Drug Use Is Showing a General Decline On a positive note, overall results from the year 2002 indicate that use of illicit drugs, alcohol, and cigarette smoking continues to decline among adolescents in the United States. Researchers attribute the noticeable decline to adolescents' perception of the dangers and hazards associated with substance abuse patterns of behavior. Johnston et al. (2003) indicated that the adolescent's perceived risk and disapproval of drug use are important factors in the reduced use. The more dangerous they perceive

the drug to be, the more decline of use is shown by statistics. This thinking pattern is often more prevalent in 8th graders who have not developed an established pattern of drug-using behavior.

Alcohol The 2002 MTF survey reported that 53% of high school seniors admit to having tried an illicit drug at least once in their lives. Lifetime use by 10th graders was 44.6%. The result for 8th graders was 24.5%. Lifetime statistics showed a slight decline for all three grades as compared to the 2001 survey (NIDA, 2003). Alcohol was the most often used illegal substance for adolescents. However, results in 2002 reflected sizeable drops at all three grade levels in the proportion of students saying they had any alcohol to drink at anytime in their life. Alcohol is considered a prohibited substance for individuals under the age of 21 in all 50 states. Lifetime use of alcohol was 47 for 8th graders, 66.9% for 10th graders, and 78.4% for 12th graders.

Cigarettes Results indicated that cigarettes were the second most often used and abused substance by adolescents in the study. It is important to note that teen use of cigarettes has been dropping steadily since the peak rates in 1996–97. In 2002, proportions of teens saying they had ever smoked fell 4 to 5% in each grade. The 8th-grade group reported 31.4% lifetime use, while 47.4% of 10th graders and 57.2% of 12th graders had tried smoking cigarettes. It is illegal for individuals under the age of 18 to smoke or even purchase cigarettes or any other tobacco products.

Marijuana Marijuana was the third most commonly abused substance. Just under 20% (19.2%) of 8th graders, 38.7% of 10th graders, and 47.8% of 12th graders reported having tried the drug at least once.

The reader is directed to the NIDA Web site, http://www.nida.nih.gov/infofax/HSYouthtrends.html for the specific statistics reported by the Monitoring the Future survey. Table 5–1 depicts a small sample of the informational statistics presented on the NIDA site.

TABLE 5–1   Sample Statistics from the 2002 Monitoring the Future Study

Lifetime	8th graders	10th graders	12th graders
Any illicit drug	24.5	44.6	53.0
Alcohol	47.0	66.9	78.4
Cigarettes	31.4	47.4	57.2
Marijuana	19.2	38.7	47.8
Inhalants	15.2	13.5	11.7
Ecstasy (MDMA)	4.3	6.6	10.5
Cocaine	3.6	6.1	7.8
Crack	2.5	3.6	3.8
Heroin	1.6	1.8	1.7

Note. *From* "Monitoring the Future National Survey Results on Adolescent Drug Use: Overview of Key Findings, 2002," *by L. D. Johnston, P. M. O'Malley, and J. G. Bachman, 2003, Bethesda, MD: National Institute on Drug Abuse.*

Drug Categories and Their Effects

This section discusses the four main categories of drugs that are commonly abused by adolescents: stimulants, depressants, hallucinogens, and narcotics. A description of each category along with examples of general behaviors that may be indicators of drug abuse is provided.

Stimulants

Stimulants generally boost the rate and output of the CNS and all the physiological systems of the body. Specifically, stimulants increase heart rate, blood pressure, body temperature, and respiration. Stimulants may give the user the feeling of having increased energy, alertness, and stamina. Stimulants provide a high that gives a temporary illusion of euphoria, of having limitless power and energy. Conversely, users also report negative feelings of paranoia. Signs of stimulant abuse that teachers might observe in students include hyperactivity, talking too fast, fever, flushed skin, elevated rate of respiration, paranoia, loss of appetite, and restlessness (Kauffman, 2001).

Stimulant Abuse   Chronic abuse of stimulants may produce both *tolerance* and *psychological dependence* or addiction. Tolerance or physical dependence means that increasing amounts of the drug are needed over time to produce the same high or reaction. The body becomes adapted to or resistant to the drug effects and continually needs more to produce the desired effect. Psychological dependence means that the individual craves the feeling of being high and keeps taking the drug because he *thinks* he needs to. Research indicates that stimulants promote more of a psychological dependence than an actual physical addiction. Stimulants are reported to promote a "possible" physical dependence but a "high" psychological dependence (Ebron, 1997; NCADI, 1997; NCSC, 1999; USDE, 1998).

Stimulant Abuse Cycle   Following the high, the user goes through a period of feeling depressed, being edgy, and craving more of the drug that will again provide the high. A stimulant abuser may need to take a "downer" or depressant (discussed in the next section) to induce relaxation or to act as a sleeping pill at night or other times to counterbalance the effects of the stimulant. This is typically how the cycle of addiction begins. Common stimulants include nicotine, caffeine, amphetamines, methamphetamine, ecstasy, cocaine, and crack. Ritalin®, a prescription medication, is a stimulant that has been used very successfully to reduce the symptoms of attention deficit hyperactivity disorder (ADHD). However, this drug can also be abused.

The Ritalin Controversy Contrary to popular belief, Ritalin does not act to slow down or calm an individual with hyperactivity. It acts to help the individual's brain function more efficiently. *Glucose* or sugar is metabolized too slowly in the brain of an individual with ADHD. Ritalin, a stimulant, acts to regulate the metabolism so it approximates the normal rate. Prescribed at the correct dosage, Ritalin allows the person to sustain attention, pay selective attention, and control hyperactivity and impulsivity. Ritalin can help the individual be more successful at school or work. However, if a person without the neurological problems related to ADHD took Ritalin, it would act like any other illegal stimulant. In other words, if a person who did not need it took Ritalin, it would work like speed (Jordan, 1998). Consequently, parents, school nurses, or anyone else responsible for dispensing medication must be sure that youth and adolescents who take Ritalin actually put the tablets in their mouth and swallow them. Illegal selling of Ritalin, a controlled stimulant medication, has become a thriving business.

Cocaine Cocaine is a white powder that comes from the coca plant grown in the Andes Mountains of South America. The natives of this region chew leaves of the coca plant. The practice is similar to the North American custom of chewing tobacco. It has also been reported that the leaves are brewed into a tea for refreshment and to relieve symptoms of fatigue, which is similar to the North American custom of drinking tea or coffee.

Pure cocaine was first used in the 1880s as a local anesthetic for eye surgery. Surgeons found it to be particularly beneficial as an anesthetic for eye, nose, and throat surgery due to its effectiveness in constricting blood vessels and limiting bleeding. However, use of cocaine as an anesthetic has become obsolete due to the development of safer drugs (NCADI, 1997).

On the street, cocaine is usually distributed illegally as a white crystalline powder or in off-white chunks called crack. The powder, usually cocaine hydrochloride, will typically be diluted with another white powdery sugar substance such as lactose, inositol, or mannitol. Lidocaine, a local anesthetic, might also be used. The other powders used for dilution are much less expensive than cocaine. Adding these powders increases the volume of the powder, thereby reducing the purity and strength of the cocaine, and results in increased profits for the dealer. Users typically snort cocaine (inhale the powder through the nostrils) or dissolve it in water and then inject it intravenously. Cocaine is rarely smoked.

Crack Crack is the crystallized solid, chunk, or rock form of cocaine. On the street it is sold in small quantities that are relatively inexpensive, usually for about $10 to $20. To make crack, powdered cocaine is mixed with baking soda and heated. During the heating process, the chemical structure changes from a powder to a crystal chuck or *rock*. This is where the term *rocks of crack* was derived. As the crystal structure changes from a powder to a solid, the substance gives off a crackling noise, hence the name crack. Smoking crack delivers large amounts of the drug to the lungs, producing immediate effects similar to those of an intravenous injection. The high is very intense and is said to be almost immediately addicting. Snorting cocaine produces the high effect within 3 to 5 minutes. Intravenous injection produces the rush within 15 to 30 seconds, while smoking crack produces an almost immediate reaction. The feeling of euphoria produced by cocaine or crack is said to be quite similar to that of amphetamine use.

The Addiction Cycle of Crack The intense high effects are usually followed by a dysphoric crash. In an attempt to avoid the fatigue and depression associated with coming down from a crack or cocaine high, the user will repeat the dose. The addiction cycle spirals out of control as the user's life starts revolving around getting money to get more crack or cocaine. The individual usually separates from family members and loved ones and loses any type of legitimate employment. This results from the abuser's lack of being able to concentrate on anything but the addiction. Lack of responsibility and dependability are primary examples of addictive behaviors. Ongoing and excessive cocaine or crack addiction may lead to seizures and death due to respiratory failure, stroke, cerebral hemorrhage, or heart failure.

The Len Bias Story   The Len Bias story is a very sad documentation of the incredible danger inherent in taking street drugs. Len Bias was an All-American basketball player from the University of Maryland. On June 17, 1986, Bias was the first-round draft pick of the Boston Celtics, a professional basketball team.

> "It feels good to be a Celtic," Bias said as the cameras clicked and the people applauded, and the future spread out before him like a long, smooth, golden expressway. What was wrong with this picture? Nothing that anyone could see. (McCallum, 1986, p. 20)

However, in less than 2 days, a mere 44 hours later, Bias was pronounced dead of cardiorespiratory arrest brought on by the use of cocaine. Bias had the reputation of being a strong, healthy athlete with good sense. He was known to have avoided drug use in the past. He had passed every routine athletic department drug test while at the University of Maryland. Medical examiners verified the fact that a user can die from trying cocaine just one time. Autopsy reports revealed that the cocaine acted to interrupt brain signals to Bias's heart. He had a seizure, respiratory failure, and ultimately cardiac arrest (McCallum, 1986). Len Bias's death is thought to be based on one-time use of cocaine.

Club Drugs: Ecstasy   The information in this section is from the U.S. Drug Enforcement Administration (2000). (Further information can be located on the DEA Web site under Intelligence Briefs found at www.usdoj.gov/dea/pubs/intel.htm).

"Club drugs" is a general term for a number of illicit drugs, primarily synthetic (artificial), that are most commonly encountered at nightclubs and *raves*. Raves are professionally produced all-night dance parties characterized by loud, rapid-tempo *techno music* (music with 140 to 200 beats per minute), light shows, smoke or fog effects, and pyrotechnics. Users report that drugs such as ecstasy heighten the user's perceptions, especially visual stimulation. Quite often, users of ecstasy will dance with *light sticks* to increase their visual stimulation. Light sticks are about 8 inches long and about 1 or 2 inches in diameter and glow with fluorescent colors.

Ecstasy or 3, 4-methylenedioxymethamphetamine (MDMA), also known as XTC, X, or Adam, is the most popular of the club drugs. Ecstasy causes stimulant and hallucinogenic effects in the user. It is also known as the *hug-drug* or the *feel-good drug*. Ecstasy reduces inhibitions, produces feelings of empathy for others, eliminates anxiety, and promotes extreme feelings of relaxation. In addition to chemical stimulation, ecstasy reportedly suppresses the need to eat, drink, or sleep. This enables the club scene or rave party participants to maintain a high level of energy or activity during all-night parties and sometimes 2- to 3-day parties. It has gained popularity primarily because of the false perception that it is not as harmful or addictive as other mainstream drugs such as heroin.

Overdose Dangers   Ecstasy is taken orally, usually in tablet form. It is a stimulant with mild hallucinogenic properties. Effects often last from 3 to 6 hours. Because individuals at dance clubs often take ecstasy, they can dance for extended periods because of the stimulant effect. Use of the drug while dancing or performing any other type of physical exertion can lead to severe hyperthermia (overheating), dehydration, heat stroke, and heart attack. An overdose is characterized by rapid heartbeat, high blood pressure, faintness, muscle cramping, panic attacks, loss of consciousness, and seizures. Repeated abuse may result in lasting neurological changes in the brain. Ecstasy causes damage to neurons that carry messages throughout the brain. The observable result of this permanent brain damage is reflected in depression, anxiety, memory loss, and general learning difficulties. One side effect is jaw muscle tension and teeth grinding. As a consequence, many ecstasy users use pacifiers to help relieve the tension.

The most critical, life-threatening response to ecstasy is *hyperthermia* (excessive body heat). Reports of ecstasy-induced deaths indicated core body temperatures ranging from 107 to 109 degrees Fahrenheit. Many rave clubs now provide cooling centers or cold showers designed to allow participants to cool off and lower their body temperature.

Monitoring the Future Survey: Ecstasy   Results of the 2002 survey indicated that the use of ecstasy is begnning to decline among 8th, 10th, and 12th graders. Lifetime use for 8th graders was 4.3%. Results indicated 6.6% lifetime use for 10th graders and 10.5% for 12th graders (Johnston et al., 2003).

Other Club Drugs   Other club drugs include Ketamine (street names: K, Special K, and Cat Valium). Ketamine is a drug primarily prescribed by veterinarians. It causes hallucinations. Chronic abuse results in delirium, amnesia, depression, cognitive and memory deficits, and fatal respiratory problems.

GHB (Gamma Hydroxybutyrate) is a CNS depressant that was banned by the Food and Drug Administration in 1990. At lower doses it causes drowsiness, nausea, and visual disturbances. Higher doses cause unconsciousness, seizures, severe respiratory depression, and coma. Of all the club drugs, GHB has been responsible for the highest incidence of emergency room visits.

Rophypnol has been called the *date-rape drug*. Street names include Roofies, Roche, Rope, Ropies, and Forget-me-Pill. It acts as a depressant, causing decreased blood pressure, drowsiness, visual disturbances, confusion, and dizziness. A significant effect of the drug is chemically induced *amnesia*; after a person takes the drug, he or she cannot remember what has happened to them for a certain period. Consequently, a person who takes this drug is easy to take advantage of. The tablets are often slipped into an unknowing victim's beverage at parties or bars. It has been reported to be a factor in many cases of rape and other incidents of sexual exploitation. Rohypnol is marketed legally in Latin America and Europe and is smuggled into the United States through mail or other delivery systems. Manufacturers are now producing a new type of this tablet containing a dye that makes it very visible if it is slipped into and dissolved in an unsuspecting person's beverage.

Methamphetamine   Street names for methamphetamine include speed, meth, and crank. Methamphetamine is taken in pill form or in powdered form by snorting or injection. Methamphetamine is a stimulant that increases heart rate, blood pressure, and respiration. Methamphetamine abuse promotes a state of hyperawareness and high levels of anxiety. It could keep a person awake for days, sometimes even weeks at a time, causing extreme paranoia and rage reactions.

Biker gangs were instrumental in setting up secret labs to produce the drug at low cost and without the added risk of having to smuggle the drug into the country. The gangs used readily available household chemicals that required little knowledge to use and generated overnight fortunes for the producers and distributors. Because recipes for meth are easy to obtain, clandestine labs have sprung up in rural areas.

Meth Labs   A person with the recipe for meth needs only about $100 worth of household chemical products and about 2 hours to produce 1 ounce or 28 grams of meth. He can then sell the meth for approximately $85 to $100 per gram on the street. The profit is significant but the associated dangers are also incredibly extreme. The chemical combinations required are volatile and highly explosive (personal communication, Sgt. Michael Inman,

District 14, Illinois State Police, 2002). The market for amphetamines has flourished dramatically.

Currently, smaller mobile labs produce a very potent form of methamphetamine called *ice*. Ice is usually colorless, odorless, and tasteless, which means it can be used without detection more easily than other drugs in the workplace, at school, in a residence hall, or at home. It is usually taken orally or injected. However, the advent of ice introduced smoking as a popular means of consumption. Ice is similar to crack; it is highly addictive and toxic.

The physical effects of meth are similar to those of cocaine, with a slower onset of the high but a longer duration. Chronic methamphetamine abuse produces behavior similar to schizophrenia. It is characterized by symptoms such as auditory and visual hallucinations; picking at the skin, which forms sores; paranoia; preoccupation with one's own thoughts; and violent or erratic behavior.

Meth Abuse Signs   Teachers in rural areas must be particularly aware of the signs because meth is more plentiful there. The following symptoms are signs of chronic methamphetamine abuse (personal communication, Sgt. Michael Inman, District 14, Illinois State Police, 2002).

- Weight loss
- Pale color in the face and skin
- Sweating from increase in body temperature
- Strong body odor or chemical smell
- Tooth decay
- Open sores (*crank bugs*) caused by scratching the itchy skin
- Paranoia
- High tolerance for physical pain
- Insomnia
- Hallucinations

Depressants

As a general category, depressants work just the opposite of stimulants. They are drugs that slow down functioning of the CNS. The CNS consists of the brain, the spinal cord, and all of the nerves that radiate through the body. Alcohol and prescription medications, including Valium, phenobarbital, and quaaludes, are examples of depressants.

Depressants inhibit or impair transmission of neurological signals throughout the CNS. Depressants sedate neurological functioning, slow physiological reaction time, and impair cognition or thinking skills. Specifically, depressants may induce muscle incoordination; cause slurred speech; reduce inhibitions and emotional control; and produce relaxation, drowsiness, and sleep. Signs of depressant abuse that teachers might observe in students include chronic drowsiness, irritability, disinhibition, extreme relaxation, or sedation (Kauffman, 2001).

The physiological symptoms resulting from the use of CNS depressants are not the same as the psychological state of "depression" (Coleman & Webber, 2002). Psychological or clinical depression is an emotional disorder characterized by sadness; inactivity; difficulty in thinking and concentrating; and feelings of dejection, hopelessness, and helplessness. Chronic use of CNS depressants may produce both psychological dependence, tolerance or physical dependence, and addiction.

The 2002 Monitoring the Future (MTF) survey reported the following statistics on high school students' abuse of depressants labeled tranquilizers. In 2000, 8th graders' abuse was reported to be 4.4%. That statistic for 8th graders is down slightly to 4.3% in 2002. Tranquilizer use by 10th graders rose from 8% in 2000 to 8.8% in 2002. Use of tranquilizers by 12th graders rose between 2000 and 2002 with percentages increasing from 8.9 to 11.4.

Medical personnel do prescribe depressants to individuals for legitimate reasons: anxiety and insomnia. Depressants may act to reduce anxiety, tension, and nervous or angry feelings. Used appropriately, depressant medications can make a person feel calmer. Alcohol and barbiturates are two of the most widely abused CNS depressants. Specific behavioral effects of stimulant and de-

TABLE 5-2 Comparison of Effects Between Stimulants and Depressants

Effects of Stimulant Drug Use	Effects of Depressant Drug Use
• Feel euphoric and powerful	• Produces drowsiness and sleep
• Experience increased energy and physical stamina	• Reduces ability to concentrate
• Feel nervous and fidgety	• Reduces memory and cognition
• Hyperactivity	• Reduces anxiety, tension, and nervous or angry feelings
• Insomnia	• Increases feelings of tiredness and apathy
• Increases heart rate	• Produces paranoia
• Increases blood pressure	• Produces hallucinations
• Increases respiration	

Note. *Ebron, 1997; U.S. Drug Enforcement Administration,* Drug Descriptions *(n.d.) and* Get It Straight *(n.d.); Johnston, O'Malley, and Bachman, 2003; Kerr and Nelson, 2002; NIDA, 2003.*

pressant drugs are compared and summarized in Table 5-2.

Alcohol

Alcohol is the most used drug in our country today and it is the #1 problem of teenagers and children. (NCSC, 1999, p. 4)

Alcohol is an illegal drug for adolescents under the age 21 in all 50 states. Alcohol abuse is a pattern of problem drinking that may result in potentially fatal health risks and lifelong social and economic problems. Alcohol is a *psychoactive* (mind-altering) drug that can affect moods, cause changes in the body, and become habit-forming. Alcohol dependence refers to a disease that is characterized by impaired or total lack of control over the amount of alcoholic beverages one drinks. Alcohol dependence has been linked to an increased risk for suicide, homicide, traffic and boat accidents, and a host of other accidents, injuries, and illnesses. Driving while intoxicated results in 650,000 accidents and 1.5 million arrests annually. Billions of dollars are spent on insurance, medical expenses, and property damage costs. Maternal drinking while pregnant is the single, and entirely preventable, cause of fetal alcohol syndrome (see Chapter 3), the leading cause of mental retardation in the United States.

Teacher and Parent Observations of Alcohol Intoxication The average age to first try alcohol is age 13 (Johnston et al., 2003). Why does 13 seem

to be the magic number? Reports indicate that when students are in middle school, peer pressure to experiment escalates while the level of supervision of social activities may begin to decrease. Also, children can learn to become secretive and manipulative in setting up occasions when they can escape adult supervision and freely experiment with drugs and alcohol.

Teachers and parents might observe the following signs if students are intoxicated by alcohol. First, they are likely to smell like alcohol. Conversely, they might smell too *minty fresh* or *spring fresh*. These suspicious odors might be apparent because students either ate an abundance of breath mints in an attempt to reduce the alcohol smell or rubbed dryer sheets all over their clothing and hair to cover the scent. This cover-up practice is also true of adolescents trying to camouflage the scent of cigarette or marijuana smoke. Students might demonstrate any of the signs listed in Table 5-3.

Barbiturates Barbiturates are barbituric acid derivatives that were first introduced for medicinal use in the early 1900s. They were primarily used for sedation or to induce sleep. More than 2,500 different types of barbiturates were synthesized. At the height of their popularity about 50 different types were marketed for human use. The different types are classified in four different categories based on the length of time a user will feel the sedative effects: (a) ultrashort-acting, (b) short-acting, (c) intermediate-acting, and (d) long-acting.

TABLE 5–3 Observable Signs of Alcohol Abuse

Short-Term Signs
- Smelling of alcohol
- Smelling too minty or spring fresh
- Slurred speech
- Impaired vision
- Disorientation

Long-Term Signs
- Change in attitude
- Decline in grades at school
- Lack of interest in past favored activities
- Lack of interest in family activities
- Secretive behavior
- New group of friends

Note. *Ebron, 1997; U.S. Drug Enforcement Administration,* Drug Descriptions *(n.d.) and* Get It Straight *(n.d.); Johnston, O'Malley, and Bachman, 2003; Kerr and Nelson, 2002; NIDA, 2003.*

Use of the ultrashort-acting barbiturates results in sedation occurring within about a minute when injected intravenously. They are currently prescribed and used legally by medical professionals. Barbiturate abusers prefer the short-acting and intermediate-acting forms of the drug. Phenobarbital (trade name Nembutal®) and secobarbital (trade name Amytal®) are popular. After taking the barbiturates orally, the desired sedation effect usually occurs within 15 to 40 minutes and can last for up to 6 hours.

Methaqualone, marketed as quaaludes and Mandrax®, was first prescribed to reduce feelings of anxiety during the day and to induce relaxation and sleep at night. The manufacturer halted production in the United States in 1984 because of the extreme hazards and abuse associated with the drug. However, the drug is still available in Canada, in Europe, and on the black market (NCSC, 1999).

Intoxication with Barbiturates Physical dependence or tolerance develops rapidly for depressant users. It is easy to become confused by the effects of the drug and forget how much has been taken. Withdrawal from the drug can be unpleasant and possibly dangerous as a result of symptoms such as convulsions, hallucinations, tremors, and even death. Teachers who observe students under the effect of depressants might observe restlessness, memory and thinking problems, loss of appetite, nausea, anxiety, blurred vision, and complaints of muscle pain.

Hallucinogens

Hallucinogenic drugs, also known as psychedelics, are used to alter human perception and mood (Ebron, 1997; NCADI, 1997; NCSC, 1999; USDE, 1998). Specifically, the individual's perceptions, sensations, thoughts, and emotions may be affected. Hallucinogens can be organic, meaning they are found naturally growing in plants and fungi. For centuries these naturally occurring substances have been used for medical, social, and religious practices. Naturally occurring hallucinogens include marijuana, peyote, mescaline, and psilocybin or psilocyn, also known as "magic mushrooms." They can also be synthetic or artificial. Synthetic hallucinogens are produced illegally in clandestine laboratories. Manufactured hallucinogens are often more potent than the naturally occurring type. Lysergic acid diethylamide, commonly known as LSD, is the most potent and the most highly studied hallucinogen. Phencyclidine (PCP), also commonly called angel dust, is another example of a powerful hallucinogenic drug illegally produced in unauthorized, secret laboratories.

Sensory affects of hallucinogens can vary widely between individuals and dosage, the environmental setting, and the user's mood, attitude, and expectations regarding the drug's effects. Researchers state that users who expect strong results from taking a drug are more likely to experience strong results. This effect is comparable to the *self-fulfilling prophecy*, meaning that one tends to get what one expects (Kaplan, 1995). Psychic effects relate to the user's individual perception of time and space. For example, time may seem to pass at either a slower pace or a much faster pace, while the color, shape, and substance of everyday common objects may appear to change and take on an altered image in the user's mind.

Flashbacks Users report the psychic experience of hallucination as ranging from extremely pleasurable to extremely frightening. Another unpredictable factor in hallucinogenic drug abuse relates to *flashbacks*. Flashbacks are described as a recurrence of the hallucinogen's effect in the absence of actually taking the drug. Weeks or even months after taking a hallucinogen, the user may experience a flashback. It is not possible to predict when a flashback might occur, but research indicates that one would be more likely to occur during times of stress and that younger individuals were more likely than older people to experience a flashback. The occurrence of flashbacks dissipates with time (Ebron, 1997; NCADI, 1997; NCSC, 1999; USDE, 1998).

No Approved Medical Use for Hallucinogens
There is currently no approved medical use for hallucinogenic drugs. Hallucinogens create sensory perceptual disorders and mood swings. They distort the user's perception of reality. Users may experience disorientation and unpredictable, erratic, and violent behaviors that can lead to serious injury or death. The effects of hallucinogens can last up to 12 hours. Hallucinogens produce physiological dependence or tolerance in the user, meaning that the dose must be systematically increased to achieve the same level of intoxication. Increasing the dose is extremely dangerous because of the unpredictability of the ingredients in the drug purchased on the street. In addition, hallucinogenic drug abuse increases the risk for convulsions, coma, heart and lung failure, and death.

Teacher and Parent Observations of Hallucinogen Intoxication Teachers and parents might observe a number of different behavioral indicators of hallucinogenic drug intoxication in students. The pupils in the eyes will be dilated. The student is likely to have hallucinations and altered perceptions of body and time. There will likely be problems focusing and sustaining attention. The student will appear to be emotionally unstable (Kauffman, 2001). Educators have reason to be

concerned. One of the most problematic side effects of hallucinogen abuse is impaired thinking skills and judgment, which may lead to poor problem solving, socially unacceptable behavior, violent behavior, and accidents. The effects of hallucinogenic drug abuse are summarized in Table 5–4.

Marijuana According to researchers (Johnston et al., 2003; NCADI, 1999), marijuana is the third most often abused substance following alcohol and cigarettes. Marijuana is produced by drying the leaves, flowers, and branches of the hemp plant. It is most often smoked for its mildly hallucinogenic and narcotic effects. It can be eaten, but a larger amount is needed and it takes longer to experience the high effects. Marijuana can be

TABLE 5–4 Effects of Hallucinogenic Drug Abuse

Physiological effects:
 Elevated heart rate
 Increased blood pressure
 Dilated pupils
 Blank stare or rapid involuntary eye movements
 Mood swings
 Convulsions
 Heart and lung failure
 Coma
 Death

Sensory effects:
 Perceptual distortions
 Auditory and/or visual hallucinations
 Disorientation
 Impaired thinking or decision-making skills

Psychic effects:
 Altered perception of time
 Altered perception of color, shape, and substance of
  common objects

Behavioral effects:
 Anxiety
 Paranoia
 Unpredictable, erratic, violent behaviors
 Serious injury, accidents

Note. *Ebron, 1997; U.S. Drug Enforcement Administration, Drug Descriptions (n.d.) and Get It Straight (n.d.); Johnston, O'Malley, and Bachman, 2003; Kerr and Nelson, 2002; NIDA, 2003.*

rolled up in *rolling papers* to a cigarette-like shape. Marijuana can also be placed in a pipe and smoked like tobacco. It is also sometimes placed in a hollowed-out cigar and then smoked. The cigar form is called a *blunt*. Finally, marijuana can be placed in an instrument called a *bong* (a type of water pipe) and smoked.

LSD Lysergic acid diethylamide (LSD) grows naturally in a fungus called ergot. LSD is by far the most potent of the hallucinatory drugs. It is odorless, colorless, and tasteless. LSD is taken orally. There are several different forms. One is in the shape of tiny tablets called *microdots*. Microdots are about one-fourth the size of an aspirin and are usually purple, but they can be any color. Another form is called a *windowpane*. Windowpanes are small thin squares of gelatin treated with LSD that look like little pieces of plastic. A third form of LSD is called *blotter paper*. This is simply a small piece of paper usually smaller than one square inch that is treated with liquid LSD. The individual chews and swallows the paper to ingest the drug. The small squares of paper often resemble children's tattoos and may be decorated with popular cartoon characters, logos or symbols, mystical drawings, zodiac signs, or unicorns (NCSC, 1999).

Phencyclidine (PCP) Phencyclidine (PCP), also known as angel dust, is a white chrystalline powder. It is easily formed into tablets or capsules. It can be mixed with other powders, water, or alcohol. It is said to have a distinctive bitter taste. PCP can be swallowed, smoked, sniffed, injected, or sprinkled on anything that will be eaten. Sometimes PCP is added to marijuana. Since PCP sold on the street is illegally manufactured, the user can never be sure of its purity or with what other dangerous chemicals it might have been combined.

PCP was initially used as a surgical anesthetic. However, it was soon replaced by safer forms of anesthesia as physicians recognized the negative side effects commonly experienced by patients.

Narcotics

A narcotic is a family of drugs derived from opium. The literal meaning of the word *opium* is *poppy juice*. Raw opium gathered from the unripened seed pods of the poppy plant is a milky white liquid that contains about 10% morphine, 0.5% codeine, 0.2% thebaine, and 1% papaverine. The rest is composed of an additional 35 *alkaloids* about which very little is known. Alkaloids are described as a variety of basic and bitter organic compounds found mainly in seed plants. An acre of poppies will produce anywhere from 3 to 5 kilograms of raw opium in a single harvest.

Narcotics include both *synthetic* (artificial) and *semisynthetic* (part naturally occurring or organic and part artificial) compounds, which produce similar results when ingested by humans. One example of a synthetic or laboratory-produced narcotic is methadone. A semisynthetic narcotic is manufactured from naturally occurring products in combination with other chemicals. One example is heroin.

Medical Use of Narcotics Morphine and codeine are extracted from the liquid opium through chemical procedures. It takes about 10 kilograms of raw opium to make 1 kilogram of morphine. Both morphine and codeine are legally produced and distributed for medical purposes. These narcotics are the most effective agents known to relieve intense pain caused by injuries and illness or disease. Narcotics can also produce a sense of well-being by reducing tension, anxiety, and feelings of anger and aggression. The medically beneficial effects of narcotics have also led to their abuse. An associated problem is that individuals build a physical tolerance for the pain medication so the dosage must be continually increased to relieve the pain.

Teacher and Parent Observations of Narcotics Intoxication Kauffman (2001) reports a variety of negative effects that teachers and parents might observe, including drowsiness, inability to concentrate, apathy, reduced physical activity, con-

TABLE 5–5 Effects of Narcotic Abuse

Medicinal use of narcotics for treatment of
- Physical pain
- Persistent cough
- Acute diarrhea

Psychological effects
- Increased feelings of general well-being
- Reduced feelings of tension, anxiety, anger, and aggression

Problematic side effects of narcotic abuse
- Drowsiness
- Inability to concentrate
- Apathy
- Reduced physical activity
- Constriction of the pupils of the eye
- Dilation of blood vessels, which may cause the skin to look flushed
- Constipation
- Nausea
- Vomiting
- Respiratory depression

Medical complications of narcotic abuse
- Skin, lung, brain abscesses
- Endocarditis (inflammation of tissue surrounding the heart)
- Hepatitis
- AIDS

Note. Ebron, 1997; U.S. Drug Enforcement Administration, *Drug Descriptions (n.d.)* and *Get It Straight (n.d.)*; Johnston, O'Malley, and Bachman, 2003; Kerr and Nelson, 2002; NIDA, 2003.

striction of the pupils of the eyes, and dilation of the blood vessels, which causes the skin to look flushed. Other problematic physical effects include respiratory depression, constipation, nausea, and vomiting. Narcotics may be taken orally, injected, or transmitted dermally with skin patches. Effects of narcotics use for medical intervention and problems related to abuse are summarized in Table 5–5.

Morphine   Morphine is the principal derivative of opium. It is one of the most effective legal drugs known for the medicinal relief of physical pain. Purity ranges from 4 to 21%, while commercial opium is standardized to contain 10% morphine. Morphine is marketed in a variety of forms including oral solutions (Roxanol®), sustained-release tablets (MSIR® and MS-Contin®), suppositories, and injectable preparations. Consequently, morphine may be administered orally, subcutaneously, or intravenously.

Morphine addicts most often use the intravenous injection method. Among users, tolerance and physical dependence on morphine tend to develop rapidly, so for a patient with an illness or an injury, dosage must be continually increased to achieve the required physical pain reduction. It is easy to develop an addiction to this pain relief medication. Similarly, as tolerance and dependence build in an illegal addict, dosage must be increased accordingly to achieve the desired feeling produced by the drug.

Heroin

Of all the illegal drugs, heroin is responsible for the most deaths. (NCADI, 1997, p. 9)

Heroin is produced from morphine and various other chemicals. It takes about 1 kilogram of morphine to produce 1 kilogram of heroin. The resulting heroin is about three to four times stronger than morphine. To make heroin, equal amounts of morphine and acetic acid are boiled at about 185° for approximately 6 hours. A number of other steps are followed to add more chemical ingredients. The final drying process yields a white powder that is between 80 and 100% pure. Dealers cut heroin with a variety of other powdered ingredients. Street heroin is reported to be only about 1 to 5% pure heroin. Again, street drugs are incredibly dangerous to users because there is no assurance of ingredients. In effect, 95 to 99% of what a heroin addict buys on the street consists of additives of unknown composition. The rest of the powder may be composed of sugar, starch, powdered milk, quinine, or any other type of powder chemical.

Heroin in its most pure form is a white, bitter-tasting powder. It can vary in color from white to dark brown due to impurities or additives left behind in the manufacturing process. A *bag* is a slang term for a single dose unit of heroin.

In the past, heroin was most often injected either intravenously (*mainlining*) or subcutaneously (*skin-popping*). Injection was the easiest, most practical way to administer lower purity heroin. However, the current availability of more pure heroin allows users to *snort* (inhale the powder from a flat surface through a short little straw) or smoke the narcotic. Snorting heroin is becoming more popular to new users because it eliminates the negative stigma of *needle tracks* associated with addiction. Tracks are a very visible sign of drug abuse made by repeated needle pricks and wounds made from multiple injections of heroin into the veins in the forearms. The fear of acquiring syringe-borne diseases such as HIV/AIDS and hepatitis has also reduced the use of injected heroin. However, snorting heroin reduces the potent effects as compared to injection. Therefore, snorting is usually only an indulgence of those who can afford the highly expensive, very pure forms of heroin.

Researchers fear a surge in adolescent heroin use because it now can be snorted or purchased in tablet form. However, the fears have not yet become a reality according to the 2002 MTF survey results. Use by 8th, 10th, and 12th graders remains relatively low and stable, with less than 2% of all adolescents admitting to heroin use. Changes in adolescent heroin use with and without a needle are documented in Table 5–6.

Medical Complications from Narcotics Abuse
Routine medical complications in narcotic abusers are mainly due to nonsterile practices of injection and inconsistent and unpredictable composition of narcotics sold on the street. There is no simple method to determine the composition or purity of drugs sold illicitly on the street. The main reason for the inconsistency of ingredients is that synthetic and semisynthetic narcotics are produced in clandestine laboratories that are not subjected to any kind of standards. In addition, workers at individual labs are free to lace the drugs with any ingredient they choose. Ingredients ranging from rat poison to drain cleaner have been found in illicit drugs (Hanson, 1997). The effects of unlawful narcotic abuse are at best unpredictable and at worst potentially fatal. Serious medical complications of narcotics abusers include skin, lung, and brain abscesses; endocarditis (inflammation of the lining of the heart); hepatitis; and HIV/AIDS.

Commonly Abused Drugs

Tables 5–7 to 5–11 contain descriptions of commonly abused drugs. The information on each chart is summarized in the following categories for each drug listed: (a) name of the drug; (b) description of the drug; (c) slang, trade, or street names of the drug; (d) how the drug is used or ingested; and (e) possible effects of the drug. The text in this section provides a narrative description of some interesting background on illegal drug use organized by drug categories.

TABLE 5–6   Heroin Use With and Without a Needle, 2001–2002

	With a Needle, 2002	2001–2002 Change	Without a Needle, 2002	2001–2002 Change
8th Graders	1.0	−0.1	1.0	−0.1
10th Graders	1.0	+0.2	1.3	+0.1
12th Graders	0.8	+0.1	1.6	+0.1

Note. From L. D. Johnston, P. M. O'Malley, and J. G. Bachman (December 16, 2002). Ecstasy use among American teens drops for the first time in recent years, and overall drug and alcohol use also decline in the year after 9/11. *University of Michigan News and Information Services: Ann Arbor, MI. [On-line]. Available:* www.monitoringthefuture.org.

TABLE 5–7 Narcotics

Drug	Description	Slang Name	How It Is Used	Possible Effects
Heroin	White to dark brown to black powder	Smack, horse, H, antifreeze, brown sugar, junk, Mexican brown, China white	Snorted, smoked (rarely), most commonly heated until liquified and then injected intravenously; also called "mainlining"	Euphoria, drowsiness, respiratory depression, constricted pupils, nausea, slow and shallow breathing, clammy skin, convulsions, coma, death

Note. *Ebron, 1997; U.S. Drug Enforcement Administration,* Drug Descriptions *(n.d.) and* Get It Straight *(n.d.); Johnston, O'Malley, and Bachman, 2003; Kerr and Nelson, 2002; NIDA, 2003.*

TABLE 5–8 Stimulants

Drug	Description	Slang Name	How It Is Used	Possible Effects
Crack/cocaine	White crystalline powder/small white to tan chunks called "rocks"	Coke, snow, nose candy, flake, big C, blow, rock	Snorted, dissolved in water and smoked; rocks of crack are smoked	Increases heart rate, blood pressure, body temperature; dilates pupils; heart attack, seizure, death
Amphetamine/ methamphetamine	White crystalline powder (pinkish tint when manufactured in areas of high humidity), resembles clear pieces of broken glass, rock candy, or rock salt; liquid form has a yellowish tint	Speed, dexies, bennies, uppers, rock candy, Hawaiian salt, ice, meth, crystal, crank, glass	Smoked, snorted, or liquefied with heat and then injected	Increases heart rate, respiration, blood pressure, body temperature; nausea, violent behavior, stroke, coma, death

Note. *Ebron, 1997; U.S. Drug Enforcement Administration,* Drug Descriptions *(n.d.) and* Get It Straight *(n.d.); Johnston, O'Malley, and Bachman, 2003; Kerr and Nelson, 2002; NIDA, 2003.*

Anabolic Steroids

Anabolic steroids are any drug or other hormonal substance chemically and pharmacologically related to testosterone (other than estrogens, progestins, and corticosteroids) that serve the purpose of enhancing extraordinary muscle growth. The Drug Enforcement Administration describes anabolic steroid abuse as a national concern. Athletes such as weight lifters, bodybuilders, football players, runners, swimmers, and cyclers use steroids as a quick fix for a number of reasons. Some athletes believe that steroid use gives them more of a competitive edge in that they can run faster, jump

TABLE 5-9   Depressants

Drug	Description	Slang Name	How It Is Used	Possible Effects
Alcohol	Liquid	Beer, wine, liquor, cooler, spritzer, booze	Orally	Addiction, dizziness, slurred speech, nausea, vomiting, hangovers, impaired motor skills, violent behavior, impaired learning, fetal alcohol syndrome, respiratory depression, death
Flunitrazepam (Rophypnol)	White tablet with no taste or odor (10 times more powerful than Valium)	Roofies, forget pill, ruffies, R2	Taken orally; "date rape" drug: individuals have been raped after someone slipped a tablet into their drink	Sedation, sleep, impaired motor functioning, memory loss, respiratory depression, death
Barbiturates	Tablets or caplets	Trade names: Valium, Thorazine, Xanax, Librium, Quaaludes, Mandrax	Orally	Highly addictive, physically and psychologically; relaxation; slower reflexes; impaired coordination, thinking, judgment, and memory

Note. *Ebron, 1997; U.S. Drug Enforcement Administration,* Drug Descriptions *(n.d.) and* Get It Straight *(n.d.); Johnston, O'Malley, and Bachman, 2003; Kerr and Nelson, 2002; NIDA, 2003.*

TABLE 5-10   Hallucinogens

Drug	Description	Slang Name	How It Is Used	Possible Effects
Lysergic acid diethylamide (LSD)	Capsules; tablets; clear, odorless liquid; liquid dropped onto blotter paper or paper tabs; sugar cubes; stamps; or dried into a clear, thin sheet called "windowpane"	Acid, boomers, yellow sunshine, cid, doses, trip, speed	Taken orally; blotter paper is licked or swallowed; microdot tablets are swallowed; windowpane is eaten	Illusions, hallucinations, altered perception of sensory impressions, psychosis, death
Phencyclidine (PCP)	Capsules, tablets, white crystalline powder	PCP, angel dust, loveboat, k-blast, wack, peace	Snorted or added to tobacco or marijuana and smoked	Hallucinations, dulled sensory perception, impaired muscle coordination, aggressive and violent behavior

Note. *Ebron, 1997; U.S. Drug Enforcement Administration,* Drug Descriptions *(n.d.) and* Get It Straight *(n.d.); Johnston, O'Malley, and Bachman, 2003; Kerr and Nelson, 2002; NIDA, 2003.*

higher, and play longer. Another reason is that steroids increase muscle mass and size in a short period, which makes athletes feel like their physical appearance has been improved or enhanced. Some steroids have been approved for medical use with humans for various skin disorders, anemia, and the replacement of inadequate levels of testosterone. In animals, steroids are prescribed for weight gain, general vigor, and skin and coat problems.

TABLE 5–11 Club Drugs

Drug	Description	Slang Name	How It Is Used	Possible Effects
Ecstasy (MDMA)	Synthetic drug in the form of tablets; herbal form as pills or tea	XTC, love drug, Adam, essence, cloud 9, X, ultimate xphoria	Tablet, taken orally	Acts as stimulant with mild hallucinogenic properties; increases body temperature, heart rate, and pulse; heart attack, stroke, hyperthermia, seizure, heat stroke, death
Ketamine	Liquid; can be evaporated to white or slightly off-white powder	K, Special K, Cat Valium	Can be injected, applied to smoking material, or consumed in drinks; powder can be smoked	Hallucinations, amnesia, depression, memory and cognitive problems, fatal respiratory problems
GHB (gamma hydroxybutyrate)	Liquid or powder	Liquid ecstasy, Soap, Easy Lay, Georgia Home Boy, Grievous Bodily Harm, Liquid X, Goop	Easily dissolved and often concealed in spring water or mouthwash bottles; flavoring is added to disguise the salty taste; may be passed off as a high-carbohydrate health drink; may be added to alcohol to increase intoxication effects	CNS depression, euphoria, possibly aphrodisiac effects, drowsiness, dizziness, nausea, visual disturbance, respiratory depression, coma

Note. *Ebron, 1997; U.S. Drug Enforcement Administration,* Drug Descriptions *(n.d.) and* Get It Straight *(n.d.); Johnston, O'Malley, and Bachman, 2003; Kerr and Nelson, 2002; NIDA, 2003.*

It is estimated that anywhere from 5 to 12% of male and 1% of female high school athletes abuse steroids. Results from the 2002 Monitoring the Future survey indicated steroid use for 8th graders was 2.5%, for 10th graders, 3.5%, and for 12th graders, 4%. These results were up slightly for 8th and 12th graders. 10th graders have remained constant, at 3.5%, for the past 3 years (Johnston et al., 2003). This is a problem that many people think affects only college and professional athletes. This growing phenomenon among high school athletes must be addressed by coaches, school administrators, and parents because of the potential dangerous side effects of steroid abuse. Anabolic steroids are typically purchased at gyms or health clubs where athletes and weight lifters go to work out, at athletic competitions, and through illicit mail order operations. Examples of commonly abused anabolic steroids include boldenone (Equipoise®), ethlestrenol (Maxibolin®), fluxymesterone (Halotestin®), and nandrolone (Durabolin® or Deca-Durabolin®). Steroids are usually taken orally or by intramuscular injection.

Negative Side Effects of Steroid Abuse Athletes combine an intensive exercise training program, a high-protein diet, and anabolic steroids with the intent of increasing muscle size; improving speed, general performance, and endurance; and decreasing recovery time between workouts or competitions.

TABLE 5–12 Effects of Steroid Abuse

Effects of Steroid Abuse on Males and Females	Effects of Steroid Abuse on Males	Effects of Steroid Abuse on Females
• Cardiovascular damage • Liver damage • Reproductive organ damage • Aggressive behavior • Elevated blood pressure • Increased cholesterol level • Severe acne • Premature hair loss • Reduced sexual functioning	• Testicular atrophy • Abnormal breast development	• Increased growth of body hair • Lower pitched voice • Reduced breast size • Inconsistent menstrual cycles

Note. *Ebron, 1997; U.S. Drug Enforcement Administration,* Drug Descriptions *(n.d.) and* Get It Straight *(n.d.); Johnston, O'Malley, and Bachman, 2003; Kerr and Nelson, 2002; NIDA, 2003.*

Negative side effects of steroid abuse relate to some general serious health problems, including cardiovascular damage, liver damage, and damage to the reproductive organs.

Specific physiological side effects for men and women include elevated blood pressure, increased cholesterol level, severe acne on the face and back, premature hair loss, and reduced sexual functioning. In males, specific side effects of steroid abuse include testicular atrophy and abnormal breast development. Females may experience various masculinizing effects, including increased growth of body hair, voice tone becoming lower pitched, reduction of breast size, and fewer or inconsistent menstrual cycles.

A major danger of adolescent steroid abuse is that steroids have been shown to stop bone growth, meaning that overall development of skeletal growth may be stunted. Once these effects occur, they may be irreversible. Further research on long-term steroid abuse is needed. The negative side effects of steroid abuse are summarized in Table 5–12.

Inhalants

Inhalants are substances that are sniffed or "huffed" to give the user an immediate high or "head rush." A diverse group of chemicals found in common, readily available products such as aerosols, office products such as indelible markers and correction

fluid, adhesives, lighter fluid, paint products, and cleaning products are abused as inhalants (Ebron, 1997; NCADI, 1997, 2003; NCSC, 1999; USDE, 1998). All of these products are easily accessible at relatively low cost, so adolescents find these drugs easy to get and use. Results from the 2002 MTF survey indicate inhalant abuse continues to decline since peak rates of around 20% were reported between 1996–98. In 2002, the percentage of lifetime use was 15.2% for 8th graders, 13.5% for 10th graders, and 11.7% for 12th graders.

Inhaling toxic chemicals can be fatal or can cause neurological, physical, and emotional problems. Effects of prolonged use include irreversible brain damage, headaches, muscular weakness, abdominal pain, CNS damage, violent and aggressive behaviors, hepatitis, nausea, nosebleeds, and a decrease in the sense of smell.

Using an inhalant even once can put an individual at risk for circulation impairment, hallucinations, severe mood swings, suffocation, and sudden death. The National Clearinghouse for Alcohol and Drug Information (2003) reports that death from inhalant abuse can occur in any of the following five ways: (a) asphyxia, which takes place when breathing stops after the inhaled chemicals severely limit availability of oxygen throughout the body; (b) suffocation, which is most often experienced by inhalers who use bags; (c) aspiration, which occurs from choking on vomit; (d) careless

TABLE 5–13 Inhalant Abuse Effects

Short-Term Effects of Inhalant Abuse

- Irregular heartbeat
- Respiratory difficulty
- Disorientation
- Headache

Long-Term Effects of Inhalant Abuse

- Irreversible brain damage
- CNS damage
- Major internal organ damage including heart, liver, lungs, kidneys
- General biochemical imbalance
- Violent and unpredictable behavior
- Decreased control of urination and bowel movements
- Nausea, abdominal pain, headache, and general muscle weakness
- Nosebleeds and loss of sense of smell

Risks for Even One-Time Abuse of an Inhalant

- Sudden death
- Circulatory system damage
- Suffocation
- Hallucinations and manic mood swings

Note. *From "Inhalants," by the National Clearinghouse for Alcohol and Drug Information Center for Substance Abuse Treatment, 2003, Substance Abuse Treatment Advisory, (3)1.*

behaviors in dangerous settings due to impaired cognitive and neurological functioning; and (e) sudden sniffing death syndrome, which is thought to be a result of cardiac arrest. The effects of inhalant abuse are summarized in Table 5–13 describing short-term effects, prolonged use effects, and risks for one-time use.

Prescription Drugs

Prescription drugs are prescribed by a medical professional to treat pain and a variety of other health problems (Ebron, 1997; NCADI, 1997, 2003; NCSC, 1999; USDE, 1998). Depressants (Valium and Tylenol with codeine) and stimulants (Ritalin) are the two categories of prescription drugs that are most often abused. Many adolescents become addicted to prescription painkillers because they can be accessed so easily at home. Some adolescents ingest the medicines themselves, while others sell the prescription doses to peers at school. The effects of depressants and stimulants vary according to the amount of the drug taken, how often it is taken, and the user's expectations of the effects the drug will produce. Prescription drugs come in a variety of different forms such as pills, capsules, liquids, sprays, and inhalants. They can be taken orally, inhaled, or injected either intravenously or intramuscularly. Prescription drugs are dangerous because they can be physically and psychologically addictive. In addition, a tolerance for prescription drugs can develop, which means the individual must keep increasing the amount of the drug taken to feel the same effects.

In addition to prescription drugs, there are over-the-counter drugs, such as cold medicines, diet pills, and painkillers, that can become addictive and are abused (Ebron, 1997; NCADI, 1997, 2003; NCSC, 1999; USDE, 1998). Even though these drugs do not require a prescription, they can be taken in abusive amounts with harmful effects.

Addicted to Prescription Pain Killers: Brett Favre, Quarterback, Green Bay Packers   National Football League quarterback sensation Brett Favre of the Green Bay Packers suffered from prescription drug abuse and addiction. Favre learned a lesson about prescription painkillers the hard way.

During the early 1990s, Brett Favre made a personal commitment to be the best quarterback in the NFL. After leading Green Bay to a runner-up title in 1996, a Super Bowl championship in 1997, and another runner-up title in 1998, it appeared as though Favre was realizing his dream. Favre built the longest starting streak among active quarterbacks, 68 games in a row. He had established new records in touchdown passes and was the league MVP for two consecutive years. However, off the field, Favre was dealing with a nightmare.

Football fans may consider Favre to lead a fascinating, charmed, and thrilling life. Many comment on how lucky he is and wish that they, too, could be quarterback for one of the leading NFL teams. However, being an NFL player is not all fun and glory.

Since 1990, Favre has had five operations. One Packer teammate, Ty Detmer, made the following comment referring to the fact that Favre routinely plays with physical pain. "Brett's not coming out of a game unless a bone is sticking out" (King, 1996, p. 27). Brett's response: "People look at me and say, 'I'd love to be that guy,' but if they knew what it took to be that guy, they wouldn't love to be him, I can guarantee you that. I'm entering a treatment center tomorrow. Would they like to do that?" (King, p. 30). Why is the MVP and leading quarterback of the NFL entering a treatment center? Playing in the NFL may look like a glamorous job. However, the injuries and pain suffered from playing football led to Favre's addiction to a prescription painkiller called Vicodin. Vicodin is a narcotic, a prescription drug that acts as an analgesic to reduce the chronic and severe aches and pains suffered in weekly football games.

Favre is not the only player or even a player in the minority to need painkillers to survive playing in the NFL. Bryan Cox, linebacker for the Chicago Bears, estimated that half of all the players in the NFL need painkillers or anti-inflammatories to make it through the season. Phil Simms, retired quarterback for the New York Giants, suggested that each NFL team would need a roster of about 250 players to make it through a season if only healthy, nonmedicated players were used.

Favre decided to take action to overcome the addiction. He expressed the hope that his public recognition of his problem would help other NFL players to admit to their own drug problems. "I am sure that there are a ton of NFL players out there—I mean it, a ton—who will watch me and come out and say to themselves, 'Man, that's me.' That's one reason I'm talking. I hope I can help some players get help. I realize how dangerous it is to keep using these things" (King, 1996, p. 29).

Risk Factors for Adolescent Drug Abuse

Longitudinal studies (Dobkin, Tremblay, Masse, & Vitaro, 1995; Dodge, 1993; Tremblay, Masse, Perron, & Leblanc, 1992) report that children may develop maladaptive behaviors at a very young age that can often be used as indicators of high risk for later substance abuse. Tremblay et al. (1992) demonstrated that early problems in the area of aggressive and hostile behavior, poor school adjustment, and low achievement were predictors of future substance abuse and other violent offenses. Dodge (1993) suggested that patterns of aggressive, hostile, and impulsive behaviors of young children are strong predictors of future substance abuse and juvenile delinquency. In addition, Dobkin et al. (1995) reported that an individual's biological and personality characteristics, including hyperactivity, oppositional behavior, likability by peers and adults, and fighting behavior, were strong predictors of future substance abuse problems.

The recommendations, based on results from this research, suggest that early intervention and prevention programs should target individual personality and behavioral characteristics and must begin in the primary grades of elementary school.

Transitions Can Be Risky

In addition, NIDA (1997) suggests that there are certain periods in students' lives that are riskier than others. Vulnerable periods tend to be those involving transitions, during which students progress from one developmental stage to the next. Examples include moving from elementary school to middle school. Studies indicate that children most often begin to experiment with drugs around age 12 or 13. Another high-risk transition period is from middle school to high school. In high school, students face an increased performance demand in social, psychological, moral and ethical, and educational venues. This is the time many adolescents succumb to substance abuse because of peer pressure or as a means to try to handle pressure, stress, and anxiety. Other difficult life changes for many children and adolescents relate to stress at home such as family discord, divorce, both parents working, living with a single parent, living with a blended family, or moving from one community to another.

Longitudinal Study on Behavior and Substance Abuse

Shedler and Block (1990) completed a longitudinal study that monitored a group of children from early elementary grades through age 18. The purpose of the study was to measure behavioral differences among adolescents who were abstinent (no first use), experimenters (substance use), and substance abusers. An outcome of the study was that the authors were able to describe problem behaviors observed in youngsters and their parents, which are now thought to be risk factors that could be used to predict future substance abuse.

For both the parents and the children, risk factor behaviors were related to communication skills, problem-solving skills, and effective interaction skills. Based on that longitudinal study, Em-bry (1997) compiled a set of behaviors that might be predictors of later substance abuse. This list of maladaptive child behaviors and ineffective parenting behaviors, summarized in Table 5–14, could be used to predict substance abuse during adolescence.

Other Problems Related to Adolescent Drug Abuse

Substance abuse has been linked to a myriad of serious and potentially fatal injuries, including an inordinately high number of falls or other injuries; boating, drowning, bicycle and automobile accidents; and other mishaps resulting in damage to the CNS. Head injuries and spinal cord damage are particularly prevalent. Almost half of all fatal car accidents involving drivers under the age of 25 also involve drug abuse, specifically alcohol intoxication. The individual's perception is drastically

TABLE 5–14 Behaviors Predicting Substance Abuse at Age 18 and Ineffective Parenting Behaviors

Behaviors of Children at Age 7
- Do not develop close social relationships with peers or adults
- Do not take pride in accomplishments
- Tend to be fearful of new experiences
- Afraid of being deprived; treated unfairly; insatiable
- Has difficulty with problem solving or decision making
- Is unable to think ahead to consequences of own actions
- Has poor verbal communication skills
- Lacks flexibility or resiliency when confronted with unexpected events
- Demonstrates lack of spontaneous behavior with parent

Ineffective Parenting Behaviors
- Demonstrates hostile behavior toward child during instructional periods
- Makes learning experiences bleak, dismal, and grim for the child
- Teaching behaviors are often confusing and bewildering to the child
- Demonstrates lack of spontaneous behavior with the child
- Does not respond to child's emotional or physical needs
- Criticizes the child's thought and behavior
- Rejects the child's ideas or suggestions
- Does not display pride in the child's accomplishments
- Does not give positive reinforcement for appropriate behavior

Note. *From* How School Climate Can Prevent or Increase Substance Abuse and Violent Crime, *by D. D. Em-bry, 1997, a paper presented at the Illinois Safe and Drug Free Schools Conference, Springfield, IL.*

impaired by the use of alcohol and other drugs, which leads to impaired cognitive processing and poor decision making. Intoxication of the victim is frequently a factor in traumatic accident situations. A history of more than an average number of injuries, emergency room visits, and/or hospitalizations may be regarded as an early indicator of substance abuse (Hoyert, Arias, Smith, Murphy, & Kochanek, 2001; Narconon, 2003; NIDA InfoFacts, 2001; Swan, 1998; U.S. Department of Health and Human Services, 2000).

Adolescent substance abuse may result in many lifelong problems. The major problems include monetary factors, deficient academic achievement, delayed adult adjustment, and lifelong medical problems. Statistics related to the costs to society and the dangers of drug and alcohol abuse have been reported by a number of research and treatment agencies (see Table 5–15).

High Cost of Substance Abuse

Drug abuse kills 14,000 Americans each year and can cost taxpayers up to $76 billion in unnecessary health care costs, additional law enforcement, traffic accidents, crime, and lost productivity in the workplace. Alcohol abuse alone costs society in excess of $99 billion annually. Substance abuse has a pervasive, negative, and detrimental effect on families, schools, neighborhoods, and communities. In the United States, the criminal justice system, health care system, and social service agencies are congested with drug abusers. The White House Of-

TABLE 5–15 Statistics on Alcohol and Other Drug Abuse

- Alcohol abuse is the number one drug problem in America.
- Alcoholism costs more than $100 million in health care and loss of productivity annually.
- Health care costs for drug abuse treatment, rehabilitation, prevention, and research are estimated at $49.9 billion annually.
- Alcohol is involved in 50% of all motor vehicle fatalities.
- Every 30 minutes at least one person is killed in a motor vehicle accident.
- Americans spend over $90 billion on alcohol annually.
- Students spend $5.5 billion on alcohol, which is more than they spend on soft drinks, tea, milk, juice, coffee, and books combined.
- Cigarette smoking is the single most preventable cause of disease and death in the U.S.
- Medical costs attributed to smoking are more than $50 billion annually.
- Methamphetamine lab seizures have increased 577% since 1995.
- Nearly half of all drug-related emergency room visits are due to cocaine abuse; alcohol is number one.
- Illicit drug overdose is the fourth leading cause of death, about the same number as motor vehicle deaths, in persons aged 25–49. Heart disease, cancer, and strokes are the top three causes of death.
- An addict may spend between $150 to $200 per day to maintain a heroin addiction.
- Marijuana is the second most common drug, after alcohol, found in the bloodstream of both nonfatally and fatally injured people.
- Reaction times for motor skills involved in driving is reduced 41% after smoking one joint and reduced 63% after smoking two.
- There have been over 7,000 published studies on marijuana. There is not a single one that suggests marijuana is safe to use.
- 75% of drug-related criminal charges are connected to marijuana.

Note. Hoyert, Arias, Smith, Murphy, & Kochanek, 2001; Naronon, 2003; NIDA InfoFacts, 2001; Swan, 1998; U.S. Department of Health and Human Services, 2000.

fice of National Drug Control Policy (ONDCP) conducted a study to determine the retail trade in illicit drugs. They wanted to learn how much money Americans were spending on illegal drugs that might otherwise have been used to support legitimate spending or saving to bolster the U.S. economy. Their results indicated that a whopping 45 to 51 billion dollars is poured down the drain of the illegal drug market each year (NIDA InfoFacts, 1998).

Deficient Academic Achievement

Substance-abusing students often show reduced academic performance. Drug abuse affects the student's overall level of comprehension and memory. Students also become preoccupied with the daily ritual of obtaining and using drugs and alcohol. A consequence is that their schoolwork suffers and they tend to develop a peer group that shares similar problems. This is how adolescents begin to develop the "everyone is doing it" mind-set. It is true in one sense. The peers they associate with are drinking and/or taking drugs. Peer pressure is extremely powerful in adolescence.

Delayed Adult Adjustment

Adolescent substance abusers may experience a delay or a total absence of successful adult adjustment. Adolescence is a time when youngsters who are progressing in a developmentally appropriate manner will learn to take on more responsibilities, become more trustworthy and independent, and learn to meet the ever-increasing performance demands as they move from elementary school to secondary school and on to college, technical school, or the workforce.

Adolescents who fall prey to substance abuse are not able to make these adjustments successfully. Their attitudes and behaviors continue to reflect the immature, irresponsible actions more typical of young adolescents. They may not finish school or be able to get or keep a job because of

their substance abuse problem. They tend to remain dependent on friends or family to support them and their habit. Friends and family members who continue to serve the drug abuser in this role are called *enablers*, which means that they enable or empower the drug addict to continue in the lifestyle of a drug abuser.

Medical Concerns

Finally, medical concerns increase dramatically in drug abusers. Cancers involving the mouth, lungs, and liver are specific problems. The NCSC (1999, p. 4) reported the following increased risk of cancer by substance abusers:

- 19% increase in cancer of the mouth and tongue
- 30% increase in cancer of the larynx (voice box)
- 24% increase in cancer of the pharynx (windpipe)
- 10% increase in cancer of the liver
- 7% increase in cancer of the rectum

Intervention Programs for Adolescent Substance Abuse

… you need top-down and bottom-up support for prevention…. You need support from every level including the mayor, the clergy, the educators, and the citizens at all levels. (NIDA, 1997, p. 5)

Recovery from substance abuse addiction is often a long-term process that can be accomplished only with a great deal of self-determination and support from family, friends, school, social services, and medical agencies. On the road to recovery, relapse is common before a patient reaches periods of abstinence. Even then, an incredibly important part of the recovery process is for the individual to want to change and be determined to change the maladaptive pattern of behavior that has become a habit. Researchers have not been able to identify any one certain type of rehabilitation program that is likely to be effective for the majority of addicts because all individuals are unique and their problems and reasons for addiction are all different (NIDA InfoFacts, 1998).

Substance abuse prevention is cost-effective. NIDA InfoFacts (1998) reports that for every dollar spent on prevention, the community saves $4.00 to $5.00 later on for treatment.

Changing Addictive Behavior Patterns Is Difficult

Think of any less than positive habit you have. How many times have you tried to change that pattern of behavior? Have you been successful? Did the results last? Can you identify your successful strategies as compared to those that were not successful and did not help you change your behavior? This is the method that needs to be used to help adolescents change patterns of dangerous behavior such as substance abuse.

First, the problem must be identified. After the behavior of the student(s) with substance abuse is identified, the new, desirable pattern must be defined. It is not enough to tell the student *not* to drink, do drugs, or smoke. The student must be referred to a source that will teach necessary new behavioral options. Professionals must teach the student alternative behaviors, the positive behaviors that will replace substance abuse activities. Examples would include any appropriate types of activities the students could do instead of substance abuse behavior. Following are some suggestions (NIDA, 1997).

Social Skills   Teach social skills that will help adolescents resist peer pressure that often leads to substance abuse. This process is based on teaching students new skills they can apply every day in their lives. The intent is for students to develop skills to reduce and eliminate substance abuse. The *Skillstreaming* series by Goldstein and McGinnis (1997) provides an excellent curriculum that all teachers or other professionals can easily use.

Cognitive restructuring is a method used in many in- and outpatient treatment facilities. Teachers in the classroom can also use this method. It is comparable to teaching social skills but it goes one step further. Cognitive restructuring teaches the students thinking skills and problem-solving skills, skills to make good decisions. Kaplan (1995) indicates that cognitive restructuring is designed to promote more independence and self-reliance. Learning the process helps students develop an internal locus of control and self-management skills for independence.

Positive Peer Interactions   Teach with interactive methods. Peer discussions, support groups, and activities to demonstrate disapproval toward substance abuse have been more productive than lecture-type classes. Students like being up from their desks and most seem to be naturally social. Rather than trying to always work against this natural energy, allow the students to use it. Use cooperative learning groups. Set up performance-based assessments rather than traditional paper and pencil tests to allow students to demonstrate their substance abuse resistance knowledge.

Teams and Activities   Provide long-term activities starting in the primary grades of elementary school that endure and are carried through the high school years. Identify high-risk students. The higher the level of risk students experience, the earlier and more intensive the intervention must be. Prevention programs should enhance students' academic skills, provide a sense of identity and achievement, and strengthen the bond students have to their school and their teachers. Set up programs where students feel like they are an integral member of the team, that they are needed and valued. Give them responsibilities to carry out that will help build success of the entire program. Heap on the positive reinforcement. Teach students to feel good about themselves. This process will reduce the chances for development of substance abuse, apathy, truancy, and dropout.

Involve Families Involve families. Prevention and intervention that focus on the family have greater impact than those that focus only on children. Teach families to talk and work together toward common goals. Make these learning sessions fun for all involved. Teach parents about drug-related behaviors, warning signs, and paraphernalia to watch for at home in children's bedrooms and backpacks. Items may include any of those noted in Table 5-16.

Community Action Plans Promote school district-wide and community-wide programs that include media campaigns for policy changes. Advocate for new laws to restrict access to illegal substances. The programs are more effective when accompanied by a combination of school and family interventions.

After-School Activities Help schools to offer opportunities to all students, particularly those at risk for substance abuse. Keep school doors open after 3:30, during the weekends, and in the evenings. Many students have no one at home and no one to supervise their time out of school. Identify those students and make an effort to involve them in extracurricular athletic, drama, music, other school clubs, part-time jobs, and with adult mentors.

Implications for Working with Youth and Adolescents

The goal of this chapter was twofold. The first was to educate teachers, parents, and other professionals who work with youth and adolescents about substance abuse and its inherent dangers. Second, educators and parents must apply the information in the classroom to identify and refer students with substance abuse problems to the appropriate resources. Education about behaviors and indicators of substance abuse without application of the knowledge at home, at school, and in the community is purposeless. The information in this chapter is meant to provide guidelines and programming to help keep youth and adolescents safe, happy, and ultimately successful in life.

TABLE 5–16 Drug Paraphernalia

Marijuana	Cocaine	Crack	LSD	Inhalants
Bong (big water pipe that looks a little like an old-fashioned clear or colored glass oil lamp), **small pipe, roach clip** (small metal utensil used to hold a marijuana cigarette that is too small to hold with the fingers), rolling papers, baggies of ground up weedy-looking material	**Small mirror** to put cocaine on, **razor blade** to divide the pile of cocaine into lines, **small straw** to snort the lines of cocaine into the nostril, small vials or tiny bags of white powder	**Crack pipes** (narrow metal or glass tubes called **stems**) used as a device for smoking crack, small chunks of crystallized powder sealed in the corners of baggies (the corner of a baggie cut off, twisted, and melted to form a seal)	**Blotter paper** (small colorful squares of paper soaked in LSD are eaten), **windowpanes** (small squares of gelatin containing LSD are eaten, look like little chips of plastic), **microdots** (tiny purple tablets), **plastic film canisters** (hold liquid or crystallized LSD)	**Balloons** (to fill with nitrous oxide to inhale), **nitrous oxide canisters** (legal for making whipped cream, etc.); any other type of **aerosol containers, glue, gas,** or other toxic-smelling products

Note. From "So You Think You Know About Teens and Drugs: 15 Clues Parents Often Miss," by A. Ebron, June 1977, Family Circle, 54–57.

Ebron (1997) summarized the warning signs of substance abuse in adolescents. If teachers, parents, and other professionals who work with youth and adolescents notice several of the following behaviors, it may indicate that the individual is having a problem with substance abuse.

Warning Signs of Substance Abuse

- Fatigue, lethargy, apathy
  - Tired all the time, asks to sleep in school
- Noticeable changes in weight, appetite, sleeping habits
- Bloodshot eyes, dilated pupils
- Chronic runny nose
- Jittery, hyperactive behavior
  - Shaky hands, dizzy spells
- Change for the worse in personality, mood swings
  - Cannot concentrate, memory problems
  - Overly defensive, hyperirritable
- Problems in school
  - Tardy/truant
  - Failing grades
  - Poor attitude
  - Asks to go to restroom a lot (to drink or take drugs)
- Change in dress
  - Poor hygiene
  - Looks rumpled/slept in clothes
- Lack of interest in family and past favored activities
  - Increased secrecy
  - Possibly with new/different peer group
  - Does not want family to meet friends
- Items of drug paraphernalia in room, locker, or backpack

Educators spend a great deal of time with students every day during the week at school. They have the time and the influence to give positive messages to students about abstinence from drugs, cigarettes, alcohol, and other illegal substances. The National Clearinghouse for Alcohol and Drug Information (2002) publishes a variety of resources on substance abuse for educators, par-

ents, and teens. It is extremely important that parents and educators be open to talking with adolescents about substance abuse issues. Teach new, more effective thinking patterns and consequently appropriate behavior (cognitive restructuring; Kaplan, 1995). Following are suggestions educators and parents can use to reinforce socially acceptable and appropriate thinking patterns in all youth and adolescents at home, at school, and in the community.

Content Knowledge for Cognitive Restructuring Regarding Substance Abuse

- Know the law: Substance abuse is illegal. Adolescents can be prosecuted and punished with fines, detention, and time in corrections.
- Be aware of the risks: Substance abuse increases the chance for illness, accidents, injury, and death—yours and others.
- Keep your edge: Substance abuse can ruin your health, your brain, and your looks. It makes you feel depressed and increases academic deficiency and creates problems with your friends.
- Play it safe and do the smart thing: One incident of substance abuse could make you do something you will regret for the rest of your life. Protect your health, family, friends, social life, and education by saying no to drugs and alcohol.
- Think twice about what you buy and wear: Are your T-shirts, hats, or jewelry walking billboards for alcohol, drugs, cigarettes, or other unhealthy habits?
- Face your problems: Substance abuse is not an escape or a method to solve problems. Substance abuse creates more problems.
- Be a real friend: Be part of the solution for others with substance abuse problems. Refer them to good sources for help.
- Remember: *Everybody else is* NOT *doing it!* Over half of all high school students have never tried any drug. Abstinence from substance abuse will contribute to making you happy, popular, and successful.

References

Coleman, M. C., Webber, J. (2002). *Emotional and behavioral disorders: Theory and practice.* (4th ed.). Needham Heights: MA: Allyn & Bacon.

Dobkin, P. L., Tremblay, R. E., Masse, L. C., & Vitaro, F. (1995). Individual and peer characteristics in predicting boys' early onset of substance abuse: A seven-year longitudinal study. *Child Development, 66*(4), 1198–1214.

Dodge, K. A. (1993). Social-cognitive mechanisms in the development of conduct disorder and depression. *Annual Review of Psychology, 44,* 559–584.

Ebron, A. (1997, June 3). So you think you know about teens and drugs: 15 clues parents often miss. *Family Circle,* 54–57.

Embry, D. D. (1997). Physiology of behavior 101: *How school climate can prevent or increase substance abuse and violent crime.* Paper presented at the Illinois Safe and Drug Free Schools Conference, Springfield, IL.

Goldstein, A. P., & McGinnis, E. (1997). *Skillstreaming the adolescent* (2nd ed.). Champaign, IL: Research Press.

Hanson, C. (1997, March). I had no idea my child was on drugs. *Ladies Home Journal, 195,* 66–70.

Hoyert, D. L., Arias, E., Smith, B. L., Murphy, S. L., & Kochanek, K. D. (2001, September). Deaths: Final data for 1999. *National Vital Statistics Report, 49*(8). Center for Disease Control and Prevention. Retrieved from www.cdc.gov/nchs/about/major/dvs/mortdata.htm

Jensen, M. M., & Yerington, P. C. (1997). *Gangs: Straight talk, straight up.* Longmont, CO: Sopris West.

Johnston, L. D., O'Malley, P. M., & Bachman, J. G. (2000a, December). *Cigarette use and smokeless tobacco use decline substantially among teens.* University of Michigan News and Information Services: Ann Arbor, MI. Retrieved from www.monitoringthefuture.org

Johnston, L. D., O'Malley, P. M., & Bachman, J. G. (2000b, December). *"Ecstasy" use rises sharply among teens in 2000; use of many other drugs steady, but significant declines are reported for some.* University of Michigan News and Information Services: Ann Arbor, MI. Retrieved from www.monitoringthefuture.org

Johnston, L. D., O'Malley, P. M., & Bachman, J. G. (2003). *Monitoring the Future national survey results on adolescent drug use: Overview of key findings, 2002* (NIH Publication No. 03-5374). Bethesda, MD: National Institute on Drug Abuse.

Jordan, D. R. (1998). *Attention deficit disorder: ADHD and ADD syndromes.* Austin, TX: Pro-Ed.

Kaplan, J. S. (with Carter, J.). (1995). *Beyond behavior modification* (3rd ed.). Austin, TX: Pro-Ed.

Kauffman, J. M. (2001). *Characteristics of emotional and behavioral disorders of children and youth* (7th ed.). Upper Saddle River, NJ: Merrill/Prentice Hall.

Kerr, M. M., & Nelson C. M. (2002). *Strategies for addressing behavior problems in the classroom* (4th ed.). Upper Saddle River, NJ: Merrill/Prentice Hall.

King, P. (1996, May). Bitter pill. *Sports Illustrated, 84*(21), 24–30.

McCallum, J. (1986). The cruelest thing ever. *Sports Illustrated, 64*(26), 20–27.

Narconon of Southern California. (2003). *Drug statistics.* Retrievable from www.drug-statistics.com

National Child Safety Council (1999). *Illusions: An informative guide about alcohol and other drugs.* Publication available from National Child Safety Council, 4065 Page Avenue, PO Box 1368, Jackson, MI 49204-1368, (517) 764-6070. www.healthy.net

National Clearinghouse for Alcohol and Drug Information (1997). *Drugs of abuse* (Publication No. RP0926). National Clearinghouse for Alcohol and Drug Information, PO Box 2345, Rockville, MD 20847-2345. 1-800-729-6686 (TDD 1-800-487-4889). www.health.org/

National Clearinghouse for Alcohol and Drug Information. (2002). *Tips for teens.* Retrievable from store.health.org/catalog

National Clearinghouse for Alcohol and Drug Information, Center for Substance Abuse Treatment. (2003, March). Inhalants. *Substance Abuse Treatment Advisory, 3*(1). Retrievable from www.samhsa.gov/centers/csat2002/pubs/ms922.pdf

National Criminal Justice Reference Service (2001a). *Club drugs resources—facts and figures.* Retrievable from www.ncjrs.org/club_drugs/facts.html

National Criminal Justice Reference Service (2001b). *In the spotlight: Club drugs—Summary.* Retrievable from www.ncjrs.org/club_drugs/club_drugs.html

National Institute on Drug Abuse (1997, March). *Preventing drug use among children and adolescents: A research-based guide* (NIH publication No. 97-4212). Retrievable from www.nida.nih.gov/

National Institute on Drug Abuse (1999). *Club drugs: Community drug alert.* Retrievable from www.drugabuse.gov

National Institute on Drug Abuse. (2003). *Commonly abused drugs.* Retrievable from www.nida.nih.gov/DrugPages/DrugsofAbuse.html

National Institute on Drug Abuse InfoFacts. (1998). *Costs to society* (NIH Publication No. 038). Retrievable from www.nida.nih.gov

National Institute on Drug Abuse InfoFacts. (2001). *Hospital visits*. Retrievable from www.nida.nih.gov/infofax/hospital.html

Shedler, J., & Block, J. (1990). Adolescent drug use and psychological health: A longitudinal inquiry. *American Psychologist*, 45(5), 612–630.

Swan. N. (1998, November). Drug abuse cost to society set at $97.7 billion, continuing steady increase since 1975. NIDA *Notes*, 13(4). Retrievable from www.nida.nih.gov

Tremblay, R. E., Masse, B., Perron, D., & Leblanc, M. (1992). Early disruptive behavior, poor school achievement, delinquent behavior, and delinquent personality: Longitudinal analysis. *Journal of Consulting and Clinical Psychology*, 60, 64–72.

U.S. Department of Education. (1998). *Growing up drug-free: A parent's guide to prevention*. Booklet available from Growing Up Drug Free, Pueblo, CO 81009 or 1-877-4EDPUBS or www.ed.gov/offices/

U.S. Department of Health and Human Services. *Healthy people*. (2000, November). Retrievable from www.odphp.osophs.dhhs.gov

U.S. Department of Justice/Drug Enforcement Administration (2000, February). *Drug intelligence brief: An overview of club drugs* (Publication No. DEA-2005). Retrievable from www.usdoj.gov/dea/index.htm

U.S. Drug Enforcement Administration. (n.d.). DEA *mission statement*. Retrievable from www.usdoj.gov/dea/agency/mission.htm

U.S. Drug Enforcement Administration (n.d.) *Drug descriptions*. Retrievable from www.usdoj.gov/dea/concern/concern.htm

U.S. Drug Enforcement Administration (n.d.) *Get it straight*. Retrievable from www.usdoj.gov/dea/pubs/straight/toc.htm

CHAPTER 6

SCHOOL VIOLENCE

After completing the chapter, the reader will be able to identify:

- Causes of school violence.
- Trends in school violence.
- Signals of potential school violence.
- Proactive strategies to reduce incidents of school violence.
- Implications for teachers, parents, and other professionals who work with youth and adolescents.

Introduction

It's Hard Growing Up

It's hard growing up knowing that going around each
corner might lead to danger.
It's hard growing up knowing that one day your little
brother or sister might get shot.
It's hard growing up knowing that your friend might
get into a gang without thinking twice.
It's hard to know that all the knowledge in the world
can't make up for a human life.
*It's hard growing up never knowing what will happen.**

Lakeisha Williams

At the time she wrote this poem, Lakeisha was a 13-year-old junior high school student in Rock Island, Illinois. She, like many youth and adolescents, has to overcome inordinate obstacles just to get to school every morning. These students live in neighborhoods that can be incredibly dangerous. Sometimes that violence transitions onto school grounds, invades the school building, and flows through students attending school and participating in school activities. All educators must be able to recognize the indicators of youth violence in order to reduce and eliminate it from schools in this country. The Center for the Prevention of School Violence (2000) defines school violence as "any behavior that violates a school's educational mission or climate of respect or jeopardizes the intent of the school to be free of aggression against persons or property, drugs, weapons, disruptions, and disorder."

The goal of this chapter is to provide an introduction to the problem of violence in the nation's schools, to make all educators more aware of the scope of school violence, and to provide some basic strategies to counteract potential violence in a

*From *Gangs: Straight Talk, Straight Up* (p. 227) by M. M. Jensen and P. C. Yerington, 1997, Longmont, CO: Sopris West. Copyright 1997 by Sopris West. Reprinted with permission.

proactive manner. The role of the student with a behavioral disorder is presented as only one component of the problem as a whole. It is beyond the scope of the chapter to provide a "how to" manual to deal with the problem of violence in schools. In collaboration with school security experts, each school district must formulate an individualized plan based on its unique population of students, geographic location, and individual problems and needs.

School Achievement Is Vital to Life Success

School achievement is a vital component of success in life. Regardless of their race or gender, students who said they had "frequent problems with their schoolwork" were more likely to use alcohol, smoke cigarettes, become violent, carry weapons, and attempt suicide. Results from the National Longitudinal Study of Adolescent Health reported that school performance, more than any other single factor, was a determinant in whether an adolescent became involved in drugs and violence. In addition, participation in supervised activities after school is highly beneficial to students. Adolescents who spend time after school in extracurricular, community, church, or recreational activities are much less likely to drink, smoke, have sex, or carry weapons as compared with students who spend their after-school hours in unsupervised settings. Educators, parents, and other professionals who work with youth and adolescents should collaborate to provide appropriate supervised activities during after-school, evening, and weekend hours for students who need them (National School Safety Center, 2001).

Schools play an important role in shaping future roles of the youth of the nation; however, educators are by no means responsible for solving the very complex problem of youth violence independently. Collaborative programs developed by schools, communities, and parents delivered to youth on a consistent basis should be the foundation for arresting the spiraling acts of violence committed by youth.

Trends in School Violence

Statistics about school safety issues are all based on self-report surveys from persons in the school environment. Because they are based on individuals' perceptions of problems, there is some variation in results. Some statistics show trends increasing while others show a decrease. In general, however, statistics on school violence seemed to be showing a pattern of improvement during the past 10 years.

Statistics on gang presence at school are divided. From 1989 to 1995 to 1999, student concerns of gang presence in their school rose from 15% to 28% to 30% (Kaufman et al., 1998; Metropolitan Life Insurance Company, 1999). Because gangs are often involved in drugs, weapons, and criminal activities, it stands to reason that their presence would increase the level of violence in schools. The Office of Juvenile Justice and Delinquency Prevention (2000) indicates that 37% of students reported a gang presence at their school. However, the U.S. Department of Education and the U.S. Department of Justice (1999) annual report on school safety indicates that student reports of gangs at school fell from 29% in 1995 to 17% in 1999.

Students' perception of violence at their school is related to their perception of teacher effectiveness. It is crucial for teachers to build positive rapport with students to help them feel safe and to learn at school. When teachers are viewed as being caring and supportive, students report lower levels of social tension and violence in their schools. For example, when Student and Teacher Perceptions' of Safety at School students describe their teachers as supportive, encouraging, and respectful, only 49% of students experience *very* or *somewhat serious* problems with violence. However, 64% of students report experiencing violence in schools where teachers are not highly rated by students, meaning the students do not perceive the teachers as being

caring or supportive (Metropolitan Life Insurance Company, 1999). It appears that teacher behavior and interactions with students can have a strong impact on levels of violence in the school.

Approximately one of every four students (24%) in the nation's schools reports experiencing hostile or negative remarks, physical fights, destructive acts, turf battles, and gang violence (Metropolitan Life Insurance Company, 1999). Physical attacks without a weapon, theft, and vandalism are much more common in schools than are more serious incidents. The Center for Prevention of School Violence (2000) reported a steady decline from 17% to 12% of the number of students who reported taking a gun to school. Interestingly, fights or attacks with a weapon are more likely to occur in middle schools or junior high schools as compared to senior high schools. There may be two main reasons for this. First, the students who have very severe aggression and hostility problems may have either dropped out or have been removed from the public school setting. Second, by the time students reach high school, they have learned more appropriate social skills and verbal interaction methods to solve their problems. Many students need to be directly taught appropriate social skills and communication skills to replace their habitual problem behaviors. Appropriate social skills are life skills. They are as critically important to successful adult adjustment as are academic and employment skills.

Assaults and Thefts in School

The good news is that, although school violence does exist, the rates of crime and violence at school have been decreasing (National School Safety Center, [NSSC] 2001). Although statistics on school safety show reductions in the number of incidents of school violence, many students and staff continue to feel unsafe at school.

The National Criminal Justice Reference Service (2000) reported that there were 133,700 violent crimes against teachers and 217,400 thefts from teachers. Based on a 12-month schedule, that averages out to about 11,000 assaults against teachers and 18,000 thefts from teachers every month in schools across the nation. The Bureau of Justice Statistics (2000) reports that there are about 83 crimes per 1,000 teachers annually.

During 1998, middle school and high school students were victims of more than 2.7 million crimes at school. Of the total, 253,000 (about 9.4%) were considered serious violent crimes (rape, sexual assault, robbery, and aggravated assault). Middle school students were more likely than high school students to be assaulted at school. On a positive note, between 1992 and 1998 violent crime against students was reduced by nearly one third—from 144 crimes per 1,000 students in 1992 to 101 crimes per 1,000 students in 1998 (Bureau of Justice Statistics, 2000).

Guns in School

Based on a self-report survey, more than one in five (21%) high school male students and 15% of middle school male students took a weapon to school at least once during the past school year (NSSC, 2001). Their reason: self-protection. These students claim school is a dangerous place. In a study conducted by the Josephson Institute of Ethics (2001), more than one in every three students (39% of middle schoolers and 36% of high schoolers) said they do not feel safe at school.

The Bureau of Justice Statistics (2000) reported that between 1993 and 1997 the number of high school students who admitted taking a weapon (gun, knife, or other) to school in the previous 30 days fell from 12% to 9%. This might not look like a big reduction at first glance. However, it is a substantial 25% decrease!

During the 1998–1999 school year, 3,523 students were expelled for bringing a firearm to school (latest year for which statistics have been reported). During the 1997–1998 school year, 3,658 students were expelled. The U.S. Department of Education and U.S. Department of Justice (2000) indicated that this figure is down from 1996–1997,

when the first report listed 5,724 expulsions. The majority of the expulsions (59%) were for handguns brought to school. Twelve percent were for rifles or shotguns, and 29% were for bombs, grenades, or starter pistols. Most expulsions (57%) were in high schools, 33% were in junior highs and, as in the previous year, 10% were in elementary schools (Malico, 2000).

Teacher Perceptions of Safety at School

The majority of public school teachers (almost 9 of every 10, or 85%) are not worried about being physically attacked in or around their school. Results from teachers who responded to the 1999 *Metropolitan Life Survey of the American Teacher, Violence in America's Public Schools*, reported that 75% felt *very safe* in or around their school. That statistic was shown to be highly correlated with teacher perception of the quality of education provided at their schools. When comparing whether teachers thought their schools were as safe as they were 5 years ago, only 37% of educators who rated their schools as providing a *fair or poor* education believed they were *about as safe*. In comparison, 60% of teachers who rated their schools as providing an *excellent* quality of education thought their schools were about as safe at they had been. Additionally, 41% of teachers who thought their school provided only *fair or poor* education also thought violence would increase over the next 2 years, while only 17% of teachers who thought their school provided an *excellent* education did. It appears that safe schools may also be associated with effective schools (Metropolitan Life Insurance Company, 1999). Complete results and all statistics from this survey may be accessed from www.metlife.com/Companyinfo/Community/Found

Definition of School Violence

How is school violence defined? How can educators recognize specific student behaviors that might be precursors to acts of school violence?

Dwyer, Osher, and Warger (1998) suggest that a broad range of potentially problematic overt behaviors and emotions comprise acts of violence that occur in schools. Examples include aggression and violent behavior toward others, suicide, abuse of illegal narcotics, and other dangerous interpersonal behaviors. These are behaviors that will negatively affect all students and school staff.

The National School Safety Center (2001) published a checklist of characteristics common to youth who commit acts of violence. This checklist may be used to help educators identify adolescents who may have the potential to create a crisis in the classroom. While there is no foolproof system for identifying potentially dangerous students who may harm themselves and/or others, this checklist provides a starting point:

_____ 1. Has a history of tantrums and uncontrollable angry outbursts.

_____ 2. Characteristically resorts to name calling, cursing, or abusive language.

_____ 3. Habitually makes violent threats when angry.

_____ 4. Has previously brought a weapon to school.

_____ 5. Has a background of serious disciplinary problems at school and in the community.

_____ 6. Has a background of drug, alcohol or other substance abuse or dependency.

_____ 7. Is on the fringe of his/her peer group with few or no close friends.

_____ 8. Is preoccupied with weapons, explosives, or other incendiary devices.

_____ 9. Has previously been truant, suspended, or expelled from school.

_____ 10. Displays cruelty to animals.

_____ 11. Has little or no supervision and support from parents or a caring adult.

_____ 12. Has witnessed or been a victim of abuse or neglect in the home.

_____ 13. Has been bullied and/or bullies or intimidates peers or younger children.

_____ 14. Tends to blame others for difficulties and problems s/he causes her/himself.

_____ 15. Consistently prefers TV shows, movies, or music expressing violent themes and acts.

_____ 16. Prefers reading materials dealing with violent themes, rituals and abuse.

_____ 17. Reflects anger, frustration, and the dark side of life in school essays or writing projects.

_____ 18. Is involved with a gang or an antisocial group on the fringe of peer acceptance.

_____ 19. Is often depressed and/or has significant mood swings.

_____ 20. Has threatened or attempted suicide[†]

The checklist may help to identify students who could be potential perpetrators of school violence. This process may also promote feelings of security at school for all students. To facilitate academic achievement and foster excellence in education, students need a school environment that feels safe and secure. School violence is detrimental to student learning. Aggression and hostile behavior in the classroom is likely to reduce student achievement due to the anxiety, tension, and disruption to the teaching/learning process. For students to achieve their highest potential, educators must spend more time teaching students and less time dealing with behavioral disruptions.

Factors That May Lead to School Violence

How might students who are at risk for committing acts of violence at school be described? Three main patterns in early behavior have been

[†]© 1998 National School Safety Center. Reprinted with permission.

described (Dodge, 1993) which are thought to be precursors of student violence at school:

- A home environment that is harsh, negative, and overly punitive
- Aggressive behavior demonstrated at a young age
- Lack of age-appropriate social skills with peers and adults

Family Factors

Two of the top four causes of school violence as determined by public school teachers who participated in the 1999 *Metropolitan Life Survey of the American Teacher* referred to family-related factors. The primary reason was lack of parental supervision in the home (77%). Second was lack of family involvement (69%). Third was negative peer group pressure (58%). Fourth was student involvement with drugs and alcohol (32%) (Metropolitan Life Insurance Company, 1999).

Family stressors, including poverty, divorce, drug and alcohol abuse, and child abuse and neglect, appear to be an early source of delayed development in children, which is often exacerbated by ineffective parenting practices (Patterson, Reid, & Dishion, 1992). Children then bring their maladaptive learned patterns of behavior to school for teachers to deal with. Some of these students may end up being referred for special education services. However, many students with a host of problems are not referred for one reason or another or do not actually qualify for special services. These are the students who may begin to show behaviors similar to those on the National School Safety Checklist. However, it is also important to understand that any student, no matter what the family background and parenting practices, can develop problem behaviors that may be disruptive at school.

It is critically important for all teachers to understand that there is a student in every classroom, in every school no matter what the size or location of the school, who has the potential to create a crisis or commit an act of violence in the classroom.

Teacher Training

The average educator was not trained to deal with the escalating levels of school violence being acted out by students in schools across the country. In the recent past, teacher training programs rightly focused on effectively preparing future educators to teach reading, writing, math, and other academic content areas. Special educators were the only teachers specifically trained in behavior management methods for the classroom. In the past, there was not such a crucial need for all teachers to be able to effectively manage crisis situations in the classroom. That need has shifted. Teacher training programs need to effectively prepare all future educators to use proactive behavior management methods in the classroom to promote more appropriate social skills, communication skills, and academic excellence.

To protect the safe and secure learning environment for all students and staff in schools across the country, every educator must be able to recognize the signal behaviors associated with school violence. All school staff should be part of the team that promotes a "no tolerance" attitude toward school violence.

A Perspective on Violence

The primary responsibility of the school is to facilitate academic achievement. Schools also need to promote appropriate social skills and well-adjusted behavioral patterns. Walker, Colvin, and Ramsey (1995) suggest that the societal and economic problems experienced by the general population are affecting children and spilling over into schools. Children learn problem behaviors as infants, toddlers, and preschoolers in the home environment. The problem behaviors are functional; they serve a purpose. Because the maladaptive behavior patterns have been successful in getting wants and needs met in the home situation, children bring deviant behaviors to school. The behaviors can be collectively referred to as *coercion* (Rhode, Jenson, & Reavis, 1992).

Coercive Behaviors

Coercive behaviors are learned and demonstrated by children at a very young age. Coercion is an escalating pattern of behavior children use when they want to get their own way or want to get adults to withdraw requests. The hierarchy of coercion described by Rhode et al. (1992) is based on noncompliance to adult requests and includes ignoring, whining, arguing, stalling or delay tactics, temper tantrums, and verbal or physical aggression. As the child's behavior escalates, many adults will back down and not require the child to follow through on a given request or command. Why? The main reason is that the child's behavior becomes intimidating and difficult to deal with. Rosemund (1998) suggested that parents often avoid dealing with a child's coercive behavior due to fear that the child will misbehave in public, they will be regarded as "bad" parents, or ultimately that their children will not like them.

Consequently, the children come to school and many use the same maladaptive behavior patterns in the schools during their primary years. The maladaptive behavior patterns demonstrated by students are greatly complicating the job of the teacher. Teachers have a hard time teaching, and students have a more difficult time concentrating and learning. Classroom disruptions influence feelings students have about their own safety and well-being. It is difficult for teachers to establish positive, caring relationships with students who demonstrate coercive behaviors. The positive rapport that teachers build with students can set the stage for increased feelings of safety at school.

Teach Positive Replacements for Violent Behaviors

Teachers can act to reduce violent and antisocial behaviors by directly teaching and consistently reinforcing socially appropriate replacement behaviors for those who are disruptive and potentially violent. This is basically a four-step process (see Table 6–1). First, teachers need to confront the problem behavior and tell students why that behavior is not appropriate for the school environment. Second, teachers need to teach the students what to do instead of the problem behavior. Many students actually do not understand what they are doing wrong. Other people in their environment who are role models all walk, talk, and act like they do. Teachers cannot control student behavior outside the school, but they can set expectations for appropriate behavior in school that will lead to increased academic achievement and improved social behavior. The third step is to prompt practice opportunities and give students feedback. Finally,

TABLE 6–1 Four-Step Process to Teach Appropriate Replacement Behaviors

1. Confront the problem behavior. Tell students why it is not appropriate for the school situation.
2. Teach the student a functional behavior to do in place of the problem behavior. Tell the student why it is important to do the new behavior and what benefit (s)he will get from doing it.
3. Prompt practice opportunities to help the student learn and internalize the new replacement behavior. Give lots of opportunities to practice. Consider giving students points or some type of bonus to motivate the student to show the new behavior. This method can provide a little incentive to help the student get back on a positive roll.
4. Give the student A LOT of positive reinforcement for trying the new replacement behavior. Prompt the student to do the new behavior in order to provide more chances to gain positive reinforcement.

Note. *From* Gangs: Straight Talk, Straight Up *by M. M. Jensen and P. C. Yerington, 1997, Longmont, CO: Sopris West. Copyright 1997 by Sopris West. Reprinted with permission.*

give a lot of positive reinforcement when the student tries the new, appropriate replacement behavior.

Cautions About Using Punishment

Punishment Is Reactive Rather Than Proactive

Unfortunately, it seems that it is basic human nature for teachers to just try to suppress or punish maladaptive behaviors students show in the classroom. Most teachers' first instinct is to simply punish problem behavior because they want to stop it. However, research does not support the use of punishment as a durable means of behavior change (Jensen & Yerington, 1997; Rhode et al., 1992). The problem with punishment is that it is merely reactive; teachers wait until a problem occurs, and then deliver an aversive consequence designed to discourage the student from repeating the problem behavior.

All teachers must be trained to be proactive, to plan and be prepared to teach the students what to do *instead* of the problem behavior. This means that for every problem behavior that teachers would like to reduce, they need to teach an appropriate replacement for the problem. This will help the students to learn how to get their wants and needs met through appropriate and acceptable means. It will teach them new patterns of behavior, resulting in higher academic achievement and improved social skills and behavior.

Students who routinely have academic and behavioral problems at school often end up dropping out. It is imperative that teachers learn proactive management strategies in order to keep students in school. Walker et al. (1995) report that 80% of all crime in the United States is committed by high school dropouts. The Bureau of Justice Statistics (2000) reports that two thirds of all prison inmates are high school dropouts (Jensen & Yerington,

1997). Schools must focus on educating all students as opposed to incarcerating uneducated criminals. If used consistently, proactive behavior management can supply one piece of the puzzle necessary to help more students stay in school and graduate with a diploma.

When Crimes Occur

One strategy that schools might use to build more positive rapport with students and to decrease crime and violence is to keep school doors open after regular hours. Results from a survey that was conducted by the Ewing Marion Kauffman Foundation (2001) indicated that juveniles are most likely to commit crimes and acts of violence between 3:00 and 8:00 P.M. This is prime time for adolescents to engage in high-risk behaviors. Statistics show that rates for juvenile crime and experimentation with drugs, sex, alcohol, and cigarettes all increase during this period if there is no supervision. For many students, this is unsupervised time before parents get home from work. Using collaborative strategies, schools, the community, and parents may be successful in decreasing crime potential by providing structured and supervised after-school activities.

Federal Legislation to Promote Safe Schools

Federal legislation has laid the groundwork for establishing school policies to reduce issues related to school violence. The laws institute a foundation that schools can build on to promote school safety and consistent policies for reducing and effectively managing potential violence. The following explanations of federal legislation are summarized from an excellent review by Kopka (1997).

Gun-Free Schools Act

The Gun-Free Schools Act (GFSA) of 1994 requires each state to formulate a state law specifying that local education agencies (LEA) expel any student who brings a firearm to school for a period of no less than one year. Each state has to enact this law in order to continue to receive funding from the Elementary and Secondary Education Act (ESEA) of 1965. However, the LEA does have the right to modify the expulsion requirement on a case-by-case basis. Specifically:

> Educators should be aware that Congress passed a law entitled the *Gun-Free Schools Act of* 1994. This law was a portion of the *Improving America's Schools Act of* 1994, which itself was part of the reauthorization of the *Elementary and Secondary Education Act of* 1965 (ESEA). Under this law, every state is required to have in effect by October 20, 1995, a state law requiring local educational agencies to expel from school any student found in possession of a gun at school. (An exception is made for students with disabilities under either the IDEA or Section 504 of the Rehabilitation Act. These students can be expelled for only 45 days.) The state laws may also permit the local education agency's chief executive officer (presumably the superintendent) to modify the expulsion requirement on a case-by-case basis. This law is currently in full effect. (North Central Regional Educational Laboratory, 1995)

Students with Disabilities and Section 504

Schools must be in compliance with Section 504 of the Rehabilitation Act of 1973, Title II of the Americans with Disabilities Act, which states that an individual cannot be discriminated against because of a disability. Herein lies a great deal of bitter controversy. Many educators believe that all students should be treated the same for committing acts of violence. If a student who has been officially labeled with a disability commits an act of violence at school, his behavior may not automatically be governed under the same restrictions as other students' behavior. A reevaluation of the student must be performed to decide whether the maladaptive behavior was related to the disability. If it was, the student is not punished according to

the state law and school policies. If a student with a disability is expelled for any period of time, an amendment to the Individualized Education Plan (IEP) is written in the form of a change in program to provide services in another setting. The LEA does have the right to seek a court order to remove any student whose behavior is deemed too dangerous for the school environment. Private schools are not governed under the GFSA. Students from private schools who participate in activities or programs at the LEA are subject to the stated provisions of the GFSA. Detailed information may be accessed at *www.ed.gov/offices*/OESE/SDFS/

The Safe and Drug-Free Schools and Community Act of 1994

The purpose of the Safe and Drug-Free Schools and Community Act (SDFSCA) of 1994 was to provide funding in the form of state grants for home, school, and community violence prevention and the reduction of drug and alcohol abuse. Grants are provided to set up training and activities on the topics of violence prevention strategies and drug and alcohol education programs for students; training and technical information for educators; and the collaborative development of violence and drug prevention programs between home, schools, and the community. *Collaboration* is the key word. All funding for programs is based on cooperation between educational agencies, parents, and community agencies to plan and present violence and substance abuse reduction programs. Detailed information may be accessed at www.ed.gov/offices/OESE/

Goals 2000: Educate America Act of 1994

Goals 2000: Educate America Act of 1994 was designed by state governors in 1989. Its purpose was to provide resources to states and communities to develop and implement education reforms. The goal of the reforms was to assist students to reach elevated academic and occupational standards. Some officials say that the national education goals are unrealistically ambitious. Baseline figures were established in 1990, and progress toward goal mastery is currently documented to be modest at best. Some comparison figures related to potential school violence are provided in Box 6–1 regarding Goal Seven: Safe, Disciplined, and Alcohol- and Drug-Free Schools. Measures of progress are charted by the National Education Goals Panel (Kopka, 1997).

Warning Signs of School Violence

Communicative Intent of Behavior

Early warning signs should be viewed as signal behaviors or indicators that a student may be on the verge of committing an act of violence and needs immediate help (Dwyer, Osher, & Warger, 1998). All educators must begin to recognize the range of possible signals that project *communicative intent*, that is, the student's outward behavior when he does not seem to be able to communicate in words. Many students do not have the actual communication skills and social skills necessary to ask for help in the usual verbal manner.

It is imperative that educators learn to translate the signal behaviors. For example, a student's need for support and encouragement to talk might come in the form of acting out, aggression, verbal threats, giving up and refusing to try, maladaptive behavior of withdrawal, reticence, or possibly making threats to hurt self or others. Teachers may need to learn to interpret what students mean, need, or want based on how they behave. Many adults will not recognize the communications for what they are; a strong plea for attention and assistance by using behavior, the only means a student has. Once teachers start recognizing that some students have deficient verbal communication skills, those students can be taught strategies to improve those skills.

There are two strategies that many teachers could use to teach effective communication skills to students. One method is to teach the students to use I *messages* (see Boxes 6–2 and 6–3). I messages are used to communicate a message to another person in a simple, straightforward manner. The other is to teach a self-instructional problem-solving format (see Box 6–4). The main idea of the problem-solving format is to teach the student a series of steps that he can go through with the goal of making a good decision or choice. It can be used as a preventive measure or it can be used in response to a problem situation.

Take All Threats Seriously

All educators must take the threat to hurt oneself or others as seriously as they would a suicide

Box 6–1 Goal Seven: Safe, Disciplined, and Alcohol- and Drug-Free Schools

Problem Description	1990 Baseline Figure	1995 Figure
Overall percentage of student drug and alcohol use	24%	33%
Sale of drugs at school	18%	24%
Victimization of tenth-grade students	40%	36%
Victimization of public school teachers	10%	15%
Tenth-grade students reporting behavioral disruptions interfere with teaching	17%	17%
Number of disruptions reported by secondary school teachers that interfere with teaching and learning	37%	46%

Note. From School Violence by D. L. Kopka (1997), Santa Barbara, CA: ABC-CLIO.

threat from a student. Effective teachers do not evaluate the potential seriousness of a suicide threat; they immediately refer the student for the appropriate services. That is the same procedure that should be followed when students make a threat of violence against another student or a staff member. Consider threats of school violence in the same light as suicide threats.

Students who take guns to school and kill classmates and/or teachers are ending their lives as unequivocally as if they had turned the guns on themselves. These students have such a huge deficit in communication and social skills that they do not have the ability to talk out problems and ask for the help they need. These seem to be students who do not feel connected to school, family, or peers.

Box 6–2 I-Message Strategy for Students

Step #1: Begin with an objective description of the behavior.
   "When you don't let me play the game…"
Step #2: Relate your personal feelings.
   "I get mad and I feel like punching you…"

Step #3: Tell the effect the misbehavior has.
   "Because I feel like nobody likes me."
Step #4: End with a specific request to redirect the behavior.
   "Please let me play the game with you guys."

Note. *Steps 1–4 from "Motivate! Managing Misbehavior,"* 1989, Creative Classroom, *13(5) p. 28.*

Box 6–3 I-Message Strategy for Educators

Step #1: Begin with an objective description of the behavior.
   "When I have to ask you to do something five times…"
Step #2: Relate your personal feelings.
   "I get very annoyed…"

Step #3: Tell the effect the misbehavior has.
   "Because I feel like you are not listening to me."
Step #4: End with a specific request to redirect the behavior.
   "Please please do what I ask you the first time or else tell me when you are going to do it."

Note. *Steps 1–4 from "Motivate! Managing Misbehavior,"* 1989, Creative Classroom, *13(5) p. 28.*

Box 6–4 Self-Instructional Strategy for Problem Solving

1. Say the problem in your own words. Explain how it affects you. How does it affect other people?
2. What was your responsibility for the problem?
3. List all of the different things you could do to try to solve the problem.
4. Write down what might happen if you did each solution.
5. Which solution would work the best? How did you did you decide on this one?
6. Think about the solution you picked. Tell step by step how you will carry out the solution.
7. What did you learn from this experience? How will it help you in the future?

They see their lives as so hopeless that a gun is the one method they think they can use to change the situation. Subsequently, they take the gun to school, carry out their threats of violence, and very effectively end any chance they might have had to become a well-adjusted, successful, and productive member of society. What kind of future is possible for an adolescent who has taken a gun to school and willfully killed and injured teachers and classmates?

In the wake of the tragic school shootings during the spring of 1998, after every single occurrence, witnesses stated that the student who did the shooting threatened that very action prior to taking the gun to school. Most people thought that type of violence would not actually be perpetrated in their community, at their school; most witnesses said no one actually expected the student would carry out his threat.

The following early warning signs of school violence were adapted from Dwyer et al. (1998). The list details specific indicators that teachers must be aware of as signals that an act of violence is imminent. Teachers who establish caring and supportive relationships with students at school are more likely to recognize these signals as the behavior patterns and emotional attitudes that precede an impending crisis. The potential for violence may be significantly reduced for students who have a positive and meaningful connection to an adult.

Early Warning Signs of School Violence

- **Social withdrawal and isolation:** Students who lack social skills and communication skills may often be peer group isolates. The problems may stem from complicating problems such as depression, feelings of rejection, bullying, or past trauma and abuse.
- **Being a victim of violence, abuse, or neglect:** Some students who have been victimized may turn their emotional distress on others and act out the violence they have experienced.
- **Lack of interest in school and low academic performance:** Students may demonstrate two

diverse patterns of academic failure. The first occurs when there is a drastic change for the worse in school performance. The second takes place when chronic school failure inhibits a student's capacity to learn and achieve at school. To determine the true nature of the problem, assess both the cognitive and the emotional foundation for the lack of progress.
- **Writing, drawing, and daily behavior that depict acts of violence:** Students who express overrepresentation of feelings of anger and rage intensely and frequently may be projecting signals of imminent violent behavior. They should be referred to a school psychologist or other counselor for professional assessment.
- **History of discipline problems such as aggression, intimidation, bully behavior, and gang membership:** Students who demonstrate these overt problem behaviors set the stage for lifelong problems, including defiance of authority, law-breaking, and criminal activity.
- **Prejudice:** Students who demonstrate intense prejudice based on racial, ethnic, religious, language, gender, sexual orientation, physical appearance, or ability may lead to violent intimidation and assaults. This behavior warrants referral to an appropriate counseling service.
- **Alcohol and other drug abuse:** Students who abuse alcohol and other drugs may be subjected to violence as perpetrators and/or victims. Drug abuse decreases self-control and successful adult adjustment in addition to being unhealthy and causes potentially fatal physiological effects.
- **Access to, use of, and/or fascination with explosives and firearms:** Students who have a history of aggression, impulsiveness, and other emotional/behavioral problems should not have access to explosives of any form. Observation of fascination with firearms must be immediately reported to the appropriate counseling service.
- **Threats of violence:** Specific threats are a reliable indicator that an adolescent is likely to

use violence toward self or others. All threats to use violence against another person should be taken seriously and reported to the appropriate counseling service.

Characteristics of Safe Schools: Intervention and Prevention

Key Characteristics of a School Violence Prevention Program

Dealing with school violence is an incredibly complex problem. To be successful, problem behaviors must be replaced with nonviolent, socially appropriate behaviors (Johnson & Johnson, 1995). School districts across the country have implemented a wide variety of violence prevention strategies, each with a different type of emphasis. Educational violence prevention strategies focus on teaching students positive replacement behaviors for problems. Curricular programs emphasize teaching appropriate replacement behaviors such as social skills, conflict resolution training, aggression management, gang prevention/intervention, and self-esteem development.

Structuring a School Violence Prevention Program

A variety of violence prevention programs are being implemented. Is there one best or most successful type? Bender and McLaughlin (1997) reported a lack of empirical research in the area of school violence prevention or violence reduction strategies simply because the field of research is relatively new. The guidelines and strategies presented are based on anecdotal data that suggest positive results.

Schools can get violence prevention programs started by laying a foundation based on current best practices. Following are seven key characteristics adapted from Kopka (1997) detailing compo-

nents of an effective school violence prevention program:

1. School staff are trained in and promote a comprehensive approach to violence prevention that views student violence as a complex problem requiring a multifaceted approach.
2. School staff are committed to early violence intervention and prevention services in the primary grades that are sustained through the secondary level.
3. School administrators provide strong leadership and enforce student disciplinary policies fairly and consistently.
4. School staff receive training in violence prevention methods that are consistently incorporated into all school-related activities.
5. The school community encourages parent participation in the violence prevention training and as volunteers in the school.
6. There is a strong and consistent effort to collaborate between school, community, and parents.
7. The school district academic curriculum is based on a foundation that promotes culturally sensitive, developmentally appropriate, relevant, and motivating content to students in all grades.

Level System to Manage School Violence

A three-level structure has been proposed (Waite, 1995) to organize a range of strategies to prevent and intervene with school violence.

Level One The first level emphasizes prevention and reduction of violence. On this level educators implement strategies within the context of the normal school day in classrooms with little extra cost. Examples include structured proactive behavior management, the use of crisis teachers or counselors, and training school staff to competently deal with school violence if and when it occurs. These level-one procedures better prepare educators to manage potentially violent behavior by using more effective behavior management techniques. Johnson and Johnson (1995) provide a list of possible activities to suppress and eliminate violence at school. These activities would be appropriate for this first level of prevention:

- Create a committee to identify sources of school violence
- Establish a threat management policy
- Eliminate weapons in school and on school grounds
- Establish a weapons of violence hotline
- Train faculty to effectively intervene early in the chain of violence
- Use positive and proactive classroom management skills to promote academic achievement and acceptable social behavior

Level Two   The second level of Waite's violence prevention strategy focuses on helping students to recognize and understand their own problem behavior through programs involving peer mediation or adult mentorship. This type of specialized training may cost more than level-one strategies. The following activities would be appropriate for the second level of prevention:

- Encourage students to abstain from violent behaviors by teaching appropriate social skills, anger management, and conflict resolution skills
- Set up mentoring relationships between students and school/community professionals
- Provide supervised activities for students on evenings and weekends

Level Three   Waite's third level requires additional equipment and personnel, including such things as metal detectors, school security cameras, and law enforcement liaison officers. Logically, these third-level strategies are much more expensive and physically intrusive than the staff training strategies described in the first two levels.

School Uniforms

School uniforms have been proposed as a strategy to reduce school discipline problems and student violence. Opponents to school uniform policies voice their disagreement, stating that uniform policies restrict the students' freedom of choice. They say that students should be encouraged to learn to make choices based on their own values rather than arbitrary rules. The U.S. Department of Education (1996) suggests that school uniform policies can enhance the learning environment, boost school safety, and improve discipline for all students. The benefits of a school uniform policy include:

- Reducing theft among students concerning designer clothing, jewelry, and costly sneakers
- Reducing the overt differences between students who are financially able to purchase expensive clothing and those who are not
- Preventing gang members from wearing gang identifiers at school
- Enhancing the learning environment and thereby increasing academic achievement
- Helping school staff recognize strangers in the building

Mandatory Dress Code Results   Administrators from the Long Beach, California, Unified School District enacted a mandatory dress code in 1994. During the intervening years, district officials claim that all categories of school crime have been reduced and that attendance is at an all-time high. Parents have responded favorably to uniform policies. In Long Beach, only 500 parents petitioned to opt their children out of the mandate. That is less than 1% of the 58,500 students in the district.

The U.S. Department of Education *Manual on School Uniforms* (1996) provided the following school crime reduction statistics for the Long Beach Unified School District. Within one year of the mandatory school uniform policy, all of the school crimes were reduced by the percentage listed:

- Overall school crime: 36%
- Fights: 51%
- Sex offenses: 74%
- Weapons offenses: 50%
- Assault and battery offenses: 34%
- Vandalism: 18%

Schools in Illinois, Florida, Georgia, Louisiana, Maryland, New York, and Virginia have made similar claims of violence reduction in their schools after instituting the uniform policy. The Manual quotes Long Beach Police Chief William Ellis: "Schools have fewer reasons to call the police. There's less conflict among students. Students concentrate more on education, not on who is wearing the $100 shoes or gang attire" (p. 7).

A 1996 survey of 306 middle school students in the Charleston, South Carolina, county school district found that school uniforms affected student perceptions of school climate. Students in a middle school with a uniform policy had a significantly higher perception of their school's climate than did students in a school without a uniform policy (Murray, 1997). Personal reactions from students who wear uniforms to school range from delight at not having to decide what to wear to indignation at looking like a "nerd." It may be important for the successful implementation of the dress code policy to obtain students' as well as parents' opinions in the uniform selection process.

Many educators seem to endorse the idea of uniforms at their school. The National Association of Secondary School Principals surveyed participants at the 1996 conference to determine school uniform preferences. Results indicated that 70% of the 5,500 middle school and secondary school principals favored adopting uniforms for their schools (Kopka, 1997).

Uniforms alone are not the answer to school violence and discipline problems. However, many school districts across the country support mandatory uniform policies as a strong contributing factor to improved social behavior and increased academic achievement. Levels of school crime are reduced, thus providing a safer and more secure learning environment for staff and students.

Early Intervention

According to the Children's Safety Network (Kopka, 1997), an essential component of an effective school violence reduction program is early intervention services to teach conflict resolution, mediation skills, critical thinking, and problem-solving skills. These skills would reduce teachers' need to interpret the students' *communicative intent* of behavior because the students would have more well-developed verbal and communication skills. Students also need to learn and practice impulse control, empathy, and resistance to negative peer pressure. For any of the programs to be successful, many teachers will require inservice training and time to teach the skills. The programs will be most effective and consistent if parents are encouraged to be involved to promote and reinforce the appropriate behaviors at home.

Students with Behavioral Disorders and School Violence

The Council for Children with Behavioral Disorders (CCBD) and the Council of Administrators of Special Education (CASE) take the official position that students with emotional and behavioral disorders (E/BD) or students receiving any other special education services are not accountable for the majority of school violence. These students definitely are adding to the daily total of disruptive acts in the school. However, they are not committing the acts of fatal violence that are becoming all too common in schools across the country. CCBD and CASE propose that true acts of violence, aggression, and destructiveness at school are most often committed by students whose behavior may be linked to a crisis situation in their lives. One reason suggested is the difference in the types of educational programming provided. Compared with students in general education classes, students in special education classes receive training in social skills and more one-to-one teaching and counseling. Consequently, they may not have the bottled-up emotions and problems that often lead to explosions of fatal school violence.

Social Skill Deficits

Research supports the assertion that students who are at risk for demonstrating violent behaviors, including drug abuse, academic failure, and dropout, often lack strong bonds or connections to positive social groups such as a biological family or a peer group (Johnson & Johnson, 1995). A major characteristic of students with E/BD is their failure to form and maintain appropriate social relationships. Programming for students with E/BD usually contains a component of social skill training. Because of smaller class sizes in special education, teachers are able to spend more one-to-one time talking to students. Professional counseling is often available or even mandated on the IEP for students with E/BD. In essence, they have the opportunity to receive a lot of assistance to deal with their problems. This may help reduce acts of violence and make school a more positive experience for students with E/BD.

Dropouts

Students with E/BD who stay in school probably spend more time with teachers than with any other adults in their environment. Therefore, school activities and teachers can have a major positive impact on these individuals if they can be persuaded to stay in school through high school. Unfortunately, they drop out at an incredibly high rate. Rhode et al. (1992) report that 65% of students with E/BD drop out of school. The prognosis for those students is not favorable; 41% are arrested within 1 year of leaving school. Educators must make a concerted effort to support and encourage students with E/BD to stay in school.

Responding to Crisis Situations

Make a Plan

Educators in every school across the country need to plan how they would react to different crisis situations. Too many school districts are still in a state of denial, thinking that school violence only happens in other schools. A routine verbal comment often expressed to the media by staff, students, and parents following an act of school violence is the common but ignorant refrain, "I can't believe it happened here." All educators must be trained to deal with school violence just as all are trained to competently manage student behavior in case of a fire or a tornado. Fire and tornado drills are routine occurrences in schools. Teachers and students know exactly what to do when the fire drill warning sounds. Now all educators need to learn to carry out that same type of drill and practice which leads to effective management of acts of school violence. Crisis situations can range from a stranger in the building, to a hostage situation, to weapons, to gang violence. There is no cookbook approach to dealing with each of these situations. Each school has a unique set of school staff, student population, building considerations, and geographic considerations to plan for.

Violence Prevention Plan Considerations

School security experts and law enforcement personnel can be of great assistance in helping to make preventative plans for reducing acts of school violence. The following considerations may be included in the plan:

1. How to set up liaisons with community law enforcement and social service agencies
2. How teachers can call for professional backup at the first sign of a crisis
3. How the teacher would evacuate the classroom in order to get students to a safe place
4. How the teacher would deal with the problem student(s) until backup arrives
5. What types of follow-up activities are carried out with the student population that may be traumatized after the incident is over
6. Who deals with the problem student(s) after the incident is over

Even though there may not be any two plans that are alike, each school should plan ahead for crisis situations. Determine a specific plan for each potential situation and then practice it just like practice is carried out for fire or tornado drills.

Implications for Working with Youth and Adolescents

Love

If you love me you would teach me the right way to live, not the wrong way.
If you love me you care, and if I love you I would do the same.
If I love you, I would respect you.
If you love me, you would make me feel special.
If you teach me right, if you love me, then you care.
I care, I love you, I respect you.[‡]

Lakeisha Williams

In this poem, Lakeisha was writing about teachers and other adults in her life who were providing

[‡]From *Gangs: Straight Talk, Straight Up* (p. 192) by M. M. Jensen and P. C. Yerington, 1997, Longmont, CO: Sopris West. Copyright 1997 by Sopris West. Reprinted with permission.

an education and guidance as she grew up. Children who feel strong positive bonds with teachers, parents, and other professionals are less likely to commit acts of violence than children who do not feel connected. Adults should take the first steps to communicate and let children know they will support, encourage, and help them solve problems.

Teachers who demonstrate kind, caring behaviors with students may actually be more successful in helping them to express feelings and emotions or to ask for help when needed. Adolescence is a turbulent time for many. It is a time when teenagers often have difficulty communicating with adults and feel disconnected and alone with their problems. Students who have more trust in teachers may be more willing to discuss problems that might otherwise lead to violent actions. Teachers should make an effort to establish close, caring relationships with students.

Parents should establish close communication patterns with their children at a very young age. It is critically important for all youth and adolescents to believe that there is someone they can talk to when a problem develops. The major cause of school violence seems to be a lack of connection to the school and a lack of strong support or bonds with the family. In addition, parents need to make sure their children are appropriately supervised. To help keep children safe, it is important for parents to know who their children spend time with and what they are doing at all times.

All educators need to receive preservice and ongoing in-service training concerning school violence. Currently most universities do not include this type of preparation in teacher training programs. In order to deal with crisis situations most appropriately, the teachers need to have drills and practice methods to deal with violent aggressive students.

Although many improvements and reductions in violent incidents have occurred, school violence continues to be a topic of grave concern across the country. Many students are making poor choices and acting out solutions to their problems using guns and other weapons against peers and school staff. The behavioral indicators of potential violence can no longer be ignored. In addition, educators must learn to use proactive strategies to prepare all students to successfully participate fully in the educational program. Proactive strategies can assist educators to promote more appropriate social behavior and help students learn to express themselves and achieve their highest potential at school and in life.

References

Bender, W. N., & McLaughlin, P. J. (1997). Violence in the classroom: Where we stand. *Intervention in School and Clinic*, 32(4), 196–198.

Bureau of Justice Statistics. (2000). *Criminal victimization 1999—changes 1998–99 with trends 1993–99.* Retrieved from www.ojp.usdoj.gov

Center for the Prevention of School Violence (2000). *Helping every student attend a safe school: The Center for the Prevention of School Violence.* Retrieved from www.juvjus.state.nc.US/cpsv/principal/ helpeveryst.htm

Dodge, K. A. (1993). The future of research on the treatment of conduct disorder. *Development and Psychopathology*, 5, 309–317.

Dwyer, K., Osher, D., & Warger, C, (1998). *Early warning, timely response: A guide to safe schools.* Washington, DC: U.S. Department of Education.

Ewing Marion Kauffman Foundation. (2001). *When school is out.* Retrieved from www.nssc1.org

Hoffman, A. M. (1996). *Schools, violence, and society.* Westport, CT: Praeger Publishers.

Jensen. M. M., & Yerington, P. C. (1997). *Gangs: Straight talk, straight up.* Longmont, CO: Sopris West.

Johnson, D. W., & Johnson, R. T. (1995). *Reducing school violence through conflict resolution.* Alexandria, VA: Association for Supervision and Curriculum Development.

Josephson Institute of Ethics. (2001). *Report card on the ethics of American youth 2000: Report #1: Violence, guns, and alcohol.* Retrieved from www.charactercounts.org

Kaufman, P., Chen, X., Choy, S. P., Chandler, K. A., Chapman, C. D., Rand, M. R., et al. (1998). *Indicators of School Crime and Safety, 1998* (NCES 98-251/NCJ-172215). Washington, DC: U.S. Departments of Education and Justice.

Kopka, D. L. (1997). *School violence.* Santa Barbara, CA: ABC-CLIO.

Malico, M. K. (2000). *Expulsions of students who brought guns to school drops for third year.* Retrieved from www.ed.gov/PressReleases/10-2000/index

McLaughlin, M. W., Irby, M. A., & Langman, J. (1994). *Urban sanctuaries: Neighborhood organizations in the lives and futures of inner city youth.* San Francisco: Jossey-Bass.

Metropolitan Life Insurance Company. (1999). *The Metropolitan Life survey of the American teacher. Violence in America's public schools.* New York: Louis Harris and Associates.

Murray, R. K. (1997, December) The impact of school uniforms on school climate. NASSP *Bulletin*, 81(593), 106–112.

National Criminal Justice Reference Service. (2000). Retrieved from www.ncjrs.org/school/safety/facts.html

National School Safety Center. (1998). *Checklist of characteristics of youth who have caused school associated violent deaths.* Retrieved from www.nssc1.org

National School Safety Center (2001, June). NSSC *review of school safety research.* Retrieved from www.nssc1.org

North Central Regional Educational Laboratory and the Midwest Regional Center for Drug-Free Schools and Communities. (1995). *The gun-free schools act.* Retrieved from www.ncrel.org/sdrs/pbriefs/95/95-s03.htm

Office of Juvenile Justice and Delinquency Prevention. Juvenile Justice Bulletin. (2000, August). *Youth gangs in schools.* Retrieved from www.ncjrs.org/pdffiles1/ojjdp/183015.pdf

Patterson, G. R., Reid, J. B., & Dishion, T. J. (1992). *Antisocial boys: A social interactional approach* (Vol. 4). Eugene, OR: Castalia.

Rhode, G., Jenson, W. R., & Reavis, H. K. (1992). *The tough kid book.* Longmont, CO: Sopris West.

Rosemund, J. (1998, December 12). Today's kids have no fear: And parents are to blame. *The Dispatch and the Rock Island Argus.* p. B1.

U.S. Department of Education. (1996). *Manual on school uniforms.* Retrieved from www.ed.gov/updates/uniforms.html

U.S. Department of Education and U.S. Department of Justice. (1999). *1999 annual report on school safety.* Retrieved from www.safeyouth.org/topics/gangs.htm#gangs_schools

U.S. Department of Education and U.S. Department of Justice. (2000). *2000 annual report on school safety.* Retrieved from www.ed.gov/PressReleases/10-2000/index.html

Waite, D. (1995). Strategies available for violence prevention. In W. N. Bender & R. L. Bender (Eds.), *Violence Prevention* (Teleconference produced by the Teacher's Workshop, Bishop, GA).

Walker, H. M., Colvin, G., & Ramsey, E. (1995). *Antisocial behavior in schools: Strategies and best practices.* Pacific Grove, CA: Brooks/Cole Publishing.

CHAPTER 7

CHARACTERISTICS AND IDENTIFICATION STRATEGIES OF YOUTH GANG MEMBERS

After completing the chapter, the reader will be able to identify:

- Gang warning signs.
- Major gang factions.
- Hand signs of the major gangs.
- Colors and graffiti of the major gangs.
- Athletic apparel adopted by the major gangs.
- Implications for educators, parents, and other professionals who work with youth and adolescents.

Introduction

Active Male Gang Member Statistics

90% are arrested by age 18
75% are arrested twice by age 18
95% do not finish high school
60% are dead or in prison by age 20
Risk for homicide is 60 times greater than average
Average life expectancy is 20 years and 5 months

(Texas Youth Commission,
Office of Delinquency Prevention, 1993)

Gangs are described as groups of individuals who associate on a regular basis, wear a common uniform, claim a turf, and usually commit various types of criminal activity (Jensen & Yerington, 1997). The Texas Youth Commission did not use an empirical format in gathering and analyzing the data given above. Survey research was used to gather information from law enforcement personnel and coroners across the country. All of the statistics relate to gang members who have been arrested or killed. The information provided as a result of the nationwide survey does provide a chilling picture of the very dangerous lifestyle that is inherent in gang membership. Gang life tends to reduce life options and presents an incredibly violent future with bleak life outcomes for youngsters who become involved. Teachers, other professionals, and parents, usually without any background training or preparation, are currently trying to cope with students who are attracted to gang culture or are members of a gang.

The purpose of this chapter is to provide educators, parents, and other professionals who work with youth and adolescents with basic strategies they can use to identify children who may become involved or are presently involved in gang activity. The main reason for this identification process is to be able to better understand which individuals will need extra support and motivation to stay in school and to achieve academic

success. These students should participate in appropriate educational, extracurricular, recreational, community, and church activities. The goal is to show all students the adventure and excitement of learning and the benefits of education. It is hoped that this will motivate them to stay in school rather than look for excitement on the street with a gang.

Reducing the number of youth and adolescents involved in gang activity will take a collaborative effort. Educators, parents, other professionals, and the community should work together to effectively manage this problem.

It has been suggested that the breakdown of the family unit may account for the epidemic rise in gang activity. It follows logically that encouraging family units to be stronger, more cohesive, and more supportive might be a viable weapon against further growth of gangs. Although that is a lovely sentiment, the family unit is not a controllable variable. The education system, social service agencies, and law enforcement bureaus, however, are controllable. Educators and other professionals who work with youth and adolescents at risk for or already involved in gang activity must be aware of how gangs fulfill basic human needs of food, clothing, shelter, belonging, identity, and self-respect for some individuals. Professionals who are aware of needs the gangs fulfill can systematically work to teach youth how to think, solve problems, and communicate to have those needs met in a socially acceptable manner.

In this chapter, specific information and illustrations are provided so that adults will be able to recognize the traditional signs, colors, and symbols of major gang factions (Jensen & Yerington, 1997). It is important to recognize the initial warning signs of gang behavior in order to provide early intervention and prevention services with the goal of preventing gang membership. The reader is directed to *Gangs: Straight Talk, Straight Up, A Practical Guide for Teachers, Parents, and the Community*, published by Sopris West for a complete and detailed book on gangs and management strategies that can be used at school, at home, and in the community (Jensen & Yerington, 1997).

Gang Prevention and Education Programs

Early education programs and prevention plans to address the violent and dangerous outcomes of gang membership may be an effective deterrent for some children to join a gang. A variety of observable behaviors that youth and adolescents demonstrate indicate gang interest or involvement. Educators, parents, and other professionals who work with youth and adolescents must be able to recognize these gang identifiers. Some gang behaviors are easier to learn because they relate to concrete visible details such as clothing items or colors, jewelry, haircuts, and tattoos. Other warning signs are more difficult to define qualitatively because they relate to abstract attitudes and personality factors.

Professionals who are knowledgeable about the variety of possible warning signs should be able to provide early prevention and intervention services to eliminate or reduce more significant gang involvement. Unfortunately, many people believe that gang awareness or gang prevention activities are most appropriate for middle school and high school students. This notion is becoming increasingly less true as gang membership rates skyrocket and the average age of gang members drops to the lower teens. Law enforcement officials report that an increasing number of children as young as 7 and 8 years old are being recruited into gangs to serve as messengers and carriers of drugs, weapons, and money for the older members. Early intervention programs in the primary elementary grades are vitally important to educate children about the dangers of gang involvement. In many school districts, the gang awareness program will be the responsibility of teachers and parents because of the lack of organized gang intervention programs in the community.

Violence Associated with Youth Gangs

These kids today, man, they don't care 'bout nothin'. Drive-bys, shootin' each other. It don't matter. It's gonna get worse before it gets better, I can tell you that. Ex-Crip gang member (Jensen & Yerington, 1997, p. 21)

Gang violence is a rampant problem that has impacted schools of all sizes across the nation. Law enforcement officials describe a virtual epidemic of youth gang violence during the past few years blasting from the inner cities, exploding through the suburbs, and shattering rural areas of the country (Jensen & Yerington, 1997; Maxon & Klein, 1990, Valdez, 2000). No community or school can declare perpetual or ongoing immunity from the onslaught of gang migration and associated violence.

A kid wants to be accepted, so he will do what the other kids are doing even if he knows it is wrong. He doesn't want to be embarrassed or disrespected by refusing to do something. On the other hand, he doesn't want to be seen doing something good or positive, then he'll get ridiculed for it. The people I hung around with would really disrespect you and sometimes hurt you if you didn't do what they wanted you to. There's a code among friends, and if you want to be with them, then you do *everything* they say and you cover up and look out for each other. That means lying and doing a lot of illegal stuff. If you don't, they will hurt you and disrespect you, ridicule you, and use you in any way they can. It is unbelievable pressure. You have to work your way up within a gang. You do this by doing everything they want. This means dressing like them, acting like them, and looking like them. (Goldstein, 1990, p. 46)

The preceding quote was by an incarcerated juvenile who claimed to be a gang member. Take note of the expressed lack of self-identity and self-esteem very common in individuals who choose to join a gang. Being a member of a peer group and having a circle of friends are considered normal and even necessary activities for individuals of all ages. Gang members, however, tend to carry this group association to unacceptable and often violent extremes. The phenomenon of *pack behavior* often becomes evident in street gang activity (Jensen & Yerington, 1997). Pack behavior takes place when groups of individuals participate in acts of aggression and violence that they would never have committed on their own. Gang members are required to carry out any and all orders from higher ranking leaders or risk a *violation*. A violation takes the form of a physical beating. Gang members are trained to carry out orders from their leader in a disciplined manner without question. A gang leader can order members to commit crimes for the gang. Following is a quote from Shannon, age 14, a young woman who became involved in gang activity to be accepted into the peer group:

> I wanted to have friends. I wasn't smart enough to get good grades. I wasn't on any of the teams. When I tried out for cheer leading, I didn't make it. I started hanging out with guys who were Vice Lords. They liked me. They accepted me. To keep up with them I did a lot of bad things. I knew they were wrong. I lied, I stole, I sold drugs, and I hurt other people. I knew it was wrong, but I did it anyway. I guess I'd do it again to be accepted—to belong to the group. (Jensen & Yerington, 1997, p. 17)

Gang Membership

The number of individuals who are gang members is difficult to quantify because definitions and methods of counting vary in different regions of the country. It is not against any law to belong to a gang. A gang is actually just another type of peer group. The problems begin to occur when members of the peer group commit intimidating, violent, and criminal activities. Many times, estimates are based on the numbers of individuals who commit gang-related crimes. There has been an effort to survey law enforcement agencies to determine the number of gang members in and around certain cities. In early 1980, there were an estimated 300,000 gang members in the United States. Current estimates suggest there are as many as two million gang members in the United States (Valdez, 2000).

The One Percent Rule

The gang membership estimates are based on the *one percent rule*. The one percent rule states that about 1% of the total population are gang members. This figure might be slightly higher in areas of the country where gang activity originated, such as southern Los Angeles. For example, as of 1998, the Cal-Gang (GREAT) intelligence system reported that there were 135,000 gang members in Los Angeles County. This represents 1.42% of the county population. In Orange County and San Diego County, there were slightly less than 1%. On average, the calculation for gang membership of 1% of any given population is considered a feasible estimate (Valdez, 2000).

Growth of Gang Membership

> Don't ever underestimate the power of the gang. Never. As a group they got power. All they need. They can control a neighborhood, a school, a city, you name it. Never underestimate them, man. Incarcerated gang member (Jensen & Yerington, 1997, p. 16)

Valdez (2000) reported the following statistics on the growth of gang membership across the country. This list shows the numbers of cities across the country reporting gang activity between 1960 and 1998:

1960:	58 cities
1970:	101 cities
1980:	179 cities
1992:	769 cities
1998:	1,200 cities (all 50 states represented)

According to Valdez (2000), the following are considered the top 10 states across the country for numbers of individuals who are gang members:

California	254,618
Illinois	76,226
Texas	67,060
Ohio	17,025
Indiana	17,005
New Mexico	16,910
Arizona	16,291
Florida	16,247
Nevada	12,525
Minnesota	12,382*

Gangs in School

It is difficult to determine the percentage of school-age students who are gang members. Many school administrators are reluctant to report a gang presence or gang-related crime in school (Trump, 2002). Apparently, school administrators think that reporting gang-related violence will reflect badly on their management capabilities (Huff, 1993; Kodluboy & Evenrud, 1993; Trump, 2002). Goldstein and Kodluboy (1998) reported that a 1991 U.S. Department of Justice Survey stated that about 15% of schoolchildren say there are gangs at their school. From 1982 to 1991, juvenile arrests for murder climbed 93% and aggravated assault rose 72% (Walker, Colvin, & Ramsey, 1995). Much of this increase can be attributed to juveniles involved in gang activity. The Council of the Great City Schools published results from a survey (1994) stating that school violence and gang-related activities were the primary concern of 82.7% of superintendents and school board members of large urban districts. Results from an 11-city survey of eighth graders indicated that 9% were currently gang members and that 17% said that they had belonged to a gang at some time in their lives (Ebensen & Osgood, 1997). Similar results were reported from other cities. Denver reported 14% and Seattle reported 15% of school-age students indicated they were active gang members on self-report surveys of school-age students (Battin, Hill, Abbott, Catalano, & Hawkins, 1998).

Youth gang members in school are likely to be from the contingent of students who are less successful academically and do not seem to feel connected or bonded with teachers. Gang members usually do not particularly like school but attend more for gang-related social purposes than for learning (Office of Juvenile Justice and Delinquency Prevention, 1996).

Lack of Teacher Preparation to Manage Violence in the Classroom

Teachers think all of us kids should respect them just because they're teachers. Well we don't. They have to earn our respect. Just like I earn my respect out on the street. Teachers who are always dissin' us won't get no respect back. We hate 'em and we give 'em hell all day long. Zack, 17 years old (Jensen & Yerington, 1997, p. 33)

Teachers often deal with the same individuals in the classroom as police officers do on the street after school hours. The major difference is that

*Gang-related statistics are gathered through survey research from police departments. Some departments do not respond to the surveys. In those cases there is no way to determine statistics for that area. For example, it may be hypothesized that states not included in the above list may actually have a larger gang problem than some that are listed. The list is as accurate and complete as possible based on returned surveys.

police officers are prepared with special training and equipment. Educators are being required to interact with and teach gang-involved youth on a daily basis with insufficient training and inadequate professional backup (Jensen & Yerington, 1997; Valdez, 2000). Police officers who deal with the presence of street gangs in their city are specially trained to handle potentially violent and aggressive individuals using a number of different methods. The preparation typically involves instruction in conflict resolution, verbal mediation, nonconfrontational de-escalation procedures, crisis intervention techniques, self-defense tactics, and weapons use. The weapons carried by patrol officers include a gun, a nightstick, and pepper mace. They also wear bulletproof vests and carry a two-way radio that enables them to call for immediate backup assistance when necessary. Teachers with dubious skills due to lack of training in self-defense or crisis intervention typically encounter potentially violent students in an isolated classroom.

Teachers' Level of Knowledge on Gang Identifiers

Jensen conducted a research project to determine preservice and practicing teachers' levels of knowledge about basic gang characteristics and management strategies in school (Jensen & Yerington, 1997). Teachers must be well trained to recognize and competently manage the associated problems in an effort to motivate and keep these students in school. The purpose of Jensen's study was to determine if teaching experience alone would lead to a gain of basic gang awareness and behavior management knowledge. Comparisons were also made between groups who had attended a previous basic gang awareness seminar or who lived or worked in an area where gangs were active.

The 374 participants in the study were surveyed with a 20-point questionnaire developed to gather the data on their level of knowledge of ba-

sic gang awareness and management strategies. Descriptive statistics were used to classify and summarize the numerical data collected. Data were analyzed using two groups: preservice teachers and practicing teachers. Frequencies and percentages were used to report teachers' awareness of gang characteristics and classroom management skills.

Survey data indicated an immediate and crucial demand for revision of teacher training curricula in the area of basic gang awareness and management strategies. Data were entered into the table as a frequency of response followed by the percentage rounded to the nearest percent (see Table 7–1). Specific results indicated that more than 50% of all survey participants said they live or work in areas where gang activity had been reported.

When asked if attending a gang awareness seminar was important for professional edification, 98 to 99% responded that it was. Results suggest that teaching experience alone does not educate or inform teachers about gangs. Of those who had not previously attended a gang awareness workshop, 88% of preservice teachers and 84% of practicing teachers could not define a youth gang. Additionally, 62% of preservice teachers and 70% of practicing teachers would not be able to recognize basic gang identifiers. Regarding behavior management strategies, 65% of preservice teachers and 40% of practicing teachers were not aware of nonconfrontational methods to use with hostile and aggressive students. Also, 91% of preservice teachers and 81% of practicing teachers did not know how to preplan or prepare to competently handle a crisis in the classroom.

The results indicate a specific need for training and knowledge that would directly affect teaching and learning in elementary, secondary, and postsecondary schools across the nation. First, teacher training programs should incorporate basic gang awareness and management into required curricula for all education majors during preservice training at the university level. To deal with all students effectively at school, educators must be knowledgeable about gang identifiers and proficient in

TABLE 7–1 Teachers' Knowledge of Gang Characteristics and School Management Strategies—Survey Results

Question	Preservice Teachers		Practicing Teachers	
1. Male/Female	M = 65	F = 194	M = 24	F = 91
2. Preservice/practicing	n = 259		n = 115	
	YES	NO	YES	NO
3. Attended previous seminar	47	212	54	61
4. Live/work in an area with active gangs	136/53	123/47	79/69	36/31
5. Importance of attending gang workshop	254/98	5/2	114/99	1/1
6. Main components that define a gang	30/12	229/88	19/16	96/84
7. Gang membership hierarchy	45/17	214/83	23/20	92/80
8. Specific gang identifiers	98/38	161/62	34/30	81/70
9. Motivation to join gangs	191/74	68/26	93/81	22/19
10. Two main Midwest factions	72/28	187/72	40/35	75/65
11. Gang migration to small towns	105/40	154/60	61/53	54/47
12. Environmental indicators of gang presence	118/46	141/54	49/43	66/57
13. Characteristics of West Coast gangs	43/17	216/83	14/12	101/88
14. Teacher behaviors to promote compliance	90/35	169/65	67/58	48/42
15. Hostile student behaviors	147/57	112/43	79/69	36/31
16. Nonconfrontational management	92/35	167/65	69/60	46/40
17. Breaking up fights	59/23	200/77	40/35	75/65
18. Establish school dress code	54/21	205/79	23/20	92/80
19. Assess gang problem at school	26/10	233/90	13/11	102/89
20. Preplan for crisis management	24/9	235/91	22/19	93/81

Note. *From* Gangs: Straight Talk, Straight Up *by M. M. Jensen and P. C. Yerington, 1997, Longmont, CO: Sopris West. Copyright 1997 by Sopris West. Reprinted with permission.*

the implementation of proactive behavior management strategies and crisis intervention techniques.

Second, school administrators must provide inservice training and seminars to educate all staff about basic gang awareness and management of aggressive, antisocial, and hostile behaviors of students. Collaboration between educators and law enforcement officials would be beneficial in sharing information to more effectively reach and teach students who are current or potential gang members.

Gang Warning Signs

Gang members dress, walk, and talk in specific ways that indicate their gang affiliation. A wide variety of visible identifiers may be present from head to toe on a gang member. Some potential gang identifiers worn in isolation may simply be an adolescent fashion statement. Many of the fashion fads the gangs have adopted are popular with youth and adolescents in general. Examples include many types of college and professional team athletic apparel and oversized or baggy clothing. Police suggest that a minimum of two specific identifiers must be present simultaneously for probable gang association (Jensen & Yerington, 1997). For example, an adolescent who is not in a gang might wear the red and black Chicago Bulls jacket and cap because he is a Bulls fan. In contrast, a Vice Lord will wear the jacket and cap because of the red and black colors. The gang member will add another gang identifier such as wearing the cap cocked to the left side, will color the left horn of the bull on the cap black, will push up the left sleeve of the jacket, or will apply the numbers 22/12 somewhere on the jacket or the cap. The 22/12 is part of the numeric alphabet code. For Vice Lords, V is the 22nd letter and L is the 12th letter of the alphabet. More information on specific gang identifiers is provided later in this chapter.

Table 7–2 summarizes gang warning signs that educators should be aware of to determine if a child's behavior is gang-related. These signs may be observed in school-age children from the early elementary grades through high school. A combination of these characteristics is usually present in every individual who eventually becomes involved with a street gang. Each of the warning signs is explained in detail in the following text.

Lacks Self-Esteem

> I was nothin' before the Crips. Nothin'. Now people know me, respect me, fear me, man. It's a real high, man. High school gang member (Jensen & Yerington, 1997, p. 44)

As demonstrated in the various quotes in this chapter, lack of self-esteem is often the common thread among all of the gang-related characteristics observed. Youngsters who have confidence in themselves and have skills and abilities that are valued by peers and adults in their environment will not often be enticed by the gang mentality. Youth and adolescents who do not have a strong family support system, who have achievement problems in school, and who have problems with peer and adult relationships are those who will look for the gang to fill the voids in their lives.

A variety of observable behaviors denote lack of self-esteem in children. In the classroom, these students may make many verbal comments discounting their own abilities. When asked to name something they are good at or a special talent they have, many students will be unable or unwilling to name even one skill. They may often resist new activities because of fear of failure. These students

TABLE 7–2 Gang Warning Signs

- Lacks self-esteem
- Lives in a gang-oriented neighborhood
- Has relatives in a gang
- Has problems at home; reserved, moodiness, abusive, etc.
- Has problems at school; disruptive, threatening, etc.
- Carries a weapon
- Lacks recreational, leisure, vocational skills
- Imitates the dress and colors of the gang
- Wears gang jewelry
- Draws gang graffiti
- Uses gang slang
- Uses gang hand signs
- Has a gang tattoo
- Carries gang paraphernalia

Note. *From Gangs: Straight Talk, Straight Up (p. 85) by M. M. Jensen and P. C. Yerington, 1997, Longmont, CO: Sopris West. Copyright 1997 by Sopris West. Reprinted with permission.*

can save face by refusing to try rather than trying and failing. They may also lack age-appropriate social skills. Group interaction skills may be problematic, resulting in a reluctance to join in group activities due to apprehension about being turned down by peers. It is common for them to be rejected or isolated from the peer group. These students may often hang around with a younger group or they will form relationships with others who tend to be peer isolates or troublemakers.

What Teachers Can Do Teachers must consistently make an effort to boost the diminished sense of self-esteem many students feel by structuring classroom expectations, curriculum, and academic assignments for increased student success. Giving high rates of genuine positive reinforcement will also help make the school environment more positive and productive for all students. Teachers who are proactive, mostly positive, and teach a motivating and relevant curriculum will be more effective with tough students (Rhode, Jenson, & Reavis, 1992). Educators also must encourage students to join school clubs, organizations, sports teams, and other extracurricular activities of interest. This will help keep students occupied with appropriate, supervised activities and off the streets and out of the gangs.

> I got into trouble a lot after school. I done robberies, muggings, I delivered drugs. It was something to do. I got money for it. If I could get a job after school, I would. If I could go somewhere, I don't know where, and work on my hobbies, or something, I probably wouldn't be a delinquent. I like music and drama and stuff. Matt, 15 years old (Jensen & Yerington, 1997, p. 42)

Seven "A's" to Encourage Student Self-Esteem   Lopez (1994) reported that proactive and positive teacher behavior can have a major impact on the self-esteem of students. She categorized suggestions for teachers that promote basic human respect and an educational environment in which students can be successful. Many students do not receive encouragement or support at home to achieve or excel in school. Teacher behavior can be an excellent motivator to increase appropriate behavior and academic achievement. It only takes a moment to follow through on one or more of the behaviors. It is important for professionals to realize that they may be the only adult in this child's life who is providing acknowledgment, ad-

miration, attention, or any of the other important behaviors. Lopez's suggestions are inexpensive, quick, and easy for teachers and other professionals to deliver. The result may be a student who enjoys school and is successful as compared to one who finds school to be such an aversive failure-oriented situation that he votes with his feet. He chooses to walk the street or walk the mall, often becoming a problem for law enforcement personnel—any place as long as it is not the classroom where he has met nothing but failure. Lopez's Seven "A's" to encourage student self-esteem are summarized in Table 7–3.

Lives in a Gang-Oriented Neighborhood

> My dad left my mom and my brother and me when I was six. I didn't have anyone to look up to. The guys on the street paid attention to me. They paid me money to carry stuff, to deliver it for them. I was just a kid. They told me if I got caught, I'd get off easy. I never got caught. Joey, 12 years old (Jensen & Yerington, 1997, p. 19)

This comment was made by a boy who grew up in a gang-controlled neighborhood. Children who show an early interest in gangs often live in

TABLE 7–3   Seven "A's" to Encourage Student Self-Esteem

1. **Acknowledgment**
   Identify and reinforce students' unique talents and abilities. Value diversity.
2. **Acceptance**
   Show basic and genuine human respect for all students.
3. **Approval**
   Provide consistent positive reinforcement and appropriate levels of constructive criticism to maintain appropriate behaviors and teach replacements for problem behaviors.
4. **Appreciation**
   Create an "appreciation list" that acknowledges desirable personality and behavioral characteristics of all students in the class.
5. **Attention**
   Make time to talk with students. The teacher should find time to give students undivided attention.
6. **Admiration**
   Make time to talk with students about individual positive qualities.
7. **Affection**
   Teachers should let students know that they care about them through the use of smiles of approval, pats on the back, supportive and encouraging comments, a warm tone of voice, and approachable body language.

Note. *From "Enhancing Self-Esteem," by L. L. Lopez, 1994, Winter,* School Safety.

neighborhoods where gangs exist. Deteriorating economic conditions have produced many neighborhoods where gang activity thrives. Subsequently, children are exposed to gang life at a very early age. Gang activity is not just a big city problem anymore. Neighborhoods in communities of all sizes across the country are now controlled by gangs. The gang leaders establish the rules or laws of the neighborhood and use violent enforcement tactics. Some children who live in neighborhoods where rival gangs are active often think they have no choice but to join one gang just to survive.

The following comment was made by an incarcerated juvenile in response to the question of how an individual's environment might cause juvenile delinquency:

> I'm not saying that the city is all such a bad place, but the city is real crowded, man. If you don't got your family behind you and you don't got nobody to go to, you gotta do it for yourself, and if you live in a broken area, you know it's even harder. You know what I'm saying? You go to school in a broken area and being constantly around violence, drugs, and abuse, no matter where you go there's no where for you to turn, you're still gonna be in the same area. There's nowhere for you to run away from it. (Goldstein, 1990, p. 68)

One of the most effective ways young children learn is through observation and imitation. If a child is surrounded by gang activity and behavior, he will soon behave like a gang member. Some children who live in gang neighborhoods become gang members because it is the only way of life they know. Often, their school is also controlled by the gangs. In that case, they are surrounded by the gang 24 hours a day with no relief from the violence of that lifestyle. Many children lack appropriate role models in their environment. Consequently, they grow up idolizing and imitating the behavior of the older gang members. They are taught very early that the neighborhood belongs to the gang and that the gang will dictate the behavior of all who live in the "hood."

The following comment was made by an incarcerated juvenile in response to the question of how environment affects a child's behavior:

> If they grew up learning that stealing, doing drugs, drinking is good, then that's what they're going to do. If they grew up learning that going to school, graduating from school, going to college is good, that's what they are going to do 'cause that's their environment. (Goldstein, 1990, p. 38)

Has Relatives in a Gang

Police departments are seeing second- and third-generation gang members from the same family. It is becoming commonplace for children to grow up under the direct influence of gang members who are their siblings or parents. As very young children, they are introduced to the gang mentality by highly trusted individuals or fellow family members. As they look up to an older member of the family, they learn to respect gang behavior. In this situation, children actually grow up under the control and guidance of the gang itself. They have great faith and trust in their own family members and believe all that they are told pertaining to the gang.

Police officials have uncovered instances in which older brothers or sisters organized and/or participated in the initiation of a younger sibling into a gang. Since this usually requires a beating, some form of physical violence, or even deviant sexual activity, it indicates strong loyalty to the gang as opposed to the biological family member.

The following comment was made by an incarcerated juvenile when asked what impact older brothers and sisters have on younger kids getting into trouble:

> I say another part, too, is not only the parents, but the older brother, older sister. You know, the young ones always admire the oldest, that's got to be a big part, too. Older brother giving the role model to the younger one, the younger one most of the time always like to follow the big brother in his steps, and if the big brother is doing negative

stuff or the big sister, eventually the young one will get into the same trouble or the same gang. (Goldstein, 1990, p. 45)

The strong family ties to gang life extend beyond the immediate family. Many times extended family members such as stepparents, stepbrothers and stepsisters, aunts, uncles, and cousins who are gang members have a direct influence on a young child. The child who spends time with these family members observes and learns to emulate their gang behavior. Children who grow up in families where gang members are present are at a much greater risk of joining the gang themselves.

The next comment was made by an incarcerated juvenile in response to the question of how families affect a child's behavior:

> From the minute they are a baby and they grow up they see what their family does, and what their family does, they are going to do. (Goldstein, 1990, p. 38)

Has Problems at Home

Children who may be attracted to gangs often experience problems at home. They tend to develop a major attitude problem with parents, teachers, and other adults in authority. This means that they may attempt to be physically and/or verbally aggressive, threatening, and intimidating in order to get what they want. Family rules suddenly mean nothing to them. These children desire too much privacy. They lose interest in typical family activities. Other children are very unwilling to tell parents where, with whom, or what they will be doing when they are out. They do not want to introduce their friends to their parents. They tend to be very secretive, almost as if they were hiding out from the rest of the family. Some children stay out later than usual and/or break curfew frequently. These children rebel against authority in general and often behave in a manner that they know will upset their parents. Parents should be constantly alert and informed as to the behavior and activities of their children. In other

words, parents must know where their children are, who they are with, and what they are doing at all times. Open, honest, and direct communication is imperative to prevent gang membership.

The next comment was made by an incarcerated juvenile in response to a question about parenting skills related to juvenile delinquency:

> I think their mother should have put a curfew on things or put her foot down or even the father put his foot down 'cause like it's hard when a parent doesn't care you can do what you want to do and nobody supervising you, nobody telling you right from wrong, you just doing what you want. (Goldstein, 1990, p. 40)

Has Problems with School

Gang members who attend school, including most wannabes and many hard-core younger members, may cause major problems for teachers and administrators. Students who are interested in gangs typically demonstrate poor academic progress at school. They are disruptive in class and often challenge a teacher's control.

Gang members are usually academic underachievers with a high rate of truancy. Refusing to participate in classroom events or simply refusing to attend school at all are common traits among school-age gang members.

The following comment was made by a former gang member relating to his impression of school and teachers:

> Some teachers think we respect them just because they are teachers. I don't. I respect those who are real and respect me. I, and most of my friends, can tell a phony teacher right away. We get sick of them. Lots of kids drop out because of them. A lot of us don't go to certain classes. Sometimes going to school is like watching a bad movie for six periods a day on television. At least when we watch TV we can switch the channel. We can't switch teachers. If possible, we just don't go to certain classes. (Arthur & Erickson, 1992, p. 47)

Carries a Weapon

Gang members often get into trouble at school for fighting and carrying weapons. Students must be aware that all weapons are prohibited in school by federal law. A weapon is described as, but not limited to, any device that can be used to attack another person. Weapons include any type of firearm, knife, club, slingshot, explosive, deadly or dangerous chemical, or any sharp or pointed instrument.

Law enforcement officers are often called to break up gang fights inside schools and on school grounds. Since it is common for members of rival gangs to attend the same school, conflicts may occur. When gang fights are preplanned, many gang members take weapons to school in anticipation of trouble.

Gang members believe that possessing a weapon in school, especially a gun, is the ultimate form of antisocial behavior. They want to show violent, antisocial behaviors to develop a rough, tough macho image. Students who have been caught with weapons in schools have told police officers that carrying a weapon gives them a feeling of power or invincibility. Some students carry weapons to satisfy a dare or a bet. Gang members may make this an initiation rite. Other students say that they need to have weapons in school to protect themselves from the harassment of gang members and other bullies.

Students who are being threatened or intimidated by gang members arm themselves for a feeling of self-protection. Police officers have been called to schools to deal with students possessing weapons. The subsequent investigation revealed that the nonmember was afraid of being hurt or even killed by gang members. The weapon was taken to school with the intent of using it to scare away the gang members.

Lacks Recreational, Leisure, and Vocational Skills

A major contributing factor that causes youth and adolescents to join gangs is the excitement they have been led to believe exists in the gang lifestyle.

Gang members who recruit new associates often target the youth who seems to spend a lot of time alone. Some youngsters admit they join gangs simply because "... it was something to do." Part of the recruiting tactic is to describe to the potential new member how much fun and excitement the gang can provide. For those who lack the socialization skills that most children automatically develop, the social features promised by the gang become very attractive. A promise of new friends is appealing to the youngster who does not have many friends of his own or who has trouble making friends.

In deciding to join the gang for the promise of a supportive peer group, the individual neglects to consider all the instant enemies who are rival gang members. Gangs members strongly support traditional rivalries. The gang will not allow a member to fraternize with or befriend rival gang members. In fact, the gang code of conduct requires members to associate exclusively with other members of the gang. This practice not only effectively limits their social circle, but also restricts the time members can spend with their biological family. Consequently, the gang leader's powerful and influential control of the members is enhanced.

Over time, many of these children begin to feel that they do not belong with anyone except members of their own gang. These children usually do not participate in sports or other extracurricular activities, do not attend or get involved in school functions, and have not developed an interest in hobbies or vocational skills. In short, many youngsters believe that they do not fit in anywhere except with the gang.

Imitates the Dress and Colors of the Gang

Youth and adolescents who are interested in a gang imitate the dress and colors of the gang. Some children may buy or want their parents to purchase only clothing of one or two particular colors such as blue, red, black, brown, or gold. They exclusively choose and wear the limited colors that show affiliation with their gang. Once youngsters have clothing in the gang colors, they typically associate with other children who are also wearing too much of the same colors.

Oversized clothing or the "grunge" look has been called "saggin' and baggin'." This is the term used to describe the baggy pants and oversized shirts that are worn by gang members. This particular type of clothing became popular in prisons, where prisoners are not issued belts for safety reasons. As a consequence, incarcerated gang members started wearing oversized denims that sagged low on the hips and exposed boxer shorts. Wearing pants very low on the hips is now considered a method of representing gang affiliation. It is important to remember that the oversized look is also a popular fashion fad.

In the early 1990s, gang members started wearing athletic apparel from college and/or professional athletic teams that use their gang colors (Jensen & Yerington, 1997). By wearing commercially produced athletic apparel, they discovered that they could wear their gang colors and symbols in places where gang identifiers had previously been banned. Many schools and businesses place rigid and uncompromising restrictions on the wearing of gang-related clothing. This has been called a *zero-tolerance policy*. Zero tolerance simply means that the school or agency does not allow gang identifiers to be worn. However, individuals of all ages like to wear athletic team apparel. This fashion fad has allowed gang members to show their affiliation simply by wearing the team clothing that fits their colors and symbols.

The important point to remember when dealing with children and sports clothing or any other type of gang-related clothing is not to conclude that a person is a gang member simply because he chooses to wear certain clothing or team apparel. At least two identifiers must be observed before suspecting an individual is showing gang allegiance.

Wears Gang Jewelry

Gang members have adopted and adapted different types of jewelry to show allegiance to their gang. Individuals involved in a gang might wear a lot of gold or silver jewelry customized with gang symbols. The symbolic jewelry might be worn as necklaces, earrings, rings, pins, or bracelets.

The Playboy Bunny emblem has been made into various forms of jewelry by both the Vice Lords and the Black Gangster Disciples. The Vice Lords wear the bunny symbol with both ears up because the ears make a "V" formation. To show disrespect to the Vice Lords, the Black Gangster Disciples wear the bunny symbol with one ear bent. People Nation gangs wear a five-pointed star and the Folk Nation gangs wear a six-pointed star. The Italian Horn is worn by the Black Gangster Disciples. To them, it represents the devil's horn, which is part of their graffiti.

The Latin People Nation gangs may wear Irish Claddagh rings. A Claddagh ring is an Irish friendship ring. The symbol on the ring is a heart held by a hand on either side and topped by a crown. The Latin People Nation gangs like the ring because one of their symbols is the crown.

Jelly bracelets and custom-made badges or buttons have been adopted by gang members. Jelly bracelets are flexible, brightly colored, "dime store" jewelry. They have been popular with many children and were subsequently adopted by the gangs. Gang members wear combinations of the bracelets in their gang colors. Gang members have also had their symbols and slogans imprinted on badges or buttons, which is a currently popular fad with other youngsters as well as retail establishments and fast-food restaurants.

Draws Gang Graffiti

Graffiti, or the drawing of the gang's signs and symbols, is one of the first gang warning signs a youngster exhibits. Any available surface in the immediate environment can be used. Teachers should pay particular attention to notebooks, book covers, lockers, clothing, and any other material the child surrounds himself with during school hours. It has been reported that a popular location for graffiti is on the toilet stalls in both the girls' and boys' restrooms. Teachers have intercepted notes and letters passed from student to student where gang signs and symbols were written or gang terminology was used. Teachers should look for letters of the alphabet written upside down and/or backward, or crossed out. This is a method of showing disrespect toward a rival gang. For example, members of the Black Gangster Disciples will write upside down or backwards "V's" and "L's" on their papers to show disrespect to the Vice Lords. Students who are involved with gangs may instinctively write letters in that fashion on their homework assignments because they are so accustomed to writing that way when communicating with each other outside school. Retaliation for disrespect between rival gang members is often brutal and violent. Retaliatory behaviors usually include some type of severe bodily harm or assault. The drive-by shooting has become the ultimate form of retaliation between gangs.

Another popular form of gang expression is to use a numeric alphabet, where numbers are used in the place of corresponding letters (e.g., A =1, B = 2, C = 3, and D = 4). Often these numeric formations will look like three-digit padlock combinations. By counting out the alphabet, the codes can be easily deciphered. Examples include 7/4, for the "G" and the "D" of the Gangster Disciples; 22/12 for the "V" and the "L" of the Vice Lords; 3/22/12 for the "C," the "V," and the "L" of the Conservative Vice Lords; or 2/15/19 for the "B," the "O," and the "S" of the Brothers of the Struggle, a Gangster Disciple affiliate. The number combinations are used in displays of graffiti.

In the home, parents should simply look around children's bedrooms to check for the presence of gang graffiti. Do not consider this an invasion of privacy, but rather a method of proactive or preventive child care. Parents report finding posters, murals, flags, and banners containing the signs and symbols of street gangs. Police advise parents to look inside their children's schoolbooks and notebooks for gang graffiti. If children think their parents will not recognize gang-related signs, they will be quite bold about writing them in obvious places about the home. Other children are more devious and write gang signs that may remain hidden on their clothing, possessions, or in secret places around the house.

The meanings of the signs and symbols that make up gang graffiti are discussed later in this chapter. Adults do not need to memorize the exact meaning of graffiti signs. However, it is important for parents and teachers to know what graffiti looks like and to recognize it as being gang-related. Box 7–1 shows examples of various types of gang graffiti from two West Coast gangs.

Uses Gang Slang

Gang members have their own distinct language. Gang slang is used and understood by other members but it may sound foreign to nongang members. There are dictionary-type lists of the jargon that has a special meaning to the gang. Some of the words are specific to certain gangs, neighborhoods, or regional areas of the country. Since new words are being added and deleted constantly, it would be difficult to try to maintain a dictionary of gang slang. Parents and teachers should listen for gang slang terminology and consider it an indicator that a child is being influenced by gang members who use it and teach it.

Some very common examples are words such as "trippin" (hanging out), "hood" (neighborhood), "homies" (friends or fellow gang members), "dis" or "dissed" (demonstrated disrespect), "slippin" (being caught alone by rival gang members), "5/0" (the term used for the police), or "packin'" (has a gun). It is not as important for parents and teachers to know the exact meanings of the words as it is for them to recognize that the terms imply affiliation with a street gang. Police caution adults not to try to talk to gang members in their own language, but rather to communicate in normal speech. The goal is to require gang members to deal with adults in the adult world rather than that of the gang. Table 7–4 provides examples of gang slang.

Box 7–1 Examples of West Coast Gang Graffiti

Crip Graffiti Examples

Blood Graffiti Examples

TABLE 7–4 Examples of Gang Slang

Term	Meaning
Are you straight?	Asking if you want drugs
Bangin'	Gang activity
Beef	Do battle or confrontation
B.G. (baby gangster)	Very young gang member
B.O.S. order	Beat on sight order
Breakdown	Shotgun
Bum rush	Mob a person, stampede, or crash an event
Comin' from the pocket	Fighting with a weapon
Comin' from the shoulders	Fighting with the hands
Crib	Apartment or home of a gang member
Demonstration	Gang fight
Double deuce	.22 caliber gun
Flying the flag	Demonstrating gang allegiance through colors, signs, symbols
Four five	.45 caliber gun
Gauge	Shotgun
Lit up	Shot with a gun
Mad dog	Stare down to challenge or intimidate
O.G. (original gangster)	An older, respected gang member
Put in work	Committing a crime for the gang
Quad seven	AK 47 (assault rifle)
Queen	Female gang member or girlfriend of a gang member
Roll-by	Drive-by shooting
Roscoe	Handgun
Smoke	Shoot someone with a gun
Strapped	Armed with a gun
Tray eight	.38 caliber gun
Violated or "V"ed	Beaten by other gang members as a punishment
What you ridin'?	What gang do you belong to?
You got four feet?	Do you want to fight?

Note. From Gangs: Straight Talk, Straight Up (pp. 97–100), by M. M. Jensen and P. C. Yerington, 1997, Longmont, CO: Sopris West. Copyright 1997 by Sopris West. Reprinted with permission.

Uses Gang Hand Signs

Gang members have also adopted their own form of sign language, which is sometimes referred to as "flagging." These signs are made by shaping the hands and fingers to depict the gang's initials, numbers, or symbols. Hand signs are "thrown up," or pointed upward, to show allegiance. They are "thrown down," or used upside down, to show disrespect. Police officers working security at teen so-cial events have reported that fights have broken out over the exchange of hand signs between rival gangs. Throwing down hand signs has been known to be the prelude to gang fights, shootings, and even deaths.

Hand signs can be used for three purposes. First, they can be flashed as a sign of allegiance to one's own gang. Second, hand signs are given to announce a specific gang's presence in an area. Third, they can be thrown down to show disrespect to or challenge a rival gang.

Teachers and parents should watch children's hands in situations in which lots of children are present, especially in and around schools. Hand signs are fairly easy to notice and always signify some type of communication. As with graffiti, it is not as important to know what the hand signs stand for as it is to know that they signify gang affiliation.

One dangerous aspect of hand signs is a practice known as "false flagging." This occurs when a gang member throws up a rival gang's hand sign in a crowd of people to see if anyone responds with the same sign. If that happens, he knows that the other person is actually a rival gang member who thinks he has identified himself with one of his own. False flagging has led to violence after the rival gang member was unknowingly lured into identifying himself to enemies.

Many schools and teen centers have banned the use of hand signs on their premises. Anyone caught using hand signs is required to leave. Educators must make the use of gang hand signs an infraction of the zero-tolerance policy for gang activity to reduce the potential for rival gang violence. Box 7–2 depicts common hand signs for major gangs.

Has a Gang Tattoo

Gang tattoos are critically important because they represent a lifelong commitment to the gang. Tattoos are permanent. Therefore, when an individual decides to get a gang symbol tattoo, he is promising to be a loyal gang member for life.

Gang tattoos usually resemble the same signs and symbols as those that are found in gang graffiti. Gang names, slogans, insignias, and initials are some of the other most common tattoo patterns.

Some gang tattoos sported by members are professionally applied in tattoo parlors. Hardcore gang members usually have enough money from the crimes they commit to afford the best.

Homemade tattoos, however, are often the variety that younger gang members settle for. Homemade tattoos are made with red-hot coat hangers, or other pieces of metal, bent to the desired pattern. This process is similar to branding cattle. Another method is to use a small sharp object to puncture the skin in the shape of a gang design. Then india ink is injected into the wound in an attempt to make gang tattoos. The least permanent form of tattooing is accomplished simply by writing on the skin with an ink pen or magic marker. Parents and teachers must be aware of any tattoo that a young person has and determine whether it is gang related.

Carries Gang Paraphernalia

The final warning sign relates to gang paraphernalia. Certain items have been characterized as being related to gang activity, including the use of pagers and cellular phones by youth and adolescents. These devices are often used for communication regarding gang meetings, drug deals, and other criminal activities. Wearing bandannas is another example. Possession of alcohol, drugs, large amounts of cash, or any type of weapon is often gang-related. Adults must not be quick to label a young person a gang member simply because he possesses these items. However, possession of such items should cause parents and teachers to start looking for other signs that could support the fact that there is a gang influence in the child's life.

Major Gang Factions

Four major factions of street gangs include the People Nation and Folk Nation gangs originating in the Midwest and the Bloods and Crips originating around Los Angeles, California. Members of these major gangs have migrated to all parts of the country. The two main gangs associated with the People Nation faction are called the Vice Lords and the Latin Kings. The major gang that comes

Box 7-2 Hand Signs of the Major Gangs

BLOODS

CRIPS

VICE LORDS

BLACK GANGSTER Disciples

LATIN KINGS

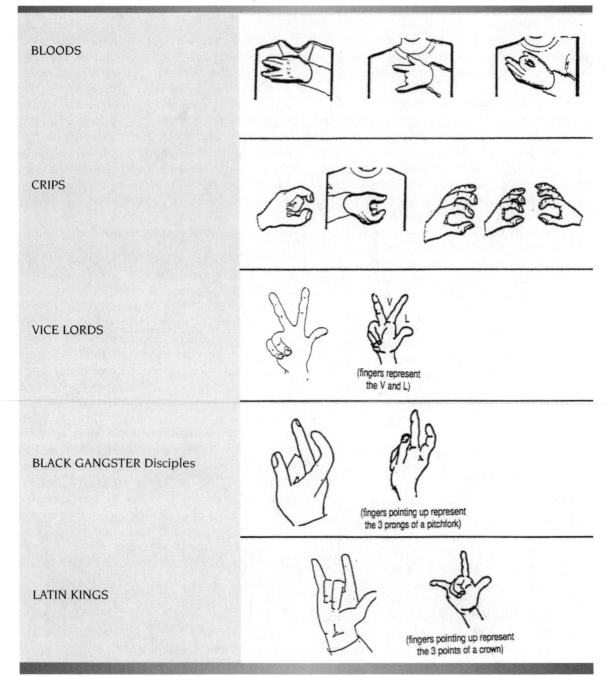

(fingers represent the V and L)

(fingers pointing up represent the 3 prongs of a pitchfork)

(fingers pointing up represent the 3 points of a crown)

Note. From Gangs: Straight Talk, Straight Up (pp. 101–103) by M. M. Jensen and P. C. Yerington, 1997, Longmont, CO: Sopris West. Copyright 1997 by Sopris West. Reprinted with permission.

under the auspices of the Folk Nation is the Black Gangster Disciples. The People Nation and Folk Nation Gangs and the Crips and Bloods have split into a multitude of subsets of the major gangs and are now active in all 50 states (Valdez, 2000).

"Representing"

Allegiance to a particular gang is demonstrated by wearing gang identifiers, including colors, signs, and symbols, or flashing gang hand signs. "Representing" means that gang members wear their gang colors and graffiti on either the right side or the left side of the body as a means to depict gang membership. Right side/left side is defined by an imaginary vertical line drawn down the center of the body.

People Nation and Folk Nation gangs from the Midwest specifically represent on either the left side or the right side of the body. The side on which the gang represents is sometimes called the "strong" side. Gang members from the People Nation faction wear all of their symbols, colors, jewelry, and tattoos on the left side. For example, the Vice Lords and the Latin Kings, both affiliates of the People Nation, wear hats tilted to the left, earrings in their left ear, and tattoos on their left arm. The side of the body on which the tattoo is located is considered to be as important as the design itself. People (left side) and Folk Nation (right side) gang members have their tattoos placed only on the strong side of the body.

The Black Gangster Disciples, part of the Folk Nation, represent all of their signs and symbols on the right side of the body. Folk Nation members represent to the right by tilting their hats to that side, buckling their belts, tying bandannas, and/or rolling up the pant leg on the right side. How gang members wear their shoes can also show gang affiliation. Some members unlace or leave partially laced the shoe on the "weak side," while wearing the "strong side" (right side—Folk Nation/ left side—People Nation) shoe completely laced and tied. Members have been known to wear gang-colored shoelaces in their strong side shoe.

The Bloods and Crips do not use the right or left method of representation. They display the colors red (Bloods) or blue (Crips) anywhere they can be easily seen. There is an interesting story behind the choice of the colors. In the Los Angeles County Jail, either red or blue bandanna handkerchiefs were issued to inmates. The Crips reportedly formed first and began demonstrating gang allegiance with the blue bandannas. The Bloods (originally called the Pirus from the name of the street in their neighborhood in Compton, California) formed to retaliate as the Crips began creating havoc and violence in the neighborhood. The Pirus adopted the red bandannas and ultimately the color red as an identifier. Color might also be worn on shirts, jackets, and hats (Bing, 1991).

Specific Gang Identifiers

Crips and Bloods

As mentioned, Crips use the color blue as their main identifier. In athletic clothing they prefer team wear that represents the Colorado Rockies because the letters "CR" appear on the team logo. They like the Los Angeles Dodgers because the Crips originated in L.A. and the uniforms are predominantly blue. British Knights apparel, especially athletic shoes, is popular for the BK emblem. Crips say the BK stands for "Blood Killer."

In sportswear, the Bloods prefer the apparel of the Cincinnati Reds, the Philadelphia Phillies, and the Kansas City Chiefs. All of these uniforms are primarily red. The Bloods interpret the Kansas City (KC) logo to stand for "Killing Crips." The graffiti is unique to each individual subset. Some examples of names include Outlaw Blood, West Side Piru Blood, Karson Pirus, Senter Park Pirus, Holly-Hood Pirus, East Coast 1 Crips, Venice Shoreline Gangster Crips, Avalon Gangster Crips, or Sixties Crips.

Vice Lords

The Vice Lords, a People Nation gang, originated and proliferated in the Illinois State Prison system during the 1960s. Early release programs and overcrowding in the prison system during the 1960s resulted in many gang members being discharged to their neighborhoods. Once back on the streets, the gang mentality flourished because of lack of educational, employment, and vocational opportunities. The Vice Lords reap financial rewards primarily through the sale of illegal narcotics such as crack cocaine on the street. Street gang sales are responsible for the epidemic explosion and widespread availability of crack cocaine (Valdez, 2000). Gangs establish their drug-selling turf and defend it at all costs, usually through violent means. The primary colors of the Vice Lord street gangs are black and red. Subsets of the Vice Lord gangs sometimes choose different colors, using yellow, orange, or one of the warmer tones or hues along with the black (Jensen & Yerington, 1997).

The Vice Lords use a variety of graffiti symbols, including but not limited to the five-pointed star, the Playboy Bunny with both ears up, the crescent moon, the pyramid, the cane, and the martini glass. Their verbal slogan is "All is well." One of the most commonly worn team uniforms for the Vice Lords is that of the Chicago Bulls basketball team. The Bulls wear red and black, the Vice Lords's colors, and also are located in the Vice Lords's home territory of Chicago. They also like the Dallas Stars and the Dallas Cowboys because of the five-pointed star on the team logos. Another intriguing identifier that the People Nation gangs, including the Vice Lords, have picked up on is the Texas Rangers baseball cap. The main color is red and the capital "T" on the cap looks like an upside-down pitchfork to them and consequently shows disrespect to the Gangster Disciples. Box 7–3 summarizes gang identifiers and graffiti that can be used to classify Vice Lord gang members (Jensen & Yerington, 1997).

Black Gangster Disciples

The Black Gangster Disciples (BGDs) also originated in the Illinois State Prison system and spread to the streets of inner-city Chicago during the early to mid 1960s. The primary motive of the BGDs is to make money through the sale of illegal narcotics, particularly crack cocaine. The BGDs have a highly organized hierarchy of leadership and are incredibly powerful on the street in major cities and small towns across the country (Jensen & Yerington, 1997).

The original colors of the BGDs are black and blue. Most of their subsets continue to use these colors. Gray and white may sometimes be used with black as the main color. Colors that suggest cooler tones or hues such as shades of blue, purple, and gray are usually preferred. Since each gang set adopts it own colors, parents and teachers should be alert for any combination.

The graffiti used by the BGDs consists of many symbols that are associated with the devil. However, this gang is not cult-oriented. Symbols used include the devil's head, horns, tail, wings, and heart. They also use the six-pointed star and the crown. Other common graffiti symbols include the flame, the sword, and the Playboy Bunny with one ear bent over. Sports team uniforms adopted by the BGDs and other Folk Nation gangs include the Duke University Blue Devils, the Georgetown Hoyas, the Georgia Tech Yellow Jackets, and the Green Bay Packers. These teams were chosen because of the colors, the team logos, and the proliferation of "G's" and "D's" on the uniforms. The verbal slogan of the BGDs is "All is one." Box 7–4 summarizes gang identifiers and graffiti that can be used to classify BGD members (Jensen & Yerington, 1997).

Latin Kings

The Latin Kings originated in the inner-city Latino neighborhoods of Chicago during the early to mid 1960s. Membership in the Latin gangs is often generational, with many family members, including fathers, brothers, uncles, and cousins, in the same gang. It is considered "macho" to be in the gang, an important part of Latino manhood. As a People Nation gang, the Latin Kings represent

Box 7–3 Vice Lord Identifiers

People Nation Gang: Represent to the left side of the body

Main Colors: Black and red

Slogan: "All is well"

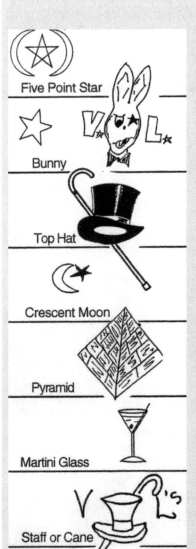

The Five-Pointed Star represents the Vice Lord Nation and its affiliates. It stands for their belief in love, truth, peace, freedom, and justice.

The Playboy Bunny with straight ears represents awareness and quickness as Vice Lords.

The Top Hat represents shelter for the Vice Lords.

The Crescent Moon represents the splitting of the Black Nation into two halves, the East and the West.

The Pyramid stands for the mystery of the construction of the Pyramid, which was constructed by Blacks. The points represent mental, physical, and spiritual strength. The 21 bricks stand for the 21 days of celebration.

The Martini Glass represents celebration and class in the Vice Lord Nation.

The Cane stands for strength in the Vice Lord Nation. Often, you see the Cane going through the top hat, this means that Vice Lords control the area.

The Circle Seven stands for the seven acts/prayers of the Holy Koran. Circle is 360 degrees of knowledge that Blacks once ruled the world and will rule the world again.
The Sun represents the rising of truth in the Black nation.

Note. From Gangs: Straight Talk, Straight Up (pp. 106–108) by M. M. Jensen and P. C. Yerington, 1997, Longmont, CO: Sopris West. Copyright 1997 by Sopris West. Reprinted with permission.

Box 7-4 Black Gangster Disciple Identifiers

Folk Nation Gang: Represent to the right side of the body

Main Colors: Black and blue

Slogan: "All is one"

Star of David	The Star of David was named after the late leader, David Barksdale. Each point stands for a concept: life of the Nation, love for the Nation, loyalty to the Nation, wisdom for leadership, knowledge for progress and direction and understanding of all things, and members of the Nation.
Crown	The Crown represents leadership and acknowledgment of the Chairmen (King Hoover, King Shorty, and King David).
Signs of the Devil	The Heart stands for the love they have for the Nation; the Devil's Horns represents the Disciples' determination to overcome all obstacles; the Pitchforks stand for the Nation's power to overcome oppression; and the Devil's Tail represents the oppression that all non-White people suffer.
Flame	The Flame stands for eternal life for the Disciple Nation.
Bunny	The Playboy Bunny logo with the one ear bent over shows disrespect to the Vice Lords.
Sword	The Sword stands for life and death within the Nation and the struggle to survive at all cost.

Note. From Gangs: Straight Talk, Straight Up (pp. 109–110) by M. M. Jensen and P. C. Yerington, 1997, Longmont, CO: Sopris West. Copyright 1997 by Sopris West. Reprinted with permission.

their gang affiliation to the left side of the body. Their colors are black and gold. Common graffiti symbols include the five-pointed star and the five-pointed crown, the cane, and the cross. The Latin Kings also tend to use a lot of anti-Disciple graffiti, primarily the pitchfork pointed down. The most favored graffiti symbol of the Latin Kings is the profile of a king, similar to that found on a deck of playing cards. Latin King graffiti, like that of other Latino gangs, tends to be very detailed and artistic when compared with the graffiti of other gangs.

Athletic team clothing adopted by the Latin Kings includes the Los Angeles Kings hockey team because the logo says, "Kings." In addition, they like the Chicago White Sox uniforms. The Chicago team logo is an example of how creative gang members can be with a very subtle identifier. On the White Sox team logo, the letters are embroidered in an ornate scripted fashion. The top of the "O" in Sox has three points, which Latin King gang members say resemble the three points of the crown used in their graffiti. In addition, the White Sox are from their home territory of Chicago. The verbal slogan of the Latin Kings is "Once a King, always a King."

Even though the Latin Kings and the Vice Lords are both People Nation gangs, they are not typically on friendly terms. If there was a reason for them to collaborate (e.g., a war against the Gangster Disciples), they would do so. After accomplishing the singular purpose, both gangs would return to being rivals. Box 7–5 summarizes the graffiti that can be used to identify the Latin Kings (Jensen & Yerington, 1997).

Look for Two Signs or Identifiers

When looking for observable gang identifiers, keep in mind that there should be at least two signs displayed simultaneously. Also be aware that some adolescents may adopt the gang look as a fashion statement or a fad. There are a variety of head to toe fashions that gang members can wear to demonstrate overt allegiance to a particular gang.

Following are examples of possible gang identifiers described from the hats down to the shoes:

- Hats are usually worn tilted to the right or the left by the midwestern gangs. Gang colors are also displayed on the head with hair beads, barrettes, and rubber bands in assorted gang-affiliated colors. The right or left representation rule is adhered to with all of the various midwestern gang symbols.
- Some gang members wear the new wave star, which is a scarf in a gang color worn under the hat that hangs down the back, similar to what has been popular with nongang members such as construction workers to keep the sun off their necks.
- Hair may be shaved or streaked in gang colors on the right side or the left side along with a cut design in one side of the hair such as a pitchfork, a star, a gang name, or a nickname.
- Jewelry is a popular method of showing gang loyalty. Any of the gang symbols can be made into jewelry. Earrings depicting gang symbols are worn in either the left or right ear. Some gang members are currently wearing gold caps engraved with gang symbols on a front tooth. Gang colors on beads or other gang-related jewelry is often worn.
- There are many different ways that details on clothing items can be used to indicate gang loyalty. Buttons on the clothes may designate gang colors, logos, or slogans. The inside of pockets may show gang colors. Gloves in gang colors may be worn on the right hand or the left hand. Fingernails may be painted in gang colors. Pant legs may be rolled up on the right side or the left side. Bandannas are worn in various ways to demonstrate gang allegiance. A bandanna in a gang color may be hung out of a pocket, tied around one leg, or tied to one side on a belt loop.
- Gym shoes may show gang affiliation both through the colors on the shoes and by the color of the laces. The shoe tongue flipped down on one side and up on the other may signify membership.

It is important to remember that gangs have adopted many currently fashionable and popular

Box 7–5 Latin King Identifiers

People Nation Gang: Represent to the left side of the body

Main Colors: Black and gold

Slogan: "Once a King, Always a King

5-pointed star

The Latin Kings fall under the Five-Pointed Star Nation of People; the points stand for love, truth, justice, freedom, and peace.

Bunny

The Playboy Bunny with the straight ears means the Kings are classy and fond of the ladies, appeal to their macho image.

Five Point Crown

The Five-Pointed Crown stands for shelter in the Latin King Nation. The points represent love, honor, obedience, righteousness, and sacrifice.

Staff or Cane

The Cane stands for strength and support for one another.

Anti-Disciple Graffiti

The Latin Kings often display anti-Disciple graffiti because they are the main rivals of the Kings. This graffiti will be written upside down or backwards.

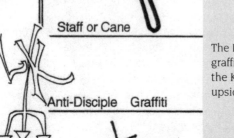

Cross

The Cross is a sign of their devotion to the gang, just as they are devoted to a family or a religion.

Note. *From* Gangs: Straight Talk, Straight Up *(pp. 111–112) by M. M. Jensen and P. C. Yerington, 1997, Longmont, CO: Sopris West. Copyright 1997 by Sopris West. Reprinted with permission.*

styles of clothing and other accessories that many children and adolescents also like to wear. Not every individual who wears one or more of these items is necessarily a gang member. A combination of two or more identifiers may suggest that an individual is demonstrating gang affiliation. It is important to look for combinations of identifiers, including colors, grafitti, and the right or left representation of symbols that is vitally important to gang members. Figure 7–1 summarizes clothing and other gang-related regalia that members might wear to school to indicate their gang loyalty (Jensen & Yerington, 1997).

Professional Athletic Clothing

Gangs have adopted and adapted many of the professional athletic teams' clothing, colors, and logos. Much of the sportswear apparel is simply adopted in its commercially produced form and worn by gang members to show gang loyalty. The gang chooses the athletic apparel to wear based on two criteria. First, it must be available in their gang colors. Second, it must have symbols or letters that correspond to or can be affiliated with their gang. Some gang members wear hooded sweatshirts with a team jacket over it. The color of the hood in combination with the color of the jacket represents the two main gang colors.

Gang members frequently personalize these items of clothing by drawing or embroidering one or more of their gang symbols and sayings. Some professional clothing manufacturers and silk screeners even custom-make gang-oriented clothing because of the potential financial profit. They know that gang members have a lot of money to spend.

For example, Black Gangster Disciples will look for apparel in black and blue colors that has symbols associated with the devil, or possibly a six-pointed object displayed on the right side of the item. The Duke Blue Devils basketball cap appears to be made to order for Gangster Disciples. It is black and blue, has a devil's head on the right side, and has a capital "D" (for Disciples) on the front.

Another example is the University of Georgia Bulldogs cap, which is also black and blue and has a bulldog on the right side with six spiky points on its collar. It also has a capital "G" (for Gangsters) on the front.

The Latin Kings adopted the Pittsburgh Pirates cap because it comes in their black and gold colors and has a "P" on the front, which they designate as standing for the People Nation. The Vice Lords have adopted the very popular Nike Air Jordans because they come in the primary VL colors of red and black. The Vice Lords have picked up on the Chicago Bulls jackets because of the red and black colors. The Vice Lords have also been known to wear Converse gym shoes because of the five-pointed star on the side. Box 7–6 provides a list of professional athletic clothing items that have been adopted by youth gangs (Jensen & Yerington, 1997).

The gangs not only have adopted sports team apparel, but also have adapted the meanings of the team names or acronyms to fit their gang's mission or image. For example, in the minds of Black Gangster Disciples, Duke (University) means "Disciples Usually Kill Everybody (or Enemies). The Orlando Magic hats have been adopted by the Vice Lords for two reasons. The hat has a five-pointed star and Vice Lord members have indicated that the MAGIC on the hat stands for "Murder All Gangsters In Chicago. (The Vice Lords and the Gangster Disciples come from opposing gang nations and are bitter rivals.)

It is interesting that so many items of apparel are made in colors and have pertinent symbols or letters on the side that are appropriate for the gang that uses the particular color and symbol. Is it simply a coincidence? It has been suggested that major sports clothing corporations are catering to gangs. Gang members make huge financial profits selling drugs and carrying out other illegal activities. They have money to spend, and retail sellers have commented "business is business" when asked if they are aware that they're selling gang-retailed items. A list of gang acronyms for athletic team names is provided in Box 7–7 (Jensen & Yerington, 1997).

GANG IDENTIFICATION
Look For at Least 2 Signs!

NEW WAVE STAR:
Sheets worn under hats that hang down from the back with gang colors or symbols

HAIRCUTS:
Shaved or streaked right or left side or in shapes such as arrows or numbers.

TEETH:
Gold caps may have gang symbols engraved on them.

SWEATSHIRTS:
Hooded sweatshirts worn under jackets with the hood out. Hood and jacket are usually gang colors.

BUTTONS:
Gang logos or slogans may be printed on them.

JEWELRY:
Gang symbols are made into jewelry, necklace, or one earring.

PANT LEG CUFFS:
Rolled up right or left side.

GYM SHOES:
Gang colors on shoes or laces. Laces tied up on one side, not in conventional way. Shoe tongue flipped down can signify membership.

HATS:
Tilted right or left. Gang colors also displayed in bandages, hairbeads, barrettes, and rubberbands.

EARRINGS:
Right or left ears. Will usually display gang symbols.

FRIENDSHIP BEADS:
Gang colors on beads. Worn on clothing, shoes, hair, or as earring.

POCKETS:
The inside of pockets colored gang colors. Bandanas in gang colors hanging out of pockets.

TATTOOS:
India-ink tattoos showing gang colors on right or left hand.

GLOVES:
Right or left hand in gang colors.

FINGERNAILS:
Two nails with gang colors on right or left hand.

BELT BUCKLE:
Worn in right or left position.

NOTE:
People wearing ANY of these identifiers are not necessarily gang members!

FIGURE 7–1 Examples of Gang-Related Clothing and Other Items

Note. *From Gangs: Straight Talk, Straight Up (p. 76) by M. M. Jensen and P. C. Yerington, 1997, Longmont, CO: Sopris West. Copyright 1997 by Sopris West. Reprinted with permission.*

Box 7–6 Athletic Teams' Apparel Adopted by Youth Gangs

Dallas Cowboys: 5-pointed star	People Nation Gangs
Boston (all teams): Brothers of the Struggle Taking Over the Nation	Black Gangster Disciples
Los Angeles Raiders Crest: Has 3 points and the Raider has his right eye covered	Black Gangster Disciples
White Sox: The "O" in Sox has 6 points or has crossed canes significant to the Vice Lords	Either People or Folk Gangs
Pittsburgh Pirates: "P" for People Nation and black and gold colors	People Nation Gangs, specifically the Latin Kings
Detroit Tigers	"D" for Disciples
Georgetown: G on bulldog's cap and 6 spikes on dog's collar	Black Gangster Disciples
Green Bay Packers: G on front of cap	Black Gangster Disciples
Notre Dame (ND)	Notorious Disciples
Adidas Shoes: 3 stripes on each side and leaf pointed up	Black Gangster Disciples and Folk Nation
Phillies: 5-pointed star and "P" on cap	People Nation Gangs and Bloods
Dallas Stars: 5-pointed star and black and gold colors	Latin Kings
Converse Shoes: 5-pointed star and crescent moon	Vice Lords
Charlotte Hornets: Stripes on bee and 4 corners on wings and feet	4 Corner Hustlers (Vice Lords)
British Knight Shoes: BK on shoes stands for Blood Killers	Crips
Colorado Rockies uniforms	Crips: Team insignia has CRIP letters as part of the logo
Orlando Magic: Blue, silver, & black	Folk Nation Gangs
Oakland Raiders: Crest has 3 points, Raider has right eye covered, colors are silver and black	Black Gangster Disciples, 3rd World Disciples, Latin Disciples
Texas Rangers: Capital "T" on cap resembles an upside-down pitchfork	People Nation Gangs

Note. *From Gangs: Straight Talk, Straight Up (pp. 78–81) by M. M. Jensen and P. C. Yerington, 1997, Longmont, CO: Sopris West. Copyright 1997 by Sopris West. Reprinted with permission.*

Box 7-7 Gang Acronyms for Athletic Team Names

DUKE University	Folks use this: Disciples Usually Kill Everybody (or Enemies)
NIKE	Nigga, I Kill Everybody (Vice Lord slogan)
Chicago BULLS	Bloods Usually Live Longer -or- Brothers United Living Lords Style (Vice Lord Slogan)
Oakland RAIDERS (formerly Los Angeles RAIDERS)	Remember After I Die Everybody Runs Scared (All Folk gangs) -or- Raggedy Ass Idiotic Disciples Everywhere Running Scared (People gangs)
ADIDAS (athletic clothing)	All Day I Despise All Slobs (Crip gangs) -or- All Day I Dream About Sex (adolescent girls)
FILA (athletic clothing)	Folks in Los Angeles
Orlando MAGIC	Murder All Gangsters in Chicago (People) -or- Men Associating With Gangsters and Incoming Crips (Folks)
University of IOWA	I Only Worship Allah (Vice Lord Islamic claim)
UNLV (University of Nevada at Las Vegas)	Written backwards = Vice Lord Nation United
Kansas City Chiefs	Bloods say KC = Killing Crips
Boston (all teams)	Brothers of the Struggle Taking Over the Nation (incarcerated members of the BGDs are called Brothers of the Struggle)
Denver Broncos	Initials reversed = Black Disciples
British Knight apparel	Crips say BK = Blood Killers
San Francisco Giants	Initials = Super Folk Gangsters (Folk Nation gangs)

Note. From Gangs: Straight Talk, Straight Up (pp. 82–84) by M. M. Jensen and P. C. Yerington, 1997, Longmont, CO: Sopris West. Copyright 1997 by Sopris West. Reprinted with permission.

Implications for Working with Youth and Adolescents

The school environment offers a "captive audience" for gang members. They can recruit, intimidate, harass, and be physically threatening to other students. Some gang members have contact only with each other during the school day because they are too young to drive to other locations. In this case, gang meetings, initiations, missions, and the exchange of literature take place within the school building, on campus, or very close to school grounds. A school environment in which the staff is uneducated about gang-related behavior allows the gang mentality to flourish. This creates significant problems for teachers and administrators who are unaware that gang members are a part of their student population and that the problems they are experiencing are gang related. It can make the school environment dangerous and frightening for other students.

This chapter was designed to provide basic gang awareness of the early warning signs of gang influence and the knowledge of their "representing" techniques. The problem cannot be managed effectively and competently if it is not acknowledged. Teachers and parents must understand how and why youth and adolescents become gang members if they are to be prevented from joining. Knowing the motivators for gang membership, the risk factors, the hand signs, the colors, and the graffiti signs and symbols will help educators, parents, and other professionals identify gang members in the school environment.

After gang members are identified, intervention tactics can be planned and implemented. Focus must be kept on providing the extra motivation and support these individuals will need to stay in school and achieve academic success. A consistent attempt must be made to counteract the strong appeal and motivation gangs provide for youth and adolescents. Schools must collaborate with community agencies to provide supervised and safe after-school, evening, and weekend programs and activities.

Parents who are aware of gang identifiers can be effective in keeping their children safe from the lure and involvement of gang activities. Parents must know where their children are, who they are with, and what they are doing at all times. Parents should know their children's friends and their parents. It is critically important for parents to verify that their children actually are where they say they will be. Parents should be vigilant about making sure their children are not wearing or creating any form of gang identifiers on their clothing, on any other possessions, in their bedrooms, or anywhere else at home.

Educators may be the key to reducing the rising numbers of gang members in this country by eliminating the supply of wannabe gang members. Wannabes are "gonnabes" unless children are provided with an alternative means to be accepted and to gain a sense of identity and self-esteem with a legitimate peer group. School achievement is a primary means of establishing an appropriate sense of self-esteem. The goal is to make youth *"don't"* wannabe in the gang. Deterring youngsters from joining will cut off the supply of youth and adolescents to the hard-core gang recruiters. In essence, this practice will keep the children in school and involved in extracurricular activities at school and in community recreation, church, and family programs.

Gangs and the violence associated with gang activity are not going to simply disappear from schools if they are denied or ignored. The ruthless criminal influence of youth involved in gang activity has reverberated from the inner city to urban and rural areas across the nation. Educators spend more time on a daily basis with these potentially violent youth than any other group of adults. To most effectively protect the safe and secure learning environment for all, every teacher must be well trained and fully prepared to recognize gang identifiers and to competently manage potentially violent students in the classroom. The major recommendation of this chapter is to educate all preservice and practicing teachers on basic gang awareness and management strategies.

Specifically, all teacher training programs should incorporate basic gang awareness and management strategies into the preservice curriculum. In addition, communities, law enforcement agencies, and school districts should collaborate to provide effective in-service training for all educators, parents, and other professionals about gangs and crisis management in school. Ongoing and successful suppression and elimination of gang violence in schools across the country must start with effective preparation and training to recognize gang identifiers and behaviors.

References

Arthur, R., & Erickson, E. (1992). *Gangs and schools.* Holmes Beach, FL: Learning Publications.

Battin, S. R., Hill, K. G., Abbott, R. D., Catalano, R. F., & Hawkins, J.D. (1998). The contribution of gang membership to delinquency beyond delinquent friends. *Criminology, 36,* 93–115.

Bing, L. (1991). *Do or die.* New York: Harper Collins.

Council of the Great City Schools (1994). *Critcal educational trends: A poll of America's urban schools.* Washington DC: Author.

Ebensen, F., & Osgood, D. W. (1997). *National evaluation of G.R.E.A.T. research in brief* (NCJ 167264). Washington, DC: U.S. Department of Justice, Office of Justice Programs, National Institute of Justice.

Goldstein, A. P. (1990). *Delinquents on delinquency.* Champaign, IL: Research Press.

Goldstein, A. P., & Kodluboy, D. W. (1998). *Gangs in schools: Signs, symbols, and solutions.* Champaign, IL: Research Press.

Huff, C. R. (1993). Gangs in the United States. In A. P. Goldstein and C. R. Huff (Eds.), *The gang intervention handbook* (pp. 3–20). Champaign, IL: Research Press.

Jensen, M. M., & Yerington, P. C. (1997). *Gangs: Straight talk, straight up.* Longmont, CO: Sopris West.

Kodluboy, D. W., & Evenrud, L. A. (1993). School-based interventions: Best practices and critical issues. In A. P. Goldstein and C. R. Huff (Eds.), *The gang intervention handbook* (pp. 257–294). Champaign, IL: Research Press.

Lopez, L. L. (1994, Winter). Enhancing self-esteem. *School safety.*

Maxon, C. L., & Klein, M. W. (1990). Street gang violence: Twice as great or half as great? In C. R. Huff (Ed.), *Gangs in America.* Newbury Park, CA: Sage.

Office of Juvenile Justice and Delinquency Prevention. (1996). *Gang suppression and intervention: Problem and response* (NCJ 149269). Chicago: National Youth Gang Suppression and Intervention Research and Development Program, School of Social Service Administration, University of Chicago.

Rhode, G., Jenson, W. R., and Reavis, H. K. (1992). *The tough kid book.* Longmont, CO: Sopris West.

Texas Youth Commission, Office of Delinquency Prevention. (1993). *Catalogs of programs and research.* Austin, TX: Author.

Trump, K. S. (2002). Gangs, violence, and safe schools. In C. R. Huff (Ed.), *Gangs in America* (3rd ed., pp. 121–129). Thousand Oaks, CA: Sage.

Valdez, A. J. (2000). *Gangs: A guide to understanding street gangs* (3rd ed.). San Clemente, CA: LawTech Publishing Company.

Walker, H. M., Colvin, G., & Ramsey, E. (1995). *Antisocial behavior in schools: Strategies and best practices.* Pacific Grove, CA: Brooks/Cole Publishing.

PART 3
CATEGORIES OF INTERNALIZED DISORDERS

Chapter 8: Anxiety Disorders

Chapter 9: Depression and Suicide

Chapter 10: Eating Disorders

8

ANXIETY DISORDERS

After completing the chapter, the reader will be able to identify:

- The characteristics of anxiety disorders.
- The characteristics of obsessive-compulsive disorder.
- The characteristics of panic disorder.
- The characteristics of phobias.
- The characteristics of post-traumatic stress disorder.
- Treatment options for anxiety disorders.
- Medications for anxiety disorders.
- Implications for educators, parents, and other professionals who work with youth and adolescents.

Introduction

Anxiety disorders are the most common mental health problem among children and adolescents (Turnbull, Turnbull, Shank, Smith, & Leal, 2002). Anxiety disorders cause difficulties for all students, not just students in special education. The severity of the disorder and the student's individual coping skills will affect academic achievement and personal adjustment to various degrees. All educators and other professionals who work with youth and adolescents must be aware of the characteristics of anxiety disorders in order to be able to provide the most appropriate interventions. As with all disorders, recognition of the symptoms and early intervention services will be most effective in reducing the negative impact for the individual.

Children with emotional and behavioral disorders (E/BD) also often have severe anxiety disorders. The federal definition of E/BD includes anxiety disorders (Gargiulo, 2003; Heward, 2003; Kirk, Gallagher, & Anastasiow, 2003). The general characteristics of anxiety disorders include excessive fear, worry, and anxiousness related to different situations. As many as 13% of youth and adolescents suffer from a variety of different types of anxiety disorders. Surprisingly, only about one third of these children receive treatment (Anxiety Disorders Association of America [ADAA], 2002; National Institute of Mental Health [NIMH], 2000). This chapter discusses a variety of anxiety disorders, including characteristics, treatment strategies, and medication. The information will assist educators, parents, and other professionals to recognize the behavioral characteristics and implement appropriate treatment strategies for youth and adolescents who have any of the following specific anxiety disorders: (a) generalized anxiety disorder, (b) separation anxiety disorder, (c) obsessive-compulsive disorder, (d) panic disorder, (e) phobias, and (f) post-traumatic stress disorder.

Characteristics of Anxiety Disorders

The *Diagnostic and Statistical Manual of Mental Disorders* (DSM-IV-TR, American Psychiatric Association [APA], 2000) provides specific characteristics to describe each of the six different types of anxiety disorders that are discussed in this chapter. The purpose of the DSM-IV-TR is to assist mental health practitioners to diagnose problem behavior in youth, adolescence, and adulthood. Educators, parents, and other professionals can also use the categories of behavior to help recognize the indicators of disordered behavior. Identifying the specific problem causing behavioral dysfunction can be helpful in planning and implementing an individualized education program. This proactive approach assists professionals in providing an effective educational and behavioral treatment approach.

When describing the characteristic features of anxiety disorders, the DSM-IV-TR states that anxiousness and avoidance behaviors are the two primary characteristics noted. Anxiousness is observed as the individual confronts and attempts to deal with problematic situations. Many persons with anxiety disorders simply try to continually avoid situations that make them uncomfortable, nervous, and anxious. Anxiety disorders can be present during childhood, adolescence, and adulthood. Most anxiety disorders are more common in females than in males, especially during adolescence (Coleman & Webber, 2002).

Causes of Anxiety Disorders

The literature has not identified a specific cause of anxiety disorders (AD) (Wicks-Nelson & Israel, 2000). It is suggested that the different types of anxiety disorders may be a result of different factors or combinations of factors in each individual's life. Both biological or genetic and environmental influences have been suggested as causation factors. Family studies do indicate that children of parents with anxiety disorders are likely to develop similar disorders. However, it has been difficult to separate the biological influence from the environmental influence. [The question remains to be answered: Do children actually inherit the potential to develop the anxiety disorder or do they learn to show the disorder from observing and imitating their parents' behavior?]

Some children may develop an anxiety disorder after experiencing or witnessing a traumatic incident. For example, a child who is bitten by a cat may develop a cat phobia. During a holiday season, a child might be frightened by a person in costume. Examples include a Santa, a monster, or a witch. That child may develop an unrealistic fear of Santas or persons in Halloween costumes. A child who endures ongoing stressful events in his life may develop a fearful and anxious pattern of behaviors (Wicks-Nelson & Israel, 2000).

Assessment of Anxiety Disorders

The assessment process for anxiety disorders is usually implemented by a mental health professional. The evaluation may be done in a clinical setting. Wicks-Nelson & Israel (2000) provide a discussion of the variety of assessments that might be used. During the process of evaluating a child's anxiety disorder, it would be important to be aware of the following three points. [First, a number of different assessment devices should be used to obtain a true picture of the child's behavior. Second, the assessor should be aware of developmental issues of concern based on the child's age. Third, the assessor must be able to separate normal fears and worries from those that are severe enough to be of clinical concern.]

A general clinical interview is often the first step in the process. This helps the clinician gain a perspective of the problem and to gather ideas for treatment program planning. Structured diagnostic interviews can be done to formulate a clinical diagnosis when warranted.

There is a self-report scale that can be completed by parents and the child with the anxiety disorder. It is called the Multidimensional Anxiety Scale for Children (MASC) (March, Parker, Sullivan, Stallings, & Conners, 1997). This evaluation instrument provides scores in four areas: (a) physical symptoms, (b) social anxiety, (c) harm avoidance, and (d) separation anxiety. Using this test, the examiner can look at several aspects of anxiety. There are also assessments that evaluate specific components of anxiety such as the Social Anxiety Scale for Children–Revised (La Greca & Stone, 1993) and the Social Phobia and Anxiety Inventory for Children (Beidel, Turner, & Morris, 1995). General behavior rating scales can also be used to determine how the child's behavior compares with a same-age population of youth or adolescents (see Chapter 2 for specifics).

The assessor may also make direct observations in various environments at home, at school, and in the community. This will help to determine which specific environmental events or people might be working to increase the child's level of anxiety.

Characteristics of Generalized Anxiety Disorder (GAD)

- You are always worried about things, even when there are no signs of trouble.
- You have frequent aches and pains that can't be traced to physical illness or injury.
- You get tired easily, yet you have difficulty sleeping.
- Your body is constantly tense (NIMH, 2000).

The preceding behaviors are all symptoms of generalized anxiety disorder (GAD).

Unrealistic Fears and Excessive Anxiety

[The primary characteristic of generalized anxiety disorder (GAD) is unrealistic or excessive anxiety about a minimum of two or more circumstances directly related to the individual's life.] In the person's real life, there is actually no legitimate reason to be so overly distressed. The extreme level of worry or fear must be present for at least 6 months and be a cause of concern almost every day of that period (APA, 1994). Examples of worries for adults might be fear of dying and leaving children alone, fear of losing one's job, or fear of personal or professional failure on the job. The fears of youths or adolescents relate more to their developmental levels. Examples include fear of social embarrassment, fear of school failure, or fear of extracurricular or athletic activity failure. In addition to the excessive level of unrealistic worry, the individual usually also displays poor coping strategies. Consequently, GAD usually has an adverse affect on the person's life. For example, an adult might miss a lot of days at work or a student might be frequently absent from school. They might not participate in social activities or they may often be unable to carry out duties or responsibilities (Gilatto, 2000).

Young children are also susceptible to GAD. It is more common in girls than in boys, and the typical age of onset is usually around 10. Estimates of prevalence suggest that GAD may affect anywhere from 3 to 15% of the school-age population (Wicks-Nelson & Israel, 2000). The prevalence rate for GAD in the general population of adolescents is estimated to be from 4 to 7%. APA (2000) reports that among adults, it is most common for GAD to occur during the ages from 20 to 30 years. Many of the individuals with GAD also have mild depression and panic disorder symptoms (APA, 2000; Wicks-Nelson & Israel, 2000). Prevalence is estimated to be about 4 to 6% of the general population, with more females than males seeking treatment (Gilatto, 2000).

Observable Symptoms of Generalized Anxiety Disorder (GAD)

Following is a list of behaviors that teachers, parents, and other professionals might observe in youth and adolescents who have GAD (ADAA, 2002; APA, 2000; NIMH, 2000; Turnbull et al., 2002; Wicks-Nelson & Israel, 2000):

- Excessive or overwhelming worry
- Unrealistic tension regarding daily events
- Anticipates the worst, even though there is little reason to expect it
- Frequent aches and pains that cannot be traced to an illness or injury
- Feeling, edgy, irritable, tired, or fatigued, but having trouble sleeping
- Body is physically tense much of the time
- Trembling, shakes, nausea, headaches

Characteristics of Separation Anxiety Disorder (SAD)

The American Psychiatric Association (2000) states that the essential behavior required for diagnosis of separation anxiety disorder (SAD) is a child's excessive anxiety and fear related to being separated from a significant individual(s). The behavior must be present continuously for at least 2 weeks for formal diagnosis. Young children with SAD are often preoccupied with thoughts of scary or bad things happening to their parents. They may refuse to attend school or participate in other age-appropriate social activities unless their parents are present. When the child is required to be separated from the significant individual, anxiety and fear usually escalate to panic. The excessive reaction is way beyond what would be expected for the child's age and developmental level.

Coleman and Webber (2002) described specifics about SAD. The prevalence rate in the general population is estimated to be from 2 to 4%. It is most prevalent in younger children, with the average age of onset around 9 years. The following fears were specific to age ranges:

- Age 5 to 8: worries and nightmares about the significant individual being harmed and reluctance to go to school
- Age 9 to 12: excessive distress at required separations from the significant individual
- Age 13 to 16: refusal to go to school and somatic complaints such as having a headache or stomachache to avoid leaving the significant individual

School Refusal Problems

Separation anxiety often relates to school attendance. Children may be fearful and anxious about separating from parents to attend school during their younger years. This may affect about 2 to 5% of the school population. It happens more during transition periods. Examples include first attending preschool, kindergarten, or first grade. The anxiety levels tend to calm down during elementary school and then escalate again during the transition to middle school.

Young children's feelings of anxiety and stress may be manifested in physical complaints such as headache, stomachache, nausea, and diarrhea. The parent perceives the child is physically ill and lets him stay home from school. If the underlying reason is separation anxiety, the parent is inadvertently reinforcing the anxiety. Separation anxiety is less common in adolescents than in younger children. However, in those adolescents who do have SAD, the fear of separation is intensified by moving from middle school to high school, peer pressure, trying to fit in socially, and academic pressure to achieve good grades. These factors may cause a student who is anxious to avoid school. As with young children, when parents allow adolescents to stay home from school, they are simply reinforcing the fear or anxiety. Teachers, parents, and other professionals can be observant to note the following fears in children,

which may be indicative of separation anxiety at school:

- Being separated from significant individuals
- Riding on the bus
- Eating in the cafeteria
- Using the school restrooms
- Being called on in class
- Changing from school clothes to uniform for gym class
- Interacting with other students and teachers
- Being picked on by peers or older students

The most effective method to reduce separation anxiety with students of any age is based on positive reassurance. Adults should consistently assure students that the feelings of anxiety and fearfulness about the situation will settle down in time and that bad things are not actually going to happen even though the child is convinced they will. Rather than forcing a fearful and anxious child to attend school all day all at once, start with short periods of time and build up. The student should be exposed to small but ever-increasing degrees of time at school. Teachers and other professionals at school can work to set up experiences that are calming and successful for students. Eventually the students will learn to gain control of and master their fears.

Characteristics of Obsessive-Compulsive Disorder

I couldn't do anything without rituals. They invaded every aspect of my life. Counting really bogged me down. I would wash my hair three times as opposed to once because three was a good luck number and one wasn't. It took me longer to read because I'd count the lines in a paragraph. When I set my alarm at night, I had to set it to a number that wouldn't add up to a *bad* number.

Getting dressed in the morning was tough because I had a routine and if I didn't follow the routine, I'd get anxious and would have to get dressed again. I always worried that if I didn't do something, my parents were going to die. I'd have these terrible thoughts of harming my parents. That was completely irrational but the thoughts triggered more anxiety and more senseless behavior. Because of the time I spent on rituals, I was unable to do a lot of things that were important to me. (NIMH, 2000, p. 2)

There are two sets of behaviors evident with obsessive-compulsive disorder (OCD). The first type of behavior relates to *obsessions*. Obsessions are described as intrusive, unwanted, repetitive, and persistent thoughts. The second type of behavior relates to *compulsions*. Compulsions are described as repetitive, purposeless behaviors that the individual feels compelled to perform (Coleman & Webber, 2002; Wicks-Nelson & Israel, 2000). DSM-IV-TR criteria for diagnosis state that the individual knows the behaviors are unreasonable and purposeless but seems to have no control over stopping the cycle of behavior (APA, 2000). Most persons with OCD have both obsessions and compulsions. Coleman and Webber (2002) reported that an additional component of OCD is that the child may sincerely believe that performing the ritualistic behaviors perfectly will somehow protect him or significant others from harm.

The average age of onset of OCD is during the transition period from childhood to adolescence, between the ages of 9 and 13 years. The disorder seems to affect males and females equally, although some studies report a slightly higher incidence in males. It is estimated that about 2% of the general population is affected (Coleman & Weber, 2002; NIMH, 2000). OCD often overlaps with other disorders, including depression, Tourette syndrome, substance abuse, attention deficit disorder (ADD), and eating disorders.

Persons with OCD experience the problems to such a time-consuming degree that the behaviors significantly interfere with their daily schedules at home, at school or work, with social activities, and with family and other social relationships. Obsessive-compulsive behaviors take up so much time that a normal routine usually is not possible (APA, 2000).

Cause and Treatment for OCD

What causes OCD? Medical research suggests that there is a neurological basis for the disorder. The dysfunction relates to a neurotransmitter called serotonin. Neurotransmitters carry messages through the brain. Serotonin regulates mood and cognitive processing.

There are two methods of treatment for OCD using medicine, behavioral therapy, or a combination of both. Doctors can prescribe several different medications to regulate the level of serotonin. The correct dosage of medicine can significantly decrease the symptoms of OCD. One of the more effective medications used is called Anafranil® (clomipramine). Others that have been approved are Prozac® (fluoxetine), Luvox® (fluvoxamine), and Paxil® (paroxetine). These medications reduce the frequency and intensity of the obsessions and compulsions. A reduction in symptoms usually begins in about 3 weeks. As the symptoms are reduced, the individual may become more susceptible to the successful implementation of behavioral therapy.

The form of behavioral therapy used to help an individual cope with OCD is called *exposure and response prevention*. During therapy, the individual is taught to deliberately and voluntarily confront or be exposed to the feared object or idea while refraining from the habitual ritualized behavioral response. For example, a compulsive hand washer would be encouraged to touch objects he believes to be contaminated without washing his hands afterward. The goal is to let several hours elapse without hand washing until the anxiety provoked has time to diminish. Treatment then proceeds one small step at a time as the individual learns to reduce the rituals. The desensitization treatment process helps many individuals with OCD to reduce obsessive thoughts and compulsive rituals. Medication will probably be necessary to regulate serotonin levels even after behavioral therapy has helped reduce the symptoms (NIMH, 2000).

Characteristic Behaviors of OCD

There are a number of observable behaviors that teachers, parents, and other professionals who work with youth and adolescents should be aware of that might signal the presence of OCD. The behaviors are divided into two groups. One is obsessions, which usually have more to do with thinking. The other group of behaviors is called compulsions, which usually relate to ritual acts. Common obsessions and compulsions follow (APA, 2000; Coleman & Webber, 2002; NIMH, 2000; Wicks-Nelson & Israel, 2000).

Obsessions

- Repetitive thoughts of violence or aggression
- Fear of dirt, germs, or contaminations (e.g., by shaking hands or touching things in public)
- Lucky or unlucky numbers
- Fear of harm to self or significant others
- Doubt (wondering if a certain behavior was actually done)
- Symmetry, order, or exactness
- Intrusive nonsense, sounds, words, or symbols

Compulsions

- Excessive hand washing, showering, bathing, toothbrushing, or grooming
- Housecleaning
- Counting items to make sure they are all there
- Checking to make sure something was done such as locking doors and windows or turning off appliances
- Ordering or arranging (making sure that a series of items are always systematically lined up in the same order)
- Repeating rituals (redoing a letter or number or any other task until it is absolutely perfect, or going back through a doorway a certain number of times until one can pass through to the room beyond)
- Straightening every object in a room until everything lines up and is in the perfect position

- Touching items of various textures
- Hoarding or collecting rituals

Characteristics of Panic Disorder

For me, a panic attack is almost a violent experience. I feel disconnected from reality. I feel like I am losing control in a very extreme way. My heart pounds really hard. I feel like I can't get my breath, and there is an overwhelming feeling that things are crashing in on me.

In between attacks there is this dread and anxiety that it's going to happen again. I'm afraid to go back to places where I've had an attack. Unless I get help, there soon won't be anyplace where I can go and feel safe from panic. (NIMH, 2000, p. 1)

not linked to other events; single

Panic attacks are described as "intense, discrete experiences of extreme fear that seem to arise quickly and often without any clear cause" (Wicks-Nelson & Israel, 2000, p. 127). Individuals who suffer from panic attacks also usually have persistent fears or intense worry about when the next panic attack may occur. There does not seem to be a specific trigger for the attacks. The unexpectedness aspect of the disorder is one of the essential features required for diagnosis (APA, 2000). A panic attack usually lasts for a few minutes. Panic attacks may occur several times a week or even daily.

Panic attacks are more common in adolescence than during the younger childhood years. This disorder is more common in girls than in boys. The prevalence rate in clinic samples is about 10 to 15%. Clinic samples relate to individuals whose problems are severe enough to warrant treatment by specialists in a clinic. It is less common in the general population, with the prevalence being estimated at about 0.6%. The common age for onset during adulthood is during the late twenties (APA, 2000; NIMH, 2000; Wicks-Nelson & Israel, 2000). Research evidence suggests that the potential for developing panic disorder may be inherited (NIMH, 2000).

DSM-IV-TR provided a list of 13 symptoms of fear that an individual may experience during a panic attack. Four of the 13 must be present for a formal diagnosis. It is common for individuals to have about six of the symptoms (APA, 2000; Coleman & Webber, 2002). Panic attacks are often preceded by an aura or a feeling of intense apprehension, or terror, almost like a sense of impending doom. The most common symptoms experienced by adolescents who were being treated at a clinic for panic attacks were *going crazy* (32%) and *fear of dying* (25%). Some persons who are victims of panic attacks develop an additional intense fear of suffering an attack in a social situation where they may be publicly humiliated. These individuals then try to stay at home where they feel safe. This avoidance behavior of being terrified to leave home is called agoraphobia (Wicks-Nelson & Israel, 2000). Following are characteristic behaviors that teachers, parents, and other professionals should be aware of related to panic disorder (APA, 2000; Wicks-Nelson & Israel, 2000).

Symptoms of a Panic Attack

1. Shortness of breath
2. Dizziness or feeling faint
3. Heart palpitations
4. Trembling or shaking
5. Sweating
6. Choking
7. Nausea or abdominal distress
8. Derealization (feelings of unreality or depersonalization, i.e., being detached from oneself)
9. Feeling numb or tingling sensation
10. Hot or cold flashes
11. Chest pain or discomfort
12. Fear of dying
13. Fear of losing control or going crazy

Interview

Following is an interview with a college student who has suffered from generalized anxiety disorder with panic attacks (personal communication,

Stephanie Ferguson, April 12, 2002). She provides an interesting personal insight to the disorder with suggestions for teachers, parents, and professionals for helping others to recognize and better manage the symptoms of the disorder.

1. *At what age did you first learn you had an anxiety (panic) disorder?*

I was 18, and a freshman here [Western illinois University] when I first found out. This mainly came about because I was having panic attacks. I kept feeling like I was going to have seizures (the aura before, with dizziness, sweating, clamminess, and impaired vision). I went to my neurologist, but we couldn't find anything, and then I talked to my dad, and he suggested that it was panic. He has anxiety problems (much worse than mine) and so do most of his brothers, and his mother. My dad started teaching me some techniques to calm myself down when I would begin to panic. Those coupled with knowing that what I was having was caused by panic instead of a medical problem, made things much better.

2. *Would you call it a generalized anxiety disorder—or specifically a panic disorder—or both?*
Both.

3. *What symptoms of anxiety disorder do you have?*
I worry about everything. Some of my main worries are:

— fear of heart stopping, or inability to breathe
— fear of having some illness, such as cancer, and that it will go unnoticed
— fear of being hurt and unable to contact anyone
— worry and anxiety about undone projects, homework, etc.
— worries when I feel "stuck" in a place and don't know how long until I can leave (such as a meeting or doctor's office)
— worry over my friends' and family's safety
— lack of self-confidence/worry over my own worth in relationships and friendships

4. *Have the symptoms gotten better or worse as you have gotten older?*

I think that the actual anxiety disorder symptoms have gotten worse. But I feel better about it now that I know why (the disorder rather than just being weird or crazy) I have these feelings.

5. *What symptoms of panic disorder do you have?*

Panic attacks! My mind feeds off of the fact that I have epilepsy from a cyst in my brain. I haven't had an actual seizure for six years, but my panic attacks usually feel the same way a seizure feels. I think what happens is that my mind knows that seizures are a scary thing for me, so when I panic, this is the scary thing it knows about. So I experience panic attacks in much the same way I experienced seizures in the past. Like…the irrational part of my mind takes over when I start to feel weak, dizzy, etc., and makes the symptoms much worse. So instead of just feeling a little bit dizzy or whatever, my imagination takes over and makes me think I am experiencing something I'm not.

6. *Have the symptoms gotten better or worse as you have gotten older?*

The symptoms first got much worse (when I was about 17), then once I learned to control them they have gotten a bit better. Once again, to know what it is gives me power. When I start to feel panicked, I can now tell myself, "This is not a seizure, it is a panic attack. You are going to be ok. Just calm down." This makes a huge difference from the way it used to be.

7. *Did you go to any special doctor for help?*

Yes. First my neurologist, now a psychologist. If I want meds I have the option to go to a psychiatrist.

8. *Do you take medication to control the symptoms?*

No. My docs and psychs have suggested the option, but I have chosen not to so far. I feel that right now, the problem is always present, but it is livable. I am already dependent on Tegretol for the seizures, and don't want another med to have to wean myself off of when I decide to have

children. If it does begin to affect my life too much, I will then consider meds.

9. *Do you use any behavioral therapy type methods to control symptoms?*

I use the method of reasoning with myself, as I said earlier. Also, if I'm feeling trapped, I tell myself that there is no situation I can't get out of. If I really want to, I can get up and walk out of a meeting or class. Somehow, just giving myself this option helps. I also have a support group in my friends and family who are there for me to talk to.

10. *What types of problems has the disorder caused in your life?*

It makes me a different person that I would be without it. I am more cautious and motherlike, never wanting to take risks or have my friends take risks that I feel are dangerous. If I feel anxious I feel different. I think only people who really know me can tell when I am feeling the beginnings of a panic attack, but to me it really changes my life. My attitude changes, and I stop having fun. I will leave a party or meeting, or avoid an activity if I panic during it.

11. *Are there any activities you used to do that you have stopped doing because of the anxiety/panic disorder? Does the disorder limit your life in any way?*

I was very into singing when I was in high school. When I came here [Western Illinois University], I was in the choir. I had never had any problems before, but choir was my fourth class in a row on Tuesdays and Thursdays, and I would be tired, hungry, and usually out of breath from running from one side of campus to the other. These things used to be quick triggers for a panic attack. I would have panic feelings sometimes becoming attacks often during choir. I started to associate my panic from being tired and weak with choir, and would panic every time I sang. This all escalated to me passing out from a panic attack during a concert, and then quitting the choir. After this I started going to the doctors and eventually found out about my disorder. Now I can sing again. This is an extreme example, but this has happened in many different situations.

12. *What advice do you have for teachers, parents, and other professionals who work with youths and adolescents who might have anxiety disorders?*

Be understanding and ask questions! If a student blows up at you or a peer, or does horrible on a test you think they should have done well on, ask for an explanation instead of just giving up on them. And if you do find a student is having lots of anxiety problems, get them to a doctor so they can be diagnosed. For me this was the moment of breakthrough. I think that once the student knows that the way they are feeling is not their fault, they can then work to change these behaviors.

Characteristics of Phobias

I'm scared to death of flying and I never do it anymore. I used to start dreading a plane trip a month before I was due to leave. It was an awful feeling when that airplane door closed and I felt trapped. My heart would pound and I would sweat bullets. When the airplane would start to ascend, it would just reinforce that feeling that I couldn't get out. When I think about flying, I picture myself losing control, freaking out, climbing the walls. I'm not afraid of crashing or hitting turbulence. It's just that feeling of being trapped. When ever I've thought about changing jobs, I've had to think about whether I'd be under pressure to fly. These days I only go places where I can drive or take a train. My friends always point out that I couldn't get off a train traveling at high speeds either, so why don't trains bother me? I just tell them it isn't a rational fear. (NIMH, 2000, p. 3)

Many adults with phobias recognize their fears as being irrational, but they still have a very difficult time controlling their acute feelings of fear and anxiety. A phobia is described as an intense fear about something such as a specific item or a situation that actually poses little or no real danger to the individual. The feared object or situation is usually avoided if at all possible or approached with an attitude of extreme and unreasonable fear or panic. The level of fear that the individual feels may vary depending on her proximity to the feared object or ability to escape from the feared situation. Being forced to face a phobia may induce a panic attack (ADAA, 2002; APA, 2000; NIMH, 2000).

Common Phobias

The most common phobias among the general population relate to animals, particularly dogs, snakes, insects, and mice. Other more common phobias relate to seeing blood, closed spaces (claustrophobia), heights (acrophobia), and airplanes (APA, 2000). NIMH (2000) provided the following list of phobias:

- Animals
- Storms
- Heights
- Water
- Blood
- Darkness
- Medical procedures

Phobias may first appear during childhood or adolescence and persist into adulthood. It is thought that some phobias may begin with a traumatic episode that severely frightens the individual. Phobias occur twice as often in females as in males. Many persons suffer little or no impairment if they can avoid the phobic object or situation. For example, a person with an alligator phobia who lives in the city will probably experience little impairment as compared with another individual with an alligator phobia who lives in the Florida Everglades (APA, 2000).

Children who have phobias seldom recognize their fear as being irrational. They will often not be able to talk about their fears; they simply try to avoid situations where they might have to face the feared object or situation. Their anxiety may be manifested by any of the following behaviors (NIMH, 2000):

- Crying
- Tantrums
- Becoming paralyzed or immobilized
- Clinging or being dependent
- Avoiding the situation or object
- Having physical aches or pains such as headaches and stomachaches

Social Phobias

- Every day you fear you will do something very embarrassing.
- You have stopped going to social activities because you are afraid to meet new people.
- When other people look at you, you break out in a sweat and shake uncontrollably.
- You want to stay home from school because you are terrified the teacher will call on you during class (NIMH, 2000).

All of these behaviors are characteristic of the anxiety disorder called social phobia. Social phobias are described as an intense fear of social situations where the individual is afraid he might be embarrassed for some reason. An estimated 4% of the general population is affected by social phobia. Onset of the disorder is usually mid to late adolescence but children have also been diagnosed. In clinic populations, the disorder is more common in males than in females. Typical symptoms in childhood and adolescence include shyness, dependent behavior, tantrums, and mutism. Academic achievement may suffer because students try to avoid attending school, the major social situation in their lives. Oftentimes the phobia relates to peer-centered settings rather than those involving adults. These children seem to feel safer among adults than peers. For a formal diagnosis, symptoms must be observed for at least 6 months. In addition, to have true social phobia, the individual must recognize that his fears are irrational, even though he does not seem to be able to control his level of anxiety related to the social situation (ADAA, 2002; APA, 2000; NIMH, 2000).

Symptoms of Social Phobias

My fear would happen in any social situation. I would be anxious before I even left the house, and it would escalate as I got closer to class, a party, or whatever. I would feel sick to my stomach. It almost felt like I had the flu. My heart would pound. My palms would get sweaty. I would get this feeling of being removed from myself and from everybody else. (NIMH, 2000, p. 6)

The main symptoms of social phobia include physical signs of fear such as heart palpitations, tremors, sweating, diarrhea, confusion, and blushing. Persons with social phobia fear that others will notice these signs and think poorly of them. The individual often experiences extreme anxiety in anticipation of a social event. As a consequence, he may either try to avoid the social situation or have a panic attack when faced with the situation.

Individuals who suffer from social phobia are often very sensitive to criticism and rejection. They may lack assertiveness skills and have a low sense of self-esteem (ADAA, 2002; NIMH, 2000). Teachers, parents, and other professionals who work with youths and adolescents should be aware of the typical behaviors associated with phobias.

Two main treatments have been effective in dealing with social phobia. Those include medication and cognitive behavioral therapy. The effective medications are from the category of antidepressants. The class of medication is called *monoamine oxidase inhibitors* (MAOIs). This type of medication works to block the effect of a brain enzyme, which then prevents the breakdown of two neurotransmitters called serotonin and norepinephrine. Both of these neurotransmitters must be at the optimal level for an individual to maintain appropriate mood and thought processing. The levels are too low in a person with social phobia or depression (ADAA, 2002).

The purpose of cognitive behavioral therapy (CBT) is to help the individual learn skills to deal with social situations that are frightening. The therapy helps the individual to change how he thinks about social situations. The goal is to develop more positive thinking patterns. CBT teaches the individual anxiety-reducing techniques, social skills, and relaxation techniques. These skills will benefit the individual at home, at school or work, and in the community.

Characteristics of Post-Traumatic Stress Disorder

Post-traumatic stress disorder (PTSD) is not a disorder that affects only victims of war, although that was how the label was initially derived. PTSD can affect persons of any age following any type of traumatic incident(s). This may include a very wide range of events from physical or sexual assault; emotional or physical abuse or neglect; serious accident; a death of a family member, friend, pet, or even a stranger; witnessing any act of violence; or a natural disaster (ADAA, 2002). When the aftermath of any traumatic incident interferes with everyday functioning and responsibilities, the individual may have PTSD. Four main symptoms are associated with PTSD:

1. The individual may relive the incident over and over again in the form of flashbacks or nightmares with intense fear, horror, and helplessness.
2. The individual may try to avoid any activities, situations, people, and conversations that may provoke memories of the original traumatic incident.
3. The individual may experience physical numbing by trying to detach or stay separate and uninvolved with other persons.
4. The individual may have difficulty sleeping, feel overanxious, be very easy to startle, have problems with concentration, and be hypersensitive and hyperirritable, and easily angered.

The symptoms of PTSD must be present for more than 1 month and must be accompanied by a reduction in ability to socialize, go to school or work, or maintain a normal productive level of duties or responsibilities related to daily functioning (ADAA, 2002). Depression, intense levels of anxiety, and substance abuse often accompany PTSD (ADAA, 2002; Wicks-Nelson & Israel, 2000).

Children often relive the experience through play (ADAA, 2002; Wicks-Nelson & Israel, 2000). They reenact various aspects of the disaster. For example, after living through Hurricane Hugo, children were observed pretending to "blow over" playhouses and other buildings as well as work at pretending to repair and reroof newly built play structures (Wicks-Nelson & Israel, 2000). Children may also show physical symptoms such as headaches and stomachaches. The symptoms usually start within 3 months of the traumatic incident. In some cases, onset symptoms may be delayed for 6 months or more. Sometimes the anniversary of the traumatic event will trigger PTSD symptoms.

Antidepressants and anxiety reduction medications can be effective in reducing the symptoms of PTSD. Stress management techniques may assist individuals to learn to reduce their own levels of anxiety regarding the traumatic event. Cognitive behavioral therapy is also used to help the individual develop new and more productive thinking patterns to cope with the traumatic experience (ADAA, 2002, Wicks-Nelson & Israel, 2000).

Implications for Working with Youth and Adolescents

A variety of anxiety disorders affect approximately 19 million Americans. Anxiety disorders affect about 13% of all children and adolescents between the ages of 9 and 17. The ADAA (2002) reports that only about one third of all victims obtain treatment.

A link has been established between anxiety disorders, depression, substance abuse, and conduct disorder (ADAA, 2002; Coleman & Webber, 2002; Wicks-Nelson & Israel, 2000). Many youth and adolescents with anxiety disorders will not have only one problem. Most treatments for these disorders are managed by mental health professionals. Teachers may be asked to compile observational data to monitor medications and daily behaviors. Teachers will also play a role in the implementation of cognitive behavioral modification programs. Teachers, parents, and family members may benefit from attending educational seminars and support group sessions. The ADAA (2002) compiled the following suggestions for parents and teachers:

- Learn as much as possible about the anxiety disorder
- Recognize and use specific verbal praise to reinforce small accomplishments made by the individual
- Modify expectations when the individual is experiencing stressful periods
- Measure progress based on individual improvement rather than against some predetermined standard
- Be flexible but try to maintain a normal family or classroom routine

Educators, parents, and other professionals should be aware of the array of treatments available that can be very effective in reducing the symptoms of anxiety disorders. Following is a short description of the variety of treatment approaches that have been used for anxiety disorders (ADAA, 2002).

Treatment Options for Anxiety Disorders

Behavioral Therapy

The purpose of the behavioral therapy process is to help the individual learn appropriate alternatives to the old problem patterns of behavior. This process helps the individual to gain control over the problem behavior. In persons with anxiety disorders, the inappropriate and unrealistic behavior usually controls them at school, at home, and in the commu-

nity. Oftentimes self-instructional strategies are used to help the individual learn a method that will help him to think and solve problems in a variety of environments throughout his lifetime. In self-instructional procedures, the student learns a series of steps in order to learn a new replacement behavior. Most social skills training programs use self-instruction procedures. The reader is directed to *Skillstreaming* (Goldstein & McGinnis, 1997) and the *Tough Kid Social Skills Book* (Sheridan, 1995).

Cognitive Therapy

The main goal of cognitive therapy is to change nonproductive or unrealistic thinking patterns. The therapist attempts to teach the individual how to restructure faulty thinking processes to reduce unrealistic fears and worries.

Cognitive Behavioral Therapy

Cognitive behavioral therapy is a combination of behavioral therapy and cognitive therapy. It teaches new alternative behaviors and thinking patterns to reduce and eliminate symptoms of anxiety. Positive self-instructional strategies are emphasized to teach the individual to gain an accurate perception of his own situation and to behave in a more productive and realistic manner.

Relaxation Therapy

The goal of relaxation therapy is to help the individual learn how to reduce feelings of anxiety and stress that are overwhelming. The individual is also taught methods to help alleviate the physical symptoms of stress such as increased heart rate, shakiness, shortness of breath, and dizziness. Training to use appropriate breathing techniques and physical exercise is emphasized.

Choosing a Therapist

A variety of mental health professionals may be beneficial in helping an individual learn to cope with anxiety disorders. The family pediatrician or general family doctor, psychiatrists, psychologists, clinical social workers, and psychiatric nurses are among the specialists who may be able to help an individual with an anxiety disorder. The severity of the anxiety disorder may be the deciding factor in who the individual sees for treatment. A family practitioner may often be the first professional to evaluate the disorder. Again, depending on the severity of the disorder, the primary care physician might refer the individual to a mental health specialist for further treatment.

Medications for Anxiety Disorders

Medication can be helpful in alleviating the symptoms of anxiety disorders. It is usually administered in combination with one of the other forms of therapeutic behavioral or counseling treatments. Use of medicine has the advantage of triggering a speedy reduction of anxiety disorder symptoms. With the reduction of stressful symptoms, the individual may be more susceptible to learning the new more appropriate behavioral alternatives. Some medicines may be prescribed for a short time, while others need to be taken on a more long-term basis.

References

American Psychiatric Association. (2000). *Diagnostic and statistical manual of mental disorders* (4th ed., text revision). Washington, DC: Author.

Anxiety Disorders Association of America (2002). Retrievable from www.adaa.org

Beidel, D. C., Turner, S. M., & Morris, T. L. (1995). A new inventory to assess childhood social anxiety and phobia: The Social Phobia and Anxiety inventory for Children. *Psychological Assessment, 7*, 73–79.

Coleman, M. C., & Webber, J. (2002). *Emotional and behavioral disorders: Theory and practice* (4th ed.) Needham Heights, MA: Allyn & Bacon.

Gargiulo, R. M. (2003). *Special education in contemporary society: An introduction to exceptionality*. Belmont, CA: Wadsworth/Thomson Learning.

Gelfand, D. M., Jenson, W. R., & Drew, C. J. (1988). *Understanding child behavior disorders*. Fort Worth, TX: Holt, Rinehart and Winston.

Gilatto, M. (2000). Generalized anxiety disorder. *The Family Physician*. Retrievable from www.findarticles.com/cf_ds/ m3225/7_62/65864095/print.jhtml

Goldstein, A. P., & McGinnis, E. (1997). *Skillstreaming* (three series—preschool, elementary, or adolescent). Champaign, IL: Research Press.

Heward, W. L. (2003). *Exceptional children: An introduction to special education* (7th ed.). Upper Saddle River, NJ: Merrill/Prentice Hall.

Kauffman, J. M. (2001). *Characteristics of emotional and behavioral disorders of children and youth* (7th ed.). Upper Saddle River, NJ: Merrill/Prentice Hall.

Kirk, S. A., Gallagher, J. J., & Anastasiow, N. J. (2003). *Educating exceptional children* (10th ed.). Boston: Houghton Mifflin.

La Greca, A. M., & Stone, W. L. (1993). Social anxiety scale for children-revised: Factor structure and concurrent validity. *Journal of Clinical Child Psychology, 22*, 17–27.

March, J. S., Parker, J. D., Sullivan, K., Stallings, P., & Conners, C. K. (1997). The multidimensional anxiety scale for children (MASC). Factor structure, reliability, and validity. *Journal of the American Academy of Child and Adolescent Psychiatry, 36*, 554–565.

National Institute of Mental Health (NIMH). (2000). *Anxiety disorders*. Retrievable from www.nimh.nih.gov/anxiety/anxiety.cfm

Sheridan, S. M. (1995). *The tough kid social skills book*. Longmont, CO: Sopris West.

Turnbull, A., Turnbull, R., Shank, M., Smith, S., & Leal, D. (2002). *Exceptional lives: Special education in today's schools* (3rd ed.). Upper Saddle River, NJ: Merrill/Prentice Hall.

Vergason, G. A., & Anderegg, M. L. (1997). *Dictionary of special education and rehabilitation* (4th ed.). Denver, CO: Love.

Walker, H. M., Colvin, G., & Ramsey, E. (1995). *Antisocial behavior in schools: Strategies and best practices*. Pacific Grove, CA: Brooks/Cole Publishing.

Wicks-Nelson, R., & Israel, A. C. (2000). *Behavior disorders of childhood* (4th ed.). Upper Saddle River, NJ: Merrill/Prentice Hall.

9

DEPRESSION AND SUICIDE

After completing the chapter, the reader will be able to identify:

- The definition and prevalence of depression.
- Causes of depression and suicide.
- Characteristic behaviors related to depression and suicide.
- Medications for management of depression.
- Assessment methods for depression and suicide.
- Implications for educators, parents, and other professionals who work with youth and adolescents.

Introduction

Ten-year-old Nicholas, a victim of childhood depression, once sat in a closet and held a toy gun to his head, screaming that he wished it were real. Fortunately, he received treatment, including counseling and medication. He describes this dark period in his life:

> I felt really scared about telling people how I felt .... I was sad and upset and angry the whole time .... I used that gun to make a point that I needed help. (Baskerville, as cited in Turnbull, Turnbull, Shank, & Leal, 1999, p. 178)

The effects of depression can be physiological as well as emotional for individuals with the disorder. The general behavioral characteristics associated with depression in children, adolescents, and adults are described as lack of motivation, extreme lethargy, lack of interest in past pleasurable activities, and profound hopelessness. In severe cases, the resultant fears, phobias, and anxiety associated with depression can culminate in suicidal ideation or attempts.

The purpose of this chapter is to describe characteristics and symptomatic behavior observable in individuals who have mood disorders with a focus on depression. Next, possible causes for depression are presented. A number of physiological, situational, and environmental causes of depression are explored. Increased levels of stress and pressure to grow up faster may be the root cause of depression in many children (Coleman & Webber, 2002; Jensen & Yerington, 1997; Kaplan, 1995). The relationship between stress and depression in children is described. Methods to assess depression are reviewed. Finally, treatment options, including medical management, and implications for educators and parents are discussed.

Mood Disorders

Difference Between Bipolar Disorders and Depressive Disorders

Kauffman (2001) describes depression as a subset of the larger category of *mood disorders*. DSM-IV-TR (American Psychiatric Association [APA], 2000) divides mood disorders into two categories: (a) bipolar disorders and (b) depressive disorders. There is a major difference between the two. With bipolar disorder, the low depressed moods are punctuated by periods of highly elevated mood described as *mania or euphoria*, a period when the individual feels an unrealistic sense of extraordinary happiness or well-being. Behavior and mood fluctuate or swing wildly between intense highs and incredible lows. Depressive disorders are *unipolar*, meaning behavior is generally in the depressed or low category without the high periods of mania. Mood swings are less extreme, usually ranging from normal to extreme *dysphoria*. Dysphoria is described as feelings of unhappiness or not being well that are inconsistent with one's circumstances. When dysphoric mood lasts for a year or more, it is called *dysthymia*.

Depression

Definition

Vergason and Anderegg (1997) provide the following succinct definition of depression: "Depression is a psychological/psychiatric term referring to dejected mood, reduced vitality/vigor, and feelings of despair." They go on to say that mild symptoms of depression may come and go with no long-term effects. However, severe depression can cause lifelong physiological, emotional, and serious mental health problems.

Depressive disorders consist of three categories, including:

- major depressive disorder (unipolar depression)
- dysthymic disorder (chronic, mild depression)
- bipolar disorder (manic depression).

Youth and adolescents who are depressed suffer an additional risk of higher than average rates of illness, accidents, injuries, academic and social skill deficits, substance abuse problems, and possibly suicide (Coleman & Webber, 2002; Kauffman, 2001; Saklofske, Janzen, Hildebrand, & Kaufmann, 1998). Harrington (1993) reports that periods of depression may occur on an episodic basis. This means that the feelings of depression are not necessarily continuous. There are breaks between episodes. However, the episodes continue to occur over a long time in the individual's life. Persons who suffer depression at one time usually experience repeated episodes. The more severe the depressive feelings, the greater the chance of future repeat episodes of depression.

Childhood Depression

Initially, mental health researchers maintained that there was no such thing as childhood depression. Early psychoanalytic theorists assumed that depression was based on the development of an overly punitive superego resulting in self-directed aggression manifested by behaviors characteristic of depression. These theorists believed that the superego did not become active until adolescence, thus making it impossible for younger children to experience feelings of depression (Coleman & Webber, 2002). It is now known that depression can and does occur in children of any age. Research currently supports the fact that many children experience depressive symptoms that are severe enough to interfere with their daily lives at school, at home, and in the community (Coleman & Webber, 2002; Kauffman, 2001; Saklofske et al., 1998).

Childhood depression parallels the symptoms of adult depression with one major difference. Rather than exhibiting adult life-stage problems related to work, family, or other social relationships, children and adolescents demonstrate behaviors of depression in age-appropriate ways for their stage in life. Kauffman (2001) provides the following examples. Younger children might be more likely to complain of physical aches and pains, be easily agitated and anxious, or be overly fearful. In contrast, adolescents tend to demonstrate antisocial and/or argumentative behavior, be more restless, and act in a hyperirritable manner. Unfortunately, many of these behavioral patterns are not recognized by educators or parents. The problems are chalked up to temperament or to a phase or stage such as the dreaded "adolescence" (National Institute of Mental Health [NIMH], 2000a).

Specific Symptoms of Childhood Depression

The following passage was written by an individual reflecting on his feelings of childhood depression. The feelings of hopelessness and failure documented are typical of children with depression:

> The story is sad. I don't know how else to put it. It is very sad to grow up feeling hopeless, worthless, alone.
>
> .... I did have some happy moments, but overall I was very, very unhappy. I thought that was the way it was supposed to be.
>
> I didn't feel human.... I didn't feel like I was like everyone else.... Somehow I deserved to feel this way. Anything I did good was luck. Anything bad that happened was my fault. Even if I had nothing to do with it. I had constant headaches, constant fatigue, body aches, especially in the back and shoulders. And why not? I was carrying the weight of the world.
>
> On and on through the darkness I aimlessly traveled, not knowing where to go, what to do. For most of my life I was literally senseless. I could not sense what was going on around me. I was living in a nearly impenetrable shell. (Fineberg, n.d.)

Two core features that usually indicate depression in children include <u>depressed mood and lack of interest in most or all normal activities</u> (Kauffman, 2001; Martin, Clarke, & Pearce, 1993; Reinherz, Hauf-Gianconia, & Carmola, 2000). The following lists of behaviors can be thought of as red flags or signals of possible depression. The first list contains behavioral descriptors common to youth, adolescents, and adults with depression. The second list consists of behaviors associated only with depression in youth and adolescents (NIMH, 2000a, p. 2).

Symptoms of Depression in Children, Adolescents, and Adults

- Persistent sad or irritable mood
- Loss of interest in activities once enjoyed
- Significant change in appetite or body weight
- Difficulty sleeping or sleeping too much
- Psychomotor agitation or retardation
- Loss of energy
- Feelings of worthlessness or inappropriate guilt
- Difficulty concentrating
- Recurrent thoughts of death or suicide

Symptoms of Depression in Children and Adolescents

- Frequent vague, nonspecific complaints such as headaches, muscle aches, stomachaches, or tiredness
- Frequent absences from school or poor performance in school
- Talk of or efforts to run away from home
- Outbursts of shouting, complaining, unexplained irritability, or crying
- Boredom
- Lack of interest in playing with friends
- Alcohol or substance abuse
- Social isolation, poor communication
- Fear of death
- Extreme sensitivity to rejection or failure
- Increased irritability, anger, or hostility
- Reckless behavior

- Difficulty with relationships
- Preference for heavy metal rock music

Categories of Depressed Behavior

Five main categories of maladaptive behavior and symptoms are described in the research on childhood depression (Coleman & Webber, 2002; "Hidden Problem," 1999; Kauffman, 2001; Kovacs & Beck, 1977). These categories include academic, emotional/affective, cognitive, motivation, and physiological indicators of depression. Behaviors characteristic of each category may be observed in an isolated manner or in combination of one or more symptoms from the remaining categories.

Academic Category

School apathy may be a sign of childhood depression. Academic indicators of depression may first be noticed when a student shows a decline in grades or general school performance that cannot be explained by illness, injury, or any other source. There also tends to be a general loss of interest in school subjects and activities previously enjoyed. Finally, students seem to give up easily on challenging school projects or simply do not finish academic assignments. Incidents of tardiness and truancy increase.

Emotional/Affective Category

Symptoms for the emotional/affective category are depressed mood and an inability to take pleasure in activities that previously were very enjoyable. Persons showing this category of symptoms might also engage in excessive, seemingly uncontrollable crying and may lack the ability to respond to humor. These children usually act sad and lonely. They do not usually have good social skills or a strong circle of friends. Their attitude is apathetic and unresponsive to activities enjoyed by the peer group.

Cognitive Category

Children with depression have higher rates of the following cognitive symptoms as compared with children who do not have depression. The indications include poor self-concept, low self-esteem, feelings of hopelessness, and excessive or undeserved feelings of guilt (Coleman & Webber, 2002). The terms *self-concept* and *self-esteem* are sometimes used interchangeably. However, they do have two different meanings (Engel, 1989). Self-concept refers to the set of images or beliefs a person has about his own self. Self-esteem is a measure of how much a person likes or values that image of himself. For example, children with depression may think they are not OK, not good, or they may feel useless or worthless. In other words, they do not like themselves very much. They have a poor self-concept. Teachers might overhear these children make frequent derogatory comments about themselves, meaning they do not value the mental image they have of themselves (Kauffman, 2001).

The link between negative self-concept and feelings of excessive guilt is relevant to depression. Children who lack an adequate self-concept are also likely to blame themselves or feel responsible when bad things happen. Hopelessness is also closely related to poor self-concept. It indicates the child's loss of hope that there is any chance of positive change in the future.

In fact, this child thinks that because he is a bad person, only more bad things will happen. Coleman and Webber (2002) warn that it is incredibly important for educators to recognize the cognitive mind-set of hopelessness because these children may resort to suicidal ideation as a means to solve their problems.

Another major cognitive symptom is an inability to concentrate. Children with depression become preoccupied with their problems and fall behind academically. Approximately 48 to 62% of students with depression were reported to also experience academic difficulties (Coleman & Webber, 2002).

Motivation Category

Two major motivational symptoms of depression include social withdrawal and suicidal ideation. Children and adolescents with motivational symptoms of depression try to avoid past pleasurable activities. Even the use of rewards or other special methods of encouragement does not seem to provide the incentive they need to get back into the normal swing of activities at home, at school, or in the community. These individuals also tend to try to avoid social situations. They are not just loners. Before the onset of depression, they did socialize with other peers and adults. Such a child should be differentiated from the child who consistently shows low social skills or has typically been rejected or is a peer group isolate. Children and adolescents with severe depression might begin thinking and talking about suicide, make threats or suicidal gestures, or ultimately attempt suicide as a means to end their problems. Because they have withdrawn to such an extreme extent, they often do not seem to have anyone to talk to about their problems.

Physiological Category

Students with depression may have more physical complaints than the average student. Examples may range from general body aches and pains to more specific illnesses. Some may feel chronic fatigue. They might say they feel tired all the time. They act lethargic. Some children and adolescents experience a change in appetite, weight, or eating patterns. They might complain of different problems associated with eating such as upset stomach or nausea. Some individuals may not be able to sleep or they might spend far too much of their days and nights sleeping.

Table 9–1 provides a summary of the five major categories of depression symptoms in youth and adolescents.

TABLE 9–1 Categories of Depression Symptoms of Youth and
Adolescents

Academic Symptoms
- School apathy
- Decline in grades or general school performance
- Loss of interest in school subjects previously enjoyed
- Giving up easily or not finishing school assignments

Affective/Emotional Symptoms
- Facial expression is dejected and unhappy
- General feeling of sadness and apathy
- Makes frequent verbal complaints of feeling sad, despondent, or tired
- Cries often in public
- Does not respond to humorous situations by smiling or laughing
- Excessive complaining

Cognitive Symptoms
- Poor self-concept
- Low self-esteem with negative self-comments
- Feelings of excessive self-blame and guilt
- Hopelessness and helplessness
- General feeling of pessimism
- Difficulty concentrating
- Forgetfulness
- Academic problems

Motivational Symptoms
- Avoidance of social situations
- Suicidal threats or ideation
- Reduction of school performance
- Has lost interest in favorite activities
- Not motivated by usual rewards or even extraordinary incentives

Physical Symptoms
- Persistent feelings of fatigue and lethargy
- Frequent complaints of body aches, pains, and illness
- Insomnia or hypersomnia
- Weight loss or gain
- Eating problems (too little or too much)

Note. *From Educational and Behavioral Disorders, by M. C. Coleman and J. Webber, 2002, Needham Heights, MA: Allyn & Bacon and Characteristics of Emotional and Behavioral Disorders of Children and Youth (7th ed.), by J. M. Kauffman, 2001, Upper Saddle River, NJ: Merrill/Prentice Hall.*

Causes of Depression

In most cases, the cause of depression cannot be specifically determined. Factors such as physiological, psychological, environmental, or situational variables may be involved. Research (Coleman & Webber, 2002; Kauffman, 2001; Saklofske et al., 1998; Schloss, Smith, & Schloss, 2001) suggests that the causes may be divided into two main categories designated as endogenous and reactive. *Endogenous* causes of depression are biological, biochemical, or genetic in nature. *Reactive* depression is described as feelings of depression that occur in response to an incident in the person's environment such as death, divorce or other family discord, child abuse or neglect, or other stressful life events.

Endogenous Causes of Depression

Coleman and Webber (2002) reviewed research studies related to the three endogenous causes of depression. Biochemical research focuses mainly on the role of two neurotransmitters, nor-epinephrine and serotonin, which are frequently associated with depression. Messages are carried throughout the central nervous system by neuro-transmitters, minute quantities of brain chemicals that are required for transmitting cognitive messages and motor activity messages throughout the brain.

There are actually about 50 different kinds of neurotransmitters. Serotonin and norepinephrine specifically relate to attention, mood, and motor activity. They regulate mood and motor activity (King, 2003). Feelings of depression occur when the brain does not produce enough of those two neurotransmitters. A low supply results in a loss of stimulation to the area in the brain stem that controls mood and motor activity which may lead to feelings of depression (Lerner, Lowenthal, & Lerner, 1995).

Genetic investigations of adopted children and twins support the theory that there is a genetic predisposition for depression. The incidence of bipolar depression in families points to a genetic link (Coleman & Webber, 2002; Kauffman, 2001; Strober & Carlson, 1982). Other researchers suggest that depression results from a combination of endogenous and reactive variables (Coleman & Webber, 2002; Hodgman, 1985; Kauffman, 2001). The combination theory explains that environmental causes must usually be in place for biological predispositions of depression to manifest themselves.

Reactive Causes of Depression

Reactive depression is sometimes also called *situational* depression. Situational depression is thought to be more short-term and related to specific problems, crisis situations, or traumas that occur in an individual's environment. The term *reactive* or *situational* is derived from the fact that the depression is part of the person's response to the difficult situation being experienced.

Seasonal Affective Disorder (SAD)

Seasonal affective disorder (SAD) is a popular term for depression that seems to start during the colder and darker months of the year. It is not an actual DSM-IV-TR category of depression. However, it can be included as it continues to be classified as a seasonal pattern for unipolar and bipolar disorders (King, 2003; Saeed & Bruce, 1998). The diagnosis is based on depressive symptoms that occur during the autumn and winter, when days are shorter and most individuals do not get much exposure to natural sunlight. When the seasons change to spring and summer and there is greater exposure to natural sunlight, the symptoms seem to dissipate (Mental Help Net Staff, n.d.). Some individuals are able to reduce or alleviate symptoms by using light therapy. Results of light therapy have been mixed (King, 2003; Saeed & Bruce, 1998). A simple strategy that might be tried at home is to replace regular light-bulbs with special bulbs that project a spectrum of light similar to real sunlight. Such lightbulbs are available in specialty catalogs.

Prevalence of Childhood Depression

The National Institute of Mental Health (2000b) reports that approximately 18.8 million Americans (about 9.5%) suffer from depression. That statistic translates into approximately 1 in 10 people. About twice as many females (12%) as males (6.5%) suffer from depression. That means about 6.7 million women and 3.2 million men may experience depression on an annual basis. Research suggests that depression is now occurring at younger ages than it had in past decades (APA, 2000). The incidence of severe depression in children is estimated to be approximately 2 to 5% for elementary school children and 4 to 8% for adolescents ("Hidden Problem," 1999; Kauffman, 2001; Saklofske et al., 1998).

Clinical statistics indicate that psychiatric disorders are the leading cause of health problems among children and adolescents in the United States. Schloss et al. (2001) report that depression in the general student population ranges from about 2 to 14%. One of every 50 school-age students may exhibit symptoms of depression (Kerns, 1992; Lamarine, 1995).

Depression may also often coexist with a variety of other psychologically based disorders. Examples include conduct disorder, eating disorders, substance abuse, and juvenile delinquency (Coleman & Webber, 2002).

Prevalence Among the Special Education Population

Research generally supports the notion that students with disabilities experience more stress at school, at home, and in the community than youth and adolescents without disabilities. However, further research is necessary to pinpoint details related to gender and age. The academic failure experienced by many students with disabilities may be the cause of elevated measures of stress. The higher than average stress levels for students with special needs have been associated with increased rates of depression and possibly suicide (Bender, Rosenkrans, & Crane, 1999).

It is particularly important for special educators to recognize the symptoms of depression. The federal definition of emotional and behavioral disorders (E/BD) includes a component directly related to mood. It states that a common trait of students with behavioral disorders is "a pervasive mood of unhappiness or depression" (PL 105-17, the Individuals with Disabilities Education Act Amendments of 1997). This component of the emotional/behavioral disorders (E/BD) definition originally stems from PL 94-142, the Education for All Handicapped Children Law, first passed in 1975. Kauffman (2001) relates that the overlap of depression with attention deficit hyperactivity disorder (ADHD) and conduct disorder is high. Researchers (Bender et al., 1999; Forness, 1988; "Hidden Problem," 1999; Schloss et al., 2001) suggest that the rate of depression is much more prevalent in students with special education needs than in the general population. The percentage is reported to be as high as 55% for students with disabilities. The Council for Exceptional Children ("Hidden Problem," 1999) reports depression in students with behavioral disorders to be about 40% and in students with learning disabilities (LD) to be about 20%. The rates for adolescents usually are higher than the rates for younger children (Coleman & Webber, 2002).

Comparative Statistics on Depression

Coleman and Webber (2002) compared results from numerous studies to document an average rate of depression for students in general and special education (see Table 9–2). The rate of adolescents with depression in the general school population was 13 to 18%. The rate for adolescents with special education needs or E/BD ranged from 21 to 55%. As can be seen, the number of students with depression is much higher in special education

TABLE 9–2 Rates of Depression for Students in General and Special Education

Rates of Depression	General Student Population	Special Education Student Population
Secondary	13–18%	21–55%
Elementary	2–5%	21–37%

Note. *From Emotional and Behavioral Disorders: Theory and Practice (4th ed.), by M. C. Coleman and J. Webber, 2002, Needham Heights, MA: Allyn & Bacon.*

programs than in general education. The results were similar when comparing elementary school populations. The average rate of depression among elementary school students ranged from 2 to 5% as compared to 21 to 37% for students in special education or psychiatric placements. Educators must be well prepared to recognize the symptoms of depression because of their relationship to potential suicidal behavior. As with most disorders, early intervention is the most successful means of remediating the problems.

Assessment Methods

When teachers observe symptoms of depression in students, it becomes their responsibility to refer those individuals for appropriate evaluations (Schloss et al., 2001). Most assessments for depression are given by psychologists or psychiatrists. A comprehensive evaluation may be based on a battery including clinical interviews, teacher observations, parent reports, student self-reports, and direct observation of the student's behavior in various environments. Standardized rating scales and structured interview methods are available to complete the assessment (Merrell, 1994). Mental health specialists may choose a variety of assessments to determine needs for therapy, counseling, and medication.

Educator's Role in Assessment

The most valuable contribution of educators is to provide accurate observations of student behavior (Kauffman, 2001). These observations are usually recorded on behavior checklists or rating scales. The results of the teacher's observations are used to document patterns or changes in behavior. Teachers are the one group of adults who spend extended time during the school day with students and are likely to be well qualified to complete checklists and rating scales to document student behavior.

DSM-IV-TR and Assessment for Depression

DSM-IV-TR is the most common assessment tool used by mental health professionals for diagnosing depression. Maag and Forness (1993) explain the process:

> DSM-IV criteria are based on the assumption that (a) depression may occur at any age, and (b) its primary features are similar across age groups. Scores on the DSM-IV range from nondepressed to severely depressed. DSM-IV criteria define a major depressive episode as one that includes five of the primary depressive disorder symptoms every day for two weeks and represents a change for the individual's previous function. In addition, the DSM-IV defines the criteria for mood disorders that are most likely to be found in school age children, namely major depression and dysthymia. Because the DSM-IV focuses on clinical syndromes or symptoms, children exhibiting "depressive like" signs may fail to meet the DSM-IV criteria for diagnosis. Therefore, these criteria should not be the sole measure for diagnosis in school children. (cited in Wright-Strawderman, Lindsey, Navarette, & Flippo, 1996, p. 267).

The primary depressive disorder symptoms are summarized from the DSM-IV-TR. They are similar to symptoms and categories of depression discussed earlier in the chapter:

- Depressed or irritable mood
- Diminished interest in previously pleasurable activities
- Significant weight loss or gain when not dieting
- Daily insomnia or hypersomnia
- Daily psychomotor agitation or retardation
- Daily fatigue or loss of energy
- Consistent feelings of worthlessness or excessive/inappropriate guilt
- Diminished ability to concentrate
- Recurrent thoughts of death, suicidal ideation, suicide attempts

Treatment Options

Depression is not "a condition that can be willed or wished away" (Wright-Strawderman et al., 1996, p. 1). Oftentimes, depression has a physiological basis in that neurotransmitters are out of balance. Depression can last from weeks to months to years and may be so severe that it is life-threatening. The symptoms of depression comprise a serious medical illness that affects the body as well as the mind. A treatment plan involving counseling and sometimes medication is as important for depression as it is for any other illness such as cancer, heart disease, asthma, or diabetes. A person can not just "snap out of" depression any more than one could snap out of cancer (NIMH, 2000a). Early and effective intervention strategies are incredibly important.

Counseling, Talk Therapy, and Behavioral Therapy

Teachers should be aware of verbal and nonverbal messages students might make regarding self-worth and suicidal ideation. Educators must take all suicide threats seriously and refer students to the ap-propriate professionals for counseling or therapy.

The purpose of counseling or *psychotherapy* for depression is to help the individual gain understanding or insight to the cause of the depressive feelings. This is usually accomplished through scheduled meetings where the therapist provides guidance through a series of verbal give-and-take sessions designed to discuss pertinent aspects and perspectives of the problem.

Behavioral therapy focuses on patterns of behavior associated with the person's depression. The goal is to assist the individual to make a self-instructional plan for handling feelings and situations in a more productive manner (NIMH, 2000a). A self-instructional plan consists of a set of behavioral steps that the person learns, role-plays, practices, and finally begins to use independently. The set of steps is used to demonstrate the new, more appropriate, and productive behavior in relevant situations. The object is to learn how to make better choices, make good decisions, learn new skills, and ultimately begin to feel more positive and satisfied with one's own life. Box 9–1 is an example of a self-instructional strategy adolescents with depression might learn to use to ask for help when they need it (Goldstein & McGinnis, 1997). This is one example

BOX 9–1 CONCENTRATING ON A TASK

Steps	Trainer Notes
1. Decide what your task is. .	Be specific. Choose one assignment or job to complete at a time.
2. Decide on a time to work on this task	Make sure that you have used good time management skills to set enough time to get the job done before it is due.
3. Decide on a place to work.	Choose a place where you can work without interruptions or distractions.
4. Gather the materials that are necessary.	Get organized with everything you need to start and finish the task.
5. Prepare yourself to concentrate on the task until it is completed.	Set aside a certain amount of time. Make positive self-comments. Tell yourself you will be successful.
6. Get started and work on the task through completion.	Plan a little reward for yourself because you did such a good job of completing your task.

Note. *From Skillstreaming the Adolescent, by A. P. Goldstein and E. McGinnis, 1997, Champaign, IL: Research Press.*

of a social skills lesson that was adapted from the *Skillstreaming* series. It provides a sample of a self-instructional strategy designed to teach students who have depression a method they can use to prepare for, begin, and concentrate on a specific task through completion.

Therapy sessions can be done on an individual, group, or family basis. While individual or small group therapy can be quite beneficial, children often benefit from family therapy. Sometimes the family-oriented therapy will get to the source of the problems causing depression when individual counseling does not. In addition, since there may be a genetic link to depression, family counseling may also alleviate depressive symptoms in other members of the family (Lamarine, 1995). Remediation or adjustment of problem situations in the home environment is usually beneficial in reducing depression in children in the family.

Medication Options for Depression

For severe cases of depression, medication in the form of antidepressants may be necessary to reduce neurological or physical symptoms. Antidepressants regulate levels of neurotransmitters, specifically serotonin and norepinephrine. Once those physiological symptoms are under control, a counselor or psychotherapist can teach the individual behavioral or coping strategies to deal with feelings and emotions.

Two often used antidepressants are Wellbutrin® and Prozac®. Lithium® is commonly prescribed for bipolar disorder (Coleman & Webber, 2002). However, Kauffman (2001) reports that medication for childhood depression remains controversial. Further research is needed to verify the effectiveness and to further study the negative side effects associated with the antidepressants.

Educational Intervention for Depression

The symptoms that accompany depression may sometimes be interpreted as willful behavior problems by some educators. Teachers must recognize the symptoms in students who suffer from depression. In the classroom, they might demonstrate lack of motivation or effort and have reduced ability to concentrate. Individualized accommodations should be provided rather than simply punishing students. Educational intervention for students with depression must be positive, encouraging, and very supportive. Teaching methods can include a comprehensive package of various lessons based on a foundation of cognitive restructuring and social skills training (Coleman & Webber, 2002; Goldstein & McGinnis, 1997; Stark, Rause, & Livingston, 1991).

Cognitive Restructuring

Cognitive restructuring means that the student is taught new and improved thinking patterns. *Social skills training*, as mentioned earlier, teaches students to demonstrate positive forms of social interaction and to inhibit nonproductive or negative social interaction patterns. In general, teachers should think *proactively*. When educators are proactive, they plan ahead and anticipate problems certain students might have in the classroom. Being proactive, the teacher then structures the classroom expectations and prepares the lesson so that the student is most likely to experience success as an outcome. This will help students who have a low self-concept and poor self-esteem feel better about themselves. Examples of activities educators can conduct with students who have depression include scheduling fun, pleasant educational activities for the student to try; teaching relaxation exercises; introducing anger-coping strategies; teaching conflict resolution skills; and using games to help students to accurately identify their feelings and emotions (Coleman & Webber, 2002).

Focusing on Strengths

There is always hope. Depression blinds us to that fact. If we can somehow hold on to our hope, just maybe we can find a way to get through. (Fineberg, n.d.)

Teachers, parents, and other professionals who work with youth and adolescents need to help children focus on their strengths. In other words, accentuate the positive! Supportively challenge the negative, self-critical comments that children make. Give frequent, genuine praise for effort and accomplishments at home and in the classroom. Teach children positive self-talk. Help them to differentiate between events in the environment that are under their control as compared with those that are not. Ask the children to write or tell about their feelings with a focus on pleasant events three or four times a day. Try to maintain a routine and predictable schedule at home and at school. Prepare children as well as possible for changes in routine.

Positive Teacher Personalities

Teachers and other adults who work with youth and adolescents should work on being viewed by them as positive and rewarding personalities. This does not mean that the teacher is considered a buddy, on the same level as the student, or in any way tolerates misbehavior. The teacher maintains the respected teacher personality. It is important for the teacher to present an attitude of willingness to listen and offer necessary support to help the student solve a problem. In other words, the teacher presents himself or herself as an educator who is caring, concerned, and willing to help students find strategies for dealing with school and personal problems (Jensen & Yerington, 1997; Rhode, Jenson, & Reavis, 1992).

Suicide

Definition

Kauffman (2005) provided a very straightforward definition of completed suicide. It is simply to intentionally and deliberately kill oneself. The term *parasuicide* is analogous to *attempted* suicide. It means that an individual tried to commit suicide but it was not completed or was unsuccessful.

Prevalence

In 1999, more young people in the 15–24 year age group died from suicide than from all of the following diseases combined: cancer, heart disease, AIDS, birth defects, strokes, and chronic lung disease. (Centers for Disease Control and Prevention, 2002)

Suicide is the third leading cause of death among young people 15 to 24 years old ("Hidden Problem," 1999). Accidents are the first and homicides are the second leading cause of death in that age group. There are approximately 2,000 completed teenage suicides annually. This means there are about 10 suicidal deaths for every 100,000 youth. For each death, there may be as many as 350 attempts (Coleman & Webber, 2002; Kauffman, 2001; Schloss et al., 2001).

Suicide rates are difficult to research for a number of reasons (Bender et al., 1999). First, data are rare. Although suicide is a very serious problem, it is not highly prevalent. Second, all suicides are studied retrospectively. Youth and adolescents who commit suicide cannot be interviewed to determine details of their state of mind or the cause of their actions. Consequently, most of the research available comes from interviewing friends and family members, who tend to be unreliable sources. The victim's sense of hopelessness, helplessness, and loneliness usually means that he did not confide his innermost feelings to others. It has been suggested that suicide notes might be a source of information. However, only about one in three suicide victims writes a note. The notes have not typically been an effective means for determining the reasons for the suicide, as they often relate what the victim wants his family and friends to believe about the suicide (Peck, 1986).

Some researchers believe that suicide statistics should be two or three times higher than what are actually reported. They hypothesize that many deaths are misreported as accidental and may be suicide cover-ups (Kauffman, 2001). Suicides may purposely be reported as accidental for three main reasons. First, there is a tendency to avoid the negative social stigma of a suicidal death. Second, many people hold the moral belief that the individual was not in a logical frame of mind and did not truly and intentionally take his own life. Third, suicides may be reported as accidents to accommodate the religious beliefs of some groups.

Prevalence of Suicide Among Special Education Population

Research on youth and adolescent suicide among students with disabilities is limited (Bender et al., 1999). There is some evidence to support the theory that a disproportionate number of students with learning and behavioral problems are at a higher risk for suicide than other students (Schloss et al., 2001). In one study, an in-depth analysis of 27 suicide notes revealed writing errors similar to those made by youth and adolescents with LD. Results from another study conducted in Los Angeles determined that 50% of successful suicides were completed by students with LD. Survey research completed by high school guidance counselors in Texas indicated that 14% of suicide-related incidents involved students with LD. Comparatively, students with LD comprise only about 5% of the total school population. Self-reports from students with behavioral disorders (BD) indicate a higher than average frequency of both suicidal ideation, parasuicide, and completed suicides (Bender et al., 1999; Coleman & Webber, 2002; McBride & Siegel, 1997).

Gender Differences

Females attempt suicide more often than males. However, males have a higher rate of completions or successful suicides because they tend to use more violent methods. Males are three times more likely to complete suicide because they use methods such as shooting or hanging. Females most often try overdosing on medications or some form of poison (Kauffman, 2001).

Causes

What causes a child to attempt to take his own life? Researchers suggest a variety of causes (Coleman & Webber, 2002; Kauffman, 2001; Schloss et al., 2001). For example, puberty and the onset of various developmental changes, feelings of social alienation, poor communication skills, conflict with peers and adults, boyfriend or girlfriend problems, or feelings of being helpless or powerless to change a problematic situation are among the causes. These variables may trigger feelings of depression that become so severe that the individual contemplates suicide (Coleman & Webber, 2002). Schloss et al. (2001) relate that youth who commit suicide have a history of personal, family, and medical difficulties.

A number of specific personality traits are closely associated with suicidal behavior. These include aggression, impulsivity, perfectionism, low self-esteem, poor problem-solving skills, lack of social skills, and hopelessness. These individuals think that no one cares about their problems (Kauffman, 2001; Kirk, Gallagher, & Anastasiow, 2003). Youth and adolescents who demonstrate these personality traits are at higher risk to attempt suicide.

The connecting thread between all suicidal factors is a feeling of deep and permanent hopelessness, loneliness, powerlessness, and despair. Individuals with these feelings believe that suicide is the one only way to stop the intense pain they feel. These youth believe that committing suicide is their only means to change what they see as a desperately hopeless future. Individuals who experience this profound hopelessness are convinced that their only release will come in the form of suicide. Thus, the stage is set. The person feels justified in ending his or her life in an attempt to resolve the seemingly insurmountable problems.

Suicide Prevention

A primary prevention for suicidal behavior is an all-school screening. This means that every student in the school is assessed for suicidal tendencies. Screening procedures present some problems because they may not be highly accurate (Kauffman, 2001). The screening procedure may identify a number of *false-positives*. False-positives are students who are identified but are not actually at high risk for suicide. The screening procedure will also identify *false-negatives*. False-negatives are those students who did not appear to be at risk according to the screening procedure criteria, but in reality they are likely to attempt or commit suicide. As Kauffman (2001, p. 483) states, the consequences of identifying a particular student as not being a suicide risk but who actually is "are obviously grim." It is of the utmost importance that school personnel implementing the screening procedure closely and carefully follow the criteria to accurately identify students who need intervention services.

After students at risk have been identified with the screening procedure, individualized therapeutic intervention services with an appropriate agency must be implemented on a consistent basis. In addition to individualized counseling or therapy, telephone hotlines and programs that help students to reduce stress, solve problems, and make good decisions may help students to gain necessary skills that will reduce the incidence of suicide attempts.

Specific Suicidal Indicators

There are specific behaviors that indicate possible suicidal intentions (Guetzloe, 1989; Kauffman, 2001; Martin, Clarke, & Pearce, 1993; Schloss et al., 2001). Adults who work with youth and adolescents must be observant for these types of behaviors demonstrated by students. Observation of these behaviors in specific students could be used to offset the incidence of false-negatives indicated by the screening criteria. They include:

_____ 1. Signs of depression, hopelessness, helplessness

_____ 2. Severe social, disciplinary, or academic problems at school, at home, and or in the community

_____ 3. A change in normal behavior or affect

_____ 4. Abnormal peer relationships, peer group rejection or isolation, or break up with a boyfriend or girlfriend

_____ 5. Situational crisis such as death of a friend or family member, divorce, pregnancy, legal arrest

_____ 6. Health problems from illness, accidents, or eating disorders

_____ 7. Substance abuse

_____ 8. Preference for heavy metal rock music

_____ 9. Suicidal threats or attempts

_____ 10. Talking about suicide plans

_____ 11. Making final arrangements such as giving away possessions

_____ 12. Unwillingness to make any plans for future activities

_____ 13. Attempting to procure the suicidal means (pills, guns, weapons)

Suicide Prevention Strategies

Take EVERY Suicide Threat Seriously! There are major suicide prevention strategies that may help to reduce the incidence of suicide among youth and adolescents (Eisenberg, 1984; Kauffman, 2001; Schloss et al., 2001). The primary prevention rule for educators is to take every suicide threat seriously. Educators must never attempt to evaluate whether a threat or talk of suicide is serious enough to refer. They simply make the referral to the appropriate agency. Educators must know and follow school policies on reporting suicide threats.

A four-step process can be used as a general means of prevention:

1. Improve observation, detection, and intervention services for students who are depressed and feeling hopeless.
2. Adults must ensure that the individual has NO access to suicidal implements. Make sure weapons such as guns, knives, razors,

and rope; any type of medicine and pills; and alcohol are completely removed from the house or the individual's environment. This does not mean "access is limited"—it means access is NONEXISTENT. Individuals with suicidal intent can be very crafty and manipulative about gaining access to their means.

3. Adults should be supportive and available to youth and adolescents. Remember, a common (faulty) thinking pattern of suicide perpetrators is hopelessness, the feeling that no one can or will help him or her. This may mean placing the individual in a restrictive environment where there are absolutely no means available and 24-hour supervision or surveillance is available.

4. Limit the media publicity given to a suicide. Suicidal behavior seems to be contagious. Media coverage often glamorizes a suicide, which then leads to copycat suicides.

Implications for Working with Youth and Adolescents

It is normal for parents and educators to become very worried when students have depression. Since depression and hopelessness correlate highly with suicide attempts, adults must recognize the symptoms early and refer students to appropriate agencies for intervention. Teachers and parents should set up close and ongoing communication systems. If a student is referred for services, the counselor or therapist must keep the other relevant adults informed of progress.

There are several methods that adults can use to help youth and adolescents cope with and conquer depression. Following are a set of strategies that educators, parents and families, and other professionals can implement on a collaborative basis (Dendy, 1995; NIMH, 2000a):

- *Learn about the symptoms of depression, suicide, and schizophrenia.* Knowledge about symptoms, duration, and intervention options all contribute to better understanding and speedy remediation and elimination of the child's depression.

- *Make sure the child and the family (when necessary) are receiving the appropriate intervention.* Help the child to consistently attend counseling sessions, keep doctor appointments, and take medication on schedule. Family counseling can offer the entire family a support system to help the child through this period of illness. As with any other biological illness, living with a child with depression, suicidal ideation, or schizophrenia can be highly stressful for the entire family.

- *Be a good listener and provide positive support.* The child will need patience, understanding and encouragement. Provide helpful suggestions that will assist the child to make good choices. Rather than dismissing feelings, point out realities of problem situations and offer guidance for positive thinking and more appropriate behaviors.

- *Take care of "little things."* The child may not be able to carry out all of his or her regular responsibilities. Think about how parents, other family members, and teachers can assist and help the child not be overwhelmed until he or she is feeling better.

- *Remember that depression and schizophrenia are truly medical and emotional conditions.* The child with depression is actually ill and is not faking being sick and is not being willfully lazy. Schizophrenia is an illness that often requires antipsychotic medication to control symptoms. Encouragement to get an appropriate amount of sleep, eat nutritionally, and get enough exercise will help the child begin to feel better. Entire families can participate in exercise and activity programs with the child to make exercising and eating fun.

- *Take all suicide threats seriously.* Youths and adolescents who talk about suicide often attempt it. Do not try to judge whether the child "really means it." Know the specific referral process at your school or in your community to obtain professional counseling services for the child.

References

American Psychiatric Association. (2000). *Diagnostic and statistical manual for mental disorders* (4th ed., text revision). Washington, DC: Author.

Baskerville, B. (1996, January 22). The turtle and the dragon: A story of childhood depression. *Mobile Press Register*, pp. 1D, 5D.

Bender, W. N., Rosenkrans, C. B., & Crane, M. (1999). Stress, depression, and suicide among students with learning disabilities: Assessing the risk. *Learning Disability Quarterly*, 22(2), 143–156.

Centers for Disease Control and Prevention. Web-based Injury Statistics Query and Reporting Systems (WISQARS) [Online]. (2002). National Center for Injury Prevention and Control, Centers for Disease Control and Prevention (producer). Available from www.cdc.gov/ncipc/wisqars [2003 March 27]. As cited in http://www.cdc.gov/ncipc/factsheets/suifacts.htm

Coleman, M. C., & Webber, J. (2002). *Emotional and behavioral disorders: Theory and practice* (4th ed.). Needham Heights: MA: Allyn & Bacon.

Dendy, C. Z. (1995). *Teenagers with ADD: A parent's guide*. Bethesda, MD: Woodbine House.

Eisenberg, L. (1984). The epidemiology of suicide in adolescents. *Pediatric Annals*, 13, 47–54.

Engel, B. (1989). *The emotionally disturbed woman*. Greenwich. CT: Fawcett.

Erickson, M. T. (1998). *Behavior disorders of children and adolescents: Assessment, etiology, and intervention*. Upper Saddle River, NJ: Merrill/Prentice Hall.

Federal Register. (1981, January 16). Washington, DC: U.S. Government Printing Office.

Fineberg, A. (n.d.). *Life with Zoloft, a personal account*. Retrievable from www.blarg.net/~charlatn/voices/Life.With.Zoloft.html

Forness, S. R. (1988). School characteristics of children and adolescents with depression. In R. B. Rutherford, C. M. Nelson, & S. R. Forness (Eds.), *Bases of severe behavioral disorders of children and youth* (pp. 177–204). Boston: Little, Brown.

Gelfand, D. M., Jenson, W. R., & Drew, C. J. (1988). *Understanding child behavior disorders*. Fort Worth, TX: Holt, Rinehart and Winston.

Goldstein, A. P., & McGinnis, E. (1997). *Skillstreaming the adolescent*. Champaign, IL: Research Press.

Guetzloe, E. C. (1989). *Youth suicide: What the educator should know*. Reston, VA: The Council for Exceptional Children.

Harrington, R. (1993). *Depressive disorder in childhood and adolescence*. New York: Wiley.

The hidden problem among students with disabilities — depression. (1999, December/January). CEC *Today*, 5 (5), 1, 5, 15.

Hodgman, C. H. (1985). Recent findings in adolescent depression and suicide. *Developmental and Behavioral Pediatrics*, 6, 162–169.

Jensen, M. M., & Yerington, P. C. (1997). *Gangs: Straight talk, straight up*. Longmont, CO: Sopris West.

Kaplan, J. S. (with Carter, J.). (1995). *Beyond behavior modification* (3rd ed.). Austin, TX: Pro-Ed.

Kauffman, J. M. (2001). *Characteristics of emotional and behavioral disorders of children and youth* (7th ed.). Upper Saddle River, NJ: Merrill/Prentice Hall.

Kauffman, J. M. (2005). *Characteristics of emotional and behavioral disorders of children and youth* (8th ed.). Upper Saddle River, NJ: Merrill/Prentice Hall.

Kerns, L. L. (1992). *Helping your depressed child*. Rocklin, CA: Prima Publishing.

King, M. W. (2003). *Biochemistry of nerve transmission*. Retrievable from www.indstate.edu/thcme/mwking/nerves.html

Kirk. S. A., Gallagher, J. J., & Anastasiow, N. J. (2003). *Educating exceptional children* (10th ed.). Boston: Houghton Mifflin.

Kovacs, M., & Beck, A. T. (1977). An empirical-clinical approach toward a definition of childhood depression. In J. G. Schulterbrandt & A. Raskin (Eds.), *Depression in childhood: Diagnosis, treatment, and conceptual models* (pp. 1–25). New York: Raven Press.

Lamarine, R. J. (1995, November). Child and adolescent depression. *Journal of School Health*, 65(9), 390–393.

Lerner, J. W., Lowenthal, B., & Lerner, S. R. (1995). *Attention deficit disorders: Assessment and teaching*. Pacific Grove, CA: Brooks/Cole Publishing.

Maag, J. W., & Forness, S. R. (1993). Depression in children and adolescents: Identification, assessment, and treatment. In E. L. Meyen, G. A. Vergason, & R. J. Whelan (Eds.), *Challenges facing special education* (pp. 341–367). Denver: Love Publishing.

Martin, G., Clarke, M., & Pearce, C. (1993). Adolescent suicide: Music preference as an indicator of vulnerability.

Journal of the American Academy of Child and Adolescent Psychiatry, 32, 530–535.

McBride, H. E. A., & Siegel, L. S. (1997). Learning disabilities and adolescent suicide. Journal of Learning Disabilities, 30(6), 652–659.

Mental Health Net Staff (n.d.). Symptoms. Retrievable from www.mentalhelp.net/poc/view_doc.php?type=doc&id=458&cn=5&clnt%3DcInt00001%

Merrell, K. (1994). Assessment of behavioral, suicidal, and emotional problems: Direct & objective methods for use with children and adolescents. New York: Longman.

Miller, D. (1994). Suicidal behavior of adolescents with behavior disorders and their peers without disabilities. Behavioral Disorders, 20(1), 61–68.

National Institute of Mental Health. (2000a). Depression in children and adolescents. Retrievable from www.nimh.nih.gov/publicat/depchildresfact.cfm

National Institute of Mental Health. (2000b). The numbers count. Retrievable from www.nimh.nih,gov/publicat/numbers.cfm

Peck, D. L. (1986). Completed suicides: Correlates of choice of method. Omega, 16, 309–323.

Reinherz, H. Z., Hauf-Gianconia, R. M., & Carmola, A. M. (2000). General and specific childhood risk factors for depression and drug disorders by early adulthood. Journal of the American Academy of Child and Adolescent Psychiatry, 39(2), 223–231.

Rhode, G., Jenson, W. R., & Reavis, H. K. (1992). The tough kid book. Longmont, CO: Sopris West.

Saeed, S. A., & Bruce, T. J. (1998). Seasonal affective disorders. Retrievable from www.aafp.org/afp/980315ap/saeed.html

Saklofske, D. H., Janzen, H. L., Hildebrand, D. K., & Kaufmann, L. (1998). Depression in children. In A. S. Canter & S. A. Carroll (Eds.), Helping children at home and at school: Handouts from your school psychologist (pp. 237–244). Bethesda, MD: National Association of School Psychologists.

Schloss, P. J., Smith, M. A., & Schloss, C. N, (2001). Instructional methods for secondary students with learning and behavior problems (3rd ed.). Needham Heights, MA: Allyn & Bacon.

Stark, K. D., Rause, L. W., & Livingston, R. (1991). Treatment of depression during childhood and adolescence: Cognitive-behavioral procedures for the individual and the family. In P. C. Kendall (Ed.), Child and adolescent therapy: Cognitive-behavioral procedures. (pp. 165–206). New York: Guilford.

Strober, S., & Carlson, G. (1982). Bipolar illness in adolescents with major depression. Archives of General Psychology, 39, 549–555.

Turnbull, A., Turnbull, R., Shank, M., & Leal, D. (1999). Exceptional lives: Special education in today's schools (2nd ed.). Upper Saddle River, NJ: Merrill/Prentice Hall.

Vergason, G. A., & Anderegg, M. L. (1997). Dictionary of special education and rehabilitation (4th ed.). Denver, CO: Love Publishing.

Wright-Strawderman, C., Lindsey, P., Navarette, L., & Flippo, J. R. (1996). Depression in students with disabilities: Recognition and intervention strategies. Intervention in School and Clinic, 31(5), 261–275.

10 EATING DISORDERS

After completing the chapter, the reader will be able to identify:

- Definition and prevalence of various eating disorders.
- Causes of eating disorders.
- Characteristics of males with eating disorders.
- The effect of the media on eating disorders.
- Characteristics of eating disorders.
- Treatment and interventions for eating disorders.
- Implications for educators, parents, and other professionals who work with youth and adolescents.

Introduction

More than half (52%) of American women think they are overweight and are on a diet. Men are also dieting; 37% of men perceive themselves to be overweight. America spends over $40 billion on diet aids every year (American Anorexia Bulimia Association [AABA], 1997*). Dieting does not appear to be overwhelmingly successful because each new generation of American women is ending up heavier in adulthood ("Eating Disorders, Part II," 1997). Ironically, each year the desirable female body image presented through various media sources becomes slimmer while the ideal male body image remains muscular and strong-looking.

Dieting is not something that only adults are concerned about. In 1996, the Council on Size and Weight Discrimination reported that 50% of 9-year-old girls and 80% of 10-year-old girls had dieted (cited in AABA, 1997; National Eating Disorders Screening Program [NEDSP] Newsletter, 1998). Results from a 1993 survey of 11,467 high school students reported that 44% of females and 15% of males were attempting to lose weight (Serdula, 1993, as cited in Schlitz, 1997).

The age at which girls start worrying about their weight seems to get younger and younger. In 1970, girls became concerned about their figures and started dieting around age 14; by 1990, the age dropped to 8 years old. Half of all girls in fourth grade are on a diet (Rader Program, 1999).

Why is this happening? Think of how often adults praise children's looks rather than their efforts, accomplishments, or character. "What a beautiful baby!" or "You look so cute!" What happens to those infants and toddlers who grow up and for one reason or another do not feel like they are so beautiful or so cute anymore? Some of them, looking for more of that type of praise, learn to strive to be thin to be appealing. Very young children have already been programmed with the message, "Thin is in!"

What Is an Eating Disorder?

Eating disorders occur when a person has a serious and ongoing problem with food and eating behavior. This behavior usually takes the form of obsessive preoccupation with food and dieting. The eating problem in some individuals is manifested as *anorexia nervosa*. Anorexia is defined as excessive intense dieting through self-imposed restriction of food. Other individuals get caught up in the addictive cycle of *bulimia*. Bulimia is defined as eating huge amounts of food and then attempting to purge the food from the body through self-induced vomiting or laxative abuse. Some individuals suffer from a combination of both. This type of problem has been referred to as *anorexic bulimia*. The anorexic stage is when the individual attempts to eat little or nothing. Then the person usually gets so hungry that she overeats. The bulimic pattern of behavior begins. After overeating, she attempts to self-induce vomiting to purge the food from her system. Then the starvation cycle begins again until extreme hunger takes over and the cycle repeats. Eating disorders were originally thought to be a physical condition, but they are now widely accepted as an addictive psychological affliction.

This chapter provides information for educators, other professionals who work with youth and adolescents, and families to help them recognize the symptoms of eating disorders. Early intervention is critical for a healthy recovery from eating disorders. First, background information including prevalence, causes, depression and eating disorders, and personality characteristics of individuals prone to eating disorders are discussed. Information about males and eating disorders is introduced. Even though the vast majority of eating disorder victims are females, there are a small number of males with the prob-

*AABA is now part of the National Eating Disorders Association (NEDA).

lem. The next segment describes the incredible impact the media has had on the increase of adolescent eating disorders. Anorexia and bulimia are explained, including descriptions of warning signs and physical complications. Finally, there are a variety of tips and implications for educators, parents, coaches, and other adults who work with youth and adolescents. The goal of the chapter is to educate adults about the problem of eating disorders so that they can make timely and appropriate referrals for necessary services. This is a problem area where early detection and early intervention are critical to remediation.

Prevalence of Eating Disorders

Initially, research indicated that eating disorders affected mostly middle-class to upper-class white females. However, the trend is now spreading to males, lower socioeconomic groups, and individuals from minority cultures. The October, 1997 *Harvard Mental Health Letter* ("Eating Disorders, Part I") provided a wealth of information on the prevalence of eating disorders. It stated that a review of 13 studies demonstrated eating disorders to be equally common among Caucasians, African Americans, and all socioeconomic classes. Males are affected by the problem but at a lower rate than females are. As many as 95% of individuals with eating disorders are thought to be female (Anorexia Nervosa and Related Easting Disorders [ANRED], 1998; "Eating Disorders, Part I," 1997; Renfrew Center Foundation, 2000).

Are eating disorders increasing? That is difficult to say. Physicians are not required to report eating disorders to a health agency, and individuals who have eating disorders are very secretive about their problem (ANRED, 1998). It is known that more cases, especially among teenagers, are being correctly diagnosed. As many as 18 to 20% of school-age students suffer from eating disorders (Phelps & Bajorek, 1991). More educators, parents, and coaches are now conscious of the overt symptoms.

This increased level of awareness is helping more adolescents obtain the medical assistance and counseling they need to overcome the eating disorder. Statistics on prevalence state that anywhere from 0.1% all the way up to 20% of the general population may have an eating disorder (AABA, 1997; ANRED, 1998; "Eating Disorders, Part I," 1997; Renfrew Center Foundation, 2000). The reason for the range of statistics is attributed to sampling a variety of groups such as only adolescents, only adults, only males, or only athletes. The most common statistic reported is 1% of the total population ("Eating Disorders, Part I," 1997). It is a difficult problem to quantify because of the denial and secrecy involved. Without treatment, 20% of individuals with eating disorders will die. For those who get treatment, that number is reduced to 2 to 3%.

Causes of Eating Disorders

Current research has not been able to identify a specific cause of eating disorders. There are a number of projected causes (AABA, 1997; ANRED, 1998; Coleman & Webber, 2002; Renfrew Center Foundation, 2000). The October, 1997 *Harvard Mental Health Letter* ("Eating Disorders, Part I," 1997) states that caution should be used when trying to determine a specific cause of eating disorders. The exact cause of anorexia or bulimia must be regarded as variable whether based on biology, family, personality, or trauma. The reason for the variability is that abnormal eating habits have an inconsistent but powerful influence on the individual. Many unique factors must be considered, such as personal biology, feelings, self-concept, family, friends, and adjustment at school or work. The impact is not predictable or consistent from one individual to the next. One very common symptom is the intense fear of weight gain or phobia about being fat that most afflicted persons express. This type of fear represents a psychological basis for the eating disorder.

Anorexia: Obsessive Dieting

Anorexia may begin with dieting that becomes an obsession (Coleman & Webber, 2002). When a person loses weight, she usually receives compliments from others. She gets a lot of positive attention. She hears a lot of comments about how great she looks. But after a while the other people stop noticing, which means that she has to lose more weight in order to keep attracting attention from friends and family. Oftentimes adolescents try to make themselves look like a favorite model or an actress without understanding that those idols usually go through daily workouts, starvation, pain, punishment, and even surgery to look the way they do (Rader Programs, 1999).

The starvation diet often continues because there is a problem with distorted body image. Having a distorted body image means that the individual sees herself as being larger or heavier than she actually is. The Rader Programs (1999) reported a study that documented this problem. Women who took part in this study overestimated the size of their hips by 16% and their waist by 25%. Those same women could accurately estimate the size of a box. In the mind of the female with anorexia, she is fat even though she is well below an acceptable body weight for her height and build. The individual simply loses all perspective of normal body weight.

Bulimia: Food Obsession

Persons with bulimia have a similar problems with distorted body image. Most are of average or just above average weight, but they have a phobia about weight gain. They see themselves as fat and food is bad; food is the enemy. As with the alcoholic and a drink, one cookie is too much but 1,000 are never enough. It seems that eating one mouthful of food that was not planned for or one cookie that is on the forbidden list is enough to set the person with bulimia off on an eating binge. Why don't they just stop? Why do they have these intense reactions and absolute fears about food? No one knows for sure.

Cause: Biological and Psychosocial Kaplan and Woodside (1987) attribute the cause to a combination of biological and psychosocial factors. Like the chicken and the egg, it is difficult to determine what came first, the biological problem or the eating disorder. Because biology is so often a factor, medical doctors should be involved in the assessment and treatment process. They can evaluate physiological causes of eating disorders. Biochemical levels are usually abnormal in the system of a person with an eating disorder. Biological considerations that a medical doctor should check include levels of neurotransmitters such as serotonin and other hormones. These biochemicals are responsible for providing a balance between energy output, maintenance of mood, and food intake. Persons with eating disorders tend to have low levels of the neurotransmitters that are needed to maintain mood and normal eating behavior. For example, adequate levels of serotonin are necessary to inhibit feeding behavior by inducing a feeling of satiation. Doctors should also check the thyroid hormones, thyroxine and triiodothyronine, and cortisol, the adrenal hormone. The levels of these hormones and neurotransmitters all tend to be lower than average for patients with eating disorders and negatively influence appetite, body weight, mood, and responses to stress.

Some individuals may have a biological predisposition to developing an eating disorder. The October, 1997 *Harvard Mental Health Letter* ("Eating Disorders, Part I") reported on a variety of biological considerations. In one twin study comparison, 9 of 16 identical twins but only 1 of 14 fraternal twins who had a parent with anorexia developed an eating disorder. Another twin study reported that if one identical twin had bulimia, the chance that the other twin would also have it was 23%. That percentage was eight times higher than the rate for nontwin siblings. If one fraternal twin had bulimia, the rate for the other twin was 9%, which is still three times higher than average. The newsletter article reported that the probability that genetics caused eating disorders was about 55%.

Temperament may also be a biological factor that causes eating disorders. Some personality types such as obsessive-compulsive or avoidant personality types or persons prone to depression seem to be more likely to develop eating disorders (ANRED, 1998). Coleman and Webber (2002) suggest that bulimia may be related to obsessive-compulsive disorder. The connection is the obsession to binge and the compulsion to purge. The person cannot seem to stop thinking about food, accumulating food, or devising how to eat secretly during the next food binge. The bulimic cycle is addictive. The craving for food or the idea of going on a food binge becomes obsessive. Once the binge is over, the individual cannot resist the compulsion to purge or rid the body of the excess food.

The avoidant personality type is described by the *Diagnostic and Statistical Manual of Mental Disorders*, (DSM-IV-TR, American Psychiatric Association, 2000) as having a pervasive pattern of social discomfort, fear of negative evaluation, and timidity. These behavioral indicators will be present in many different situations with family, at school or work, and in the community. The individual must show at least four of the behaviors summarized in Table 10–1.

Cause: Emotional or Psychological Other sources suggest that eating disorders are a pattern of behavior that develops over time but also seems to have an emotional or psychological basis ("Eating Disorders, Part II," 1997; National Eating Disorders Association, 2002); Renfrew Center Newsletter, 1996). It is hard to determine whether an individual has an eating disorder from casual observation. ANRED (1998) describes the outward personality of persons with anorexia and bulimia. Individuals with anorexia were often well-behaved, good children. They grow up to be conscientious, hard-working, high-achieving students and adults. They tend to be people-pleasers who seek approval and avoid conflict with others. Individuals with bulimia have most of the characteristics of people with anorexia. In addition, they often are described as having problems with depression and anxiety. Some have problems with impulsivity and lack of self-control, resulting in problem behaviors such as shoplifting, drug and alcohol abuse, or binge shopping. Many have problems trusting other people and consequently develop mostly superficial relationships.

Persons with eating disorders become experts at covering up problems. Some may appear to be living well-adjusted lives, have friends, and are successful in school or at their job. Others seem more withdrawn and introverted. Both groups, however, confess that they often feel like they do not fit in, feel unhappy, and think that they have no true friends. The person tries to take control, to fix things to feel better. Since our culture places so much value on thinness, the individual makes a misguided and ineffective attempt to be in control and to fit in by dieting to be thin, thinner, thinnest. Dieting to extremes and the resulting physical and emotional hunger are strong triggers for developing the addictive cycle of binging and purging—bulimia.

The trigger of the eating disorder may be an ongoing experience or emotional pain that is so severe and debilitating that the individual cannot deal with it appropriately. The person feels helpless, out of control, and unable to manage the situation. The buildup of unmanageable emotional pain that could trigger an eating disorder may occur in any of the following ways (ANRED, 1998; National Eating Disorders Association, 2002):

TABLE 10–1 Avoidant Personality Type Characteristics

- Is easily hurt by criticism or disapproval from others
- Has no close friends other than first-degree family members
- Does not get involved with others unless certain of acceptance
- Avoids social or occupational activities that require more socializing
- Is reticent in unfamiliar situations for fear of making a mistake ↳ holds back
- Fears showing outward signs of anxiety such as crying or blushing
- Exaggerates the probability of potential difficulties in unfamiliar situations and uses that as an avoidance tactic

- A single traumatic event such as death, divorce, onset of puberty, leaving home for the first time, breakup of an important relationship, starting college, starting a new job, getting married, rape, or abortion.

- A combination of any of the preceding events that takes place over a 2- or 3-year period.

- A person may live with the emotional pain of any or a combination of traumatic events until a point is reached where he or she cannot take it any more.

- The onset of depression or other mood swings may trigger an eating disorder.

- A person who was a very sensitive child often tries to cover up or forget painful situations or experiences. Many things may have affected the child who was hypersensitive that would not have made a lasting impression on another child. The sensitive child who did not have the coping strategies to effectively manage the stress may become an adolescent or an adult with an eating disorder.

- A child who grows up in a controlling environment may develop an eating disorder. Some children, adolescents, and even adults feel as though they do not have their own identity. It is lost while always trying to live up to the expectations of another person, whether a parent, spouse, friend, or coach. The eating disorder may be a way of taking control in one aspect of their lives.

- Comments about the body, weight, or physical appearance may trigger an eating disorder if the person believes that he or she does not measure up.

Many persons with eating disorders simply did not learn to express feelings in a way that promotes support and encouragement to solve problems while they were growing up. Consequently, family dynamics may also play a role in the development of problems with eating. ANRED (1998) reported on family dysfunctions that might result in eating disorders. Daughters of mothers with eating disorders seem to be more prone to developing their own eating disorders. Children learn to walk and talk through observation and imitation. They can also learn eating disorders by seeing what their mothers or sisters do.

Mothers who have eating disorders themselves often project their biases about eating and weight to their children. They handle food issues differently than those who have normal weight and eating patterns. They may make frequent comments about their diets and lack of satisfaction with their own bodies.

Some families are smothering or overcontrolling. Conversely, some families are so loosely structured that the child has no sense of support or family unity. Some parents put a great deal of emphasis on physical appearance. A critical comment, even in jest, about a child's appearance or body may have long-term negative effects. Any of these family behaviors can unwittingly push children into an eating disorder.

Interview with an Individual with an Eating Disorder

The following interview was conducted with a young adult female who developed an eating disorder while in high school.

Q: At what age were you when the eating disorder began?

A: I was a junior in high school.

Q: Do you know what caused it?

A: It is hard to say. I have been in sports since I was little. I always remember thinking I was big, or that I was fat. I was in gymnastics and volleyball and track. I really liked sports. But I was always self-conscious wearing my leotard or the short shorts that seem to be the uniform in girls sports—but not boys. I didn't have a flat stomach. My thighs always looked fat to me. It seemed to me like all the other girls were so nice and thin. I just always felt fat and ugly and self-conscious.

I had very long hair when I was in high school. I got it cut really short—just for a change. My boyfriend at the time remarked after I got my hair cut, that girls had to be really skinny to look good with hair that short. I remember how awful I felt, thinking I must look big and fat.

Then another boy made a comment once when he was describing the appearance of another girl. He said that she wasn't exactly fat—that she was just big like… and he pointed to me. I was humiliated.

I was desperate to be thin. My older sister was thin, popular, and pretty. I was not any of those things. Then, one day reading the newspaper there was a column in "Ann Landers" about how a girl was making herself throw up after she ate and she was losing weight. I tried it. I have never been able to stop.

Q: *Have you ever had any help or counseling?*

A: No, I have thought about it many times because I just hate myself for doing this. But I am too embarrassed to go to tell anyone. I never want to look in the mirror because I hate what I see. I don't want to see my face or my body because I hate myself.

Q: *Have you heard that eating disorders are a type of addiction?*

A: Yes, I have read everything I can find. I think I have a combination of anorexia and bulimia. I will eat very little for periods of time. Then I binge and make myself vomit when I know no one else will be around.

Q: *Do you think you are overweight?*

A: Honestly, I think I have that distorted body image problem we talked about before we started this interview. I feel like I look ugly, unattractive. I don't know what I look like to other people.

Q: *How has the eating disorder affected your life?*

A: I hide things a lot. I try to hide my real feelings a lot. I don't really have close friends. I have always been shy with other people. I don't

like to be in crowds. I like to be alone. I wish I could stop this. I hope I do someday.

I have been able to keep going to school. I don't miss my classes and I get all my work done. People have said I am a perfectionist. I guess I would agree with that.

I hate to eat around other people. I avoid it whenever I can. Unless I know what everyone else is eating is something I know I like and can eat. I only have certain foods that I like—that are OK. If I have to eat other food that I don't really like or don't want to eat, or is too fattening, it makes me feel sick.

Q: *What do you think would help you to stop?*

A: Probably going to a good counselor. I wish I could go to some type of anonymous group or something. I might have a hard time talking to a counselor—or a doctor. I don't really want to tell anyone this.

Q: *Have you tried to stop on your own?*

A: Yes. My mother knows I have had this problem, but she doesn't know that it is as bad as it is. She tries to help me. She usually knows when I lie about throwing up. She said if I can't stop, I have to go to the doctor. So I am trying. I mark stars on a calendar for my good days when I don't binge.

Q: *Is that helping?*

A: I think it does. I really don't want to disappoint my mother.

Q: *Do you have anything else you want to add?*

A: I have one thing for other high school students. Try to be nicer to each other. Think about how other people might feel if you make a mean comment about how they look. Don't say things that will make other people feel bad. Don't make fun of other people whether they are your friends or not.

Don't ever let yourself start having an eating problem. It doesn't help you lose weight. It just makes you sick; it makes you hate yourself. If you are thinking about it, talk to someone right away who can help you. It is too hard to stop; it takes over your life.

Q: *Thanks for taking the time to do this interview. Hopefully this will help other girls and boys who might have this problem.*

A: You are welcome. I hope it does help.

Eating Disorders and Depression

Eating Disorders Go Hand in Hand with Depression

The characteristic behaviors that indicate the presence of an eating disorder often overlap with symptoms of depression. It is estimated the 40 to 50% of individuals with eating disorders also suffer from depression (ANRED, 1998; "Eating Disorders, Part II," November, 1997). Eating disorders seem to go hand in hand with depression. It is hard to tell if the person is depressed because (s)he has an eating disorder or if she developed an eating disorder because of the depression (Pale Reflections Newsletter, 1999). Biochemical discrepancies between the two problems have been shown to be similar. The 1997 *Harvard Mental Health Letter* ("Eating Disorders, Part II") described the similarities. Persons with eating disorders and those with depression seem to have the same type of hormonal and neurotransmitter abnormalities. Serotonin, a neurotransmitter that regulates mood, is lower than average in both groups. Women with clinical depression show twice the rate of bulimia and eight times the rate of anorexia compared with the average woman. Additionally, 40% of people with anorexia also had suffered from depression at some time.

Eating Disorders Are Addictive

ANRED (1998) reported that brain chemistry can change as a result of an eating disorder. Once an individual gets caught up in the starve–binge–purge cycle, biochemicals are altered in such a way that the disorder is physiologically prolonged. The starving and binging activate brain chemicals that produce feelings of peace and euphoria. The feelings of well-being temporarily dispel anxiety and depression. Persons with eating disorders may learn to use food as medication. The food reduces painful feelings and distressing moods.

The cycle of compulsive overeating is related to depression (ANRED, 1998; "Eating Disorders, Part II," 1997; Rader Programs, 1999). This is how it works. Persons who binge or who are compulsive overeaters eat because they feel bad or are depressed. They think eating will be comforting; hence the term *comfort food*. However, after eating, they know that the immense quantity of food consumed was really bad for them. Those with bulimia purge. Then they feel more guilty and become more depressed and resolve, "...never to do that again...." They often make a resolution to diet or fast to make up for the episode of binge eating. The stringent diet usually is impossible to maintain, and they reach the point where they feel ravenous and starving. They become more depressed and stressed out. Then they lose control and go on another binge. Hence, the cycle of addiction begins. Therapy must address the feelings of depression that often trigger the hunt for comfort food.

Personality Characteristics of Persons with Eating Disorders

Overachievers

Personality characteristics seem to play a major role in the development of eating disorders. The *Harvard Mental Health Letter* (November, 1997) describes women with eating disorders as being "...serious, well-behaved, orderly, perfectionist, hypersensitive to rejection, and inclined to irrational guilt and worry... before, during, and after treatment..." ("Eating Disorders, Part II," p. 3). Individuals often have what is generally known as "perfectionist" tendencies. These individuals are usually hard-working overachievers who are very compliant to authority figures. They have a great need to please others. They are often shy and introverted.

It is thought that some people develop anorexia as a means to gain a sense of power and control in their lives. They gain power by restricting their food intake. If they are forced to eat or they eat a food that was not "safe" or planned, they may self-induce vomiting. About 50% of patients with anorexia are also prone to bulimia (ANRED, 1998). They try to be so controlled that they will attempt to purge the unwanted food from their bodies by self-induced vomiting or abuse of laxatives or diuretics.

The Pitfalls of Perfectionism   The Counseling Center at the University of Illinois (1988) and ANRED (1998) have published information describing the pitfalls of perfectionism and strategies for remediation. Perfectionism seems to be a very common trait of individuals with eating disorders. The term relates to a series of self-defeating behaviors aimed at mastering incredibly high and unrealistic goals.

Perfectionists often have to feel like they are the best or none of their effort is worthwhile. Society promotes perfectionism as a desirable trait for success. But there is a major difference between setting realistic and attainable goals and the often destructive behavior of the perfectionist. ANRED (1998) gave this analogy of how a perfectionist might think about weight. If fat is bad and thin is good, thinner is better and thinnest is best—even if thinnest is 68 pounds in a hospital bed on life support.

A person can have excellent time management skills, complete tasks with a high degree of accuracy and creativity, and achieve much success in life while maintaining a healthy lifestyle. That is not a description of a problem-type perfectionist. The desire to be perfect, or always the best, can actually interfere with success. It is likely that perfectionists learned early in life that they were valued

by others because of how they looked or what they accomplished or achieved. That leads to basing one's self-worth on the approval of others. These individuals lack a sense of identity. Their self-worth is based on their looks, their accomplishments, their weight, or their eating habits. It is not a healthy psychological characteristic. That is exactly what people with eating disorders do. Their self-esteem is precariously balanced on external and constantly changing standards. When self-esteem plummets because of an unfeeling statement or a casual remark of another person, eating-disordered behavior skyrockets. It becomes an addictive, vicious cycle that can easily spiral out of control.

The Cycle of Perfectionist Problems   The cycle is composed of a number of interrelated steps. First, the perfectionist sets an unrealistic goal. For example, the person with an eating disorder sets as a goal an unrealistically low weight. Second, the perfectionist fails to meet the goal. The person with the eating disorder can no longer maintain the starvation diet to lose the unrealistic amount of weight and goes on an eating binge. Third, day-to-day productivity and effectiveness are reduced because of the faulty thinking process of constant pressure and chronic failure. The person with the eating disorder becomes depressed. Fourth, the failure to achieve the unrealistic goal leads to self-blaming, feelings of inferiority, and reduced self-esteem. The person with the eating disorder hates herself for her perceived lack of control and lack of success with the diet. She keeps thinking, "If I only try harder, I can do it." Consequently, she gets back on the diet merry-go-round.

Eating Disorders and Males

Males make up only from 5 to 10% of individuals afflicted with eating disorders. However, males comprise about 25% of individuals who are binge eaters or compulsive overeaters (NEDSP Newsletter, 1998). Binge eating is not the same as bulimia. Binge eaters do not attempt to purge; they just have episodes where they consume inordinately large amounts of food ("Eating Disorders, Part I," 1997).

Males binge on different types of food than females do. Men are more apt to binge on protein foods like hamburgers or huge steaks, while women are more likely to binge on carbohydrate-rich foods such as doughnuts, pastries, and candy. This is not written in stone. It is just a generality. It can vary for each incident of the starve–binge–purge cycle (ANRED, 1998).

Society expects men to be big and strong. One of the major reasons males do not suffer the high rates of eating disorders that women do is that they feel a lot less pressure to be sleek and slim. They also have a higher ratio of lean muscle mass to fat ratio as compared to females (AABA, 1997). That means they use calories more efficiently and consequently do not gain weight as easily as females do. A list of interesting facts on males and eating disorders is provided by national organizations (AABA, 1997; ANRED, 1998; NEDSP, 1998):

- The signs, symptoms, and treatment methods for males are similar to those for females.
- Male athletes, especially swimmers, weight lifters, gymnasts, jockeys, dancers, rowers, and wrestlers, are more susceptible to eating disorders.
- Males are generally more likely than women to exercise compulsively and excessively as a manifestation of an eating disorder.
- Males may not be as preoccupied with actual weight as with fitness and muscle development.
- Males may be very unlikely to pursue treatment because of the social stigma of having a problem so highly associated with females.

Eating Disorders and the Media

Bigger is better, right? Everyone who is anyone is on the fast track. Everyone wants a better job, higher pay, bigger house, bigger car. Right? Society expects men to be big strong, powerful, and protective. So bigger is better, right? Wrong! Bigger is not better when it concerns the shape of women's bodies. Females are supposed to be tiny, waiflike, and thin—the thinner the better. The statement "You can never be too rich or too thin" has been popular for generations.

Eating disorder organizations (AABA, 1997; ANRED, 1998: Rader Programs, 1999) across the country place blame on various media sources for the rise of eating disorders among adolescents. Children and youth are bombarded by images and messages that relate, "You have to be thin to be beautiful, happy, and successful." Children learn to prefer the thin, slender physique at a very young age.

The Rader Programs (1999) reported studies of young children and their preferences relating to body size. In one study, preschoolers were offered their choice of dolls to play with that were identical in every respect except one: weight. Nine of 10 preschoolers picked the thin doll. Another study asked children to pick which pictures of other children were more attractive to them. A child in a wheelchair, a child with a facial deformity, and a child with a missing limb were all rated more attractive than an overweight child.

Movies, television shows, and advertisements bombard youth and adolescents with actors and actresses whose body size and build are not the norm and are virtually unattainable for the average person. Overweight people are portrayed as lazy or bad. Overweight females are not prevalent or very popular on TV. Thin women and muscular men are viewed as successful, popular, and powerful. It is extremely difficult to overcome the power of the media to give children the message that appropriate behavior, good manners, kindness, and generosity to others are qualities that really matter.

Television and movie actresses Rosie O'Donnell, Oprah Winfrey, and Camryn Manheim have made great strides in projecting the message that women can be of average or above-average body weight and still be happy and incredibly successful. When a doctor appeared on Oprah's show to discuss the topic of women and weight, he said the average adult female weighs 140 pounds and wears size 14. Oprah and the audience stood and cheered. Oprah has also made great strides to educate females about the importance of a healthy diet and consistent exercise. In addition, one of her most important contributions relates to all the programs she has created and presented to women on the importance of self-esteem—to be proud of who you are and what you have accomplished. Oprah deserves a cheer! She is a positive role model for women everywhere.

On Rosie O'Donnell's former television show, Rosie actually ate candy. Plus she enjoyed it. She frequently asked guests about their favorite candy or whether they could remember certain candies from their childhood. It was so wonderful! She also ate other treats that guests brought in. It was refreshing to see a celebrity acting like a normal person. Think how often you see actors or actresses actually eating. Once in a while Rosie lamented the fact that she was a little overweight, but she did not constantly talk about trying to be on a diet. Rosie started the incredibly popular "Chub Club," which had almost 200,000 male and female members, including children, teenagers, and adults. The motto of the Chub Club was, "Move More, Eat Less: Get Healthy for the Millennium." The goal was to help people create a healthier lifestyle. Rosie spoke very honestly about her attempts to exercise more and the difficulties she experienced in trying to change her habits. She talked about the struggle to follow through to try and be healthier and to have more energy for herself and her children. She related that when the Mattel Toy Company approached her about producing a Rosie Barbie® Doll, she responded with the directive that it had to be of normal female proportions, not like the usual Barbie. Hopefully, more media celebrities will begin to follow Rosie O'Donnell's approach to food and treats that she encouraged while her program was on the air.

Characteristics of Anorexia Nervosa

Anorexia nervosa is described as a self-imposed restriction of food. Anorexia extends well beyond the boundary of ordinary dieting. It is an obsession with being thin. An individual with anorexia goes to great lengths to avoid consuming food, has a very limited number and types of food that are acceptable to eat, and attempts to eat as little as possible. This self-starvation may result in life-threatening weight loss. Anorexia nervosa is reported to have a 20% mortality rate. This is the highest rate of any psychiatric diagnosis (AABA, 1997). According to the DSM-IV-TR (APA, 2000), dangerous weight loss is defined as total body weight that is a minimum of 15% below that which is considered normal. It is estimated that 1% of teenage girls may suffer from anorexia. Fifteen percent of these girls die from starvation complications or suicide each year (Coleman & Webber, 2002; Hsu, 1980). Anorexia does occur in males, albeit at a much lower rate. It is estimated that about 5 to 10% of all individuals with anorexia are males (ANRED, 1998; "Eating Disorders, Part II," 1997; Renfrew Center Newsletter, 1996).

The most striking feature of an individual with anorexia is a gaunt, emaciated physical appearance. It is not unusual for individuals with anorexia to lose 15 to 35% or more of normal body weight for their height and build. Persons with anorexia often exercise to an extreme. Their obsession with limiting food and diet may be accompanied by a manic need to exercise. Despite their emaciated appearance, they maintain a regimen of excessive exercise and continue to starve themselves. Individuals with anorexia often do not recognize their disordered eating patterns. They eat exactly what they want to and believe that they are doing what they need to do to be in control and lose weight.

Warning Signs of Anorexia

A number of observable patterns of behavior are demonstrated by individuals with anorexia (AABA,

1997; Coleman & Webber, 2002; "Eating Disorders, Part I,", 1997; Renfrew Center Foundation, 2000). The major indicator of anorexia is significant weight loss. Being a minimum of 15% below normal body weight is a guideline for anorexic behavior. The individual often has a distorted body image. The person continues to feel fat and continues severe food restriction to the point of physical starvation. The gaunt, emaciated physical stature is usually accompanied by a pasty complexion. The poor coloring may be due to underlying anemia (Kaplan & Woodside, 1987). Even though many of these individuals have lost anywhere from 15 to 35% of normal body weight, they continue to compulsively diet and exercise at an excessive rate.

Observable Behavioral Indicators   An individual with anorexia may make verbal statements about fearing weight gain and talk about being fat even though she definitely is not. Another recognizable signal is that food, diet, and exercise become the focus of life. People with anorexia have unusual eating habits. They categorize foods as being "good or safe" and "bad or dangerous." This means they will allow themselves to eat only a few types of food in small amounts. For example, they may limit themselves to one piece of bread for breakfast, a dish of lettuce or one apple for lunch, and lettuce and a small amount of rice for dinner. If another person tries to make them eat more types of foods or larger amounts, they use different methods to avoid eating. Some pocket the foods or hide food in napkins. Some just cut the food into tiny bits and move them around on the plate. Others avoid the meal table situation by saying they ate earlier or in another place. Some simply say over and over again that they are not hungry. Most will avoid restaurants and any type of situation where they have to eat with others. As many as 50% of individuals also show bulimic symptoms. If forced to eat, they induce vomiting to purge the unwanted food from the body (ANRED, 1998).

Control Issues   People with anorexia sometimes use the illness as a means of gaining some control or power in their lives. If they feel out of control, taking charge of the food they eat or do not eat may be the one way they can feel as though they have some form of power. Dieting to an extreme also may be a means of attracting attention. Most people notice when another individual loses weight and compliment the person on the weight loss. The individual with anorexia might then go overboard with the diet as a means to continue to try to gain that type of attention.

Being Thin Will Make Me Happy   Most females with anorexia are of average to above-average intelligence. However, they demonstrate faulty thinking patterns. They seem to have a very simplistic way of thinking about happiness. It is common for girls with anorexia to think, "If I am thinner, I will feel better about myself." They do not think logically or objectively about their eating patterns and the choices they are making. Some will become highly irritated and irrational with a person who tries to help them. Because of poor nutrition, incredibly low food intake, and the resulting physical complications, many have trouble concentrating at school or on the job. They obsess about food and weight. They hold themselves and others to rigid, perfectionist standards (ANRED, 1998).

Their social relationships tend to be superficial. Some present themselves as needy and dependent while others act fiercely independent, rejecting all attempts from others to help. Most have trouble talking about feelings and insist that "Everything is OK. I'm just tired or stressed out." They then attempt to reduce the stress through anorexic rituals of not eating, exercising too much, or binging and purging (ANRED, 1998).

Persons with anorexia may develop lanugo, a fine hair growth all over the body (Pale Reflections Newsletter, 1999). Lanugo develops after prolonged periods of starvation or minimal caloric intake. It is the body's attempt to keep warm or maintain heat when most of the subcutaneous fat layer has been lost. People with anorexia also wear baggy clothes or many layers of clothing to hide weight loss or stay warm. In addition, many young women weigh themselves multiple times each day. They spend time inspecting their bodies in a mirror and usually find something to criticize. Most of them say they hate their bodies. Most females with anorexia do not feel good about themselves unless they are very thin. However, the distorted body image causes a problem because an anorexic individual is never thin enough to satisfy herself. Table 10–2 summarizes the warning signs of anorexic behavior.

Physical Complications of Anorexia

Along with the potential of life-threatening weight loss, there are a number of physiological complications of anorexia (AABA, 1997; Coleman & Webber, 2002; "Eating Disorders, Part I," 1997; Kaplan & Woodside, 1987; Renfrew Center Newsletter, 1996). Depending on the amount of weight loss, the individual will have gaunt, hollow facial features and sharply protruding bones. Many people with anorexia bruise easily because of the loss of the insulating subcutaneous fat layer. These problems are a result of malnutrition and starvation. Many suffer from dry skin and hair loss. Being overly sensitive to cold is another complication. The individ-

TABLE 10–2 Warning Signs of Anorexia

- Significant weight loss
- Excessive exercise
- Distorted body image
- Frequent excuses for not eating meals
- Unusual eating habits
- Limited types of food eaten
- Perfectionist
- Needs frequent approval from others
- Needs to have feelings of control or power of own life
- Very secretive about eating habits
- Difficulty with eating in public
- Wears baggy clothes to hide body/weight loss
- Frequently checks weight on scale
- Pale, pasty complexion
- Self-worth is determined by what is eaten

ual has lost the necessary layer of body fat that helps to maintain normal body heat. They also tend to have a lower than average basal body temperature. Their bodies do not compensate for changes in temperature, so they often feel cold.

Depending on the age of onset of anorexia, some individuals with anorexia experience delayed puberty. Preadolescent females fail to menstruate and develop breasts at a normal age. In males, testosterone levels may remain low, resulting in impotence. In later adolescence, menstruation hormone levels drop, bringing about disruptions or cessation (amenorrhea) of menstrual periods. This can result in temporary or permanent infertility. Approximately 17% body fat is required for a normal cycle of menstruation, and 23% body fat is necessary for a normal cycle of ovulation in females (Frisch & McArthur, 1974).

Many people with anorexia also experience erratic mood swings and insomnia. As a result, these individuals may be irritable, unpredictable, depressed, and possibly suicidal. Other dangerous physiological complications include premature bone loss, deterioration of the kidneys, low blood pressure, and heart failure.

On February 4, 1983, singer Karen Carpenter died of chronic anorexia nervosa. Karen fought a public battle with anorexia from 1975 to 1983. She and her brother Richard were a popular worldwide musical duo, selling nearly 100 million records. Karen suffered heart failure at the end of her struggle with anorexia. Unfortunately, Karen had been making progress toward overcoming anorexia when her heart, weakened by the condition, simply gave out.

Characteristics of Bulimia Nervosa

The October, 1997 *Harvard Mental Health Letter* defines bulimia nervosa as "oxlike hunger of nervous origin" ("Eating Disorders, Part I," 1997). Specifically, the individual who has had two or more episodes of binge eating every week for at least 3 months is considered to be bulimic. A person with bulimia will binge on abnormally large amounts of food and then attempt to purge the food from the body before digestion. Self-induced vomiting and abuse of laxatives or diuretics are the most common methods of purging. Some individuals indulge in extensive exercise regimens to burn off calories. Compulsive exercise and fasting between binges are also common symptoms. If the individual tries to fast, binges become common because the body is starved for food. Then the sufferer believes overeating is acceptable because she can purge after eating. This is how the cycle of addiction begins. It is estimated that 3% of women have had bulimia for a period at some point in their lives (Pale Reflections Newsletter, 1999). Symptoms can develop at any time, but they most commonly appear during adolescence.

Another method some use to purge is with syrup of ipecac (Pale Reflections Newsletter, 1999). Syrup of ipecac is a type of medicine intended to induce vomiting in a person who has swallowed a toxic substance. As with most medicines, ipecac can be dangerous to the individual who abuses it by taking large or frequent doses.

Individuals with bulimia may be loners or have only superficial social relationships with others. They may be shy and introverted. It is not easy for them to make friends. They spend a lot of time thinking about food and where and when their next binge will take place. It must be done very secretively. They feel ashamed and guilty about their inability to control the binges. Thus, they spend a lot of time alone rather than in peer group activities or with a friend.

Danger Signals of Bulimia

There are a number of observable behaviors indicating bulimic tendencies that parents, educators, coaches, and others should be aware of (AABA, 1997; Coleman & Webber, 2002; "Eating Disorders, Part I," 1997; Kaplan & Woodside, 1987; Renfrew Center Newsletter, 1996). First, people with bulimia have an intense preoccupation with their weight. It

is common for them to have a distorted body image. They think they look fat and overweight even though they are not. They think others must see them as being overweight. Many are of normal or just above normal weight for their height and build. However, they verbalize phobias about weight gain, feelings of being fat, and fear of being overweight, and they constantly talk about food and dieting. Like those with anorexia, they have a distorted body image.

Second, individuals who have bulimia show peculiar eating patterns. They may be secretive about eating and may not want to eat in public or around others because they may be binge eating or trying to fast or eat very little. During nonbinge periods, they may allow themselves a very limited range of foods, meaning there are only certain foods that they think are acceptable. Such foods may be different for every individual.

Third, they may exercise compulsively. They often become upset if their exercise routine is interrupted and insist on exercising to the exclusion of all other activities. Exercise is a way of purging calories from the body.

Fourth, bulimia seems to be accompanied by severe psychological problems. Persons with bulimia are their own worst critics. They have a low sense of self-esteem and low self-concept. Their self-worth is often determined by what they ate or what they weighed the last time they got on the scale. They have a fear of not being able to stop eating voluntarily. Self-deprecating thoughts following eating, no matter what the amount eaten, are common. Unlike individuals with anorexia, persons with bulimia recognize their disordered eating patterns as a problem. Many experience guilt and self-hate over their inability to control their food cravings. The out-of-control behavior results in high levels of anxiety and depression.

Fifth, persons with bulimia will often go directly to the bathroom after eating. They self-induce vomiting to purge the food. Many will run the faucets in the sink, bathtub, or shower to disguise or cover the vomiting noises. If it is not possible to use a restroom, some go to an isolated location and vomit into some type of container that can be disposed of. Many develop red marks or scars on the hands or knuckles from inducing vomiting. The marks are due to skin irritations made by the teeth during repeated attempts to induce vomiting with the fingers down the throat. They may also have bloodshot eyes and a sore throat from the vomiting. They may also complain often about feeling cold. Table 10–3 summarizes behavioral danger signals that are possible indicators of bulimia.

Physical Complications of Bulimia

Bulimia is not thought to be as dangerous to health as anorexia is, but it is associated with many undesirable physical effects that could be life-threatening or fatal (Kaplan & Woodside, 1987; Renfrew Center Newsletter, 1996). Clinical depression is common because people with bulimia recognize that they have a severe problem in their eating patterns. They recognize their addiction and feel helpless to stop it. They feel too ashamed to seek help. Gastrointestinal problems may occur, including irritation of the esophagus, stomach, salivary glands, and throat from persistent vomiting. There may be damaged or discolored teeth because gastric acids erode dental enamel. Some

TABLE 10–3   Danger Signals of Bulimia

- Preoccupation with weight and dieting
- Verbalizes fear of weight gain
- Peculiar or secretive eating habits
- Binging/purging
- Laxative/diuretic/ipecac abuse
- Going to the bathroom shortly after eating
- Compulsive exercise
- Mood swings or depression
- Dental problems
- Red marks or scars on the knuckles from self-induced vomiting
- Bloodshot eyes
- Wears baggy clothes to hide body
- Frequent self-deprecating comments
- Perfectionist
- Needs approval from others
- Loner/introverted

TABLE 10–4   Physical Complications of Bulimia

- Depression
- Gastrointestinal problems affecting the salivary glands, esophagus, and stomach
- Damaged tooth enamel
- Lung irritation
- Chronic dehydration
- Bowel problems from laxative abuse
- Heart and kidney problems

people with bulimia may suffer from lung problems due to choking on vomitus. Food particles may lodge in the lungs and cause inflammation.

Binging and purging may cause chronic dehydration. Vomiting causes a decrease in body fluids, resulting in reduced levels of potassium, sodium, and chloride. When these biochemical levels are low, muscle spasms, general body weakness, and fatigue are common. Extensive abuse of laxatives can cause critical problems, such as bloody diarrhea. At a later stage, individuals may become laxative-dependent and unable to have a bowel movement without a laxative. Finally, an extreme result of chronic laxative abuse may be life-threatening in the form of a completely flaccid and nonresponsive bowel. Heart problems and kidney damage can occur in severe cases (NEDA, 2002; U.S. Department of Health and Human Services, n. d.). Table 10–4 summarizes physical complications of bulimia.

Treatment of Eating Disorders

The preferred treatment for both anorexia and bulimia is regulating the amount of calories consumed and returning weight to normal levels for height and body build.

Anorexia is particularly difficult to treat because most people with anorexia do not recognize their disordered eating patterns. Their distorted body image makes them feel as though they still need to diet. Two main treatments that have been used to manage anorexia include medication and behavior modification. There is no drug that simply cures symptoms of anorexia. However, antidepressants have been used with some success to reduce the number of binging incidents. The medications used are often the some antidepressants that are used to treat depression. One drug commonly used is Prozac® (fluoxetine). The medications act on the brain to increase serotonin levels. Persons with anorexia and bulimia are frequently found to have lower than average levels of serotonin. Serotonin is a neurotransmitter that acts to balance or regulate mood. A low level may result in feelings of depression.

Cognitive behavior modification is used to help individuals with anorexia change not only their eating habits but also their faulty thinking patterns. They need to change how they think about eating, their body image, and improve their self-concept. Sometimes contingency contracting is used to formalize the agreement between the individual with anorexia and the physician or therapist. The purpose of the contract is similar to that of any behavior modification plan. It outlines what behaviors the individual will demonstrate and what the reward or incentive will be for following through. In the case of the individual with anorexia, the behavior might be to show a regular pattern of eating a normal amount of food with sufficient calories to return to a safe body weight.

If the individual will not attempt to take in an amount of calories that will promote healthy weight gain and normal body weight, she may need to be placed in residential treatment or a hospital situation for treatment of the eating disorder. Forced feedings, either intravenously or directly into the stomach, may be mandated by the physician in cases where the individual has reached a potentially fatal weight loss. Calculating body mass index (BMI) may be more realistic than calculating actual weight. BMI is a measure of *body fat or obesity*. BMI is calculated by percentage in a range for height and weight.

How Can Men Help to Prevent Eating Disorders in Females?

The majority of individuals with eating disorders are female. Although the specific cause for eating disorders is not known, prevention strategies can be implemented to reduce the chances that young girls will develop eating disorders (Renfrew Center Newsletter, 1996).

First, recognize that adolescence is a very challenging time both for the adolescent and for the adults who live or work with them and coach and/or teach them. Adolescence is also a period when male approval is critical to girls and young women. They develop ideologies about men that may stay with them for the rest of their lives. Fathers and male teachers and coaches should understand how important they are to young girls. Fathers who are separated or divorced should make an effort to be a part of the daughter's life. All men who interact with female adolescents should demonstrate positive interaction methods that will contribute to their emotional and physical health. Understanding contributing factors to eating disorders is critically important for males.

Second, evaluate attitudes and messages projected about females and weight, dieting, body, and beauty. Make sure conversations relate to acceptance and value of the young woman as a person and a personality rather than simply her appearance. Be sure that undue pressure is not placed on girls to make drastic changes to measure up to some other image. Talk about the pressures that women feel to change their looks and to lose weight in order to please others. Be aware of negative or degrading talk about women's bodies that are not like those portrayed on the pages of fashion magazines. Convey respect, trust, approval, and admiration for accomplishments to help increase girls' self-esteem.

Third, set good examples in the areas of diet and exercise. Emphasize the need to set healthy eating patterns rather than eating to diet and lose weight. Focus on teaching youngsters to make healthy eating and exercise choices. Show girls that they can attain control and power by being strong, healthy, and physically fit. They will learn they do not have to diet to be powerful, successful, or beautiful. Participate in fun activities that require physical fitness.

Fourth, show respect for women in general. When women are put down or degraded, even if it is meant as a joke, the female adolescent will also feel put down simply by association. The young girl's sense of self-concept and self-esteem is still in an emerging state. It is bound to be a little shaky and will be affected by those "jokes" in poor taste. During conversation, listen to her and show her respect as an equal. Help girls to define values and determine what is really important in life. Don't just try to impose your values or views. Show appreciation for her unique characteristics and traits even when her opinions are different. Show a willingness to share responsibilities that might be considered "women's work." Give her the same opportunities that a boy might have. Be careful not to send messages suggesting that women are less important, that there are things she cannot accomplish, or that there is information she does not need to know because she is a girl. Show that men and women can respect each other and work together as equal partners.

Things Parents Can Do to Prevent Eating Disorders

There are a number of proactive strategies that parents can use to prevent the occurrence of eating disorders in their children. Levine and Smolak (2002) compiled a number of pertinent suggestions. First, they recommend that parents be aware of their own thoughts, attitudes, and behaviors related to food, eating, and body image. There is a higher incidence of eating disorders among children of parents who verbalize dissatisfaction with their own bodies, have eating problems, and/or diet rigidly. Some parents may need to make modifications in their own be-

liefs and behaviors if their children are to develop positive body images and eating behaviors.

Second, parents should make an effort to control judgmental verbal remarks about children's body size or shape. Try to avoid stereotyping of "fat is bad" or "thin is good." Parents should convey an attitude of acceptance of healthy body size, shape, and eating behaviors. If a child does have a weight problem, the family physician, nurse practitioner, or a registered dietitian may assist the family in learning and establishing healthier eating behaviors.

Third, discuss healthy eating and exercise plans. Try to have meals and do exercise activities together as a family. Emphasize the benefits of nutritious, well-balanced meals and moderate, fun types of exercise. Focus on the pleasure involved in activities rather than on the appearance of participants.

Fourth, educate children about various forms of prejudice, including degrading those who are overweight, smaller than average, or simply different. Teach children to show genuine human respect for others. Be a good role model of kind, caring, generous, and accepting behaviors.

Fifth, promote healthy self-esteem and self-respect in children by expressing positive comments about their intellectual, social, and athletic efforts. Focus more on character than on outward looks or appearance. Provide boys and girls with an equal variety of activities and opportunities. Levine and Smolak (2002, p.1) conclude with the comment that "A well-rounded sense of self and a solid self-esteem are perhaps the best antidote to dieting and disordered eating."

The IMAD Approach

Levine and Hill (1991) proposed a strategy called IMAD to help deal with an individual who may have or be developing an eating disorder. The strategy prescribes a series of steps that may be used as a method to informally assess whether an individual has an eating problem. The acronym stands for:

Inefficiency: Is the individual suffering from lapses in strength, energy, and concentration?

Misery: Is the individual suffering emotional problems such as anxiousness, anger, depression, obsession, or sadness?

Alienation: Does the individual have a pervasive or all-encompassing concern with eating, weight, exercise, and/or body image that is separating her from friends, family, and past favorable activities?

Disturbance: Has the individual developed new or different habits that are frightening, upsetting, or generally disturbing to herself and/or others?

After establishing that there is a concern about the presence of an eating disorder, the following strategies may be used to discuss the problem:

- **Time to talk:** Set aside a mutually convenient time to talk. Make an effort to present feelings of concern to the individual in an open and honest manner that conveys kindness and caring.

- **Show your concern:** Describe specific behavioral incidents to communicate to the individual why you are concerned about her behavior. Avoid using statements that project blame, shame, or guilt. Relate your feelings of support and encouragement to seek professional assistance from qualified medical, nutrition, or other health professionals.

- **Avoid conflict:** If the individual denies or refuses to acknowledge an eating problem, reaffirm your reasons for believing that there is a problem and offer your continued support if she would like to talk or seek other assistance.

Implications for Working with Youth and Adolescents

There are a number of tactics that adults can use if an eating disorder is suspected in an adolescent (Renfrew Center Newsletter, 1996). First, learn about the signal behaviors that may indicate an eating disorder. Adults must recognize the symptoms in order to provide referrals, care, and treatment. Second, let the teen know that his or her well-being is of primary concern. Third, try to get the teen to talk about feelings and emotions related to daily living. Stress builds as problems accumulate that the teen cannot manage. Teenagers live in a fast-paced, tumultuous world. They may not always take the initiative in discussing their problems with adults. Fourth, encourage the adolescent to talk to a counselor or a therapist who specializes in eating disorders. The individual needs to attend the counseling sessions consistently and must learn to take responsibility for his or her own behavior.

Early Intervention Is Important

Early intervention is critical to remediation of eating disorders. If an adult recognizes the symptoms and suspects that an adolescent may have an eating disorder, a referral can be made to a school counselor, school nurse, or local mental health center. It is important that the referral be made to a source with experience in assessing and treating individuals with eating disorders. Table 10–5 lists questions to ask a potential therapist. The answers to the questions can help to make a decision as to whether a particular therapist would be appropriate (Renfrew Center Newsletter, 1996). In addition, many communities have support groups for adolescents with eating disorders and their parents.

Try to keep a positive attitude. People of all ages do recover from eating disorders. Try not to make the person feel guilty. Most adolescents with eating disorders already feel guilty enough. Try not to focus on weight, food, or exercise when casually

TABLE 10–5 Questions to Ask a Potential Therapist

- How did you get interested and involved in treating eating disorders?
- How long have you been working in this area?
- What is your background, education, training (psychiatrist, psychologist, social worker, nurse, etc.)?
- Are you affiliated with any hospital and/or other organization?
- What percentage of the people you have seen have eating disorders?
- Are there any former or current patients I might be able to talk to?
- How much time will be focused on talking about food, weight, and diet issues?
- Will you restrict any of my behaviors in order for me to see you (i.e., Can I come to therapy if I throw up, do drugs, exercise, etc.)?
- Do you believe people can make a complete recovery from eating disorders or will I always have this problem?
- What is your opinion of the self-help support groups (OA, ACOA, AA, etc.)?
- What is important for me to know about you? Why should I see you?
- Do you think you would be able to successfully work with me?
- What can I expect during a session?
- How interactive are you?
- Will you monitor my weight?
- When, if ever, do you hospitalize?
- Will you involve my family?

Note. From the Renfrew Center Newsletter, 1996, Philadelphia, PA.

interacting with the individual with an eating disorder. This becomes the responsibility of the doctor and the therapist.

The Renfrew Center Newsletter (1996) presents qualities of a good therapist. All good therapists should have sound educational and training credentials. Interview the therapist before making a commitment to therapy. Check to make sure the therapist has the appropriate degree and make sure that all training regulations for the field of therapy have been met. Consult your physician for a recommendation for a board-certified therapist. The effective therapist is a professional who works with the client to establish therapy goals. The therapist maintains confidentiality of information shared in each session. The therapist should create an environment where the client feels safe to bring up uncomfortable or unpleasant feelings and experiences. The therapist should individualize and tailor the therapy sessions to each client's specific needs. The competent therapist empowers the client. Through therapy, clients should learn to recognize and make a plan for their own problem solving.

References

American Anorexia Bulimia Association. (1997). Informational packet available from AABA. Phone: (212) 575–6200; www.aabainc.org

American Psychiatric Association. (2000). *Diagnostic and statistical manual of mental disorders* (4th ed., text revision). Washington, DC: Author.

Anorexia Nervosa and Related Eating Disorders. (1998). Information available from www.anred.com

Coleman, M. C., & Webber, J. (2002). *Emotional and behavioral disorders: Theory and practice* (4th ed.). Needham Heights, MA: Allyn & Bacon.

Counseling Center (1988). *Perfectionism.* University of Illinois, Urbana–Champaign.

Frisch, R. E., & McArthur, J. W. (1974). Menstrual cycles: Fatness as a determinant of minimum weight for height necessary for their maintenance or onset. *Science*, 185, 949–951.

Eating Disorders, Part I. (1997, October). *Harvard Mental Health Letter*, 14(4).

Eating Disorders, Part II. (1997, October). *Harvard Mental Health Letter*, 14(5).

Hsu, L. K, (1980). Outcome of anorexia nervosa: A review of the literature (1954–1978). *Archives of General Psychology*, 37, 1041–1043.

Kaplan, A. S., & Woodside, D. B. (1987). Biological aspects of anorexia nervosa and bulimia nervosa. *Journal of Counseling and Clinical Psychology*, 55(5), 645–653.

Levine, M., & Hill, L. (1991). How to help a friend: The IMAD approach. Retrievable from www.nationaleatingdisorders.org

Levine, M., & Smolak, L. (2002). 10 things parents can do to prevent eating disorders. Retrievable from www.nationaleatingdisorders.org

National Eating Disorders Association. (2002). *Causes of eating disorders*. Retrievable from www.nationaleatingdisorders.org

National Eating Disorders Screening Program Newsletter. (1998). Available from NEDSP, One Washington Street, #304, Wellesley Hills, MA 02181-1706. www.nmisp.org

Pale Reflections Newsletter. (1999). Retrievable from www.pale-reflections.com

Phelps, L., & Bajorek, E. (1991). Eating disorders of the adolescent: Current issues in etiology, assessment, and treatment. *School Psychology Review*, 20(1), 9–22.

Rader Programs. (1999). Special information available from Rader Programs, Washington Medical Center, 12099 W. Medical Center, Los Angeles, CA 90066. Phone: 1-800-841-1515; Fax: (310) 391-6295; www.raderpro.com

Renfrew Center Foundation. (Spring, 2000). *Perspective*, 5(2).

Renfrew Center Newsletter. (1996). Published by the Renfrew Center, 475 Spring Lane, Philadelphia, PA 19128. Phone: 1-800-RENFREW; www.renfrewcenter.com

Schlitz, T. (1997). *Suggestions for improving body image*: Handout 7.1, *Eating concerns support group curriculum*. Greenfield , WI: Community Recovery Press.

Serdula, M. K., Collins, M. E., & Williams, D. F. (1993). Weight control practices of US adolescents and adults, Part II. *Annals of Internal Medicine*, 119(7), 667–671.

U.S. Department of Health and Human Services, Office on Women's Health. (n.d.). *Frequently asked questions about eating disorders*. Retrievable from www.4woman.gov/faq/eatingdi.htm

4
CATEGORIES OF EXTERNALIZED DISORDERS

ATTENTION DEFICIT HYPERACTIVITY DISORDER (ADD)

After completing the chapter, the reader will be able to identify:

- Historic points in the treatment of ADD.
- Definition and prevalence of ADD.
- Causes of ADD.
- Medications for management of ADD.
- Characteristics of ADD.
- Assessments for ADD.
- Allergies and nutrition related to ADD.
- Implications for educators, parents, and other professionals who work with youth and adolescents.

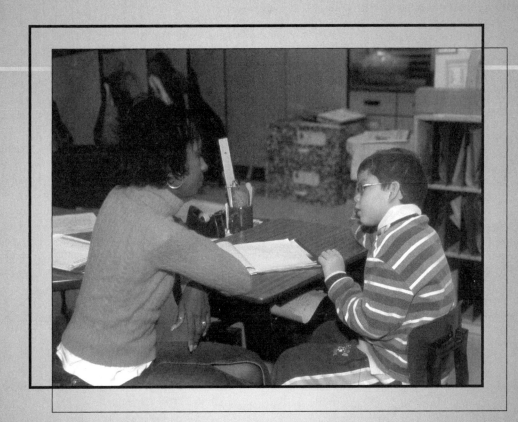

Introduction

I was always getting into stuff. I was always curious about things and had to explore or check out everything. My mom must have thought I was a terror. Once I vacuumed all the water out of the toilet. One time I got a can of mace and accidentally sprayed it in my face.

I stuck rings in light sockets and knives in the toaster… I got shocked. I did it at least four more times even though I got shocked. Once I played in a big bed of fire ants. I was covered with bites. I ran in the house and jumped into the bathtub.

I used to talk a lot when I was little. Kids in school called me "motor mouth." If I thought of something, I just said it. I wouldn't think twice. It would just come out.

When I was growing up, people say I was in constant motion. I guess some people thought I was "hyper." Some people thought I was downright "crazy." I couldn't sit down for a long time. I had trouble sitting down even when I wanted to. I couldn't sit still for school, reading, or even watching TV.

Teachers have told me they can see I will be famous some day. I had long talks with my teachers while I was standing in the hall. Since I was in the hall almost every day, I had my own special spot. I would peek in the room and make faces. The other students would laugh a lot. I would wander off and peek in the bathroom. I would run in, flush all the toilets, put soap in all the sinks and on the mirrors, and run back to my spot in the hall.

Usually teachers seated me up front near their desk or back in the cubbyhole. Sometimes I had to sit in the corner. I'd get mad. It didn't work. I'd still turn around and get someone's attention. I had to sit in a cubicle with high sides in third through seventh grade. They put me there so I wouldn't disturb the other students. (Dendy, 1995, p. 333)

So goes the life of a student with attention deficit disorder. Children with attention deficit hyperactivity disorder can be both a joy and a challenging, frustrating puzzle to their parents and teachers. The goal of this chapter is to help educators learn the typical signs and behavioral symptoms in the hope that no more students spend their days at school standing in the hall, sitting in the corner, or being placed in a cubicle isolated from the rest of the class for long periods.

This chapter follows the policy standard set by the U.S. Department of Education (1991) and uses the term *attention deficit disorder* (ADD) to cover both ADD and ADHD. It is recognized and accepted that ADD and ADHD are two disorders with differing types of observable behavior. The primary feature of ADD is typically thought of as inattentiveness. ADHD usually implies that inattentiveness is compounded by hyperactivity. More details are provided later in the chapter comparing and contrasting specific behaviors associated with ADD and ADHD (Jordan, 1998).

The major goal of the chapter is to provide information about the characteristic behaviors of individuals with ADD for educators and other professionals who work with youth and adolescents. First, a short summary of the history and background of ADD is presented. Second, typical behavioral characteristics and a formal definition of ADD are discussed. Behavioral criteria for diagnosis are reviewed. Sections are presented relating to causes of ADD, common overlapping problems such as conduct disorder (CD), learning disabilities (LD), and oppositional defiant disorder (ODD); use of medication; and nutritional therapy for individuals with ADD. Finally, implications for educators and other professionals are summarized. The information is focused on assisting those who teach or work with youth and adolescents to gain information about the disorder and to recognize the signs and symptoms of ADD.

Other Health Impairments Category

ADD is not recognized as a separate category under the Individuals with Disabilities Education Act (IDEA) of 1997 (Heward, 2000). However, it is included under the category Other Health Impairments. To qualify for special education services, a battery

ADD –

of assessment results must document that the individual has a deficit in attentiveness that significantly and adversely impacts educational achievement. Additionally, individuals with ADD may be eligible to receive special education services under Section 504 of the Rehabilitation Act (PL 93-112), 1973. This law declared that a person cannot be excluded on the basis of disability alone from any program or activity receiving federal funds (Heward, 2000, p. 28). An individualized 504 plan documents adaptations and modifications that will be provided to a specific student in the general education classroom. These plans are written for students who have some type of educational need (academic or behavioral) but do not meet the full requirements for special education placements.

ADD Is a Neurobiological Condition

ADD is a neurobiological condition, which means the individual has a dysfunction in the central nervous system (CNS). The CNS consists of the brain, the spinal cord, and all the nerves that radiate throughout the body. All thoughts and body movements are controlled by the CNS. When the CNS is not functioning appropriately, the individual has difficulty processing and producing expressive, receptive, and written language as well as controlling motor activities. *Expressive language* relates to how well one is able to use spoken language to convey thoughts, feelings, wants, and needs. *Receptive language* relates to how well one is able to listen and comprehend communications from others. For many individuals with ADD, CNS difficulties may affect the individual's ability to achieve academically at school, to be successful in the workplace, and to establish social relationships with others. All of these issues are common characteristics of ADD. Barkley (1990) classified the basic maladaptive behaviors associated with ADD into the following five categories:

1. lack of persistence of effort to complete tasks;

2. behavioral impulsivity such as acting or talking before thinking;
3. hyperactivity;
4. failure to follow through on rules or directives;
5. fluctuation in the quality of work output.

These signal behaviors are particularly important for educators to be aware of because they are indicative of ADD and often cause behavioral problems and academic underachievement in the classroom. The five areas are discussed in detail in later sections of the chapter.

History and Background Information

Individuals who showed disruptive, impulsive, and overactive behavioral symptoms of ADD were noted in history as far back in time as that recorded by the ancient Greek philosophers and physicians (Jordan, 1998). The behaviors were nonconforming to the societal mores of the times and made successful adjustment and acceptance by others almost impossible. At that time, the Greeks thought that the nonconforming behaviors were caused by "body humors" being out of balance. It is remarkable how close the ancient Greeks were to understanding the neurological basis of ADD known today.

The neurological impairment theory of ADD has been studied by researchers from the ancient Greeks through current times. Jordan (1998) provided a complete and detailed history of ADD from the early 19th century to the present. This history continues to support the concept of a neurological basis for ADD. Following is a short summary of Jordan's (1998) historical perspective:

1890   William James developed a theory that persons with attention deficits and behavior that was socially disruptive, impulsive, and immoral must suffer from an underlying neurological deficit. Since that time a number of researchers have added to the knowledge base.

1908   Alfred Tredgold provided medical evidence that brain deficits contributed to disruptive behavior and established a platform supporting the use of medication to help control behavioral problems.

1934   Eli Kahn and Leonard Cohen suggested that ADD-type behavior had an organic cause.

1937   William Bradley prescribed Benzedrine (a stimulant medication) to effectively reduce disruptive behavior resulting from organic problems such as brain stem deficits.

1940   Kahn, Cohen, Bradley, Strauss, and others introduced the term *minimal brain damage syndrome* (MBDS). It became the most widely used label for the cluster of behaviors that included hyperactivity, impulsivity, attention deficits, mood swings, explosive emotional behaviors, and inappropriate social behavior.

1942   Lauretta Bender introduced the concept of "maturational lag" to describe disruptive behavior not due to actual brain damage but instead related to delayed maturation of portions of the central nervous system. This research theorized that some children who were thought to have MBDS might actually outgrow some of the symptoms.

1957   Morris Laufer, Ernest Denhoff, and George Solomon introduced the term *hyperkinetic impulse disorder* (HID) to label children with hyperactivity. They suggested the overactivity was caused by nerve pathway deficits in the section of the midbrain called the diencephalon.

1962   Samuel Clements and John Peters proposed the concept of minimal brain damage (MBD). This model included factors such as home environment, school performance, social behavior, health history, and emotional temperament for diagnosis. MBD replaced MBDS as the customary label for individuals with ADD behaviors.

1968   The second edition of the *Diagnostic and Statistical Manual of Mental Disorders* (DSM-II, American Psychiatric Association [APA], 1968) introduced a new diagnostic category, "Hyperkinetic Reaction of Childhood Disorder." This label replaced MBDS.

1980   The third edition of the *Diagnostic and Statistical Manual of Mental Disorders* (DSM-III, APA, 1980) replaced "Hyperkinetic Reaction of Childhood Disorder" with a new term, Attention Deficit Disorder with and without hyperactivity. There was ADD+H (Attention Deficit Disorder with Hyperactivity) and ADD–H (Attention Deficit Disorder without Hyperactivity). Three categories of symptoms for diagnosis were (a) inattention, (b) impulsivity, and (c) hyperactivity.

1987   A revised third edition of the *Diagnostic and Statistical Manual of Mental Disorders* (DSM-III-R, APA, 1987) made a change in the definition of attention deficit disorders. It replaced ADD+H/ADD–H with a single label of ADHD. The category of ADD–H was changed to Undifferentiated ADD.

1994   The fourth edition of the *Diagnostic and Statistical Manual of Mental Disorders* (DSM-IV, APA, 1994) changed the definition once again. ADD–H was reinstated with three clinical categories for attention deficit problems:

314.01   Attention Deficit Hyperactivity Disorder, Combined Type

314.00   Attention Deficit Hyperactivity Disorder, Predominantly Inattentive Type

314.01   Attention-Deficit/Hyperactivity Disorder, Predominantly Hyperactive/Impulsive Type

2000 The ADD–H definition in the latest revision of the *Diagnostic and Statistical Manual of Mental Disorders* (DSM-IV-TR, APA, 2000) was unchanged.

Some researchers (Barkley, 1998; Jordan, 1998) were still not satisfied with the DSM-IV classification terminology for ADD-type problems. Their argument against the phrasing was based on the idea that children who are inattentive but not hyperactive should not have a confounding and confusing label that amounts to "Attention Deficit/Hyperactivity Disorder—without Hyperactivity." Further research would be needed to fine-tune the classification terminology of the ADD category of special learning needs.

Definition of ADD

DSM-IV-TR Definition

The formal diagnosis of ADD is based on the definition from the DSM-IV-TR (APA, 2000). ADD is described as a persistent pattern of developmentally inappropriate levels of inattention, impulsivity, and hyperactivity. A behavioral symptom is considered to be significant in the diagnosis only if it occurs at a higher than average rate for most people of the same age as the subject being tested. Persons with ADD typically show more severe symptoms in situations in which sustained attention is required and little physical activity is allowed. For example, such students have trouble in a classroom where a great deal of "sitting still" is required. Other times when students with ADD might be frustrated and experience lack of success include (a) listening to the teacher present a long class lecture, (b) taking notes, (c) attending a lengthy meeting, (d) completing a long paper-and-pencil-type task at a desk, or (e) working on any repetitive, monotonous task. Note the common factors. Students with ADD have difficulty in general with tasks that require sustained listening or

concentrated attention with little flexibility for movement or variability in the task or the product produced.

Behavioral Indicators

Behavioral symptoms that might be observed in individuals with ADD vary from fidgeting, blurting out responses, being unable to focus or sustain attention, being out of the seat and talking in class without permission, to being unable to complete tasks. In addition to the behavioral symptoms, the DSM-IV-TR criteria also require the following five conditions for an official diagnosis of ADD:

1. The onset of symptoms must occur no later than 7 years of age (although people can be and are diagnosed through the life span).
2. The symptoms must occur in at least two out of three environments, including home, school or work, and the community.
3. The problem behaviors must cause clinically significant stress and disturbance in the individual's life.
4. The ADD symptoms are not a result of pervasive developmental disorder; a mood disorder; schizophrenia; or any other type of anxiety, dissociative, or personality disorder.
5. The disturbance in behavior must last at least 6 months during which at least six (or more) symptoms of inattention and six (or more) symptoms of hyperactivity-impulsivity are present.

Table 11-1 relates the criteria and the behaviors used to diagnose ADD.

Prevalence

Wide Range of Statistics

Despite many technology and assessment advancements, no accurate figure is available to document the exact number of school-age students

TABLE 11–1   Diagnostic Criteria for ADD

A. Either (1) or (2)

(1)   Six (or more) of the following symptoms of inattention have persisted for at least 6 months to a degree that is maladaptive and inconsistent with developmental level:

Inattention

 (a) often fails to give close attention to details or makes careless mistakes in schoolwork, work, or other activities
 (b) often has difficulty sustaining attention in tasks or play activities
 (c) often does not seem to listen when spoken to directly
 (d) often does not follow through on instructions and fails to finish schoolwork, chores, or duties in the workplace (not due to oppositional behavior or failure to understand instructions)
 (e) often has difficulty organizing tasks and activities
 (f) often avoids, dislikes, or is reluctant to engage in tasks that require sustained mental effort (such as schoolwork or homework)
 (g) often loses things necessary for tasks or activities (e.g., toys, school assignments, pencils, books, or tools)
 (h) is often easily distracted by extraneous stimuli
 (i) is often forgetful in daily activities

(2)   Six (or more) of the following symptoms of hyperactivity-impulsivity have persisted for at least 6 months to a degree that is maladaptive and inconsistent with developmental level:

Hyperactivity

 (a) often fidgets with hands or feet or squirms in seat
 (b) often leaves seat in classroom or in other situations in which remaining seated is expected
 (c) often runs about or climbs excessively in situations in which it is inappropriate (in adolescents or adults may be limited to subjective feelings of restlessness)
 (d) often has difficulty playing or engaging in leisure activities quietly
 (e) is often "on the go" or acts as if "driven by a motor"
 (f) often talks excessively

Impulsivity

 (g) often blurts out answers before questions have been completed
 (h) often has difficulty waiting for a turn
 (i) often interrupts or intrudes on others (e.g., butts into conversations or games) (DSM-IV, pp. 83–84)

B. Some hyperactive-impulsive or inattentive symptoms that caused impairment were present before age 7 years.

C. Some impairment from the symptoms must be present in two or more situations (e.g., at school [or work] and at home).

D. There must be clear evidence of clinically significant impairment in social, academic, or occupational functioning.

E. The symptoms do not occur exclusively during the course of a Pervasive Developmental Disorder, Schizophrenia, or other Psychotic Disorder, and is not better accounted for by another disorder (e.g., Mood Disorder, Anxiety Disorder, Dissociative Disorder, or a Personality Disorder).

Code based on type:

 314.01 Attention-Deficit/Hyperactivity Disorder, Combined Type: If both criteria A1 and A2 are met for the past 6 months [or this subtype should be used if six (or more) symptoms of inattention and six (or more) symptoms of hyperactivity-impulsivity have persisted for at least 6 months].

 314.00 Attention-Deficit/Hyperactivity Disorder, Predominately Inattentive Type: If Criterion A1 is met but Criterion A2 is not met for the past 6 months [or this subtype should be used if six (or more) symptoms of inattention (but fewer than six symptoms of hyperactivity-impulsivity have persisted for at least 6 months].

 314.01 Attention-Deficit/Hyperactivity Disorder, Predominately Hyperactive-Impulsive Type: If Criterion A2 is met but Criterion A1 is not met for the past 6 months [or this subtype should be used if 6 (or more) symptoms of hyperactivity-impulsivity (but fewer than six symptoms of inattention) have persisted for at least 6 months].

Note. *Reprinted with permission from the* Diagnostic and Statistical Manual of Mental Disorders, Text Revision, *Copyright 2000. American Psychiatric Association.*

with ADD. ADD, as with all other disorders, is manifested by a variety of associated problems that may be categorized as mild, moderate, or severe. Several studies report that approximately 3 to 5% of the general school population is considered to have ADD (APA, 2000; Bender, 1997; DuPaul & Stoner, 1994; Lerner, Lowenthal, & Lerner, 1995; Rief, 1993). That statistic can be interpreted to mean that about 2 million students in schools across the country have attention deficits, hyperactivity, impulsiveness, and social skill problems. It averages out to about 2 or 3 students in a classroom of 30. However, other studies report an even wider estimate with a much higher upper limit for the percentage. Research statistics from Barkley (1998), Bender (1997), and Lerner et al. (1995) range anywhere from as low as 1% to as high as 23% of students.

Maag and Reid (1994) suggest that the differences in estimates of ADD prevalence rates result from using a variety of assessment tools and different populations of educators, parents, medical personnel, and other professionals when gathering data on youth and adolescents with ADD. When studies depend on gaining their information from parents' and teachers' perceptions and the family physician's possibly questionable expertise in the area of ADD, percentages of students with ADD are lower as compared with studies that are actually conducted in clinics, hospitals, or other research settings. Percentages tend to be much higher in those environments.

Why does this happen? Professionals in clinic or research settings who specialize in treating individuals with ADD are more likely to see the very subtle indicators of ADD. Additionally, students who are referred to clinics or hospitals tend to have more severe levels of ADD as compared with those students who find adequate assistance in their home schools.

Another reason for the wide range of prevalence estimates may be due to variability in assessment criteria. Professionals in schools and clinics around the country have different interpretations of the assessment criteria used for referrals and eligibility requirements for special services. Schools, clinics, or other agencies that have a lower standard or more loosely structured assessment and evaluation criteria may be reporting higher numbers of students who meet the ADD criteria and qualify for special services. Other agencies with more strict standards may have lower numbers of students who are eligible. Although there may be higher percentages of referrals in some areas and lower percentages referred in others, Guyer (2000) reports that the nationwide average of students actually diagnosed and labeled with ADD has never been higher than 3%.

Male vs. Female ADD Ratios

As with most disorders in special education, ADD occurs much more frequently in males than in females. Studies (APA, 2000; Bender, 1997; DuPaul & Stoner, 1994) report that anywhere from three to nine boys have ADD for every one girl who is diagnosed. The lower ratios of 3:1 or 5:1 are more common in community and school placements. Clinic referrals usually have higher male to female ratios of 7:1, 8:1, or 9:1 because mild or moderate cases of ADD can be managed efficiently in the school and home environment. Students with severe ADD are referred to clinics or treatment centers for more in-depth, rigorous assistance. More boys than girls tend to have severe ADD. Consequently, the clinic ratio of males to females is much higher. Rief (1993) reported that girls are more likely to have attention deficits without hyperactivity.

Causes

ADD as an Inherited Condition

Much current research documents ADD as a neurobiological disorder. This means that structures and functioning of the brain are different in individuals with ADD as compared with those who do not have

ADD symptoms (Bender, 1997; Guyer, 2000; Jordan, 1998; Lerner et al., 1995; Rief, 1993). The neurobiological basis for ADD also strongly suggests that ADD is *genetically linked*, meaning it is an inherited condition. Generational patterns or heredity are actually considered to be the primary predictor of ADD (Parker, 1992). DSM-IV-TR (APA, 2000) identifies ADD as the most common inherited childhood disorder. The link is strongest among males. It is estimated that 40% of all youth with ADD have at least one parent with the condition (Dendy, 1995). Goldstein (1991) suggests that he could identify 80% of children classified as ADD by age 4 based on parental history alone. Thus, research supports the inherited cause or genetic link for ADD transmission.

In addition to neurological disfunction, several other factors might cause attention deficits (Rief, 1993):

- Complications or trauma during pregnancy or birth may result in damage to the brain.
- A child may have been exposed to poisonous levels of lead that caused brain damage.
- ADD symptoms may be linked to a diet high in artificial flavors, colors, and preservatives, as well as food allergies.
- Severe illness, accident, or traumatic brain injury may cause ADD.

Rief (1993) went on to explain that ADD symptoms may be apparent in children who were prenatally exposed to drugs and alcohol. Scientific research does not currently support a direct link between prenatal drug exposure and ADD symptoms. However, prenatally exposed children seem to demonstrate neurological dysfunction and behavioral problems that are incredibly similar to those of children with ADD.

Twins and Adopted Children

Gilger, Pennington, and DeFries (1992) used twin studies to document heredity as a cause of ADD. Their results showed that identical (monozygotic) twins had ADD in 92% of cases studied while only 33% of fraternal (dizygotic) twins had ADD. Studies of adopted children lend more credence to the heredity theory. Silver (1992) reported that the incidence of ADD in adopted children occurred five times more often than would be expected in biological children. It is suspected that the biological parents of the adopted children probably also had ADD. The University of Minnesota Twin Studies (Goodman & Stevenson, 1989) reviewed behavioral characteristics of twins who were separated and raised in different environments for various reasons. The results showed that hyperactivity was common in identical twins even when they were reared separately. There was not a high correlation for fraternal twins. Again, the implication points to a genetic basis for ADD.

Neurobiological Research and Assessment of ADD

Several types of technology allow scientists to study brain structures and functioning, and researchers have been able to view the internal structures in the brains of individuals with ADD. Researchers are concerned with three areas of the brain as they relate to ADD (Dendy, 1995):

- First is the frontal area of the brain. Placing the hand on the forehead is an effective method to locate the frontal area of the brain, which is called the prefrontal lobe, or premotor cortex. This is the section of the brain that controls the ability to pay attention and inhibit responses.
- The second area is the limbic system, which is in the middle or central part of the brain. It includes a structure called the hippocampus, which specializes in memory abilities. The purpose of the limbic system is to influence emotion, memory, and motivation.
- The third area of the brain that relates to ADD is called the posterior area: reticular formation. This is toward the bottom and back of the brain. It controls the level of brain arousal and the ability to pay attention to important stimuli and ignore distractions.

Scientists can use technology to study the brain while it is actively functioning. They are actually able to see the brain of an individual at work. This firsthand observation also allows researchers to note changes in brain functioning that result from medication. The technology can also be applied to determine the effectiveness of medication (Lerner et al., 1995).

Positron Emission Tomography (PET) Positron emission tomography (PET) has been heralded as the leading scientific research method documenting a neurobiological basis for ADD (Zametkin et al., 1991). Scientists can use PET to show unequivocally that glucose metabolism in the brains of individuals with ADD is much slower than average. To test brain metabolism, scientists inject glucose colored with a radioactive chemical into a vein of the test subject. The PET scanner measures how much glucose the brain uses during a specific amount of time. That measurement is then compared with the metabolism rate of a control group of individuals whose brains function within normal parameters. During the years that Zametkin et al. collected data, the rate of metabolism was consistently slower in the brains of individuals with ADD. Additionally, individuals with ADD used less glucose, particularly in the right frontal area and the posteromedial orbital areas of the brain. These two regions in the brain are responsible for purposeful movement (related to hyperactivity) and impulse control.

Magnetic Resonance Imaging (MRI) Magnetic resonance imaging (MRI) allows scientists to look at the internal structures of the brain on a video screen (Lerner et al., 1995). MRI technology provides them with the ability to look at different sections of the brain to ascertain the size and location of different structures. MRIs have shown that in persons with ADD, the frontal regions of the brain are more symmetric and smaller than those of individuals without ADD.

Brain Electrical Activity Mapping (BEAM) Neuroscientists also use a procedure called brain electrical activity mapping (BEAM) to monitor brain activity. This procedure replaces electroencephalography (EEG) (Lerner et al., 1995). Computers are used to map brain waves that occur as a response to different stimuli such as sound, sight, taste, touch, and so on. Results have shown that electrical activity in the brains of individuals with ADD occurs at a different rate than in people without ADD.

All of these scientific procedures can be done to document the neurobiological basis of ADD. They can be used to remove some of the guesswork and personal bias from the assessment and diagnosis process. The advanced use of technology to diagnosis ADD is one means of determining more specific prevalence rates for ADD than was previously possible, although it is not a foolproof method.

In summary, some specific structures in certain portions of the brain look and function abnormally in individuals with ADD (Jordan, 1998). The malfunctioning in the brain is thought to be genetically linked because ADD seems to run in families. How the brain works in individuals with ADD is also different as compared with brain functioning in those who do not demonstrate ADD. Neurological metabolism of glucose (sugar), a procedure necessary for normal thought processing and motor actions, actually takes place more slowly in the brains of individuals with ADD. This slower than average glucose metabolism causes inattentiveness and impulsivity.

Neurotransmitter Deficiencies

What is the basis of the neurological problem? What is the neurological dysfunction? *Neuroscientists*, or researchers who study the brain and how it works, relate that the main problem has to do with neurochemical imbalances in the brain. Messages are carried throughout the CNS by neurotransmitters, which are minute quantities of brain chemicals that are required for transmitting cognitive messages and for motor activity. Cognition relates to the ability to think and process information. Mental processes such as memory, reasoning, comprehension, and judgment are all cognitive processes (Vergason & Anderegg, 1997).

There are actually about 50 different kinds of neurotransmitters. The three that relate to attention, mood, and motor activity are serotonin, norepinephrine, and dopamine, which specifically control attention, impulsivity, and hyperactivity (Busch, 1993). Problems occur because the brain does not produce enough of those neurotransmitters. A low supply results in a loss of stimulation to the area in the brain stem that controls attention and motor activity (Lerner et al., 1995). Stimulant medications have been used in an attempt to regulate the production of serotonin, norepinephrine, and dopamine.

Use of Medication

Up until my ADD was diagnosed, I had never done very well in school. During class I tended to be real tired and sleep a lot. I guess I thought I was lazy and stupid. Since I started taking Ritalin, I'm mostly making A's and B's. Shawn, age 16 (Dendy, 1995, p. vii)

Highly Controversial Issue

Bradley (1937) documented early positive results of using stimulant medication to deal with behaviors common to ADD. Since it was first proposed, the use of medication to "calm down" problem behavior has been a topic of controversy and debate among researchers, educators, other related professionals, and parents. More than 50 years later, it remains one of the most hotly contested and controversial issues concerning children, behavior, and education.

Joint Decision for Parents and Physicians

Rief (1993) provided suggestions to facilitate the use of medication. Parents and physicians should jointly make the decision on the use of medication to control ADD symptoms. It is not an easy decision

to make. Parents usually agonize over the advantages and disadvantages of giving their child a "drug." Educators do not diagnose ADD or prescribe medication. The teacher's job at this point is not to influence the parents in this decision. Rather, it is to provide helpful information to determine the need for or the effectiveness of the medication. The educator's role may involve observing and documenting the student's behavior, communicating with parents and physicians, and helping to make sure that if necessary, the student receives the medication from office personnel or the school nurse on schedule.

Try Environmental Modifications First

Medication should be used to manage the symptoms of ADD only after educators and parents have collaborated to provide structured and consistent environmental modifications. Environmental modifications combined with a proactive, individualized behavior modification plan can be highly effective in reducing behavior problems associated with ADD. Some students with mild to moderate symptoms may not need medication at all. A behavioral intervention plan that is consistently implemented may be all the student needs to function appropriately. Medication by itself should not be exploited as a "quick fix" for an individual's problem behavior.

Medicine Can Be Effective

Some personal anecdotes from three parents after their children with ADD began taking stimulant medications follow:

Shawn's memory has improved so much since he has been on medication. . . . He remembers to do his chores and to bring his laundry down to be washed. He never could do this before. It is like the difference between night and day.

The most amazing observation to me was the day I saw Steven sit down at a desk and study for over 3 hours. Before it would have been rare for him to study for even 15 minutes.

Lewis's grades are much improved since starting on Ritalin. No F's this semester. He even had his second A this year. Quite an achievement! (Dendy, 1995, pp. 87–88)

Some individuals absolutely require medication for the brain to function efficiently and appropriately enough to allow learning to take place. Medication often gives the student the ability to respond appropriately to environmental modifications and proactive behavior change plans. Medication does help approximately 70% of the individuals with ADD who take it consistently. It has been shown to improve attention; decrease impulsivity, hyperactivity, aggression, and noncompliance; increase academic achievement; and increase appropriate social interactions (Bender, 1997; Dendy, 2005; DuPaul & Stoner, 1994; Hinshaw, 1995).

Medications for Managing ADD Symptoms

Two main categories of medication are used to manage behavioral symptoms associated with ADD. The first category includes stimulant medications, and the second is a group known as tricyclic antidepressants (Rief, 1993).

Stimulant Medications Stimulants are the most common medication given to reduce problematic behaviors of ADD. They mainly help individuals to focus and maintain attention and to regulate motor activity levels. How do they work? To put it simply, in a person with ADD, stimulant medications correct the level of necessary neurotransmitters and regulate the use of glucose in the brain. Stimulant medications do not "calm down" the individual, as is commonly thought. They help bring neurological activity into balance so that all parts of the CNS function efficiently.

In contrast to their effectiveness for ADD symptoms, stimulant medications are not effective in treating the symptoms of learning disabilities. Some educators and other professionals automatically link LD and ADD. They consider the categories synonymous, or they assume that if a student has LD, he or she automatically has ADD (Goldstein & Goldstein, 1990). This is not true because different areas of the brain are affected by the two disorders. Students who have ADD and those who have LD both have learning difficulties, but they cannot be treated similarly because the cause of the problem differs. However, many students do have coexisting disorders of LD and ADD.

Types of Stimulants Dendy (2005) provides easy-to-follow and very detailed explanations of medications for ADD and their effectiveness. Stimulant medications such as methylphenidate (Ritalin®, Concerta®, Focalin®, Metadate®, Methylin®), dextroamphetamine (Dexedrine®, Adderall®, DextroStat®), and pemoline (Cylert®) are effective in managing symptoms of ADD because they stimulate those parts of the brain that are not functioning efficiently; specifically, they regulate the amount of neurotransmitters and the rate of glucose metabolism (Dendy, 2005; Jordan, 1998). They are all CNS stimulants which work to enable individuals with ADD to stay on task, concentrate, produce more schoolwork, behave more appropriately, and demonstrate more stable moods. Ritalin and Adderall are the two most common stimulants used (Dendy, 2005). In a side note, a new nonstimulant drug called atomoxetine (Strattera®) was released in 2003 that is effective for some individuals in controlling ADD symptoms.

Even though media suggest that Ritalin is being overprescribed and controversial, it has been effective in approximately 80% of individuals with ADD. If Ritalin does not work and trials of either Dexedrine or Cylert are used, effectiveness jumps to an incredible 90 to 95%! Despite the proliferation of nightmare accounts of drug use for ADD, the majority of individuals do respond quite well. Medical research studies document that stimulant medications are the single most effective treatment to benefit individuals who have ADD (Dendy, 2005).

Exactly why is medication effective? The stimulants each affect the brain a little differently. Stimulant medications increase the production of three neurotransmitters called dopamine, norepinephrine, and serotonin. It is necessary for these neurotransmitters to be available in the correct amounts in order for the CNS to function appropriately. The nonstimulant Strattera works in a similar fashion to balance the level of norepinephrine. The reader is directed to Jordan (1998) and Dendy (2005) for a detailed, scientific explanation of how stimulant medications act to bring about balanced and efficient neurological functioning in persons with ADD.

How Is Medication Dosage Prescribed? Medications for ADD have traditionally been prescribed based on the weight of the individual. Physicians try to get the most effect at the lowest dose to prevent side effects. However, some younger children with more severe problems may actually need higher doses than teenagers or young adults. The dosage may be based on severity of symptoms, strength of the type of medication used, and the individual's unique response to the medicine rather than body weight alone. Medication trials may be used to determine the most appropriate dosage. All medication needs to be prescribed and carefully monitored on an individualized basis.

Table 11–2 shows the typical dosage prescribed for Ritalin and Dexedrine. Dendy (2005) provided some interesting information concerning Ritalin and Dexedrine. First, some individuals may have an adverse reaction to the 5 mg tablets of Ritalin. Their behavior may become more active and agitated. Researchers tracked the problem to the yellow dye contained in the 5 mg tablets but not in the 10 or 20 mg tablets of Ritalin. The second interesting fact is that when taking the 20 mg sustained-release tablets, only 5 to 10 mg of the dose are actually released. Also, Dexedrine is considered to be twice as potent as Ritalin (Dendy, 1995).

A disadvantage of the short-acting medicine is that the individual must remember to take the dose three times a day. The benefit of the newer intermediate and long-acting medications is that the individual and his/her family have options to best meet personal needs. One major benefit is that the long-acting medicines eliminate the need for students to have to take a dose at school.

How do physicians decide which stimulant medication to prescribe? Ritalin has been the most widely prescribed and effective medicine for ADD symptoms. Current research shows that Adderall and Dexedrine are just as effective (Dendy, 2005). As stated previously, each of the three main stimulants will affect individuals and neurotransmit-

TABLE 11–2 Commonly Prescribed Stimulant Medications

Short-Acting Stimulants (Begin within 15–30 minutes and last 4–6 hours)		
Ritalin	5, 10, or 20 mg tablets	Lasts 4 hours
Methylin	5, 10, or 20 mg tablets	Lasts 4 hours
Focalin	2.5, 5, 10 mg tablets	Lasts 4–6 hours
Dexedrine	5 mg tablets	Lasts 4 hours
DextroStat	5 or 10 mg tablets	Lasts 4 hours
Intermediate-Acting Stimulants (Begin within 1 hour and last 4–8 hours)		
Ritalin SR	20 mg tablets	Lasts 4–6 hours
Dexedrine SR	5, 10, or 15 mg capsules	Lasts 6–8 hours
Adderall	5 to 30 mg tablets	Lasts 6–8 hours
Metadate ER	10 or 20 mg tablets	Lasts 6–8 hours
Long-Acting Stimulants (Begin within 1 hour and last 8–12 hours)		
Ritalin LA	20, 30, or 40 mg capsules	Lasts 8–10 hours
Methylin ER	10 or 20 mg tablets	Lasts 8 hours
Adderall XR	5–30 mg capsules	Lasts 8–10 hours
Metadate CD	20 mg capsules	Last 8 hours
Concerta	18, 27, 36, or 54 mg tablets	Last 10–12 hours

Note. From Teenagers with ADD and ADHD: A Parent's Guide (2nd edition), by C. Z. Dendy, 2005, Bethesda, MD: Woodbine House. Adapted with permission of the author.

TABLE 11–3 Neurotransmitters and Related Behaviors

Neurotransmitter	High Level	Low Level
Dopamine	Undistracted Works intensely on tasks	Inattentive Distractable, moves from one thing to another Difficulty completing job Difficulty thinking ahead Difficulty delaying response Cognitive impulsivity
Norepinephrine	Thrill seeker Seeks new activities Impulsive aggression	Indifferent Low energy; apathy Depressed Planned aggression
Serotonin	Satisfaction Sense of well-being Focus on one thing Helps with sleep	Dissatisfaction Irritability Aggression to self/others Impulsivity Obsessive compulsive Suicide risk Fire setting

Note. From Teenagers with ADD and ADHD: A Parent's Guide (2nd edition), by C. Z. Dendy, 2005, Bethesda, MD: Woodbine House. Reprinted with permission of the author.

ters in a little different way. Table 11–3 provides a summary detailing what types of behavior are associated with high or low levels of each neurotransmitter. Based on evaluation of behavioral deficits, appropriate medication is prescribed.

Antidepressant Medications Tricyclic antidepressants also increase attention, stabilize mood, and reduce levels of hyperactivity. Tricyclic antidepressants could be used in place of stimulants for two reasons. First, some individuals cannot tolerate stimulant medications. One of the main problems with giving a stimulant medication to a child with ADD is the side effect of developing motor or vocal tics. The second reason is that some persons have clinical depression in addition to ADD. They gain the benefit of improving attentiveness as well as the antidepressant effect. Tricyclic antidepressants include imipramine (Tofranil®), desipramine (Norpramin®), and amitriptyline (Elvail®).

Another less commonly used medication is catapres (Clonodine®), which is used to treat adults with high blood pressure. This medicine may be effective for individuals who were not able to be treated effectively with other more commonly used prescription drugs.

There is no substantiated research that documents why catapres seems to be effective for some individuals with ADD. It has been successful for children who have aggressive and/or hyperactive behaviors or for those with Tourette syndrome (a neurologically based tic disorder) who cannot tolerate stimulant medications because they cause an increase in tics (Rief, 1993).

Medication Side Effects

Rief (1993) reported the side effects of medication that teachers should be aware of. When keeping observational logs or checklists of behavior during medication trials, it is important to keep a record of any different or unusual behaviors noted during the school day. Side effects include loss of appetite, insomnia, stomachache, or headache. Some children may show more emotional instability, such as hypersensitivity to criticism, irritability, or mood swings, as the medication begins to wear off. This may be alleviated by adjusting the dose or the time of day when the medication is taken.

Sometimes these side effects diminish over time. If they persist, the physician should reevaluate and adjust the dose or change the medication.

Cases have been documented in which stimulant medications for ADD actually made coexisting conditions or problems worse (Palmer, 1992). If children have tic disorders, Tourette syndrome, or anxiety disorders in addition to ADD, stimulant medications may not be appropriate. A small percentage of children develop tics in response to stimulant medications. Tics are defined as involuntary muscle movements that may include sniffling, throat clearing, eye twitches, or facial grimaces. Tics are the most common symptom of Tourette syndrome (see Chapter 12).

The Educator's Role in the Medication Process

Teachers probably spend more time with a school-age child during the week than any other adults, including the child's parents. Even though they do not live with the child or prescribe medication, educators have a central role in assessing the effectiveness of medication for students in the classroom. Bender and Mathes (1995) succinctly described the responsibility of the teacher in the medication process (see Table 11–4). The teacher's responsibilities are not inordinately difficult, but they do require some extra planning, time, and effort. The time invested will pay off in the long run. The student will ultimately be able to function more independently and will require less of the teacher's time and attention.

First, educators are involved in the assessment of behavior while providing support to both student and parents throughout the process. During the assessment phase, teachers may be asked to complete some type of assessment device, such as a rating scale, a checklist, or a narrative log to document levels and types of behavior observed at school.

Second, following the assessment, the physician will make recommendations for a medical trial. Medication is most effective when used in conjunction with a proactive behavioral plan. The plan should be positively oriented and based on teaching students appropriate alternatives to problem behavior. A high

TABLE 11–4 Teacher's Responsibilities in the Medication Process

❑ Complete a behavioral assessment
❑ Plan an individualized behavior intervention program
❑ Collect data on frequency of behavior
❑ Analyze data to determine behavioral change and need for intervention plan revisions

Note. *From "Students with ADHD in the Inclusive Classroom: A Hierarchical Approach to Strategy Instruction," by W. N. Bender and M. O. Mathes,* Intervention in School and Clinic, 30, *pp. 226–234.*

rate of positive reinforcement should be used. Rhode, Jenson, and Reavis (1992) suggest that teachers incorporate at least four to six genuine positive reinforcers and social praise for every reprimand given. The teacher is primarily responsible for planning and carrying out the behavioral intervention. However, parents are an incredibly important link in the success of the plan. Whenever possible, the teacher should collaborate with the parents to plan the behavioral intervention. Parents should be encouraged to implement the behavior plan at home—after school, evenings, and on weekends and vacations. This collaborative strategy results in a more pervasive behavior intervention plan with consistent expectations and programming for the student.

The third component of the educator's responsibility in the medication process is to collect data and monitor the effectiveness of the medication trial and behavior intervention plan. Frequency recording is a quick and easy method that teachers can use to count the number of times certain behaviors occur. The teacher keeps a tally of the number of times specific behaviors occur. This can be done during short (20 to 30 minute) specified periods during the day or all day long.

Different Types of Attention Deficits

Attention Is a Multifaceted Concept

The concept of "attention" or "paying attention" is multifaceted. Students with ADD usually experience problems when they try to "pay attention." There are many ramifications to consider when attempting to develop interventions for these students. Rooney (1993) described some terms associated with attention problems. The differentiation would be helpful for educators to pinpoint what specific type of attention problem a student may be demonstrating. First, attention is divided into two categories. The first category is called *encoding*, which is defined as an attentional weakness based on the inability to process and store incoming stimuli. The second category is based on the concept of *selection*. When there is attentional weakness with selection, the individual has difficulty automatically choosing which stimuli to process and which stimuli to ignore. Each of the two categories is further broken down to pinpoint attentional weaknesses.

Encoding   Students with encoding problems may experience difficulty in a number of different areas when they try to pay attention in class. The deficit areas are described as (a) attention span, (b) focusing attention, (c) dividing attention, (d) sustaining attention, (e) using the appropriate intensity of attention, and (f) using sequential attention. A short explanation of each follows:

- *Attention span*: The length of time an individual can concentrate on a task without a break in attention.
- *Focusing attention*: The ability to ignore distracting or irrelevant stimuli and concentrate on appropriate stimuli.
- *Dividing attention*: The ability to split attention between two or more sources of incoming stimuli when necessary. Speed and accuracy of task completion are increased with mastery of this skill.
- *Sustaining attention*: The ability to maintain focus of attention through task completion. Students with ADD may not be able to sustain attention because they use so much energy trying to filter out distractions that they can't keep their attention on the task until they are finished.
- *Using the appropriate intensity of attention*: This relates to factors such as interest, motivation, and novelty. When these

elements are greater, students demonstrate an increased ability to sustain attention. They tend to do poorly on tasks that are long, routine, and boring.
- *Using sequential attention*: The ability to focus attention on the stimuli in the correct and necessary order to successfully complete a task. Following directions for a specific task in the correct order is an excellent example.

Selection   Students in the classroom are bombarded by different types of stimuli. In the typical classroom, the teacher talks and moves around; other students talk, fidget, or move around the classroom; and there are a variety of incoming sounds from the hallway and outside the windows.

Selective attention is a process that requires the individual to choose the appropriate stimuli on which to focus. As distracting noise and activities increase in the classroom, the students must choose the stimuli on which to focus and sustain attention. Then they have to choose what stimuli need to be further processed. For example, vocabulary words are often listed at the beginning of a chapter. This is a clue to students that these words are important. Students who have satisfactory selective attention skills will notice and learn the vocabulary words. Selection has important ramifications in the area of study skills and taking tests.

Selective attention has a number of component factors, including (a) involuntary attention, (b) voluntary attention, (c) filtering, and (d) response set. Each of these factors is described in more detail:

- *Involuntary attention*: An immediate attentional response that is described as an automatic response. An example is looking in the rearview mirror of the car when one is driving and hearing a siren.
- *Voluntary attention*: Attention that is both deliberate and intentional. Conscious thought is required to choose the stimuli on which the individual focuses attention. With practice this process can become more automatic on tasks that an individual repeats many times.

Examples include math computations, writing checks, or driving a car.

- *Filtering*: The process whereby an individual is able to separate irrelevant stimuli from relevant stimuli.
- *Response set*: A second process of filtering that occurs when the individual chooses to select stimuli to attend to based on the similarity to his or her preconceived notion. For example, if someone tells a child to watch for the school bus to come down the street, he must have previous knowledge of the big orange or yellow bus in order to know which vehicle to attend to of the many that might pass by. The child is actually filtering or sifting through the known set of vehicles, or the schema, in order to pay attention to the school bus. Children with ADD have difficulty with schemas. It is hard for them to filter out distractions and zero in on and use the previous knowledge they acquired.

Behavioral Characteristics of ADD

Inattention, impulsivity, hyperactivity, and social skill problems are most often listed as maladaptive behavioral patterns of ADD. According to the DSM-IV-TR (APA, 2000), the three primary characteristics of individuals with ADD are inattention, impulsivity, and hyperactivity (Lerner et al., 1995; Weyandt, 2001). However, Barkley (1993) proposed an innovative theory based on the idea of disinhibition of behavioral response. He suggested that individuals with ADD simply are not able to delay (or inhibit) behavioral responses to various stimuli from the environment. This theory is based on neurological functioning, meaning that the maladaptive behaviors and characteristics of ADD are all due to the individual's lack of ability to control behavioral responses.

Although this chapter uses the term ADD to describe the entire gamut of attention, learning, and behavioral problems associated with attention problems, researchers do note differences between inattentiveness and impulsivity with and without hyperactivity.

The DSM-IV-TR (APA, 2000) does differentiate between symptoms that are *predominantly inattentive* and *predominantly hyperactive*. Table 11–5 shows typical behaviors that might be observed in individuals with each of the three types of ADD described in the DSM-IV-TR (APA, 2000). Note the multitude of social skill difficulties. As Dr. Dale Jordan has related (Jordan, 1998), children with hyperactivity-type symptoms seem to pay attention to everything while children with inattentive type symptoms do not seem to pay attention to anything. Table 11–5 also provides some suggested interventions to assist individuals with ADD.

In most cases, whether the students have the predominantly inattentive, hyperactive, or combined type of ADD, learning how to get along with others in the school, community, and at home may be an area in need of remediation. Four program manuals, *Skillstreaming* (Goldstein & McGinnis, 1997); *The Tough Kid Social Skills Book* (Sheridan, 1994); *Bully-Proofing Your School: A Comprehensive Approach for Elementary Schools* (Garrity, Jens, Porter, Sager, & Short-Camilli, 1994); and *Bully-Proofing Your School: A Comprehensive Approach for Middle Schools* (Bonds & Stoker, 2000), provide fully prepared lessons that teachers can use for social skills instruction.

ADD Assessments

Multimethod Assessment

The social, behavioral, and academic difficulties of ADD are not a unique characteristic of attention deficit disorder. Many students without a formal diagnosis of ADD also have attention deficits, social skill problems, and impulsivity, or hyperactivity. The overt manifestations of ADD can be mirrored in other physiological, educational, behavioral, or emotional disorders such as learning disabilities, conduct disorder, substance abuse, and depression. Children with no diagnosed disorders of any type may show transient phases of

TABLE 11–5 Observable Behavior Comparison Chart

Characteristic	Predominantly Hyperactive Type	Predominantly Inattentive Type	Proactive Intervention
Decision making Problem solving	Tends to be impulsive or reactive; acts without thinking first	May appear to be lethargic; slow to react; has difficulty making a choice or choosing an option	Teach a structured choice-making procedure to help students consider options and think ahead to consequences
Personal space boundaries of others and limitations of rules or laws	Tend to be physically intrusive; verbally interrupt; rebellious; do not understand that rules apply to them	Recognize personal space boundaries; tend to be polite to others and obedient, but do not voluntarily participate in academic and social activities	Teach social skills in a consistent and structured format with many opportunities for practice and positive reinforcement
Assertiveness skills	May be overly competitive, bossy, irritating to others	Are likely to be underassertive, vulnerable to bullies, docile	Teach social skills that promote balanced assertiveness skills and skills to deal with bullies
Attention-seeking behavior from adults and peers	Often demonstrate provocative behavior that is irritating and disruptive	Tend to be more introverted; shy, quiet, possibly dependent on adult, with little voluntary participation in activities	Teach students appropriate participation skills; focus on providing consistent positive reinforcement to build on student's strengths
Acceptance by peers	May be able to make friends but seems to change often; does not seem to bond; other children quickly tire of the demanding, bossy attitude	Often has difficulty making friends; does not initiate social interactions, but can bond with others	Teach friendship-making skills

Note. *Data in the first three columns are based on* Helping Your Hyperactive ADD Child *by John F. Taylor, 1997, Rockin, CA: Prima.*

some of these behaviors at different points in their development. It is very important to conduct a thorough *multimethod assessment* to determine the presence of ADD in a particular student. A multi-method assessment is one in which several different types of valid and reliable testing materials are used, a number of different sources of information are studied, and several different informants from the child's environment participate (Weyandt, 2001).

A multimethod assessment for ADD may contain as many as eight different components. A suggested strategy from DuPaul and Stoner (cited in Weyandt, 2001) includes the following steps:

- Step 1: Screening
  The teacher screens all the students in the classroom for behaviors that might indicate the presence of ADD.

- Step 2: In-Depth Assessment
  For those students identified in the screening, further specific and focused assessment is conducted. These assessments may take the form of parent and teacher interviews, school record reviews, behavior rating scales to determine how the target student's behavior is perceived by others in the environment, a medical examination by a physician who is familiar with the symptoms of ADD, and direct observation of school behavior and academic skills. Additionally, direct assessments with the student may be conducted at this stage of the process. Direct student assessments can take the form of IQ tests, achievement tests, structured interviews, observations in multiple settings, and self-report interviews. Structured interviews with the parents can be used to obtain developmental milestones in the areas of medical, educational, social-emotional, and family history. Parents can offer information about the relative success of past treatments if there were any.

- Step 3: Analyze and Interpret Results
  All of the assessment tools must be analyzed and interpreted. The results can determine the number and presence of specific behaviors related to ADD, the age at which the behaviors became apparent, how chronic and severe the behaviors are across environments, how much the behaviors differ from the norm, and to what degree functional behavior is impaired. Other overlapping disorders can also be ruled out or included at this point.

- Step 4: Plan an Individualized Program
  The information interpreted from the multimethod assessment is used for program planning. The pertinent aspects of the treatment plan may be based on severity of symptoms, range of the student's functional behaviors, the presence of overlapping disorders, response to prior treatment, and available community-based treatment options. School programming must include both academic and behavioral objectives (Barkley, 1998; Hallahan & Kauffman, 2000).

- Step 5: Collect Data and Evaluate
  Teachers should consistently collect data to determine the effectiveness of the intervention plan. When teachers consistently collect data, students consistently achieve at higher levels. More frequent data collection is most effective in determining students' progress. The data must be reviewed to determine students' rate of progress and to decide if it is necessary to revise the program. The multimethod assessment steps are summarized in Table 11–6.

TABLE 11–6 Multimethod Assessment Process

Step 1	Screening	Teacher screens all students for potential ADD problems
Step 2	Multiple Assessments	A variety of assessments are conducted with numerous persons and the student himself
Step 3	Interpretation of Results	Severity, age of onset, chronicity of ADD problems are determined
Step 4	Treatment Plan Development	An individualized treatment plan is designed based on the unique results of the multiple assessments
Step 5	Evaluate Treatment Plan	Periodic collection of data is conducted to determine ongoing effectiveness of the treatment plan

Note. From An ADHD Primer, by L. L. Weyandt, 2001, Needham Heights, MA: Allyn & Bacon.

Medical Examination

During Step 2 of the assessment process, the purpose of the medical examination is to determine if there are any medical conditions that need to be treated. Hallahan and Kauffman (2000) report that, although rare, there are some physiological conditions that may mirror the inattentiveness and hyperactivity of ADD. Those conditions include but are not limited to brain tumors, thyroid problems, and seizure disorders. A neurologist may be involved to determine whether there is a neurobiological basis for the individual's problems. In essence, the medical examination can either establish the presence of ADD or rule it out based on other medical conditions diagnosed.

Clinical Interview

A specially trained clinician may complete an interview with the parents and the child for the purpose of gathering information about the child's physical and psychological characteristics. The clinician usually takes an ecological approach to review a wide range of functional behaviors. "Ecological" refers to relevant situations, adults, and peers in the child's entire environment. Home, school, and community perspectives would be considered.

Observational and Behavior Rating Checklists

Observational or behavior rating checklists are used to gain an observer's perception of a particular student's behavior. The observer should be a person who interacts frequently and has a relationship with the student. There are specific forms for teacher, parent, and peer rating scales. There are also checklist and rating scales for student self-reports.

Parent rating scales are used to gather information about the parents' perspective of their child's behavior. The behaviors on these scales relate to the student's behavior at home and with the family. Some typical sample behaviors from the Parent Response section of the *Jordan Executive Function Index for Children* (Jordan, 1998) are:

- Remembers what to do after school without being reminded or supervised.
- Remembers phone messages and messages from teachers to parents.
- Cleans up own room without supervision.
- Does routine chores without being reminded.

The specially devised scales for teachers focus on typical behaviors educators would observe with students. Teachers can be an excellent resource for completing observational and behavior rating checklists. They can supply information about the student in the areas of academic and social-emotional history, situations in which problems occur, duration of the problems observed, and relative success of interventions that have been tried.

Some typical sample behaviors from the Teacher Response section of the *Jordan Executive Function Index for Children* (Jordan, 1998) are:

- Tunes out or ignores what goes on nearby in order to concentrate on necessary tasks.
- Follows rules without having to be reminded multiple times.
- Notices how others respond to his or her behavior. Picks up cues as to how own behavior should be changed.

Student self-reports provide information regarding the student's own perception of his or her behavior. Sample statements from the *Behavior Rating Profile* (Brown & Hammill, 1990) are:

- My teacher often gets angry with me.
- Other students don't like to play or work with me.
- I am not interested in schoolwork.
- I can't seem to concentrate in class.

Most behavior rating scales attempt to determine how often behavior occurs by using response categories such as "Always," "Usually," "Sometimes," and "Never." Using the ecological approach and incorporating teacher, parent, and student scales can help provide a wide-range picture of the student's behavior.

The ACID Test

Jordan (1998) reported that a sawtooth pattern on the profile summary chart of the Wechsler Intelligence Scale for Children (WISC-III) may be an indication of ADD. The 12 different components of the WISC-III are based on formal academic tasks. There are 4 subtests that require ability to concentrate, sustain attention, and use memory skills in order to successfully answer the test questions. The 4 subjects include:

A = Arithmetic
C = Coding (digit symbols)
I = Information
D = Digit span

These are the 4 subtests on which students with ADD tend to do relatively poorly compared to the rest of the subtest components. Thus, Jordan calls this the ACID test (1998). A sawtooth (very up and down, widely spaced) pattern develops on the profile of the WISC-III because those 4 areas tend to be very low while the other 8 areas tend to be higher. Students with ADD-type problems tend to do poorly on the ACID subtests on which a higher level of concentration and perseverance to the task is necessary to obtain a higher score. The attention problems combined with impulsivity and hyperactivity of students with ADD make it difficult for them to successfully complete these portions of the WISC-III.

Severity Levels of ADD

The various symptomatic behaviors of ADD can be rated on a scale from mild to severe (Jordan, 1998).

The severity of the symptoms dictates what type of special services and support services (if any) the individual needs. The combination of these characteristics in an individual with severe symptoms has challenged even the most patient of parents, educators, and other professionals who work with youth and adolescents. Individuals with ADD often have lifelong problems in three main areas: (a) being able to pay attention for an age-appropriate, required amount of time; (b) completing tasks at school, at home, in the community, and in the workplace; and (c) establishing appropriate and lasting social and personal relationships.

Jordan Executive Function Index for Children

Jordan (1998) emphasizes that there are degrees of ADD behavior in students that can be rated from mild to severe. Different types of behavioral and/or medical interventions are required based on the rating of severity. For further information, the reader is directed to the rating scales Jordan (1998) has developed to accurately assess the level of ADD. The Jordan Executive Function Index for Children consists of a Parent Response Section and a Teacher Response Section. The two sections should be completed by teachers and parents separately. The sections should not be filled out collaboratively, and the scores should not be mixed. School and home are two distinctly different environments with different functional requirements. Educators and parents may observe different patterns of behavior.

Jordan Executive Function Index Components
Each section of the Jordan Executive Function Index contains three components. The first component relates to observable behavior, the second component relates to self-organization, and the third component relates to self-control skills. The Parent Response Section has questions related to parents' impression of home behavior. The Teacher Response Section has questions pertain-

ing to the teacher's impression of school-related behavior.

Each question is scored by placing a check mark to rate the child's behavior on a scale including "Never" (0 points), "Sometimes" (1 point), "Usually" (2 points), or "Always" (3 points)." All of the questions are written as positive behaviors, for example, "Tunes out (ignores) what goes on nearby in order to keep on doing necessary tasks" or "Can take part in group activities without being called back to attention over and over" (Jordan, 1998, p. 159).

Weighted scores are added for each component. For example, a check mark under the rating "Usually" counts for 2 points and a check mark under "Always" counts for 3 points. After the scores are totaled, the rater simply transfers them to the Summary of Behaviors profile page, which indicates five categories of Severe, Moderately Severe, Moderate, Mild, or No problems in the three areas of (1) behavior, (2) self-organization, and (3) self-control. Because of the positive framing of all the questions, lower scores indicate more severe ADD problems. The Summary of Behaviors page suggests general interventions for different levels of severity of the problem. This is an informal, easy-to-use assessment tool that can help parents and educators determine how severe the ADD problem is and make some initial decisions for an intervention program. A summary of characteristic behaviors for each of the three categories adapted from Jordan (1998) follows:

- **Mild ADD:** Mild symptoms of ADD may be described as more of an annoyance to the individual and to others than a serious problem. Auditory and reading comprehension may be inconsistent and unpredictable. It is better to pair written directions with verbal instructions. The individual may become restless soon after starting a task and may display a higher than average amount of body movement.

- **Moderate ADD:** The individual who has moderate symptoms of ADD needs constant supervision. The teacher, supervisor, or boss must provide frequent reminders and prompts

in order for the individual with moderate ADD to follow through and complete assigned tasks. As long as the person has this type of guidance, he usually will be successful in completing responsibilities. Classroom achievement, workplace performance, social skills, and personal relationships will continue to be a lifelong problem. Individuals with ADD tend to think impulsively and emotionally rather than logically. A person with moderate ADD may acquire a reputation for being difficult to work with or to get along with.

- **Severe ADD:** Persons with severe ADD face lifelong challenges in the areas of academic achievement, workplace adjustment, and social relationships. They often show behaviors that make them very difficult for the average person to deal with at school, in the workplace, and in the community, as well as to live with at home. The thinking and behavioral problems they demonstrate result in their being hypersensitive and hard to get along with, undependable, and irresponsible. They may become outcasts. They may not be accepted by society in general because their behavior can be aggressive, self-centered, and immature. They do not seem to learn from past mistakes or be able to take advice from others.

Differences Between ADD/ADHD

Jordan (1998) does differentiate between ADD and ADHD. For the purposes of this section, the two abbreviations are used and explained in terms of observable behavior. Students who have ADD (attention deficit without hyperactivity) may be dreamers and tend to be more withdrawn, underactive, and rather shy with peers. In contrast, those with ADHD (attention deficits and hyperactivity) usually act in a manner that is more disruptive, show task completion difficulties, and display more acting-out and impulsive behavior such as calling out in class or not being able to wait or take turns (Lerner et al., 1995).

Jordan (1998) has a unique description to differentiate ADD from ADHD. He states that students with ADD have problems learning because they do not pay attention to anything. They drift along through life in a dreamworld of their own making. In contrast, students with ADHD have problems learning because they pay attention to everything. They are highly distractable. Any noise, any movement, any other person in the environment can grab this student's attention and take it away from the teacher's directions or the task he should be completing. In effect, there is always competition for the teacher to engage and keep the attention of the student with ADHD.

Jordan does note one interesting common characteristic of the two groups. He suggests that students with ADD and ADHD want to learn; they intend to pay attention. The problem is that they initially "plug in" to the activity or the speaker; however, through no fault of their own, all the "plugs keep falling out." The experience of all the "mental plugs falling out" can be used to explain the irregular patterns of testing results and academic achievement for individuals with ADD.

Jordan (1998) and Rief (1993) presented a list of behavioral characteristics that differentiate attention

TABLE 11–7 Behavioral Characteristics of Attention Deficit Disorder Without Hyperactivity (ADD)

- Quiet, drifting, daydreamers
- Passive, quietly confused
- Easily distracted by extraneous stimuli
- Slow to process information
- Difficulty listening and following directions
- Difficulty focusing and sustaining attention
- Inconsistent performance in schoolwork
- Tunes out, may appear "spacey," forgetful
- Disorganized (loses or can't find belongings); desk at school and room at home is a disaster area
- Poor study skills, often late
- Difficulty working independently
- Easily bored
- May also be depressed

TABLE 11–8 Behavioral Characteristics of Attention Deficit Disorder with Hyperactivity (ADHD)

- High activity level
- Appears to be in constant motion
  - Highly emotional and sensitive
  - Insatiable, hard to satisfy, claim unfairness
  - Roams around classroom; great difficulty staying in seat
  - Aggression, impulsivity, and lack of self-control
  - Blurts out verbally, often inappropriately
  - Can't wait for his/her turn
  - Poor listener, often interrupts or intrudes on others
  - Easily bored, doesn't finish tasks
  - Noisy, often talks excessively
  - Gets in trouble because he/she can't "stop and think" before acting (responds first/thinks later)
  - Often engages in physically dangerous activities without considering the consequences (for example, jumping from heights, riding bike into street without looking); hence a high frequency of injuries
- Difficulty with transitions/changing activities
- Aggressive behavior/easily overstimulated
- Socially immature
- Low self-esteem and high frustration

deficits with and without hyperactivity. The characteristics are presented in Tables 11–7 and 11–8.

ADD, Residual Type

Researchers disagree as to whether ADD is outgrown. Jordan (1998) reported that the third edition of the *Diagnostic and Statistical Manual of Mental Disorders* (DSM-III, APA, 1980) included a subtype of attention deficit disorder under the code 314.80, Attention Deficit Disorder, Residual Type. This category has not been represented in subsequent revisions of the manual. It was eliminated in the DSM-III-R edition published in 1987. Three possible diagnostic protocols were provided in the DSM-III:

1. The individual once met the criteria for Attention Deficit Disorder with Hyperactivity.
2. Signs of hyperactivity are no longer present, but signs of the illness have

persisted to the present without periods of remission, as evidenced by both signs of attention deficits and impulsivity (e.g., difficulty organizing work and completing tasks, difficulty concentrating, being easily distracted, making sudden decisions without thought of consequences).

3. The symptoms of inattention and impulsivity result in some impairment of social or occupational functioning. (Jordan, 1998, p. 36)

Current researchers estimate that 70 to 80% of individuals with ADD do outgrow their symptoms (Barkley, 1995; Jordan, 1998). On an encouraging note, Jordan (1998) reports that children with mild to moderate ADD who do outgrow their symptoms can go on to become independent, well-educated, well-adjusted, and productive adults. Persons who do not outgrow ADD can continue to take medication to control the problematic symptoms, use behavioral coping strategies, and grow up to be very well adjusted and successful in life. Often, individuals with ADD do well in occupations that provide a high level of supervised direction and allow a lot of freedom for activity and movement.

Associated Behavior Problems with ADD

Individuals with ADD often have other types of complicating problems. ADD does not seem to exist very often in isolation. Approximately 50% or more of children with ADD also have other types of learning and behavioral problems. Researchers indicate that anywhere from 44 to 65% of students with ADD also have conduct disorder, oppositional defiant disorder, learning disabilities, significant levels of aggression, and other overt problem behaviors (Barkley, DuPaul, & McMurray, 1990; Dendy, 2005; DuPaul & Stoner, 1994; Fletcher, Shaywitz, & Shaywitz, 1994; Guyer, 2000; Weyandt, 2001).

When ADD is a primary condition, learning disabilities seem to be a very common coexisting disorder. Specifically, Fletcher et al. (1994) report a coexisting rate of 15% for ADD and LD. Furthermore, Barkley et al. (1990) indicate 19 to 26%, Silver (1998) states 30 to 50%, and McKinney, Montague, and Hocutt (1993) count up to a whopping rate of 63% overlap between ADD and LD. The wide range in percentages is due to individual interpretation of the criteria and assessment methods for the diagnosis of ADD and LD in schools and clinics across the country.

When looking at LD as a primary area of need, a high percentage of students have coexisting ADD. Students with diagnosed learning disabilities are seven times more likely than the average child to also have ADD (DuPaul & Stoner, 1994). Silver (1998) reported that 20% of students with LD also have ADD.

Another condition related to behavior that appears to have a high correlation with ADD is oppositional defiant disorder (ODD). The DSM-IV-TR (APA, 2000) describes ODD as "a recurrent pattern of negativistic, defiant, disobedient, and hostile behavior toward authority figures that persists for at least 6 months" (p. 100). DuPaul and Stoner (1994) suggest that it is the most common disorder occurring with ADD. More than half (65%) of children with ADD are reported to have ODD. Another excessive behavior problem, verbal and physical aggression, is a complicating factor for 40% of students with ADD (Barkley et al., 1990).

McKinney et al. (1993) report that children with ADD tend to be so aggressive that they are rejected by other children more often than children without ADD. As many as 65% of children with ADD also have conduct disorder (CD) (Jordan, 1998; Weyandt, 2001). The DSM-IV-TR (APA, 2000) describes conduct disorder as "a repetitive and persistent pattern of behavior in which the basic rights of others or major age-appropriate societal norms or rules are violated" (p. 98).

The criteria include such problems as (a) aggression to people and animals, (b) property destruction,

(c) deceitfulness or theft, and (d) serious rule and curfew violations. CD is a potentially much more serious problem than ODD even though some of the symptoms may appear the same. When ADD and CD coexist, it might be difficult to separate the two. One differentiating factor is the voluntary aggression, hostility, and anti-social behavior commonly apparent in CD. In contrast, the person with only ADD tends to be more "accidentally rude and intrusive" (Jordan, 1998, p. 103).

Food Allergies and Nutritional Therapy

Inattention, hyperactivity, and other symptoms of ADD may be linked to the individual's diet and allergic reactions to food or other elements of the environment. Researchers are divided on opinions that food or allergies actually trigger ADD behavior (Feingold, 1975; Friedman & Doyle, 1992; McGee, Stanton, & Sear, 1993; Rapp, 1986). In the past it was often thought that hyperactive children simply needed more discipline, that they needed to "learn a lesson." One medical researcher (Rapp, 1986) reports that children with behavioral problems may simply be hypersensitive to certain elements of the environment. If so, all the best laid and consistent disciplinary plans in the world will not have a positive effect on this physiological problem.

List of Allergens Is Extensive

What are some possible allergens? The list is almost endless, but it may include various foods and drinks; artificial colorings, additives, and preservatives; dust, molds, and pollen; pets or animals; and other environmental chemicals. Dr. Lendon Smith (Rapp, 1986) relates the following about children with hyperactivity and sensitivity or allergies to food and/or the environment:

They notice everything and must respond to each stimulus. Telling them to "Stop it" is like telling the ocean to stop roaring. If children only hear negatives while they are growing up, they are more likely to develop a poor self-image.... Seventy-five percent of prisoners in our jails were hyperactive children; seventy-five percent of them were battered children. I think I know why some of them were battered. They were rude, mouthy, did not mind, and could not sleep. (p. xii)

It appears that allergies to food and other environmental substances may cause some major behavioral and social interaction difficulties. It is important for educators, other professionals, and parents to recognize allergy symptoms to ensure that they are not punishing behavior that children cannot voluntarily control. Children with ADD may have allergies that exacerbate their condition. In addition, children with allergies alone may demonstrate behavior that makes them look as if they have ADD. How can you recognize symptoms of allergies?

Physiological Signs

Certain facial clues may show that a child is allergic to something she inhaled or ingested. Rapp (1986) states that red earlobes; red, rougelike cheek patches; dark blue, black, or red under-eye circles; wrinkles below the eyes; and nose wrinkles from rubbing nose upward are signs to watch for. The gesture children make as they rub their itchy noses up with one hand has been called the "allergy salute" (personal communication, 1995, Angie Jeter, mother of Emma, who has dairy and wheat allergies).

Children who have the facial characteristics just mentioned might also demonstrate some of the following behaviors (Rapp, 1986). They might appear sleepy, tired, or "spacey" and be unable to concentrate or focus on a task or activity through completion. Some might be fidgety and unable to sit still. Some children show symptoms of depression.

Other physical symptoms include headaches; coughing or wheezing; stuffy nose with lots of throat clearing; itchy, watery eyes; itchy skin rashes; gastrointestinal problems; excessive thirst; and generally "not feeling well." Table 11–9 lists foods that might cause allergic reactions. Sugar alone is not thought to be a culprit (Conners, Caldwell, & Caldwell, 1985; Jordan, 1998; Rapoport, 1982/83; Wolraich et al., 1994). The problem is that sugar is often found in foods that also contain artificial colors, flavors, preservatives, and caffeine. The list contains many foods that kids like. It is easy to see why it would be difficult and frustrating to keep a child with an allergy well-fed and happy.

The Feingold Diet

Jordan (1998) summarized the research findings of Dr. Ben Feingold, who wrote *Why Your Child Is Hyperactive* in 1975. Feingold reported astonishing results of positive behavior change using nutrition therapy for children with ADD. His findings were based on clinical experience using a special, rather stringent food diet rather than empirical research (Guyer, 2000). Unfortunately, no other scientist has been able to replicate Feingold's advantageous effects

TABLE 11–9 Substances That Might Cause Allergic Reactions

Artificial colors
Artificial flavors
Preservatives
    Sweet colored beverages
    Candy
    Cereal
    Corn or popcorn products
Chocolate
Peanut butter
Tomato products (including pizza)
Dairy products
Baked goods
Raisins
Fruits
Apple, grape, or orange juice

Note. *Summarized from* Attention Deficit Disorder: ADD and ADHD Syndromes *by D. R. Jordan, 1998, Austin, TX: Pro-Ed.*

(Barkley, 1995; Friedman & Doyle, 1992; Green & Chee, 1994) so there are no other research data to support his claims. Additionally, the federal government sponsored multiple major research projects to try to either substantiate or counter Feingold's claims. All of the results were synthesized to conclude that there was a small subset (possibly 1%) of children who would respond favorably to Feingold's diet (*Defined Diets and Childhood Hyperactivity*, 1982). Conclusions stated that the diet would not have a positive effect on the vast majority of children with hyperactivity (Guyer, 2000). However, it is still good to know what substances Feingold identified that might be causing problems for children with ADD.

Eliminate Natural Salicylates Feingold advocated the elimination of two types of food groups to reduce ADD symptoms. Group 1 consisted of foods that contained naturally occurring salicylic acid, which is a certain type of plant chemical. He hypothesized that eating foods or drinking beverages containing salicylic acid could trigger hyperactive and disruptive behavior. Table 11–10 lists common fruits, vegetables, and foods that contain salicylic acid.

Eliminate Food with Artificial Chemicals The Group 2 foods in the Feingold study contained artificial chemical additives, preservatives, and colorings. Some of the chemical additives in prepared foods include sorbates, sulfites, benzoates, nitrates, nitrites, antioxidants, and propionates. To keep up with this diet, the food shopper would have to memorize the names of the chemicals in question and become a food-label-reading detective. Table 11–11 lists some common foods that contain artificial colors, preservatives, and flavorings.

Feingold Diet Was Unrealistic Think about trying to implement this diet at home with a family! It would probably be a very healthy diet, even if it were done only part of the time. The problem is that the list of forbidden foods is almost endless. A family trying to consistently follow the Feingold diet would practically have to buy basic, organic

TABLE 11–10 Fruits, Vegetables, and Other Foods That Contain Salicylates

Apples (cider or cider vinegars)
Apricots
Blackberries
Strawberries
Oranges
Cherries
Raspberries
Gooseberries
Peaches
Nectarines
Prunes, Plums, Grapes, Raisins, Currants
Any product with grape extract
 Grape juice
 Wine and wine vinegars
 Sweeteners
 Flavors
 Coloring agents
Almonds
Cloves
Mint flavor, oil of wintergreen
Tea (all varieties)
Tomatoes and tomato products (tomato sauce, ketchup, pizza sauce)
Cucumbers and pickles
Bell peppers

Note. *Summarized from* Attention Deficit Disorder: ADD and ADHD Syndromes *by D. R. Jordan, 1998, Austin, TX: Pro-Ed.*

TABLE 11–11 Representative List of Foods That Contain Artificial Flavors, Colors, and Preservatives

Bacon/sausage/hot dogs
Lunch meat
Ice cream
Margarine/butter/shortening
Vitamins/cough drops/syrup
Mustard/ketchup/mayo/tartar sauce
Cereal
Soft drinks (diet and regular)
Cake/cookie/brownie/muffin mixes
Any other dessert mixes
Bakery goods
Pudding/jello/yogurt
Chocolate syrup/chocolate powder
Candy
Instant beverage drinks (Tang/other fruit drinks)
Frozen fish
Chips/crackers/snacks

Note. *Summarized from* Attention Deficit Disorder: ADD and ADHD Syndromes *by D. R. Jordan, 1998, Austin, TX: Pro-Ed.*

ingredients and make everything from scratch. There probably would be no convenience foods, no fast foods, no bakery treats, no candy, no pizza (can you even imagine!?!), and no ice cream and cake at birthday parties. And then what do you do when you go on vacation, visit relatives, or your children go to their friends' homes for sleepovers? Based on the research, this probably is a very healthy diet that would help children with ADD, but the difficulties for parents in trying to implement the diet may cause more stress, frustration, and unhappiness in the family than it is worth.

Proactive Behavior Management Strategies

Academically, school wasn't challenging. I didn't get any gratification out of the academics. I always felt I could do the work. The work was always easy but I couldn't concentrate. I'd get attention from [doing] academics but everyone got the same attention. But I could get limitless attention if I misbehaved. I always had good intentions. I always wanted attention but I hated bad attention. But it was the only attention I could get.

You forget things when you have ADD. So you forget to take your medicine, which is supposed to help you remember things. Dang, if I could just remember to take my medicine I would be fine. When I was younger, people would say "Why? Why? Why?" And now I know why I had problems in school. But I still can't remember to take my medicine. Robert, age 18 (Dendy, 1995, p. vii)

When planning behavior management, disciplinary, and reward strategies for students with ADD, it is important to differentiate between *not being able to remember* and *choosing not to be responsible.* Parents and teachers must be able to determine which is which. When the determination is made that the student just cannot remember, the adults can think of ways to supply prompts, hints, and reminders for that individual. When the student does respond to the prompt, positive reinforcement should be given.

Confront Inappropriate Behavior

If the student is choosing not to be responsible, the adult should confront that particular problem behavior. It might be helpful to try to learn why the student is behaving in a particular, unacceptable way. There may be a simple solution to the problem if the student is willing to discuss it. The teacher or parent can supply a positive redirection when the student is not making an independent choice to be responsible; meaning the student is told how to do the behavior and is verbally prompted to do it. Compliance should be rewarded. If the student continues to choose not to be responsible and the adult cannot determine why, there may be a need to effect a mild punishment such as cost response, timeout, limiting an activity at home such as computer or TV time, or setting an early bedtime. It is more important to try to teach and promote the responsible behavior than it is to punish the problem behavior.

Implications for Working with Youth and Adolescents

If one person would have interceded on my behalf. If one person would have said, 'This is not a stupid person we are dealing with. . . . There is something more involved here that we need to get to the bottom of,' the weight of the world would have been lifted from my shoulders. Joe, age 41, just diagnosed with ADD and LD (Rief, 1993, p. 11)

Early Intervention

ADD is not a condition that can be cured, and for many it will not be outgrown. Unfortunately, there is a strong link between ADD and failure throughout the lifespan (Rief, 1993). A major goal for parents and educators of students with ADD is to identify them early and teach coping strategies. Recognize behavioral and academic strengths in addition to areas of need. Build on

their strengths and teach alternatives or new skills for deficit areas. Teach students systems and strategies to get organized and complete tasks. This format may help reduce and eliminate the failure cycle in which many individuals with ADD find themselves trapped.

There are certain classroom and home management and organization techniques that teachers and parents can use to help students with ADD to be more successful. The classroom and the home environment should be both structured and predictable but also flexible enough to meet the needs of individual students. Parents and teachers should collaborate to provide a structured and consistent set of expectations regarding school and home behavior, academic achievement, and management methods. The system should be basically positive and proactive. This means that realistically high expectations will be set for the student's behavior and achievement. Positive consequences will be established for the student to earn contingent upon demonstrating the required behaviors both academically and behaviorally.

Parent/Teacher Communication

Consistent communication between parents and teachers can be established using a "home note" system (Jenson, Rhode, & Reavis, 1994). Home notes are a quick and easy form of communication with a three-part responsibility for successful use. First, the teacher is responsible for completing the note on a daily or weekly basis. Second, the student is responsible for delivering the note to parents and then back to the teacher. Third, the parents are responsible for reading the note and following up on agreed-upon responsibilities based on the note's content.

The information in this chapter included a number of proactive management procedures that parents and educators can use with students with ADD (Jensen & Yerington, 1997; Rief, 1993); these are summarized in Table 11–12.

TABLE 11–12 Proactive Management Procedures for the Classroom

- Provide clear expectations for academic work and appropriate behavior
- Provide a predictable schedule and routine with needed flexibility
- Provide four to six praise statements for each reprimand (Rhode, Jenson, & Reavis, 1992)
- Be sensitive to students' fragile egos and self-esteem. Avoid ridicule, sarcasm, and comments or practices that might embarrass or humiliate
- Be proactive; reduce the chances for problems to occur with analytic, preventive management methods
- Provide consistent consequences that are fair and respectful to students
- Demonstrate understanding, empathy, flexibility, and patience with students' problems
- Plan ahead to create tasks that set students up for success with academic achievement and appropriate behavior
- Teach organization and study skills
- Work to make homework a manageable and positive experience
- Demonstrate caring behavior and genuine human respect for students

References

Achenbach, T. M. (1986). *Manual for the Child Behavior Checklist—Direct Observation Forum.* Burlington–University of Vermont, Department of Psychiatry.

Achenbach, T. M., & Edelbrock, C. (1983). *Manual for the Child Behavior Checklist and Revised Child Behavior Profile.* Burlington–University of Vermont, Department of Psychiatry.

American Psychiatric Association. (1968). *Diagnostic and statistical manual of mental disorders* (2nd ed.). Washington, DC: Author.

American Psychiatric Association. (1980). *Diagnostic and statistical manual of mental disorders* (3rd ed.). Washington, DC: Author.

American Psychiatric Association. (1987). *Diagnostic and statistical manual of mental disorders* (3rd ed., revised). Washington, DC: Author.

American Psychiatric Association. (1994). *Diagnostic and statistical manual of mental disorders* (4th ed.). Washington, DC: Author.

American Psychiatric Association. (2000). *Diagnostic and statistical manual of mental disorders* (4th ed., text revision). Washington, DC: Author.

Atkins, M. S., Pelham, W. E., & Licht, M. H. (1985). A comparison of objective classroom measures and teacher ratings of attention deficit disorder. *Journal of Abnormal Child Psychology, 13*(1), 155–167.

Barkley, R. A. (1990). *Attention deficit hyperactivity disorder: A handbook for diagnosis and treatment.* New York: Guilford Press.

Barkley, R. A. (1993). A new theory of ADHD. *The ADHD Report, 1*(5), 1–4.

Barkley, R. A. (1995). *Taking charge of ADHD: The complete, authoritative guide for parents.* New York: Guilford Press.

Barkley, R. A. (1998). *Attention deficit hyperactivity disorder: A handbook for diagnosis and treatment* (2nd ed.). New York: Guilford Press.

Barkley, R. A., DuPaul, G. J., & McMurray, M. B. (1990). Comprehensive evaluation of attention deficit disorder with and without hyperactivity as defined by research criteria. *Journal of Consulting and Clinical Psychology, 58,* 775–789.

Bender, W. N. (1997). *Understanding ADHD: A practical guide for teachers and parents.* Upper Saddle River, NJ: Merrill/Prentice Hall.

Bender, W. N., & Mathes, M. O. (1995). Students with ADHD in the inclusive classroom: A hierarchical approach to strategy instruction. *Intervention in School and Clinic, 30,* 226–234.

Bonds, M., & Stoker, S. (2000). *Bully-proofing your school: A comprehensive approach for middle schools.* Longmont, CO: Sopris West.

Bradley, W. (1937). The behavior of children receiving benzedrine. *American Journal of Psychiatry, 94,* 577–585.

Brown, L. L., & Hammill, D. D. (1990). *Behavior rating profile: An ecological approach to behavioral assessment.* Austin, TX: Pro-Ed.

Busch, B. (1993). Attention deficits: Current concepts, controversies, management, and approaches to classroom instruction, *Annals of Dyslexia, 43,* 5–25.

Conners, C. K. (1969). A teacher rating scale for use in drug studies with children. *American Journal of Psychiatry, 126,* 884–888.

Conners, C. K., Caldwell, J. A., & Caldwell, J. L. (1985). Effects of breakfast and sweetener on the cognitive performance of children. *Psychophysiology, 22,* 573.

Costello, A. J., Edelbrock, C. S., Kalas, R., Kessler, M., & Klaric, S. (1982). *The* NIMH *Diagnostic Interview Schedule for Children* (DISC). Pittsburgh, PA: Authors.

Defined Diets and Childhood Hyperactivity. (1982). Bethesda, MD: National Institutes of Health Consensus Development Conference Summary, Vol. 4, No. 3.

Dendy, C. Z. (1995). *Teenagers with ADD: A parent's guide.* Bethesda, MD: Woodbine House.

Dendy, C. Z. (2005). *Teenagers with* ADD *and* ADHD: *A Parent's Guide* (2nd ed.). Bethesda, MD: Woodbine House.

DuPaul, G. J., & Barkley, R. B. (1992). Situational variation of attention problems: Psychometric properties of the revised Home and School Situations Questionnaires. *Journal of Clinical Child Psychology*, 21(2) 178–188.

DuPaul, G. J., & Stoner, G. (1994). ADHD *in the schools*: Assessment and intervention strategies. New York: Guilford Press.

Edelbrock, C. S., & Achenbach, T. M. (1984). The teacher version of the Child Behavior Profile: Boys aged 6–11. *Journal of Consulting and Clinical Psychology*, 52, 207–217.

Feingold, B. F. (1975). *Why your child is hyperactive.* New York: Random House.

Fletcher, J. M., Shaywitz, B. A., Shaywitz, S. E. (1994). Attention as a process and a disorder. In G. R. Lyon (Ed.), *Frames of reference for the assessment of learning disabilities: New views on measurement issues.* Baltimore: Paul H. Brookes.

Friedman, R. J., & Doyle, G. T. (1992). *Management of children and adolescents with attention deficit-hyperactivity disorder.* Austin, TX: Pro-Ed.

Garrity, C., Jens, K., Porter, W., Sager, N., & Short-Camilli, C. (1994). *Bully-proofing your school: A comprehensive approach for elementary schools.* Longmont, CO: Sopris West.

Gilger, J., Pennington, B., & DeFries, J. (1992). A twin study of the etiology of comorbidity: Attention deficit hyperactivity disorder and dyslexia. *Journal of the American Academy of Child and Adolescent Psychiatry*, 31, 343–348.

Goldstein, A. P., & McGinnis, E. (1997). *Skillstreaming.* Champaign, IL: Research Press.

Goldstein, S. (1991, January). Young children at risk: The early signs of attention deficit hyperactivity disorder. CHADDer BOX, pp. 3–4.

Goldstein, S., & Goldstein, M. (1990). *Managing attention disorders in children.* New York: Wiley.

Goodman, R., & Stevenson, J. (1989). A twin study of hyperactivity: II. The etiological role of genes, family relationships, and perinatal adversity. *Journal of Child Psychology and Psychiatry*, 30, 691–709.

Green, C., & Chee, K. (1994). *Understanding* ADD: *Attention deficit disorder.* New York: Doubleday.

Guyer, B. P. (2000). ADHD: *Achieving success in school and life.* Needham Heights, MA: Allyn & Bacon.

Hallahan, D. P., & Kauffman, J. M. (2000). *Exceptional learners: Introduction to special education* (8th ed.). Needham Heights, MA: Allyn & Bacon.

Heward, W. L. (2000). *Exceptional children: An introduction to special education* (6th ed.).Upper Saddle River: Merrill/ Prentice Hall.

Hinshaw, S. (1995). An interview with Steven Hinshaw. Attention! 1(4), 9.

Hyman, I. A. (1997). *School discipline and school violence.* Needham Heights, MA: Allyn & Bacon.

Jensen, M. M., & Yerington, P. C., (1997). *Gangs. Straight talk, straight up.* Longmont, CO: Sopris West.

Jenson, W. R., Rhode, G., & Reavis, H. K. (1994). *The tough kid tool box.* Longmont, CO: Sopris West.

Jordan, D. R. (1998). *Attention deficit disorder:* ADD *and* ADHD *syndromes.* Austin, TX: Pro-Ed.

Lerner, J. W., Lowenthal, B., & Lerner, S. R. (1995). *Attention deficit disorders: Assessment and teaching.* Pacific Grove, CA: Brooks/Cole.

Maag, J, W., & Reid, R. (1994). Attention deficit hyperactivity disorder: A functional approach to assessment and treatment. *Behavioral Disorders*, 20(1), 5–23.

McCarney, S. B. (1989). *Attention Deficit Disorder Evaluation Scale* (ADDES). Columbia, MO: Hawthorne Educational Services.

McGee, R., Stanton, W. R., & Sears, M. R. (1993). Allergic disorders and attention deficit disorder in children. *Journal of Abnormal Psychology*, 21, 79–88.

McKinney, J. D., Montague, M., & Hocutt, A. M. (1993). Educational assessment of students with attention deficit disorder. *Exceptional Children*, 60(2), 125–131.

Palmer, O. (1992). Medical treatments and professionals (pp. 53–70). In T. Haerle (Ed.), *Children with Tourette syndrome: A parent's guide.* Rockville, MD: Woodbine House.

Parker, H. C. (1992). *The* ADD *hyperactivity book for schools.* Plantation, FL: Impact.

Quay, H. C., & Peterson, D. R. (1987). *Manual for the Revised Behavior Problem Checklist.* Unpublished manuscript. University of Miami: Coral Gables, FL.

Rapoport, J. (1982/1983). Effects of dietary substances in children. *Journal of Psychiatric Research*, 17, 187–191.

Rapp, D. J. (1986). *The impossible child at school and at home: A guide for caring teachers and parents*. Buffalo, NY: Practical Allergy Research Foundation.

Rhode, G., Jenson, W. R., & Reavis, H. K. (1992). *The tough kid book*. Longmont, CO: Sopris West.

Rief, S. F. (1993). *How to reach and teach ADD/ADHD children*. New York: The Center for Applied Research in Education.

Rooney, K. J. (1993). Classroom interventions for students with attention deficit disorders. *Focus on Exceptional Children*, 26(4), 1–16.

Shaywitz, S. E., Schnell, C., Shaywitz, B. A., & Towle, V. R. (1986). Yale Children's Inventory (YCI): An instrument to assess children with attention deficits and learning disabilities: Scale development and psychometric properties. *Journal of Abnormal Child Psychology*, 14, 347–364.

Sheridan, S. M. (1995). *The tough kid social skills book*. Longmont, CO: Sopris West.

Silver, L. B. (1992). *The misunderstood child: A guide for parents of children with learning disabilities*. Blue Ridge Summit, PA: Tab Books.

Silver, L. B. (1998). *The misunderstood child* (3rd ed.). New York: Times Books.

Turnbull, R., Turnbull, A., Shank, M., & Smith, S. J. (2004). *Exceptional lives: Special education in today's schools* (4th ed.). Upper Saddle River, NJ: Merrill/ Prentice Hall.

U.S. Department of Education. (1991, September 16). Clarification of policy to address the needs of children with attention deficit disorders within the general and/or special education. Memorandum.

Vergason, G. A., & Anderegg, M. L. (1997). *Dictionary of special education and rehabilitation* (4th ed.). Denver, CO: Love Publishing.

Walker, H. M., Colvin, G., & Ramsey, E. (1995). *Antisocial behavior in schools: Strategies and best practices*. Pacific Grove, CA: Brooks/Cole Publishing.

Weyandt, L. L. (2001). *An ADHD primer*. Boston: Allyn & Bacon.

Wolraich, M., Lingren, S., Stumbo, P., Stegink, L., Applebaum, M., & Kiritsky, M. (1994). Effects of diets high in sucrose or aspartame on the behavior and cognitive performance of children. *New England Journal of Medicine*, 330(5), 301–306.

Zametkin, A. J. (1991). The neurobiology of attention deficit hyperactivity disorder. CHADDER BOX, 5(1), 10–11.

Zametkin, A. J., Nordahl, T. E., Gross, M., King, A. C., Semple, W. E., Rumsey, J., et al. (1990, November 15). Cerebral glucose metabolism of adults with hyperactivity of childhood onset. *New England Journal of Medicine*, 323, 1361–1364.

12

TOURETTE SYNDROME

After completing the chapter, the reader will be able to identify:

- The definition of Tourette syndrome.
- Services provided by the Tourette Syndrome Association.
- Prevalence and characteristics of Tourette syndrome.
- Related conditions that overlap with Tourette syndrome.
- Medication and other intervention strategies for Tourette syndrome.
- Behavior management and classroom strategies for Tourette syndrome.
- Implications for educators, parents, and other professionals who work with youth and adolescents.

Introduction

In my second year of high school, I was sitting in a class where my seat was in the back. I could hear all of my classmates, including a girl who had been my friend, laughing. I wondered what they were laughing at. Suddenly I realized that I was blinking my eyes and twitching my mouth over and over, and I could not stop. I knew that this was what they were laughing at and I tried to cover my face with my hair. I cut that class the next day. I continued to cut school a lot that semester, each day hoping that the terrible twitching would stop, but it never did. Then my father began to hassle me at home, telling me I was "doing that" again and nagging me to stop. So I had to avoid being seen by my father, and all of my friends began to subtly avoid me. (Smith, 1987, p. 1)

Tourette syndrome (TS) is a neurological disorder of unknown cause (Bruun, Cohen, & Leckman, 2001). Although TS is not formally recognized as an emotional or behavioral disorder, the disorder is included in this text for two reasons. First, TS can potentially cause numerous and varied frustrating problems at school, at home, and in the community for the individuals who have it. Second, in many cases the initial symptoms of TS go unrecognized as being an involuntary, neurological disorder. Educators, parents, and community members often punish individuals for demonstrating the tics because they are seen as being willful, disruptive, and annoying. The goal of this chapter is to provide a foundation that will assist educators, parents, and other professionals who work with youth and adolescents to more readily recognize TS symptoms in order to provide early intervention services, including the most appropriate educational programming, medical treatment when necessary, and other required social services.

This chapter provides the reader with information concerning the typical observable symptoms of TS. Background information on the cause and prevalence of TS along with descriptions of tics are discussed. Examples of both simple and complex motor and vocal tics are provided. The method used to diagnose TS is presented along with a convenient checklist that educators and parents can use to keep track of possible symptoms. The overlap between TS and other disorders such as ADD and obsessive-compulsive disorder (OCD) is discussed. At this time, there is no cure for TS. A variety of intervention strategies, including medical, psychological, and behavioral, are provided. Finally, implications for educators, parents, and other professionals who work with youth and adolescents conclude the chapter.

History of Tourette Syndrome

Tourette syndrome was first reported in the medical literature in 1885 by a physician named Gilles de la Tourette (Hearle, 1992; U.S. Dept. of Health and Human Services, 1995). Dr. Tourette, a French neurologist, had an 86-year-old patient, the Marquise de Dampierre, who demonstrated multiple involuntary tics, both motor and vocal. The most common symptoms of TS are various motor and vocal tics. Tics range from mild to moderate to severe. Diagnosis is made primarily through observation of the variety and duration of the tics.

The Tourette Syndrome Association (TSA)

Much of the information in this chapter comes from the Tourette Syndrome Association (TSA). Additionally, a number of researchers have written books, guides, website papers, and articles for various journals and magazines, most of which are distributed by the TSA. The national TSA is located in Bayside, New York, and there are many state chapters throughout the country. Contact information is listed at the end of the chapter. The TSA is an all-volunteer not-for-profit agency that offers many services at no cost. It can provide assistance and information in a number of areas, including:

Supportive Services
- Assistance to help families deal with the day-to-day problems of living and coping with TS.
- Advocacy and guidance to help families and schools provide the most appropriate educational program for the student with TS.
- Networking to help individuals and families communicate with each other to discuss mutual concerns and provide support.
- A physicians' referral list, including doctors, psychiatrists, psychologists, and counselors who are experienced in dealing with persons who have TS.

Information and Education
- Workshop presentations to educate people of all ages and all professions about TS.
- Conferences on various topics related to TS with lectures presented by professionals in the areas of medicine, psychology, education, and other related fields.
- Maintenance and distribution of library/ literature on TS.

Outreach
- Promoting the establishment of TSA support groups in communities across the country.
- Appointment of regional liaison people to assist and support families.

Research
- Encouraging and participating in research on TS to develop more effective medications, alleviate effects, discover causes, and find a cure.

Statistics
- Maintaining an up-to-date census of diagnosed cases of TS.

The TSA provides literature, books, videos, and other guides and pamphlets to educate the public about TS. They also have lesson plans to assist teachers to work most effectively with students who have TS. Do not hesitate to contact them for further information.

What Is Tourette Syndrome?

Definition

Tourette syndrome is a neurologically based disorder characterized by vocal tics, motor tics, and other behavioral manifestations (Bruun et al., 2001). Persons with TS have a chemical imbalance in the brain; it is not a form of mental illness (Colligan, 1989; Hansen, 1992; Shapiro & Shapiro, 1989). The biochemical imbalance in the brain is related to an excess of or an oversensitivity to a neurotransmitter called dopamine.

Neurotransmitters are bits of biochemicals that carry messages along neurons through the brain. Dopamine carries messages related to the control of muscular movements. Medication can be given that acts to block or reduce the individual's sensitivity to dopamine. Medications have been used to reduce the symptoms of TS and are described in more detail later in this chapter.

Autosomal Gene Disorder

Neurological and biological research on the cause of TS is in an emerging state. Researchers report that TS and other tic disorders are most likely genetically linked conditions (Bruun et al., 2001; Hansen, 1992; Shapiro & Shapiro, 1989; TSA, 1994). TS is classified as an *autosomal gene disorder*. An autosomal gene disorder means at least one parent must carry the genetic information for TS on a chromosome in order for the child to inherit the disorder. A child has a 50% chance of inheriting TS if one or both of the parents are carriers. There is a catch, though. A parent can carry the gene for TS without ever showing any of the symptoms. Genetic testing for TS has not yet advanced to the stage where evaluations can be done to determine if a person who does not show symptoms could be a carrier. Tic disorders, including TS, do seem to run in families.

Researchers (Bruun et al., 2001) say that the *vulnerability* for TS is passed from one generation to the next. A person who is vulnerable receives the genetic material to potentially develop TS. This is similar to inheriting the potential to develop the symptoms. However, not every child who receives the genetic material actually develops characteristics of TS. In addition, for those who do, the exact type and severity of symptoms cannot be predicted. Vulnerability can be carried by mothers or fathers and can be passed on to sons or daughters.

There is a difference in percentage between sons and daughters who inherit the genetic vulnerability for TS to actually show symptoms of the disorder. Only 70% of females who inherit genetic vulnerability actually express symptoms while 99% of males do. The degree of severity of symptoms expressed is called *penetrance*. The idea of penetrance is comparable to severity. Because penetrance is higher in males, they are more likely to show the symptoms than females are. Males also tend to have more severe TS characteristics.

Variety of Symptoms and Overlapping Conditions

The gene for TS can cause a variety of different symptoms. This is called *variable expression*. Symptoms can be demonstrated in a range from mild to moderate to severe (or full-blown TS), to milder tic disorders, to OCD, to attention deficit hyperactivity disorder (ADD), and to other learning and behavioral disorders. Males and females can also develop overlapping conditions between tic disorders, OCD, and ADD in a range from mild to moderate to severe. Males are more likely to develop TS or other tic disorders, while females are more likely to show concomitant symptoms of OCD. The majority of individuals who inherit TS

vulnerability have mild cases and do not require medical assistance or special services during their lives.

Prevalence of Tourette Syndrome

How many people have TS? Because of the wide range of symptoms, it is difficult to specifically count the number of individuals with TS. Other tic disorders are very difficult to separate from TS. Prevalence statistics are really just estimates. The TSA (1994) reported that full-blown TS occurs in about 1 of every 2,000 to 3,000 individuals. This means that these individuals have very severe symptoms. Three times that number of people may be afflicted with partial expressions of TS, including chronic tic disorders and OCD. About 75% of people diagnosed with TS are male (Shapiro & Shapiro, 1989). Other forms of tic disorders are called transient tics of childhood, chronic tic disorders, and multiple tic disorders. None of these are actually TS. About 1 in every 200 Americans may have some sort of tic disorder (TSA, 1994).

Difference Between TS and Other Tic Disorders

Bruun et al. (2001) relate descriptions of transient and chronic tic disorders that are not actually TS. Transient tic disorders may affect up to 15% of students during the early school years. These disorders tend to last only a few weeks and usually do not result in associated school or behavioral problems. Examples of transient motor tics include eye blinking, nose puckering, grimacing, squinting, and licking the palm. Common transient vocal tics include throat sounds, nose sounds, and humming. These tics increase when the child is excited or fatigued. Approximately 3 to 4 times more boys than girls are affected. Transient tics usually do not last more than 1 year. However, it is not uncommon for a student to demonstrate a variety of tics over several years.

Chronic tic disorders do not change over time as transient tics do. The same tic may persist over many years. Persons with chronic multiple tics usually have several chronic tics or series of tics that last for many years. There is a very fine line separating these tic disorders. Medical personnel make the diagnosis. It is not easy for a physician to differentiate TS from other tic disorders.

Tourette Syndrome Characterized by Tics

The major observable symptoms of TS are tics. The Tourette Syndrome Association (1994) describes tics as fast, involuntary vocalizations or movements that occur rapidly and repeatedly (but with no certain rhythm). As with any other type of disorder, the tics may be classified as mild, moderate, or severe. People with mild TS may function normally without the need for medication, behavioral therapy, or special education services. Others with severe tics may need medication, special services, and behavioral therapy or counseling to learn to manage their disorder and cope with the reactions of others to their symptoms.

Hansen (1992) related that tics can occur many times each minute or only a few times a day. The tics might be so mild that they are barely noticeable to others or so extreme that they are highly distressing and even debilitating to the individual. Tics are classified as mild, moderate, or severe based on their complexity and the degree to which they interfere with an individual's daily activities. Some tics occur 20 to 30 times per minute. Examples include eye blinking, grimacing, neck jerks, or mouth twitches. Other complex tics can be much more disruptive. Examples include loud barking or howling, other verbal utterances and phrases, kicking, deep

knee bends, and touching or smelling other people or objects.

Meaning of "Involuntary"

"Involuntary" refers to the person's inability to control the occurrence of the tics. Some people do have the ability to postpone tics for anywhere from a few seconds to hours at a time. But as one "Touretter," as they refer to themselves, stated, "Ultimately, one must tic. Tics are as irresistible as the urge to sneeze or scratch a mosquito bite" (personal communication, Dr. Avril VonMinden, 1998). Some Touretters may be able to delay tics until after school or work so they can release their symptoms in privacy. This usually results in more severe tic outbursts. Tics seem to get worse if a person is tense or under more stress or pressure. They are reduced in situations where the individual is relaxed or able to concentrate on a specific task (TSA, 1994).

Researchers have provided a fount of information on the vocal and motor tics associated with TS (Colligan, 1989; Hansen, 1992; Hearle, 1992; Shapiro & Shapiro, 1989). Vocal tics, also called phonic tics, relate to any type of sound, including speech. Vocal tics come from the muscles that form speech sounds. Motor tics come from muscles in the body that produce involuntary muscle movements. Motor tics are any type of involuntary muscle movement.

Simple Tics and Complex Tics

Tics are divided into two categories: simple or complex. Tics that are brief, isolated, and involve only one part of the body or one vocalization are classified as simple. Simple motor tics can affect isolated body parts such as the eyes or the mouth. Examples include a mouth twitch, an eye blink, a shoulder shrug, a simple sound like a grunt, humming, puffing breath, clearing the throat, or nasal snuffling. Complex tics involve more complicated movements or sounds. Examples include coordinated muscle movements like hitting, kicking, and deep knee bends; touching certain objects or textures; smelling objects or items of interest; or saying words or phrases. Complex motor tics usually affect larger muscle groups or the whole body.

Persons with TS can have any number of simple and complex vocal and/or motor tics at any time. It is reported that tics seem to come and go, or wax and wane. This waxing and waning phenomenon relates to the varying kinds or types of tics expressed and their severity.

Variety of Tics

Shapiro and Shapiro (1989) conducted long-term studies that categorized patients' tics. About one third of patients developed between 2 and 10 symptoms during their lives. Forty-four percent demonstrated between 11 and 20 different tics. The rest of the persons studied (about 25%) expressed 21 or more tics. The largest number of tics that any one participant of the study displayed was 60. The most common simple motor tic, exhibited by 80% of the participants in the study, was an eye movement. Other common motor tics were horizontal neck movements, arm movements, grimaces, mouth opening, hand and finger movements, leg movements, lip motions, and movements of the torso. The most common simple vocal tics were throat clearing, grunts, squeals, shrieks, yelps, and other high-pitched cries, sniffing, coughing, screaming, and snorting. As can be seen from this long-term study, there certainly is no lack of variety of tics.

Coprolalia is a complex vocal tic that has been sensationalized by the media. Coprolalia manifests as the utterance of socially inappropriate or unacceptable words or phrases. It is an extremely socially unacceptable complex vocal tic. Bruun et al. (2001) define coprolalia as an explosive utterance of inappropriate or foul language, typically swear words and sometimes racial or ethnic slurs. Something about the "forbiddenness" of the words or phrases seems to compel individuals with coprolalia to say them, apparently against their will. This tic is rare, but unfortunately it is one of the most well known tics of TS. It occurs in a minority of persons with TS. The

estimate is anywhere from 5 to 30% based on the clinic population being assessed (Hansen, 1992; Wang & Curry, 1993). Table 12–1 summarizes the variety of tics associated with TS.

Intellectual Functioning

Persons with TS have intelligence levels similar to those of the general population. Mental retardation or reduced cognitive functioning is not a common symptom. However, it is estimated that many school-age children with TS have a variety of learning problems. ADD has been reported as a common overlapping condition in as many as 50 to 60% of individuals with TS. Learning problems include attention deficits, hyperactivity, lack of concentration, lack of attention to detail, distractibility, reading deficits, handwriting deficits, and impulsivity (TSA, 1994).

Progression of Symptoms

Importance of Early Diagnosis

At 8 years of age, Mitch Vitello (1992) knew he was different from other kids. He could not sit still and his arms and legs violently jerked all over. His head jerked so much that he got migraine headaches. Mitch's family did not know what to make of his peculiar behavior. They usually tried to help him by ignoring the movements and simply referred to them as "Mitch's habits."

TS is a baffling disorder. Many individuals go for years without a diagnosis being made. The symptoms are usually mildly annoying to all-out aggravating for the Touretter and others around him. An early diagnosis is critical to the sense of self-esteem of the person with TS.

All too often Touretters are yelled at, ridiculed, or humiliated because they have a disorder that they cannot control. The child with undiagnosed TS may be threatened, rejected, and excluded from

TABLE 12-1   Tics Associated with Tourette Syndrome

Simple Vocal (or Phonic) Tics
Nose sniffling or snuffling or snorting
Throat clearing
Coughing
Grunting
Teeth clicking
Puffing expirations
Sucking inspirations
Humming
Squeaking
Whistling
Hiccuping
Belching

Complex Vocal (or Phonic) Tics
Animal sounds
Barking or howling
Cow, chicken, rooster
Repeating phrases
Repeating words or parts of words
Speaking in a falsetto voice
Stuttering
Muttering to oneself
Palilalia
   Repeating one's own words over and over again such as, "Oh my
   goodness!" or "I have to do my math!"
Echolalia
   Repeating an advertising slogan or jingle over and over again or another
   person's words; for example "clean my room, my room, my room, my
   room …" after a parent has asked the child to clean up the messy bedroom
Coprolalia (rare)
Repeating or bursting out with foul language or swear words

Simple Motor Tics
Eye blinking
Neck or head jerking
Shoulder shrugging
Facial grimacing
Squinting
Eye rolling
Sticking tongue out

Complex Motor Tics
Jumping or hopping
Deep knee bends
Twirling
Pinching or poking
Shoulder and arm movements
Finger movements (drumming, flexing, shaking)
Clapping

continued

TABLE 12–1 (Continued)

Flexing or shaking feet
Fiddling with own clothing
Smelling or touching other people or things
Echopraxia
    Imitating movements of others
Copropraxia (rare)
    Using obscene gestures
Writing the same letter or word over and over again
Stabbing pencil into paper or book page
Pressing pencil or pen down into paper and pulling back, tearing the page

Any combination of motor movements

Other Behavioral Manifestations
Attention deficit hyperactivity disorder (ADD)
Obsessive-compulsive disorder (OCD)
Emotional instability
Irritability
Impulsivity
Aggression
Self-injury (rare)
Hitting, biting, skin picking, or head banging
Learning disabilities

Note. *Tourette Syndrome Association. (n.d.).* Guide to the Diagnosis and Treatment of Tourette Syndrome, *retrieved November 10, 2003, from http://www.tsa-usa.org and the National Institute of Neurological Disorders and Stroke. (2001). NINDS Tourette Syndrome Information, retrieved November 10, 2003, from http://www.ninds.nih.gov/health_and_medical/disorders/tourette.htm*

activities by peers, parents, teachers, neighbors, and even strangers who do not understand the basis of the behavior. Parents may be overwhelmed by their child's strange behavior. The disorder is frequently misunderstood. Oftentimes, because of the wide range of variability and the waxing and waning of symptoms, others do not believe that the individual with TS cannot control the behavior. Many individuals with TS are punished for their tics. Oftentimes, parents or educators do not realize that the symptoms are related to an uncontrollable tic disorder. Many students get into trouble at school because their tics are viewed as willful, disruptive, or voluntary behaviors. Here is a parent's comment about the child's behavior at school:

> We knew about TS, and the lip smacking, and the way he flipped his head like he was trying to get the hair out of his eyes, but we didn't know about the echoing. He started repeating the last two or three words of each sentence. At first it was a whisper and then out loud. We had four very tough months before someone told us that the repeating (by this time he would repeat things we said out loud) was also part of the TS. He got in so much trouble at school because of this, and we weren't able to help him at home because we didn't know. (Hearle, 1992, pp. 24–25)

One set of parents related that their son Andrew's first symptom was sniffling and throat clearing. They thought he just had a lingering cold (personal communication, Melody and Walter Dow, 1996). Other parents mistake those types of early symptoms as signs of allergy or asthma (Shapiro & Shapiro, 1989). Andrew also had an early tic of shoulder shrugging. When asked about it, he simply replied that he was "shaking off the germs." At the time, Andrew's parents did not think too much about their son's behavior. They had older daughters and thought he was just showing more typical boylike behavior. As time went on, there were more symptoms and a frustrating search for information and medical assistance.

The stigma of TS gets worse when the child becomes an adolescent. Adolescence is unquestionably a trying period under the best of circumstances. An individual with TS could be scarred for life by negative social interactions with others who do not understand the disorder. Early diagnosis and treatment are crucial to the individual's well-being and successful adjustment. In addition, appropriate medical treatment and behavioral therapy can greatly reduce the severity of symptoms as well as the individual's ability to cope.

Onset of Tics

Tics usually start to occur around age 6 or 7, and 90% of all individuals with TS demonstrate tics by age 10 (Shapiro & Shapiro, 1989). Tics may begin as early as 1 year of age (APA, 2000). It is rare for TS to be diagnosed after age 21 but it has happened (Bruun et al., 2001). The most common first motor tic is a facial movement such as eye blinking, mouth twitching, or grimacing. More than half of all children with TS develop an eye tic first (Hansen, 1992). Early vocal tics include throat clearing, grunting, or nose noises such as sniffling, snuffling, or snorting.

Shapiro and Shapiro (1989) discussed the progression of symptoms. There does not seem to be a common pattern. The frequency, severity, and types of tics are unique to each individual. About one fourth (27%) of persons with TS will experience a reduction or elimination of symptoms for various periods of time while others suffer throughout their entire lives.

Tics also change. One may disappear and then another starts (waxing and waning). Tics may become less severe during puberty or adolescence. In about 35% of cases, the tics become much less severe during early to mid adolescence. Some individuals even recover completely and permanently during this stage. Why does this happen? During

adolescence, biochemical changes occur in the body and appear to have a positive effect on TS symptoms. Many adults have milder symptoms than they did as youth and adolescents. Conversely, some adults who previously had milder symptoms have more severe tics in their early 20s and 30s. It is impossible to predict what will happen to each individual.

How Is Tourette Syndrome Diagnosed?

Currently, there is no genetic or biological test that can specifically pinpoint a diagnosis of TS, determine whether a person is a carrier, or diagnose TS prenatally. In order to do those tests, researchers must locate the TS gene on a chromosome. Scientists are actively searching for the gene at this time. After the gene is located, tests may become available. Now, the best assessment is observation of behavior. What symptoms or characteristics should parents and educators be watching for? For a formal diagnosis of TS, at least two motor tics and one vocal tic must be observed for a minimum of 1 year (TSA, 1994).

Family members, educators, and classmates are often aware of a child's funny, weird, or strange habits. However, many of them do not make the connection between those abnormal patterns of behavior and TS until they see a television program or read a magazine article. These media sources have been helpful in educating the public about TS.

Media Coverage of TS

National statistics report that 80% of TS cases are not initially discovered by the family physician. Rather, they are diagnosed after a family member sees a television program or reads a magazine article and brings the symptoms to the attention of the doctor (Colligan, 1989). Sometimes parents take their child to the physician only to encounter the same situation many of us have been in when we take the car into the mechanic because it has been making a funny noise. The car runs very smoothly while the mechanic is test-driving it. You vainly try to imitate the noise as the honest mechanic is telling you he cannot find a problem. Same in the doctor's office. Parents vainly plead for their son or daughter to "show the doctor what you do at home" while the child "just doesn't feel like doing them" or "can't do the tics on command" (Bruun et al., 2001). It is a frustrating situation all-around. The physician cannot diagnose what she cannot see. One pediatrician who was unfamiliar with symptoms of TS told Mr. and Mrs. Dow that their son "was just being a boy." When a diagnosis of Tourette syndrome was finally made, the Dows were able to understand and link all of the early symptoms.

Evaluation Process

Hansen (1992) provided an excellent summary of the evaluation process used for TS. As mentioned earlier, in order to be diagnosed, an individual must show a minimum of two motor tics and one vocal tic for at least 1 year. It is not always easy to make a diagnosis for three main reasons. First, tics have tendency to wax and wane, meaning they change over time. It might take a while to get a complete picture of an individual's symptoms. Second, many individuals will suppress their symptoms when they are around a stranger or when they are in the doctor's office. This means the physician or therapist never gets a firsthand view of the symptoms. Videotaping typical behavior at home can be very beneficial to offset this problem. Finally, other conditions have symptoms that are similar to and can be confused with TS.

The *Diagnostic and Statistical Manual of Mental Disorders*, (DSM-IV-TR, APA, 2000) provides the official criteria for diagnosing TS. The following four points are required:

1. Both multiple motor and one or more vocal tics have been present at some time during the illness, although not necessarily concurrently. (A *tic* is a sudden, rapid, recurrent, nonrhythmic, stereotyped motor movement or vocalization.)

2. The tics occur many times a day (usually in bouts) nearly every day or intermittently throughout a period of more than one year, and during this period there was never a tic-free period of more than 3 consecutive months.
3. The onset is before age 18 years.
4. The disturbance is not due to the direct physiological effects of a substance (e.g., stimulants) or a general medical condition (e.g., Huntington's disease or postviral encephalitis). (p. 114)

A physician will use the DSM-IV-TR criteria in addition to making what is called a "differential diagnosis." A differential diagnosis compares the individual's behavior with the behaviors of others who have other types of tic disorders. The purpose of this procedure is to rule out disorder(s) the individual does not have. Since there is no test that can tell if an individual actually does have TS, the doctor may run tests on some other conditions, including but not limited to Duchenne muscular dystrophy, head trauma, brain tumor, epilepsy, and autism, simply to rule them out.

Direct Behavioral Observations

Observation of behavior takes center stage in the diagnosis of TS. Parents and educators can keep checklists or logs of behavior, and they should share information. The average teacher may not know about the symptoms of TS. If parents suspect TS, they should share what they know with educators. Teachers may have materials and knowledge they can convey to parents. Knowledgeable parents and teachers could present an in-service workshop to help other teachers spot students with abnormal behavior patterns or habits that might be TS. Educators and parents can make an effective team to help the school-age child, family members, and classmates effectively cope with TS. A checklist such as the one shown in Figure 12–1 would be useful for teachers and parents to note and monitor any tics that are occurring. If parents and teachers both kept track of tics on a checklist, it could easily be used to communicate information about

FIGURE 12–1 Teacher's Checklist of Symptoms for TS

Student's Name: _____ Teacher's Name: _____ Date: _____

Vocal Tics	☆	T/D	Severity	Motor Tics	☆	T/D	Severity	Other Behaviors	☆	T/D	Severity
Nose sniffling				Eye blinks				ADD			
Throat clearing				Facial grimace				OCD			
Coughing				Shoulder shrugs				Emotional instability			
Grunting				Head/neck jerks				Irritability			
Teeth clicking				Eye rolls/squints				Impulsiveness			
Puffing expirations				Jumping/hopping				Aggression			
Humming				Knee bends/twirls				Self-injury			
Whistling				Smells/touches				Head banging			
Barking/howling				Clap/pinch/poke				Skin picking			
Palilalia				Hand/arm movement				Learning disability			
Echolalia				Foot/leg movements				Medications?			
Coprolalia				Echopraxia							
*				Copropraxia				*			
*				*							

☆ = For a quick frequency count, simply place a check in the box to denote occurrence of the tic.

T/D = Time of Day. Write the time that the tic was observed.

Severity = Mild, Moderate, Severe. Mild symptoms are described as those that have little or no disruption to the student, peers, or teachers. Moderate symptoms are those that cause only a little disorder but the teacher is able to redirect easily. Severe symptoms are those that stop the learning/teaching process and interrupt the student, peers, and teachers from the regular classroom routine. The students are unable to work and the teacher is unable to teach due to dealing with the tics.

* = List any motor, vocal, or other behaviors not already given. In column three, list prescription medications taken by the student.

Note. Data from "Recognizing Tourette Syndrome in the Classroom," by N. Colligan, 1989, School Nurse, 5(4), pp. 8–12.

TABLE 12–2 Summary of Information Doctors Need to Diagnose TS

❑ Checklist of symptoms
❑ Frequency and severity of each tic
❑ How disruptive each tic is to daily activities
❑ At which times of the day tics are better or worse
❑ In what types of environmental situations tics are better or worse
❑ Extended family history of tics, OCD, ADD, and LD

Note. *Adapted from "Recognizing Tourette Syndrome in the Classroom," by N. Colligan, 1989, School Nurse, 5(4), pp. 8–12.*

the student's behavior between home, school, and the therapist or doctor's office.

Providing a checklist will help the physician make a diagnosis. In addition to specifying which tics are occurring, the completed checklist can be used to document the frequency, severity, and extent to which the tics disrupt the individual's daily activities. It can also be used to note when the tics are better or worse. The doctor will also want to know about the extended family's history of tics, OCD, ADD, or other learning problems. Table 12–2 summarizes information that parents and educators can help gather for the doctor to use in making a diagnosis of TS.

Multidisciplinary Team Evaluation

A number of specialists will examine the individual to help asses symptoms for TS. After completing their own evaluations, the specialists consult with each other and share their findings to determine a diagnosis and need for special services. This group of individuals is commonly called a multidisciplinary team. This is not a new or an uncommon approach. Multidisciplinary teams typically get together when diagnosing other disorders such as autism, mental retardation, learning disabilities, or cerebral palsy. It is a new approach for TS, though. Medical personnel are in the early stages of learning about TS, and scientists are just beginning to develop assessment methods to test for TS. Specialists and their roles in the evaluation may include but are not limited to:

- **Pediatric (or regular) neurologist:** This physician is a medical doctor who specializes in diagnosing and treating neurological disorders. A pediatric neurologist specializes in working with children. Neurological disorders can include problems with the brain, the spinal cord, and the nervous system. The neurologist will perform tests that rule out other specific disorders and try to pinpoint specific impairments or weaknesses. Some of the tests neurologists conduct might include blood tests or an EEG (electroencephalogram) to measure the electrical activity of the brain and to check for seizure activity. The neurologist will also ask questions to obtain information for a family medical history.

- **Neuropsychiatrist:** This person is a medical doctor who specializes in diagnosing and treating neurological disorders such as OCD, depression, and ADD. The neuropsychiatrist can also perform an EEG and blood tests. Another test this doctor might do is called a CAT (computerized tomography) scan. The CAT scan compiles a series of X-rays to make a computerized picture of the brain at different levels. Looking at the picture of the brain can assist doctors in ruling out other problems and pinpointing abnormalities. It seems as though the neurologist and the neuropsychiatrist complete a similar type of evaluation. However, because neuropsychiatry is a narrower medical field, the neuropsychiatrist probably would be more familiar with the effective medications to treat disorders such as TS.

- **Psychologist:** The psychologist is a professional who specializes in assessing human behavior, emotions, and thinking patterns. The psychologist then can provide therapy and determine management methods to deal with problem situations. A psychologist is not a medical doctor and does not diagnose TS or prescribe medicine. The psychologist helps the individual and the family come to terms with the diagnosis and assists the individual with other issues such as management strategies, self-esteem, and social skills.

- **Occupational therapist:** This professional specializes in helping people with various disorders to learn or improve motor skills needed to carry out daily activities. An occupational therapist performs tests to determine specific motor problems that might be related to neurological impairment.
- **Educator:** The teacher spends a great deal of time on a daily basis with school-age children. Teachers can help with behavioral checklists and records of frequency and severity of tics and other problem behaviors. Teachers are able to comment on a student's self-esteem, social skills, academic skills, and fine or gross motor skills.

After all evaluations are completed, the multidisciplinary team meets with the family to share the results of the assessment. The team uses the results to make a diagnosis. After the diagnosis is made, a treatment plan is developed. The plan usually involves medication for those with symptoms severe enough to warrant it, possibly counseling therapy, and behavioral intervention when necessary. The correct type and dosage of medication can act to quickly bring symptoms under control. However, medication must always be closely monitored for effectiveness and side effects. The type of medication and dosage may need to be changed or adjusted to achieve the right combination. Counseling and behavioral intervention provide coping skills for successful adjustment.

Related Conditions or Problems

Behavior Problems and Tourette Syndrome

A number of debilitating conditions may overlap with TS and result in various behavior problems. These behavior problems often cause further complications in everyday living for patients with TS.

Frankel (1989) outlined three main types of behavior problems that may be evident:

1. Some behaviors are simply a result of the neurological condition. These behaviors include increased irritability, low tolerance for frustration, attention problems, and hyperactivity. Also included are obsessive-compulsive and ritualistic behavior patterns. Some individuals also show self-destructive or self-abusive behaviors, often in response to their increased sense of frustration and irritability.

2. Some behavior problems relate to complications or undesirable side effects of medications. Medication does not cure the symptoms, but will often help to reduce the incidence or severity of tics. Some side effects include depression, lack of motivation, sedation, restlessness, and cognitive difficulties. Shapiro and Shapiro (1989) report additional side effects of muscle spasms, tremors of the hands and feet, sluggishness, and abnormal posture. Parents have informally reported serious weight gains of 20 to 60 pounds in less than a year (U.S. Department of Health and Human Services, 1995). One parent stated that he thought the weight gain did more to damage his son's self-esteem than the tics did. As with all medication, positive and negative effects must be closely monitored.

3. Some behavior problems relate to the tics and behavioral manifestations of TS in general. These problems are wide-ranging and difficult to define specifically. There are many different types of problems because each person reacts to and copes with the daily challenges of TS in unique ways. Examples range from difficulties with social relationships and interactions with others, learning problems, stress management problems, self-esteem and self-concept problems, and problems getting and keeping a job.

Problems occur as the individual reacts to growing up and living with a biological condition over which one has no control. Think how frustrating that would be! TS is not only socially disruptive but also often physically painful. As one man with TS stated, "Necks just aren't supposed to move the way mine does 10,000 times a day!" (I'm a Person, Too [video]). He does daily exercises to strengthen neck muscles to counteract the muscular pain caused by the tic.

A further complication relates to the fact that tics wax and wane. Individuals can go through periods when symptoms almost seem to disappear. Think how relieved and hopeful they would feel that they might somehow be more "normal" and more socially accepted only to find one day either that tics that had disappeared were back or that a new tic was developing. Shapiro and Shapiro (1989) reported that tics disappeared in their patients for anywhere from 1 week to an extraordinary 7 years.

TS and Overlapping Conditions

TS and ADD

Researchers (Lowe, Cohen, Detlor, Kremenitzer, & Shaywitz, 1982; TSA, 1994) indicate that many children with TS also exhibit deficits in attention and increased levels of behavioral activity. In many children, the attentional problems were apparent before the tics of TS. Shapiro and Shapiro (1989) presented some interesting facts related to the apparent overlap of characteristics of ADD and TS. As many as 60% of patients seen by specialists for severe TS also had symptoms of ADD. Severe, as compared to mild or moderate indicators, is the key. The mannerisms of persons with severe cases of ADD and severe TS often overlap.

TS and Learning Disabilities

When milder cases of ADD and TS are studied, the percentage of patients with both handicapping conditions was substantially reduced. Students who have ADD often have learning problems in school. The same is true for students with TS. Burd (1992) reported that as many as 40% of students with TS are also diagnosed with learning disabilities. A learning disability is described as a 2-year discrepancy between actual and expected academic achievement. The most common areas for problems to occur are reading, math, spelling, and handwriting.

TS and Obsessive-Compulsive Disorder

A link has been established connecting TS and obsessive-compulsive disorder (OCD). Bruun et al. (2001) documented that a high percentage of persons with TS also have OCD; a specific percentage was not given. In most cases, the tics of TS seem to appear before the compulsive behaviors of OCD. It may be difficult to separate the symptomatic behaviors of OCD and TS because both show repetitive, maladaptive behaviors that the person cannot seem to stop doing. Shapiro and Shapiro (1989) describe a person with OCD as having uncontrollable thoughts that are intrusive and unwanted. These thoughts then create tension and anxiety in the person's mind. The anxiety can be relieved only by completing meaningless repetitive actions like hand washing; checking doors, windows, and appliances; following certain patterns without deviation to complete tasks; or possibly developing an eating disorder such as compulsive eating or bulimia.

The behaviors of OCD are slightly different from tics. They tend to be more involved than the complex motor or vocal tics. There is a similarity in that the ritualistic, compulsive behaviors of OCD tend to hinder social relationships and school or job performance to the same degree, if not more so, than the tics of TS.

Gaffney and Ottinger (1995) provided a list and description of OCD behaviors common in patients with TS (Table 12–3). The list is divided into behaviors described as "obsessions" and those defined as "compulsions." *Obsessions* are stereotyped, irresistible thoughts or ideas that make a person feel anxious. The person who has the obsessive thoughts is capable of recognizing that they do not make any sense and can try to suppress and control behavior related to the thoughts. *Compulsions* are defined as voluntary, but often irresistible, behaviors that are usually acted out in response to obsessive thoughts. The purpose of the action is to relieve stress or to keep something bad (e.g., contamination that might occur without excessive hand washing) from happening. As with the obsessions, the person usually realizes that the compulsive behavior is often unreasonable. But he still cannot stop doing it.

Additional research is needed to study the relationship between OCD and TS (Bruun et al., 2001; Gaffney and Ottinger, 1995; Shapiro & Shapiro, 1989). Caution must be taken to ensure that the ostensible OCD behaviors are not simply complex tics. Intensive investigation is necessary to determine whether OCD and TS occur together at a rate higher than in the general population of persons who do not also have TS. Researchers have suggested that OCD behaviors may actually be another form of expressing the TS gene and therefore may be an integral component of the disorder (Bruun et al., 2001). This is another facet of TS that requires further study of patients with TS and OCD to determine their rate of co-occurrence.

TS and Social or Emotional Skill Deficits

When I was eight. I noticed I was different from the other kids. I made strange movements. It got to the point where the other kids noticed. They started to laugh and look at me strangely. I felt bad inside and sometimes I cried. I didn't know what was wrong with me. My parents didn't know, The doctors didn't know either. (Vitello, 1992, p. 11)

Persons with TS may have difficulty forming social relationships with others. They are often ridiculed, humiliated, and ostracized by peers and adults (Bass, 1996; Seligman & Hilkevich, 1992;

TABLE 12–3 Obsessive and Compulsive Behaviors That Are Common in Persons with TS

Obsessions
- Contamination: Germs, chemical, and other contaminants
- Disease: Skin disorders
- Sexual: Aggressive sexual impulses toward others or self
- Harm: Self or others, particularly spouse or children
- Doubting reality: Unrealistic perceptions that might lead to disaster or death if unchecked such as checking locked doors, windows, stove or iron turned off, or fears that one hit a pedestrian
- Perfectionist: Everything must be "just right"

Compulsions
- Skin picking or hair pulling in response to skin obsession
- Hand washing or continually wearing gloves in response to contamination obsession
- Touching self, others, or objects (haphemania)
- Checking and rechecking locks, alarms, windows, stove, iron in response to doubting obsession
- Hoarding objects or food
- Perfectionist: Everything must be redone until it is perfect

Note. Adapted from *Tourette Syndrome*, by G. R. Gaffney and B. Ottinger, 1995, University of Iowa: Virtual Hospital. Retrieved from http://www.vh.org/adult/patient/psychiatry/tourettesyndrome/tourettesyndrome.html. Adapted with permission.

Smith, 1987). TS is an enigma for the uninformed. As stated earlier, many people think the individual with TS is simply behaving in a willfully inappropriate manner. Because TS is often such a misunderstood condition, it is frequently difficult for the individual with TS to be accepted into the peer group at school and in the community.

Intervention Strategies for Tourette Syndrome

Treatment for symptoms of TS must be multifaceted (Frankel, 1989; Hearle, 1992). The physician who treats a patient with TS should be mindful of the fact that TS is an illness with both physiological and psychological ramifications. Medication is one facet of treatment used for TS symptoms that are severe enough to interfere with the person's daily activities. Some individuals do not need medication because their symptoms are milder and less frequent.

Behavioral therapy is another facet of treatment for TS. Therapy or counseling would benefit many persons and families with TS. Behavioral therapy can help the individual and the family cope with TS, the problems that the disorder presents in daily life, and the reactions of others to the individual with TS.

Behavioral intervention is a third facet of treatment that may be employed. Positive and proactive behavior management strategies can be used to teach a wide variety of skills to the individual and family with TS. The procedures taught will vary with the needs of the individual. Some examples include teaching control of impulses, improved social interaction skills, and time management.

A treatment plan that combines medication when necessary, counseling or therapy, and individualized behavioral intervention strategies can help the individual with TS to feel that he has more power and control over his own life.

Medication for TS

Medication Is Not a Cure

Medication will not cure TS, but it can help to reduce and possibly eliminate tics and behavioral manifestations, including OCD and ADD. The positive effects on reduction of symptoms will last only as long as the medication is taken. Bruun et al. (2001) and Palmer (1992) described the different types of medications that are used, how they help, and the side effects that might occur. Palmer's chapter, "Medical Treatments and Tourette Syndrome," provides valuable information on TS and medications for children and is written in an easy to read format for parents, educators, and other professionals (Palmer, 1992).

Mild Symptoms May Not Require Medication

Some individuals with TS do not require medications. They have symptoms that are mild and do not interfere with daily activities. The mild symptoms can often be controlled by counseling or behavioral intervention strategies to reduce stress and help the individual cope with the symptoms. For students, classroom modifications can also help reduce the effects of TS. Such modifications are discussed in a later section of this chapter.

Specific Medications Used for TS Symptoms

Many different types and combinations of medications are used to reduce the symptoms of TS. Each medication has the ability to produce desired effects plus, unfortunately, unwanted side effects. The individual must be closely monitored by a team, including medical personnel, family members, educators, and other professionals. The goal is to ensure that the medication is producing the majority of positive effects and is not resulting in side effects that are debilitating or even worse than the TS itself. Three main categories of prescription medication used to treat TS include (a) anti-tic drugs, (b) anti-ADD drugs, and (c) anti-OCD drugs. Each of the three types of medication works to reduce symptoms of TS by interacting with different neurotransmitters that carry messages to the brain.

Anti-tic Medications The purpose of anti-tic medications is to block the activity of the neurotransmitter called dopamine. Neurotransmitters can be described as chemical messengers. They help move messages smoothly through the pathways of neurons in the brain (Dendy, 1995). Dopamine is found in minute portions in the blood and helps to carry messages about muscle movements throughout the brain. It is believed that tics are caused either by too much dopamine or by the individual's hypersensitivity to it. Anti-tic medications have been very successful in reducing the frequency and severity of tics. However, they have also been totally ineffective for some individuals. No one seems to know why. The only way to find out if a medication will work for a particular person is to try it (Palmer, 1992).

Two anti-tic medications that have been used with success are Haldol® (haloperidol) and Orap® (pimozide) (Palmer, 1992). The optimal dosage for each individual is critical with these two drugs because the potential side effects can be debilitating. Documented side effects include cognitive difficulties with memory and basic thinking skills, restlessness, sedation, drowsiness, decreased coordination, dry mouth, blurred vision, constipation, weight gain, depression, and school phobia. The physician should give the lowest dose possible to avoid side effects. For Haldol, the dose ranges from 0.25 mg for a child to 5 mg for an adult. A similar dose is used for Orap but adults may take up to 8 mg.

Anti-ADD Medications Anti-ADD medication increases the level of norepinephrine in the brain.

Norepinephrine is a neurotransmitter that helps the individual to inhibit impulses to an appropriate degree. As many as 60% of children with TS also have ADD. A medication that can help manage the symptoms of both would be ideal. Similar to anti-tic medications, anti-ADD drugs vary in effectiveness from one individual to the next. However, they can be very effective at reducing some or all of the symptoms of ADD: poor attention, hyperactivity, and impulsivity.

The most often used anti-ADD drug is Ritalin® (methylphenidate). Ritalin is a stimulant that acts to increase the flow of norepinephrine and dopamine (Dendy, 1995). A negative side effect is associated with Ritalin for some individuals. While it reduces the ADD behaviors, it can *increase* the tics of TS because some individuals with TS already have too much (or an oversensitivity to) dopamine (Dendy, 1995; Lowe et al., 1982; Palmer, 1992). Prescriptions of Ritalin for ADD behavior in an individual with TS must be carefully monitored because it can actually make the tics worse (Lowe et al., 1982; Palmer, 1992). It is critical that Ritalin be carefully prescribed and monitored for effectiveness. A typical dose of Ritalin can be anywhere from 5 mg to 60 mg a day. Some doctors propose that patients receiving Ritalin take a break from the medication for short periods. This is called a *drug holiday*. Drug holidays may be scheduled during vacations or on weekends. Ritalin, if taken continuously, can stunt growth. Other side effects include sedation, reduced appetite, insomnia, and nervousness (Dendy, 1995; Lowe et al., 1982; Palmer, 1992).

Tricyclic Antidepressants For an individual with TS and ADD who cannot take Ritalin, an alternative medication from a group called *tricyclic antidepressants* may be tried. Antidepressants serve to improve the functioning of neurotransmitters in the brain. They have been shown to reduce ADD behaviors without making the tics worse. Two examples are Norpramin® (desipramine) and

Tofranil® (imipramine) (Dendy, 1995; Palmer, 1992). These drugs are often prescribed in combination with Haldol or Orap. Doses can range from 10 mg or 25 mg up to 100 mg per day. The physician will start with the lowest dose and then gradually increase if necessary to determine the optimal level for a *maintenance dose* of the drug for each individual. The maintenance dose is the level at which optimal positive effects are achieved with the fewest side effects.

Side effects that have been documented for these drugs include sedation, dry mouth, blurred vision, light-headedness, and mild memory difficulty. In addition, the side effects are worse at the beginning of the medication trial. Negative side effects can be offset by taking the dose at bedtime (Palmer, 1992).

Anti-OCD Medications Anti-OCD medications bring the level of the neurotransmitter serotonin into proper balance. Proper levels of serotonin are essential to stabilize mood and reduce obsessive-compulsive behaviors. Individuals who have TS complicated by OCD may benefit from this type of medication. The specific purpose of anti-OCD drugs is to reduce and possibly eliminate unwanted, disturbing, obsessive thought patterns and compulsive behavior. A positive result is that the person will be able to concentrate more effectively on tasks and daily activities (Palmer, 1992).

Two of the most often used medications for TS and OCD are Anafranil® (clomipramine) and Prozac® (fluoxetine). Higher doses of Anafranil are required to treat OCD as compared to ADD, which means the chances for negative side effects are greater. Prozac does not seem to have the same or as many negative side effects as Anafranil. Some individuals experience energizing effects or nervousness for the first 3 or 4 weeks of taking Prozac, but that usually disappears. Other documented side effects include nausea, heartburn, headaches, diarrhea, and insomnia (Palmer, 1992).

Currently, Prozac is manufactured only in a 20 mg capsule. For individuals who need a smaller dose, the capsule can be opened and emptied into 8 ounces of juice. It must be stirred well to dissolve it. Drinking 2 ounces of the Prozac-juice mixture is equivalent to a 5 mg dose. The juice can then be covered and stored in the refrigerator. If necessary, the dose can be increased by 5 mg every 4 to 5 days until the optimum maintenance dose is achieved. The ideal dose may be between 10 and 40 mg for children and 60 and 80 mg for adults. It is recommended that Prozac be taken in the morning to minimize insomnia (Palmer, 1992).

Children with TS and aggressive behavior problems may benefit from a medication called Tegretol® (carbamazepine) or from Lithonate® (lithium carbonate). These two medications have a mood-stabilizing effect (Dendy, 1995). They can help the individual to control aggressive urges, impulsive reactions, and explosive emotions (Palmer, 1992).

Parent/Physician Collaboration Is Imperative

Parents and physicians should work closely to monitor appropriate doses of medication. As children grow up and mature, the doses may need to be modified. Teachers can be very helpful in keeping logs and checklists of behavior during the day at school. Some individuals will continue to need medications all their lives. However, for about 75% of persons with TS, the tics begin to decrease between the ages of 16 and 18. At that time, medication can be decreased gradually. Abruptly stopping the medication might result in a rebound effect. This means the symptoms might temporarily worsen, or the person could develop tired, run-down feelings similar to symptoms of the flu or a virus. About 50% of adults eventually discontinue medication completely. The symptoms subside, and individuals can use behavioral coping techniques to effectively manage those symptoms that remain (Palmer, 1992).

Behavioral Management Methods for TS

Proactive Behavioral Intervention

A number of behavioral concerns are associated with TS. In addition to the problems of ADD and OCD, there are other problems that can cause adversity in daily life, at school, at home, in the community, and on the job. Examples include difficulty coping with or self-managing any or all of the following: (a) impulse control, (b) quick temper, (c) overreactions, (d) mood swings, and (e) oppositional and defiant behavior (Gaffney & Ottinger, 1995).

All children must learn limits and conform to the rules, laws, and general expectations of society. The culture in which one lives defines the limits of acceptable behavior. Some are more strict and some are more lenient. Many children simply learn these limits, follow the rules, and obey the laws of the community with no special services or programs other than effective parenting and a solid education. However, other children, some with TS or other types of handicapping conditions, do not automatically learn to conform to and respect the limits of the society. These children need extra assistance and guidance in the form of a well-structured, positive, and proactive behavioral intervention plan. The main purpose would be to learn positive alternatives for old patterns of problem behavior. Each individualized behavior plan should have self-reliance and independent functioning as an ultimate goal. In addition, graduating from high school is essential for successful adult adjustment. The high school graduate then has the choice of entering the world of work or going on for further education.

There is a general strategy (covered in Chapter 2 in great detail) that educators, parents, or others who work with youth and adolescents can use to change any problem behavior. The plan is based on a behavioral model that has two main assumptions: first, that all behavior is learned; second, that consequences from the environment can shape and maintain new, appropriate behaviors. Here are the steps:

1. Identify the problem behavior using observable, measurable terms.
2. Identify a functional, appropriate behavior that is incompatible with the old problem behavior.
3. Teach the student the new behavior.
4. Use a lot of positive reinforcement to help the student internalize the new behavior.

This four-step strategy can be of great benefit in helping individuals with TS cope with any of the associated behavioral problems. In addition, there are a number of classroom-based strategies that can assist students to successfully adjust to the educational environment. The behavior plan must be proactive, positive, individualized, and consistently implemented. This strategy can help students with TS show increased rates of achievement, improved social skills, and generally acceptable behavior.

Classroom Strategies for Students with TS

Special Education Services

Students who are formally diagnosed with TS by a physician qualify for special education services under the special education category of *Other Health Impairments* (Colligan, 1989). Because students with TS have average intelligence and many have mild symptoms, there may not be a need for special education services. However, Davidovicz (1995) reported that 30% of students with TS also have various forms of learning disabilities. Many students with TS also have learning problems as a result of the specific patterns of cognitive dysfunction common to persons with TS. The general learning problems are based on difficulties with *expressive* and *receptive language*. Expressive language relates to how well one is able to use spoken language to convey thoughts, feelings, wants, and needs. Receptive language relates to how well one is able to comprehend communications from others. The severity of the learning problems that may overlap with TS do not correlate with the intensity of the TS symptoms.

If needed, the student should receive a full psychoeducational evaluation by the multidisciplinary team at the school. Based on assessment results, the team decides which special services are necessary and is responsible for writing an Individualized Education Program (IEP) to document the academic and behavioral goals, objectives, and special services for the student for the school year.

Students with TS may have various academic difficulties that could keep them from achieving up to their expected ability level in school. The most obvious basic signs to watch for are low grades and academic achievement below expected potential (Davidovicz, 1995). It is important to identify specific areas of academic or behavioral concern. Areas where students with TS might experience difficulty in the classroom include (a) organization of work and materials, (b) listening skills (auditory processing), (c) rule/direction following behavior, (d) visual motor skills, (e) completing tasks within time limits, (f) memory, and (g) taking notes (Colligan, 1989; Conners, 1994; Davidovicz, 1995; Favish, 1995; Gaffney & Ottinger, 1995). After identifying areas of concern, educators and parents can collaborate to set up a plan to help the student learn acceptable alternative behaviors. Ultimately, the goal is for the student to independently cope and show the new patterns of behavior.

Educate Classmates About TS

Parents and medical personnel can be instrumental in helping teachers learn about TS and management methods. Depending on the individual preferences of the student with TS and the family, it might also be helpful to educate classmates

about TS. There are a number of techniques educators can use to help students with TS to be more successful at school. Instruction in social skills is one suggestion for teachers to try. Teaching prosocial skills will benefit all students, not just students with TS. The *Skillstreaming* series (Goldstein & McGinnis, 1997) has programs for preschoolers, elementary school students, and adolescents. Each program manual is divided into 60 age-appropriate social skills. The social skills lessons are all based on a self-instructional model that requires students to remember three to five steps to implement the skill. Each lesson consists of expert role-modeling of the skill, student role-plays, performance feedback from teachers and classmates, and transfer of training, including homework assignments to practice the skill.

Classroom Strategies

A variety of strategies may be used in the classroom. The teacher should analyze the situation and use any strategies that may be beneficial to individual students. Table 12–4 summarizes suggestions compiled from various sources related to school-oriented concerns of students with TS. Students with TS may experience a higher than average number of problems in school because of their neurological disorder. The tics often leave them feeling helpless and powerless due to their lack of control. Students with TS do not want to be out of control. They do not want to be different. They want to fit in with the rest of the class. Consequently, they are easily frustrated by their lack of control over their own bodies.

Students with TS can be hypersensitive, easily distracted, and hyperirritable. It is easy for them to be overstimulated by large groups, noisy situations, and disorganization in the classroom. Educators and parents can use the following suggestions to help teach students with TS impulse control to increase academic achievement and improve social behavior and acceptance from others.

TABLE 12–4 Strategies for Effectively Managing Academic Problems of Students with TS

Interventions for the General Environment

- Educate school staff and students about symptoms and behaviors of TS
- Attempt to create a calm classroom environment
  - Reduce stress and distractions
  - Create a carrel or other area to help the student concentrate
- Allow movement to burn off energy
  - Run errands, do classroom chores, incorporate activity breaks
  - Allow student to go to a place to release tics
- Set up the classroom for student success academically and behaviorally
  - Develop proactive expectations and behavior plans to address areas of concern
  - Teach appropriate replacements for problem behaviors
- Set up a three-ring notebook with organized sections for each class
  - Color code folders to match notebook covers for each class
  - Three-hole punch zipped bags and insert assignments to keep all together
  - Attach a pencil case with extra school supplies
- Provide a duplicate set of books to keep at home during the school year for homework
- Provide an age-appropriate daily or weekly assignment sheet to organize and facilitate completion of daily assignments and homework
- Modify classwide expectations for individual student needs
- To facilitate transitions, alert student with reminders several minutes apart when changing from one activity or classroom to another

Interventions for Social/Emotional/Behavioral Problems

- Model acceptance of the child and the symptoms of TS
- Modify school/classroom expectations that might discriminate against a student with a neurological disorder
- Establish daily routine and attempt to stick to it
- Set expectations and reinforce them consistently
- Use a high level of genuine positive reinforcement for accomplishments and effort
  - For example, reward student for remembering all required materials instead of punishing him for forgetting
- Allow student to voluntarily leave the classroom and go to a predetermined safe place when under high stress or having severe tics
- Set goals for the student to realistically challenge abilities
- Look for special talents and interest to develop and reinforce in the school setting
- Seat student next to student to be a buddy or to be a good role model
- Develop a system, gesture, or code word to let student know when behavior is not appropriate

Interventions for Academic Learning Problems

- Teach age-appropriate study skills and strategies for time management and organization
- Allow student to wear headphones to block out distracting noise
- Alert students to important information
  - Say "This is important" or "Listen carefully" or "Write this down" or "Put a star by this" or "This will be on the test"
- Use visual aids in lessons to help the student focus on important details
  - Color highlight
  - Arrows that point to important sections
  - Check off blanks or boxes in front of each step of directions
- Break assignments into smaller segments
- Shorten assignments based on mastery of key concepts
- Provide a marker to follow along when reading
- Hand out written assignments with due dates typed along with requirements
- Provide typed copy of blackboard work so the student does not have to recopy
- Allow student to tape-record or give answers orally rather than writing answers

continued

TABLE 12–4 (Continued)

- Provide books or reading passages on tape for the student to listen to as he follows along visually
- Teach keyboarding skills
- Provide student with computer time to type assignments
- Provide typed outlines to accompany videotapes
- On assignments and tests, mark answers that are correct
  - Help students correct answers that are incorrect so that material is learned
  - Allow students to improve grades by reworking incorrect answers

Interventions for Note Taking

- Prepare a skeleton outline where the student follows along and fills in the blanks
- Allow student to tape-record the lesson
- Provide another student with carbon paper to make a copy of the notes

Interventions for Tests

- Type tests; do not handwrite them
- Grade content separate from spelling and punctuation
- Read the test to the student and have him answer questions aloud
- For multiple-choice tests, allow the student to simply circle the correct answer rather than using Scantron answer sheets
  - Many students will have difficulty filling in the circles of a Scantron sheet for machine scoring
- For tests that require reading a selection and answering comprehension questions, provide an index card with a window cut out so the student can focus on small sections of print
- For math computation tests, try folding the paper into eighths or fourths and put only one problem in a section. This helps the student to focus and minimize distraction and keep all work related to one problem in one section
- When testing math computations that involve columns, such as long division or multiplication of multidigit numbers with regrouping, use lined paper but set the paper up so the lines run vertically. This will help the student keep computations lined up correctly.
- PL 94-142 mandates that students with formally labeled special education services (TS qualifies under *Other Health Impairments*) be allowed unrestricted time to take tests *no matter what instructions for the standardized test state*. Teachers can note on the student's test that unrestricted time was allowed to complete the test due to the presence of a handicap.

Note. *Burd, 1992; Conners, 1994; Favish, 1995; Hearle, 1992; Walls, 1995.*

Implications for Working with Youth and Adolescents

Educators, parents, and other professionals who work with youth and adolescents who have TS should project calm acceptance of the various tics associated with the disorder. This general strategy will help others in the environment to interact appropriately with the individual who has TS. Following is an example of some very beneficial advice that one father gave his 12-year-old son with TS. This bit of guidance and wisdom related from the son's viewpoint turned out to be very

helpful to him in learning to feel comfortable in social situations:

The time I learned to deal with my problem [TS] was the summer I went to camp in Boston. It was 1987 and I was twelve and a half. I looked forward all the months before going and the Tourette seemed not to be acting up. Suddenly, just before leaving for camp, I had an allergy attack that always seemed to start the Tourette's problem up. I was angry because I knew people would make fun of me at camp just like they did at school. It was frightening.

On the first day of camp no one would even talk to me. I called home and told my parents that

I had no friends. I was down and lonely. My mother wanted to come and pick me up. She thought the Tourette syndrome was the worst it had ever been. It was. But my father said he had something very important to tell me. He said I had to learn to deal with the condition no matter how bad it got. "If you act like it bothers you, it will bother other people. How you deal with your problem is how other people will deal with it." (Vitello, 1992, pp. 12–13)

Mitchell Vitello followed his father's advice the next morning at the camp breakfast. When other boys at his table remarked on the peculiar movements, Mitch calmly told them, "it's just a condition I have that acts up sometimes and makes me move differently. It's nothing major. It comes and goes. I can't help it. You'll get used to it" (p. 13). Mitch gave the other boys this explanation with a friendly smile on his face and, sure enough, they did get used to it. He found out that if he acted like the tics didn't matter, the other kids didn't care either (Seligman & Hilkevich, 1992).

All individuals with TS should learn this beneficial lesson in dealing with the general public. Most people do not know about TS until they either see a TV program about it, read a popular magazine article about TS, or encounter a person who has it.

To help individuals with TS achieve their highest potential and to become successfully adjusted adults, educators and parents should form collaborative and mutually beneficial partnerships. The partnerships can be helpful in a number of ways. The more people know about TS, the less stigma there will be educating the public about it.

In conclusion, TS is a neurologically based handicap that is characterized by motor tics and vocal tics. Although researchers are not yet completely certain what causes TS, they think it is probably due to a malfunction of one or more neurotransmitters in the brain. It is estimated that 100,000 persons in the United States may have full-blown TS while as many as 1 in 200 have some type of tic disorder. Unfortunately, the motor and vocal tics that characterize TS are often misunderstood by the uneducated or uninformed public. The result is a very negative stigma for persons with TS who have no control over the tics.

Teachers, medical personnel, and parents of children with TS should help educate the public about the disorder. Early intervention is critical to determine the most appropriate intervention and to help the individual and his family effectively manage the disorder. Any child who has a tic disorder should have a complete medical examination. Schools must ensure that all students with TS receive the most appropriate education and any other necessary special services. A united approach that combines medical, educational, behavioral, and social skill intervention for persons with TS is essential. This strategy will help each individual be accepted in society and achieve to his or her highest potential.

References

American Psychiatric Association. (2000). *Diagnostic and statistical manual of mental disorders* (4th ed., text revision). Washington, DC: Author.

Bass, M. (1996). *Tic, tic, tic: Tourette syndrome and me.* Santa Barbara, CA: Marlea Press.

Bruun, R. D., Cohen, D. J., & Leckman, J. F. (2001). *Guide to the diagnosis and treatment of Tourette syndrome.* Retrievable from www.tsa-usa.org

Burd, L. (1992). Educational needs of children with Tourette syndrome. In T. Hearle (Ed.), *Children with Tourette syndrome: A parents' guide* (pp. 169–205). Rockville, MD: Woodbine House.

Colligan, N. (1989, December). Recognizing Tourette syndrome in the classroom. *School Nurse* 5(4), 8–12. Available from the Tourette Syndrome Association, Inc., 42-40 Bell Boulevard, Bayside, NY 11361. (718) 224-2999 or (800) 237-0717.

Conners, S. (1994). *Specific classroom strategies and techniques for students with Tourette syndrome.* Available from the Tourette Syndrome Association, Inc. 42-40 Bell Boulevard, Bayside, NY 11361. (718) 224-2999 or (800) 237-0717.

Davidovicz, H. (1995). *Learning problems and the TS child.* Available from the Tourette Syndrome Association, Inc., 42-40 Bell Boulevard, Bayside, NY 11361. (718) 224-2999 or (800) 237-0717.

Dendy, C. Z. (1995). *Teenagers with ADD: A parent's guide.* Bethesda, MD: Woodbine House.

Favish, J. (1995). *Helpful techniques to aid the student with Tourette syndrome in the completion of written assignments in the classroom and at home.* Available from the Tourette Syndrome Association, Inc., 42-40, Bell Boulevard, Bayside, NY 11361. (718) 224-2999 or (800) 237-0717.

Frankel, M. (1989). *Behavioral problems in Tourette syndrome.* Paper distributed by the Tourette Syndrome Association, Inc., 42-40 Bell Boulevard, Bayside, NY 11361. (718) 224-2999 or (800) 237-0717.

Gaffney, G. R., & Ottinger, B. (1995). *Tourette syndrome* [Web document]. University of Iowa: Virtual Hospital. www.vh.org/adult/patient/psychiatry/tourettesyndrome/tourettesyndrome

Goldstein, A. P., & McGinnis, E. (1997). *Skillstreaming* (Three Series—Preschool, Elementary, or Adolescent). Champaign, IL: Research Press.

Hansen, C. R. (1992). What is Tourette syndrome? In T. Hearle (Ed.), *Children with Tourette syndrome: A parents' guide* (pp. 1–25). Rockville, MD: Woodbine House.

Hearle, T. (1992). *Children with Tourette syndrome: A parents' guide.* Rockville, MD: Woodbine House.

Lowe, T. L., Cohen, D. J., Deltor, J., Kremenitzer, M. W., & Shaywitz, B. A. (1982). Stimulant medications precipitate Tourette syndrome. *Journal of the American Medical Association, 247*(12), 1729–1731.

Palmer, O. (1992). Medical treatments and Tourette syndrome. In T. Hearle (Ed.), *Children with Tourette syndrome: A parents' guide* (pp. 53–70). Rockville, MD: Woodbine House.

Seligman, A. W., & Hilkevich, J. S. (1992). *Don't think about monkeys.* Duarte, CA: Hope Press.

Shapiro, E., & Shapiro, A. K. (1989). Gilles de la Tourette syndrome and tic disorders. *The Harvard Medical School Mental Health Letter, 5*(11).

Smith, J. (1987, November–December). The need to know. *The Exceptional Parent.* Distributed by the Tourette Syndrome Association, Inc., 42-40 Bell Boulevard, Bayside, NY 11361. (718) 224-2999 or (800) 237-0717.

Tourette Syndrome Association (1994). Questions and answers about Tourette syndrome. Pamphlet distributed by the Tourette Syndrome Association, Inc., 42-40 Bell Boulevard, Bayside, NY 11361. (718) 224-2999 or (800) 237-0717.

U.S. Department of Health and Human Services. (1995). *Tourette syndrome* (NIH Publication No. 95 2163). Washington, DC: U.S. Government Printing Office. Pamphlet and more information available from Office of Science and Health Reports, National Institute of Neurological Disorders and Stroke, PO Box 5801, Bethesda, MD 20824. (301) 496-5751 or (800) 352-9424.

Vitello, M. M. (1992). *Doing it differently.* In A. W. Seligman, & J. S. Hilkevich (Eds.), *Don't think about monkeys.* Duarte, CA: Hope Press.

Walls, R. (1995). *Children and Tourette syndrome:* Teacher handout. Communique/National Association of School Psychologists.

Wang, C., & Curry, L. (Eds.). (1993). *Tourette syndrome: A continuing education course for registered nurses.* Reseda, CA: Tourette Syndrome Association–Southern California Chapter (TSA–SC).

Videos

The following videos are available from the Tourette Syndrome Association, Inc., 42-40 Bell Boulevard, Bayside, New York 11361. Contact them at (718) 224-2999, (800) 237-0717, or www.tsa-usa.org. The association can also provide contact information regarding state associations and materials.

I'm a Person, Too. Video documentary featuring five people from diverse backgrounds with TS.

Stop it—I Can't! This video, narrated by William Shatner, provides a fast-paced, up to-date documentary depicting young people with TS. The individuals in the video have learned to cope with TS and are achieving their goals. The purpose of the video is to help children understand about individual differences.

Be My Friend. This video explains the symptoms of TS, associated behavioral problems, educational issues, and services provided by the TSA.

CHAPTER

13

CONDUCT DISORDER

After completing the chapter, the reader will be able to identify:

- The components used to define conduct disorder.
- The APA (2000) diagnostic criteria required for the official label of conduct disorder.
- Components of oppositional defiant disorder and antisocial personality disorder and their relation to conduct disorder.
- Characteristics of students who are bullies and victims.
- Causes of conduct disorder.
- Assessment methods for conduct disorder.
- Prevention and intervention strategies for conduct disorder.
- Implications for educators, parents, and other professionals who work with youth and adolescents.

Introduction

Ritchie, a second grader, had been referred for special services. Problems included frequent behavioral patterns of coercing peers, dominating playground activities, making his own rules for games, breaking rules, verbally abusing and ridiculing others, and physically provoking and overpowering smaller, younger children. One day at recess, the playground supervisor observed that Ritchie began choking a kindergartner for no apparent reason. He appeared to have a clear goal of hurting the smaller child. When the counselor who was assigned to deal with the problem asked Ritchie why he was choking the other student, he replied in amazement, "Well, it was recess!" (Walker, Colvin, & Ramsey, 1995)

Ritchie's actions and total lack of guilt or remorse about hurting another person are common characteristics among students with conduct disorder (CD). Their classroom behavior tends to be so disruptive that teachers have a hard time presenting lessons, and the other students in the class are distracted from learning. Most other students do not want to be on the same team, work on a group project, or even be friendly with students with CD. The student with CD is typically on the fringes of or excluded from the normal, same-age peer group. The isolated or rejected students then look for another group with whom to associate. They usually end up with others who have problems like theirs or with younger children whom they can boss around or dominate.

Behavior Associated with CD

The general behavior problems associated with CD include aggression, property destruction, deceitfulness and theft, and serious rule violations (APA, 2000). To avoid confrontation, some teachers merely allow students with CD to sit in the back of the room and sleep during class, hoping they will just keep quiet. Students with CD can be so difficult to deal with in the classroom that many teachers fervently hope that the disruptive student(s)

will be absent. (As one gains experience in teaching, it might be noted that they are hardly ever absent and, in fact, they are almost always early!)

Students who show the antisocial and aggressive behaviors characteristic of CD are usually referred for special education services at school. Based on the severity of their problem behavior, some students may be in resource rooms or self-contained classrooms in the public schools. Others may require a more restrictive environment and may be placed in a residential treatment, hospital, or corrections environment. Walker, Colvin, and Ramsey (1995) report that the number of students with CD in the schools is increasing dramatically. They estimate that approximately half of all students referred for behavioral disorders show externalizing behaviors similar to CD. As with many disorders, more males than females are diagnosed with CD. This means that the most typical student for teachers in emotional/behavior disorder (E/BD) classrooms is liable to be a male with excessive, aggressive, antisocial behavior common to CD.

CD Compared to More Transient Problems

Many children show a variety of problems as they grow up. However, there is a difference between CD and the more transitory problems some children experience. Transient problems are the kind that just seem to work out with time and without the need for individualized, special services. What differences might educators observe that would help screen for the existence of CD? One main difference is that the maladaptive behaviors of children with CD tend to be much more frequent and intense than the more temporary types of behavior problems that might be just a phase or a stage that the child is going through (Morgan & Jenson, 1988; Walker et al., 1995). That is, true CD behaviors occur much more often and are much more severe than the average child's problem behavior. CD behavior is also very persistent; it tends to be resistant to even the most well-planned and consistent behavioral intervention. This aspect of CD behavior is frequently very frustrating for teachers and parents. It is difficult and often exhausting to try to teach class or have any type of normal family life and activities with these children.

Most educators and other professionals who work with youth and adolescents have observed firsthand the more serious behaviors of CD. Examples include temper tantrums; coercion in the form of whining, arguing, and making excuses; fighting with their siblings and peers; cheating, lying, or stealing; cruelty to people or animals without showing guilt; violating curfew; extreme noncompliance to adult requests; verbal and physical intimidation or assault; or destroying the property of others (Kauffman, 2001; Rhode, Jenson, & Reavis, 1992). All these coercive behavior problems may be included under the general label of CD.

Terminology and Labeling

A phenomenon reported by Coleman and Webber (2002) is the varying terminology used by different agencies to classify youth and adolescents with the antisocial and aggressive behavioral patterns characteristic of CD. Mental health agencies or clinics and many educational systems use the term *conduct disorder* as defined by the DSM-IV-TR (APA, 2000).

The legal system uses the term *adjudicated delinquents* for minor children who demonstrate lawbreaking behavior. Because of the aggressive and antisocial nature of the behaviors characteristic of CD, breaking the law is a frequent occurrence. Those individuals then become participants (albeit unwilling) of the juvenile justice system. Walker et al. (1995) relate evidence suggesting that antisocial behavior at a young age has a poor prognosis for remediation in later life. They stated that a pattern of antisocial behavior during the elementary school grades resulting in the label of CD is the number one predictor of adolescent delinquency. Juvenile delinquency is the single best predictor of adult criminality. Walker et al. go on to say that children who display antisocial behavior at a very young age are labeled CD while older youth who show the same patterns of behavior are arrested and labeled delinquent. Approximately half of youth labeled with CD are also labeled delinquent.

Finally, the educational system may use the terms *conduct disorder, emotional or behavioral disorder,* or *social maladjustment.* Use of the term *social maladjustment* prompts a controversial discussion on labeling practices. Currently, students who are labeled socially maladjusted can be legally excluded from receiving any type of special education services at school. It has been suggested that some schools actually use the social maladjustment label to legitimately exclude some problem students from special education services. This means that they are not subject to the 10-day maximum suspension rule for special education students mandated by IDEA (see chapter 1). Additionally, students with social maladjustment can be expelled from school for chronic misbehavior. Students in special education cannot be expelled for disruptive behavior that is a manifestation of their handicapping condition. However, as discussed in chapter 1, the Individualized Education Plan (IEP) team can meet and determine whether a change of placement may be more appropriate than the present situation if multiple problems were occurring.

All of the labels for deviant and aggressive behavior seem to have one common factor: antisocial behavior. Whether the individual is labeled with CD, social maladjustment, or delinquency, educators and other professionals who work with youth and adolescents must be prepared to effectively manage the problems associated with aggression and antisocial behavior. The terms *conduct disorder* and *antisocial behavior* may be used interchangeably in this chapter.

Definition of CD

The most readily observed behavior related to CD is antisocial behavior. Specifically, the individual repeatedly violates rules or laws and the rights of others or age-appropriate social norms. Individuals with CD often display aggressive behavior toward others and react in a very hostile manner during interactions with peers and adults (APA, 2000). Specific problem behaviors range from physical fights and deliberate cruelty to people and animals to property destruction and fire setting to theft and other serious rules violations such as running away, school truancy, and curfew violations. A formal diagnosis of CD is often based on the severity or intensity and duration of the behavior problems (Morgan & Jenson, 1988; Walker et al., 1995). The *Diagnostic and Statistical Manual of Mental Disorders*, Fourth Edition, Text Revision (APA, 2000) provides the definition for conduct disorder that is often used by professionals for diagnosis. It includes both characteristics of behavior and a time element (see Table 13–1). The DSM-IV-TR states that a minimum of three characteristic behaviors listed in the definition must be present for at least 12 months and there must be at least one behavior evident during the 6 months before diagnosis. These behaviors would be demonstrated in a variety of environments such as home, school, and community.

CD Subtypes

The subtypes of CD (APA, 2000) are generally concerned with the age of onset of the problem behaviors demonstrated by the individual. The subtypes can occur at the mild, moderate, or severe level. In addition to the age of onset, differences between the subtypes relate to characteristic problem behaviors demonstrated, developmental progression and prognosis of the disorder, and gender of the individual.

Childhood-Onset Type   Childhood-onset type of CD is defined by the existence of at least one characteristic behavior before the age of 10 years. These individuals are typically hyperaggressive male children who lack social skills and may have shown behaviors typical of oppositional defiant disorder (ODD) in early childhood. These children usually develop behaviors characteristic of full-blown CD as they reach adolescence. Because the problem behaviors of these individuals are so innate and severe, many children will go on to develop antisocial personality disorder as adults.

Adolescent-Onset Type   The adolescent-onset type is a milder form of CD. It is diagnosed when there are no characteristic behaviors apparent before the age of 10. These individuals do not demonstrate the higher level of aggression or the serious social skill deficits of the childhood-onset type. Because the conduct problems develop later, they are not as ingrained. These individuals are less likely to have persistent CD or develop antisocial personality disorder as adults. When females are diagnosed, they are more likely to have the adolescent-onset type.

Oppositional Defiant Disorder

Coleman and Webber (2002) relate that oppositional defiant disorder (ODD) often coexists with CD. The two conditions are not distinctly different. However, CD is considered to be a more serious lifelong condition. Both conditions tend to be intensely annoying and frustrating to peers, family members, and other adults in the environment. The main difference is that while students with ODD are inclined to be antagonistic and defiant to others, they do not violate society's norms or the rights of others. A progression of this disorder may begin with ODD in early childhood. If the symptoms become worse, the diagnosis may be changed to CD as the student gets older (APA, 2000).

Antisocial Personality Disorder

Individuals who are diagnosed with CD at a young age are likely to have the most severe symptoms (Coleman & Webber, 2002). These individuals' symptoms often continue into adulthood, and then the individuals are labeled with antisocial personality disorder (APD). The DSM-IV-TR (APA, 2000) changes the label from CD to APD when characteristic antisocial behaviors persist past age 18. These problems are manifested by criminal behavior; family, social relationship, and employment difficulties; and generally elevated levels of aggression. Table 13–2 lists typical symptoms of ODD and APD.

TABLE 13–1   Diagnostic Criteria for Conduct Disorder

A. A repetitive and persistent pattern of behavior in which the basic rights of others or major age-appropriate social norms or rules are violated, as manifested by the presence of three (or more) of the following criteria in the past 12 months, with at least one criterion present in the past 6 months:

Aggression to people and animals
  (1)   often bullies, threatens, or intimidates others
  (2)   often initiates physical fights
  (3)   has used a weapon that can cause serious physical harm to others (e.g., a bat, brick, broken bottle, knife, gun)
  (4)   has been physically cruel to people
  (5)   has been physically cruel to animals
  (6)   has stolen while confronting a victim (e.g., mugging, purse snatching, extortion, armed robbery)
  (7)   has forced someone into sexual activity

Destruction of property
  (8)   has deliberately engaged in fire setting with the intention of causing serious damage
  (9)   has deliberately destroyed others' property (other than by fire setting)

Deceitfulness or theft
  (10) has broken into someone else's house, building, or car
  (11) often lies to obtain goods or favors or to avoid obligations (i.e., "cons" others)
  (12) has stolen items of nontrivial value without confronting a victim (e.g., shoplifting, but without breaking and entering; forgery)

Serious violations of rules
  (13) often stays out at night despite parental prohibitions, beginning before age 13 years
  (14) has run away from home overnight at least twice while living in parental or parental surrogate home (or once without returning for a lengthy period)
  (15) is often truant from school beginning before age 13 years

B. The disturbance in behavior causes clinically significant impairment in social, academic, or occupational functioning.

C. If the individual is 18 years or older, criteria are not met for Antisocial Personality Disorder.

Code based on age at onset:
  312.81 Conduct Disorder, Childhood-Onset Type: onset of at least one criterion characteristic of Conduct Disorder prior to age 10 years
  312.82 Conduct Disorder, Adolescent-Onset Type: absence of any criteria characteristic of Conduct Disorder prior to age 10 years
  312.83 Conduct Disorder, Unspecified Onset: age at onset is not known.

Specify severity:
  Mild: few if any conduct problems in excess of those required to make the diagnosis **and** conduct problems cause only minor harm to others
  Moderate: number of conduct problems and effect on others intermediate between "mild" and "severe"
  Severe: many conduct problems in excess of those required to make the diagnosis **or** conduct problems cause considerable harm to others.

Note. *Reprinted with permission from the* Diagnostic and Statistical Manual of Mental Disorders, *Text Revision, Copyright 2000. American Psychiatric Association.*

TABLE 13–2   Problem Behaviors of ODD and APD

ODD

- Problem behaviors are usually evident before age 8
- Temper problems
- Argumentative, defiant, and noncompliant to adult requests
- Irritable, touchy, easily annoyed
- Angry and resentful
- Spiteful, vindictive, deliberately annoys others

APD

- Evidence of CD before age 15
- Pattern of irresponsible and antisocial behavior after age 15
- Inconsistent work behavior, unemployment, repeated absences
- Failure to conform to expected social norms
- Social relationship problems, fighting, other aggression
- Failure to honor financial responsibilities
- Transience and irresponsibility related to family and future
- Dishonest; cons others
- Reckless regarding own and others' safety

Note. From the Diagnostic and Statistical Manual of Mental Disorders, *Fourth Edition, Text Revision, American Psychiatric Association.*

Bully and Victim Behavior

Many children are victims of occasional teasing behavior, but some children are repeatedly targeted. Bully behavior is an insidious problem that is chronic and pervasive in schools across the nation (Bonds & Stoker, 2000; Garrity, Baris, & Porter, 2000; Garrity, Jens, Porter, Sager, & Short-Camilli, 1994; Newman, Horne, & Bartolomucci, 2000). Without adult intervention, bullies can inflict emotional and physical harm on many other students. Statistics indicate an average range from about 15 to 20% of students who may be affected by bullies during their school years. Some studies show a much more frequent and higher incidence of bully behavior. Results of a survey conducted with high school students reported that 80% of students had been bullied during their school years. When fourth and fifth graders were surveyed, 90% reported being the victim of bully behavior at some time during their early school years (Bonds & Stoker, 2000).

Definition

Bully behavior occurs when one individual deliberately and repeatedly uses power over another person in a willful manner with the aim of hurting the other person. There is a definite imbalance of power in this situation. The bully has all the power and control; the victim has none. It is interesting to note how close that definition is to the definition of CD (. . . a persistent and willful violation of the rights of others and the rules or laws of a society . . .).

Tattletales

As a teacher or other professional who works with youth and adolescents, have you ever been annoyed by frequent *tattletales*? How did you deal with it? Did you intervene with the situation or did you tell the adversaries to "fight your own battles?" Oftentimes tattling is the way a child who is being repeatedly targeted and victimized tries to obtain assistance from an adult. The victim of a bully typically does not have the social skills required to "fight their own battles" or make the bully stop. It is critically important that adults intervene when an altercation occurs more than once between two students who are not friends (Garrity et al., 1994).

Teach students who tattle a problem-solving strategy for determining what types of situations are necessary to tell the teacher. Then teach the students what to say if they believe they are being bullied by others so they get help to deal with the situation. The *Teacher's Encyclopedia of Behavior Management* (Sprick & Howard, 1995) provides multiple detailed intervention plans for dealing with tattle-tales and bully behavior.

Difference Between Bully Behavior and Normal Conflict

Garrity, Baris, and Porter (2000) provided a set of criteria to use as a guideline to determine whether a conflict situation might actually be bully behavior. If there is a situation between two or more children, ask the following questions:

1. Does the bully pick on the same child day after day consistently without letting up?
2. Does the bully win or have more power because the other child is smaller, younger, less socially able, or different in any other way?
3. Is the child being victimized afraid and very upset emotionally?
4. Does the bully see the entire situation as "no big deal" or as the other child is "asking for it" or "deserves" it?
5. Does the bully actually seem to enjoy making the other child upset? (p. 17)

Answering yes to even one of these questions is a strong indicator that bully behavior is occurring. Bonds and Stoker (2000) suggest that teachers use the *Double I/R* criterion to determine whether bullying is taking place. To apply this criterion, review the incident and decide whether the altercation involved behavior that was *Intentional*, *Imbalanced*, and *Repeated*. If a problem behavior occurs more than one time between children who are not friends and there is unequal power in the situation, the adult should intervene. Adult intervention is the only reliable method that will make the bully behavior stop. The child being victimized does not have the ability to show the behaviors necessary to stop the other child from being a bully.

Bullies Can Be Boys or Girls

The New Kid on the Block[*]

> There's a new kid on the block.
> And boy that kid is tough,
> that new kid plays real hard,
> that new kid is real tough,
> That new kid's big and strong,
> with muscles everywhere,
> that new kid tweaked my arm,
> that new kid pulled my hair.
>
> That new kid likes to fight,
> and picks on all the guys,
> that new kid scares me some,
> (that new kid's twice my size)
> that new kid stomped my toes,
> that new kid swiped my ball,
> that new kid's really bad,
> I don't care for her at all.
>
> Jack Prelutsky

There is a fallacy that bullies are always boys. Not true! Both girls and boys can be bullies. Boys tend to show more overt, physically harmful behaviors. They either directly inflict harm or threaten a victim with later harm. Girls tend to use social alienation, which is often much more sly, sneaky, and devious. Females often bully with social alienation tactics such as malicious gossip, humiliation, and peer group rejection tactics. All bully behavior may take the form of physical, emotional, or sexual abuse. The harm may range from mild to moderate to severe abuse.

Characteristics of Bullies

Garrity et al. (2000) related an informal method that might be used to screen for bullies. It involves asking children two questions:

> Do others sometimes pick on you? The child who answers, "Nobody ever picks on me" may be a bully. (p.8)

Children who are bullies will not admit to even occasional conflicts with others.

> How do you feel when you see someone else getting picked on? The child who answers, "He probably got what he deserved" may be a bully. Most children will feel badly if they see another child being picked on even if they aren't brave enough to do anything about it. Children who lack that feeling are at risk for doing emotional or physical harm to others because they lack empathy or the ability to relate to others. (p. 8)

Garrity et al. (1994, 2000) provided the following checklist of observable characteristics of children who are bullies:

Bully Behavior Checklist
- May be boys or girls
- Average to just below average academic skills
- Tend to have a peer group that empowers/supports bully behavior
- Values power rewards of aggressive behavior
- Lacks empathy, compassion, guilt, remorse
- Likes to dominate, control others, must win at any cost
- Often has aggressive adult role models
- Does not take responsibility for behavior; projects problems onto others
- Sincerely believes that it is acceptable to be cruel and hurtful to others
- Thinks that it is OK to be abusive to get own needs met
- Avoids interactions with adults and likes to play in areas that cannot be easily observed by those supervising

Bullies choose their victims for a specific reason. They target victims based on how they look, dress, walk, talk, and act. There is always an imbalance of power. The victim is usually very emotionally upset, while the bully feels more powerful and reinforced by tormenting others. The victim will typically be very anxious and nervous. This child may appear to be fearful and may cry easily. The bully tends to be very unemotional and shows no remorse for hurting another person. The bully thinks he is totally justified in his actions. Frequently, the bully verbalizes statements such as:

"He got just what he deserved...."
"She asked for it...."
"He had it coming...."
"She made me mad...."

Characteristics of Victims

All victims of bully behavior suffer from the stress and anxiety of the situation. Most victims show disrupted academic performance. Some are tardy on a daily basis so they will not have to walk to school or be on the playground or in the hallways during the less well structured and supervised periods before school starts. They lose interest in school activities and academic achievement. Many lose trust in teachers because they think the teachers do not help and do not try to stop the bully. Victims of bully behavior have recounted situations many years later with the same signs of post-traumatic stress syndrome as do war victims (Garrity et al., 1994).

Passive Victims   Two types of victims have been identified (Garrity et al., 1994, 2000): *passive* victims and *provocative* victims. Passive victims are children who are shy, insecure, and deficient in social skills. They seem to be on the fringe of the peer group. They may play alone at recess time, which makes them easy targets for bullies. They usually are honestly afraid of the bully, so they just give in rather that try to stick up for themselves. That is how the cycle of bully behavior begins. Many of these children may also have suffered past trauma or abuse. There may be five times as many children with special education needs who are victimized as compared to children without special needs.

Provocative Victims   Provocative victims show a different set of behaviors that can make them targets for bullies. They are often impulsive and reactive and also lack social skills. Rather than being on the fringe of the peer group, they are usually right at the center trying to participate, although they may not have any close friends. They are rarely quiet and they do not like to be alone. They tend to push, shove, and try to use aggression to get attention. They often make inappropriate verbal remarks to others because they lack impulse control. These students are victimized because they so often irritate and annoy others. Some may mistake the behavior of the provocative victim as bully behavior. Garrity et al. (2000) provided the following differences:

1. A provocative victim is not intentionally cruel to others.
2. A provocative victim typically loses and cannot overpower others.
3. A provocative victim usually does not have friends; a bully does. (pp. 6–7)

The following checklist cites observable characteristics of children who are victims (Garrity et al., 1994, 2000):

Victim Behavior Checklist
___ Shy, anxious, insecure
___ Lack ability to defend themselves verbally or physically
___ Physically weak, cry easily
___ May have suffered past abuse or trauma
___ Walk with head down and slumped shoulders; little eye contact with others
___ Play alone at recess time
___ Are on the fringe of the peer group without close friends
___ May be hyperactive, impulsive children who tease and provoke
___ Burst into other children's activity without knowing how to ask to join
___ Make many impulsive, inappropriate verbal remarks
___ Do not respect, rules, boundaries, or others' personal space
___ May use aggression to try to get attention

Behaviors of Neutral Students: The Silent Majority

Many students at school are not involved in bully behavior or victim behavior. This is a group of students who have good social skills. They know how to interact appropriately with others. They have the skills to make friends, solve problems, make good decisions, bargain, negotiate, and compromise. Even though many of the students in this group are aware of bully behavior incidents taking place, they do not often intervene. Most are too afraid of the bully. They believe that they will become the next victim if they get involved and try to help the current victim. All students in school should learn the skills necessary to stand up to bullies, to help others who are being victimized. To do this, schools must set up a zero-tolerance policy for bully behavior. All students should learn how to go to an adult to report the bully behavior. All adults who work with youth and adolescents should be proactive in recognizing the signs of bully behavior. Garrity et al. (1994) and Bonds and Stoker (2000) provide excellent resources to educate teachers, other professionals, parents, and students about bully and victim behavior.

Bully Behavior and Fatal Violence

During a 15-minute shooting spree, a junior high student in the state of Washington killed three students and his teacher. Unfortunately, this is not a unique or isolated situation. In the aftermath, classmates described this student as being shy and serious, studious, a loner, and a person who was often the target for harassment. Apparently his larger than average feet, gangly physical build, studiousness, and cowboy style clothing made him a target for bullies. The first student killed was popular, athletic, and a known bully (Walls, n.d.). Following the rash of tragic school shootings that have taken place in schools during the past 5 years, bully behavior has become an area of increasing concern in education. Dr. Ronald Stephens, Executive Director of the National School Safety Center, suggests that the majority of violence perpetrators were frequently first victims of bullying and harassment (National School Safety Center, n.d.). These children mistakenly think using a gun will stop the bullying and solve their problems.

School shooters have voiced feelings of ostracism, humiliation, isolation, and rejection from the peer group and often from teachers and administrators at school. Some have indicated feeling rejection from parents and family. The extreme violence used was their misguided attempt to get back at the parents, teachers, and peers who, in their minds, had bullied them. All parents, educators, and other professionals who work with youth and adolescents must be aware of the signals of bully behavior. There is a great need to make sure that all children are included and feel a bond to both school and family.

Walker, Ramsey, and Gresham (2004) report that bully behavior has been identified as a common factor in many of the fatal school shootings that occurred in U.S. schools during the 1990s. As media coverage sensationalized the stories of school violence, the number of individuals killed and wounded by the shooters seemed to increase with each episode. In the aftermath, the majority of shooters verbalized their perceptions of having been the victims of peer and adult humiliation, rejection, harassment, and bully behavior. The shootings were their misguided attempts to take revenge on others. It is critically important that parents, educators, and other professionals who work with youth and adolescents be aware of the characteristics of bully and victim behavior. Adults should be proactive and intervene. The victim does not have the skills or the power to make the bully stop.

Intervention

It is important for educators, parents, and other adults to identify and acknowledge the signs of bully behavior and set up a program to deal with the bullies, the victims, and the neutral students. All three groups must learn appropriate assertiveness skills. The basic idea is to teach the bully social skills so that she can get along with others in an appropriate manner. The victim must learn social skills in the areas of assertiveness and obtaining adult support. Students who are neutral should learn how to intervene when appropriate and gain adult assistance. There are comprehensive manuals on bully and victim behavior programs for educators, parents, and other professionals (Bonds & Stoker, 2000; Garrity et al., 1994, 2000; Newman et al., 2000) that can be used to set up in-service training programs and provide specific methods of intervention on bully behavior. These manuals include materials for teaching others about bully and victim behavior. They also provide information on separate small-group lesson plans for bullies, for victims, and for students in the silent majority. Garrity et al. (2000) wrote a manual defined specifically for parents.

Prevalence of Conduct Disorder

Conduct disorder is one of the most frequently diagnosed conditions of children at mental health facilities across the country. Prevalence rates seem to be higher in urban areas than in rural areas. Rates also vary due to the population sample and method of assessment (APA, 2000). The percentage rates are higher for males than for females. The range for males diagnosed with CD is from 6 to 16% (APA, 2000; Coleman & Webber, 2002; Phelps & McClintock, 1994), while females with CD comprise approximately 2 to 9% of the school-age population. It is estimated that there are about eight times as many boys as girls with CD (Coleman & Webber, 2002; Morgan & Jenson, 1988). Kauffman (2001) reports that the overrepresentation of boys with antisocial behavior may be due to a number of factors, including biological sensitivity, societal expectations for boys, parenting practices, role models, and reinforcement of aggressive and antisocial behavior.

Students who demonstrate the chronic, highly aggressive, and antisocial behavior of CD greatly outnumber the students labeled with serious emotional disturbance (SED). The federal government uses the label SED for students with behavioral disorders. Walker et al. (1995) report that students with SED comprise only about 1% of the total school-age population.

Causes of Conduct Disorder

The following comment was made by an incarcerated juvenile when asked how he thought some children learned antisocial patterns of behavior:

> Some neighborhoods kids live in are wild. Stealing is normal and a way of life. If you need food or clothing, you just steal. When little kids are growing up, they see this going on all the time and think it's normal and that's the way it should be.... It's mainly the environment around you. The people that you're with, the people that live round you. For instance, if you go outside and everyone around you is a delinquent, the only value you have is to be a delinquent because that's how everybody is. (Goldstein, 1990, p. 50)

Research shows that CD is a result of multiple causes (Coleman & Webber, 2002; Erickson, 1998; Walker et al., 1995), ranging from genetic or biological to environmental. It is most common for there to be more than one factor that precipitates the problem behaviors of CD. The individual who develops CD typically was exposed to a combination of deviant or abnormal family, community, and genetic influences. The debate about causes for different types of mental illness usually focuses on the *nature versus nurture* controversy. Nature is considered to be traits that are biological or genetic, while nurture refers to home, family, early life experiences, and social interactions (Black, 1999).

Developmental Pathways

The behavioral problems evidenced by children with CD may follow one of three common devel-

opmental pathways that result in the manifestation of minor to severe antisocial acts. The patterns of developing behaviors are described as overt, covert, or disobedient (Loeber et al., 1993; Walker et al., 1995):

- Overt problem behaviors may be described as impulsive or reactive. They are crimes specifically directed toward harming people such as assault, coercion, bullying, robbery, or rape.
- Covert problem behaviors are directed more toward property and are of a more concealed or surreptitious nature. Examples include arson, theft, lying, drug and alcohol abuse, or vandalism.
- The disobedience pathway consists of oppositional behaviors whereby children show high levels of noncompliance to adult requests and behavioral expectations.

Youth and adolescents with CD may display any one or all three types of behavior. Demonstrating all three behaviors makes them highly at risk for the development of delinquency and ongoing adult criminal behavior. Being diagnosed with severe CD behavior during the elementary school years is the number one predictor of delinquency during adolescence and then continuing to develop APD during adulthood (Kauffman, 2001; Patterson, Reid, & Dishion, 1992; Wahler & Dumas, 1986).

Age of Onset as a Causation Factor

The age of onset of antisocial behavior appears to have a predictable effect on future deviant behavior. Researchers (Walker et al., 1995) divide the individuals into one of two groups described as either early starters or late starters. Early starters are defined as those children who are socialized to violence and aggression from infancy by the family environment and ineffective parenting practices. Late starters are thought to be introduced to antisocial behavior through the peer group and peer pressure as opposed to maladaptive family situations. Logically, it is much more difficult for educators and other professionals to successfully intervene when children have an early start on CD behaviors.

Temperament as a Factor

It has been suggested that the behaviors associated with CD may begin as early as infancy (Kauffman, 2001). Infants with difficult temperaments often later show behaviors associated with early starters of CD. Children with hyperirritable temperaments are at elevated risk for developing antisocial behavior. Some infants do show coercive social interactions with caregivers. Irregularity of biological processes, difficult adaptation to change, intensity of reaction, and quality of mood are all areas that may affect how positive the interactions are between caregivers and infants. In addition, early high levels of noncompliance and oppositional behaviors are two problems that may evolve during the early childhood years.

Temperament is an inherited personality style or a trait that predisposes an individual to act in certain ways (Gelfand, Jenson, & Drew, 1988). Research has been conducted to determine the link between early temperament and the development of behavioral disorders (Chess & Thomas, 1983; Thomas & Chess, 1977). A large group of children ($n = 136$) were studied to determine how temperament during infancy affected later development of behavior problems. The children were assessed in nine areas (Gelfand, Jenson, & Drew, 1988):

1. Activity level: the proportion of daily active and inactive periods.
2. Rhythmicity: the regularity of biological functioning.
3. Approach or withdrawal: the initial response to new or unfamiliar stimuli.
4. Adaptability: response to new or altered situation after initial response.
5. Threshold of responsiveness: intensity level of stimulation necessary to evoke a response.
6. Intensity of reaction: the energy level of the response to stimulation.

7. Quality of mood: the amount of appropriate, friendly behavior compared to the amount of inappropriate, crying, negative behavior.
8. Distractibility: the effectiveness of extraneous stimuli to alter ongoing behavior.
9. Attention span and persistence: the length of time and continuation of an activity when presented with distraction.

Using the nine categories, the children were all rated during infancy on a 3-point scale of high, medium, or low. Then, at age 2 years, the children were reassessed. At that time, 10% of the children were rated as having a *difficult temperament*. These children cried frequently; showed irregular biological functions; had a high rate of negative moods and intense reactions; and were easily frustrated. They tended to negatively withdraw from new situations and showed slow adaptations to change. Another 15% of the children were grouped in a category called *slow to warm up*. These children showed low activity levels and were slow adapters whose first reaction was to withdraw from change in daily routines.

The largest group (40%) in the sample were categorized as *easy temperament*. These children demonstrated regularity of habits; they were generally happy and adaptable to new people, situations, and change in the environment. Another 35% of the children were difficult to type because they showed variability across all three categories. The findings were tabulated when the population sample reached adulthood. Seventy percent of the *difficult temperament* children developed behavioral disorders, while only 18% of the *easy temperament* children did so. This study supports the biological theory of causation for CD patterns of behavior.

It is important to remember that children with difficult temperaments do not automatically develop CD. Teachers and parents must be aware that these students are more vulnerable to inconsistency in the environment and to situations that produce stress and frustration, and that they have more difficulty adjusting and adapting to change.

Be proactive, plan ahead; analyze what might cause difficulties for these students. Prepare classroom activities and assignments to increase the likelihood of success for all students.

Link Between Delinquency and APD

Black (1999) reviewed a longitudinal study by Robbins (1966) of 542 individuals who were counseled as adolescents in a child guidance clinic for severe forms of juvenile delinquency. The goal was to determine the link between juvenile delinquency and APD in adulthood. Results showed that some of the individuals who participated in Robbins's study showed improved, positive adjustment as adults. Many more did not. Specifically, statistics provided indicated that 12% were considered to be remitted and showed no problem behavior at all as adults. Another 27% had demonstrated improved behavior as they grew up but were still getting into trouble as adults. The largest group, 61%, had not improved at all. In fact, some individuals were exhibiting more serious deviant behavior as adults. The individuals who did continue to have more serious problems through the lifespan would be classified as early starters. Following is a synopsis from Black (1999):

> Those who continued to make trouble had an earlier onset of behavior problems and showed a greater variety of problems than the others. Their childhood behaviors were more severe and their first arrests occurred at earlier ages. Robbins observed that only those who showed at least six kinds of antisocial behavior and had four or more episodes of such behavior—or at least one episode serious enough to result in a court appearance—were later diagnosed as sociopathic personalities. In milder cases, behavior problems were eventually outgrown. (p. 82)

Biological Factors

Kauffman (2001) reports that genetic and biological factors are almost always correlated with the most severe forms of CD. However, the link is not as strong with more mild to moderate cases. In mild to moderate patterns of CD, parenting methods, family interactions, and the social environment seem to have a stronger effect on shaping behavior. Researchers who favor the genetic theories refer to cyclical symptoms over generations in families who seem to produce offspring with similar type problems. They suggest that there is an organic or biological component of causation. Controversy abounds over whether there are actually any genes linked to hyperaggressive and antisocial behaviors.

The XYY Chromosome Theory There has been little empirical support for a genetic hypothesis to explain generational patterns of aggressive behavior in families. Erickson (1998) examined the XYY chromosomal hypothesis on aggression in men. Supposedly, the XYY pattern results in increased levels of aggression in men. This hypothesis has not been supported by research replication. It had been suggested that men who had an extra Y chromosome (and a total of 47 rather than 46) were overrepresented in prisons and mental institutions because of their hyperaggressive behavioral patterns. However, further study revealed that the majority of men with the XYY chromosome configuration were not incarcerated. Furthermore, the men who were in prison had committed more crimes against property than crimes against persons. Property crimes are considered to be less serious than crimes against persons. Finally, the amount of crime committed by men with the XYY chromosome pattern is not a significant percentage of total crime. Consequently, the XYY chromosome pattern seems to play only a minor role in influencing aggressive or antisocial behaviors.

Heredity and Genetics Research studies on twins indicate a weak but significant link between genetics and antisocial behavior at different ages (Erickson, 1998). Researchers (Christianson, 1977; Cloninger & Gottesman, 1987; Crowe, 1983) have established the fact that there is a slightly (4%) higher correlation in the rates of criminal behavior between identical twins than between fraternal twins. However, this correlation seems to be true only for *adult criminal behavior*. There was no difference between identical twins and fraternal twins for rates of juvenile delinquency. Those scientists who support the nurture theory take the same cyclical patterns of deviant behavior and contend the cause to be related to generational family interaction patterns of abuse; neglect; and harsh, inconsistent punishment (Black, 1999). Adoption studies have shown that antisocial behavior occurs more frequently in children adopted by parents with antisocial behavior patterns (Crowe, 1974). In summary, most researchers would agree that genetics or biology may supply the potential for aggression and antisocial behavior. However, family upbringing, nurturing, and environmental variables can either increase or decrease the potential.

Environment and the Nurture Theme

The nurture theme is strongly based in social learning theory (Bandura, 1973, 1977). Social learning theory appears to play an incredibly important role in shaping children's behavior. It may be one of the strongest influences on the development of behavioral patterns. The environment some individuals live in could be responsible for producing symptoms of CD. Three main environmental causal factors might include any of the following: (a) parenting and discipline in the early home environment that is harsh, punishing, and inconsistent; (b) demonstrating aggressive behavior in the primary elementary grades; and (c) early social rejection by peers due to antisocial or other problem behavior.

The following comment was made by a juvenile while in detention, who had been asked about harsh, punitive discipline in the family:

Parents, they think they be helping a kid by beating them, and it makes them worse, all the anger, he can't do nothing about being beat, so that anger just stays inside him. Because the kid is getting beat from being a toddler on. It could

make the kid feel like beating and violence is what life is all about. ... And he could think it is normal and then when he goes to school... he might fight. And when the teacher or principal gets that kid to the side and says, "listen, you can't do that in my school," the kid might not understand. He might be like, "Why can't I fight? My parents told me that it is right to fight," and he might not know any different. (Goldstein, 1990, pp. 38–39)

Learning may be considered a two-step process. First, behavior is learned and demonstrated for certain reasons. Specific behaviors are functional; they serve to get wants and needs met. Second, behaviors that are reinforced are repeated.

Children learn a great deal about social behavior through the observation and imitation of role models from their environment. Following behavior, consequences from the environment increase, decrease, or maintain those actions of the individual. Consequences sound like a bad sort of thing.... However, consequences can be considered either positive or negative. Positive reinforcement is an effective consequence used to increase a desired behavior.

Punishment is a negative consequence designed to reduce the recurrence of a problem behavior. When the behaviors observed and imitated are positive, individuals repeat those specific behaviors and learn socially acceptable behavior. If the role models are negative, children are likely to learn deviant patterns of behavior. It is just as easy for children to learn positive behaviors as it is for them to learn problem behaviors. Inappropriate behaviors are learned because they are reinforced by certain persons or events in the environment. When that happens, the problem behavior will be repeated. That is how many children learn aggressive, antisocial behaviors. Children are most likely to imitate a model who appears to be rewarded for his behavior. There are currently many inappropriate role models on television, in the movies, and in video games who are rewarded for extremely inappropriate and violent behavior.

The immediate consequences of behavior strongly affect whether behaviors are repeated often enough to internalize specific patterns of behavior for the purposes of meeting the needs of the individual. Adults can interrupt the problem behavior and redirect it to more positive patterns followed by consistent and continuous schedules of positive reinforcement for the new pattern of appropriate behavior.

The following response was given by an adolescent who was sentenced to a corrections facility for delinquent behavior. The individual was interviewed and asked for an opinion on what could be done to stop juvenile delinquency:

> From the minute they're a baby and they grow up they see what their family does, and what their family does they're going to do. Yeah, that's their environment, that's how they grew up. If they grew up learning that stealing, doing drugs, drinking is good, then that's what they're going to do. If they grew up learning that going to school, graduating from school, going to college is good, that's what they're going to do 'cause that's their environment (Goldstein, 1990, p. 38).

The environment in which a child grows up and the adult role models he often observes obviously play a very strong role in shaping personality, character, and behavior.

Consequences Shape Behavior

Social learning theory asserts that all behavior, including antisocial behavior or aggressive behavior, is learned through direct consequences of the behavior. Bandura (1973) explained that three major factors influence the occurrence of aggressive behavior. First, there are environmental conditions that prompt certain behaviors. Second, there is the nature of the behavior itself. Some behaviors that are positive and appropriate naturally solicit positive reinforcement from the environment. Other behaviors that may be antisocial, aggressive, noncompliant, or illegal can be reinforced or supported by the environment. That happens when the individual who acts out the inappropriate behavior is rewarded by

getting away with it or getting something he wants. All behaviors are consequated in some way; they are either reinforced or punished after they occur. Third, there are other people in the environment, described as the cognitive or affective variables, who influence the occurrence or repetition of the behavior. This means that the individual learns through repetition and reinforcement of behavior that he can use aggression to get wants and/or needs met.

The reciprocal effects of all three components and the individual's social history with family, peers, and other adults determine whether an aggressive pattern of behavior is repeatedly demonstrated (Kauffman, 2001). Thus, the individual learns to control the environment and others in it with aggression, hostility, and intimidation. Although these are maladaptive behaviors, they continue to be used because the individual is rewarded for using them. He learns that aggression is an effective means to intimidate others, to get his own way, or to get what he wants. As a result, the individual continues to demonstrate antisocial behavior and aggression rather than to learn and use more appropriate problem-solving and decision-making skills.

Common Characteristics of Students with CD

Kauffman (2001) summarized a number of environmental factors that appear to be common in students with CD. The factors relate to family, school, and peers. However, there is no one single causative factor when diagnosing CD. It is a multiply caused condition. Each person with a disorder must be considered as a unique individual. However, common characteristics have been identified.

Family

Some families have a child who has problems despite effective parenting and strong family bonds. However, the more typical family with a child who has CD might be described as chaotic, unsupportive, and generally dysfunctional in nature. There frequently are many children spaced closely together. Divorce, abandonment, and high levels of interpersonal conflict are routine. Family interactions and parental supervision tend to be lax to nonexistent. There may be extended family members living in the home who also have problems. Discipline is described as harsh, punitive, inconsistent, and unpredictable. Many times a single parent is head of the household. For one reason or another, the child with CD may not receive enough positive attention. When asked what caused problems for children in a family, an incarcerated juvenile commented:

> Like not being around your parents or gettin' love like you see other kids get; and you start saying nobody cares about me. You just do things to get attention because it's the only way you could get it. (Goldstein, 1990, p. 42)

The adults in the home environment also tend to lack social skills and child-rearing skills. They may use coercive interactions to settle differences. Examples of the coercive behavioral patterns that might be used during an argument or discussion involving a difference of opinion include fighting, yelling, hitting, and slamming the door on the way out. Since these are common patterns of behavior observed by young children with CD, they imitate those patterns in similar situations. They tend to imitate behaviors that are easy and familiar to them (Kaplan, 1995). Thus, the generational, antisocial patterns of behavior may be perpetuated.

School

Growing up in a chaotic home situation often leads to academic and behavioral difficulties at school. The majority of students with antisocial behavior experience a variety of problems in school related to academic underachievement or failure and social skill deficits. Disciplinary strategies at school that are erratic, inconsistent, and highly punitive are likely to make the problems worse.

Educators who are very well versed and highly competent at teaching academic content area sub-

jects are often at a loss when it comes to managing problem behavior in the class. Most teachers resort to exclusionary forms of punishment: send the student out in the hall or down to the office and give a detention or a suspension. This form of punishment is ineffective over the long term because it does not teach the student what to do instead of the problem behavior.

Another factor that may lead to students' disruptive behavior in the classroom is an academic curriculum that is neither motivating, relevant, nor appropriate for the individual strengths and weaknesses in skill levels of the students. This phenomenon leads to lack of motivation and increased levels of apathy, being off-task, and escalating problem behavior.

Human nature seems to focus on problem behavior and ignore positive, appropriate behavior. Too often, no one pays any attention to the nonaggressive behaviors or attempts to achieve academically at school that students with CD demonstrate on occasion. When they do behave and try to achieve, no one notices. Then, as soon as they deviate even the slightest bit or break the most trivial rule, punishment comes crashing down. Thus, they tend to view school as a highly aversive failure situation.

CD Affects Academic Achievement   The average student with a behavior disorder is already 2 years behind academically (Morgan & Jenson, 1988). Walker et al. (1995) reported further academic underachievement among boys labeled either antisocial or at-risk. Boys labeled antisocial had more severe problem behaviors than boys who were labeled at-risk. The results were documented by longitudinal data gathered across 3 years. Percentile scores from standardized math, reading, and total achievement during the fifth, sixth, and seventh grades were charted. In all cases, the academic scores for the group of boys with at-risk behaviors ranged above the 50th percentile. This means their scores were better than at least 50% of the other students who took the achievement tests. Their percentile scores extended from a low of 52.18 percentile on math in the seventh grade to a high of 58.88 on the total achievement score during the sixth grade. All of the academic achievement scores for the group of boys with antisocial behavior were below the 50th percentile. Their scores ranged from a low of the 23.80 percentile on math in the seventh grade to a high of the 43.36 percentile on reading in the sixth grade. These scores mean that about 60–80% of other students scored higher on the achievement test.

Both of the highest percentile scores for the two groups occurred during the sixth grade and both of the lowest percentile rankings occurred for math during the seventh grade. It is clear that both groups could benefit by a boost in academic achievement. Even the high of scoring in the 58th percentile means that 42% of the students, which is almost half, are achieving at higher levels than the group studied. What is not clear, however, is exactly which came first (sort of like the chicken or the egg). Is the academic underachievement a result of the CD? Conversely, might the aggression and antisocial behavior be a result of the learning frustrations experienced by the student? Proactive and positive educational practices may be just the tool necessary to reduce antisocial behaviors and teach students positive, socially acceptable alternatives.

Social Skills and the Peer Group

Students who have so many problems both at home and at school usually show extreme social skill deficits. Demonstrating antisocial behaviors at a young age is highly predictive of future adult social interaction problems later in life (Kauffman, 2001). When children show multiple forms of antisocial behavior problems with a high frequency of occurrence across multiple settings, they are almost guaranteed to be rejected by peers and adults (Walker et al., 1995). At a very young age, children will reject another child who shows highly aggressive and disruptive forms of behavior. The social rejection usually leads directly to isolation from the normally developing peer group and concomitant academic failure.

These excluded children often gravitate toward a negative peer group. This group usually is composed of other students with the same type of problems. The prime time for this to happen is around fourth and fifth grades. Seventy percent of the children who become involved with a deviant peer group experience their first felony arrest within 2 years of becoming an active member of that peer group (Walker et al., 1995). In adolescence, lack of parental supervision combined with other negative family factors and academic failure merge to lure them into more serious forms of antisocial behavior. Delinquency, substance abuse, gangs, and other criminal activities become commonplace for them. If the delinquent pattern of behavior continues, it becomes highly predictive of adult criminality (Walker et al., 1995). In addition, this type of maladaptive behavior then seriously limits future opportunities in education, employment, and positive social relationships.

CD Symptoms Are Persistent

CD is not a stage or a phase that children just grow out of as they mature. CD tends to be very persistent and resistant to intervention. The progression of the disorder tends to run from the diagnosis of CD in childhood, to juvenile delinquency in adolescence, to APD in adulthood. The label *juvenile delinquent* refers to a minor child who has broken the law (Vergason & Anderegg, 1997).

Stability of CD Compared to IQ Scores

CD behaviors have been shown to be so persistent that they are compared to the stability of IQ scores. Walker et al. (1995) reported that the correlation factor on consistency of IQ score over a decade was approximately .70 while the coefficient for aggressive behavior was approximately .80. This means that both IQ score and aggression are relatively constant and do not tend to change very much during the life span (does not tend to increase or decrease as a person ages).

A coefficient of 1.0 means that the behavior would remain totally invariable as the individual passed through developmental stages during the life span. For example, regarding IQ, this means that smart students tend to become smart adults. Pertaining to CD, this means that young children diagnosed with CD are likely to maintain antisocial, aggressive behaviors through adulthood. The coefficients of .70 and .80, being very close to 1.0, show that both IQ and aggression are stable behaviors over a given period (Quay, 1986; Reid, 1993).

Approximately 50% of children with the most severe cases of CD are later diagnosed with APD (Phelps & McClintock, 1994). Kutner (1993) reported almost the same results for students who demonstrate bully behavior. About half of the students who were under age 10 and got in trouble at school for being overly aggressive with others went on to demonstrate more serious maladaptive behavior during adolescence. Kazdin (1987) recommends that when individuals over the age of 8 demonstrate severe rates of behaviors characteristic of CD, it should be considered an incurable, chronic condition.

However, even though some people consider CD to be a lifelong disorder, the individual can be taught self-management and coping strategies. With consistent intervention, problem behaviors can be managed with an appropriately structured and effective behavior management plan. Because of the developmental progression of CD, early identification and intervention services take on incredible importance and may be the most direct route to successfully arresting the process.

Assessment for CD

Assessment methods to diagnose CD can take many forms. Screening at an early age is vital for remediation of antisocial behavior. A significant mistake made by early childhood educators is to assume that young children who show aggressive behaviors will simply improve or outgrow those behaviors on their own. This pivotal misconception leads teachers to do nothing about the prob-lems during the early childhood years, when intervention has the most potential to be effective and successful at reducing antisocial behavior.

The early childhood years are absolutely the most critically important time to screen for and intervene with antisocial behavior. Without effective early intervention, children with antisocial behaviors tend to show escalating rates of deviant behaviors, often with increasingly harmful results to themselves and to others (Walker et al., 1995). Individuals with CD usually begin to show more serious, criminal types of behavior as they get older if there is no structured intervention. Kazdin (1987), as cited in Walker et al. (1995), predicted after about age 8, antisocial behavior and conduct disorder should be viewed as a chronic disorder (like diabetes) for which there is no cure (pp. 4–5).

Screening

Early intervention begins with screening all children for antisocial behaviors. Drummond (1993) relates that any screening instrument for antisocial behavior should meet the following criteria to make it most effective. The instrument should be brief, quick, and easy for educators to use. It should be comprised of approximately 10 research-based, reliable, and valid behavioral descriptors. Research-based means the test has previously been used to efficiently identify students who are truly at risk for developing antisocial behaviors. Reliable means that if the test was given to the same students multiple times, it would identify the same students with antisocial behavior each time. Valid means that the device actually screens for antisocial behaviors and not for a variety of other handicapping conditions. Behavioral descriptors are definitions of behaviors that would be seen in children with CD.

Important Components of a Screening Program

There are four important points to keep in mind when setting up a screening program (Walker et al., 1995). In general, the points relate to the idea that educators must be on the lookout for the types of behavior that indicate CD in young children:

- Use a *proactive* approach rather than a *reactive* approach for screening.
- Gain a broad-based perspective of the student's behavior with an ecological screening procedure.
- Screen at-risk students early, ideally in preschool or kindergarten.
- Use sociometric screening devices supplemented by direct observations, school records, and teacher/peer/parent ratings.

There is no need to wait for a major problem to occur. That is known as the reactive or "wait and see what happens" approach. Instead, work to effectively manage and eliminate small problems as they crop up. Observe and analyze behaviors of all children in a variety of environments. Chances are if the student has a problem in one area, he is also having that problem or other problems in a variety of classroom or educational environments. Plan structured intervention to deal with problems as they first appear no matter what the age of the child. Do not sit back, wait, and hope the antisocial behavior of young children will go away. The *train and hope* method rarely accomplishes anything positive (Morgan & Jenson, 1988). Usually, problems that are ignored just become worse.

Student Risk Screening Scale (SRSS)

One example of a screening device specifically designed to assess for antisocial behavior is the *Student Risk Screening Scale* (SRSS, Drummond, 1993). It contains the following seven items related to antisocial behavior:

1. Stealing
2. Lying, cheating, sneaking
3. Behavior problems
4. Peer rejection
5. Low academic achievement
6. Negative attitude
7. Aggressive behavior

Each of the seven behavioral items is scored on a 3-point scale where 0 = never occurs, 1= occasionally occurs, and 3 = frequently occurs. The total score on the SRSS can range anywhere from 0 to 21, with higher scores showing more serious behavior. Drummond then established categories based on total scores for levels of risk as follows:

High risk = 9–21
Moderate risk = 4–8
Low risk = 0–3

Students with high-risk scores should be further evaluated to determine specific behavioral problems. The results of the SRSS will show teachers precise areas of behavioral risk for all students screened. Based on the areas of risk, educators can design individualized behavior change plans to reduce those behaviors and teach new, appropriate, positive replacement behaviors. Study skills to improve academic performance, social skills to increase appropriate interactions with others, health awareness to identify consequences of high-risk lifestyle, and strategies for resisting the temptations of drug and alcohol abuse are focus areas for program planning (Kauffman, 2001). These and other forms of intervention can then be implemented to intervene in individualized problem areas.

Functional Assessment

Functional analysis is an assessment procedure to determine what purpose a student's aberrant behavior serves (Kauffman, 2001). To implement functional analysis, the observer completes an anecdotal-type observation in which a running narrative of behaviors is recorded. Then, to analyze the narrative, the observer organizes the information into A, B, and C categories. The A stands for antecedent, the B for behavior, and the C for consequence. The antecedent is what happens just before the problem behavior. It can be thought of as a trigger or a cause of the behavior. The behavior is the action(s) of the student noted in observable, measurable terms. The description should be objective and not judgmental. Finally, the consequence is what happens right after the behavior. Consequences usually serve to increase, decrease, or maintain behavior.

Knowing the antecedents and consequences derived by the behavior is useful for planning redirection. The redirection is the new, appropriate behavior to teach as an alternative to the problem behavior. Sometimes identifying the antecedent, and then eliminating it, will help to reduce the occurrence of the problem behavior. Functional analysis can provide a basis to plan and implement behavior change strategies for making environmental modifications. Examples include tasks required, rules and limitations imposed on the student, and types of reinforcement used to help remedy the maladaptive behavior. In summary, the main purpose of functional behavioral analysis is to determine what purpose the student's problem behavior serves. The student is then taught a socially acceptable replacement behavior that he can use to meet his needs. It is an effective method for teachers to use with behavior change plans.

Multidimensional Behavior Rating Scales

In addition to generally antisocial behavior, students with CD are likely to show problems in a number of situations. Multidimensional rating scales such as the *Child Behavior Checklist* (CBCL, Achenbach & Edelbrock, 1991), the *Revised Behavior Problem Checklist* (RBPC, Quay & Peterson, 1987), or the *Behavior Rating Profile* (BRP, Brown & Hammill, 1990) can be used to assess a variety of behavior problems. Some of the other challenging areas that often overlap with CD include hyperactivity, depression, and other home or school problems. Table 13–3 provides a sample of the array of behaviors covered on multidimensional rating scales.

Predicting the Future

The ability to forecast impending serious behavior problems in specific young children could aid in providing early intervention for those who need it. Walker et al. (1995) reported a relatively simple,

TABLE 13–3 Behavioral Descriptors from Multidimensional Rating Scales

Attention seeking (show-off)
Daredevil (thrill-seeker)
Disruptive, annoying to others
Fights with others
Has a delinquent peer group
Steals, lies
Verbally expresses disrespect for morals, values, laws
Short attention, distractible
Tense, restless
Sluggish, lethargic
Fearful, anxious, depressed
Hypersensitive (feelings are easily hurt)
Self-conscious, easily embarrassed
Repetitive speech, expresses unrealistic thoughts and ideas

Note. *From Manual for the Child Behavior Checklist and Revised Child Behavior Profile, by T. M. Achenbach and C. S. Edelbrook, 1991, Burlington, VT: University of Vermont, Department of Psychiatry; Manual for the Revised Behavior Problem, by H. Quay and D. R. Peterson, 1987, Coral Gables, FL: Author; and Behavior Rating Profile: An Ecological Approach to Behavioral Assessment, by L. L. Brown and D. D. Hammill, 1990, Austin, TX: Pro-Ed.*

but astoundingly accurate method of predicting future delinquency using a sample of fifth graders. The authors used three simple methods to record measures. First, a 5-minute observation using anecdotal recording to document classroom related social skills was completed. Second, the number of discipline referrals in the student's cumulative file was quantified. Third, the number of negative peer interactions that occurred during two 20-minute observations on the playground during recess was recorded. Children with low social skills, numerous discipline referrals, and many negative peer interactions were considered high risk. The authors were then able to use the data collected to predict the arrest record of the students 5 years later at age 15 to 16. Their predictions were accurate in 80% of the cases.

Prevention Strategies

The following response was given by an adolescent who was sentenced to a corrections facility for delinquent behavior. The individual was interviewed and asked for an opinion on what could be done to stop juvenile delinquency:

> The best thing to do to stop juvenile delinquency would be to have structured delinquency classes set in regular city classrooms to learn about the problems of delinquency. Have regular normal classrooms for all the students who have similar problems; a required class that the court makes them take. Before graduation you would have to take a test, role-play, et cetera, and eventually move back into a regular classroom setting. After graduation, you should have follow-up and aftercare emergency numbers you can call if you are thinking of getting into trouble again. Additionally, halfway delinquent houses could be set up throughout the community. (Goldstein, 1990, p. 132)

Three Forms of Prevention

Three types of prevention can be instituted to deter antisocial behavior in youth and adolescents (Kauffman, 2001). The three methods of prevention tactics are categorized as primary, secondary, and tertiary:

- Primary prevention might also be called early intervention. Its purpose is to preclude serious antisocial behavior from occurring in very young children. It takes place *before* the problem behavior pattern can become established.
- Secondary prevention strategies are designed to remediate problem behaviors *after* they occur. This might be accomplished with behavior change plans, counseling, therapy, or other special services.
- Tertiary strategies are developed to reduce the negative affects of antisocial behavior patterns that are resistant to change or unlikely to be changed. The meaning of tertiary is simply "third in order." Tertiary strategies are the least desirable to use, but they should be employed as a means to try to reduce harmful negative effects. An example is counseling or a support group for a family with a child who has CD. Another example is residential treatment, in which students with serious behavior

problems are placed in order to work on behavioral goals and objectives.

Intervention Strategies

Exclusionary Strategies

Detention, in-school suspension, out-of-school suspension, expulsion—all of these disciplinary tactics are exclusionary punishments. Schools tend to use exclusionary punishment to deal with any and all problem behavior. It is quicker and easier for staff members to use than structured and consistent intervention tactics. Students who are not successful in the classroom are typically viewed as behavior problems and subsequently are punished by removal from class or school for a specified period of time. Increasingly severe punishment in the form of more days of suspension or ultimately expulsion are commonly employed for students who cannot seem to conform. Lack of motivation and disruptive behavior problems have been used as grounds for permanently removing certain students from the school system (Sprick, Sprick, & Garrison, 1996).

This punishment-by-removal-from-school form of discipline is based on the fallacy that all students *want* to be in school. Many students learn to use the system to earn a free pass out of school—to legally be absent from school for any number of days. Additionally, the students often are not required to make up the academic work missed; in fact, many are not even allowed to. This exclusionary system stems from the following rationale:

> Learning is a privilege. If the privilege is abused, you will be sent out of the classroom. If your behavior doesn't improve, you will be sent to the office. If your behavior doesn't improve, then you will be suspended. If your behavior still doesn't improve, you will be expelled. (Sprick et al., 1996, p. 4)

Disadvantage to Exclusionary Policies The main disadvantage of the exclusionary system is that it is incredibly negative. It makes school and teachers seem very aversive to tough students—

students who have learning, behavioral, and motivational problems (Rhode, Jenson, & Reavis, 1992). In addition, the punishment system does not teach any new replacement skills. Remember, all behavior is learned. All behavior is functional. Certain behavioral patterns result in wants and needs being met. If students are not taught functional, positive, appropriate replacements for problem behavior, they will keep repeating the same old mistakes.

Prison Recidivism   Recidivism rates for federal prison inmates reflect problems associated with exclusionary punishment. After serving time and being released from prison, 62% of prison inmates commit another crime within 1 year and are then again incarcerated (Bureau of Justice Statistics, 1999). The problem is that the inmates did not learn any new behaviors while they were in prison. Once they get out, they tend to fall back on old, familiar behaviors and commit crimes again. On average it costs about $20,142 each year to incarcerate an inmate for 1 year in a state prison. This figure does not include costs to buy the land, build the prison, or any legal and court costs of the prisoners. The expenditures per inmate were determined by dividing the amount spent on salaries, wages, supplies, utilities, transportation, contractual services, and other current operating items paid for during the fiscal year by the average daily inmate population (U.S. Department of Justice, n.d.). The average cost to educate a public school student is about $6,000, while average cost of private education is about $3,000 (National Center for Policy Analysis, 1996). Based on those cost comparisons, it makes a lot more sense to educate all students, using alternative means and individualized strategies necessary for students who have learning and behavioral problems.

Dropout Rate   The ultimate and ideal goal in education is for all students to graduate, get a high school diploma, and be employable or go on for further education. Currently, that is not happening. The general dropout rate in the United States is about 7 to 29% depending on ethnicity and geographic location. The rates provided by the National Center for Education Statistics in August 2000 indicated that the dropout rate was about 7% for White students, about 13% for African American students, and about 29% for Hispanic students (U.S. Department of Commerce, Bureau of the Census, 2000). About two thirds of all prison inmates across the country are high school dropouts (Jensen & Yerington, 1997).

Current popular exclusionary discipline policies repeatedly exclude students with problems. This practice makes school such an aversive situation that the students often simply drop out, which makes them more likely to fall into the lure of criminal activity. Rhode et al. (1992) reported that 41% of students who drop out are arrested in the first year after separating from school. When that happens, they become a burden for all taxpayers and the legal system. Therefore, either schools can work consistently and effectively to educate all students or we can all pay the big bucks later to incarcerate criminals.

Proactive and Positive Behavior Management

Behavior management practices for students who show aggressive and antisocial behavior must have a proactive and positive orientation. Most students with chronic problem behavior have been through every type of punishment procedure a school can dish out, with no positive effect. What is a more viable alternative? Think positive; think proactive! Educators must be prepared to teach students what to do in place of the old antisocial behaviors that keep getting them into trouble. Each time a problem behavior is reduced or eliminated, there must be a redirection or a teaching component to help the students learn new positive behaviors to replace the inappropriate behavior (Jensen & Yerington, 1997; Rhode et al., 1992). Punishment alone does not result in long-term, durable behavior change. At best, it simply stops the behavior momentarily, usually only while the punisher is present (Kaplan, 1995). Students must be taught alternative, positive replacement behaviors.

Intervention for CD

Educators can use the basic assumptions of the behavioral learning model as a foundation for designing a proactive and mostly positive intervention plan (Jensen & Yerington, 1997; Kaplan, 1995; Kauffman, 2001; Rhode et al., 1992). There are three main components to include: (a) determine specific target behavioral objectives; (b) select strategies for changing behavior to teach and reinforce new appropriate alternative behaviors; and (c) consistently use a precise and accurate data collection method to analyze, measure, and document behavioral change.

Use of all three components in the intervention plan allows the teacher to quantitatively and qualitatively measure the behavior change outcome for each individual student. To be most effective, the behavior change techniques should be employed by adults and peers who have ongoing contact with the student. Yes, peers! Peer pressure can be used in a very positive manner. Teach children how to be good role models. Teach them how to be helpers to reinforce and encourage positive behavior for other children who need to learn to show improved and more appropriate behaviors at school, in the community, and at home. This group could include parents, other caretakers, coaches, other group leaders, teachers, siblings, and classmates. Involving all of these individuals provides a very pervasive and much more more consistent behavior change program. The main focus of the program is on teaching and reinforcing new appropriate alternatives to reduce antisocial behavior.

Some children will not automatically know what to do in place of a misbehavior even though they have been repeatedly punished for the behavior. They do not automatically learn from their mistakes. In fact, it seems like they keep making the same mistakes over and over. This is why these children need to be consistently taught alternative behaviors. It is important to remember to use specific verbal praise and lots of positive reinforcement to encourage the child to keep showing the new replacement behavior. This process can be used to help students be more successful at school, at home, and in the community.

Cognitive Behavior Modification (CBM)

Cognitive behavior modification (CBM) focuses on the student's observable behavior as well as on how he thinks and solves problems. The strategy teaches new thinking behavior. CBM is based on self-instructional training to teach the individual new thinking patterns and good decision-making and problem-solving skills. Self-instructional training simply means that the individual is taught a series of steps to follow to learn a new behavior. The goal of CBM is self-management. The student has gained the ability to control his own behavior (internal locus of control) rather than being dependent on an outside source such as a teacher or a parent for control (external locus of control). Figure 13–1 is a structured method adults might use with youth and adolescents to teach new thinking patterns.

School-Based Interventions

Interventions to modify antisocial behavior at school can be based on a wide variety of strategies. Teachers who are designing the intervention plan can use the method best suited to the needs of each student. A variety of intervention techniques for teachers to use individually or in combination to help reduce problem behavior in the classroom are presented in this section. These are proactive interventions that any teacher could implement in the classroom. They are relevant for both general education and special education.

Classroom Expectations Determine a set of classroom rules or expectations. Develop about five rules, stated in a positive fashion, to tell students what TO DO rather than what NOT to do (Rhode et al., 1992). It may be more effective for the teacher to present them to the students as expectations rather than rules. Many students with ODD and CD view rules as simply something to break or something that does not apply to them. The teacher can state that these expectations will be in place so that all students can learn and be successful in the classroom.

FIGURE 13–1   A Strategy to Teach a New Thinking Pattern

Cognitive Behavior Modification Problem-Solving Activity

1. Say the problem in your own words. Explain how it affects you. How does it affect other people?

2. What was your responsibility for the problem?

3. List all of the different things you could do to try to solve the problem.
   a.
   b.
   c.

4. Write down what might happen if you chose each solution.
   a.
   b.
   c.

5. Which solution would work the best? Why did you decide on this one?

6. Look at the solution you picked. Tell step-by-step how you will carry out the solution. Tell exactly what you will do and what you will say. Write what you will do first, second, third, and so on.
   a.
   b.
   c.
   d.
   e.

I pledge to carry out this plan next time this problem occurs. I understand that this plan will help me solve problems in an appropriate way.

_____   _____
Student's Signature   Date   Teacher's Signature   Date

The set of rules or expectations are the very foundation upon which all the rest of the behavior management principles are built. It is important to talk to the students about the expectations: teach, role-play, and periodically review the expectations just like any other concept the students need to learn. The students will not learn the expectations if the teacher only refers to them on the first day of class. The expectations should be taught in a fashion similar to any other important subject or skill.

Finally, post the expectations in LARGE letters on a 3″ × 5″ piece of tagboard. Remember to give students positive reinforcement for following the expectations. Have a predetermined consequence all ready to apply if students do not follow rules.

Examples of Effective Classroom Expectations

Do what your teacher asks the first time.
Be at desk ready to begin class when the bell rings.
Raise hand and wait for permission before talking in class.

Work on assignments during time provided in class.

Turn in completed assignments on time.

Positive Reinforcement: IFEED Teachers must actively plan to use a great deal of positive, genuine, teacher praise and positive reinforcement for appropriate behavior. The classroom must have a positive climate for tough students to be successful (Rhode et al., 1992). Aim for about four to six positive praise statements for each reprimand given during class time. Rhode et al. (1992) described five teacher behaviors to practice when giving students praise. The acronym IFEED was used to help teachers remember this strategy:

I = Immediate
F = Frequent
E = Eye conact
E = Enthusiasm
D = Description

- **Immediately** praise the appropriate behavior. Reduce the amount of time that lapses between the behavior and the teacher's verbal reinforcement. This helps the student connect his own appropriate behavior with the positive reinforcement.

- **Frequently** praise behavior. Look for opportunities to give students a pat on the back, some praise, or to tell them how well they are doing. For some students, the teacher may have to look hard for tiny good behaviors. It is important to find the little bits of gold in every student. Some students might have nice-sized chunks of gold; some might have little nuggets; others have a little gold dust that is not found until the teacher gets through all the crusty stuff on the outside. Teacher attention is so incredibly reinforcing to students that a little positive attention goes a long way toward encouraging academic excellence and improved social behavior.

- Use direct **Eye Contact** with the student being praised. Look the student right in his beady little eyes! Eye contact helps ensure the

students knows he is being spoken to, listens to the teacher, and comprehends the message. It's not a guarantee; it just makes it more likely!

- Be **Enthusiastic** when praising behavior. Make it fun and exciting for students. When the teacher's behavior is enthusiastic and motivating, students are more likely to be engaged and motivated. Motivation is contagious; it is catching like a cold or the flu. If the teacher has it, the students are going to have it. Teaching is like a sales job. What works in a classroom works because the teacher sold it with enthusiasm and motivation.

- Give praise **Descriptively**. Rather that simply saying, "good job" or "good work," tell the student precisely what she did well. Here is a descriptive example: "You must have really studied for the math test this week! You have every single problem computed and labeled correctly. I am so proud of you for putting in so much effort to study your multiplication facts!"

It takes a little longer, but it is so much more effective for the student to be able to connect his behavior with the reinforcement. When used consistently, the IFEED method works very well on its own. It can be combined with tangible rewards, including token reinforcement or point systems. These systems provide an immediate reinforcer in the form of points or tokens that can be traded at a later time for preferred activities, privileges. or tangible reinforcers. The distribution of tokens and points or other tangible rewards should always be paired with verbal praise like the IFEED method.

Verbal Positive Reinforcement It is important for teachers and parents to consistently give verbal feedback to the student regarding her behavior and academic achievement. Some students are not accustomed to receiving positive reinforcement from adults. One reason may be that they do not show many appropriate behaviors. It is important to start small. Make note of small appropriate behaviors such as good eye contact, appropriate facial expression, participation, effort on tasks, or memory skills to reward. Try to use mostly positive redirection and feedback to help prompt and shape the prosocial replacement behaviors. These positive consequences are crucial to helping students learn and internalize the new behaviors.

Antecedents and Consequences Be aware of antecedents and consequences coming from the environment. Antecedents come just before a behavior and can be thought of as the cause or trigger of a problem. A consequence happens right after and usually serves to increase, decrease, or maintain a behavior.

It is important to recognize small signals or subtle indicators of problem behavior brewing. Some overt difficulties students exhibit are easier to observe than others. Subtle behaviors are much more difficult to spot. Making an effort to become an expert at analyzing student behavior will help teachers learn to recognize the more subtle signals of imminent problem behavior. Skill at observation and interpretation will help teachers to recognize small problems that may be ready to escalate. It is much easier to deal with small problems than major explosions. Every behavior has an antecedent, whether it is readily observable or not. A crisis situation usually results from a series of smaller storms that can be tracked by observant teacher radar.

Teachers must be aware of specific consequences that occur right after student behavior. It is very easy to inadvertently reward misbehavior with teacher attention. Teacher attention is powerful and highly rewarding for students. Peer attention can also be very reinforcing. For some students who are usually not targets of positive teacher attention, negative attention will do just fine. They will take whatever they can get. This is how some teachers unintentionally reinforce the very behaviors they want to reduce. Rather than using negative attention or punishment, the teacher should be ready to redirect misbehavior to a positive alternative.

Contingency Contracts Teachers might want to set up a contingency contract to formally designate the agreement regarding appropriate behavior and positive reinforcement between the teacher and/or parents and the student. The contract sets the terms for expected behavior in writing. It usually designates the positive reinforcement that will be given and a specific period for duration of the contract. Jenson, Rhode, and Reavis (1994) provide a variety of ready-made contracts for teachers in the *Tough Kid Tool Box*. There are sample contracts to promote more appropriate general behavior, to follow rules, to increase academic achievement, to be more successful at recess or on the bus, to complete homework, and to behave properly in the cafeteria.

Modeling and Imitation Children learn a lot by watching models and imitating what they do. This method is called observational learning. Teachers and parents should be good, consistent models of desired student behaviors. To begin this learning process, the teacher may need to work in private on-to-one sessions with the student. The student must be able to recognize and perform the behavior in order to consistently imitate or model the behavior himself.

Peers can also be used as good role models. Teach classmates and siblings to use *positive peer pressure* at school and at home. Pairing a student who is a good role model with a student who needs to learn the appropriate replacement behavior can be an effective method of behavior change. It is important to consistently reinforce students for imitating the appropriate behaviors. Adults and peers can provide verbal positive reinforcement.

Shaping Shaping is a procedure that teachers can use for behavioral intervention. The teacher task analyzes a specific skill to determine all the steps between the student's current level of performance and the desired mastery level of the skill. The process is based on rewarding successive approximations of the desired target behavior. Successive approximations are described as each behavioral step. To use shaping, the teacher promotes new student responses by building on behavioral skills the student already has. The teacher then reinforces successive approximations of the desired behavior. The key to effective shaping is to identify and reinforce specific steps toward behavioral improvement.

The teacher reinforces progress toward the behavioral goal. However, if the student should backslide for any reason, the teacher does not reinforce behavior that regresses to a previous successive approximation. Only forward progress is rewarded.

Social Skills Instruction   Systematic social skills training is incredibly important for students with CD. The social skills curriculum will help students learn to initiate and maintain appropriate social relationships. It will help the students learn how to make friends and cope with a variety of situations in the social environment. Like the antisocial behavior problems that are associated with CD, social skill deficits are not a stage or a phase that children just outgrow. Kauffman (2001) identified peer isolation as a child as the number one predictor of future adult adjustment problems. An effective social skills training program not only teaches students to demonstrate appropriate social behavior and social decision-making skills, but also teaches students to inhibit behaviors that are likely to cause problems.

Self-Management Skills

Self-management, self-reliance, and independence are an ultimate goal of education. To practice effective self-management, students should be able to apply the following three steps (Kaplan & Carter, 1995). First, the students should be able to self-assess their behavior. This means they have to know when they are doing the behavior and when they are not. For example, they would need to comprehend what constituted *rule-following* behavior as opposed to *rule-breaking* behavior in order to *follow the rules* at school or at home.

Second, students must be able to self-monitor their behavior. Self-monitoring means that the student keeps track of the behavior. This might be done by marking a chart or graph, placing a token in a can, or giving himself points on a score sheet.

Finally, the student should be able to self-reinforce herself for following through on behavioral goals. Most individuals who are successful in their personal lives and careers know how to plan to get work done and follow through on responsibilities

before rewarding themselves with fun and desirable activities. Teaching self-management procedures to students will help them learn to function independently and to be successfully adjusted adults.

In summary, the old punitive, exclusionary disciplinary strategies act as tools to weed the less desirable, less motivated students out of school. It is a known fact that many students who drop out of high school, who leave without a diploma, end up on the wrong side of the law. Rhode et al. (1992) reported that 65% of students with behavioral disorders drop out of high school. Of those students, 41% are arrested within 1 year of separating from school. Additionally, remember that two thirds of all prison inmates across the country are high school dropouts (Jensen & Yerington, 1997). Tough kids need effective educational programming. All educators should motivate and educate these students to help shape them into well-adjusted and productive adults. As one teacher said, "My ultimate goal is for all of my students to be taxpayers" (personal communication, Jeff Radosh, 2001). The proactive approach to intervention—based on teaching new, appropriate, and positive behaviors and improved thinking, problem-solving and decision-making skills—is the most effective intervention for remediating CD behavior.

Implications for Working with Youth and Adolescents

The following response was given by an adolescent who was sentenced to a corrections facility for delinquent behavior. The individual was interviewed and asked for an opinion on what could be done to stop juvenile delinquency:

> One thing I thought about is like give some kind of privileges. Like school, they should give, like, every month or maybe every semester some kind of thing for people who haven't skipped or missed much school. Like maybe an hour lunch ... I don't know—something that most students would want, something that most students would work

for, you know, if you didn't take that skip day ....
Maybe the same for the community .... Maybe like
a carnival or something where, like, students that
weren't in trouble or anything ... or have kept
themselves out of trouble .... Some kind of privileges like that. I don't know exactly, it would be
kind of hard, but like a carnival or a fair. (Goldstein,
1990, p. 143)

Most students are looking for structure and discipline. They want to be successful. They like to
earn rewards, do fun things, feel like they are part
of the team, and successfully accomplish tasks.
Youth and adolescents with CD are no different
from others with normally developing behavior.

It is the responsibility of educators, parents, and
other professionals to guide these students through
the obstacle course of education and social interactions to achieve to their greatest potential. It is often a very difficult job. Students who have learned
antisocial and aggressive behavior are not always
pleasant or very fun to work with. However, many
students just need the right teacher to find the right
way to teach them. The author has been asked on
several occasions why she chooses to work with students with CD and other types of antisocial and aggressive behavior problems. My answer? "I see a
great deal of untapped potential in these students.
There is so much talent just waiting to be discovered. In many cases, a lot of it is "street smarts." But
that just goes to show what they can learn when
they are strongly motivated. There is gold in every
one of those students. I just have to find the way to
get through to each individual student!"

An individualized, well-planned, patient, and
generally positive approach is the foundation for
an excellent start to motivating these students to
show more appropriate behavior and higher levels
of academic achievement at school. That way,
many of the students who might have become
high school dropouts, gang members, or criminals
may just end up being the next success story with
a high school diploma, a college education, and a
good job.

Identification and early intervention with antisocial behavior is the key to remediation of this
chronic and lifelong problem. Teachers must learn
basic identifiers for CD. Then it will be important
for educators, particularly early childhood teachers and other elementary grade teachers, to be familiar with quick and easy-to-administer screening
devices to determine which students may be showing early signs of CD. Following the screening procedure, identified students should have a positive
and proactive individualized behavior management
plan to provide intervention and remediation for
antisocial behaviors. Reducing problem behaviors
and teaching new positive replacement behaviors
must be a priority in program planning and intervention for students with CD behavior.

References

Achenbach, T. M., & Edelbrock, C. S. (1991). *Manual for the Child Behavior Checklist and Revised Child Behavior Profile*. Burlington, VT: University of Vermont, Department of Psychiatry.

American Psychiatric Association. (2000). *Diagnostic and statistical manual of mental disorders* (4th ed., text revision). Washington, DC: Author.

Bandura, A. (1973). *Aggression: A social learning analysis*. Englewood Cliffs, NJ: Prentice Hall.

Bandura, A. (1977). *Social learning theory*. Englewood Cliffs, NJ: Prentice Hall.

Black, D. W. (1999). *Bad boys, bad men*. New York: Oxford University Press.

Bonds, M., & Stoker, S. (2000). *Bully-proofing your school: A comprehensive approach for middle schools*. Longmont, CO: Sopris West.

Brown, L. L., & Hammill, D. D. (1990). *Behavior Rating Profile: An ecological approach to behavioral assessment*. Austin, TX: Pro-Ed.

Bureau of Justice Statistics. (1999). www.ojp.usdoj.gov/bjs/

Chess, S., & Thomas, A. (1983). *Origins and evolutions of behavior disorders: From infancy to early adult life*. New York: Brunner/Mazel.

Christianson, K. O. (1977). A review of studies of criminal-ity among twins. In S. S. Mednick & K. O. Christianson (Eds.), *Biosocial basis of criminal behavior* (pp. 45–88). New York: Gardner Press.

Clonninger, C. R., & Gottesman, L. L. (1987). Genetic and environmental factors in antisocial behavior disor-ders. In S. A. Mednick, T. E. Moffitt, & S. A. Stack

(Eds.), *Causes of Crime: New biological approaches* (pp. 92–109). New York: Cambridge University Press.

Coleman, M. C., & Webber, J. (2002). *Emotional and behavioral disorders: Theory and practice* (4th ed.). Needham Heights, MA: Allyn & Bacon.

Crowe, R. R. (1974). An adoption study of antisocial personality. *Archives of General Psychiatry, 31*, 785–791.

Crowe, R. R. (1983). Antisocial personality disorders. In R. E. Tarter (Ed.), *The child at psychiatric risk* (pp. 214–227). Oxford, England: Oxford University Press.

Drummond, T. (1993). *The Student Risk Screening Scale (SRSS)*. Grants Pass, OR: Josephine County Mental Health Program.

Erickson, M. T. (1998). *Behavior disorders of children and adolescents: Assessment, etiology, and intervention* (3rd ed.).Upper Saddle River, NJ: Merrill/Prentice Hall.

Garrity, C., Baris, M., & Porter, W. (2000). *Bully-proofing your child: A parent's guide.* Longmont, CO: Sopris West.

Garrity, C., Jens, K., Porter, W., Sager, N., & Short-Camilli, C. (1994). *Bully-proofing your school: A comprehensive approach for elementary schools.* Longmont, CO: Sopris West.

Gelfand, D. M., Jenson, W. R., & Drew, C. J. (1988). *Understanding child behavior disorders.* Fort Worth, TX: Holt, Rinehart and Winston.

Goldstein, A. P. (1990). *Delinquents on delinquency.* Champaign, IL: Research Press.

Jensen, M. M., & Yerington, P. C. (1997). *Gangs: Straight talk, straight up.* Longmont, CO: Sopris West.

Jenson, W. R., Rhode, G., & Reavis, H. K. (1994). *The tough kid toolbox.* Longmont, CO: Sopris West.

Kaplan, J. S. (with Carter, J.). (1995). *Beyond behavior modification* (3rd ed.). Austin, TX: Pro-Ed.

Kauffman, J. M. (2001). *Characteristics of emotional and behavioral disorders of children and youth* (7th ed.). Upper Saddle River, NJ: Merrill/Prentice Hall.

Kazdin, A. (1987). *Conduct disorders in childhood and adolescence.* London: Sage.

Kutner, L. (1993, January). Young bullies often get worse. *Eugene Register Guard.*

Loeber, R., Wung, P., Keenan, K., Giroux, B., Stouthamer-Loeber, M., Van Kammen, W., et al. (1993). Developmental pathways in disruptive child behavior. *Developmental and Psychopathology, 5*(1/2), 103–134.

Morgan, D. P., & Jenson, W. R. (1988). *Teaching behaviorally disordered students: Preferred practices.* Upper Saddle River, NJ: Merrill/Prentice Hall.

National Center for Policy Analysis. (March 26, 1996). *Private Education Costs Less.* Retrievable from www.ncpa.org

National School Safety Center. (n.d.). *Safe school planning: The art of the possible.* Retrievable from www.nscc1.org.

Newman, D. A., Horne, A. M., & Bartolomucci, C. L. (2000). *Bully busters: A teacher's manual for helping bullies, victims, and bystanders.* Champaign, IL: Research Press.

Patterson, G. R., Reid, J. B., & Dishion, T. J. (1992). *Antisocial boys: A social interactional approach* (Vol. 4). Eugene, OR: Castalia.

Phelps, L., & McClintock, K. (1994). Conduct disorder. *Journal of Psychopathology and Behavioral Assessment, 16*(1), 53–66.

Quay, H. (1986). Conduct disorders. In H. Quay & J. Werry (Eds.), *Psychopathological disorders of childhood.* (pp. 35–72). New York: Wiley.

Quay, H., & Peterson, D. R. (1987). *Manual for the Revised Behavior Problem Checklist.* Coral Gables, FL: Author.

Reid, J. (1993). Prevention of conduct disorder before and after school entry: Relating interventions to developmental findings. *Development and Psychopathology, 5*(1/2), 243–262.

Rhode, G., Jenson, W. R., & Reavis, H. K. (1992). *The tough kid book.* Longmont, CO: Sopris West.

Robbins, L. N. (1966). *Deviant children grown up.* Baltimore: Williams & Wilkins.

Sprick, R. S., & Howard, L. M. (1995). *Teacher's encyclopedia of behavior management.* Longmont, CO: Sopris West.

Sprick, R. S., Sprick, M., & Garrison, M. (1996). *Foundations: Establishing positive discipline practices.* Longmont, CO: Sopris West.

Thomas, A., & Chess, S. (1977). *Temperament and development.* New York: Brunner/Mazel.

U.S. Department of Commerce, Bureau of the Census (2000). Current Population Survey, unpublished tabulations; and U.S. Department of Education, National Center for Education Statistics, Dropout Rates in the United States. Retrievable from nces.ed.gov/pubs2002/droppub_2001/

U.S. Department of Justice. (n.d.). *State prison expenditures, 1996.* Retrieved from http://www.ojp.usdoj.gov/bjs/abstract/spe96htm.

Vergason, G. A., & Anderegg, M. L. (1997) *Dictionary of special education and rehabilitation.* Denver, CO: Love.

Wahler, R., & Dumas, J. E. (1986). "A chip off the old block": Some interpersonal characteristics of coercive children across generations. In P. Strain, M. Guralnick, & H. M. Walker (Eds.), *Children's social behavior: Development, assessment, and modifications* (pp. 49–91). Orlando, FL: Academic Press.

Walker, H. M., Colvin, G., & Ramsey, E. (1995). *Antisocial behavior in schools: Strategies and best practices.* Pacific Grove, CA: Brooks/Cole.

Walker, H. M., Ramsey, E., & Gresham, F. M. (2004). *Antisocial behavior in schools: Evidence-based practices* (2nd ed.). Belmont, CA: Wadsworth/Thompson.

Walls, L. *Bullying and sexual harassment in schools.* (n.d.). Retrievable from www.cfchildren.org/article_wallsl.shtml.

PART 5

CATEGORIES OF PERVASIVE DEVELOPMENTAL DISORDERS

Chapter 14: **Autism Spectrum Disorders and Schizophrenia**

CHAPTER

14

AUTISM SPECTRUM DISORDERS AND SCHIZOPHRENIA

After completing the chapter, the reader will be able to identify:

- The definition of autism spectrum disorders, including autism, Rett's disorder, childhood disintegrative disorder, and Asperger's syndrome.
- Causes and prevalence of autism spectrum disorders.
- Typical behaviors related to specific autism spectrum disorders.
- The meaning of autistic savant.
- Assessment methods for autism spectrum disorders.
- Characteristic symptoms and treatment options for schizophrenia.
- Implications for educators, parents, and other professionals who work with youth and adolescents.

Introduction

When you first understand that your child's been diagnosed with autism, part of the frustration is that people always ask you, "Well, what causes that? What's the cure?" There are no answers. And it is frustrating for us to have to know that initially, but even harder for us to try to have to explain it. (Greenbough, 1989, p. 29)

The situation is frustrating but true. Currently, there are no specific answers. Using autism as one example of a pervasive developmental disorder (autism spectrum disorder), it is a baffling and often disheartening disorder for researchers, educators, parents, and other family members. Until one encounters a disorder of this type firsthand, most people either do not know anything about autism or have a vague notion of the affliction based on television programs and magazine articles. More commonly, the public knows about autism through Dustin Hoffman's Academy-Award-winning portrayal of Raymond Babbit, a man with autism, in the movie *Rainman*.

The Autism Society of America (ASA) is a resource that can be used to obtain realistic and current information on autism. ASA was founded in 1965 by a small group of parents. The society has grown to more than 24,000 members connected by over 200 chapters across the United States. The ASA provides information and education on autism, supports ongoing research, and advocates for programs and services for individuals with autism. For further information:

Autism Society of America
7910 Woodmont Avenue, Suite 300
Bethesda, MD 20814-3067
Phone: (301) 657-0881; Fax: (301) 657-0869
www.autism-society.org

Although the American Psychiatric Association (APA, 2000) uses the umbrella term *pervasive developmental disorder*, some professionals have begun to use the term *autism spectrum disorder* (Gargiulo, 2003; Heward, 2003; Simpson & Zionts, 2000; Turnbull, Turnbull, Shank, Smith, & Leal, 2002). The goal of this chapter is to define the subtypes of pervasive developmental disorder (autism spectrum disorder), including autism, Rett's disorder, childhood disintegrative disorder, and Asperger's syndrome. Information is provided on the possible causes, prevalence, and characteristics of the disorders. In addition, assessment methods and a number of general treatment options are presented.

Pervasive Developmental Disorder

Definition of Pervasive Developmental Disorder

What is a pervasive developmental disorder (autism spectrum disorder)? *The Diagnostic and Statistical Manual of Mental Disorders* (DSM-IV-TR, APA, 2000) defines a pervasive developmental disorder as a qualitative impairment in the areas of imaginative activities and social interaction skills, including verbal and nonverbal communication skills and social behaviors. The observer will note concurrent inadequate development of academic, language, speech, and motor skills to a severe degree. It is estimated that approximately 10 to 15 children in every 10,000 show the more general behavioral symptoms of this disorder (APA, 2000; Simpson & Zionts, 2000).

Autism Spectrum Disorders and Pervasive Developmental Disorder

Autism has been historically referred to as a *pervasive developmental disorder*. The constellation of neurologically based disorders with characteristics somewhat like autism are being labeled *autism spectrum disorders*. This still means that the disorders have pervasive wide-ranging symptoms, a variety of characteristics, and skill levels from very low to very high. To reduce confusion, the meaning remains the same; only the label has been changed by researchers. How do researchers differentiate between a diagnosis of autism spectrum disorder and autism or any of the other associated disorders? The label *autism spectrum disorder* is used when the child shows *general* pervasive maladaptive behavior related to social interaction and communication skills but lacks the specific characteristics of autism. The distinctive attributes of autism are presented later in the chapter. Other autism spectrum disorders, including Rett's syndrome, childhood disintegrative disorder, and Asperger's syndrome, are also discussed. Schizophrenia, a disorder that was confused with autism (Kauffman, 2001) during the early years of research, is also addressed.

Domino Theory and Autism Spectrum Disorders

Think of the domino theory. A person can set up an intricate pattern of dominoes so that the edge of each one will slightly overlap the next if it were to fall over. If the first domino in line is tapped over, every other domino of the pattern will topple. That is comparable to what happens when an individual has an autism spectrum disorder. If cognitive skills are delayed, social skills probably will be delayed. If social skills are delayed, the individual probably will have communication deficits. When an individual has a communication deficit, frustration often sets in and behavior problems develop. After behavior problems become apparent, the individual has a difficult time forming effective social relationships and will have problems with academic achievement and later employment skills.

In general, autism spectrum disorders are like a vicious cycle or a snowball effect. A delay in one area seems to impact many other areas of functioning for the individual. However, every individual with an autism spectrum disorder has unique characteristics. Some have greater or lesser deficit areas of functioning. Some may have specific deficits in certain areas but may be normal or even above average in others.

Autism

Early History of Autism

Researchers are progressing in the quest to figure out why some babies are born with autism. As long-term studies are conducted, researchers are also determining the most effective types of lifelong treatment options. What they do know is that autism is a neurologically based disorder of unknown cause. It is a permanent, lifelong condition. There is no cure (personal communication, Dr. Gary Sasso, University of Iowa, 1996).

Much has been accomplished with empirical studies in the past 50 years or so since early researchers first promoted a *psychogenic* (psychologically caused) basis for autism (Rimland, 1997). This means that scientists thought something or someone caused children to become autistic after birth. In spite of the progress, however, many questions remain unanswered.

During the early 1940s and the 1950s, Kanner (1943) and Bettelheim (1959) promoted a psychogenic theory stating that autism was actually induced after birth by the negative personality characteristics of parents. More specifically, autism was said to be caused by a mother who was emotionally cold and distant with her infant. Hence, the *refrigerator mom* theory arose (Bettelheim, 1959). Just imagine what a boatload of guilt those parents, especially the mothers, must have felt.

Bettelheim went so far as to advocate a *parentectomy* (Bettelheim, 1959; Gargiulo, 2003; Heward, 2003; Simpson & Zionts, 2000). This is like an appendectomy, a tosillectomy, or a hysterectomy. But in this case, rather than surgically cutting out an organ that is causing a physical problem or an illness, the parent (specifically the mother) is cut out of the child's life. Bettelheim's theory focused on the assumption that the child would recover and be cured if all contact was severed between the child and the mother. Thankfully, these psychogenic theories were never credited with empirical research support. Researchers were able to demonstrate a lack of significant difference between parenting styles of children who were developing normally and those who had children with autism (Gargiulo, 2003; Heward, 2003; Turnbull et al., 2002). In addition, other causation theories, primarily based on an organic neurological chemical imbalance, have been developed with follow-up research-based support (Gargiulo, 2003; Heward, 2003; Simpson & Zionts, 2000; Turnbull et al., 2002).

Here is a comment from a parent:

> The strain on our marriage was a lot worse before we knew what was wrong. Even though we didn't say anything, we were always trying to put blame on each other. Once we knew that we didn't cause the problem, it was easier. (Powers, 2000, p. 64)

Definition

Autism is a neurological disorder that causes a wide array of developmental disabilities. Researchers suggest that the maladaptive behaviors associated with autism are caused by a neurological condition, possibly a biochemical imbalance in the brain. It is considered to be a lifelong handicap with no known cure (Simpson & Zionts, 2000). The DSM-IV-TR (APA, 2000) reports the essential feature of autism to be deviant, delayed, or nonexistent communication and social interaction skills. This maladaptive pattern of behavior is usually accompanied by an inordinately restricted assortment of activities and interests. This is why persons with autism do so many repetitive behaviors.

Developmental Delays

Many developmental skills, including social skills, behavioral skills, and the interest in or ability to communicate, do not develop during normally expected periods in children who have autism. The term *developmental delay* refers to the fact that children

with autism are slower in reaching developmental milestones compared with the normally progressing child. It can also mean that the skill never develops at all or that the child lost a previously learned skill (Simpson & Zionts, 2000). Autism is the fourth most common of all developmental disabilities. Only mental retardation, epilepsy, and cerebral palsy occur more often. Simpson and Zionts (2000) explained how the developmental delays can be grouped into three main categories: cognitive delay, social adaptation delay, and motor delay.

Manifestations of cognitive delay might include mental retardation and learning deficits. However, this does not mean that all children with autism have mental retardation or learning problems. Symptoms of autism range from mild to moderate to severe. Persons with autism may have average to above average intelligence with marked potential for learning and education. However, the DSM-IV (APA, 1994) reported that 75% of individuals with autism function in the moderate range (IQ 35–50) of mental retardation.

Developmental delays in social adaptation and communication skills are one of the most noticeable and problematic areas associated with autism. A major indicator is extreme social withdrawal and severe social skill deficits. Individuals with autism often actively avoid interactions with others (Gargiulo, 2003; Heward, 2003; Simpson & Zionts, 2000; Turnbull et al., 2002).

Individuals with autism often demonstrate motor delays. Motor activities are any type of body movements. The word *motor* specifically refers to any motion that uses muscles. Simpson and Zionts (2000) report that motor delays are not as common as cognitive and social adaptation delays. Some children with autism have completely normal motor development (Gargiulo, 2003; Heward, 2003; Simpson & Zionts, 2000; Turnbull et al., 2002).

Etiology of Autism

Organic Disorder   Current research has not been able to establish any exact or specific *etiology* (cause) for autism (Fisher et al., 1999). What is known for a fact is that parents do not cause or prompt a child to become autistic after birth. Most researchers agree that autism is *organic* in nature (Bigler, 1988; Damasio & Maurer, 1978; Fisher et al., 1999; Rutter, 1965). "Organic" means that infants are born with the potential to develop the symptoms. Before birth, there is some type of biochemical imbalance in the neurological system. The discrepancy might result from prenatal brain damage, a genetic accident, or birth trauma (Gargiulo, 2003; Gelfand, Jenson, & Drew, 1988; Heward, 2003; Simpson & Zionts, 2000; Turnbull et al., 2002). These problems are thought to increase a child's vulnerability to autism, but they are not thought to be a definitive factor in causing the condition.

Using neurotechnology, researchers have been able to compare the brains of individuals with autism to the brains of those who have no neurological disorders (Coleman & Webber, 2002; Ornitz, Atwell, Kaplan, & Westlake, 1985; Simpson & Zionts, 2000). They have made two important discoveries. First, individuals with autism tend to have higher than average levels of serotonin in the blood. Serotonin is a neurotransmitter that facilitates the transmission of nerve impulses, which are carried on platelets through the bloodstream. Some individuals have been found to register as much as 100% higher than average levels. However, this finding requires further empirical replication to support the theory that it is a universal feature of autism. The second discovery revealed abnormalities in the brain stem and cerebellum of children with autism.

Another biochemical substance may be responsible for causing some of the problem behaviors related to autism (Simpson & Zionts, 2000). It seems that too much of a naturally occurring opiate, called opioids, is produced in the brain of many individuals with autism. Opioids are thought to regulate a number of social behaviors and interest in social interactions and human bonding. Emerging research indicates that a medication designed to reduce opioid levels has been successful in reductions of self-abuse, self-stimulation, and social withdrawal in some persons with autism.

With further research, the overabundance of opioids may explain why persons with autism are so withdrawn and isolated and seem to have little interest in or need for communicating and interacting with other people.

Genetic Link Innovative research is being conducted to locate and identify a possible genetic link for autism in families. APA (2000) reports that after a family has one birth child with autism, siblings have an increased risk to also be born with the disorder. Powers (2000) reported that the chance of having multiple children with autism is about 2 to 3%. This does not seem like a very big chance. It is, though, when one considers that the figure is actually 50 times higher than for parents who do not have any children with autism. Twin studies show a higher rate of concordance (meaning both twins are affected) for autism in identical twins compared with fraternal twins (Gelfand et al., 1988). Ritvo, Freeman, Mason-Brothers, Mo, and Ritvo (1985) used the UCLA Registry for Genetic Studies in Autism to compare 61 sets of twins. The concordance rate for identical twins was 95.7% as compared to 23.4% for fraternal twins. The genetic link may be through a recessive gene, meaning both parents must be carriers for the disorder to be inherited by their children (Gelfand et al., 1988). Ongoing research is necessary to gather conclusive evidence to determine an undisputed cause for autism (Gargiulo, 2003; Gelfand et al., 1988; Heward, 2003; Simpson & Zionts, 2000; Turnbull et al., 2002).

Prevalence of Autism

There are no socioeconomic, racial, cultural, or ethnic boundaries for autism. Simpson and Zionts (2000) report that there is not a country or a region of the world where autism has not been observed. The DSM-IV-TR (APA, 2000) provided a summary of information on both the prevalence of autism and the typical developmental course of the disorder. Heward (2003) reports that prevalence of autism among school-age children in the late 1990s has increased as much as three times the figures reported in the 1970s. It is estimated that approximately 15 to 16 children in every 10,000 develop autism (Baron-Cohen, 1995; Gillberg, 1995; Wing, 1993). ASA (2000) has estimated that as many as 1 in every 500 children has autism. However, the higher figures may also include individuals who have autistic spectrum disorders, but not enough to qualify under the DSM-IV-TR criteria (Powers, 2000). Simpson and Zionts (2000) relate that approximately 360,000 people currently have a diagnosis of autism. They break this figure down into two groups. About 110,000 have full-blown symptoms of autism and meet the eligibility criteria in the DSM-IV-TR. The remaining 250,000 exhibit most, if not all, of the symptoms required for diagnosis.

Male/Female Ratio As with most handicapping conditions, more males than females have autism. The ratio is about 4 or 5 males for each female (Fombonne, 1999; Heward, 2003). Powers (2000) stated that when girls have autism they tend to have more severe symptoms and have lower IQs than the average boy with autism. Some researchers have suggested that firstborn males are the most likely individuals to have autism, but to date, evidence is not conclusive.

Developmental Course of Autism

Parents often have to learn their way by trial and error through the unfamiliar and uncertain course of development with their child who has autism (APA, 2000). Unfortunately, there is not much predictability. Sandy, the mother of a child with autism, Alex, tells how she learned to deal with "night time terrors":

> Every night, remembers Sandy, Alex could not fall asleep. The buzz of an insect, the flash of a light, the whir of a fan, filled him with terror. He'd begin to scream and shake his hands in front of his face. We had a ritual. We'd play the Beatles tape with which he was familiar, put the headphone on him, cover him with a blanket, and tiptoe out. That shut out the scary world, but only for a little while. Finally, when he and we were just exhausted, we'd just try to leave him in his room. He'd circle and circle endlessly, walking and running for hours.

> Later on, we hit upon buying him a tent, setting it up on his bed, and finally he felt safe. But until then I was frantic. There was nothing I could do to help him and the doctors would say there was nothing wrong. He'd outgrow the stage. Stage? It was a nightmare. (Cohen, 1989, p. 95)

Onset of Symptoms The onset of autism usually appears by age 2 1/2 or 3. However, some parents indicate that they were aware of their child being "different" from birth (Powers, 2000). One of the comments made by parents is that the infant with autism was an especially easy baby to care for: quiet, complacent, happy just to be left alone (personal communication, Mrs. Janet Schleissman, mother of Tanner, a child with autism October, 1996). It is incredibly frustrating for many parents to have a feeling that something is wrong with their child, but not be able to come up with a definitive diagnosis. Because of the range and variability of symptoms, many parents are told by professionals that the child is going through a difficult stage, to be patient, that he will just grow out of it, or that he is just acting like a "real boy" (personal communication, Mrs. Janet Schleissman, October, 1996). The most often recalled early symptom was the infant's lack of curiosity and lack of attention to social interactions. Babies with autism are reported to be aloof, withdrawn, and generally uninterested in bonding with caregivers.

Regression of Skills Regression of previously mastered skills is another maladaptive pattern of development in some children whose parents observed no symptoms of autism during infancy. With these children, parents reported normal general development for anywhere from 12 to 24 months. Then the child began showing some significant signs of autism. This heartbreaking phenomenon occurs only in a minority of cases. Behavioral indicators of autism that parents might see at this time include social withdrawal and losing previously learned skills such as language skills, play skills, and bowel and/or bladder control. The children continue on a path where previously mastered developmental skills appear to regress and other skills are not learned. Following is a quote from parents who thought their son, Robbie, showed normal behavior for most of his first year but then seemed to regress:

> Robbie was a handsome blonde boy who stopped talking at age twenty-one months.... Robbie stood at six months, said his first word at ten months, walked by his first birthday, and could name about thirty-five objects by the time he was a year and a half old .... He spoke less and less, until there were times when he would go for weeks without saying a word. He would, however, babble, shriek, laugh, and cluck his tongue frequently throughout the day. More and more, his parents suspected a hearing problem or even deafness because he no longer responded to his name. They weren't sure about this though, because sometimes it seemed as if Robbie would stop whatever he was doing to listen to a train whistle blowing ever so faintly in the distance. (Powers, 2000, pp. 1–2)

Autism seems to follow a persistent course through childhood and adolescence, although characteristic behaviors and associated problems differ for each individual. Progression of the disorder and prognosis for the future are as unique as each individual. Some children will show increases in certain skills while others show decreases in those same skills during the same phase of life. The individual's IQ and the presence of interest in communicative speech appear to be the two strongest factors related to maximum progress.

Independent Living Skills for Adults with Autism Some adults with autism can learn skills to live independently or semi-independently. *Independent living* means they are able to acquire the functional skills for employment, to use transportation systems, and to take care of their own personal needs. If an individual lives *semi-independently*, he lives outside a parent's home or an institution but does receive close supervision and structure from a specially trained individual (Simpson & Zionts, 2000). It is esti-

mated that about one third of most highly functioning adults with autism can live independently. However, many continue to experience problems, particularly with social interaction and communication skills.

Diagnostic Criteria for Autism

Professionals in the mental health system are often called upon to assess young children for autistic-like behavior. They typically use the DSM-IV-TR (APA, 2000), which lists criteria pertinent to the diagnosis of autism (see Table 14–1).

Characteristics of Autism

As with all other disorders and handicapping conditions, symptoms of autism can range from mild to moderate to severe. Individuals with the most severe symptoms of autism make up about 2 to 3% of the total. Table 14–2 shows common symptoms of autism arranged in a hierarchy from mild to severe for each of the three areas specifically affected by the disorder.

Major Symptoms of Autism

The three main areas of dysfunction for individuals with autism were broken down and explained in more detail by Powers (1999). He described six major symptoms of autism. Each of the six categories is presented with a description and examples of behavioral manifestations. The six predominant observable characteristics include:

1. Failure to develop normal socialization;
2. Disturbances in speech, language, and communication;
3. Abnormal relationships to objects and events;
4. Abnormal responses to sensory stimulation;
5. Developmental delays and differences;
6. Begins during infancy or childhood.

TABLE 14-1 Diagnostic Criteria for 299.00 Autistic Disorder

A. A total of six (or more) items from (1), (2), and (3), with at least two from (1), and one each from (2) and (3):

  (1) qualitative impairment in social interaction, as manifested by at least two of the following:
- (a) marked impairment in the use of multiple nonverbal behaviors such as eye-to-eye gaze, facial expression, body postures, and gestures to regulate social interaction
- (b) failure to develop peer relationships appropriate to developmental level
- (c) a lack of spontaneous seeking to share enjoyment, interests, or achievements with other people (e.g., by lack of showing, bringing, or pointing out objects of interest)
- (d) lack of social or emotional reciprocity

  (2) qualitative impairments in communication as manifested by at least one of the following:
- (a) delay in, or total lack of, the development of spoken language (not accompanied by an attempt to compensate through alternative modes of communication such as gesture or mime)
- (b) in individuals with adequate speech, marked impairment in the ability to initiate or sustain a conversation with others
- (c) stereotyped and repetitive use of language or idiosyncratic language
- (d) lack of varied, spontaneous make-believe play or social imitative play appropriate to the developmental level

  (3) restricted repetitive and stereotyped patterns of behavior, interests, and activities, as manifested by at least one of the following:
- (a) encompassing preoccupation with one or more stereotyped and restricted patterns of interest that is abnormal either in intensity or focus
- (b) apparently inflexible adherence to specific, nonfunctional routines or rituals
- (c) stereotyped and repetitive motor mannerisms (e.g., hand or finger flapping or twisting or complex whole body movements)
- (d) persistent preoccupation with parts of objects

B. Delays or abnormal functioning in at least one of the following areas, with onset prior to age 3 years: (1) social interaction, (2) language as used in social communication, or (3) symbolic or imaginative play.

C. The disturbance is not better accounted for by Rett's Disorder or Childhood Disintegrative Disorder.

Note. *Reprinted with permission from the* Diagnostic and Statistical Manual of Mental Disorders, *Text Revision, Copyright 2000. American Psychiatric Association.*

TABLE 14-2 Symptoms of Autism

Social Interactions	Communication	Behavioral Symptoms
Little or no interest in making friends	Has speech skills but does not converse	Is physically passive and tends to be inactive
Prefers own company to others	Reverses "you" and "I" pronouns	Does not respond to requests by familiar people
Does not imitate other's actions at an early age	Has echolalia	Has picky eating habits
Does not interact playfully with others	Lacks imagination and ability to "pretend"	Throws frequent tantrums for unknown reason
Avoids eye contact	Does not use symbolic gestures (Bye bye)	Behaves aggressively
Does not smile at familiar people	Does not communicate with words or gestures	Physically attacks or injures others
Does not differentiate between family and strangers		Self-abuse behavior: head banging/eye gouging

Note. *Based on* Autism Information and Resources for Professionals and Parents, *by R. L. Simpson and P. Zionts, 2000, Austin, TX: Pro-Ed.*

Symptom #1: Failure to Develop Normal Socialization Lack of social interaction is one of the most prominent characteristics of autism. Individuals appear to live in their own little isolated world. They seem uninterested in forming even the most basic bonds or attachments with other people. Caregivers have noticed that when they try to cuddle or hug children with autism, the child may arch her back and stiffen as if the hug were distressing. Another characteristic is the active avoidance of eye contact. They seem to "look through" others. Powers (2000) describes how children with autism use other people "as tools." They may use people mechanically as a "means to an end" (p. 4). For example, if a child wants juice from the refrigerator, she may take a grown-up by the arm and herd him over to the refrigerator without a word or a glance. The grown-up is treated like any other tool. This pervasive inability to relate to others in the social environment is the most common symptom of autism.

Symptom #2: Disturbances in Speech, Language, and Communication The second major symptom of individuals with autism is their inability and seeming disinterest to use language or communicate productively with others. Simpson and Zionts (2000) relate that practically all individuals with autism demonstrate significant speech and language problems. Speech is defined as the mechanism by which people communicate orally, while language refers to the verbal, nonverbal, and written processes humans use to communicate. Communication is the combination of being able to receive as well as express oneself using speech and language. Needless to say, for individuals with autism, the lack of communication skills and social interaction has a detrimental affect on their ability to express wants and needs, to relate to others, and to learn.

Echolalia Powers (2000) reports that 40% of individuals with autism do not speak at all. Others use a nonproductive form of speech called *echolalia*.

This means that they simply echo words, phrases, sentences, jingles, or other forms of speech that others say to them or they hear. Note the frustration inherent in learning how to raise a child with autism as a parent asked the following question about echolalia: "The way Patrick repeats whatever I say is extremely annoying. Sometimes he says the whole sentence; at other times he might repeat part of what I say. What is the purpose? (Simpson & Zionts, 2000, p. 74).

This scenario triggers an interesting memory. Remember when you were younger and one of your brothers or sisters tried to irritate you by mimicking or repeating every single word you said until you were in a frenzy of anger and at the point of tears? Think what it would be like for parents who live with a child who has this type of verbal behavior all the time and cannot control it.

Echolalia may be immediate or delayed by any period of time ranging from minutes to days to weeks or even months. Using echolalia is not thought to be an attempt to communicate. It is suggested that the parrot-like verbalizations are simply an involuntary reaction to some type of environmental stimulus, meaning that it gives some type of sensation or feedback to the individual. Echolalia may occur more often in unfamiliar, anxiety-provoking situations (Simpson & Zionts, 2000). Most attempts to communicate with individuals who have autism are very frustrating. They are not interested in conversation with others, and they do not make or maintain eye contact or attention with the communicator. Children with autism rarely understand abstract concepts. They are not able to comprehend body language or gestures. They cannot seem to control pitch or volume of vocalizations. Another characteristic is repetitive use of jargon or words or phrases out of context. Powers (2000, p. 5) provided the following example: "... One child said, 'Time to be heading home,' with great agitation whenever asked to do something she didn't want to do. Rimland (1997) wrote the following description of his son's verbal behavior before he knew anything about autism:

Mark began speaking at about eight months. Pronouncing with perfect diction, words like "spoon," "all done," "teddy bear," and "come on, let's play ball." At age two he could repeat anything said to him with remarkably clear pronunciation. His uncle tried him on "hippopotamus" and Mark replied "hippopotamus" with no hesitation. ... It soon became evident that Mark's speech was like that of a tape recorder— just repetition of words, phrases, sentences, and even nursery rhymes without any real idea of what they meant. (p. xi)

"The number one piece of advice I'd give to another parent is to get support. I could not go it alone" (Powers, 1997, p. 53). This quote illustrates a parent's need for hope and guidance to help deal with a child with autism. It is critical for educators and other professionals who work with children who have autism and their families to remember that the child is part of a family. Learning to raise a child who does not communicate easily and who seems to have no interest in others can be an extremely frustrating and frightening endeavor. Most parents and other family members are totally bewildered and looking for answers and assistance to help deal with their child most appropriately.

Symptom #3: Abnormal Relationships to Objects and Events Individuals with autism usually interact with items in their environment and events in a nonfunctional or nonproductive manner. Most children with autism do not play with toys in a conventional manner. They seem to have their own preferred methods. Examples include spinning objects, arranging and rearranging objects according to some pattern, or using toys or other objects in a repetitive but nonpurposeful manner.

There is also a need for a predictable routine. Individuals with autism may become agitated and anxious if daily events and the usual schedule are modified. This great need for routine could be an advantage or a disadvantage. It may be an advantage in that it could help some individuals to learn a pattern of behavior that they can later use at home, at school, or for a paying job or competitive employment.

However, the need for a routine that never varies can also be detrimental in that the individual lacks necessary flexibility to accommodate in a home, educational, or employment environment where routines cannot always be kept the same. In that situation, the individual may not be able to live, learn, or work effectively or successfully. Following is an account of a personal experience I had with an individual without at first knowing he had autism:

I was working as a teaching assistant at UW–Madison helping to give tests at a university clinic. I didn't know that the young man who brought the mail around to the offices had autism. He appeared to do his job well, was well dressed, very nice looking, and did not have outstanding symptoms of autism. However, my first clue was when I passed him in the hall and said hello. He quickly ducked his chin down to the side on one shoulder and responded with "Hi" in a monotone, robotic type voice. Later, when I tried to engage him in conversation in the elevator where we were the only two passengers, he huddled toward a back corner and acted very shy and nervous. Finally, one day when he brought the mail into my office, I smiled at him and reached out my hand to take it. He would only place it in the mail basket. That was his routine. After the third incident with the mail basket, I asked about him and was told he had autism. He was considered very high functioning. He was able to live in a semi-independent fashion. He had an apartment with a another adult male who had a developmental disability. He learned the city bus system and was successful with his job at the clinic.

The following example relates how Jim, a verbal, high functioning adult with autism, felt about change of routine:

As a child, Jim would get very upset about the loss of familiarity that came with new paint, new furniture, and so forth. "When my parents got a new car, I experienced it almost as intensely as the loss of a family member." Possibly, Jim continues, "even more intensely; the cars were familiar, comfortable, and not intrusive, while family members were often intrusive. . . ." (Cesaroni & Garber, 1991)

Even though many individuals with autism show a need for specific and unpredictable routines, it can be modified. With a combination of proactive education, training, and systematic positive reinforcement, they can learn to adapt to routine and schedule changes. They can learn to use a variety of objects for their intended purpose in a functional manner.

Symptom #4: Abnormal Responses to Sensory Stimulation   Sensory stimulation in the environment relates to what people see, hear, taste, smell, and touch. The brain processes incoming stimuli, focuses on what is important, and filters out what is unnecessary. It appears that the neurological system in persons with autism does not work this way. Some may overreact to certain sensory stimuli while others show no reaction at all. This unpredictable behavior can be highly frustrating and often baffling to caregivers and educators. Here is an example of one such incident. Parents of a child with autism in London, England, got to the point where they did not want to take their child out in public because of her unpredictable, nerve-shattering, screaming temper tantrums. They finally figured out what the problem was after working with a professional interventionist. Guess what it was? The color red. For some reason this child processed red as being terrifying and scary. Think of how red is used in England. In addition to red being used randomly on buildings, houses, and advertising signs, the phone booths are red and the buses in London's public transportation system are red.

Children may show a fascination with lights, patterns of color, shapes, textures, jingles, logos, buildings, or other structural patterns. Remember Raymond's fascination with the steel beams of the big bridge, how he watched the spinning roulette wheel, watched the dryer spin, and repeated phrases from the Judge Wapner show in *Rainman*? Cesaroni and Garber (1991) interviewed

a verbal, high functioning individual with autism and gained firsthand information about this person's unique sensory processing. Jim, a 27-year-old man with autism, was working on graduate studies in developmental psychology at the time of the interview. Jim's parents noted that he was never cuddly as a child and still appears to be uncomfortable with physical touching of any sort. Jim told the interviewers that "touching the lower part of his face produces a sound-like sensation in addition to the tactile sensation" (p. 305). Jim related that touching in general is not a pleasant sensation. He said that it was "not necessarily painful but was very intense and could be overwhelming and confusing" (p. 305).

Jim further related that he found it difficult to discuss his own sensory processing for two reasons. First, the vocabulary used is subjective and tends to be abstract. Second, in order for others to understand, he must use verbal descriptions developed by and for people whose sensory processing is different from his own. Following is a list of some of Jim's sensory differences. The differences provide a fascinating contrast to the average person's sensory impressions of the world:

- Sometimes the channels got confused and one sensory impression came through another channel. For example, sound might be processed as color.
- Certain sounds seemed menacing such as low-frequency musical notes. The sound itself was not scary, but it triggered some loss of orientation that felt unpleasant and frightening.
- Jim was not scared by loud noises. He always thought he had a premonition that something sensory was going to come through.
- Jim noticed that auditory stimuli sometimes interfered with other sensory processes. He gave an example of turning off the car radio while trying to read road signs. In the kitchen, he would turn off noise-making appliances while trying to taste something.
- Sound was often accompanied by color, shape, texture, movement, scent, or flavor.

Another intriguing explanation of sensory differences comes from Dr. Temple Grandin (Shopler & Mezibov, 1992). Dr. Grandin is a person with autism who is considered to be incredibly high functioning. She has a Ph.D. and is a professor of animal science at the University of Colorado–Fort Collins.

Dr. Grandin related that while she was growing up, church behavior was often a problem. She figured out why. Some textures of clothing give her an irritating sensory impression. Her mother dressed her up in pretty little dresses with starched lacy petticoats. The church clothes felt different from her everyday clothes. The petticoats itched. As an adult, Dr. Grandin has learned that some clothing textures still give her very negative sensory impressions. She buys clothes that all have a similar texture and says that as a youngster, her church behavior could have been improved by a few simple changes in clothing. Noises can also cause sensory difficulty. Dr. Grandin states,

> My hearing is like having a hearing aid stuck on super loud. It is like an open microphone that picks up everything. I have two choices: turn the mic on and get deluged with sound. Or shut it off. Mother reported that I sometimes acted like I was deaf. . . .I can't modulate incoming sound. (p. 107)

Symptom #5: Developmental Delays and Differences Children develop social, behavioral, and cognitive skills at a relatively even pace as they grow. Some mature faster while others are slower. There is a range of variability that is considered normal. However, children with autism tend to show very uneven rates of development. Their rate of development for cognitive, social, and communication skills tends to be much slower than average. Some of these skills, such as speech and communication, never develop. They may show partial development, which then seems to disappear or regress. In comparison, large and fine motor skills may develop at an average pace.

Symptom #6: Begins During Infancy or Early Childhood Symptoms of autism become apparent during infancy or early childhood. Most parents obtain a diagnosis by the time the child is 3 years old. Some children may not be correctly diagnosed at such a young age. Other diagnoses such as mental retardation or pervasive developmental disorder may be used and later changed to autism. In some children, symptoms may appear to be reduced around age 5 or 6. During adolescence, the symptoms improve for some and worsen for others. However, if the disorder truly is autism, there is no cure, as some rather sensationalized TV programs and magazine stories have claimed. Researchers consider autism to be a lifelong disorder (Gargiulo, 2003; Gelfand, Jenson, & Drew, 1988; Heward, 2003; Powers, 2000; Simpson & Zionts, 2000; Turnbull et al., 2002).

Checklist of Common Behaviors

Following is a checklist of common behaviors that might help teachers, parents, and other professionals identify symptoms of autism in young children. Children may show some or all of the symptoms. It is a simple-to-use checklist that can function as a screening device (Rendel-Short, 1978).

_____ 1. Is not interested in playing with other children

_____ 2. Acts as though he does not hear others

_____ 3. Resists learning new skills

_____ 4. Shows no fear of dangerous situations

_____ 5. Resists change in routine

_____ 6. Indicates needs by gestures

_____ 7. Laughs and giggles inappropriately

_____ 8. Does not like to cuddle or be physically close to others

_____ 9. Shows repetitive, meaningless body movements

_____ 10. Does not show normal eye contact with others

_____ 11. Shows inappropriate attachment to objects

_____ 12. Spins objects
_____ 13. Does not play with toys in a conventional manner
_____ 14. Is aloof and withdrawn from other people
_____ 15. Is not sensitive to pain
_____ 16. Echoes words or phrases

Stereotypic Behaviors of Autism

A parent of a child with autism made the following comment about his child's behavior:

> Lawrence self-stimulates constantly. Rocking, weird breathing patterns, hand waving, rolling his eyes—he's in constant motion. Out in public, people are always watching him. We try to see the humor in it. He *is* a funny-looking little guy! (Powers, 1997, p. 164)

In addition to communication and social interaction deficits, there is a set of behaviors common to individuals with autism. These are often termed *stereotypic* behaviors. They are described as repetitive or ritualistic behaviors that have no apparent meaning. Examples include body rocking, hand flapping, spinning items, tasting and touching inappropriately, finger waving, head banging, or light filtering. Other than *light filtering*, most of the stereotypic behaviors are quite self-explanatory. Light filtering happens when the individual "reflects light by moving his hands back and forth in front of his eyes" (Simpson & Zionts, 2000, p. 6).

Why do individuals with autism perform these self-stimulatory behaviors over and over and over again? It is thought that they provide some sort of sensory feedback to the individual. In addition, the sensory feedback possibly provides a calm or comforting sensation. For example, rocking is a common stereotypic behavior of individuals with autism. Think about how calming and soothing rocking in a rocking chair is for persons of any age. Since most individuals with autism do not express themselves well using speech, it may never be known what purpose the stereotypic behaviors serve.

Mystery of the Autistic Savant The majority of individuals with autism test in the range of mental retardation throughout their lives. As in the general population, IQ scores are relatively stable through the life span. Most people with autism (74%) score below 50 with only a few (2 to 3%) scoring above 85 (Gelfand, Jenson, & Drew, 1988). Some individuals with autism show *splinter skills* in very isolated or unique areas. These are amazing skills of brilliance or genius ability. Such individuals are sometimes called *autistic savants*. Only a small percentage of people with autism have these skills, possibly 1 in 10 (Blake, 1989; Simpson & Zionts, 2000). It may be more common for persons with true autism to have savant skills as compared with individuals who have autistic spectrum disorder.

How can a person who has mental retardation, autism, and multiple developmental delays count hundreds of items with lightning speed, multiply huge numbers in his head, play complex musical compositions, know the days of the week for any date given, or show gifted artistic ability? The most common savant skills relate to music, art, math, mechanics, calendar calculations, coordination, and pseudolanguage.

The following are examples of some of these areas:

- **Counting:** In *Rainman*, Raymond was able to count hundreds of toothpicks that fell on the floor in a matter of seconds.
- **Coordination:** One toddler was able to walk the rail of his crib without falling.
- **Pseudolanguage:** This is described as the ability to produce or reproduce material verbally or in writing with limited or no comprehension. One young girl can type passages from memory totally free from errors. The girl once typed a page of complicated directions she had heard only once after more than 1 year had passed.
- **Calendar Calculators:** These people have a rather mind-boggling skill. When given any calendar date during any time in history, they can tell the weekday on which that date falls.

Development of Savant Skills After years of research, the mystery of the autistic savant remains unsolved (Blake, 1989; Simpson & Zionts, 2000). Some have suggested reasons for the splinter skills of brilliance. Ritvo (cited in Blake, 1989) has studied savant skills and does not think they are actually as outstanding as they seem at first. He says they only seem to be so unusual because of the other problems and developmental delays that accompany autism. Ritvo states, "... If they put their minds to it, other people can, for instance, learn to do the calendar trick." He thinks that the savant skills are simply developed with practice by a person who has no other interests. This supposition is based on the reasoning that individuals with autism do not have a variety of interests. Some people become preoccupied with a certain habit to the point that they perseverate on that one isolated skill, which then develops to the genius level.

In contrast, Blake (1989) also references Dr. Bernard Rimland, who believes practice does indeed play a role but that practice alone could not account for the astounding savant skills. The basic reasoning is that some skills appeared so early in life that there was not enough time to practice to perfection. A case was cited of a child who could draw brilliantly at age 6 without ever going through the typical scribbling stages that are normal for young children. In another case, a 6-month-old child was able to hum complex musical arias. One young child was able to dismantle and perfectly reassemble clocks, radios, TVs, and vacuum cleaners.

How can these skills be explained? Where do they come from? In general, they do seem to involve memory. Rimland says unique neurological functioning plays a role in the development of autistic savant skills. Another component is that persons with autism may exist in a *hypodistractible* state. That is, they are not distracted by anything in the surrounding environment. They have no drive for variety or novelty. Consequently, they are attracted to repetition, sameness, and familiarity. Then practice comes in and plays a role. They practice one skill to the total exclusion of all other skills. They never develop varied or flexible interests.

One specific part of the brain, called the hippocampus, may play a role in the development of savant abilities. The hippocampus controls emotions and memory, helps screen out irrelevant stimuli, and assists in mapping out spatial relations and learning processes. Blake (1989) contends that *hyper-hippocampus functioning* could account for both the abilities and the problems of the savant. The hyperfunctioning may be the brain's method of compensating for another deficiency, particularly in the *amygdala*, the area of the brain that is responsible for emotional tone of memories.

Assessment Methods for Individuals with Autism

You may have been most concerned because your child never smiled, or continually flapped his hands, or because he learned to talk, but then mysteriously seemed to forget how. But whatever your worries, nothing could have prepared you for your child's actual diagnosis.

In our case, we were informed after a week of intensive testing that our son was autistic-like. You may have been told that your child is autistic or that he has early infantile autism or a pervasive developmental disorder. However the news is phrased, it is usually a devastating shock to parents already buffeted by months of worry and foreboding. For many parents this pain is so searing that even years later, the memory automatically causes tears. Very few things indeed are worse than learning that your child has autism. You want to go back in time, to change things somehow.... You feel so desperately helpless and overwhelmed that you can't imagine ever laughing or feeling good about anything ever again. (Tommasone & Tommasone, 2000, p. 33)

Professional Evaluation Teams ASA reports that there are no actual medical tests that can be used to diagnose autism (www.autism-society.org). The formal diagnosis is based on observation of the individual's communication, behavioral, and developmental levels. Medical evaluation can be used to rule out other possible causes of the symptoms observed.

To make a diagnosis of autism, a variety of assessments may be completed. It is important for professionals to remember that this can be a very scary, anxiety-provoking process for parents. The evaluations can be completed in a number of different settings, depending on the needs of the child. Evaluations might take place in private clinical settings; university medical centers; mental health associations; at city, county, state, or other public facilities; at public schools; or in the family home. There is no specified format for the evaluation. Each evaluation will be specifically designed for the individual child. There should be a twofold purpose of each assessment battery. One purpose may be for diagnosis if it has not already taken place. The second purpose of assessment is for intervention and program planning.

An assessment battery for autism is usually completed by a team of professionals who have special skills and expertise. Each person evaluates a special area. Professionals who participate in the assessment process may include the following (Simpson & Zionts, 2000):

- **Psychologist:** School psychologists or clinical psychologists can give tests to assess a number of different areas. These areas might include IQ, language, academic achievement, perceptual and neurological strengths and weaknesses, behavior and social skills, and functional skills. They might use standardized tests, interviews, or direct observations. Once the tests are given, they calculate the scores and make program recommendations to parents and educators.
- **Psychiatrist:** Psychiatrists also do testing but concentrate more on interviews and observations. Because they hold a medical degree, they can prescribe any necessary medications.

- **Educators:** Educators give tests to determine academic ability, functional skills, and social skills. The information from these tests is used to plan the most appropriate educational program for school-age students.
- **Social Worker:** School and community social workers serve as a link between educators, families, and community agencies. They will usually gather a complete life history on the child. This document will contain information from parents, educators, physicians, and any community agencies involved.
- **Speech Pathologist:** Speech pathologists assess communication areas, including receptive and expressive language. This information is particularly important because most children with autism have severe communication delays and deficits.
- **Audiologist:** An audiologist uses testing procedures to assess the child's ability to hear.
- **Physical Therapist:** Physical therapists use direct observations and standardized tests to determine fine and gross motor skills.
- **Occupational Therapist:** Occupational therapists also look at motor skills but are most interested in how the motor skills are used to complete self-help and functional daily living skills.
- **Medical Personnel:** Medical professionals complete evaluations in any area that may be of concern. A nurse, pediatrician, opthomologist, or family practitioner may be involved. (Simpson & Zionts, 2000)

Reporting to Parents Following the evaluation, the team meets with the parents to provide results and possibly a diagnosis. During the testing procedure and the follow-up meeting, it is of utmost importance that the team treat the parents in a kind, tactful, and respectful manner. As noted in the opening parental quote from the assessment section, this is an incredibly stressful, difficult, and sensitive experience for parents. One of the main tactics that professionals should use as they work through the testing procedures is to always use plain English explanations of tests and results during discussions with parents. The parents must have clear and concise information about their child's strengths; areas of need; and recommended methods to achieve behavioral, social, and learning goals. Parents will not benefit or even be able to comprehend the necessary information if professionals use technical jargon.

Variety of Assessments

The following comment was made by a parent of a child with autism in regard to assessment:

> They shouldn't try to do all the testing at one time because children get frustrated just like parents—taking a test for two or three hours straight. After the first half hour or 45 minutes, the child gets frustrated and he just doesn't want to be there anymore. I really think if they are going to put him through a battery of tests, they should break it up, even if it has to be over a week's time. Don't try to cram everything into two or three days, because that's really not enough time and you can't get the child to perform his best. (Powers, 1997, p. 201)

There are many tests that can be given to determine specific levels of functioning for individuals with autism. Tests run the gamut from cognitive functioning for IQ scores to qualitative data of family and social histories to rating scales of commu-nication, behavioral, and social skills to medical evaluations. Simpson and Zionts (2000) provide the following descriptions of the variety of tests that may be used to assess the skills and abilities of children who have autism.

Tests of Cognitive Ability A test of cognitive ability is used to assess *cognitive functioning*, defined as the ability to think and solve problems. This term is often used interchangeably with intelligence level or IQ. Cognitive tests are a very common component of the assessment battery because they are used to determine an individual's mental processing abilities. Table 14-3 lists tests of cognitive ability that can be used with children who have autism. These tests are administered by a specially trained examiner. The scope of test items included can range from reasoning and memory to comprehension and judgment.

Some tests of cognitive functioning are paper/pencil-type assessments given in a group format. However, the tests used to assess the skills of children who have autism would be more performance-based individualized tests. The scores from the test allow the examiner to compare the skills or developmental levels of a child with autism to a sample of normally developing same-age peers. Cognitive ability or IQ level is thought to be the best predictor of an individual's general prognosis, or future outcomes. IQ is relatively stable throughout the life span. Logically, young children who show

TABLE 14-3 Tests of Cognitive Ability for Children with Autism

Name of Test	Description
Wechsler Preschool and Primary Scale of Intelligence (WPPSI)	Designed for children age 4 to 6 years
Revised Wechsler Intelligence Scale for Children (WISC-R)	Designed for youth and adolescents age 6 to 17 years
Revised Wechsler Adult Intelligence Scale (WAIS)	Designed for adolescents and adults age 17 years and older

higher IQ scores have an increased chance to overcome developmental delays associated with autism. Cognitive test results provide three separate IQ scores: (a) performance, (b) verbal, and (c) full-scale. Full-scale scores are the combined verbal and performance scores. Verbal scores assess skills in vocabulary, general information, and ability to understand social situations. Performance scores indicate level of skills for nonverbal areas such as block designs or putting together puzzles.

Cognitive Tests for Individuals Who Are Nonverbal

Because so many children with autism are nonverbal, the Wechsler-type IQ tests may not be appropriate. A good alternative for children who are lower functioning and have severe communication deficits are tests that determine developmental functioning levels in a variety of areas. The tests are often based on normative sample populations of children who are younger than the child with autism who is being tested. That gives the tester an idea of the child's general age-equivalent skills.

Four tests that can be used to gain an age equivalency score for children who are lower functioning and have severe communication deficits include (a) the Bailey Scales of Infant Development, (b) the McCarthy Scales of Children's Abilities, (c) the Stanford-Binet Intelligence Scale, and (d) the Leiter International Performance Scale.

Family and Social Environmental History The social worker usually compiles this history in a narrative report. The goal of the report is to provide a view to the child's world and background. Information in this report can be wide-ranging. The assessment usually covers prenatal and birth information, developmental milestones, parenting practices, educational strengths and weaknesses, personality and genetic factors, and family and other environmental considerations. The information is typically gathered in a direct interview with parents and other caregivers. The informational report is used to help with remediation of deficit areas and future program planning.

Medical Evaluations Medical evaluations vary based on symptoms, developmental levels, age, and abilities. If a medical evaluation is indicated, the type is individualized based on observed areas of need for each child. Some children with autism need prescription medication to assist in reducing problematic symptoms. Some general areas of development that are usually assessed and then compared to normal milestones include physical, language, cognitive, and emotional. Specific medical exams might cover any or all of the following:

- EEG (electroencephalogram to examine the brain's electrical functioning)
- Neurological functioning
- Cranial nerve functioning (12 nerves that control bodily functions)
- Sight
- Smell
- Symmetry (balance across parts of the body)
- Balance and coordination
- Sensory sensitivity (response to light and touch)
- Deep tendon reflexes
- Hand and foot dominance
- Motor activities (hop, skip, bounce a ball)

Behavioral and Social Development Evaluation The most common type of behavioral or social assessment appropriate for children with autism is direct observation of behavior. To obtain a well-rounded picture of the child's skills, observations may be completed at home, at school, and in a variety of community settings. This information can be gathered in two different ways. First, an anecdotal or narrative format can be used. The narrative report of behavior and social interaction is simply a running account of all the behaviors noted during the observation period. The second method is to use a behavior checklist or rating scale. As with other types of standardized assessments, behavior rating checklists allow the evaluator to compare the child's behavior to a normed sample of same-age peers.

To complete a behavior scale, a person who is familiar with the child's behavior evaluates behavior on a structured form. Usually ratings are either *yes* or *no* or they relate to the frequency of behavior such as *always*, *sometimes*, or *never*. The results are used for both diagnosis and program planning.

There are a variety of standardized behavior rating checklists and evaluation scales on the market. One example, the Informational Observation Data Sheet (Simpson & Regan, 1986) allows evaluators to observe and compare behaviors in six areas of functioning: (a) stereotypic/self-stimulation behaviors, (b) aggressive behavior, (c) speech and language, (d) self-help/independent living skills, (e) social skills, and (f) independent work habits. Other behavior rating scales appropriate for children with autism include the Behavior Checklist (Simpson & Regan, 1986) and the Autism Screening Instrument for Educational Planning (2nd ed., Krug, Arick, & Almond, 1993).

Speech and Language Assessment Evaluations for skills and abilities in speech and language may take a number of different forms. Tests, interviews, observations, or other clinical methods might be used. Clinical methods are procedures used by speech pathologists. The professionals who evaluate speech and language are most interested in how the child uses speech to communicate needs, relate feelings, and interact with others. The results of the assessment are used for planning intervention programs designed to make communication systems more functional for both the individual and others in his environment. The main purpose is to determine a child's strengths and weaknesses regarding communication methods. Then the professionals can plan an intervention program to increase or improve the child's communication skills.

The speech and language assessment may be conducted in a variety of formats. First, interviews with family and educators may be conducted. Sec-

ond, the child might be directly observed in a variety of environments at home, at school, or in the community. This type of observation allows the observer to note specific communication strengths, weaknesses, and strategies that the child uses. Finally, children may be tested in a clinic setting by a professional speech and language clinician.

Academic Assessments The skills and abilities of children with autism vary widely depending on whether they have mild, moderate, or severe symptoms and what level of mental retardation they have. Some children are able to learn to read and pursue an academic curriculum, but many more children are not. The child's IQ can help determine whether an academic assessment would be appropriate. When an academic curriculum is not appropriate, emphasis can be placed on functional skills. Examples include social skills, vocational training, and independent living skills.

Education and Treatment Options

Even though autism is a lifelong disorder with no known cure, early intervention, behavior interventions, program planning, and education are of the utmost importance. Simpson and Zionts (2000) indicate that the majority of children with autism can make progress to overcome some of the deficits of the disorder. Social, communication, academic, and behavioral improvements do not happen by chance. Autism is not a stage or a phase that children will outgrow. Early intervention is one of the keys to overcoming deficits and developmental delays. Parents should get assistance and treatment immediately when they suspect a problem. This will help ensure that their child receives the most appropriate services from the start.

Educators and other professionals specifically trained in the area of education and intervention with autism can be of great assistance in helping children overcome deficits. Dr. Temple Grandin was diagnosed with autism as a child. She gives credit to teachers and other professionals for the achievements and progress she has made as an adult and now an incredibly successful professional person with autism. "I am deeply grateful to the dedicated teachers and therapists who worked with me. They were responsible for my improvement and their importance can not be overemphasized (1981, p. 1).

Facilitated Communication   During the early 1990s, a number of researchers and practitioners began to study a possible innovation to teach communication skills to individuals with autism. The method was called *facilitated communication*.

Facilitated communication is a process whereby an individual, the facilitator, uses light arm support to teach students with autism to type communications (Biklen, Morton, Gold, & Berrigan, 1992; Spake, 1992). The facilitator is trained to provide emotional and physical support for typing or pointing at letters. The facilitator support is meant to help the students maintain focus during the communication process but *not* type. Additionally, the physical support of the facilitator was meant to be faded from the process so that eventually the individual with autism would be able to type without any external means of support (Biklen & Schubert, 1991). It was reported that the individuals revealed all sorts of unexpected literacy and number skills.

Initially, researchers claimed that facilitated communication was a viable method to assist individuals with autism to read, write, and express their thoughts by typing letters on a keyboard. Researchers claimed that this method was being used successfully with individuals who previously had no ability to communicate.

ASA has taken a neutral stand on the controversial practice of facilitated communication, neither condeming nor condoning the method (www.autism-society.org). They suggest that all types of treatment should be individualized and that caregivers must carefully evaluate the pros and cons of all treatment options. However, it is important to note that currently there is no scientific evidence supporting facilitated communication as a valid communications technique for individuals with autism or mental retardation (APA, 1994, cited in www.autism-society.org).

Highly Controversial Method   The facilitated communication method has been fraught with controversy from the onset (Levine, 1994, Levine, Shane, & Wharton, 1994). Facilitator influence has been a recurring problem through a series of studies that sought to replicate early research claims. This means that the facilitator, rather than the individual with autism, is more likely to be doing the typing (Cabay, 1994; Eberlin, 1993; Hirshorn & Gregory, 1995; Myles, 1996; Myles & Simpson, 1994; Simpson & Myles, 1995; Smith, 1994; Wheeler, 1993). The general problem that kept recurring was that most participants were not able to give correct responses unless the facilitator knew the correct and expected response. In summary, it is important to remember that facilitated communication may be a method that could potentially assist some individuals to communicate. Effective use of the facilitated communication method should be decided on a case-by-case basis.

Professional Organization Positions   Many professional organizations, including ASA, the American Academy of Child and Adolescent Psychiatry, the American Academy of Pediatrics, the American Association on Mental Retardation, and the American Psychiatric Association, agree that facilitated communication should not be used for:

(a) actions related to nonverbal communications of abuse and mistreatment;
(b) actions related to nonverbal communications of personal preference, self-reports about health, test and classroom performance, and family relations;
(c) client response in psychological assessments using standardized assessment procedures;
(d) client–therapist communication in counseling or psychotherapy, taking therapeutic actions, or making differential treatment decisions. (Biklen et al., 1992, p. 9)

The American Association on Mental Retardation (AAMR, 1994, as cited in www.autism-society.org) does not support facilitated communication but encourages the use and further development of augmentative and alternative methods of communication.

Augmentative Communication A strategy that seems to have more credence as an alternative method of communication among researchers is to teach individuals to use *augmentative communication* strategies (Levine et al., 1994). Examples include communication boards or sign language. Communication boards consist of pictures or symbol representations normally used in verbal communication. The individual is taught to point to one or more symbols on the board to convey thoughts, wants, or needs to others. Communication boards can be manual or computerized. Some electronic boards now use voice synthesizers with prerecorded verbalizations that include an extensive vocabulary with high-quality speech output (Turnbull et al., 2002; Ysseldyke & Algozzine, 1995).

ASA (www.autism-society.org) summarizes the following educational approaches. Children with autism may be educated in public schools, alternative day schools, residential treatment centers, or hospital-like institutions, depending on the severity of symptoms. Educators and parents must collaborate to determine the most beneficial educational program based on the student's individual needs. School-age students with autism may be in inclusion classrooms. This means that they are placed part-time in special education classrooms and part-time in general education classes. Inclusion placements are based on the individual needs, academic skill levels, social behavior, and the student's communication abilities.

The Lovaas Method Dr. Ivar Lovaas piloted this intensive treatment method based on the behavioral model at UCLA in the 1960s. The behavioral model uses positive consequences to shape new appropriate behavior. It continues to be a research-based and effective method for teaching children with autism. Replications of research report that children achieve gains in IQ, language comprehension and expression, and adaptive and social skills. The goal is to teach children how to learn by focusing on developing attention, language, social, and self-help skills. There is some concern because this is such an intensive treatment program with a heavy emphasis on the behavioral approach. Critics suggest that children develop *prompt dependence*. This means that the child may not actually be learning or internalizing the skill. In effect, the teacher's verbal or physical prompt and then immediate reward for behavior is what elicits the desired behavior. Educators are encouraged to use the Lovaas method along with other research-based teaching methods.

TEACCH The acronym TEACCH stands for Treatment and Education of Autistic and related Communication-Handicapped Children. The goal of TEACCH is to provide the individual with functional coping strategies throughout the life span. Empirical studies have supported the efficacy of the approach since it was first implemented over 30 years ago.

TEACCH has been successful in helping individuals to learn functional skills that can be *generalized* to a variety of environments. Generalization means that the individual is able to apply what is taught in the classroom to a real-life setting. The curriculum varies between individual students, based on their unique abilities and needs. The TEACCH method is easily compatible with a variety of other teaching methods for individuals with autism. This program was founded in the state of North Carolina, which reports the lowest parental stress rates, the lowest rate of requests for out-of-home placements, and the highest rate of employment for individuals with autism.

PECS PECS stands for Picture Exchange Communication System. This program combines in-depth speech therapy with real-life communication methods to help students truly communicate their thoughts, needs, and feelings, as opposed to simply *talking words* that do not achieve a purpose. The goal is to help the individual learn to spontaneously initiate communication, to help understand the function of communication, and to develop communication competency. This program is highly compatible and often overlapped with the TEACCH method.

Greenspan Greenspan has also been referred to as the DIR (Developmental Individual-Difference, Relationship-Based) Model. Using the developmental model, this program targets emotional development and personal interactions to foster the individual's skills that are developmentally delayed. The focus for skills training centers on the areas of sensory modulation, motor planning and sequencing, and perceptual processing. Reported outcomes suggest that this method allows parents and educators to engage the child in a more relaxed and happy atmosphere. When used as an early intervention technique, it is also thought to lay the groundwork for future neurological and cognitive development.

Social Stories This program uses stories or scripts that are personalized for each individual to help him or her learn social skills. The stories are designed to address specific social behaviors that are problematic to the individual. The skills are taught and practiced in a structured setting so that the individual can later independently use the learned skill as a guide for conduct or self-management in the specific social situation. The advantage of the approach is the individualization, which is reported to assist in improving social skills, reducing frustration and anxiety for the individual, and improving behavior when the approach is used consistently.

Other Autism Spectrum Disorders

Autism spectrum disorder is a general term for a number of disorders that affect a wide range of human behavior. The term *spectrum* is used because of the varied array of characteristic behavior disorders common to these conditions. The symptoms of these disorders seem to be pervasive and tend to impact every area of personal functioning, including cognitive, speech and language, behavioral and social, and physical development. Each

autism spectrum disorder has its own set of specific characteristics. Three examples of autism spectrum disorder—Rett's disorder, childhood disintegrative disorder, and Asperger's syndrome—are described next.

Rett's Disorder

Rett's disorder is a handicapping condition with symptoms similar to autism. An interesting fact that makes this disorder very different from other handicapping conditions is that all reported cases to date have been diagnosed in females.

The DSM-IV-TR (APA, 2000) describes the common pattern of development for Rett's disorder. The child shows normal prenatal and perinatal development up to around 5 months of age. Head circumference is usually of normal size at birth. Then, between the ages of 5 and 48 months, two main problems begin to occur. First, normal growth of head circumference begins to decelerate. This means that normal neurological development is not taking place. As a result, receptive and expressive language skills are impaired along with severe psychomotor retardation. Psychomotor links psychological functioning with motor skills. This means that the cognitive deficits in the sensory and perceptual parts of the brain have a detrimental impact on motor coordination (Vergason & Anderegg, 1997). Individuals with Rett's disorder usually have severe to profound mental retardation.

A second major indicator of Rett's disorder during this period is the loss of previously acquired purposeful hand movements and fine motor skill control. Stereotypic hand movements for Rett's disorder are described as hand wringing or hand washing (without water) motions. Other gross motor skills problems develop later, along with poor coordination of gait or body trunk movements.

Social skills are negatively impacted during the onset and course of Rett's disorder. The individual tends to lose interest in the social environment as the disorder progresses. Rett's disorder is a lifelong affliction with no known cure. The progressive loss of skills tends to be consistent during the life span, with only a few individuals showing small improvements in developmental delays and increased interest in the social environment during late childhood or adolescence.

Childhood Disintegrative Disorder

Childhood disintegrative disorder is rare and occurs much less often than autism. It is diagnosed most frequently in males. Onset usually begins after a period of normal development anywhere from 2 to 4 years of age but before 10 years. Then a clinically significant regression of previously acquired skills begins to occur. Common initial behavioral indicators include hyperactivity or irritability and are followed by loss of speech and other skills. For diagnosis, at least two of the following skills would be affected: (a) expressive or receptive language, (b) social skills or adaptive behavior, (c) bowel or bladder control, (d) play skills, or (e) motor skills (APA, 2000, p. 79). Severe mental retardation is common.

Asperger's Syndrome

Compared to Autism The DSM-IV-TR (APA, 2000) lists Asperger syndrome (AS) as a separate category from autism. This has caused a minor controversy in that some researchers think AS is merely a representation of one point on the continuum of autistic-like disorders while others indicate that the cognitive, communication, and lifelong prognosis are distinctly different from those of autism (Gargiulo, 2003; Heward, 2003; McLaughlin-Cheng, 1999).

Those who believe that AS is a component of the autism continuum closely compare it to "high functioning" autism (Bloch-Rosen, 1999). Although there are a number of similarities, there are differences. Both autism and AS involve impairments of social functioning and stereotypic repetitive patterns of behavior. However, there is a major difference in that persons with AS do not show the devastating communication and cognitive deficits common to individuals who have autism.

The meta-analysis completed by McLaughlin-Cheng (1999) indicates that students with AS tend to perform at a significantly higher level than students with autism on tests of cognitive ability and adaptive functioning. Some researchers (Frith, 1991; Gargiulo, 2003; Heward, 2003) suggest that many parents find the diagnosis of AS much less negative and devastating than a diagnosis of autism. The symptoms of AS tend to be milder and easy to manage.

Definition AS is a pervasive developmental disorder that severely affects formation of normal social interaction skills. There are distinct differences between the two disorders. Unlike autism, persons with AS do not show significant delays in language development or cognitive functioning (Heward, 2003). They do tend to have poor communication, motor, and social skills; show repetitive and stereotyped behaviors; and have an intense preoccupation with mechanical things or parts of things (Heward, 2003; Kauffman, 2001). Individuals with AS often demonstrate an intensely restricted range of interests (Bloch-Rosen. 1999). The DSM-IV-TR (APA, 2000) diagnosis requires clinically significant impairment of social and occupational functioning and severely restricted interests and activities. The criteria for the diagnosis of AS are found in Table 14–4.

Common Behaviors Lord (1999) provided an interesting description of the typical behavioral patterns that might be observed in persons with AS. Following is a summary of behaviors one might observe:

Social Interactions
- Do not accurately read social cues of others
- Lack motivation to interact and share conversation
- Tend to be peer group isolates
- May focus on small details rather than on whole picture

Communication
- Language acquisition may be delayed
- May use memorized phrases out of context

TABLE 14-4 Diagnostic Criteria for 299.80 Asperger's Disorder

A. Qualitative impairment in social interaction as manifested by at least two of the following:

   (1) marked impairment in the use of multiple nonverbal behaviors such as eye-to-eye gaze, facial expression, body postures, and gestures to regulate social interaction

   (2) failure to develop peer relationships appropriate to developmental level

   (3) a lack of spontaneous seeking to share enjoyment, interests, or achievements with other people (e.g., by lack of showing, bringing, or pointing out objects of interest to other people)

   (4) lack of social or emotional reciprocity

B. Restricted repetitive and stereotyped patterns of behavior, interests, and activities, as manifested by at least one of the following:

   (1) encompassing preoccupation with one or more stereotyped and restricted patterns of interest that is abnormal either in intensity or focus

   (2) apparently inflexible adherence to specific nonfunctional routines or rituals

   (3) stereotyped and repetitive motor mannerisms (e.g., hand or finger flapping or twisting, or complex whole-body movements)

   (4) persistent preoccupation with parts of objects

C. The disturbance causes clinically significant impairment in social, occupational, or other important areas of functioning.

D. There is no clinically significant general delay in language (e.g., single words used by age 2 years, communicative phrases used by age 3 years).

E. There is no clinically significant delay in cognitive development or in the development of age-appropriate self-help skills, adaptive behavior (other than in social interaction), and curiosity about the environment in childhood.

F. Criteria are not met for another specific Pervasive Developmental Disorder or Schizophrenia.

Note. *Reprinted with permission from the* Diagnostic and Statistical Manual of Mental Disorders, *Text Revision, Copyright 2000. American Psychiatric Association.*

- May have difficulty with receptive and expressive language
- Language needs to be precise and concrete
- May not understand figures of speech, metaphors, or smiles
- Spoken language may have odd patterns
- May be too loud, lack local accent, use monotonous tone, pedantic speech style
- May talk incessantly on a topic of self-interest without recognizing boredom of the listener
- May seem to talk "at" rather than "to" others
- Body language and facial expression may appear stiff
- May use eye gaze rather than eye contact

Narrow Interests / Preoccupations
- Obsession with certain, very narrow topics
- Schedules, maps, trains, computers, dinosaurs, etc.

Repetitive Routines / Inflexibility
- May insist on rigid adherence to routines
- May have outstanding rote memory skills (check for comprehension)
- May lack spontaneous imagination and creative thinking skills

A More Down-to-Earth Description of Asperger's Syndrome

Asperger's syndrome is a term used when a child or adult has some features of autism but may not have the full-blown clinical picture. There is some disagreement about where it fits in the autism spectrum disorder spectrum. A few people with Asperger's syndrome are very successful and until recently were not diagnosed with anything but were seen as brilliant, eccentric, absent minded, socially inept, and a little awkward physically.

Although the criteria state no significant delay in the development of language milestones, what you might see is a "different" way of using language. A child may have a wonderful vocabulary and even demonstrate hyperlexia but not truly understand the nuances of language and have difficulty with language pragmatics. Social pragmatics also tend be weak, leading the person to appear to be walking to the beat of a "different drum." Motor dyspraxia can be reflected in a tendency to be clumsy.

In social interaction, many people with Asperger's syndrome demonstrate gaze avoidance and may actually turn away at the same moment as greeting another. They may have a desire to interact with others but have trouble knowing how to make it work. They are, however, able to learn social skills much like you or I would learn to play the piano.

There is a general impression that Asperger's syndrome carries with it superior intelligence and a tendency to become very interested in and preoccupied with a particular subject. Often this preoccupation leads to a specific career at which the adult is very successful. At younger ages, one might see the child being a bit more rigid and apprehensive about changes or about adhering to routines. This can lead to a consideration of OCD but it is not the same phenomenon.

Many of the weaknesses can be remediated with specific types of therapy aimed at teaching social and pragmatic skills. Anxiety leading to significant rigidity can be also treated medically. Although it may be difficult, adults with Asperger's can have relationships, families, happy and productive lives. (Freisleben-Cook, n.d.)*

Causes   The DSM-IV-TR (APA, 2000) suggests that research on the cause of AS is in an emerging state. At this time it is termed a neurobiological disorder of unknown cause. Regarding developmental course, AS seems to appear later than symptoms of autism. The child usually exhibits quite normal patterns of development through the preschool period. At that time children with AS begin to show some motor skill deficits. Awkwardness or clumsiness may become apparent. Significant difficulties with social interactions are usually recognized

*Lois Freisleben-Cook's description was originally a post to the bit.listserv.autism newsgroup/listserv.

when the individual begins attending school. During this period the restricted range of interests, activities, and stereotypic behaviors is usually first observed.

Prevalence   Prevalence of Asperger's syndrome is estimated to occur at a rate of about 3 to 7 children per 1,000 children aged 7 to 16 years, and AS occurs about five times as often as autism (Bloch-Rosen, 1999; Ehlers & Gillberg, 1993). The DSM-IV-TR (APA, 2000) reports that AS is more common in males than in females. It is considered to be a lifelong disorder with no known cure.

Assessment Methods   Assessment of symptoms for a diagnosis of AS begins, as do many evaluations, with a comprehensive history of physical development, medical issues, educational milestones, and family factors. Bloch-Rosen (1999) details areas most relevant to the assessment of AS. These include specifics such as age of onset of symptomatic behaviors, the individual's ability to use language for communication, and unique or narrow range of personal interests. Particular emphasis should be placed on the individual's social interaction skills, level of cognitive functioning, and use of repetitive rituals or inflexible routines.

Educational Interventions for Asperger's Syndrome   To provide the most effective services, parents and educators must be aware of the child's personal strengths and areas in need of intervention. Some students with AS may be referred and placed in special education classes, while others may receive education services in the general classroom. Placement options depend of the unique characteristics of each individual.

Kiln and Volkmar (1997) reported successful teaching methods for students with AS. Individualization of learning strategies should be based on assessment and current level of academic skills. Successful instruction of academic concepts may be based on a more concise, explicit, and rote approach. A general strategy employing a parts-to-whole verbal instructional method may be successful.

Since social interaction skills appear to be a major deficit for most individuals with AS, learning activities designed to improve conversation, general communication, and social skills are imperative. Specific concepts include understanding body language and nonverbal cues in others, skills for carrying on a conversation, and increasing awareness of one's own verbal and nonverbal behavior. While Asperger's syndrome has many behaviors and symptoms in common with autism, they are treated as separate entities. Because individuals with AS often have normal to above normal levels of cognitive functioning, educational and lifelong options are very different. Persons with AS must be provided with services that focus on remediation of social and communication skill deficits.

Schizophrenia

Schizophrenia is a complex, extremely puzzling condition that was originally closely linked with autism (Gargiulo, 2003; Simpson & Zionts, 2000). Some children who are diagnosed with autism or another autism spectrum disorder at a young age are later diagnosed with schizophrenia (Kauffman, 2001).

Schizophrenia is described as an illness manifested by *psychotic* conditions. Psychotic refers to a broad classification of severe emotional, behavioral, and/or mental disorders that are characterized by a persistent ignoring of reality; a lack of ordered, organized behavior; and an inability to function adequately in daily living (Vergason & Anderegg, 1997). Specifically, patients with schizophrenia seem to be unable to separate real events from unreal experiences. Sometimes the psychotic symptoms may develop as a result of an undetected medical disorder. A thorough medical examination should always be a precautionary treatment used to rule out other biological causes for the abnormal behavior before diagnosing schizophrenia. Three million Americans may develop schizophrenia during their lives (about 1%) and as many as 100,000 individuals have severe schizophrenia resulting in institutionalization.

About 1 of every 100 adults may have schizophrenia. It is increasingly more rare in persons under age 18 (Kauffman, 2001). Because schizophrenia develops at an age when most students are leaving high school, there typically are no school screening procedures or other general testing methods used to detect the disorder. Clinics and medical centers are the likely options for testing and treatment. The disorder equally affects males and females. Schizophrenia is not a split personality or multiple personality disorder.

Characteristics of Schizophrenia

Psychotic episodes may involve *delusions, hallucinations*, and other specific types of abnormal emotional and cognitive processes (APA, 2000). The disordered thinking and processing problems may be observed by the following symptomatic behaviors: (a) incoherence, (b) catatonic behavior, (c) flat or grossly inappropriate affect, and (d) anxiety and confusion (APA, 2000; Heward, 2003; Kauffman, 2001). The first symptoms may begin to show up between the late teenage years and the early 30s. There have been exceedingly rare cases of schizophrenia being diagnosed in childhood. Some less obvious symptoms that might precede psychotic behaviors include social isolation or withdrawal and unusual speech, thinking, or behavioral patterns. Functional thinking patterns are negatively affected by the disorder.

The person may endure many hours of not being able to "think straight." Thoughts may come and go so rapidly that it is not possible to "catch them." The person may not be able to concentrate on one thought for very long and may be easily distracted and unable to focus attention. The person may not be able to sort out what is relevant and what is not relevant to a situation. He may be unable to connect conversations into logical sequences, as thoughts may become disorganized and fragmented, jumping from topic to topic in a way that is totally confusing to others. This can make conversation very difficult and may contribute to social isolation. If other people cannot make sense of what an individual is saying, they are likely to become uncomfortable and tend to leave that person alone (Shore, 1986, pp. 3–4).

Persons with no mental illness may occasionally do strange things, have periods of anxiety, or be unable to think clearly. This does not mean they are developing schizophrenia. Comparatively, persons with schizophrenia can also appear quite normal much of the time.

Delusions   Delusions are false thoughts or mental images that an individual believes to be true even though they have no actual basis in reality. There are two types of delusions. *Delusions of grandeur* are characteristic of persons who have psychotic disturbances. This means an individual has an exaggerated misconception of his own importance, position, ability, wealth, or accomplishments. *Delusions of persecution* are evident in a psychotic condition when an individual believes that another person(s) is trying to humiliate, injure, or harm him in some way. Shore (1986) provided the following example of delusions:

> Some delusions in schizophrenia are quite bizarre—for instance, believing that a neighbor is controlling the schizophrenic individual's behavior with magnetic waves, or that people on television are directing special messages specifically at him or her, or are broadcasting the individual's thoughts aloud to other people. Delusions of persecution, which are common in paranoid schizophrenia, are false and irrational beliefs that a person is being cheated, harassed, poisoned, or conspired against. (p. 3)

Hallucinations   Hallucinations are an abnormal mental condition in which the individual believes that imaginary things are real or that real things are immensely distorted. The person may sense things, feel things, see objects, or hear sounds that do not actually exist (Vergason & Anderegg, 1997). Hearing voices that other people do not hear is the most common type of hallucination. The voice may describe the patient's activity, carry on a conversation, warn of impending dangers, or tell the person what to do (Shore, 1986, p. 3).

Three Phases of Schizophrenia

The three phases of schizophrenia are called *prodromal, active,* and *residual* (APA, 2000).

Stage One: Prodromal   During the prodromal stage, a number of behavioral indicators may be noticed by family members and friends. There usually is a clear deterioration from what is considered normal behavior for the individual. Those behaviors include (a) social withdrawal, (b) neglect in personal hygiene and grooming, (c) flattened or lack of appropriate emotional responses or communication difficulties, (d) bizarre ideation and perceptions, (e) lack of initiative, (f) loss of interest in former pleasurable activities and friends, (seeming lack of ability to follow through on familiar role functions (school, work, social relationships, and self-care).

Stage Two: Active   Behavior becomes more severely dysfunctional during the active stage, when delusions, hallucinations, communicative incoherence, and even *catatonic* behaviors appear. Catatonic behaviors are a manifestation of mental illness characterized by a trancelike immobility, or stupor, that may cause rigidity of the muscular system. There may also be purposeless restless activity and unwarranted levels of excited behavior (Vergason & Anderegg, 1997).

Stage Three: Residual   The third phase of schizophrenia, referred to as the residual phase, usually involves more affective and role function disorders. It is not common for individuals to be able to return to their preprodromal phase behaviors. There is almost always permanent deterioration of behavior and functioning. Many family members and friends notice the personality deterioration that is evident in the early stage of schizophrenia. Common observations indicate that there is a definite change in personality, that the person just "isn't himself." Teachers and parents should refer adolescents and young adults who are showing symptoms of the schizophrenic stages for psychiatric evaluation. It is important to obtain a diagnosis and early intervention to reduce symptomatic behaviors and keep the individual's life as normal as possible.

Onset and Treatment of the Illness

The cause of schizophrenia is not known. It is thought to be primarily due to heredity (Kauffman, 2001). Medical research suggests that genetic factors produce a vulnerability that may be influenced by environmental triggers. However, no specific gene has been identified, no biochemical factor has been proven responsible, and no specific pattern of stressful environmental events has been recognized. Neurotransmitters, bits of biochemicals that carry messages between nerve cells, may be a link to understanding the cause of schizophrenia (Shore, 1986).

Research does support the fact that the illness runs in families (National Institute of Mental Health, 2000). Close relatives of patients with schizophrenia have an increased probability of developing the illness. For example, children with parents with schizophrenia have a 10% possibility of developing it while the general population has only a 1% chance (Shore, 1986). APA (2000) indicates that the typical age of onset for schizophrenia is during adolescence or young adulthood. The diagnosis requires that symptoms be apparent for at least 6 months. Treatment options for schizophrenia may involve antipsychotic medications, rehabilitation strategies, and talk therapy. The following treatment options are summarized from Shore (1986):

Medication   Medication does not cure a patient with schizophrenia. Many individuals do not benefit from medication and some do not require it. For those who do need it, medication can help reduce symptoms, which allows the person to function more effectively and appropriately. Antipsychotic medications (also called neuroleptics) have been very effective in reducing hallucinations and delusions. These medications do not produce an addiction. They can be very beneficial in that they help the individual differentiate between psychotic symptoms and the real world. In addition, there may be an increased ability to think clearly and to make informed choices and decisions with medication.

Rehabilitation   Rehabilitation programs are defined as nonmedical programs. They often involve training in the areas of social skills, management and organizational skills, vocational skills, and problem solving. Talk therapy may focus on issues such as current or past problems, thoughts, feelings, and relationships. Researchers have yet to identify a preferred or generally successful treatment method. Treatment is individualized based on symptoms. This facet of treatment is important because it helps the patient develop skills necessary for successful adjustment outside the confines of an institution.

Talk Therapy or Psychotherapy   Talk therapy or psychotherapy involves regularly scheduled meetings between the patient and a specially trained mental health professional. This group may include psychiatrists, psychologists, psychiatric social workers, or nurses. The therapy process may be successful in helping individuals to better understand themselves and their illness. It can also be used to help them cope in the real world.

Family therapy is often prescribed to help the family understand and cope with a member who has schizophrenia. This is a beneficial strategy to use in treatment planning. The family can provide a much-needed support system for the patient.

Implications for Working with Youth and Adolescents

The following advice is from a parent with a child who has a pervasive developmental disorder:

> My best advice; GET INVOLVED. The best thing you can do for yourself is become friends with other people who have children who also spit 200 times in an hour. They understand you and where you are coming from. (Powers, 1997, p. 251)

The symptomatic behaviors of autism spectrum disorders indicate a general pervasive delay in a number of different functioning areas. Autism spectrum disorder is a label for a general delay in cognitive, behavioral, communication, and social functioning skills. However, there are a number of specific autism spectrum disorders, including autism, Rett's disorder, childhood disintegrative disorder, and Asperger's syndrome. Although all are considered autism spectrum disorders, each has specific and unique criteria for diagnosis. All of the autism spectrum disorders are considered to be lifelong disabilities with no known cure. Parents, educators, medical personnel, and social service agency workers should provide early, intensive treatment. The goal is to help the child, parents, and other family members cope with the problems inherent for persons with autism spectrum disorders.

Early intervention is critical to address the array of global functioning problems experienced by children with pervasive developmental disorders. Parents, teachers, and other professionals should collaborate to provide the most effective program to help these children achieve to their highest potential.

> When I first heard about full-day school and long bus rides for a 2-year-old, I cried. But he loved school right from the beginning. And once he started school, he progressed so quickly. (Powers, 1997, p. 199)

This quote was from a parent of a child with a pervasive developmental disorder. It emphasizes the importance of an individualized and effective educational program for all students with handicaps. For many students, early childhood special education classes are highly beneficial. They provide the foundation necessary for each individual child to develop and progress academically and socially as they grow up. All children need an individualized program to help them achieve to their highest potential.

References

American Psychiatric Association. (1994). *Diagnostic and statistical manual of mental disorders* (4th ed.). Washington, DC: Author.

American Psychiatric Association. (2000). *Diagnostic and statistical manual of mental disorders* (4th ed., text revision). Washington, DC: Author.

Autism Society of America. (2000). Retrieved from www.autism-society.org.

Baron-Cohen, S. (1995). *Mind blindness: An essay on autism and theory of mind.* Cambridge, MA: MIT Press.

Bauer, S. (1999). *Asperger syndrome.* Retrievable from *www.udel.edu/bkirby/asperger/aspergerpapers.html*

Bettelheim, B. (1959). Joey: A mechanical boy. *Scientific American, 200,* 116–127.

Bigler, E. D. (1988). *Diagnostic clinical neuropsychology.* Austin, TX: University of Texas Press.

Biklen, D., Morton, M. W., Gold, G., & Berrigan, C. (1992). Facilitated communication: Implications for individuals with autism. *Topics in Language Disorders, 12*(4), 1–28.

Biklen, D., & Schubert, A. (1991, Nov.–Dec.). New words: The communication of students with autism. *Remedial and Special Education, 12*(6), 46–57.

Blake, A. (1989). Real "Rain Men": The mystery of the savant. *Autism Research Review International, 3*(1), 1–2, 7.

Bloch-Rosen, S. (1999). *Asperger's syndrome, High functioning autism, and disorders of the autistic continuum.* Retrievable from www.udel.edu/bkirby/asperger/aspergerpapers.html

Cabay, M. (1994). A controlled evaluation of facilitated communication using open-ended and fill-in questions. *Journal of Autism and Developmental Disorders, 24*(4), 517–527.

Cesaroni, L., & Garber, M. (1991). Exploring the experience of autism through firsthand accounts. *Journal of Autism and Developmental Disorders, 21*(3), 303–313.

Cohen, S. S. (1989, May 9). He's not broken. *Woman's Day,* pp. 90–98.

Coleman, M. C., & Webber, J. (2002). *Emotional and behavioral disorders: Theory and practice* (4th ed.). Needham Heights, MA: Allyn & Bacon.

Damasio, A. R., & Maurer, R. G. (1978). A neurological model for childhood autism. *Archives of Neurology, 35,* 777–786.

Eberlin, M. (1993). Facilitated communication: A failure to replicate the phenomena. *Journal of Autism and Developmental Disorders, 23*(3), 507–530.

Ehlers, S., & Gillberg, C. (1993). The epidemiology of Asperger syndrome: A total population study. *Journal of Child Psychology and Psychiatry, 34,* 1327–1350.

Fisher, E., Van Dyke, D. C., Sears, L., Matzen, J., Lin-Dyken, D., & McBrien, D. M. (1999). Recent research on the etiologies of autism. *Infants and Young Children*, 11(3), 1–8.

Fombonne, E. (1999). The epidemiology of autism: A review. *Psychological Medicine*, 29, 769–786.

Frith, U. (Ed.) (1991). *Autism and Asperger syndrome*. Cambridge, UK: Cambridge University Press.

Gargiulo, R. M. (2003). *Special education in contemporary society: An introduction to exceptionality*. Belmont, CA: Wadsworth/Thomas Learning.

Gelfand, D. M., Jenson, W. R., & Drew, C. J. (1988). *Understanding child behavior disorders*. Fort Worth, TX: Holt, Rinehart and Winston.

Gillberg, C. (1995). *Clinical child neuropsychology*. Cambridge, MA: Cambridge University Press.

Grandin, T. (1981). Teaching tips from a recovered autistic. *Focus on Autistic Behavior*, 3(1), 1–8.

Greenbough, B. S. (1989). *Children with autism*. Bethesda, MD: Woodbine House.

Guber, P., & Peters, J. (Executive Producers). (1988). *Rainman*. [Motion picture]. (Available from MGM/UA Home Video, Inc, 1000 Washington Blvd., Culver City, CA 90232).

Heward, W. L. (2003). *Exceptional children: An introduction to special education* (7th ed.). Upper Saddle River, NJ: Merrill/Prentice Hall.

Hirshorn, A., & Gregory, J. (1995). Further negative findings on facilitated communication. *Psychology in the Schools*, 32(2), 109–113.

Kanner, L. (1943). Autistic disturbance of affective contact. *Nervous Child*, 2, 217–250.

Kauffman, J. M. (2001). *Characteristics of emotional and behavioral disorders of children and youth* (7th ed.). Upper Saddle River, NJ: Merrill/Prentice Hall.

Kiln, A., & Volkmar, F. R. (1997). Asperger's syndrome. In D. J. Cohen & F. R. Volkmar (Eds.), *Handbook of autism and pervasive developmental disorders* (2nd ed.). New York: Wiley.

Krug, D., Arick, J., & Almond, P. (1993). *Autism Screening Instrument for Educational Planning* (2nd ed.). Austin, TX: Pro-Ed.

Levine, K. (1994, August). What if … A plea to professionals to consider the risk-benefit ratio of facilitated communication. *Mental Retardation*, 32(4), 300–304.

Levine, K., Shane, H. C., Wharton, R. M. (1994, August). Response to commentaries on risks of facilitated communication. *Mental Retardation*, 32(4), 317–318.

Lord, R. (1999). *Asperger syndrome*. Retrievable from www.udel.edu/bkirby/asperger/aspergerpapers.html

McLaughlin-Cheng, E. (1999). Asperger syndrome and autism: A literature review and meta-analysis. *Focus on Autism and Other Developmental Disabilities*, 13(4), 234–245.

Myles, B. S. (1996, Spring). Impact of facilitated communication combined with direct instruction on academic performance of individuals with autism. *Focus on Autism and Other Developmental Disabilities*, 11(1), 37–44.

Myles, B. S., & Simpson, R. L. (1994, July). Facilitated communication with children diagnosed as autistic in public school settings. *Psychology in the Schools*, 31(3), 208–220.

National Institute of Mental Health. (2000). *Depression in children and adolescents*. Retrievable from www.nimh.nih/gov/publicate/depchildresfact.cfm

Ornitz, E. M., Atwell, C. W., Kaplan, A. R., & Westlake, J. R. (1985). Brainstem dysfunction in autism. *Archives of General Psychiatry*, 42, 1018–1025.

Powers, M. D. (1997). What is autism? In M. D. Powers (Ed.), *Children with autism: A parents' guide*. Rockville, MD: Woodbine House.

Powers, M. D. (2000). What is autism? In M. D. Powers (Ed.), *Children with autism: A parents' guide* (2nd ed.). Rockville, MD: Woodbine House.

Rendle-Short, J. (1978). *Infantile autism diagnosis*. Washington, DC: National Society for Autistic Children.

Rimland, B. (1964). *Infantile autism: The syndrome and its implications for a neural theory of behavior*. New York: Appleton-Century-Crofts.

Rimland, B. (1978, August). Inside the mind of an autistic savant. *Psychology Today*, pp. 68–80.

Rimland, B. (1997). Introduction. In M. D. Powers (Ed.), *Children with autism: A parents' guide* (pp. 1–29). Rockville, MD: Woodbine House.

Ritvo, E. R., Freeman, B. J., Mason-Brothers, A., Mo, A., & Ritvo, A. (1985). Concordance for the syndrome of autism in 40 pairs of afflicted twins, *American Journal of Psychiatry*, 142, 74–77.

Rutter, M. (1965). The influence of organic and emotional factors on the origins, nature, and outcome of childhood psychosis. *Developmental Medicine and Child Neurology*, 7, 518–528.

Shopler, E., & Dalldorf, J. (1980, June). Autism: Definition, diagnosis, and management. *Hospital Practice*, 64–73.

Shopler, E., & Mezibov, G. B. (1992). *High functioning individuals with autism*. New York: Plenum Press.

Shore, D. (1986). *Schizophrenia: Questions and answers.* U.S. Department of Health and Human Services. DHHS Publication No. (ADM) 86-1457. Washington, DC: U.S. Government Printing Office.

Simpson, R. L., & Myles, B. S, (1995, Winter). Effectiveness of facilitated communication with children and youth with autism. *Journal of Special Education,* 28(4), 424–439.

Simpson, R. L., & Regan, M. (1986). *Management of autistic behavior.* Austin, TX: Pro-Ed.

Simpson, R. L., & Zionts, P. (2000). *Autism: Information and resources for professionals and parents.* Austin, TX: Pro-Ed.

Smith, M. D. (1994). Facilitated communication: The effects of the facilitator. *Journal of Autism and Developmental Disorders,* 24(3), 357–367.

Spake, A. (1992, August). Breaking the silence. *Teacher Magazine,* 3(4), 14–21.

Tommasone, L., & Tommasone, J. (2000). Adjusting to your child's diagnosis. In M. D. Powers (Ed.), *Children with autism: A parents' guide* (2nd ed.). Rockville, MD: Woodbine House.

Turnbull, A., Turnbull, R., Shank, M., Smith, S., & Leal, D. (2002). *Exceptional lives* (3rd ed.). Upper Saddle River, NJ: Merrill/Prentice Hall.

Vergason, G. A., & Anderegg, M. L. (1997). *Dictionary of special education and rehabilitation* (4th ed.). Denver, CO: Love.

Wheeler, D. L. (1993). An experimental assessment of facilitated communication. *Mental Retardation,* 31(1), 49–60.

Wing, L. (1993). The definition and prevalence of autism: A review. *European Child and Adolescent Psychiatry,* 2, 1–14.

Ysseldyke, J. E., & Algozzine, B. (1995). *Special education: A practical approach for teachers* (3rd ed.). Boston: Houghton Mifflin.

PART 6
THE FUTURE OF SPECIAL EDUCATION

Chapter 15: Best Practices in Working with Students with Emotional and Behavioral Disorders (E/BD)

BEST PRACTICES IN WORKING WITH STUDENTS WITH EMOTIONAL AND BEHAVIORAL DISORDERS (E/BD)

After completing this chapter, the reader will be able to identify:

- The importance of using a collaborative approach that is proactive and positive to educate students with E/BD.
- Inclusion practices that stress preparation of staff and students.
- Ongoing research to document effective educational practices.
- Life skills preparation for students with E/BD.

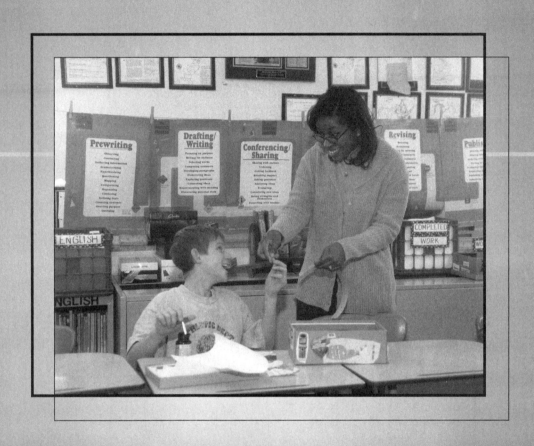

Summary

In the long run, permanent behavior changes are maintained only by basic positive procedures. (Rhode, Jenson, & Reavis, 1992, p. 2)

This is a basic three-step process:

1. Confront problem behavior.
2. Teach an appropriate replacement.
3. Heap on the positive reinforcement.

Basically, it's a "teach 'em what to do instead" program.

Proactive Positive Procedures

The emphasis throughout this text has been on the proactive and positive use of the behavioral model to reduce problem behavior and teach students socially appropriate replacement behaviors. Proactive teachers think ahead. They analyze, plan, and prepare. Proactive teachers use behavior management and classroom management procedures that will help students achieve at higher levels and show the most appropriate behavior. These teachers use mainly positive approaches with students who have E/BD.

The use of verbal positive reinforcement to teach and maintain appropriate behavior cannot be stressed enough. Students with E/BD have a high risk for dropping out of school. The current dropout rate is estimated to be about 65%, with a 41% arrest rate. School should be a positive and rewarding environment. Educators, parents, and professionals must collaborate to provide the most effective educational programming for students with E/BD. The goal is to inspire and encourage these students to stay in school, graduate, and be employable adults.

All teachers should work together to provide students with a motivating, relevant, and challenging curriculum. Students should view teachers as being rewarding, positive personalities. A classroom with a positive climate is the foundation necessary to begin the process of educating students who have E/BD with academic, social, and behavioral skills for lifetime success (Jensen & Yerington, 1997; Jensen, Rhode, & Reavis, 1996; Kaplan, 1995; Rhode et al., 1992). Social skills instruction is as important as academics for students with E/BD (Goldstein & McGinnis, 1997; Sheridan, 1995). Social skills are essential life skills that will help students achieve academically as well as maintain relations on the job. A consistent program of social skills instruction will assist youth and adolescents to learn to get along with peers and adults—at school, at home, and in community activities. The key to successfully teaching students with E/BD is proactive and positive management strategies.

Inclusion

The trend of integrating persons with disabilities into the mainstream of society began in the 1960s and continues in schools today with mainstreaming and inclusion practices. Youth and adolescents with E/BD present unique challenges for educators, parents, and other professionals. In addition to the wide range of emotional and behavioral problems these students demonstrate, many also have overlapping learning, attention, and conduct problems. The education of students with E/BD requires a collaborative approach.

A pivotal point regarding successful inclusion of students with E/BD relates to the incredibly important collaborative relationship between educators, parents, and other professionals who work with youth and adolescents. Suggestions have been provided at the end of each chapter of the text to facilitate this process.

Many schools across the nation have either willingly or unwillingly adopted an inclusion model of educating students who have disabilities. Unfortunately, some schools have embraced the inclusion model without adequate preparation of staff or students. To implement the inclusion model without a great deal of disruption, preparation must take place in three areas:

1. General and special educators need training and time to collaborate.
2. General and special educators must learn specialized teaching methods. General educators must learn more about individualization of academic instruction and behavior management while special educators must learn about content area instruction and teaching to larger groups. Both may need to learn team teaching skills.
3. Students must be prepared. Students with E/BD must have a satisfactory level of academic and behavioral skills necessary for success in the inclusion classroom.

After the preparation has been completed, inclusion or mainstreaming should take place on an individualized basis.

Ongoing Research on Effective Education

There is an ongoing need for continuing research to determine successful educational models for students with E/BD. To date, educational practices have not been highly effective for students who have behavioral difficulties and additional learning problems. School tends to become a very aversive experience for students with E/BD. When school is punishing and failure-oriented, students vote with their feet. Many drop out of school.

Educators must be aware of the importance of using positive approaches for students with E/BD. The best predictor of lifetime success for students with E/BD is a solid foundation of basic academic skills (Rhode et al., 1992). To learn basic academic skills, the students must be in school.

References

Goldstein, A. P., & McGinnis, E. (1997). *Skillstreaming the adolescent* (2nd ed.). Champaign, IL: Research Press.

Jensen, M. M., & Yerington, P. C. (1997). *Gangs: Straight talk, straight up.* Longmont, CO: Sopris West.

Jenson, W. R., Rhode, G., & Reavis, H. K. (1996). *The tough kid toolbox.* Longmont, CO: Sopris West.

Kaplan, J. S. (with Carter, J.). (1995). *Beyond behavior modification* (3rd ed.). Austin, TX: Pro-Ed.

Rhode, G., Jenson, W. R., & Reavis, H. K. (1992). *The tough kid book.* Longmont, CO: Sopris West.

Sheridan, S. M. (1995). *The tough kid social skills book.* Longmont, CO: Sopris West.

AUTHOR INDEX

SUBJECT INDEX

Abnormal relationships to objects
and events, 320–321
Abnormal responses to sensory
stimulation, 321–322
Abruptio placentae, 67, 71
Academic achievement
alternative day schools and, 47
anxiety disorders and, 166
assessment and, 24, 25
attention deficit disorder and,
223, 242
conduct disorder and, 294–295, 297
correctional facilities and, 52–53
depression and, 184, 185, 186, 188
educational placement options
and, 41
emotional and behavioral disorders
and, 4, 5, 8
gang activity and, 140, 143, 161
inclusion and, 42
IQ and, 7, 8
pervasive developmental disorder
and, 312
prenatal drug exposure and, 76
residential schools and, 52–53
school violence and, 114–115, 117,
118, 124, 128
self-contained classrooms and, 47
social phobias and, 175
substance abuse and, 102, 105
Tourette syndrome and, 272, 273–274
victim behavior and, 286
ACID test, 240
Acrophobia, 174
Active schizophrenia, 336
ADD. See Attention deficit disorder
(ADD)
Adderall, 231
ADHD. See Attention deficit
hyperactivity disorder (ADHD)
Adjudicated delinquents, 281
Adolescent-onset conduct disorder, 282
Adolescents and adolescence
anxiety disorders and, 166
conduct disorder and, 282, 295

depression symptoms and, 183,
184, 186
drug abuse risk factors, 102–103
Monitoring the Future survey and,
85–86
prenatal drug exposure and,
76–77, 78
schizophrenia and, 335
stress and, 82
substance abuse and, 82, 83, 90, 91,
93, 94–95, 103, 108
Tourette syndrome and, 261
Adoption studies
attention deficit disorder and, 228
conduct disorder and, 292
depression and, 187
Adult criminal behavior, 292
African Americans, 15
After-school activities, 107, 114, 120,
161
Age factors. See also Adolescents and
adolescence; Early childhood
Asperger's syndrome and, 334
autism and, 316, 322
conduct disorder and, 282,
289–290, 296
depression and, 182, 183–184, 186,
187–189, 191
drug use/addiction and, 65
schizophrenia and, 335
Aggression. See also School violence;
Violence
alternative day schools and, 47
attention deficit disorder and, 243
behavioral model of intervention
and, 31
conduct disorder and, 280, 281, 282,
288, 289, 291, 292, 293,
295–296, 306
as externalizing behavior, 6
gang activity and, 136
inclusion and, 42
prenatal drug exposure and, 72, 73
social maladjustment and, 5
substance abuse and, 102

suicide and, 193
Tourette syndrome and, 270
Agoraphobia, 172
AIDS, 66, 96
Alcohol-related birth defects
(ARBD), 70
Alcohol use/addiction. See also Fetal
alcohol effects (FAE); Fetal
alcohol syndrome (FAS);
Prenatal drug exposure
alcohol as depressant, 90
as commonly abused substance,
82–83
costs to society, 66, 104
effects of, 91, 92, 98
observable signs of use, 92
as overlapping condition, 8
parenting and, 16, 91
statistics on, 85
synergistic effects of, 64
Alternative day schools, 44, 47–48
Alternative education, 18–19
American Academy of Child and
Adolescent Psychiatry, 329
American Academy of Pediatrics, 329
American Association on Mental
Retardation, 329
American Psychiatric Association, 329
Amphetamines, 84, 97
Amygdala, 324
Anabolic steroids, 97–100
Animal phobias, 174
Anorexia nervosa
characteristics of, 202, 207–211
definition of, 200
physical complications of, 211
warning signs of, 209–211
Anorexic bulimia, 200
Antecedents, 29, 304
Antidepressants, 191, 214, 233,
269–270
Antisocial behavior, 281. See also
Conduct disorder
Antisocial personality disorder, 282,
284, 291, 296

Developmental delays, 314, 322
Developmental Individual-Difference, Relationship-Based (DIR) Model, 331
Dexedrine, 231, 232
Dextroamphetamine, 84, 231
Diagnostic and Statistical Manual of Mental Disorders (DSM-II), 224
Diagnostic and Statistical Manual of Mental Disorders (DSM-III), 224, 242–243
Diagnostic and Statistical Manual of Mental Disorders (DSM-III-R), 224, 242
Diagnostic and Statistical Manual of Mental Disorders (DSM-IV-TR)
  anorexia nervosa and, 209
  anxiety disorders and, 166
  Asperger's syndrome and, 332, 333, 334
  attention deficit disorder and, 224–225, 228, 236
  autism and, 314, 315–316, 317, 318
  conduct disorder and, 281, 282, 283
  depression and, 189
  eating disorders and, 203
  mood disorders and, 182
  obsessive-compulsive disorder and, 170
  oppositional defiant disorder and, 243
  panic disorder and, 172
  pervasive developmental disorder and, 312
  Rett's disorder and, 331
  Tourette syndrome and, 262
Difficult temperament children, 12, 290
DIR (Developmental Individual-Difference, Relationship-Based) Model, 331
Direct observation, 24, 28, 262, 264
Disobedient pathway, 289
Dividing attention, 235
Domino theory, 313
Dopamine, 230, 231, 233, 255, 269
Dow, Andrew, 260, 262
Dow, Melody, 260, 262
Dow, Walter, 260, 262
Dropout rates
  alternative day schools and, 48
  conduct disorder and, 300
  emotional and behavioral disorders and, 7, 8–9

prenatal drug exposure and, 76
proactive behavior management and, 120, 344
school violence and, 128
Drug Enforcement Administration, 97
Drug holidays, 269
Drug use/addiction. *See also* Prenatal drug exposure
  adolescent risk factors for, 102–103
  anabolic steroids and, 97–100
  commonly abused drugs, 96–102
  costs of, 104
  demographic changes in, 65–66
  depressants and, 90–92
  hallucinogens, 92–94, 98
  history of, 83–85
  inhalants, 100–101, 107
  narcotics, 84, 94–96, 96, 97, 117, 152
  as overlapping condition, 8
  parenting and, 16, 93, 94–95
  prescription drugs, 101–102
  stimulants and, 86–90, 91, 97
  synergistic effects of, 64
Dysphoria, 182
Dysthmia, 182
Dysthymic disorder, 183

Early childhood
  conduct disorder and, 296
  pervasive developmental disorders, 338
  prenatal drug exposure and, 74–75
Early intervention
  anxiety disorders and, 166
  attention deficit disorder and, 247
  autism and, 328
  conduct disorder and, 296, 298, 306
  eating disorders and, 200, 201, 216–217
  gang activity and, 135
  prenatal drug exposure and, 72–73
  schizophrenia and, 335
  school violence and, 127
  substance abuse and, 102
  Tourette syndrome and, 254, 275
Easy temperament, 12, 290
Eating disorders
  anorexia nervosa, 200, 207–211
  bulimia nervosa, 200, 202–204, 211–213, 214
  causes of, 201–204
  definition of, 200–201

depression and, 188, 203, 204, 206, 213
IMAD approach to, 215–216
implications for educators, 216–217
interviews and, 204–206
males and, 207–208
media and, 201, 208–209
obsessive-compulsive disorder and, 170, 203
personality characteristics and, 206–207
prevalence of, 201
prevention of, 214–215
treatment of, 213–216
Echolalia, 319–320
Ecological approach, to assessment, 25
Ecological model of intervention, 35–36
Ecstasy, 87–88, 99
Educational interventions
  for Asperger's syndrome, 334–335
  for autism, 328
  for depression, 191
Educational placement options
  alternative day school, 47–48
  correctional facilities, 52–54
  history of, 40–41
  implications for educators, 54–55
  inclusion, 41–43, 344–345
  least restrictive environment and, 40, 43–46
  mainstreaming, 41, 43
  prenatal drug exposure and, 75
  residential schools, 49–52
  special education services and, 46–47
Education for All Handicapped Children Act, 41, 188
EEG (electroencephalogram), 264, 327
Electroencephalogram (EEG), 264, 327
Elementary and Secondary Education Act (ESEA) of 1965, 121
Ellis, William, 127
Emotional/affective factors
  depression and, 184–185, 186
  eating disorders and, 203
  Tourette syndrome and, 267–268, 273
Emotional and behavioral disorders (E/BD)
  causes of, 11–17
  characteristics of, 6–7

Gang activity, *continued*
  teacher preparation and, 134,
    137–138, 161–162
  violence and, 134, 135–136, 142,
    144, 146, 149, 162
  warning signs, 135, 139–149
Gang graffiti, 145–146, 147, 152, 155
Gang hand signs, 148–149, 150
Gang jewelry, 145, 155
Gang-oriented neighborhoods,
  141–142
Gang paraphernalia, 149
Gang slang, 146, 148
Gangsters, 84
Gangs (West), 134–135
Gang tattoos, 149, 151
GED (high school equivalence
  degree), 53
Gender
  anorexia nervosa and, 209
  Asperger's syndrome and, 334
  attention deficit disorder and, 227
  autism and, 316
  bully behavior and, 285
  childhood disintegrative disorder
    and, 332
  conduct disorder and, 280, 288
  drug use/addiction and, 65
  eating disorders and, 200–201,
    207–208
  generalized anxiety disorder
    and, 168
  phobias and, 174
  prevalence rates and, 11
  Rett's disorder and, 331
  suicide and, 193
  Tourette syndrome and, 256
General education classrooms
  Asperger's syndrome and, 334
  autism and, 330
  conduct disorder and, 301–302
  effective classroom expectations,
    302–305
  inclusion and, 41, 42
  least restrictive environment and,
    43, 44, 46
  mainstreaming and, 41, 43
  Tourette syndrome and, 272,
    273–274
General education teachers
  inclusion and, 42, 345
  least restrictive environment
    and, 45

  mainstreaming and, 41
Generalization, 330
Generalized anxiety disorder (GAD),
  167–168, 172
Genetic factors
  attention deficit disorder and,
    227–230
  autism and, 315
  causes of emotional and behavioral
    disorders and, 12
  conduct disorder and, 289, 291–292
  depression and, 12, 186, 187, 191
  eating disorders and, 202
  prenatal drug exposure and, 63
  schizophrenia and, 12, 337
  Tourette syndrome and, 255–256
GFSA (Gun-Free Schools Act) of 1994,
  120–121
GHB (Gamma Hydroxybutyrate),
  89, 99
Girls and Boys Town, 51–52
Girls and Boys Town National
  Hotline, 51
Glucose metabolism, 229, 231
Goals 2000: Education America Act of
  1994, 121–122
Graham, Elizabeth, 66
Grandin, Temple, 322, 328–329
Greenspan, 331
Growth retardation, 69
Gun-Free Schools Act (GFSA) of 1994,
  120–121
Guns. *See also* Weapons
  gang activity and, 144
  school violence and, 116

Hallucinations, 335, 336
Hallucinogens, effects of, 92–94, 98
Harrison Narcotic Act of 1914, 84
Harvard Mental Health Letter, 201, 202,
  206, 211
Head circumference measurement,
  69, 71, 72, 331
Head/facial deformities, 69, 70
Hepatitis, 96
Hepatitis B, 66
Heroin, 83, 84, 94, 95–96
High school equivalence degree
  (GED), 53
Hippocrates, 83
HIV, 66, 96
Hoffman, Dustin, 312
Homebound instruction, 44, 46

Home note system, 33, 247–248
Hostility, 6
Hug-drug, 88
Hunger, 15
Hyper-hippocampus
  functioning, 324
Hypersensitive behavior
  attention deficit disorder and, 244
  eating disorders and, 204
  medication side effects and, 233
  prenatal drug exposure and,
    67–68, 71
  temperament and, 12
  Tourette syndrome and, 269, 272
Hyperthermia, 88, 89
Hypodistractible state, 324

IAES (individualized alternative
  education setting), 18
Ice (methamphetamine), 90
IDEA 1997
  assessment and, 24
  assumptions of, 17
  attention deficit disorder and, 222
  definition of emotional and
    behavioral disorders and, 4–5, 6,
    11, 188
  least restrictive environment
    and, 40
  manifest determination and, 17–19
  traumatic brain injury and, 13
IEP. *See* Individualized Education Plan
  (IEP)
IFEED method, 303
IMAD approach, 215–216
I messages, 122, 123
Imitation, 304
Implications for educators
  anxiety disorders and, 176–177
  assessment and, 37
  attention deficit disorder and,
    247–248
  conduct disorder and, 305–306
  depression and, 195
  eating disorders and, 216–217
  educational placement options
    and, 54–55
  emotional and behavioral disorders
    and, 19
  gang activity and, 161–162
  intervention models, 37
  pervasive developmental disorder
    and, 337–338

prenatal drug exposure and, 72–78
substance abuse and, 107–108
Tourette syndrome and, 274–275
Inclusion
autism and, 330
as educational placement option,
41–42, 344–345
least restrictive environment and,
43–45
problems with, 42–43
self-contained classrooms and, 47
Inclusion classrooms, 44
Independent living skills
autism and, 317, 328
fetal alcohol syndrome and, 70–71
prenatal drug exposure and, 76, 77
Individualized alternative education
setting (IAES), 18
Individualized Education Plan (IEP)
assessment and, 24
behavior intervention strategies
and, 45
manifest determination and, 17–18
Tourette syndrome and, 272
transition programs and, 77
Informational Observation Data
Sheet, 328
Inhalants, 100–101, 107
Injuries, 13, 103–104, 183, 228
Intensity of attention, 235
Internalized disorders. See Anxiety
disorders; Depression; Eating
disorders; Suicide
Internalizing behaviors
characteristics of, 7
labels and, 9
poverty and, 15
prevalence rates and, 11
Internal locus of control, 301
Interpsychic conflict, 30
Intervention. See also Early
intervention
behavioral intervention plans, 7, 18,
19, 45
bully behavior and, 288
conduct disorder and, 297,
299–305
educational interventions, 191, 328,
334–335
positive reinforcement and, 301,
303–304
substance abuse and, 105–107
Tourette syndrome and, 268

Intervention models
behavioral model, 30–35, 344
biophysical model, 29–30
ecological model and, 35–36
implications for educators, 37
observation and, 33–35
proactive methods and, 29, 32
psychodynamic model, 30
research-based behavior
management strategies and,
28–29
social learning theory model,
36–37, 292
Interviews
anxiety disorders and, 167
assessment and, 24, 27, 28
attention deficit disorder and, 239
eating disorders and, 204–206
panic disorder and, 172–174
Involuntary attention, 235
Involuntary tics, 257
IQ
academic achievement and, 7, 8
assessment and, 24, 25
autism and, 316, 317, 323, 326–327,
328, 330
conduct disorder and, 295–296
prenatal drug exposure and, 72, 76

James, William, 223
*Jordan Executive Function Index for
Children*, 239, 240–241
Juvenile justice system, 281

Kahn, Eli, 224
Ketamine, 89, 99

Labels, 9, 10, 281
LaDue, Robin, 74
Language skills, 75–76
Lanugo, 210–211
Latin Kings, 149, 150, 151, 152, 155,
156, 157
Latinos, 15
Latin People Nation, 145
Laudanum, 83
Laufer, Morris, 224
Law enforcement officers
gang activity training of, 137–138
gang graffiti and, 146
gang hand signs and, 148
gang violence and, 135
relatives in gangs and, 142

teachers' collaboration with, 139
weapons and, 144
Lead levels, 228
LEA (local education agencies), 121
Learning disabilities
attention deficit disorder and, 222,
231, 243
correctional facilities and, 53
fetal alcohol syndrome and, 69
as overlapping condition, 8
residential schools and, 49
suicide and, 193
Tourette syndrome and, 266, 271
Least restrictive environment (LRE)
definition of, 43
educational placement options
and, 40, 43–46
inclusion model, 43–45
Leiter International Performance
Scale, 327
Light filtering, 323
Light sticks, 88
Light therapy, 187
Local education agencies (LEA), 121
Lovaas, Ivar, 330
Lovaas method, 330
Low birth weight, 71, 72
LSD (lysergic acid diethylamide), 92,
94, 98, 107

Magnetic resonance imaging
(MRI), 229
Mainstreaming, as educational
placement option, 41, 43
Major depressive disorder, 183
Maladaptive behavior
attention deficit disorder and, 223
autism and, 314
behavioral model of intervention
and, 32
conduct disorder and, 280–281, 293,
295, 298
depression and, 184–185
prenatal drug exposure and,
68, 74
residential schools and, 49
school violence and, 118–119, 122
substance abuse and, 102, 103
Tourette syndrome and, 266
Mandatory dress codes, 126–127
Manheim, Camryn, 208–209
Mania, 182
Manifest determination, 17–19

as externalizing behavior, 6
inclusion and, 42
Norepinephrine, 187, 191, 230, 231, 233, 269

Observational checklists, 239–240, 262, 263, 264
Observational learning, 304
Obsessions, 170, 171, 267
Obsessive-compulsive disorder (OCD)
  bulimia nervosa and, 203
  characteristics of, 169–171
  Tourette syndrome and, 170, 256, 266–267, 268, 270
  treatment for, 170
Occupational therapists, 265, 325
OCD. *See* Obsessive-compulsive disorder (OCD)
ODD (oppositional defiant disorder), 222, 243–244, 282, 284, 301
O'Donnell, Rosie, 208–209
ONDCP (White House Office of National Drug Control Policy), 104–105
One percent rule, 136
Open head injuries, 13
Opioids, 315
Opium, 84, 94, 95
Oppositional behavior, 6
Oppositional defiant disorder (ODD), 222, 243–244, 282, 284, 301
Outdoor adventure programs, 36, 52
Overachievers, and eating disorders, 206–207
Overlapping conditions
  anxiety disorders as, 8, 166, 177
  attention deficit disorder and, 8, 222, 243–244
  depression as, 188, 206
  emotional and behavioral disorders and, 7–9, 344
  obsessive-compulsive disorder as, 170
  residential schools and, 49
  Tourette syndrome and, 256, 266–268
Oversized clothing, 145
Over-the-counter medications, 84, 101
Overt problem behaviors, 289

Pack behavior, 136
Panic attacks, 171, 172–174
Panic disorder, 168, 171–174

Parasuicide, 192
PARC (Peoria Association for Retarded Citizens), 74, 75
Parentectomy, 313–314
Parent rating scales, 239
Parents and parenting. *See also* Families; Family dysfunction
  adolescents' alcohol intoxication and, 91
  adolescents' hallucinogen intoxication and, 93
  adolescent's narcotics intoxication, 94–95
  after-school activities and, 114
  assessment process and, 25
  attention deficit disorder and, 227, 230, 234, 239, 240
  autism and, 313, 315, 320, 322, 323, 325–326
  bully behavior and, 288
  causes of emotional and behavioral disorders and, 13
  coercive behavior and, 191
  conduct disorder and, 281, 288, 289, 291, 292, 293–294
  eating disorders and, 214, 215
  gang activity and, 16, 134, 143, 146, 149, 161
  poverty and, 16–17
  prenatal drug exposure and, 74, 75
  prereferral methods and, 25
  school uniforms and, 127
  school violence and, 118
  school violence prevention and, 125, 129
  single-parent households, 14, 16, 294
  substance abuse of adolescents and, 83, 103, 108
  Tourette syndrome and, 260, 262, 270, 272
Parent/teacher collaboration
  attention deficit disorder and, 247–248
  behavioral model of intervention and, 33
  dropout rates and, 344
  inclusion and, 344
Passive victims, 286–287
PCP (phencyclidine), 92, 94, 98
PECS (Picture Exchange Communication System), 330
Pediatric neurologists, 264

Peer group isolates, 7, 185, 332
Peers
  alcohol use and, 91
  conduct disorder and, 280, 282, 292, 295, 301, 305
  depression and, 185
  emotional and behavioral disorders and, 7
  gang activity and, 136, 140, 144
  inclusion and, 42
  outdoor adventure programs and, 52
  peer attention, 304
  prenatal drug exposure and, 76
  residential schools and, 51
  school violence and, 118, 127
  substance abuse and, 82, 102, 105
  substance abuse prevention and, 106
  Tourette syndrome and, 260, 267
Pemoline, 231
Penetrance, 256
People Nation, 145, 149, 151, 152, 153, 155, 157
Peoria Association for Retarded Citizens (PARC), 74, 75
Perfectionism, 206–207
Pervasive developmental disorder. *See also* Autism
  autism diagnosed as, 322
  autism spectrum disorders and, 312–313, 316, 331–335, 337–338
  definition of, 312
  domino theory and, 313
  implications for educators, 337–338
Peters, John, 224
PET (positron emission tomography), 229
Peyote, 92
Phencyclidine (PCP), 92, 94, 98
Phenobarbital, 90, 92
Phobias, 174–176
Physical dependence
  on narcotics, 95
  on prescription drugs, 101
Physical therapists, 325
Physiological factors
  anorexia nervosa and, 211
  bulimia nervosa and, 213
  depression and, 185, 186, 190
  food allergies and, 244–245
  prenatal drug exposure and, 71–72

models of, 50–52
 prenatal drug exposure and, 75
Residual schizophrenia, 336
Resource rooms, 44, 46, 280
Response set, 236
Retaliatory behaviors, 146
Rett's disorder, 313, 331–332
Revised Behavior Problem Checklist
 (RBPC), 298
Revised Wechsler Adult Intelligence
 Scale (WAIS), 326
Revised Wechsler Intelligence Scale
 for Children (WISC-R), 326
Rice, Haymes, 65
Rimland, Bernard, 324
Ritalin, 87, 101, 230, 231, 232, 269
Robert Wood Johnson
 Foundation, 66
Role models, 292–293, 301, 304
Rolling papers, 94
Roosevelt, Theodore, 83–84
Rophypnol, 89, 98
Rule-breaking behavior
 attention deficit disorder and, 244
 boot camps and, 54
 conduct disorder and, 280,
  281–282, 305
 residential schools and, 49
 Tourette syndrome and, 271
Rule-governed behavior, 31

SAD (seasonal affective
 disorder), 187
SAD (separation anxiety disorder),
 168–169
Safe and Drug-Free Schools and
 Community Act (SDFSCA) of
 1994, 121
Safe schools
 characteristics of, 125–127
 federal legislation and, 120–122
Salicylates, 245, 246
Sasso, Gary, 313
Schizophrenia
 autism and, 313, 335
 characteristics of, 335–336
 definition of emotional and
  behavioral disorders and, 5
 genetic factors and, 12, 337
 implications for educators, 195
 phases of, 336
 treatment of, 337
Schleissman, Janet, 316
Schleissman, Tanner, 316

School districts
 assaults and thefts, 115–116
 manifest determination and, 19
 prevalence rate variances and, 10–11
School psychologists, 25
School refusal problems, 169
School Social Behavior Scales (SSBS), 28
School uniforms, 126–127
School violence. *See also* Violence
 academic achievement and,
  114–115, 117, 118, 124, 128
 crime and, 120
 definition of, 114, 116–117
 factors leading to, 117–118
 federal legislation and, 120–122
 guns in schools, 116
 level system for school violence
  management, 125–126
 maladaptive behavior and,
  118–119, 122
 positive replacement for violent
  behaviors, 119–120, 125
 prevention of, 125–129
 punishment and, 120
 responding to crisis situations,
  128–129
 safe school characteristics, 125–127
 school uniforms and, 126–127
 threats of violence, 122–125
 trends in, 115–116
 warning signs of, 122–125
Schultz, Dutch, 84
Screening
 assessment and, 25
 attention deficit disorder and, 238
 conduct disorder and, 296–297, 306
 suicide and, 194
SDFSCA (Safe and Drug-Free Schools
 and Community Act) of
 1994, 121
Seasonal affective disorder (SAD), 187
Secobarbital, 92
Section 504 of the Rehabilitation Act
 of 1973, 24, 121, 223
SED (serious emotional
 disturbance), 289
Selection, attention deficit disorder
 and, 235–236
Self-assessment, behavioral model of
 intervention and, 33
Self-concept, 185, 201, 212, 215, 265
Self-contained classrooms, 44,
 46–47, 280
Self-control, 33

Self-esteem
 bulimia nervosa and, 212
 depression and, 185
 eating disorders and, 207, 209, 215
 gang activity and, 140–141, 161
 prenatal drug exposure and, 77
 school violence and, 125
 self-contained classrooms and, 47
 seven "A's" for, 141
 social phobias and, 175
 suicide and, 193
 Tourette syndrome and, 265
Self-fulfilling prophecy, 36, 92
Self-instructional problem-solving
 format, 122, 123
Self-instructional strategies, 177,
 190–191, 301
Self-management, 31, 301, 305
Self-monitoring, 33
Self-reinforcement, 33
Self-report scales
 anxiety disorders and, 167
 assessment and, 24, 26
 attention deficit disorder and, 239
 depression and, 189
 suicide and, 193
Semisynthetic narcotic compounds,
 94, 96
Separation anxiety disorder (SAD),
 168–169
Sequential attention, 235
Serious emotional disturbance
 (SED), 289
Serotonin
 attention deficit disorder and,
  230, 233
 autism and, 315
 bulimia nervosa and, 202, 214
 depression and, 187, 191, 206
 eating disorders and, 206
 obsessive-compulsive disorder and,
  170, 270
Seven "A's" for self-esteem, 141
Severe behavior, 5
Sexually transmitted diseases, 66
Shaping, 304–305
Signal behavior, 33
Simms, Phil, 102
Simple tics, 257–258
Single-parent households, 14, 16, 294
Situational depression, 187
Skillstreaming series (Goldstein &
 McGinnis), 106, 177, 191,
 236, 272